[redacted]

MICROECONOMICS
A Modern Treatment

ECONOMIC THEORY AND MATHEMATICAL ECONOMICS

Consulting Editor: Karl Shell

UNIVERSITY OF PENNSYLVANIA
PHILADELPHIA, PENNSYLVANIA

Franklin M. Fisher and Karl Shell. **The Economic Theory of Price Indices: *Two Essays on the Effects of Taste, Quality, and Technological Change***

Luis Eugenio Di Marco (Ed.). **International Economics and Development: *Essays in Honor of Raúl Presbisch***

Erwin Klein. **Mathematical Methods in Theoretical Economics: *Topological and Vector Space Foundations of Equilibrium Analysis***

Paul Zarembka (Ed.). **Frontiers in Econometrics**

George Horwich and Paul A. Samuelson (Eds.). **Trade, Stability, and Macroeconomics: *Essays in Honor of Lloyd A. Metzler***

W. T. Ziemba and R. G. Vickson (Eds.). **Stochastic Optimization Models in Finance**

Steven A. Y. Lin (Ed.). **Theory and Measurement of Economic Externalities**

David Cass and Karl Shell (Eds.). **The Hamiltonian Approach to Dynamic Economics**

R. Shone. **Microeconomics: *A Modern Treatment***

In preparation

C. W. J. Granger and Paul Newbold. **Forecasting Economic Time Series**

MICROECONOMICS
A Modern Treatment

R. SHONE

Esmée Fairbairn Research Fellow at the University of Sheffield
United Kingdom

ACADEMIC PRESS New York San Francisco
A Subsidiary of Harcourt Brace Jovanovich, Publishers 1976

ACADEMIC PRESS, INC.
111 Fifth Avenue, New York, New York 10003

ISBN 0–12–641350–9

Library of Congress Catalog Card Number: 76–25738

PRINTED IN GREAT BRITAIN

CONTENTS

Preface ix
Acknowledgements xii
Notation xiii

PART I METHODOLOGY 1

CHAPTER 1 ECONOMIC SCIENCE 3
1.1 Introduction 3
1.2 Classifying Economic Propositions 4
1.2 (i) Classification of the First Kind 4
1.2 (ii) Classification of the Second Kind 7
1.3 Introduction of a γ-class 9
1.4 Refutation and Verification 11
1.5 Axiomatics and Model Building 13
1.6 A Summing Up 14

PART II CONSUMER THEORY 15

CHAPTER 2 THE THEORY OF CHOICE 17
2.1 The Problem Stated 17
2.2 The Choice Set and Attainable Set 18
2.3 Relations and Orderings 19
2.4 The Relations *P*, *R* and *I* 22
2.5 The Axioms of Choice Theory 24
2.6 Continuity of Preferences 28
2.7 'The' General Economic Problem 29
2.8 Some Unsettled Questions 32

APPENDIX 2A CHOICE UNDER UNCERTAINTY 34
APPENDIX 2B SOCIAL CHOICE 38

CHAPTER 3 PREFERENCE AND UTILITY APPROACHES TO CONSUMER THEORY 45
3.1 Introduction 45
3.2 The Consumption Choice Set 45
3.3 Important Properties of $\mathbf{R}^n$ and $\mathbf{E}^n$ 47
3.4 A New Look at Elementary Indifference Curves 54

3.5 Convex Sets, Convex/Concave and Quasiconvex/Quasiconcave Functions 56
3.5 (i) Convex Sets 57
3.5 (ii) Convex and Concave Functions 59
3.5 (iii) Quasiconcave and Quasiconvex Functions 59
3.6 The Axiom of Convexity 61
3.7 The Utility Function 64
3.8 Some Deductions from Neoclassical Utility Theory 67
3.9 Separability of the Utility Function and Some Extensions 69
3.10 Revealed Preference Theory 73

CHAPTER 4 NEOCLASSICAL AND MODERN CONSUMER CHOICE COMPARED 78
4.1 Neoclassical Optimisation 78
4.2 Restrictions on the Demand Equations 82
4.2 (i) Aggregation Restrictions 88
4.2 (ii) Symmetry 88
4.2 (iii) Homogeneity 89
4.2 (iv) Negativity 90
4.3 Compensated Demand Curves 91
4.4 Groups of Commodities 92
4.5 Prices in the Utility Function 94
4.6 The Kuhn–Tucker Conditions for an Optimal Solution 95
4.7 Neoclassical Optimisation Reconsidered 101
4.8 A New Look at Consumer Optimality 103
4.9 The Generalised Substitution Theorem 107
4.10 Revealed Preference Theory Revisited 109

APPENDIX 4A THE KUHN–TUCKER THEOREMS 111

PART III PRODUCTION THEORY 121

CHAPTER 5 THE THEORY OF PRODUCTION 123
5.1 Introduction 123
5.2 Axioms of Production 123
5.3 Convex Cones 132
5.4 The Production Set of the Economy 137
5.5 Profit Maximisation 140
5.6 Continuity and Semi-continuity of Functions and Correspondences 143

CHAPTER 6 LINEAR THEORIES OF PRODUCTION 153
6.1 Introduction 153
6.2 Ricardian Model 153

6.3 Input–Output Model 160
6.3 (i) Closed Leontief Model 162
6.3 (ii) Open Leontief Model 166
6.4 Decomposability and Perron–Frobenius Theorem 170
6.5 Activity Analysis 174
6.6 Conclusion 180

CHAPTER 7 NON-LINEAR PRODUCTION THEORY 183
7.1 Introduction 183
7.2 The Production Function 183
7.3 Homogeneous and Homothetic Production Functions 189
7.4 Equilibrium of the Firm 193
7.5 Comparative Statics of the Firm 196
7.6 A Critique of Traditional Production Theory 197

PART IV GENERAL EQUILIBRIUM THEORY 201

CHAPTER 8 THEORY OF MARKET DEMAND AND SUPPLY 203

8.1 Introduction 203
8.2 Derivation of Individual Demand Curves 203
8.3 Derivation of Individual Supply Curves 206
8.4 Market Demand 214
8.5 A First Introduction to Equilibrium 214
8.6 Normalised Price Set 218
8.7 The Mathematics of Equilibrium Points 221

CHAPTER 9 THEORY OF EXCHANGE AND GENERAL EQUILIBRIUM 227
9.1 Introduction 227
9.2 Axioms of Exchange 227
9.3 Pure Exchange Model – Neoclassical Version 233
9.4 Existence of Equilibrium in a General Exchange Model 236
9.5 Existence of Equilibrium in an Open Leontief Model 244

CHAPTER 10 WELFARE ECONOMICS 249
10.1 Introduction 249
10.2 Pareto Optimality 251
10.3 The Social Welfare Function 263
10.4 Interdependent Utilities 267
10.5 Public Goods 269
10.6 Theory of Second Best 271
10.7 The Core of an Economy 274

PART V INTRODUCTION TO DYNAMICS 281

CHAPTER 11 STABILITY AND INTRODUCTORY DYNAMICS 283
11.1 Introduction 283
11.2 Static Stability 284
11.3 Dynamics 291
11.4 Stability in an Open Leontief Model 299
11.5 Conclusion 303

Notes 309
Bibliography 317
Author Index 325
Subject Index 327

PREFACE

Microeconomics has been moving rapidly in a direction of greater analytical sophistication. Part of this change has given rise to new questions and if not to new questions certainly new ways of answering old questions. The time has come for synthesis and part of the purpose of the present text is to give a consistent thread to what appears to be a variety of approaches to microeconomics.

We can, for convenience, distinguish two approaches to microeconomics which, for want of any better label, we shall call *traditional* and *modern.* The distinction between these is often a matter of degree only but we can broadly consider them under six headings. Traditional theory tends to consider microeconomics in terms of individual elements either as consumers or as firms. Although this must always be true the modern approach concentrates more on how these basic elements interact. Thus, modern microeconomics is concerned with the economy besides the elements which compose that economy. Because of this, modern microeconomics is *general* equilibrium economics whilst traditional microeconomics has largely remained in the realm of *partial* equilibrium theory. The third distinction is only a matter of degree and rests on the extent to which microeconomics is grounded in the theory of choice and behaviour. Modern microeconomics starts with a clear statement of the theory of choice and shows how propositions are based upon this. We see, therefore, that the first chapter of Part II consists of the theory of choice. Closely associated with this is a fourth distinction which amounts to the use of an axiomatic approach to the subject. Most modern texts in microeconomics have an axiomatic approach which is rarely seen in the traditional texts. This does not imply that the former is superior to the latter but that there is a preference for the former as a means of study. A fifth distinction rests on the degree to which microeconomics is tied to welfare. Although traditional microeconomics by no means neglects welfare, the link in modern microeconomics is far clearer, as Chapter 10 will show. Finally, there is the difference in the type of mathematics employed. Traditional microeconomics rests almost wholly on classical calculus whilst modern microeconomics makes greater use of set theory and topological concepts. Part of the aim of this book, therefore, is to aid in 'translating' the traditional into modern microeconomics and vice versa.

Part of the impetus in the modern approach is the desire to obtain general theories. This has always been true of sciences and although not wholly successful in economics it has been one impetus behind recent developments in microeconomics. In the first chapter, therefore, we discuss to what extent economics can be treated as a science. The approach taken there is philosophical and does not consider in the least the sociological view of a science as highlighted by T. S. Kuhn [70] and elaborated by B. Ward [124]. The methodology of economics took a new turn with Friedman's now famous essay on *Positive Economics* [40], but interest waned until very recently when methodological issues once again became prominent, as typified by Worswick [127] and Kaldor [64].

The approach taken in this book, which is by no means the only one, is to set down as clearly as possible the axioms from which the conclusions are derived. Alternative systems are discussed such as input–output analysis as against neoclassical production theory..

The book is divided into five parts. Part I is concerned with methodology and Chapter 1 gives the thinking lying behind the remainder of the text. The reader may find it beneficial to give this chapter a quick initial reading and return to it when the remainder of the book has been read.

Part II, on consumer theory, is composed of three chapters. The first sets out the axioms of choice under certainty for an individual. Appendices give brief comments on axiomatic approaches to choice under uncertainty and social choice respectively. We then move into consumer choice and highlight the utility as against the preference approach to consumer theory. Finally, we set out a number of results derived in the neoclassical model of consumer demand. The appendix to Chapter 4 presents the theorems of Kuhn and Tucker. Throughout we start from the least restrictive assumptions to the more specific. It is for this reason that neoclassical analysis, both in demand and in production theory, appears in the final sections.

The third part is composed of the axiomatics of production, linear theories of production – Ricardian, input–output and activity analysis – and finally non-linear production theory.

Part IV turns to general equilibrium with a discussion of market demand and supply, which includes a discussion of equilibrium in a modern setting and gives an intuitive introduction to the fixed point theorems. Both pure exchange and general exchange models are discussed. The final chapter of Part IV discusses the developments in welfare economics including Pareto optimality, the social welfare function, interdependent utilities, public goods, the theory of second best and finally the core of an economy.

The final part of the book gives an introduction, and no more than an introduction, to the application of dynamics to microeconomics. It discusses static and dynamic stability, tatonnement and stability for some of the models discussed earlier in the book.

Inevitably a choice had to be made of what went into the book. The intention is that the material should be suitable for a postgraduate course in microeconomics. Where areas have been ignored they occasionally appear in the questions which accompany all but the first chapter. The main impetus behind the text has been a view that there has been no book that takes a student from the undergraduate to the postgraduate. There is a lacuna which it is hoped this work goes part way to filling. Also it is believed that the subject should be 'toyed' with and consequently over 110 exercises, which generally incorporate solutions, are provided for this purpose.

Although the book is intended for postgraduates undertaking a course in microeconomics it is also suitable in part for advanced undergraduates pursuing courses in 'advanced economic theory' or mathematical economics. It is not intended to be a book in mathematical economics but rather microeconomics approached from a mathematical standpoint. For this reason alone it is difficult to give the requirements essential for the present text. However, anyone who has worked through books such as Ferguson [37] or Bilas [17] will find the economics manageable; and through Allen [3] or Chiang [22] will not find the mathematics too difficult. There is one major difference, however: this is that the present work uses matrix algebra quite liberally. Furthermore, matrix differentiation is used particularly in Chapters 4 and 7. A short, but excellent, summary of matrix algebra (which includes matrix differentiation) can be found in J. Johnston's, *Econometric Methods* [60, ch. 4]. Where specialist techniques are required references will be given to mathematical texts which the reader may consult. However, a good introduction to analysis and topology for the mathematically mature student is Simmons's *Introduction to Topology and Modern Analysis* [114].

To help the reader on seeing the interrelationships between subject areas and different approaches to the same subject a consistent notation is used. Also vectors and matrices are in bold type and elements of a set formed by a Cartesian product are printed in cursive script. Besides the list of notation given at the outset, the more important or unusual are also explained when they first arise in the text.

R. SHONE

ACKNOWLEDGEMENTS

It is undoubtedly true that a person is a product of both his former teaching and his reading and, on rare occasions, an element of individuality. The present book owes much to my former teachers, particularly those resident in Essex in the year 1968–9 for it was here that I found the greatest stimulus to pursue economic theory. The greatest debt of all is to Professor Morishima, whose encouragement and stimulus enabled me to understand some of the delights that economic theory can offer. My debt to the literature will be patently obvious.

The present book has been in part used for a course in Mathematical Economics for third-year undergraduates at the University of Sheffield during the years 1971–4. I would like to thank those students who encouraged me to improve my exposition. In particular, I would like to thank Martin Knapp, who has read nearly the whole manuscript both as an undergraduate and now as a postgraduate. His exacting comments on nearly all chapters were most appreciated. Also a large debt is owed to Professor Nicholson, who read almost the entire manuscript in its next-to-final stage. Although I have not taken all his advice the final draft is much improved as a result of his scrutiny. I am also greatly indebted to friends and colleagues, in particular, R. S. Love, G.C. Reid, B. J. McCormick and F. Neal. Secretarial assistance from P. Garside, R. Miller, M. Tunnell, I. Berry and Linda Henderson at the final stage was most appreciated. Finally, I am indebted to Macmillan for their editorial job on a rather complex manu-manuscript in time of rapid cost increases.

September 1974 R. SHONE

NOTATION

Quantifiers and Logic

$\forall$	for all
$\exists$	there exists some
$\sim$	negation of
$\Rightarrow$	implies
$\Leftrightarrow$	implies and is implied by
iff	if and only if
s.t.	subject to
or	non-inclusive or
$\veebar$	inclusive or

Set Notation

$\in$	belongs to ($\notin$ does not belong to)
$\cap$	intersection
$\cup$	union
$\subseteq$	subset
$\subset$	proper subset
$\bar{A}$	complement of the set A
$\emptyset$	null set

Consumer Demand

k^{th}	*Individual* ($k = 1, \ldots, m$)
P^k	strictly preferred to
R^k	at least preferred to
I^k	indifferent to
P_k^*, R_k^*, I_k^*	Pareto rankings
$\mathbf{X}^k$	consumer's choice set
$\mathbf{B}_0^k$	better set associated with $\mathbf{x}_0$
$\mathbf{W}_0^k$	worse set associated with $\mathbf{x}_0$
A	attainable set

Society

P	strictly preferred to
R	at least preferred to
I	indifferent to
P^*, R^*, I^*	Pareto ranking by society
$\mathbf{X} = \sum_k \mathbf{X}^k$	society's choice set

General

$A\mathbf{x}$	$\mathbf{x}$ is attainable ($\sim A\mathbf{x}$ $\mathbf{x}$ is not attainable)
$C\mathbf{x}$	$\mathbf{x}$ is chosen ($\sim C\mathbf{x}$ $\mathbf{x}$ is not chosen)
$\mathbf{x}R\mathbf{y}$	$\mathbf{x}$ is in this relation to $\mathbf{y}$
$\mathbf{x}RP\mathbf{y}$	$\mathbf{x}$ is revealed preferred to $\mathbf{y}$
$\alpha(a, b)$	action a is chosen with probability α and b with probability $1 - \alpha$

Production

j^{th}	*Firm* ($j = 1, \ldots, l$)
$\mathbf{Y}_j$	production set
$\mathbf{Y}_j^*$	dual cone of $\mathbf{Y}_j$

Economy

$\mathbf{Y} = \sum_{j=1}^{l} \mathbf{Y}_j$ economy's production set

$\mathbf{Y}^*$ dual cone of $\mathbf{Y}$

$\hat{\mathbf{Y}}$ and $\hat{\mathbf{Y}}^*$ truncated cones of $\mathbf{Y}$ and $\mathbf{Y}^*$

Pro $(\mathbf{Y})$ the projection of $\mathbf{Y}$

$\mathbf{Y}^{\perp}$ dual cone orthogonal to $\mathbf{Y}$

Int $(\mathbf{Y})$ interior points of the cone $\mathbf{Y}$

General

$\mathbf{x}T\mathbf{y}$ x is transformed into y

$\mathbf{x}RT\mathbf{y}$ x and y is a reversible transformation

$\mathbf{p}$ price vector

$\mathbf{x}$ input vector

$\mathbf{y}$ *either* an output vector or an input/output vector

a_{ij} input i used to produce one unit of j — both within the system

b_{ij} basic i^{th} input used to produce one unit of jth output

$\mathbf{c}$ final demand vector

$\mathbf{A}$ inter-industry input/output matrix

$(\mathbf{I} - \mathbf{A})$ transactions matrix

$\mathbf{B}$ input/output matrix of basic factors

General Equilibrium

$\mathscr{x} = (\mathbf{x}^1, \mathbf{x}^2)$ particular consumption allocation

$\mathscr{X} = \mathop{\times}_{k=1}^{m} \mathbf{X}^k$ total set of consumption allocations

$\mathscr{X}^*$ efficient consumption allocations

$\mathscr{y} = (\mathbf{y}_1, \ldots, \mathbf{y}_l)$ particular production allocation

$\mathscr{Y} = \mathop{\times}_{j=1}^{l} \mathbf{Y}_j$ total set of production allocations

$\mathscr{W} = \mathscr{X} \times \mathscr{Y}$ total set of allocations (consumption and production)

$t_0, t_1, \ldots$ trading positions

$\mathbf{T} = \{t / t \in \mathbf{B}^1 \cap \mathbf{B}^2\}$ trading set

$\mathbf{T}^*$ efficient set of trades (same as CC'', the contract curve)

$\mathbf{T}^k$ trading curve of kth individual

$\mathscr{U}(\mathbf{y}) = \mathop{\times}_{k=1}^{m} u^k$

$\hat{\mathscr{U}} = \bigcup_{\mathbf{y} \in \hat{\mathbf{Y}}} \hat{\mathscr{U}}(\mathbf{y})$

$\mathbf{z}(\mathbf{p})$ excess demand function

$\mathbf{M}(\mathbf{p})$ modulated excess demand function

$\mathbf{S}_n = \{\mathbf{p} / \iota'\mathbf{p} = 1, \mathbf{p} > 0\}$ unit simplex

Mathematical

$f(\mathbf{X})$ image set of $\mathbf{X}$

$d(\mathbf{x}, \mathbf{y})$ a metric or distance function

$[a, b]$ interval including a and b

(a, b) interval excluding a and b

$[a, b)$ and $(a, b]$ interval including one end-point only

$N_\epsilon(\mathbf{x})$ ϵ-neighbourhood (or ϵ-ball) of $\mathbf{x}$

$N'_\epsilon(\mathbf{x}) = N_\epsilon(\mathbf{x}) - \{\mathbf{x}\}$ deleted neighbourhood of $\mathbf{x}$

$I(\mathbf{A})$ interior points of the set $\mathbf{A}$

$B(\mathbf{A})$ boundary points of the set $\mathbf{A}$

$C(\mathbf{A}) = \mathbf{A} \cup B(\mathbf{A})$ closure of $\mathbf{A}$

$\{\mathbf{x}_n\}$ or $\{\mathbf{x}^\nu\}$ sequences

Some Important Vectors and Matrices

Vector Inequalities

$\mathbf{x}^0 > \mathbf{x}^1$ $x_i^0 \geqslant x_i^1$ $\forall i$ and for at least one i $x_i^0 > x_i^1$

$\mathbf{x}^0 \geqslant \mathbf{x}^1$ $x_i^0 \geqslant x_i^1$ $\forall i$

$\mathbf{x}^0 \gg \mathbf{x}^1$ $x_i^0 > x_i^1$ $\forall i$

$\mathbf{x}'$ and $\mathbf{A}'$ denote the transpose of $\mathbf{x}$ and $\mathbf{A}$ respectively

Vectors

From $u(\mathbf{x})$ and $\mathbf{p}'\mathbf{x} = y$

$$\mathbf{u}_x = \frac{\partial u}{\partial \mathbf{x}}$$

$$\boldsymbol{\lambda}_p = \frac{\partial \lambda}{\partial \mathbf{p}}$$

$$\mathbf{x}_y = \frac{\partial \mathbf{x}}{\partial y}$$

From $u(\mathbf{x}, \mathbf{p})$ and $\mathbf{p}'\mathbf{x} = y$

$$u_p = \frac{\partial u}{\partial \mathbf{p}}$$

$$\mathbf{E}_y = y\,\hat{\mathbf{x}}^{-1}\,\mathbf{x}_y$$

Matrices

From $u(\mathbf{x})$ and $\mathbf{p}'\mathbf{x} = y$

$$\mathbf{U} = \frac{\partial \mathbf{u}_x}{\partial \mathbf{x}'}$$

$$\mathbf{X}_p = \frac{\partial \mathbf{x}}{\partial \mathbf{p}'}$$

$$\mathbf{S}_p = \left.\frac{\partial \mathbf{x}}{\partial \mathbf{p}'}\right|_{u\,=\,\text{const.}}$$

From $u(\mathbf{x}, \mathbf{p})$ and $\mathbf{p}'\mathbf{x} = y$

$$\mathbf{U}_x = \frac{\partial \mathbf{u}_x(\mathbf{x}, \mathbf{p})}{\partial \mathbf{x}'} \qquad \mathbf{U}_p = \frac{\partial \mathbf{u}_x(\mathbf{x}, \mathbf{p})}{\partial \mathbf{p}}$$

$$\mathbf{E}_p = \hat{\mathbf{x}}^{-1}\,\mathbf{X}_p\hat{\mathbf{p}}$$

$$\mathbf{Z}_p = \frac{\partial \mathbf{z}}{\partial \mathbf{p}'}$$

From $q = f(\mathbf{x})$

$$\mathbf{q}_x = \frac{\partial q}{\partial \mathbf{x}}$$

$$\mathbf{q}_w = \frac{\partial q}{\partial \mathbf{w}}$$

$$\mathbf{q}_w = \frac{\partial q}{\partial \mathbf{w}}$$

$$\mathbf{x}_p = \frac{\partial \mathbf{x}}{\partial p}$$

From $q = f(\mathbf{x})$

$$\mathbf{Q} = \frac{\partial \mathbf{q}_x}{\partial \mathbf{x}'}$$

$$\mathbf{X}_w = \frac{\partial \mathbf{x}}{\partial \mathbf{w}'}$$

Scalars

$\lambda_y = \partial\lambda/\partial y$

$\phi = \lambda_y^{-1} \lambda y^{-1}$ income flexibility parameter

Part I
METHODOLOGY

1

ECONOMIC SCIENCE

1.1 Introduction

This chapter is methodological. Its aim is to set down, in the most general terms, the approach to economic science that will be taken in this book. As a consequence this chapter will freely call on other branches of knowledge from which clearer and more penetrating examples can readily be drawn, leaving the remainder of the book to supply in detail the economic examples.

The essential message of this chapter is the importance of establishing a clearly defined set of postulates on which the whole edifice of economic knowledge rests. Such an edifice materialises as the subject develops and, unlike a building, it is not laid down first. Science develops in a piecemeal fashion, formulating hypotheses which, even if not wholly true, will remain fruitful after the necessary corrections have been made. Science in this sense can be conceived of as 'successive approximations to the truth'.[1]* In an attempt therefore to clearly define such a set of postulates we employ, quite freely, formal logic and pure mathematics. It is important to point out now that these two branches of knowledge do not in themselves establish any assertions about matters of empirical fact; what they do provide is an efficient and indispensable machinery for deducing from abstract theoretical assumptions, theorems specific enough to be accessible to direct empirical test.[2] We shall say more on this below.

But is there such a subject as *economic science*? In order to answer this question we must be clear by what we understand by the term 'science'. One of the most influential philosophers on the history of science has put it as follows:

It is the desire for explanations which are at once systematic and controllable by factual evidence that generates science; and it is the organization and classification of knowledge on the basis of explanatory principles that is the distinctive goal of the sciences. More specifically, the sciences seek to discover and to formulate in general terms the conditions under which events of various sorts occur, the statements of such determining conditions being the explanations of the corresponding happenings. This goal can be achieved only by distinguishing or isolating certain properties in the subject matter studied and by ascertaining the repeatable patterns of dependence in which these properties stand to one another. [88, p. 4]

This statement is far reaching, and has behind it many distinctions of substance. In the sections to follow it is hoped that we can bring out how economic science fits into this scheme. To the extent that economics can be a science the scientific method is applicable, i.e. a body of canons which are used for judging the

* See pp. 309–16 for Notes to Chapters 1–11.

reliability of the procedures adopted and also by which evidential data are obtained and the criterion for assessing the evidence on which conclusions are drawn. [88, p. 13]

It is important to stress that advancement depends more on the correct method than on the correct result obtained by the wrong method: the latter is likely to lead to isolated developments whilst the former to a cornerstone for all future developments. It is, therefore, essential that economics be put under the microscope and its tendencies and hypotheses critically examined and tested with unfailing exactitude and detail. No proposition should be uncritically accepted, and all the methods of science that are possible to bring to bear on the problem should be so applied. Alfred Marshall was well aware of this:

> All the devices for the discovery of the relations between cause and effect, which are described in treatises on scientific method, have to be used in their turn by the economist: there is not any one method of investigation which can properly be called the method of economics; but every method must be made serviceable in its proper place, either singly or in combination with others. [83, p. 24]

The formulation too is to be investigated in order to see what vistas may be opened by alternative formulations: for one such arrangement may be incapable of falsification but an alternative capable of falsification. The criterion throughout is the method which does not violate the 'rules' but which will further our knowledge the greatest.

Economics employs both the *deductive* and *inductive* methods. Deduction is basically reasoning which allows statements to be made which are not obvious but which have been obtained from a set of postulates each of which in themselves are simple.[3] Induction is a process which infers something about the general from experience of the particular. In this book we shall be concerned almost wholly with the deductive method. A discussion of the contribution of induction to economic science would require another book.

1.2 Classifying Economic Propositions

We shall denote the totality of propositions that exist in economic science, as so far understood, by the set $P = \{P_1, \ldots, P_n\}$. But once we have these propositions we must categorise them in some useful way, for only then can our analysis proceed. By useful we mean that the categorisation increases our understanding of economic phenomena which is contained within the propositions. We shall in fact carry out a two-way classification, both of which are important, and both of which have been discussed in the economic literature.[4]

1.2 (i) Classification of the First Kind

Two classes of propositions can be usefully distinguished which shall be designated the α-class and the β-class, i.e.

$$P_\alpha = \{P_{\alpha 1}, P_{\alpha 2}, \ldots, P_{\alpha k}\} \quad \text{and} \quad P_\beta = \{P_{\beta 1}, P_{\beta 2}, \ldots, P_{\beta m}\}$$

denote respectively all those propositions belonging to the α-class and the β-class. The α-class constitutes the fundamental propositions of the science which in themselves cannot be deduced from any other set of propositions. Any propositions belonging to P_α therefore, cannot be deduced either from another proposition belonging to P_α or deduced from propositions belonging to the β-class.[5] The β-class consists of those propositions which follow logically from some, or all, the P_α.

The question arises as to whether we can treat the propositions in the α-class as axioms. To do this, however, we must be clear as to how we are using the term 'axiom'. It can be used in two senses, and these two senses can lead to a different view of the axiomatic treatment of economic science. The first interpretation of an axiom is that it is a necessary truth which is clearly apparent to any rational mind; in other words, the propositions are self-evident. Lord Robbins in his *Essay on the Nature and Significance of Economic Science* gives explicit recognition to this view and is therefore worth quoting in full:

> The propositions of economic theory, like all scientific theory, are obviously deductions from a series of postulates. And the chief of these postulates are all assumptions involving in some way simple and indisputable facts of experience relating to the way in which the scarcity of goods which is the subject-matter of our science actually shows itself in the world of reality. . . . These are not postulates the existence of whose counterpart in reality admits of extensive dispute once their nature is fully realised. We do not need controlled experiments to establish their validity: they are so much the stuff of our everyday experience that they have only to be stated to be recognised as obvious. . . . It is on postulates of this sort that the complicated theorems of advanced analysis ultimately depend. And it is from the existence of the conditions they assume that the general applicability of the broader propositions of economic science is derived. [104, pp. 78–9]

The present author shares this view to the extent that he considers the propositions belonging to P_α can be interpreted in this way. But the interpretation is too narrow. It is clear that the axioms of Euclidean geometry are treated in this way, as are the axioms of revealed preference theory (see Section 4.10); but a perusal through any science will reveal many axioms which are far from self-evident, even though they must belong to the α-class. For example, we shall show later that the proposition 'a firm's objective is to maximise profits' is a member of P_α, but this is by no means self-evident; so much so that it has come under strong criticism.

The second interpretation of axiom, which is implicit in much of the economic literature, is that it is a proposition which asserts the generally accepted convention of the meanings attached to fundamental terms, i.e. the *primitives* of a subject.[6] In any axiomatic approach to a subject there must be some basic or fundamental terms which are undefined. However, these terms are themselves used to define others in the system. For example, the letters of the alphabet are the fundamental terms (primitives) of a language. These are combined to form (define) words which in turn are combined to form sentences. Conversely, the smallest fundamental unit into which a sentence can be broken down is in terms of the letters of the alphabet. Such primitives in economics include utility, preference, firm, production, cost, and so on. In other words, the axioms, conventions, limit what can be said or cannot be said about these fundamental ideas. Friedman, for example, in his essay on *Positive Economics,* puts forth this under the heading: 'Use of Assumptions in Stating a Theory'. He argues that the assumptions, axioms, specify the domain for which the model is applicable [40, pp. 23–30].

In order to clarify the meaning of 'primitive' terms consider the theory of preferences which has as a primitive term R meaning 'at least preferred to'. Since R is a primitive we cannot define it as such, but we can define other relations in terms of this primitive. For example, we can define indifference, I, to be the state where $\mathbf{x}R\mathbf{y}$ and $\mathbf{y}R\mathbf{x}$ are both true. Furthermore, we can define strictly preferred, P, in terms of R and I; namely, $\mathbf{x}P\mathbf{y}$ is the state where $\mathbf{x}R\mathbf{y}$ but $\mathbf{x}$ and $\mathbf{y}$ are not indifferent. There is no fundamental reason why we take R as a primitive of preference theory. We could equally well have taken P, strictly preferred to, as our primitive. In this instance we could not define P as we could before but we can define indifference in terms of P; namely, $\mathbf{x}$ is not preferred to $\mathbf{y}$ and $\mathbf{y}$ is not preferred to $\mathbf{x}$. We could then define R as the state where $\mathbf{x}$ is preferred to $\mathbf{y}$ or $\mathbf{x}$ is indifferent to $\mathbf{y}$. This is just the way in which Euclidean geometry is built up, being based on the primitives point, line, parallel, etc.

It has been argued that the first interpretation of axioms is that they are necessarily true. Can the same be said of axioms which take the form of conventions? An example from probability theory brings out a number of aspects of importance here. To establish a probability model we would proceed as follows:[7]

Let S be the sample description space, i.e. the space over which all the possible events are defined, and let A and B be two events; then the axioms of probability are:

Axiom 1 For any $A \in S$ there is a real number $p(A)$ associated with A such that $p(A) \geqslant 0$

Axiom 2 $p(S) = 1$

Axiom 3 For any $A \in S$, $B \in S$ and $A \cap B = \emptyset$

$$p(A \cup B) = p(A) + p(B)$$

Let us list a number of points which are brought out by this illustration. (1) The postulates, which we can call P_1, P_2 and P_3, all belong to P_α. (2) The class S to which these postulates apply is not defined – this is typical of an axiomatic treatment. (3) The number p is defined only implicitly by the three axioms, this 'probability' being a primitive. (4) As so far laid down it is meaningless to ask whether P_1, P_2 and P_3 are true or false or to ask whether $p(A) = ½$ is true or false. However, if p is associated with a relative frequency of some physical phenomena it is meaningful, in a probability sense, to ask both questions. This correspondence between an abstract or pure set of postulates with a physical representation is what economists mean when they demand *operational theories.*[8] Only when there is a physical correspondence can their implications be, in principle, tested.[9]

In what sense, however, do we take some of the P_α as conventions? We shall in Chapter 2 take P as a primitive of choice theory, where this means 'is preferred to'.

From this we define the relation of indifference, which we denote by I. The first axiom, the axiom of comparability, states that all elements of a choice set can be taken in pairs and that the choosing agent can say whether he prefers one to the other or he is indifferent. This means all elements of the choice set can in fact be compared. This is by no means a self-evident truth. But it is a convention adopted to limit the range of application: in this instance it limits the choices to only those elements for which full information is known, in other words to choices under certainty.[10] More importantly, we shall see that the general theory of consumer choice, and, to a large extent, production theory, includes the axiom of convexity. This amounts to indifference curves and isoquants being convex to the origin. Once again this is by no means self-evident. In fact, if there were either externalities in consumption, or increasing returns to scale in production, both consumption and production sets would lose their convexity. The axiom of convexity is effectively saying that the convention of the author will be to exclude as outside the domain of study problems involving externalities in consumption and production. The fact that convexity is stated as an axiom emphasises that it is a fundamental proposition, for it cannot be deduced from any other propositions in P_α nor from those belonging to P_β.[11] It is a convention adopted by economists to enable them to establish a model and carry out analysis.

The β-class consists of lemmas, propositions (but propositions deduced from those in P_α), and theorems. To the extent that we follow the rules of deductive logic the propositions of the β-class are tautological in the sense that they are implied by the P_α propositions and hence inevitably follow from these. The distinction between lemmas, propositions and theorems is purely a convention, a theorem being a deduction which is considered of some importance.

1.2 (ii) Classification of the Second Kind

The second form of classification which has been given great attention is that between normative and positive propositions in economics. The class of normative propositions, designated P_N, comprises those which involve value judgements; they involve statements of what ought to be. The class of positive propositions, P_P, on the other hand, comprises those which do not involve value judgements: they refer to states that are and not what ought to be.

It is clear from the discussion of the first classification that all propositions in economic science can be placed in one of two mutually exclusive subsets, namely, P_α or P_β.[12] Can this be said of P_N and P_P? It would appear that all premises, so long as they can be narrowed down to a single statement, can be classed either as belonging to P_N or to P_P, at least in principle. Positive premises must give a positive conclusion; only normative premises can give a normative deduction; mixed premises must implicitly involve a normative deduction. The following schema illustrates the links:

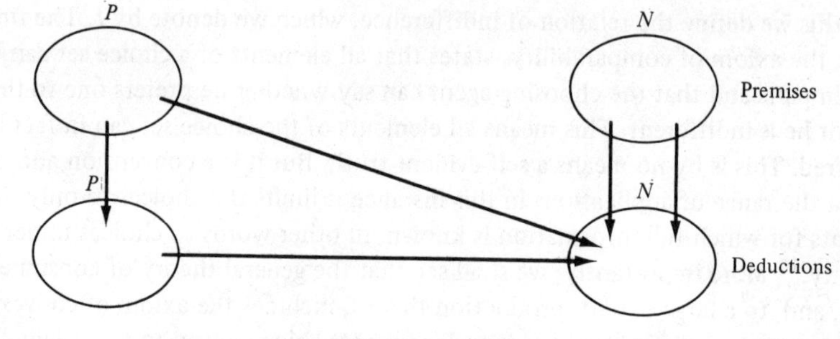

Fig. 1.1

How then does this classification aid our understanding? Consider the schema in Fig. 1.2. This says that the participants agree on the deduction but start from a different normative premise, even though the positive premise is the same. Taking

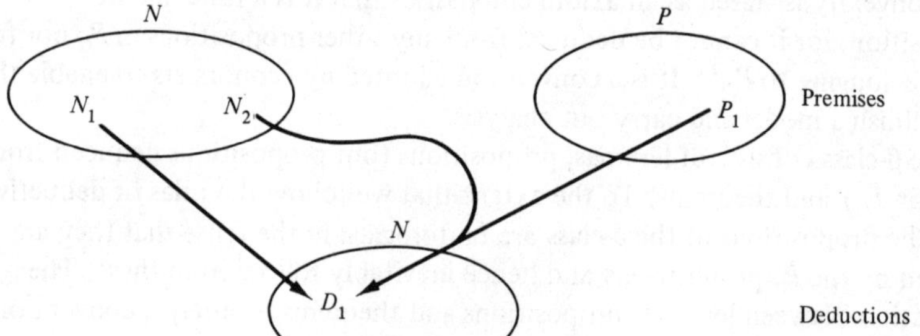

Fig. 1.2

the statements in the form 'if p and q then r' we have:

Individual 1 If N_1 and P_1 then D_1
Individual 2 If N_2 and P_1 then D_1

What this reveals is the different implicit value judgement involved in the same prediction, or deduction, D_1. As Friedman states this would appear the situation of much government policy [40, p. 5]. Each of labour, conservative, and liberal may agree on the policy conclusion, D_1, but some may reject it and others accept it on the basis of the implied value judgement embodied in the premises N_1 and N_2.

We can use the above formulation to make another of Friedman's arguments explicit. The schema in Fig. 1.3 pictures two alternative predictions dealing with the same subject. The question now arises can a choice be made between D_1 and D_2, and, if so, does the act of choice involve only positive or does it involve normative issues? Friedman would argue: 'Any policy conclusion necessarily rests on a prediction about the consequences of doing one thing rather than another, a prediction that must be based – implicitly or explicitly – on positive economics'

[40, p. 5]. As the schema in Fig. 1.3 makes clear both D_1 and D_2 are normative, but what Friedman appears to be saying is that scientific method as such, which allows us to make choices, belongs to the realm of positive science.[13] To what extent choices are positive or not will be made clear in Chapter 2, which is concerned with the general theory of choice.

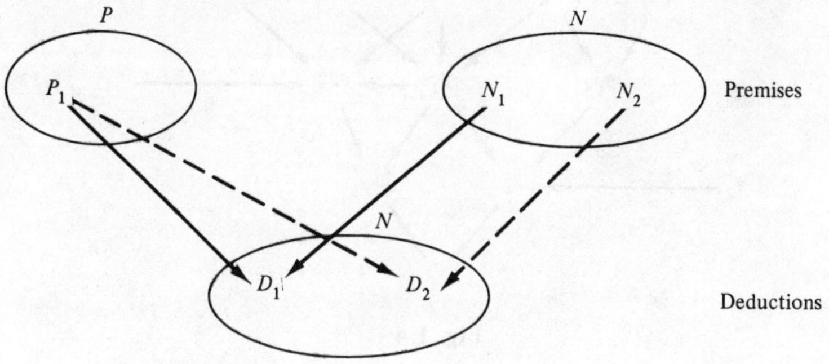

Fig. 1.3

Having discussed briefly the second classification the next question that arises is: to what extent are the two classifications interdependent? It was argued that so long as the premises are narrowed down to single statements they could be allocated either to P_N or to P_P. But the propositions belonging to P_α will be single statements and can therefore be subdivided into positive and normative. This will not generally be true of the propositions in P_β, because some will be positive conclusions based on positive premises; some normative conclusions based on normative premises; and others, probably the larger part, normative conclusions based on positive and normative premises. A classification of P_β into normative and positive propositions is possible only if all the mixed deductions can be clearly identified. A large part of economics is an attempt to differentiate these three subsets of P_β.[14]

1.3 Introduction of a γ-class

Thus far all propositions can be allocated to the subsets P_α and P_β. However, in practice theorising takes a somewhat different form which we have schematically illustrated in Fig. 1.4. This shows that in order to establish proposition (lemma or theorem) β_3 an additional assumption, γ_1, had to be introduced which was either explicitly, but more usually implicitly, in β_3. Similarly, to establish theorem β_4 another proposition, γ_2, had to be invoked.

A point to note is that every theorem in the β-class from β_3 onwards rests on the accepted convention of γ_1 and γ_2. In particular, β_6 implicitly requires the acceptance of both γ_1 and γ_2. It is important, therefore, to know what interpretations can be given to the *γ-class.* Two interpretations are useful. First we can consider the γ-class as consisting of all *simplifying postulates.* Second, the γ-class consists of those propositions introduced so that analysis can be taken further. Let us take each in turn.

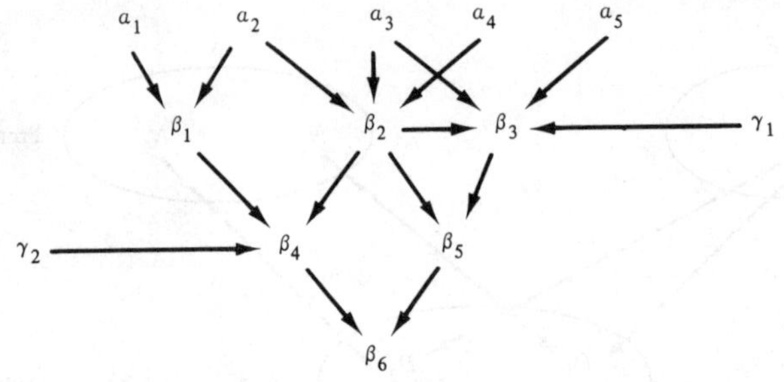

Fig. 1.4

A simplifying proposition, such as 'the economy produces only two commodities', cannot be deduced from any other proposition and is therefore like those in the α-class. However, unlike those in the α-class they are not fundamental. We could postulate the economy has *n* goods with no change in our conclusions. It is this which gives content to the meaning of 'simplifying'. There is difficulty in this, however. Sometimes, what appears to be a simplifying proposition is in fact not: it is more fundamental than at first appears. For example, the early theoretical literature on the *Pure Theory of International Trade* assumed that the world was composed of only two countries, that each country produced only two goods and that these two goods were produced by means of only two factors of production. If this was a purely simplifying postulate the conclusions so derived would equally hold in an *m* country, *n* commodity and *r* factor world. However, Professor Pearce has forcefully argued that this is not the case, that such a proposition is fundamental to the conclusions [98]. Such a proposition, although appearing to belong to the γ-class, in actuality belongs to the α-class. In this instance it is not a simplifying postulate. Economics is replete with simplifying assumptions some of which conform to the use employed here and therefore belong to the γ-class, whilst others are not simplifying and belong to the α-class.

The second interpretation that can be given to the γ-class is to the effect that analysis cannot continue unless we introduce further assumptions – and as the schema in Fig. 1.4 illustrates they are likely to be of an *ad hoc* nature, being introduced in order to arrive at, say, postulate β_4 from β_1 and β_2. For example, we might have, for an oligopolist, the proposition 'the market reacts differently for a rise in price than for a reduction in price' (kinked demand curve). Such a postulate belongs to the γ-class. It is not fundamental in the sense employed above for the α-class, nor is it a deduction from the fundamental propositions, but it is invoked to give rise to a proposition such as 'a firm will maintain a fixed price', a proposition which belongs to P_β.[15] The scheme in Fig. 1.4 also illustrates what Leontief has called the 'implicit' theorising of the Neo-Cambridge economists [74].

Science develops partly by trial and error. It is not hard to find examples of propositions of the γ-class which have become part of the a-class. The only problem with this procedure is that the a-class loses its distinctive property of being the *minimum* number of fundamental postulates on which thinking in a discipline rests.[16]

1.4 Refutation and Verification

It may be asked why we have taken such pains to elaborate as we have done so far. The reason is because a scientific approach requires specificity in the linguistic expressions used in stating its propositions. This leads us naturally into the problem of refutation or verification. Whether we wish to test only the predictions of a theory (*à la* Friedman) or also its assumptions, in both instances it is true that the more precise are the linguistic expressions the greater is the likelihood of refutation than the vague common-sense hypotheses: and this applies to both assumptions and predictions. Put more strongly, it is often the vagueness of linguistic expression which has enabled a theory to stand for any length of time. As a simple illustration consider the following two propositions:

P.1 *A firm operates at minimum average cost.*
P.2 *A firm operates in the region of minimum average cost.*

Proposition 1 is more specific than Proposition 2 and accordingly is more likely to be refuted. Furthermore, Proposition 2 begs the question: What is an 'acceptable region'? Also note, the first may be refuted but the second may still be true, but not conversely.

The conclusion to be drawn from this is that we should not praise a theory just because it has withstood the test of time, a statement sometimes made, because this may just be a result of its vagueness and difficulty in refutation.[17] On the other hand, if a theory is not vague and has stood the test of time it deserves our praise, e.g. Ricardo's theory of comparative advantage.[18]

A distinction is sometimes made between refutation and verifiability. If we hypothesise consumers buy more when the price falls, is this verified when we find a set of circumstances when this is true? If it is true on the first, second, . . . , occasions we cannot guarantee it will be true on the next occasion. Even if it is true for the one-million it may be untrue for the one-million-and-one. It is claimed, therefore, that the hypothesis cannot be verified. We can argue, however, that a set of circumstances is consistent with a hypothesis, i.e. it does not refute the hypothesis. This will then allow for the possibility that the next may refute the hypothesis.

But this brings out a further consideration. If one million do not refute a hypothesis but one does, do we reject the hypothesis? Clearly not. But this does raise the problem of the margin of disagreement one will be prepared to tolerate. This is a matter of degree only, and we feel it is a problem between the scientist and his knowledge of the subject matter.[19] What this does raise is the inherent stochastic or probabilistic element in a deterministic set of postulates. If some of the postulates are themselves probabilistic then an even greater degree of uncertainty enters into the rejection of a hypothesis.

It has been argued, particularly by Friedman [40], that we should test a theory's predictions rather than its assumptions. Let us consider this more closely with the help of the analysis so far presented. We can greatly simplify the difficult concepts if we concentrate purely on the issue at hand, and this is best done by using the *propositional calculus* of logic. Most hypotheses can be put in the form (or variant of this): If p then q. p is the *antecedent* proposition or clause, and q the *consequent*. For example: 'If the market is perfect then price will be at minimum average cost'; where the antecedent and consequent are readily identifiable.

It is to be observed that the antecedent clause contains a theoretical term, namely, 'perfect competition'. Suppose we naïvely attempt to test whether perfect competition exists, we would undoubtedly come to the conclusion that it does not. Must we therefore suppose that price is not at minimum average cost? Theoretical terms cannot be defined explicitly; furthermore, they do not exist in any spatiotemporal region: 'point', 'plane', 'vacuum', 'elasticity at a point', etc., have no spatiotemporal region. Under these circumstances the consequent can be tested for its falsity independently of the obviously untrue antecedent assumption on which it is based. In other words:

> If a hypothesis embodies a theoretical term and if that hypothesis is included in the antecedent clause of a propositional schema, then to show that the antecedent does not exist in any spatiotemporal region does not invalidate the truth or falsity of the consequent.

This proposition is put in precise terms in that it refers only to hypotheses which embody theoretical terms. It was argued above that a number of axioms are of the kind which limit the domain of application for which the theory is to predict. Take once again the axiom of convexity. This can be operationalised by giving it a physical correspondence and so, in any field of research, such as consumer demand, we can test whether it is true or false. We make such an assumption because we believe it is more often true than false, which in itself is testable. To this extent the predictions derived from this will be more often true than false. If the antecedent clause of this kind can be replaced by one which is true on more occasions, without being vague in its linguistic expression, it follows that the consequent (prediction) must also be true on more occasions. It could be argued that the antecedent may be true and, although the consequent logically follows, it is refuted in the real world. But this would be true under the original and the replaced antecedent clause. For example, in the oligopoly case referred to above, the truth of the consequent clause 'price will remain unchanged' is very much dependent upon the truth of the antecedent clause 'the market reacts differently for a rise in price than for a reduction in price'. Considerations of this kind should be borne in mind when we discuss the differences between *traditional* and *modern* microeconomics.

What can be said about simplifying assumptions which invariably take the form of antecedent clauses? 'A world composed of two commodities' requires only observation to reject, but would we reject the conclusions because of this? Clearly not. The argument here is that the consequent would follow if one of the antecedent clauses referred to two commodities or referred to n. To the extent, therefore, that hypotheses whose antecedent clause belongs to P_γ, and are of a simplifying nature as indicated above, the truth or falsity of the consequent is independent of the truth or falsity of the antecedent. But what of the other elements of P_γ which are not simplifying, which although not fundamental are important for the rest of the analysis. These propositions have the same characteristics in this regard as the axioms of P_α which delimit the applicability of a theory, i.e. the frequency of true predictions will be dependent upon the frequency of truth in the assumptions.

It should be apparent that when we refer to an 'assumption' it can be a proposition belonging to P_α, P_β, or P_γ and that the interpretation given to such an assumption will differ according to which class it belongs.

1.5 Axiomatics and Model Building

So far it has been supposed that from a set of α-propositions, and employing deductive logic, a whole set of β-propositions can be derived. It was in this way that Euclid built up his Geometry. Just such a self-contained system can be considered as a *closed* system. Consider the schema in Fig. 1.5. The five propositions in P_α and

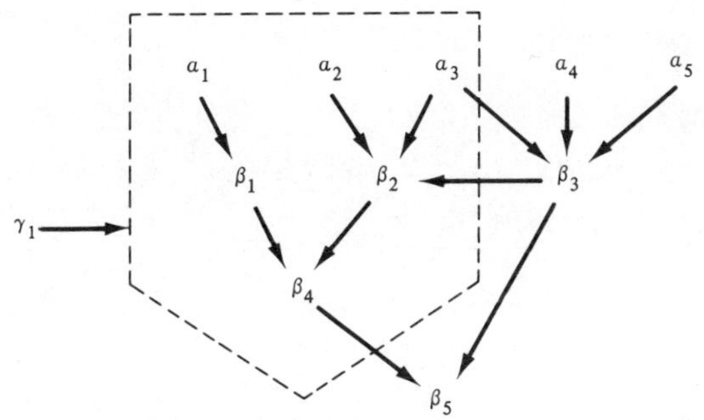

Fig. 1.5

the five deductions P_β constitute a closed system. However, suppose we consider this system too complex to look at because it involves either too many variables or too many interactions. Accordingly, we decide to consider a subsystem contained in the dotted area. This subsystem is *open:* open in the sense that it requires proposition β_3, which in turn requires axioms α_4 and α_5. Since deductions β_2 and β_4 depend upon β_3, and hence α_4 and α_5, the analyst, in order to arrive at a subsystem to approximate reality, introduces proposition γ_1, i.e. γ_1 is needed because we are considering only a part of the system: γ_1 in effect 'replaces' the set (β_3, a_4, a_5). However, differences of opinion can arise as to the appropriateness of proposition γ_1 which makes the subsystem a viable one. A different γ_1 may produce a subsystem which is a better approximation to reality.

An obvious question to pose is whether a theorist must always begin his analysis with the fundamental propositions contained in P_α. It would be foolhardy to contemplate such a procedure if one is interested in propositions β_{205} and β_{206}. Let us consider this in terms of Fig. 1.5. Suppose a theorist in wishing to obtain theorems β_4 and β_5 states as his 'axioms' β_1, β_2 and β_3. In what sense is this a valid procedure? If the interest of the theorist is in β_4 and β_5 and if the above schema holds, then in taking as 'axioms' propositions β_1–β_3 the theorist is considering a closed system. In such a case the procedure is a valid one. However, suppose he had considered only propositions β_2 and β_3 as 'axioms'. The system now being considered is open; and it is now that the debate begins. One disputant may say proposition a_1 is required to deduce β_4; another that β_4 requires proposition β_1; and yet another that even β_5 requires a_1; and so on. Since most theories involve many propositions and many interrelationships this problem is even more likely to occur, the disputes becoming longer and more heated. Only by clearly formulating our theories can we hope to avoid such wasteful disputes; but, more importantly, only by so doing will our understanding progress.

The point of this section is no more than to make the reader aware of theorising which may be poor, and as a help in sorting out the many doctrinal debates. To do this one must have a clear conception of:

(1) the system or subsystem, and
(2) knowledge of whether the system or subsystem is open or closed.

1.6 A Summing Up

This chapter has laid the foundation for those which follow. The reader should always be conscious of his methodology, because it is too easy to slip into incorrect theorising. Also this chapter has refrained from giving elaborate economic illustrations because these will follow in greater detail; but to the extent that the bare elements have been given each subject-area can be viewed in the light of this chapter.

We must now turn to establishing the axioms of P_α on which economic science rests. There is not one foundation of economic science but many alternatives and part of our job is to see how we can choose between them.

Part II

CONSUMER THEORY

In this part we set out to define a set of axioms which define the choice behaviour of consumers. By starting with a primitive 'preference' we establish seven axioms which must be fulfilled by any choice problem whether it be a consumer, a society or a firm. In so far as these axioms are based on what mathematicians and logicians call order relations then these relations are discussed first so that a rigorous foundation can be laid. More to the point, we can be extremely specific in our statements concerning consumer demand. The questions we are trying to answer include the following. Can we always make a choice? Does it always follow. that the item we most prefer is the one actually chosen? What do we mean by rational behaviour and consistent behaviour in economics?

Consumer theory in traditional microeconomics has been based on utility. However, we can analyse consumer demand either in terms of preferences or in terms of utility. The basic question we face here is whether the theory of choice based on preferences is the same as that based on utility. We therefore discuss both and establish the link between them. In so far as utility is a function defined over a commodity space we must be clear on which theorems in mathematics we can call upon to discuss our economic problem. For example, can the commodity space be unconnected (contain holes)? Chapter 3, therefore, contains a certain amount of mathematics which allows us to be precise on the properties possessed by the commodity space; and secondly, by what types of functions will be suitable representations of utility which satisfy the axioms previously discussed.

Economics has often been reduced to the statement that it is no more than optimising (i.e. maximising or minimising) some objective function subject to a number of constraints. This form of the economic problem is first discussed in Chapter 2 and then applied specifically to demand theory in Chapter 4. Of particular note in this formulation is whether the constraints are in the form of equalities or inequalities.

Hence we first set out to obtain the principles of rational choice. However, only choices under certainty are discussed in detail, although Appendix 2A discusses briefly choices under uncertainty. Furthermore, we deal only with individual choice, leaving social choice to be briefly discussed in Appendix 2B. From such rational choice we obtain demand behaviour. Thus Chapter 4 sets out to answer what predictions of demand theory are implied by our theory of choice. Another problem is: Can we deal with economic problems, such as rationing, which places a consumer inside his (money) budget line? In attempting to answer such questions it is particularly important to specify the constraints suitably to take account of their inequality feature. Since dealing with inequalities has become more pronounced we have presented in Appendix 4A the theorems of Kuhn and Tucker.

Other questions dealt with include: Is the theory of choice based on indifference curve analysis too rigid? Is revealed preference theory superior to other theories of choice? If prices as well as commodities enter the utility function does this alter the predictions of our theory?

Finally, part of the analysis presented in this section is preparing the way to discuss general equilibrium theory in Part IV. This includes Appendix 2B besides the analysis of Chapter 4.

2

THE THEORY OF CHOICE

2.1 The Problem Stated

The student learns very early that economics is concerned with choice. It is argued that because goods are scarce or because income is limited an individual or an economy must make choices. In the standard textbook of Lipsey we see the phrase, 'Choices are necessary because resources are scarce' [76, 3rd ed., p. 50]. He goes on to say, 'Because resources are scarce, we are forced to choose. A choice means that you have one thing or the other [but not both]' (p. 51). The same argument can be found in Samuelson [108, 9th ed., pp. 17–30]. The argument appears to be that goods which are not scarce will not command a price, or that their price will be zero.[1] Choice is then illustrated for an economy as in Fig. 2.1 by the use of a production possibility boundary showing that a country, when on the boundary, must choose between x_1 and x_2, and to the extent that it gives up x_2 for more x_1 the slope denotes the opportunity cost of choosing x_1 in place of x_2.

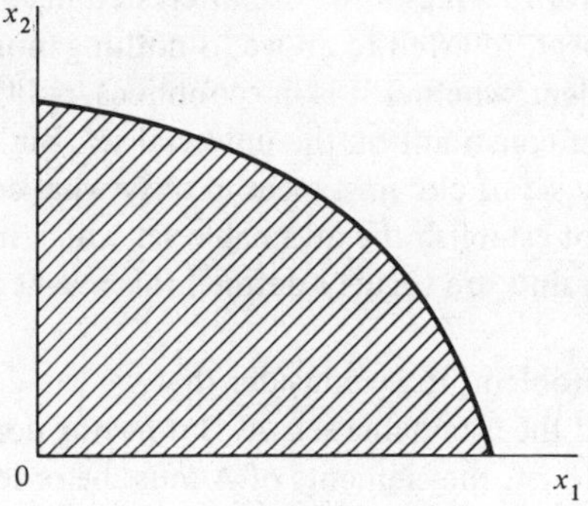

Fig. 2.1

However, in order to embark on a discussion of economic problems of this type we must be absolutely clear on what is involved when choices are made, i.e. we must consider the theory of choice. The purpose of this chapter, therefore, is to lay the foundations and principles of choice theory; to see what they are and how they are related so that we do not misuse them when we consider the economic problem. In order to keep the discussion within reasonable bounds this chapter will consider only choice theory under certainty. Those interested in choice theory under uncertainty will find some brief notes in Appendix 2A to this chapter.

2.2 The Choice Set and Attainable Set

We can conceive of a set χ as composed of all the objects a choosing agent can have the possibility of selecting, i.e. $\chi = \{x_1, \ldots, x_s\}$. This universal set is deliberately left vague and will take on significance within the set of axioms we are about to elaborate. However, for any particular problem χ must be known to the choosing agent, in other words, we assume complete knowledge on the part of the choosing agent about the state of nature so that he knows all the objects over which he can make choices. In any given situation some of these choices will be attainable whilst others will not. It may be that all x_i $(i = 1, \ldots, s)$ are attainable or that no x_i is attainable; but for any problem the choice set can be divided into two mutually exclusive subsets: (1) the attainable set, **A**; and (2) the unattainable set, $\bar{\mathbf{A}}$, where $\mathbf{A} \cup \bar{\mathbf{A}} = \chi$. For example, suppose we are considering the choice of Prime Minister. The universal set is composed of all members of the House of Commons belonging to the party in power, since technically they all have the possibility of becoming Prime Minister. However, for one reason or another a certain number will be ruled out as ineligible, and the effective choice set is the remainder – this is the attainable set **A**. Or alternatively, a consumer with a fixed income may have the choice of, say, two goods, but his attainable set will be the maximum of each taken separately or in combination which he can obtain with his fixed income.

What in fact these two examples illustrate is that a constraint of some kind is imposed on the choosing agent which reduces the effective choices open to him to a subset of the total. It is for this reason we are interested in constraints. In particular, the scarcity aspect, referred to above, is nothing more than a result of this constraint. Each problem, whether it is in economics, politics, philosophy, etc., will impose its own type of constraint on the universal set. But one thing is clear, until we can specify in any set of circumstances exactly what constitutes the constraints, then we cannot establish the attainable set which includes the effective choices. Also, if the constraints are vaguely defined this means the attainable set is equally vague.

Let us summarise the problem. If we consider that we can define the constraints then we have distinguished the attainable set, **A**. But having done this, in order to choose from this attainable set, the elements of **A** must be ordered. But in what sense do we order the elements of the attainable set? If we can rank the elements of **A**, say from highest to lowest, or most preferred to least preferred, with no two the same, then we have a *strong ordering.* But there is no reason to suppose that there will be no two or more elements ranked the same. If this is the case then we have a *weak ordering.* But this is not sufficient; we require the ordering to be *transitive* so that if x_i is ranked higher than x_j and x_j is ranked higher than x_k we can take it as reasonable (consistent) to suppose x_i is ranked higher than x_k. Given the attainable set and a transitive relation defined on it then it will be possible to choose one element of **A** which is ranked at least as high, or at least as preferred, as any other element in **A**. In the examples referred to above such an element would consist of the member of parliament chosen as Prime Minister and the desired combination of the two goods on the part of the consumer, respectively. This does not preclude the possibility that the Prime Minister is chosen arbitrarily from a number of parliamentarians who were considered of equal rank. Nor does it preclude the possibility that a number of commodity bundles were equally ranked with the one chosen. What matters is that there is no more preferred Prime Minister or more preferred commodity bundle which belongs to **A**. We must now look at this more rigorously, for we must be clear in what sense we can say '**x** is preferred to **y**'. Is transitivity the only requirement for rationality? Are there some elements of **A** which cannot be compared? Can we guarantee that the element most preferred is the one actually chosen? Can we even say that there always will exist a most preferred element of **A**?

2.3 Relations and Orderings

A choice involves a comparison between two or more objects which we can always consider as being taken two at a time, i.e. in binary form. We are concerned with a relation that exists between two such objects. Let us consider this generally with the help of Fig. 2.2. Let the two choices, objects or elements, be denoted **x** and **y**.

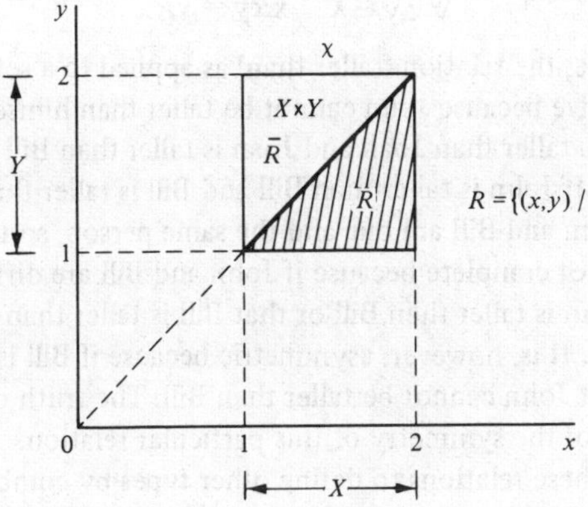

Fig. 2.2

We can consider $\mathbf{x} \in \mathbf{X}$ and $\mathbf{y} \in \mathbf{Y}$, where **X** and **Y** are subsets of χ. A relation is no more than a restriction imposed on the Cartesian product $\mathbf{X} \times \mathbf{Y}$, which defines some association between **x** and **y**.[2] For example, the relation $x > y$ defines the set $R = \{(x, y) / x > y\}$ and the set R is a subset of $X \times Y$. More formally:

Definition 2.1

Given $\mathbf{X},\mathbf{Y} \subseteq \chi$, where χ is the universal set, then a *relation* with domain **X** and range **Y** is defined to be any subset **R** of $\mathbf{X} \times \mathbf{Y}$. If $(\mathbf{x},\mathbf{y}) \in \mathbf{R}$ we write $\mathbf{x}R\mathbf{y}$, and if $\mathbf{X} = \mathbf{Y}$ we say that R is a *relation on* χ.

A relation can be considered in two ways each of which has its uses. Fig. 2.2 illustrates that we can consider a relation as a set, generally of the form $\mathbf{R} = \{(x,y)/\ \phi(x,y)\}$ where $\phi\,(x,y)$ is a statement about **x** and **y**, e.g. '**x** is greater than y'. However, as the definition indicates, we can write the relation between **x** and y in the form xRy. This way of presenting a relation is particularly useful because we can readily write its negation as $\sim(xRy)$, i.e. '**x** is not in this relation to **y**'. In terms of the figure it would be the complement of R, viz. $\bar{R}$.

In much of the discussion to follow, both in this chapter and the next, we shall be concerned with particular types of relations because each type has desirable or undesirable properties. For ease of reference we shall define the major six basic relations:

Definition 2.2

A relation R on χ is

1. Reflexive if $\quad \forall x \in \chi \quad xRx$
2. Transitive if $\quad \forall x,y,z \in \chi \quad (xRy \;\&\; yRz) \Rightarrow xRz$
3. Anti-symmetric if $\quad \forall x,y \in \chi \quad (xRy \;\&\; yRx) \Rightarrow x = y$
4. Complete if $\quad \forall x,y \in \chi \quad (x \neq y) \Rightarrow (xRy \veebar yRx)$
5. Asymmetric if $\quad \forall x,y \in \chi \quad xRy \Rightarrow \sim(yRx)$
6. Symmetric if $\quad \forall x,y \in \chi \quad xRy \Rightarrow yRx$

Consider, for example, the relation 'taller than' as applied to a set of university students. It is not reflexive because John cannot be taller than himself. It is transitive since if John is taller than Joan and Joan is taller than Bill then John must be taller than Bill. If John is taller than Bill and Bill is taller than John are both true this must imply John and Bill are one and the same person, so that the relation is anti-symmetric. It is not complete because if John and Bill are different people it does not follow that John is taller than Bill or that Bill is taller than John, they may be both the same height. It is, however, asymmetric because if Bill is taller than John then it follows that John cannot be taller than Bill. The truth of asymmetry must rule out the truth of the symmetry of this particular relation.

We can use some of these relations to define other types by combining Definitions 1–6 in various ways. We shall consider first an *order relation.* It is unfortunate that this relation has grown in economics in a haphazard fashion and different writers have used different interpretations of order. Table 2.1 sets out the interpretations given by Debreu [30], Arrow [7], Lancaster [73] and Sen [111].

The important distinction, however one wishes to define each, is that between a *quasi-ordering* and an *ordering.*

Definition 2.3

1. A relation R on χ is a *quasi-ordering* on χ if it is reflexive and transitive.
2. A relation R on χ is an *ordering* on χ if it is reflexive, transitive, and anti-symmetric.

TABLE 2.1

Relation numbers	*Debreu*	*Arrow*	*Lancaster*	*Sen*
A. 1 and 2	Preordering		Quasi-ordering	Quasi-ordering
B. 1, 2 and 3	Ordering		Ordering	Partial ordering
C. 1, 2 and 4	Complete preordering	Weak ordering	Complete quasi-ordering	Ordering
D. 1, 2, 3 and 4	Complete ordering		Complete ordering	Chain
E. 1, 2, 4 and 5		Strong ordering		

The quasi-ordering and ordering relations in Definition 2.3 are sometimes considered as *partial.* The addition of the completeness condition gives rise to a *complete* quasi-ordering and a *complete* ordering. In making a distinction between weak and strong orderings the condition of asymmetry is introduced. In this book we shall take a weak ordering to be synonymous with a complete quasi-ordering and a strong ordering to include, in addition to those of a complete ordering, the condition of asymmetry.[3] The following schema, Fig. 2.3, is useful in keeping these distinctions clear. The lower half refers to the more general conditions, the upper half to the more rigid conditions, and the numbers refer to the list of relations given in Definition 2.2.

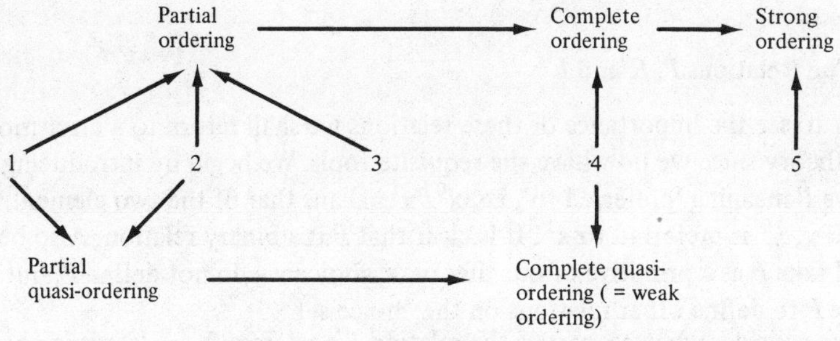

Fig. 2.3

It is well to realise that the reason why we are interested in orderings is because consistency in behaviour requires that an individual has an ordering. A quasi-ordering has attracted the attention of economists because it requires the least objectionable relations, viz. reflexivity and transitivity. What holds for quasi-orderings must hold for an ordering but not necessarily the converse. Similarly, what holds for a complete quasi-ordering holds for a complete ordering but not necessarily the converse. An ordering, as defined in Definition 2.3.2, is used particularly by logicians and mathematicians. As far as economics is concerned interest centres on quasi-orderings and whether they are partial or complete. The reason for this is because for an individual we need only assume reflexivity and transitivity whilst for a group (society) social preferences (see Appendix 2B – Axiom 2B.1) must be complete. Even when we consider an individual's preferences, if we wish that a choice is always to be made then, as will be made clear below, preferences must give rise to a complete quasi-ordering.

A second most important type of relation which we shall make constant use of in consumer theory and production theory, is the *equivalence relation.*

Definition 2.4

A relation R on χ is an *equivalence relation* if it is reflexive, symmetric, and transitive.

Take for example the set **U** of all the students in a university. Let the relation R denote 'is the same sex as'. Then R is reflexive because Sue is clearly the same sex as Sue. It is symmetric because if John is the same sex as Bill then Bill is the same sex as John. Finally, R is transitive because if Jane is the same sex as Sue and Sue is the same sex as Pamela then Jane and Pamela are of the same sex. Hence, R denoting 'is the same sex' is an equivalence relation. It is also apparent that this particular equivalence relation partitions the set **U** into two classes, namely the class of males, **M**, and the class of females, **F**. Notice also that each element of **U** belongs to one or other of the equivalence classes and for R to be a *partition* of **U** (in the mathematical sense) we also require that $\mathbf{M} \cup \mathbf{F} = \mathbf{U}$ and $\mathbf{M} \cap \mathbf{F} = \mathbf{L}$, which is clearly true.

2.4 The Relations *P*, *R* and *I*

In order to see the importance of these relations we shall return to a discussion of choice theory since we now have the requisite tools. We begin by introducing the primitive P meaning 'preferred to', i.e. $\mathbf{x}^0 P \mathbf{x}^1$ means that of the two elements $\mathbf{x}^0, \mathbf{x}^1 \in \chi$, $\mathbf{x}^0$ is preferred to $\mathbf{x}^1$. It is clear that P is a binary relation. Also because we shall take P as a primitive of our theory of choice we do not define P, but we shall use P to define other relations on the choice set.

Let us consider what properties the relation P possesses. It is clear it is not reflexive, for it is not true that $\mathbf{x}P\mathbf{x}$, i.e. it is true that $\sim(\mathbf{x}P\mathbf{x})$. It is not complete because if $\mathbf{x}^0$ is not equal to $\mathbf{x}^1$ in the choice set, then it is possible that neither $\mathbf{x}^0 P \mathbf{x}^1$ and $\mathbf{x}^1 P \mathbf{x}^0$. It may or may not be transitive, but it is anti-symmetric. The truth of the asymmetry implies the truth of anti-symmetry and asymmetry is clearly true. Finally, P is not symmetric. In that P is not reflexive we cannot have a quasi-ordering or an ordering by the relation P alone.[4] This follows from the truth of the condition for $\mathbf{x}^0, \mathbf{x}^1 \in \chi$, $\sim(\mathbf{x}^0 P \mathbf{x}^1)$ and $\sim(\mathbf{x}^1 P \mathbf{x}^0)$. To take account of this we use the equivalence relation to define indifference in terms of the primitive P:

Definition 2.5

(Indifference) $\forall \mathbf{x}^0, \mathbf{x}^1 \in \chi \; \mathbf{x}^0 I \mathbf{x}^1 \Leftrightarrow [\sim(x^0 P x^1) \,\&\, \sim(x^1 P x^0)]$, where $\mathbf{x}^0 I \mathbf{x}^1$, is read $\mathbf{x}^0$ is indifferent to $\mathbf{x}^1$, i.e. that $\mathbf{x}^0$ and $\mathbf{x}^1$ are ranked equally.

We must take note of three things. First, as we pointed out in Chapter 1, p. 6 we do not require to introduce *I* as a primitive because we can define *I* in terms of *P*, therefore we require only *P*. Second, we have *not* introduced the notion of utility; and in particular $\mathbf{x}^0 I \mathbf{x}^1$ does not necessarily mean that the elements $\mathbf{x}^0$ and $\mathbf{x}^1$ have equal utility. The concept is quite general; all we are supposing is that they are ranked equally. Third, *I* is reflexive, transitive, and symmetric and hence is an equivalence relation. However, it is not anti-symmetric, complete, or asymmetric.

Having defined *I* in terms of *P* we can define *R*, meaning 'at least preferred to', in terms of *P* and *I*, thus:

Definition 2.6

$$\forall \mathbf{x}^0, \mathbf{x}^1 \in \chi \; \mathbf{x}^0 R \mathbf{x}^1 \Leftrightarrow [\mathbf{x}^0 P \mathbf{x}^1 \text{ or } \mathbf{x}^0 I \mathbf{x}^1].$$

For ease of reference Table 2.2 sets out which relations in Definition 2.2 are satisfied by *P*, *R* and *I*.

TABLE 2.2

Relations	*P*	*R*	*I*
1. Reflexive	Not true	True	True
2. Transitive	True	True	True
3. Anti-symmetric	True	Not true	Not true
4. Complete	Not true	True	Not true
5. Asymmetric	True	Not true	Not true
6. Symmetric	Not true	Not true	True

The relation *I*, in being reflexive and transitive, establishes a partial quasi-ordering on the elements of the set χ. Therefore, by applying the equivalence relation on the set χ we can obtain a set of indifference sets, $\mathbf{I}_1, \mathbf{I}_2, \ldots, \mathbf{I}_k$, where each set is composed of no elements, one element, or many elements each of which are ranked equally. These sets must be mutually exclusive for, otherwise, if one element from one indifference set also belonged to a second indifference set, by definition of indifference, the two sets would be indifferent and they would therefore be one set. Hence *I* partitions χ into the equivalence classes $\mathbf{I}_1, \ldots, \mathbf{I}_k$. Now apply the relation *P* to the sets $\mathbf{I}_1$ to $\mathbf{I}_k$. Since we have for $\mathbf{I}_1 \neq \mathbf{I}_2$ the condition $\{\mathbf{I}_1 P \mathbf{I}_2 \text{ or } \mathbf{I}_2 P \mathbf{I}_1\}$ then *P* completely orders $\mathbf{I}_1, \ldots, \mathbf{I}_k$. Furthermore, *P* applied to $\mathbf{I}_1, \ldots, \mathbf{I}_k$ is both transitive and asymmetric and therefore anti-symmetric. An *induced* strong ordering over the sets $\mathbf{I}_1, \ldots, \mathbf{I}_k$ is thus established.

2.5 The Axioms of Choice Theory[5]

We are now in a position to state our first axiom of choice theory, the axiom of comparability.

Axiom 1 (Comparability) $\forall \mathbf{x}^0, \mathbf{x}^1 \in \chi \qquad (\mathbf{x}^0 P \mathbf{x}^1 \text{ or } \mathbf{x}^1 P \mathbf{x}^0 \text{ or } \mathbf{x}^0 I \mathbf{x}^1)$

This axiom says no more than of two things offered for choice we either prefer one of them or we are indifferent between them. It means that $\mathbf{x}^0$ and $\mathbf{x}^1$ can be compared. This is by no means a self-evident truth and yet it clearly belongs to the class P_α of fundamental propositions referred to in section 1.2. The question arises: Under what conditions is it not possible to compare $\mathbf{x}^0$ and $\mathbf{x}^1$? The usual answer is lack of information concerning the objects $\mathbf{x}^0$ and $\mathbf{x}^1$. The argument being that in a world of certainty the two elements $\mathbf{x}^0$ and $\mathbf{x}^1$ can be ranked, i.e. they can be compared. This does not mean that the choosing agent is necessarily faced with all choices; it means only that if any two choices are offered to him he can always state a preference or an indifference.

This does mean that indifference and lack of completeness are logically distinct. If one is indifferent then choosing something is preferable to choosing nothing, and if truly indifferent whichever is chosen will give rise to no loss and therefore no regret in having chosen one rather than the other. However, in the case of incompleteness of preferences no decision can be made [112]. It will, therefore, be assumed that Axiom 1 is a convention which limits the range of application of the theory to *choice under certainty.* It is possible to consider choice under uncertainty, but to do this we must introduce probabilistic propositions. Some comments on an axiomatic treatment of uncertain choices will be found in Appendix 2A to this chapter.

Given that any three points can be compared we must introduce some 'thread' to the preferences and to do this we assume that preferences are transitive:

Axiom 2 (Transitivity) $\forall \mathbf{x}^0, \mathbf{x}^1, \mathbf{x}^2 \in \chi \qquad (\mathbf{x}^0 P \mathbf{x}^1 \;\&\; \mathbf{x}^1 P \mathbf{x}^2 \Rightarrow \mathbf{x}^0 P \mathbf{x}^2)$

It is important to be clear that transitivity applies to discrete points besides continuous preferences; in other words, transitivity does not presuppose the continuity of preferences. The converse is true however; continuity implies transitivity (see Section 2.6 below). At this stage we do not wish to restrict the range of application too greatly and consequently we do not take as our axiom that of continuity. This is an important point because we shall see when we come to discuss economic choices that neoclassical theory assumes continuity and hence eliminates from analysis the study of indivisible goods.

To make explicit the fact that P is a partial ordering we introduce the axiom of asymmetry which emphasises the fact that indifference can arise.

Axiom 3 (Asymmetry) $\forall \mathbf{x}^0, \mathbf{x}^1 \in \chi \qquad [\sim(\mathbf{x}^0 P \mathbf{x}^1) \,\underline{\vee}\, \sim(\mathbf{x}^1 P \mathbf{x}^0)]$

i.e. $\mathbf{x}^0$ is not preferred to $\mathbf{x}^1$ or that $\mathbf{x}^1$ is not preferred to $\mathbf{x}^0$ or the fact that both $\mathbf{x}^0$ is not preferred to $\mathbf{x}^1$ and $\mathbf{x}^1$ is not preferred to $\mathbf{x}^0$; in other words, you cannot have both $\mathbf{x}^0$ preferred to $\mathbf{x}^1$ and $\mathbf{x}^1$ preferred to $\mathbf{x}^0$, but in saying this we do not rule out indifference. This means P cannot give a strong ordering on χ. However, we have established that with the aid of the equivalence relation, I, we can establish an *induced* strong ordering.

So far we have the situation that the choice set χ can be divided into the attainable set $\mathbf{A}$ and the unattainable set $\bar{\mathbf{A}}$. That all the elements of χ can be compared and, with the aid of the relations P and I, an induced strong ordering of the elements in χ can be obtained. Let us suppose, then, that the highest indifference set consists of only one element. Can it be said that this element will be the chosen one? From Axioms 1–3 alone we cannot guarantee this! We must therefore introduce further axioms which will guarantee that whatever object(s) are ranked highest are the ones actually chosen. These are referred to as the *axioms of rationality*.

In order to discuss the axioms of rationality we must introduce into our analysis two further primitives, the characteristic of being attainable A, and the act of being chosen, C. Thus $A\mathbf{x}$ will denote that the element $\mathbf{x}$ is attainable ($\sim A\mathbf{x}$ will denote that $\mathbf{x}$ is not attainable), and $C\mathbf{x}$ will denote that the element $\mathbf{x}$ is chosen (and $\sim C\mathbf{x}$ that $\mathbf{x}$ is not chosen), where $\mathbf{x} \in \chi$.

We have argued above that the attainable set arises because of a constraint on choices; it would appear reasonable therefore to argue that any actual choice must come from an element in the attainable set. If we can choose between jam and shoes but cannot even contemplate the choosing of a Rolls-Royce, given our budget, then our behaviour must be reflected in our assessment of jam and shoes. If a Rolls-Royce is unattainable, for this given budget, then it makes sense to say that whatever is chosen we know that it will not be a Rolls-Royce. Hence, all choices actually made must be possible or attainable. To guarantee this we introduce Axiom 4:

Axiom 4 $\quad \forall \mathbf{x} \in \chi \qquad (C\mathbf{x} \Rightarrow A\mathbf{x})$

This says no more than for any $\mathbf{x} \in \chi$, if $\mathbf{x}$ is chosen then it must be that $\mathbf{x}$ is also attainable.

Suppose jam and marmalade are both attainable and suppose further that marmalade is strictly preferred to jam. The axioms so far presented will not guarantee that if jam and marmalade are offered as a choice that marmalade will be the item actually chosen. If a consumer is to be rational we require that of all the objects attainable he will in fact choose the most preferred or, alternatively, he will never choose the less preferred – thus allowing for indifference. We therefore introduce the following axiom:

Axiom 5 $\quad \forall \mathbf{x}^0, \mathbf{x}^1 \in \chi \qquad [(\mathbf{x}^0 P \mathbf{x}^1 \;\&\; A\mathbf{x}^0) \Rightarrow \sim C\mathbf{x}^1]$

i.e. if we have two choices $\mathbf{x}^0$ and $\mathbf{x}^1$, the least preferred will not be chosen when the more preferred is attainable. The reason for stating Axiom 5 in what appears a negative way is because we do not wish to state the following:

$$\forall \mathbf{x}^0, \mathbf{x}^1 \in \chi \qquad [(\mathbf{x}^0 P \mathbf{x}^1) \;\&\; A\mathbf{x}^0) \Rightarrow C\mathbf{x}^0]$$

since this implies more than $x^0 P x^1$; it implies that x^0 is the most preferred of all $x \in A$, rather than just preferred to x^1. It is clear then that Axiom 5 will not in itself guarantee that a choice will be made. Furthermore, if **A** consists of only one element, x^0 say, then by Axiom 5 we cannot say that x^0 will be chosen even though it is attainable. We accordingly overcome this difficulty with Axiom 6.

Axiom 6 $\quad \exists x \in \chi \quad Ax \Rightarrow \exists x \quad Cx$

i.e. if there exists at least one **x** which is attainable then there will always be some **x** chosen. Thus, if something is attainable the less preferred will never be chosen, and that something *will* be chosen.

The final axiom is somewhat technical but we can approach it in stages. Suppose the boundary of **A**, as drawn in Fig. 2.4, does not in fact belong to the attainable

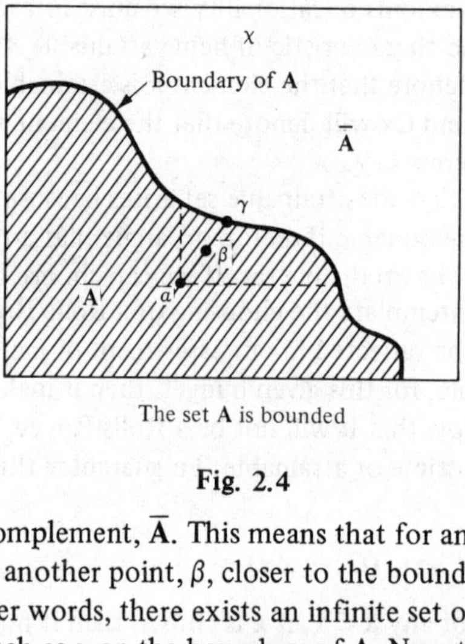

The set A is bounded

Fig. 2.4

set but rather to its complement, $\bar{A}$. This means that for any point in **A**, such as α, we can always find another point, β, closer to the boundary such that β is preferred to α. In other words, there exists an infinite set of points between a given point α and a point such as γ on the boundary of **A**. Now the axioms so far only ensure that if there exists an **x** then an **x** is chosen and that the least preferred will not be chosen. But in the present case the choosing agent would not make a choice because there does not exist a most preferred element. The same situation arises if the set **A** is an infinite set. In Fig. 2.5 we have let $A = \chi$ and supposed χ to be the whole non-negative quadrant. Once again we cannot stipulate that there exists a most preferred point.

The first case we say that the set **A** is *open,* meaning it does not contain its boundary; while the second is *unbounded,* meaning it cannot be enclosed in a finite figure (say a square or a circle).[6] Notice that the attainable set in Fig. 2.4, although open, is none the less bounded. In order to eliminate this problem of infinite spaces we introduce Axiom 7 which limits our domain of study to finite spaces, i.e. it restricts our analysis to closed and bounded attainable sets.

Axiom 7 $\quad \exists x^0 \in \chi \qquad [Ax^0 \;\&\; \forall x^1 \,(Ax^1 \Rightarrow x^0 P x^1 \text{ or } x^0 I x^1)]$

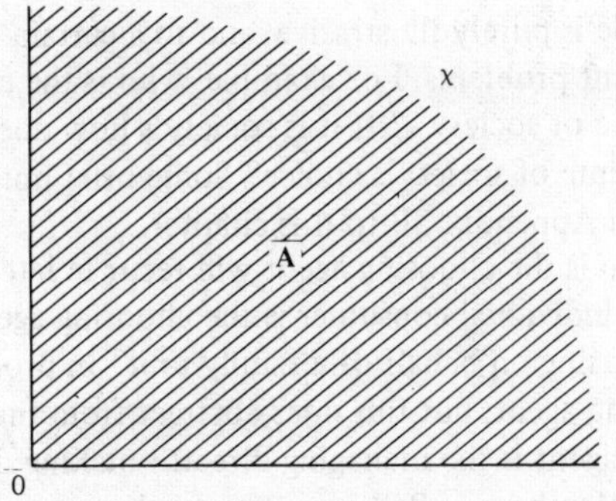

The set A is unbounded

Fig. 2.5

i.e. there exists at least one $\mathbf{x}^0$ such that $\mathbf{x}^0$ is attainable, and for all $\mathbf{x}^1$, if $\mathbf{x}^1$ is attainable then $\mathbf{x}^0$ is either preferred to $\mathbf{x}^1$ or is indifferent to $\mathbf{x}^1$.

Axioms 1–7 are the foundations of the general theory of choice under certainty. They guarantee that for any choice problem the universal set of choices can be divided into two mutually exclusive sets: the attainable set and the unattainable set. The attainable set is closed and bounded and consists of at least one element. All the elements of the universal set can be compared, and with the application of P and I an induced strong ordering can be established. Since the attainable set is non-empty there will be a chosen element and, by the rationality axioms, this chosen element will come from the most preferred indifference set. Take, for example, a choice to be made by the government between inflation and unemployment. Axioms 1–7 imply that these can be compared, that there exists an attainable set which is closed and, although not bounded, is bounded from below by the Phillips curve, which is all we require in this instance. We can establish a complete quasi-ordering and, assuming the government is a rational decision-making body as here defined, there will exist a most preferred, i.e. least objectionable, unemployment–inflation combination.

Take as another example the choice of Prime Minister. The choice set χ is the members of the House of Commons of the party in power. Of these we shall suppose only five belong to the attainable set, and further suppose that these are denoted by the first five elements of χ. Thus $\chi = \{x_1, x_2, \ldots, x_s\}$ where s is the total number of members of the ruling government.

$$\mathbf{A} = \{x_1, x_2, x_3, x_4, x_5\} \text{ and } \bar{\mathbf{A}} = \{x_6, x_7, \ldots, x_s\}.$$

The set **A** is non-empty, closed and bounded. Suppose we have

$$\mathbf{I}_1 = \{x_1\},\ \mathbf{I}_2 = \{x_2, x_3\},\ \mathbf{I}_3 = \{x_4\},\ \mathbf{I}_4 = \{x_5\} \text{ with } \mathbf{I}_1 P \mathbf{I}_2 P \mathbf{I}_3 P \mathbf{I}_4,$$

then clearly by Axioms 1–7, member x_1 will be chosen as Prime Minister.

This second example is purely illustrative, and to a certain degree is also avoiding some important problems. For example, who is the chosing agent? Is this just one person's choice or society's? If it is society's how does the individual's choice fit into the scheme of society's choice? Some brief notes on community choice will be found in Appendix 2B to this chapter.

The problem of who is the choosing agent will recur in later chapters. In consumer demand the individual consumer is the choosing agent, but is it as simple as this, is he not purchasing on behalf of a family unit? In production theory the producer is the choosing agent, but this does abstract from the joint stock company in which the choosing agent is the managing director making decisions on behalf of the shareholders. The Members of Parliament make decisions on behalf of the people. To the extent that preferences are left undefined, we do not need to go into the psychology of the choosing agents. In other words, by employing P as a primitive, rather than something else, we are undertaking a positive act of limiting the theory to observed behaviour, and take the psychology of such acts as outside the province of study. We must, however, be quite clear about who the choosing agent represents because a different choosing agent will have a different ranking of the elements of the choice set.

2.6 Continuity of Preferences[7]

Continuity is generally considered as a purely mathematical problem and yet Axioms 1–7 do not involve this concept at all; nowhere have we said that the preference ordering must be continuous (to be defined rigorously below). Why then consider continuity at all? The reason lies in the economist's interest not in choices *per se,* which is the content of this chapter, but in the choices by consumers for economic goods and by producers in choosing the best technique of production. For such problems continuity of preference is considered an essential element in their theoretical treatment. Most of the literature invariably takes the preference ordering to be continuous from the outset, and the axiom of continuity will be found in such works as G. Debreu's *Theory of Value* [30, p. 52].

Unfortunately there are a number of interpretations of continuity used in the literature. We shall list here the three most common alternatives.

Definition 2.7 (i)

> A preference relation P on χ is continuous if in going from a position where $\sim(\mathbf{x}P\mathbf{y})$ to one where $\mathbf{x}P\mathbf{y}$ the agent passes through a position where $\mathbf{x}I\mathbf{y}$.

Definition 2.7 (ii)

> A preference relation P on χ is continuous if for $\mathbf{x}^0$, $\mathbf{y}^0$ and $\mathbf{x}^0P\mathbf{y}^0$ we have the condition that for any $\mathbf{x}$ close to $\mathbf{x}^0$ it is preferred to $\mathbf{y}^0$, and for any point close to $\mathbf{y}^0$, $\mathbf{x}^0$ is preferred to this.

Definition 2.7 (iii)

A preference relation P on χ is continuous if for any $\mathbf{x}^0$ the set $\{\mathbf{x}/\ \mathbf{x} \in \chi, \mathbf{x}^0 P \mathbf{x}\}$ is an open set.[8]

Definition 2.7 (i) is employed by Wald and Marschak [82] and it is the one most frequently used in the discussions of choice under uncertainty, e.g. Baumol [13, 14]. Definition 2.7 (ii) has been employed by Pearce [95, p. 24]; whilst Definition 2.7 (iii) has been used by more modern writers such as Uzawa [121].

As pointed out above, the interest in continuity arises from the economist's concern most particularly with consumer theory. As we shall see in the next chapter, to establish an order preserving function we must have the condition of continuity. However, to take the discussion further requires the application of some mathematical tools employed by the more recent writers on economic theory, and these we shall investigate in the first part of the next chapter.

2.7 'The' General Economic Problem

Lionel Robbins in his *The Nature and Significance of Economic Science* has said that 'Economics is the science which studies human behaviour as a relationship between ends and scarce means which have alternative uses' [104, p. 16]. Such scarce means limit our choices to those that can be attained and in terms of the present discussion amounts to the attainable set **A**. On the other hand, the ends reflect the preferences of the choosing agent which can be represented either by a preference relation, as outlined in the present chapter, or by a preference function. In modern parlance, therefore, 'the' economic problem is one of optimising (i.e. either maximising or minimising) some preference function subject to a set of constraints.

However, the principles of choice we have considered so far are very general and in order to consider any particular choice problem we must be more specific. This specificity arises in two directions. First, in order to designate our attainable set we must be very clear on the restrictions we impose on the choices to be made by a choosing agent. Second, in order to rank the elements of our choice set we require a clear statement of how this is to be done. Furthermore, the criterion for ranking will change from problem to problem, e.g. we use utility in consumer theory and profits in production theory. We see, therefore, that this chapter has directed our attention to two considerations:

(1) What is the form of the attainable set, i.e. what restrictions are imposed on the choice set?

(2) Can we establish a *preference function* which will give us our criterion for ranking the elements of the choice set?

Let us consider these two questions a little more formally. Suppose that our choice set is given by S and that we wish to rank the elements $\mathbf{x} \in S$. Suppose further that we have a preference function or objective function as it is sometimes called. There is no reason why the preference function should be defined over all the elements of the choice set. Therefore, let χ be a subset of S, i.e. $\chi \subseteq S$, and let this denote the set of elements of the choice set over which the preference function is defined. In other words,

$$\mathbf{Y} = \{y/y = F(\mathbf{x}), \mathbf{x} \in \chi\}$$

denotes the preference function. Our problem amounts to maximising or minimising the preference function subject to the fact that the element **x** must belong to the attainable set **A**. We have in more general terms (where we have stated only a maximum) the constrained optimisation problem

$$\begin{aligned} &\max.\ y = F(\mathbf{x}) \\ &\mathbf{x} \in \chi \\ &\text{s.t. } \mathbf{x} \in \mathbf{A} \end{aligned}$$

where s.t. denotes 'subject to'.

Even this general formulation is revealing. No matter what we take as the objective function, the constraints remain the same for these are given by the problem under discussion. In the theory of the firm, for example, we have production, cost, and resource constraints; but whatever they are they remain the same whether we have as our objective function that of profits or whether we have total revenue.[9] What does matter when we take alternative preference functions are the values obtained in the solution to the constrained optimisation problem. There is no reason to suppose that, with the same constraints but a different preference function, the solutions will be the same. This is the essence of the various theories of the firm. Different preference functions, i.e. goals of the firm, have been proposed but these cannot alter the constraints although they will alter the solution values. Take, for example, the three alternative objectives: (1) profit maximisation, (2) revenue maximisation and (3) to break-even. It is well known from elementary economics that the first has the smallest output and the highest price of the three listed. Revenue maximisation has a higher output and a lower price compared with profit maximisation. Finally, for those who have as an objective to break-even, their output will be greater and their price the lowest of the three forms of behaviour (see Exercise 9).

We can go a little further. The constraints can generally take two forms which must be clearly appreciated because the mathematical technique for handling them is quite different. These are:

(1) equality constraints,
(2) inequality constraints.

Also the preference function may take special forms, e.g. linear, quadratic, etc. For ease of reference we classify in Table 2.3 some of the most common situations met with in economics and allied disciplines. Also, in order to keep the table compact, we have set the alternatives in terms of matrix notation and throughout the book we shall refer back to this table. $F(\mathbf{x})$ denotes the objective function, which can take any form in classical and non-linear programming. However, in linear programming, as its name implies, the objective function is linear,

$$F(\mathbf{x}) = \mathbf{c}'\mathbf{x} = c_1x_1 + \ldots + c_nx_n;$$

while in quadratic programming the objective function is expressed as a quadratic equation, e.g.

$$F(\mathbf{x}) = b_{11}\, x_1^2 + 2b_{12}\, x_1\, x_2 + b_{22}\, x_2^2$$

(where we have assumed that **B** is a 2 x 2 symmetric matrix).

$$\mathbf{g}(\mathbf{x}) = \mathbf{b},\, \mathbf{x} \geqslant 0 \text{ or } \mathbf{g}(\mathbf{x}) \leqslant \mathbf{b},\, \mathbf{x} \geqslant 0$$

is the constraint set. In other words, it gives an algebraic form to the attainable set, **A**. Classical programming has equality constraints although the attainable set can take on any shape. In the case of non-linear programming the attainable set takes the same shape as classical programming, but the latter is merely the boundary of the former. In the case of linear and quadratic programming the boundaries of the attainable sets are linear. These will become clearer as we proceed.

TABLE 2.3

Name	*Form of* $F(\mathbf{x})$	*Form of constraint*	
1. Classical programming	$F(\mathbf{x})$	$\mathbf{g}(\mathbf{x}) = \mathbf{b}$	$\mathbf{x} \geqslant 0$
2. Non-linear programming	$F(\mathbf{x})$	$\mathbf{g}(\mathbf{x}) \leqslant \mathbf{b}$	$\mathbf{x} \geqslant 0$
3. Linear programming	$F(\mathbf{x}) = \mathbf{c}'\mathbf{x}$	$\mathbf{A}\mathbf{x} \leqslant \mathbf{b}$	$\mathbf{x} \geqslant 0$
4. Quadratic programming	$F(\mathbf{x}) = \mathbf{x}'\mathbf{B}\mathbf{x}$	$\mathbf{A}\mathbf{x} \leqslant \mathbf{b}$	$\mathbf{x} \geqslant 0$

To conclude this section let us illustrate the importance of distinguishing between equality and inequality constraints by means of an example. Suppose we have a profit function which is expressed in terms of output, i.e.

$$\pi(y) = 8y - y^2 - 12.$$

Let

$$\mathbf{Y} = \{y/0 \leqslant y < +\infty\}$$

denote the set of all possible outputs. The objective is to maximise profits. However, we shall suppose output is constrained. Consider two alternative constraints, (1) an equality constraint $\mathbf{A}_1 = \{y/y = 5\}$ and (2) an inequality constraint $\mathbf{A}_2 = \{y/0 \leqslant y \leqslant 5\}$. Since the solution to the maximisation problem must be contained in the constraint set then the solution under $\mathbf{A}_1$ can be nothing other than at output $y = 5$ with $\pi(y) = 3$. Where the constraint set takes the form of $\mathbf{A}_2$ then the solution can lie anywhere in the set $\mathbf{A}_2 = \{y/0 \leqslant y \leqslant 5\}$. In this instance the solution is interior at $y = 4$ and $\pi(y) = 4$. Notice, however, that if $\mathbf{A}_1 = \{y/y = 3\}$ and $\mathbf{A}_2 = \{y/0 \leqslant y \leqslant 3\}$ then both optimisation problems would give

$\mathbf{Y} = \{y / 0 \leqslant y < +\infty\}$ $\qquad$ $\mathbf{Y} = \{y / 0 \leqslant y < +\infty\}$

$\mathbf{A}_1 = \{y / y = 5\}$ $\qquad$ $\mathbf{A}_2 = \{y / 0 \leqslant y \leqslant 5\}$

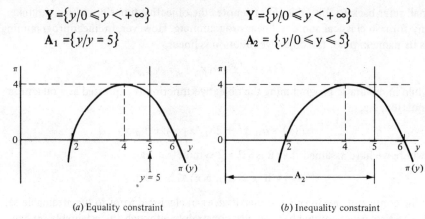

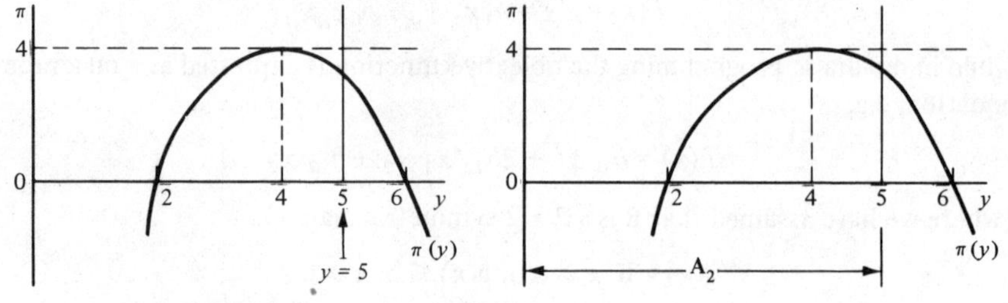

(*a*) Equality constraint $\qquad$ (*b*) Inequality constraint

Fig. 2.6

the same solution. The reader should reflect on this by asking himself whether in consumer theory a consumer always settles on his budget line or at an interior point to it?[10] Also, if one is considering under-capacity utilisation how must the constraint set be specified?

2.8 Some Unsettled Questions

There are a number of issues in the theory of choice which have not yet been resolved. The fact that we set out our axiom set so boldly does not necessarily mean that everything is now known about choice. The reason why there is still disagreement is because we use axioms not as necessary truths but more in terms of conventions (see Section 1.2 (i)). There is no reason why such conventions should be the same! However, to some degree we can account for differences in the axiom set. To the extent that some might argue that completeness (comparability) is not a necessary axiom they often imply choices are made in uncertain circumstances. If one cannot choose between a holiday in Spain or a holiday in Greece is this because one's knowledge about these places is insufficient to make a choice? There is certainly a growing interest in transactions costs which are encountered in obtaining information [72]. How we deal with such problems, however, is still being debated.

Transitivity has always been a debated axiom. This seems to be one of those axioms which are 'obvious-truths' rather than a convention. It is the vital ingredient that gives us consistency. (However see Exercise 6.) But it is not clear to what extent we can do away with this axiom. Psychologists have attempted to carry out experiments in order to see whether this in fact is true [87]; some economists have seen how far they can take the theory of consumer behaviour under the assumption of intransitive choices, such as Sonnenschein [117] and Chipman [24]. However, both areas of investigation have had little success.

In this text we have taken a rational person to be one satisfying, in particular, Axioms 4–7, the rationality axioms. But can we discuss choices which are irrational? Is it not possible to require only consistency and not necessarily rationality? Irrational behaviour has been studied by such economists as Arrow [7], Becker [16] and Richter [103].

With these reservations in mind, along with those discussed in Appendices 2A and 2B, we now turn to consumer theory as our first particular application of the theory of choice.

Appendix 2A

CHOICE UNDER UNCERTAINTY*

Axioms 1–7 of Chapter 2 concern only certain choices in which the *state of the world* is complete, i.e. every consequence of every action is known to the choosing agent. In conditions of certainty, therefore, every action implies a unique consequence and hence choices among consequences is equivalent to choices among actions. However, some choices involve imperfect knowledge which inevitably introduces the element of uncertainty. Furthermore, the rules of choice under certainty would not explain such phenomenon as insurance. In both cases it is the uncertainty as seen by the individual and this is subjective. In the situation of uncertainty, therefore, an action may not uniquely determine the consequences of an agent. It follows from this that a structure of choices among consequences is not sufficient to determine choices among actions because there no longer exists a one-to-one correspondence between consequences and actions [9].

The choice we have just alluded to is in fact only one interpretation. The stochastic element in this analysis lies in the act of choice, and it is therefore referred to as *stochastic act of choice* by G. Debreu [28]. An alternative analysis used by D. Davidson and P. Suppes [27] introduce the stochastic element into the objects of choice, and this is referred to as *stochastic objects of choice.* In the latter case the universal set χ is composed of sure prospects such as commodities, and the problem is deciding on even chance mixtures of pairs of sure prospects. The former gives a different interpretation to the universal set χ. In this case χ is the set of all actions. In the stochastic act of choice if a and b are two actions belonging to χ then the choosing agent is asked to choose one. He chooses action a with probability α and action b with probability $1 - \alpha$. In what follows we shall confine ourselves to stochastic acts of choice.

Let us now introduce some notation. Let the set χ be composed of all actions and is given for any problem. A choosing agent is presented with a pair (a, b) and is asked to choose one. He chooses action a with probability α, written $\alpha(a, b)$, and action b with probability $1 - \alpha$, written $\alpha(b, a) = 1 - \alpha(a, b)$. The relation $\alpha(a, b) > \frac{1}{2}$ is taken to mean 'a is preferred to b', i.e. aPb if and only if $\alpha(a, b) > \frac{1}{2}$. If we write $\alpha(a, b) > \alpha(c, d)$ this is read as 'a is preferred to b more than c is preferred to d'. Our present problem amounts to establishing the axioms required to order the elements of the set χ so we can, even under uncertainty, predict the choices made by the choosing agent. It is to be noted, however, that the choice under certainty is a special case of the present problem. In the case of certainty all probabilities are either 0 or 1, hence $\alpha(a, b) = 1$ is the condition that aPb with certainty.

*This appendix presupposes a knowledge of the material in Chapter 3, and ideally should not be read until Chapter 3 has been completed.

Stemming from the work of von Neumann and Morgenstern [89] the issue has been to find a utility function U defined on (χ, a). It is not readily apparent that such a function exists and the set of axioms discussed by a number of authors, such as Herstein and Milnor [51], G. Debreu [28], Marschak [82], and K. J. Arrow [9] to name but a few, have supplied different alternatives. These alternatives arise from the different interpretations of choice discussed above. However, the axioms of order, continuity, and indifference are common to most.

In all cases the axioms are stated by means of a utility function which is real valued. The following definitions present explicitly the ideas of a real-valued function, an order-preserving function, and a linear function.

Definition 2A.1

A utility function for (χ, a) is a real-valued function U on χ such that

$$[a(a, b) \leqslant a(c, d)] \Leftrightarrow [U(a) - U(b) \leqslant U(c) - U(d)] .$$

We also require the utility function to be order preserving:

Definition 2A.2

A utility function U on χ is order preserving if

$$\forall\ a, b \in \chi \quad U(a) > U(b) \text{ iff } aPb.$$

Furthermore, it can be shown that any utility function which satisfies the axioms to follow must be linear, where we mean by linearity:

Definition 2A.3

A utility function U on χ is linear if

$$\forall\ a, b \in \chi \text{ and } 0 \leqslant a \leqslant 1 \qquad U[aa + (1 - a)b] = aU(a) + (1 - a)U(b)$$

Let us now state the axioms for choice under uncertainty.

Axiom 2A.1 (Complete ordering) χ is completely ordered by R.
This we have discussed already in Chapter 2.

Axiom 2A.2 (Continuity)

$$\text{If } \forall\ a, b, c \in \chi \quad aPbPc \text{ then } \exists\ a \quad 0 < a < 1 \quad bI[aa + (1 - a)c]$$

Notice how this axiom of continuity uses the concept of continuity contained in Definition 2.7(i) on p. 28.

Axiom 2A.3 (Indifference)

$$\forall\ a, b, c \in \chi \quad \text{if } aIb \text{ then } \exists\ a \quad [aa + (1 - a)c]\,I\,[ab + (1 - a)c] \text{ for any } c.$$

Axiom 2A.4 (Unequal probability) $\forall\ a, b \in \chi$ and α, α' if aPb then

$$[\alpha a + (1-\alpha)b]\ P[\alpha' a + (1-\alpha')b] \quad \text{iff } \alpha > \alpha'.$$

i.e. if other things are equal we always choose the action with the greatest probability of a favourable consequence.

Axiom 2A.5 (Compound probability) $\forall\ a, b \in \chi$ and probabilities $\alpha, \alpha', \alpha''$ we have

$$\alpha[\alpha' a + (1-\alpha')b] + (1-\alpha)\ [\alpha'' a + (1-\alpha'')b]\ I\ [pa + (1-p)b]$$
$$\text{where } p = \alpha\alpha' + (1-\alpha)\alpha''.$$

i.e. given two alternative probabilities α' and α'' that action a will be chosen such that there is a probability of α that α' holds and $1-\alpha$ that α'' holds, then we have a compound probability of $\alpha\alpha' + (1-\alpha)\alpha''$ that action a will be chosen. Alternatively, using our earlier notation $\alpha\ [\alpha'\ (a, b), \alpha''(a, b)] = p(a, b)$, where $p = \alpha\alpha' + (1-\alpha)\alpha''$. Axioms 2A.1–2A.5 allow us to write:

$$U[\alpha a + (1-\alpha)b] = \alpha U(a) + (1-\alpha)U(b).$$

Given such a real-valued order preserving linear function U defined on χ, we can establish α by asking the choosing agent when he is indifferent between the certainty of $b \in \chi$ and the uncertainty of the pair $(a, c) \in \chi$. We have then $\alpha(b, d) = 1$ for any $d \in \chi$ and $0 < \alpha(a, c) < 1$, further that $U\ [\alpha a + (1-\alpha)c] = \alpha U(a) + (1-\alpha)U(c)$, hence:

$$1 \cdot U(b) = \alpha U(a) + (1-\alpha)U(c)$$

As Ellsburg neatly points out [36], if we rearrange the left-hand side to $\alpha U(b) + (1-\alpha)U(b)$ then we can readily see that measurability requires comparison of differences:

$$\alpha U(b) + (1-\alpha)U(b) = \alpha U(a) + (1-\alpha)U(c)$$
$$\text{i.e.}\quad \alpha\ [U(a) - U(b)] = (1-\alpha)\ [U(b) - U(c)].$$

In other words, the amount of utility the choosing agent stands to win by taking a gamble multiplied by the probability of success is equal to the utility of what he stands to lose multiplied by the probability of losing the gamble.

It is also clear that we can obtain α from $U(b) = \alpha U(a) + (1-\alpha)U(c)$

$$\text{i.e.}\quad \alpha = \frac{U(b) - U(c)}{U(a) - U(c)}.$$

We shall conclude this discussion with an important point made by Ellsburg [36]. A number of people over the years have discussed measurable utility, each with the same aim in mind and often using the same symbolism. However, their results in fact differ. Unfortunately, it is not easy to see in what way the differences arise. We can illustrate the problem in the following manner. For cardinal utility the utility function must be defined up to a linear transformation (since only this form of monotone transformation preserves ratios), i.e. $V = a + \beta U$. Now all approaches must obtain this functional form, but since the constants a and β in the function $V = a + \beta U$ are arbitrary, there is no reason to suppose each approach will give the same constants. In particular, since the classical approach and the von Neumann and Morgenstern (N–M) approach did differ it is then likely that the constants from each would also differ. Thus we might have:

Classical	$V^* = a^* + \beta^* U$
N–M	$V = a + \beta U$

There would be no differences in the two if V were a linear transformation of V^*, but it is more likely that it would be a monotone transformation. Hence, 'In general, the order of magnitude of the differences between corresponding numbers would be different for the two indices [i.e. the Classical and N–M]; therefore, prediction based on the rule of maximising moral expectations [i.e. the expected utility equalling $aU(a) + (1 - a)U(b)$] would differ for the two approaches' [93, p. 272].

The approach outlined in this appendix is by no means the only one. A fairly comprehensive stochastic choice model was proposed by Luce in his *Individual Choice Behaviour* [78]. The analysis is based on a fundamental axiom which states a condition that holds among the probabilities of choice from related sets of alternatives. His analysis shows that this axiom implies a ratio scale (a γ-scale). One important aspect of his approach is that some of the predictions are capable of being put to the test (i.e. capable of being falsified). A discussion of various stochastic models will be found in two survey articles by W. Edwards [34, 35].

Appendix 2B

SOCIAL CHOICE

So far we have been dealing with individual choice. Consider now a group of m people each with a ranking relation $P_1, \ldots, P_m$ from which we obtain $R_1, \ldots, R_m$ and $I_1, \ldots, I_m$. The obvious next question is whether we can talk of a ranking relation for the group as an entity. For example, if the group is a whole society can this society rank the states of nature? But immediately we raise this question we must face up to the fundamental philosophical consideration which it entails. We could conceive of the group as having an entity on to itself and is not viewed in terms of its individual members. In this instance social preference is independent of the preference of its members. We could alternatively view the same situation in the sense that there is a connection between individual and social preference but we abstract from it. The fundamental issue is whether society's preferences should or should not depend upon individual preferences. This is not idle speculation. In the history of Western culture we find periods when states of nature were considered 'good' or 'bad' according to some religious decree and decided not by its members but (supposedly) by some omnipotent and omnipresent being. The age of reason and enlightenment brought forth an alternative view which was that man was in large part in control of his own destiny and the members of society can in and of themselves decide whether a state of nature is 'good' or 'bad'. This view is very much with us today and it is at the heart of the American Constitution. What we have concluded, then, is to take as a basic value judgement the following proposition, which we shall call the *Ethical postulate.*

Proposition

(Ethical Postulate) Society's preferences depend upon the preferences of the individuals in that society and on none outside that society.

The first part of this proposition is generally accepted but the additional statement that society's preferences should be independent of members outside of that society is not usually stated. It is, however, important and by no means trivial. For example, if by society we mean a political entity then this proposition rules out choices made by this society which is based on, say, the Pope's decree. The birth pill is an obvious case in point.

The work of Arrow, to which we now turn, is based on the acceptance of this proposition. As we shall see, Arrow established five conditions to show *how* the individual's preferences are to count in society's choices. In other words: What is the rule which uniquely determines the preference ordering of society in terms of the given individual preference orderings? It will be useful to introduce some notation at this point. Let P_i, R_i, and I_i be the relations we have so far discussed which are for the ith individual, noting that only P_i is a primitive, R_i and I_i being defined in terms of P_i. Let the group, sometimes called a society, be composed of m individuals. Let $(P_i) = (P_1, \ldots, P_m)$, $(R_i) = (R_1, \ldots, R_m)$, and $(I_i) = (I_1, \ldots, I_m)$ denote the sets of individual order relations. We shall use analogous notation for the order relations for the group. P will denote the group's strict social preference; R the relation 'at least preferred to by society'; and I the group's indifference.

In order to begin the analysis we must supply some definitions:

Definition 2B.1

A collective choice rule is a functional relation $\emptyset$ such that for any set of m individual orderings (R_i), one, and only one, social preference relation R is determined, i.e. $R = \emptyset(R_1, \ldots, R_m)$.

Definition 2B.2

A social welfare function is a collective choice rule $\emptyset$, the range of which is restricted to the set of *orderings* over χ, where χ is the universal choice set.

In terms of our definitions, Arrow was interested in finding a social welfare function $\emptyset$ such that the social preference relation R, determined uniquely by (R_i), reflected rational choice-making in the sense that R also satisfies Axioms 1–7. It is to be noted that it must satisfy all seven and not just Axioms 1–3. Rationality in Arrow's terms included only the first three axioms but he does require the element chosen to come from the choice function and this means that Axioms 4–7 are applicable. The rationality discussed by M. K. Richter [103] is also in conformity with Axioms 1–7.

We shall now state Arrow's five conditions as five axioms [7, ch. 3; 111, ch. 3*].

Axiom 2B.1 (Completeness) Given any three states, the social ranking R must completely order the preferences of society for any set of individual preference rankings defined over those states, i.e. the domain of the rule $\emptyset$ must include all logically possible combinations of individual orderings.

Axiom 2B.2 (Responsiveness) Let (R_i) and (R'_i) be two sets of order relations defined over two states of the economy **x** and **y**. Let (R'_i) rank **x** higher for some individuals and no lower for all individuals relative to (R_i). Then if under (R_i), $\mathbf{x}P\mathbf{y}$ it implies $\mathbf{x}P'\mathbf{y}$.

Axiom 2B.3 (Independence of irrelevant alternatives). Let (R_i) and (R'_i) be any two sets of individual orderings with R and R' their associated social orderings, and $C(\chi, R)$ and $C(\chi, R')$ their associated choice functions. If for all pairs of alternatives $\mathbf{x}, \mathbf{y} \in \chi$ $\mathbf{x}R_i\mathbf{y} \Leftrightarrow \mathbf{x}R'_i\mathbf{y}$ for all i then $C(\chi, R) = C(\chi, R')$.

Axiom 2B.4 (Nonimposition) The social ranking R is not to be imposed.

Axiom 2B.5 (Nondictatorship) The social ranking R is not to be dictatorial i.e. there is no individual k such that for every element in the domain of rule $\emptyset$

$$\forall \mathbf{x}, \mathbf{y} \in \chi \qquad \mathbf{x} P_k \mathbf{y} \Rightarrow \mathbf{x} P \mathbf{y}$$

regardless of all other members' orderings.

Of these five axioms only Axiom 2B.1 is value free since it only defines the domain over which the social ranking is applicable. Axioms 2B.2–2B.4 are Arrow's value judgements and formulate precisely in what way the ethical postulate stated above is to be understood. Axioms 2B.2 and 2B.4 taken together amount to the condition of consumer's sovereignty. This is made clear if we define precisely what is meant by imposing a social ranking R.

Definition 2B.3

A social ranking R is said to be imposed if, for some distinct pair of alternatives $\mathbf{x}$ and $\mathbf{y}$, $\mathbf{x} R \mathbf{y}$ for *any* set of individual orderings (R_i).

If we negate this condition we obtain

$$\forall (R_i) \quad \sim \exists \mathbf{y} \qquad \mathbf{y} P \mathbf{x}$$

In other words, the economy can never express a preference for $\mathbf{y}$ over $\mathbf{x}$ even if for each individual we have $\mathbf{y} P_i \mathbf{x}$. As Arrow says, some preferences are taboo [7, p.28]. An example of an imposed social ranking would be the Pope's decree that The Pill should not be used by Catholics.

Axiom 2B.2 as stated has a Paretian flavour and we can in fact replace Axioms 2B.2 and 2B.3 with what Arrow calls the Pareto condition.

Axiom 2B.P (Pareto) If $\forall\, i \;\; \mathbf{x} P_i \mathbf{y} \Rightarrow \mathbf{x} P \mathbf{y}$

i.e. if every member of society prefers $\mathbf{x}$ to $\mathbf{y}$ then so does society.

Axiom 2B.3 requires that the social welfare function gives rise to a choice made by society from a given environment and to depend only on the orderings of individuals among the alternatives in that environment. In other words, the choice function $C(\chi, R)$ for given χ depends only on χ and not on the complement of χ. This in essence reduces social choice to a type of voting. It also rules out interpersonal comparisons.

Having set up these five axioms Arrow proved the following theorem:

Theorem 2B.1 (Arrow Possibility Theorem) Given Axioms 2B.1–2B.5 there exists *no* social ranking R which satisfies all axioms simultaneously.

A proof of this theorem can be found in Arrow [7, ch. 5]. We shall here only give a flavour of the theorem. Consider an economy composed of only two individuals and there are three states of nature. Using the above Axioms 2B.1 – 2B.5 we can establish the following two lemmas:

Lemma 2B.1 $xP_1y \;\&\; xP_2y \Rightarrow xPy$

Lemma 2B.2 $xP_1y \;\&\; yP_2x \Rightarrow xIy$

i.e. when both members prefer **x** to **y** then so does society; when both members rank **x** and **y** in reverse order then society is indifferent between them.

Now suppose we have the following individual rankings:

Individual 1 xP_1yP_1z

Individual 2 yP_2zP_2x

Employing Lemmas 2B.1 and 2B.2 we establish the following conditions:

(1) $yP_1z \;\&\; yP_2z \Rightarrow yPz$

(2) $xP_1y \;\&\; yP_2x \Rightarrow xIy$

(3) $xP_1z \;\&\; zP_2x \Rightarrow xIz$

But, by transitivity, if yPz and xIy then it follows xPz, but this contradicts the result in (3). In other words, the assumption that there exists a social welfare function compatible with Axioms 2B.1–2B.5 has led to a contradiction.

There are a number of social rankings which we can derive from the individual rankings according to which criteria we wish to be fulfilled. This follows immediately from the Arrow Possibility Theorem. In order to get a consistent set one axiom must be given up. We shall consider this further in our discussion of welfare, but we can at this point define a Pareto ranking which will be of particular interest.

Definition 2B.4

(Pareto ranking) We have a Pareto ranking with P^*, R^*, and I^* if $\forall\, x, y \in \chi$.

(a) $\forall\, i\;\; xR_iy \;\&\; \exists\, k\;\; xP_ky \Rightarrow xP^*y$

(b) $\forall\, i\;\; xR_iy \Rightarrow xR^*y$

(c) $\forall\, i\;\; xI_iy \Rightarrow xI^*y$

It also follows that Pareto optimality as met in elementary economics can now be defined rigorously in terms of a Pareto ranking:

Definition 2B.5

(Pareto optimum) $x^* \in \chi$ is Pareto optimal if

$$\sim \exists\, x \in \chi \qquad xP^*x^*$$

The Pareto ranking is only partial because some states are not (Pareto) comparable. Suppose two individuals are faced with a fixed endowment of a good.

The set can be represented by the triangle OAB in Fig. 2B.1, where (1, 0) represents individual 1 having all the endowment, and (0, 1) individual 2 possessing all the endowment. The boundary set AB is the Pareto optimal set. Consider, however, a point a in the interior of χ. All the points in the south-west quadrant are inferior to a, all those in the north-east quadrant are preferred to a. However, points in the south-east and the north-west denoting positions of preference for one individual

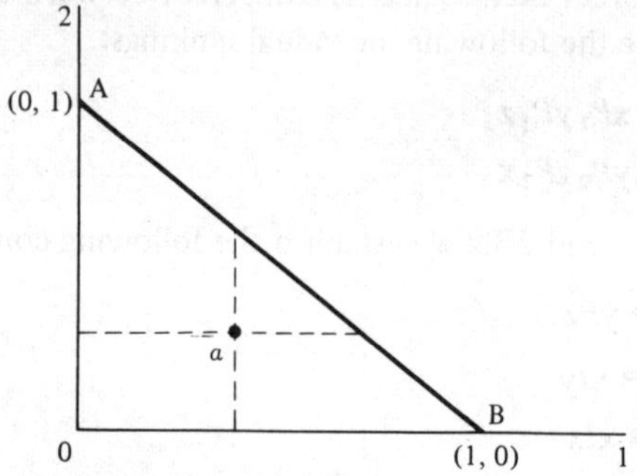

Fig. 2B.1

but not for the other means, by Definition 2B.4, these points cannot be compared by means of a Pareto ranking relative to a. It is clear, therefore, that the relation R^* violates Axiom 2B.1 of a complete ordering; the Pareto ranking satisfies Axioms 2B.2–2B.4 only.

Collective choice is a vital area of study and it is only recently that economists have shown any real interest in it. Arrow, of course, is the basic reference [7] but Professor Sen has also made attempts at clarifying some of the issues [111]. Of particular interest is the relationship between social choice and the means by which such choices are made; for example, dictatorship or by some type of voting. The relationship between the theory of voting and public choice is a rapidly developing one and discussions have taken a number of directions [100].

This appendix has only hinted at the beginnings of this large and important area of study and the interested student (and, one might argue, all students should be interested in such an area of study) will find Phelp's *Reading in Economic Justice* a good beginning [99].

EXERCISES

1. Let $\tilde{\mathbf{I}}$ be the set of all equivalence classes $\mathbf{I}_j$ of a set χ. Prove that $\tilde{\mathbf{I}}$ is a partition of χ.

2. There are six men in line for company manager $M_1, \ldots, M_6$. Let $M = \{M_1, \ldots, M_6\}$. Each man possesses three attributes from a total of five, $a_1, \ldots, a_5$ as follows:

$$M_1 = (a_1, a_2, a_3) \quad M_4 = (a_1, a_4, a_5)$$
$$M_2 = (a_2, a_3, a_4) \quad M_5 = (a_2, a_4, a_5)$$
$$M_3 = (a_3, a_4, a_5) \quad M_6 = (a_2, a_3, a_5)$$

The choosing body ranks the five attributes as follows:

$$a_1 I a_2; a_2 P a_3; a_3 P a_4; \text{ and } a_4 I a_5.$$

(i) List the elements of the choice set and the attainable set.
(ii) Derive all the indifference sets (equivalence classes).
(iii) Which man becomes company manager?

3. Suppose that R, 'at least preferred to', is used as a primitive. Rewrite Axioms 1, 2, and 3 in terms of R; and define P in terms of R and I.

4. Prove that asymmetry $\Rightarrow$ anti-symmetry but not conversely.

5. Given the following lexicographic ordering, where $\mathbf{x}^0 = (x_1^0, x_2^0)$ and $\mathbf{x}^1 = (x_1^1, x_2^1)$

$$\mathbf{x}^0 P \mathbf{x}^1 \text{ if } \quad \forall\, x_2^0, x_2^1 \quad x_1^0 > x_1^1$$
$$\mathbf{x}^0 P \mathbf{x}^1 \text{ if } \quad x_1^0 = x_1^1 \quad x_2^0 > x_2^1$$
$$\mathbf{x}^1 P \mathbf{x}^0 \text{ if } \quad x_1^0 = x_1^1 \quad x_2^0 < x_2^1$$

(i) Illustrate this in Euclidean two-space.
(ii) What constitutes the indifference set $\mathbf{I}^0$?
(iii) Is this ordering a quasi-ordering or an ordering as defined in Definition 2.3?
(iv) Does this ordering satisfy Axioms 1–3?

6. In an experiment by K. May (*Econometrica,* 1954) three potential marriage partners were endowed with three qualities, a 'bundle' of qualities. Other than the problem of majority voting, he found that seventeen individuals out of sixty-two displayed the cycle of preferences $\mathbf{x}^0 P \mathbf{x}^1$, $\mathbf{x}^1 P \mathbf{x}^2$, but $\mathbf{x}^2 P \mathbf{x}^0$. Would this suggest that the axiom of transitivity is an unacceptable axiom on which to base a theory of choice?

7. Prove that if R is transitive then it follows that P and I are both transitive; but that if P is transitive it is possible for I to be intransitive.

8. Given the following definitions of semi-transitivity of a binary relation, Q

$$\mathbf{x}^0 Q \mathbf{x}^1 \;\&\; \mathbf{x}^1 Q \mathbf{x}^2 \Rightarrow \forall\, \mathbf{x}^3 \quad (\mathbf{x}^0 Q \mathbf{x}^3 \;\text{ or }\; \mathbf{x}^3 Q \mathbf{x}^2)$$

show that if P satisfies semi-transitivity then P is also transitive but that I is not necessarily transitive.

9. Given the following revenue and cost functions, in terms of output y

$$R(y) = 80y - y^2$$
$$c(y) = 1{,}000 + 10y$$

show that the following solutions hold, where p denotes the price of output

(*a*)	Profit maximisation	$y = 35$	$p = 45$
(*b*)	Revenue maximisation	$y = 40$	$p = 40$
(*c*)	Break-even behaviour	$y = 50$	$p = 30$

What would be the result if in addition there was a minimum profit constraint of $\pi = 150$?

3

PREFERENCE AND UTILITY APPROACHES TO CONSUMER THEORY

3.1 Introduction

In the last chapter we discussed the general theory of choice. Like general systems theory, which is now becoming increasingly studied, the general theory of choice provides a common set of concepts which apply to consumers' choices as equally as to producer choices. However, it is now time to turn to some applications and consumer theory is a fitting start because in its early development it was taken to be almost synonymous with choice theory.

The purpose of the present chapter is twofold. The less economic purpose is to lay down some mathematical concepts which have become increasingly used by modern writers on consumer theory. Hence Sections 3.3 and 3.5 are predominantly mathematical. The sections have deliberately been segregated so that reference can be made back to them because the mathematical concepts outlined there are not specific to consumer theory but arise repeatedly in other branches of micro-economics. The second purpose is to discuss the utility approach to consumer theory which dominated until the early 1950s. Even today indifference curve analysis is still with us; as a tool of logical thinking it is still valuable even if non-operational. Another aspect which will be discussed is to what extent the preference approach and the utility approach are the same. Finally, the behavioural approach of Revealed Preference Theory is discussed and compared with subjective preference and utility approaches to consumer theory. Since it is only when the various theories are brought to a common basis that their similarities and differences can be most highlighted then our aim, in this chapter, is to reinterpret the traditional approach to consumer theory in the light of the general theory of choice; and to compare this with the subjective and behavioural preference approaches which are already expressed in what we have called a 'modern' viewpoint. Throughout we are concerned only with the individual, although a brief mention of a Paretian welfare function will be found in section 3.9.

3.2 The Consumption Choice Set

The choice set of the consumer unit comprises all the commodities, goods and services, which he faces. We shall denote the consumer's choice set by **X**. Since we are considering choices we are concerned only with commodities which the consumer has at his disposal. This may of course vary, e.g. if the country begins international trade, thus importing goods which before were not in the choice set of the choosing agent. What can be said, however, is that the number of choices must be finite (but probably large). Let us assume that the number of commodities available to our representative choosing agent are n, and if we consider an axis representing each commodity then the commodity choice set will be the non-negative orthant of an n-dimensional space.[1]

Let us indicate the situation diagrammatically. Consider a consumer agent who has only two commodities open to him, which we shall call x_1 and x_2, the commodity bundle will be $\mathbf{x} = (x_1, x_2)$ which can be considered as a 2-tuple. A particular commodity bundle chosen by the consumer, say $\mathbf{x}^0 = (x_1^0, x_2^0)$, can be represented by a point in the non-negative orthant of a two-dimensional space, as illustrated in Fig. 3.1.

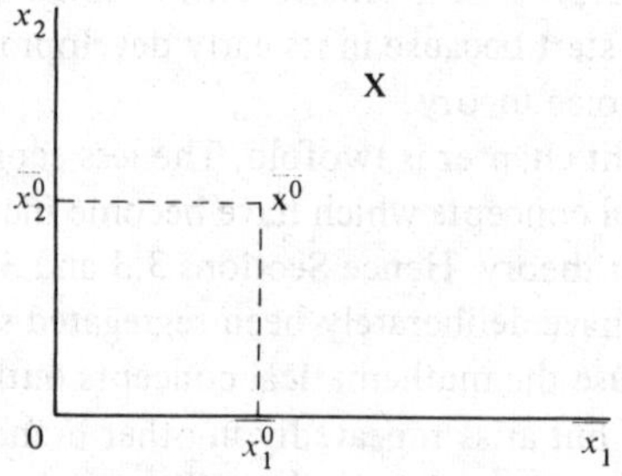

Fig. 3.1

Now as far as economics is concerned we are interested only with commodities which, in mathematical terms, constitute *real* variables. In other words, if we are going to represent commodities x_1 and x_2 we do so by giving them a correspondence with the real line, the distance from the origin denoting the quantity of each commodity. In other words, commodities are cardinally measurable. This is important as we shall see when we come to discuss utility. Since utility is not cardinally measurable it cannot be exhibited in a Euclidean space since this space implies a cardinal measure of distance as defined by Euclid (which is made clear following Definition 3.1). To be explicit, commodities are represented in a Euclidean space because they are cardinally measurable whilst utility is represented in real space which is non-Euclidean because utility is an ordinal variable. A real space is denoted **R** and a Euclidean space is denoted **E**. $\mathbf{R}^2$ or $\mathbf{E}^2$ represent real or Euclidean two-dimensional space respectively. In Fig. 3.1, therefore, $\mathbf{x}^0 \in \mathbf{E}^2$. More generally, for $\mathbf{x} = (x_1, \ldots, x_n)$ we have $\mathbf{x} \in \mathbf{E}^n$ (or $\mathbf{X} = \mathbf{E}^n$).

Let us generalise this a little further, which will be useful later, and suppose the choosing agent makes choices between n commodities which are a subset of k commodities at his disposal, hence $n \leqslant k$. We do this so we can deal with the situation of a consumer who wishes to consume only some of all goods, i.e. he consumes $n < k$. This is important because in neoclassical consumer demand he consumes some of every good ($n = k$). We shall, therefore, make this explicit in our first axiom of consumer choice theory:

Axiom 8 $\mathbf{X} \subseteq \mathbf{K}$ $(n \leqslant k)$

where **X** is an n-dimensional commodity space and **K** a k-dimensional commodity space. What we have effectively done is explicitly made a correspondence between commodities and points on the real line. In so far as this is valid we can then establish theorems on the real line which, because of this correspondence, holds in the relation between the commodities. Consequently, if we are to appreciate at all what we have done, we must investigate briefly the properties of a real n-dimensional space. In order to convince the reader that this is an important exercise, it can be mentioned here that a similar correspondence is made in production theory also, and so most of economics is dependent upon the properties of real n-dimensional space.

3.3 Important Properties of $\mathbf{R}^n$ and $\mathbf{E}^n$

A real n-dimensional space becomes a metric space when a real distance function, d, is defined on it. Let us be more rigorous:

Definition 3.1

A set **S** is a metric space if and only if a real-valued function $d(\mathbf{x}, \mathbf{y})$, called a metric, is defined on the Cartesian product $\mathbf{S} \times \mathbf{S}$ such that $\forall \mathbf{x}, \mathbf{y}, \mathbf{z} \in \mathbf{S}$:

(1) $d(\mathbf{x}, \mathbf{y}) \geqslant 0$ and $d(\mathbf{x}, \mathbf{y}) = 0$ if and only if $\mathbf{x} = \mathbf{y}$
(2) $d(\mathbf{x}, \mathbf{y}) = d(\mathbf{y}, \mathbf{x})$
(3) $d(\mathbf{x}, \mathbf{z}) \leqslant d(\mathbf{x}, \mathbf{y}) + d(\mathbf{y}, \mathbf{z})$

We call $d(\mathbf{x}, \mathbf{y})$ the distance between **x** and **y**. There are a number of metrics but the most common is the Euclidean distance:

$$d(\mathbf{x}, \mathbf{y}) = \left[\sum_{i=1}^{n} (x_i - y_i)^2\right]^{1/2}$$

For example, with two points $x = 4$ and $y = 8$ in one-dimensional space then $d(\mathbf{x}, \mathbf{y}) = |x - y| = |4 - 8| = 4$. Whilst for the points $\mathbf{x} = (1, 1)$ and $\mathbf{y} = (4, 5)$ in two-dimensional space then $d(\mathbf{x}, \mathbf{y}) = d(\mathbf{y}, \mathbf{x}) = [(3)^2 + (4)^2]^{1/2} = 5$. (The reader is advised to draw this second case.)

If we consider this Euclidean metric then $\mathbf{R}^n$ becomes $\mathbf{E}^n$.

Mathematicians have established that the spaces $\mathbf{R}^n$ and $\mathbf{E}^n$ are *connected* but not *compact*. These terms will appear repeatedly and so we shall look into them here.

Definition 3.2

An open subset $\mathbf{G} \subseteq \mathbf{X}$, where **X** is a metric space, is said to be connected if there are no two non-empty open sets $\mathbf{G}_1$ and $\mathbf{G}_2$ such that

$$\mathbf{G}_1 \cap \mathbf{G}_2 = \emptyset \text{ and } \mathbf{G}_1 \cup \mathbf{G}_2 = \mathbf{G}$$

Rather than prove some of the theorems of connected spaces, an intuitive idea will probably be more revealing at this stage. Fig. 3.2 shows a set **G** which is open and which can be represented by the two open sets $\mathbf{G}_1$ and $\mathbf{G}_2$ such that $\mathbf{G}_1 \cap \mathbf{G}_2 = \emptyset$ and $\mathbf{G}_1 \cup \mathbf{G}_2 = \mathbf{G}$, and consequently **G** is *not* connected.

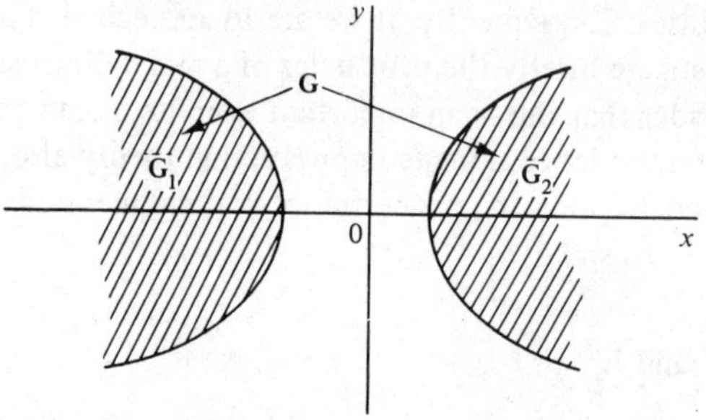

$$\mathbf{G} = \{(x, y)/x^2 - y^2 < 1\}$$

$$\mathbf{G}_1 \cup \mathbf{G}_2 = \mathbf{G}$$

$$\mathbf{G}_1 \cap \mathbf{G}_2 = \emptyset$$

Fig. 3.2. A non-connected set

We shall list some important theorems concerned with connected sets:

Theorem 3.1 A necessary and sufficient condition for a non-empty set in $\mathbf{R}^1$ to be connected is that it is an interval, i.e. the interval $[a, b]$ is connected and conversely the only connected sets in $\mathbf{R}^1$ are intervals.[2]

Theorem 3.2 A necessary and sufficient condition for a non-empty open set in $\mathbf{R}^n$ to be connected is that any two of its points may be joined by a polygonal path lying entirely in the set.

A polygonal path is one in which two points are joined by a set of straight line segments, as illustrated in Fig. 3.3. Theorem 3.2 also means that $\mathbf{R}^n$ is connected as

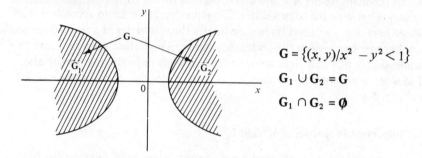

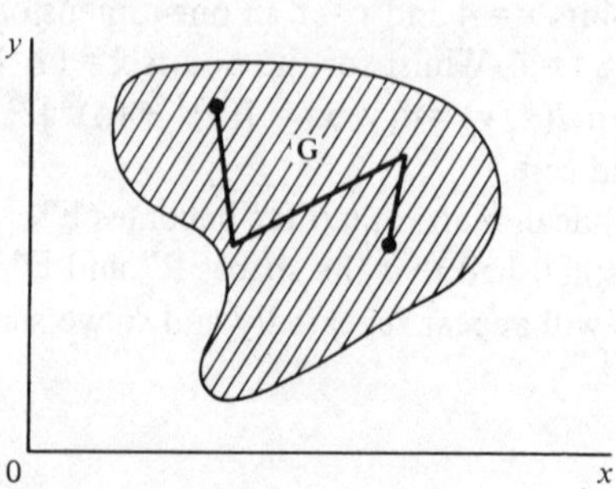

Fig. 3.3. A connected set

is illustrated in this figure. Also compare Fig. 3.2 which has points which cannot be joined by a polygonal path lying entirely within the set.

Theorem 3.3 If the domain of a continuous function is connected so is the image.[3]

This theorem is most important because as we shall show presently, the choice set is connected, and the preference function is defined on this set and so the image is itself connected. A graphical illustration will help to clarify this. Let f be the mapping of **X** *into* **Y**, where **X** is the domain, **Y** is the range and $f(\mathbf{X}) \subset \mathbf{Y}$ is the image of **X** under the mapping f. Then if **X** is an interval on the real line $\mathbf{R}^1$ it is connected by Theorem 3.1, and by Theorem 3.3 we have that the image set $f(\mathbf{X})$ is also connected; this is illustrated in Fig. 3.4 because the image set is also an interval which by Theorem 3.1 is connected.

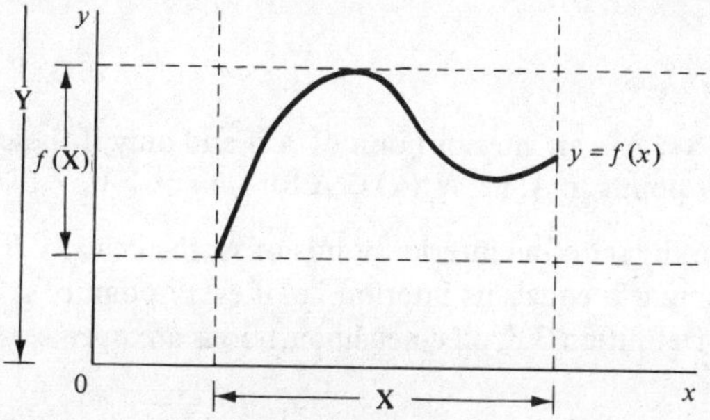

Fig. 3.4

A more important concept than connectedness is that of compactness, at least for the economist. But in order to define this we require some other mathematical concepts. These too will be repeatedly referred to and so we shall explain them fully here so reference can be made back to them if desired. We first require the definition of a neighbourhood of a point.

Definition 3.3

Given a metric space **X** and a distance $d(\mathbf{x}, \mathbf{y})$ defined on $\mathbf{X}^n$, an ϵ-neighbourhood (or ϵ-ball) of the point $\mathbf{x} \in \mathbf{X}$ is given by:

$$N_\epsilon(\mathbf{x}) = \{\mathbf{y} \in \mathbf{X} / d(\mathbf{x}, \mathbf{y}) < \epsilon\}$$

and ϵ is a real finite positive number (usually small).

Fig. 3.5 (*a*) shows an ϵ-neighbourhood in $\mathbf{E}^1$, and Fig. 3.5 (*b*) in $\mathbf{E}^2$.
We also define a deleted neighbourhood of **x** as $N'_\epsilon(\mathbf{x}) = N_\epsilon(\mathbf{x}) - \{\mathbf{x}\}$, i.e. the ϵ-neighbourhood minus the point **x** itself.

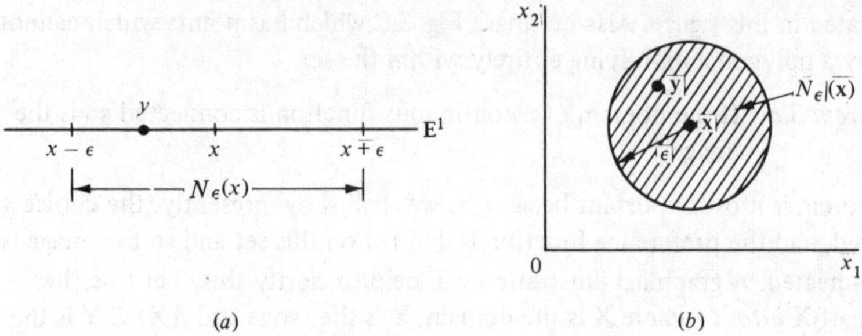

Fig. 3.5. ϵ-neighbourhoods

The definition of neighbourhood requires us to be concerned with a metric space, and this we defined earlier. We now use the definition of ϵ-neighbourhoods to define two other points: (1) an *interior point*, and (2) a *boundary point.*

Definition 3.4

If $\mathbf{A} \subset \mathbf{X}$ then $\mathbf{x} \in \mathbf{A}$ is an interior point of $\mathbf{A}$ if and only if there is some $N_\epsilon(\mathbf{x})$ containing only points in $\mathbf{A}$, i.e. $N_\epsilon(\mathbf{x}) \subset \mathbf{A}$ for some $\epsilon > 0$.

Let $I(\mathbf{A})$ denote the set of all interior points of $\mathbf{A}$, then clearly $I(\mathbf{A}) \subset \mathbf{A}$. The set $\mathbf{A}$ is *open* if and only if it equals its interior, i.e. if every point of $\mathbf{A}$ is an interior point. Notice, by Definition 3.3, all ϵ-neighbourhoods are open sets.

Definition 3.5

If $\mathbf{A} \subset \mathbf{X}$ then $\mathbf{x} \in \mathbf{A}$ is a boundary point of $\mathbf{A}$ if and only if every $N_\epsilon(\mathbf{x})$ contains at least one point in $\mathbf{A}$ and at least one point in $\bar{\mathbf{A}}$, i.e.

$$N_\epsilon(\mathbf{x}) \cap \mathbf{A} \neq \emptyset \text{ and } N_\epsilon(\mathbf{x}) \cap \bar{\mathbf{A}} \neq \emptyset \qquad \epsilon > 0$$

Definitions 3.4 and 3.5 are illustrated in Fig. 3.6

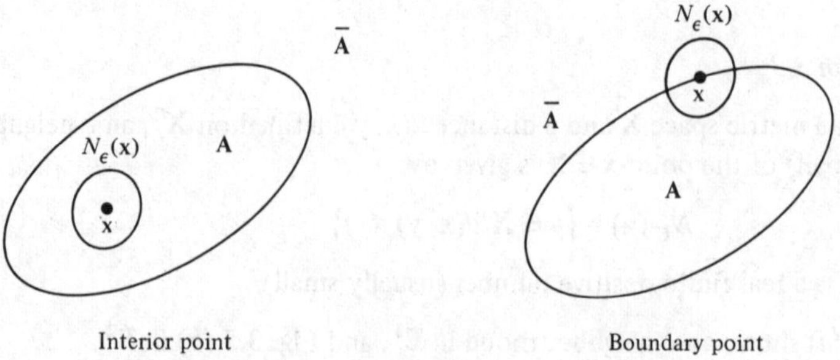

Fig. 3.6

The set of all boundary points of **A** is denoted $B(\mathbf{A})$. The *closure* of **A** is the union of **A** and its boundary, i.e. $C(\mathbf{A}) = \mathbf{A} \cup B(\mathbf{A})$. The set **A** is closed if $\mathbf{A} = C(\mathbf{A})$, i.e. if and only if **A** contains all its boundary points. Let us consider two simple examples to illustrate these mathematical concepts.

Example 3.1 $\mathbf{A} \subset \mathbf{X}, \mathbf{X} = \mathbf{E}^1$ and $\mathbf{A} = \{x/0 < x < 1\}$

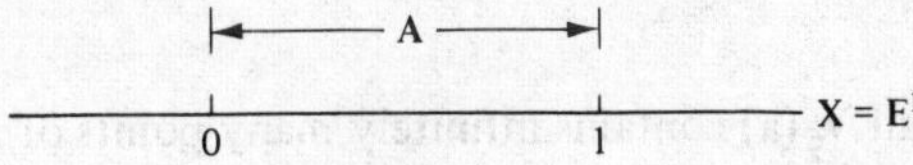

Fig. 3.7

$I(\mathbf{A}) = \{x/0 < x < 1\}$

$B(\mathbf{A}) = \{0, 1\}$

$C(\mathbf{A}) = \{x/0 \leqslant x \leqslant 1\}$ $\quad C(\mathbf{A}) \neq \mathbf{A}$, hence **A** is open.

Example 3.2 $\mathbf{A} \subset \mathbf{X}, \mathbf{X} = \mathbf{E}^2$ and $\mathbf{A} = \{(x, y)/x^2 + y^2 \leqslant 4\}$

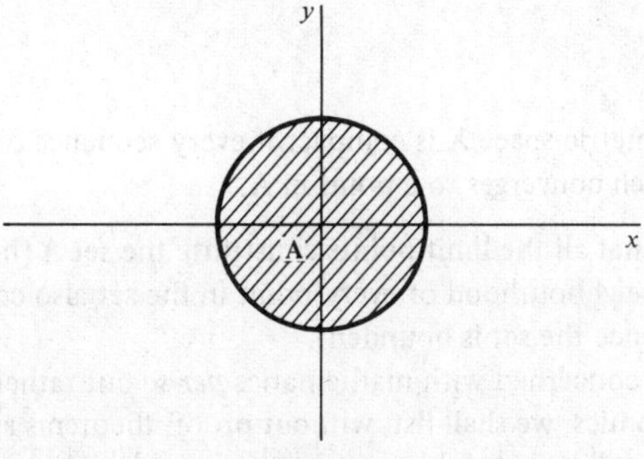

Fig. 3.8

$I(\mathbf{A}) = \{(x, y)/x^2 + y^2 < 4\}$

$B(\mathbf{A}) = \{(x, y)/x^2 + y^2 = 4\}$

$C(\mathbf{A}) = \{(x, y)/x^2 + y^2 \leqslant 4\}$ $\quad C(\mathbf{A}) = \mathbf{A}$, hence **A** is closed.

A set $\mathbf{A} \subset \mathbf{X}$ is *bounded* if and only if given any two points in **A**, the distance between them is finite. Alternatively, for some point $\mathbf{x} \in \mathbf{X}, \mathbf{A} \subset N_\epsilon(\mathbf{x})$.

Definition 3.6

The sequence $\{\mathbf{x}_n\}$ in the metric space **X** is said to converge to the point $\mathbf{a} \in \mathbf{X}$ if

$$d(\mathbf{x}_n, \mathbf{a}) \to 0 \text{ as } n \to \infty$$

$$\text{i.e.} \quad \lim_{n \to \infty} \mathbf{x}_n = \mathbf{a}$$

Definition 3.7

Given a subset **A** of **X**, the point $\mathbf{a} \in \mathbf{X}$ is a limit point (or point of accumulation) of **A** if every deleted neighbourhood $N_\epsilon(\mathbf{a})$ contains a point of **A**; i.e. **a** is a limit point of **A** if every neighbourhood $N_\epsilon(\mathbf{a})$ contains a point of **A** other than **a** itself.

Other ways of defining a limit point (which are useful for some theorems but not for others) are:

(i) Every ϵ-ball $N_\epsilon(\mathbf{a})$ contains infinitely many points of **A**.
(ii) There is a sequence of points $\mathbf{x}_n \in \mathbf{A}$ such that $\mathbf{x}_n \neq \mathbf{a}$ and $\mathbf{x}_n \to \mathbf{a}$ as $n \to \infty$.

Consider, for example, the use of (ii) to define a closed set. A set **A** is closed if $\mathbf{x}_n \to \mathbf{a}$ and $\mathbf{a} \in \mathbf{A}$, i.e. $\lim_{n\to\infty} \mathbf{x}_n = \mathbf{a} \in \mathbf{A}$. This interpretation of a limit point, although conceptually more difficult than Definition 3.7, is used in the definition of compactness. Let us therefore turn to this awaited definition of compactness.

Definition 3.8

A subset **A** of a metric space **X** is compact if every sequence of **A** has a subsequence which converges to a point in **A**.

What this means is that all the limit points constitute the set **A** (hence the set is closed), and every neighbourhood of every point in the set also contains other points in the set (hence the set is bounded).

Since we are not concerned with mathematics *per se* but rather with its application in economics, we shall list, without proof, theorems associated with compact sets which will be helpful in our economic analysis.[4]

Theorem 3.4 Let $\mathbf{X} \subset \mathbf{E}$ where **E** is a metric space,
(i) If **X** is compact, then **X** is bounded and closed.
(ii) If **E** is compact and if **X** is closed, then **X** is compact.

Corollary In $\mathbf{R}^n$ a set is compact if and only if it is bounded and closed.

Theorem 3.5 If the domain of a continuous function is compact, then the range is also compact.

Corollary (i) If the domain of a continuous function is compact, then the range is bounded and closed.

Corollary (ii) If the domain of a real-valued continuous function is compact, then the function is bounded and attains its upper and lower bounds.

The next theorem requires discussion but follows naturally from the previous two.

Theorem 3.6 (Weierstrass Theorem) If **X** is a non-empty compact set, and $F(\mathbf{x})$ is a continuous function defined over the set **X**, then $F(\mathbf{x})$ has at least one maximum (minimum) either in the interior of **X** or on the boundary of **X**.

We shall discuss this theorem with the help of Figs 3.9 and 3.10, and shall pay attention only to a maximum. In both figures **X** is a closed bounded set and is thus compact. By Theorem 3.5, since $F(\mathbf{x})$ is a continuous function, the image set

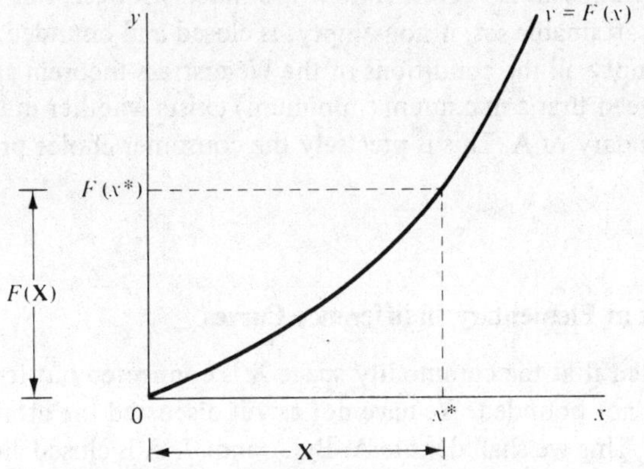

Fig. 3.9. Boundary maximum

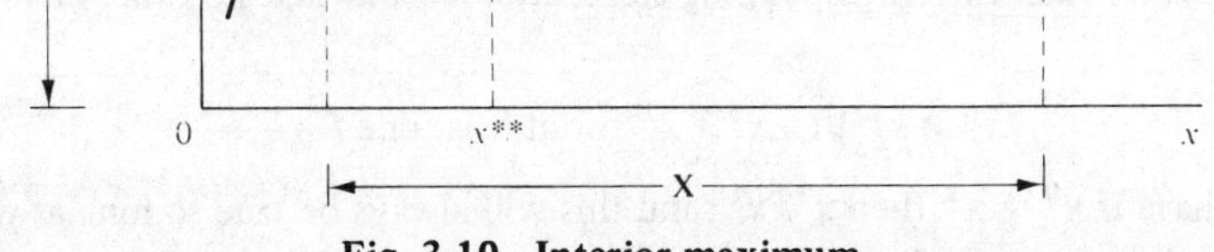

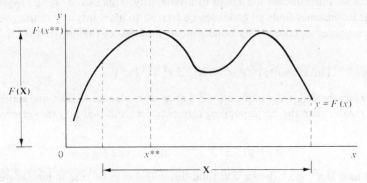

Fig. 3.10. Interior maximum

$F(\mathbf{X})$ is also compact. We see from Fig. 3.9 that the image set reaches a maximum at the boundary, i.e. $F(\mathbf{x})$ is a maximum at $\mathbf{x} = \mathbf{x}^*$ and $\mathbf{x}^*$ is a boundary point of **X**. Fig. 3.10 illustrates an interior maximum with $F(\mathbf{x})$ being a maximum at $\mathbf{x} = \mathbf{x}^{**}$ and $\mathbf{x}^{**}$ being an interior point of **X**. Note also that in Fig. 3.10, $F(\mathbf{x})$ reaches another maximum also at a value of x which is an interior point, thus explaining the statement 'at least one maximum' in the theorem.

In Section 2.7 we discussed the fact that many economic problems amount to a situation of optimisation. In other words, maximising or minimising some objective function subject to a set of constraints. Now the objective function which arises in most economic problems is nearly always continuous. If we are to apply the Weierstrass theorem, therefore, we have to establish whether the attainable set **A**, over which the objective function is restricted, is a non-empty closed and bounded set. In most economic problems the attainable set is non-empty, but none of the axioms will guarantee this; Axiom 6 only guarantees that if it contains just one element this will be chosen. However, Axiom 7 is much stronger; this does guarantee that the attainable set, if non-empty, is closed and bounded. Therefore, so long as **A** is non-empty all the conditions of the Weierstrass theorem are satisfied and we are guaranteed that a maximum (minimum) exists whether in the interior of **A** or at the boundary of **A**. This is precisely the consumer choice problem as we shall now show.

3.4 A New Look at Elementary Indifference Curves

So far we have stated that the commodity space **X** is connected but it is not compact since it is not bounded. We have not as yet discussed the attainable set of the consumer unit. This we shall denote **A**. By Axiom 7, **A** is closed and bounded and hence is compact; to the extent that it is a subset of **X** it is also connected. But our knowledge of **X** and **A** does not tell us anything about the preference function, in particular whether it has properties of continuity and connectedness. But before we do this we must discuss the axiom of insatiability. This axiom says no more than that a consumer finds all goods scarce relative to his wants and so there will always exist another commodity bundle more preferred to the one he already has, i.e.

Axiom 9 (Insatiability) $\forall\ \mathbf{x}^0 \in \mathbf{X} \quad \exists\, \mathbf{x}^1\ (\mathbf{x}^1 P \mathbf{x}^0)$

Axiom 9 has the following implication.[5] Let $\mathbf{x}^0 > \mathbf{x}^1$ denote at least one element of $\mathbf{x}^0$ is greater than the corresponding element of $\mathbf{x}^1$ and that no other element is less, i.e.

$$x_i^0 \geqslant x_i^1 \ \forall i, \ \ x_i^0 > x_i^1 \text{ for at least one } i.$$

We then have if $\mathbf{x}^0 > \mathbf{x}^1$ then $\mathbf{x}^0 P \mathbf{x}^1$; and this will always be true so long as we have the non-satiation axiom. Put briefly, we always prefer more to less.

But Axiom 9 is more restrictive than it first appears. In terms of our general optimisation problem of maximising $F(\mathbf{x})$ subject to $\mathbf{x} \in \mathbf{A}$ it amounts to restraining the set of functions F to those which are monotonically increasing. Since Axiom 9 is introduced specifically for the consumer, and since there is no reason it will be imposed for other economic optimisation problems, let us label the preference function $u(\mathbf{x})$ and refer to it as a utility function. However, why introduce Axiom 9 at all? Part of the reason is that it reduces our area of ignorance. More to the point, it allows us to consider preferences solely from a knowledge of the quantities contained in the commodity bundles; which, it is important to note, is an objective assessment.

In order to see the importance of many of the statements so far made we shall assume that the reader has been introduced to elementary indifference curve analysis (e.g. Lipsey [appendix to ch. 15]), and we shall discuss this in the light of what we have done thus far. In the neoclassical theory of consumer choice the frontier of the attainable set **A** is a straight line and denotes the budget constraint open to the consumer. Let us look into this more closely. We have said that the constraint can take two forms: either that of an equality or of an inequality. Which we choose makes a difference in the present context. Fig. 3.11 (*a*) shows **A** as a budget line whilst Fig. 3.11 (*b*) shows it as a triangle contained in the non-negative orthant.

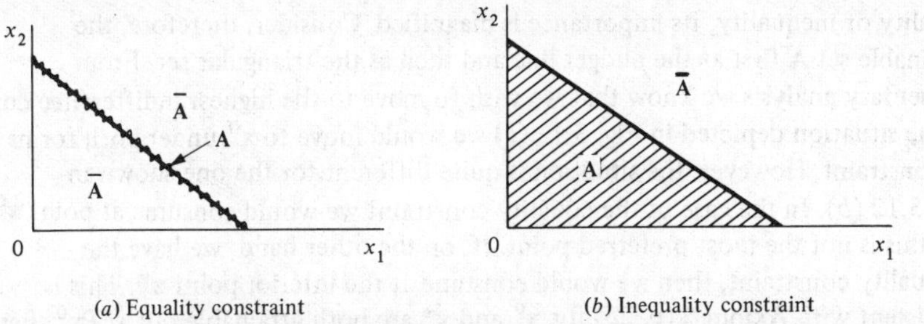

Fig. 3.11

Two points are worth noting. First, to argue that the slope of the budget line denotes the ratio of prices presupposes a price mechanism exists. We can have a constraint in consumer demand theory without there necessarily being a price mechanism in existence. We could conceive of the slope of the line, which denotes the boundary of the attainable consumption set as in Fig. 3.11 (*b*), or the consumption set as in Fig. 3.11 (*a*), as denoting how x_1 is substituted for x_2 by consumers. In this example the rate is fixed. Second, the two figures are depicting different behaviour assumptions. Fig. 3.11 (*a*) is saying in effect that the consumer will spend all his income either on x_1 or x_2 in which case he will always be on the budget line. Fig. 3.11 (*b*) is saying he can consume anything within the shaded region, whether he will consume on the budget line or not can only be ascertained by introducing the consumer's preferences, for this will establish whether the most preferred point does or does not arise on the budget line. To summarise so far, to pose the constraint as an equation means that one is restricting the choice set to correspond with the budget line, and hence the chosen element, or most preferred point(s), must lie on this line by construction. On the other hand, if the constraint is specified by an inequality then we have no way of knowing, by the axioms so far laid down, whether the most preferred point(s) will lie on the budget line, but at least this formulation does allow the possibility that it will not.[6]

We saw in Chapter 2 that the relation P will enable us to obtain equivalence classes $\mathbf{I}_j$. In traditional microeconomics these equivalence classes are drawn as smooth continuous curves. Such indifference curves can only be drawn under very special conditions. Axioms 8 and 9, along with the assumption that the relation P on $\mathbf{X}$ is continuous, are not sufficient to obtain such traditional indifference curves. The remainder of this chapter is addressed to the question of the sufficient conditions which must be imposed in order to obtain the neoclassical indifference curves. We shall take great pains to elaborate on each so that the full implications of our assumptions are fully realised.

Let us suppose for the moment that we have smooth indifference curves $\mathbf{I}_j$, as shown in Fig. 3.12. Fig. 3.12 (*a*) and (*b*) violate the axiom of insatiability (Axiom 9) having satiation points at $\mathbf{x}^*$; Fig. 3.12 (*c*) has its satiation point at infinity, and so satisfies the insatiability axiom.[7] Violation of Axiom 9 itself is not so detrimental to the analysis but when taken in conjunction with the type of constraint, whether equality or inequality, its importance is magnified. Consider, therefore, the attainable set $\mathbf{A}$ first as the budget line and then as the triangular set. From elementary analysis we know that we wish to move to the highest indifference curve. In the situation depicted in Fig. 3.12 (*a*) we would move to $\mathbf{x}^0$ under both forms of constraint. However, the situation is quite different for the one shown in Fig. 3.12 (*b*). In the case of the equality constraint we would consume at point $\mathbf{x}^0$, but this is not the most preferred point. If, on the other hand, we have the inequality constraint, then we would consume at the interior point $\mathbf{x}^*$. This is consistent with Axiom 5 (p. 25) for $\mathbf{x}^0$ and $\mathbf{x}^*$ are both attainable but $\mathbf{x}^* P \mathbf{x}^0$, hence we must choose $\mathbf{x}^*$ over $\mathbf{x}^0$. However, if we choose $\mathbf{x}^*$ over $\mathbf{x}^0$ we do not spend all our income. As Fig. 3.12 (*a*) and (*c*) illustrate, so long as the point of satiation is well outside the attainable set the solution will always be a boundary solution. There is no great loss, therefore, if we accept the axiom of insatiability.

Even if we accept the insatiability axiom this still does not exclude the possibility that the boundary solution is such that one of the two goods is not consumed. We shall return to this once we have investigated the concept of convexity in Section 3.5 (i).

3.5 Convex Sets, Convex/Concave and Quasiconvex/Quasiconcave Functions

Modern microeconomic analysis quite frequently uses the concept of convexity. The beginning student of consumer theory learns very early that indifference curves are convex to the origin. In the 'modern' approach such a statement is replaced by some *set* or other being convex. In production theory too we shall find that the production sets are assumed to be convex.

Functions too, whether they are utility functions or production functions, are distinguished by convex and concave features. Since the precise properties of each come to have economic significance (see, for example, Exercises 4 and 11), we preface our economic discussion with a somewhat (economically) barren set of

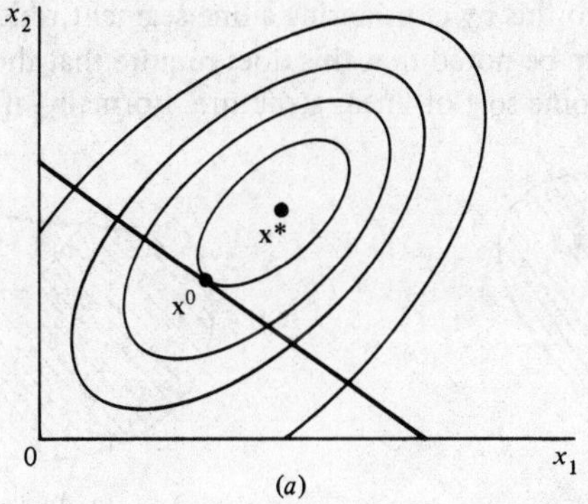

(*a*)

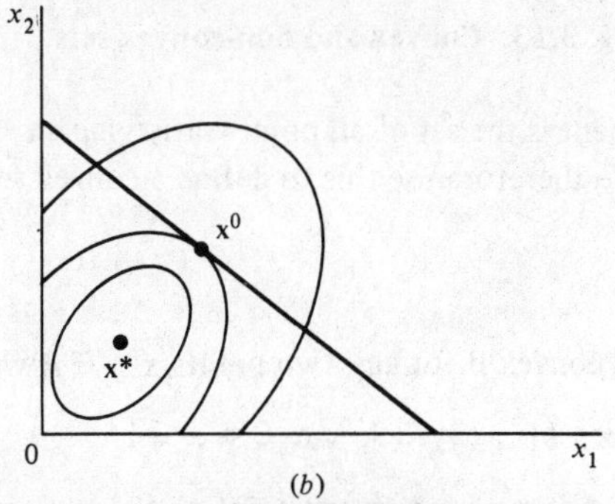

(*b*)

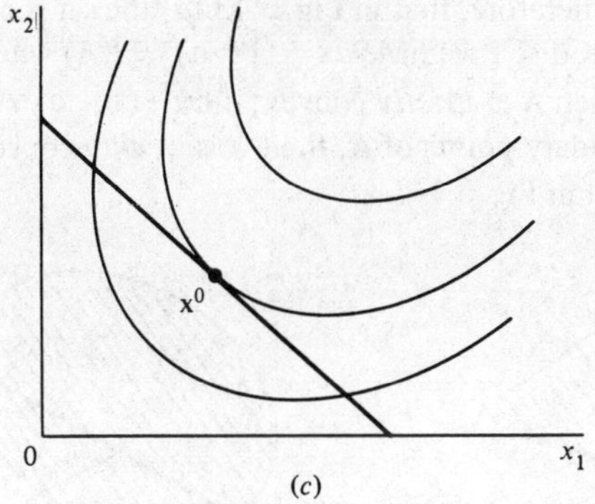

(*c*)

Fig. 3.12

mathematical statements concerning such sets and functions. This approach at least has the advantage that the reader can constantly refer back to this section.

3.5 (i) *Convex Sets*

Intuitively, the idea of a convex set is that it has no hollows. Consider the two diagrams in Fig. 3.13; our problem is to establish a rigorous criterion by which to distinguish them. We do this by considering a line segment which joins any two points in the set. It is to be noted that this does require that the space in which the set is defined has some sort of linear structure. Formally, if **x** and **y** are two

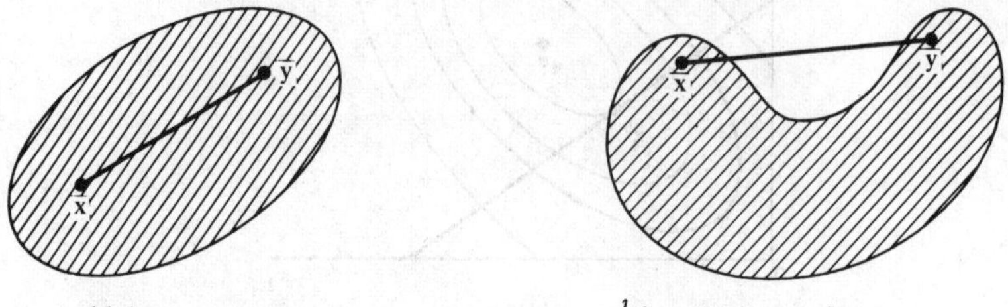

(*a*) A convex set (*b*) A non-convex set

Fig. 3.13. Convex and non-convex sets

points then a line segment is the set of all points satisfying $a\mathbf{x} + (1 - a)\mathbf{y}$, $0 \leqslant a \leqslant 1$, also denoted $[\mathbf{x}, \mathbf{y}]$. We therefore use this to define a convex set.

Definition 3.9

A subset **A** of $\mathbf{R}^n$ is convex if for any two points $\mathbf{x}, \mathbf{y} \in \mathbf{A}$ we have

$$a\mathbf{x} + (1 - a)\mathbf{y} \in \mathbf{A} \;\; \forall a \;\; 0 \leqslant a \leqslant 1$$

In other words, the set **A** is convex if every point on the line segment $[\mathbf{x}, \mathbf{y}]$ also belongs to **A**. We see, therefore, that in Fig. 3.13 (*a*) the set is convex but not in Fig. 3.13 (*b*). If for $0 < a < 1$ we have $a\mathbf{x} + (1 - a)\mathbf{y} \in I(\mathbf{A})$ where $I(\mathbf{A})$ denotes the interior points of **A**, then **A** is *strictly* convex; if $a\mathbf{x} + (1 - a)\mathbf{y} \in B(\mathbf{A})$, $0 < a < 1$ and $B(\mathbf{A})$ denotes the boundary points of **A**, then **A** is *weakly* convex. These two concepts are illustrated in Fig. 3.14.

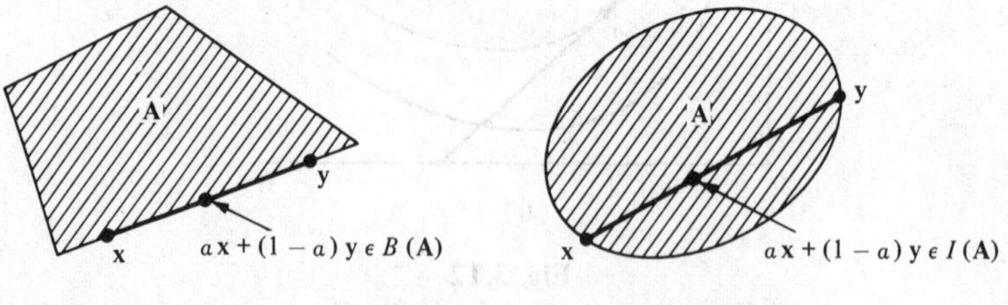

(*a*) Weakly convex (*b*) Strictly convex

Fig. 3.14

The following present important examples of convex sets, where **x** and **y** are vectors.

Example 3.3 $\mathbf{R}^n$ is convex, and $\mathbf{E}^n$ is convex.

Example 3.4 A linear subspace in $\mathbf{R}^n$ is convex. $\mathbf{L}$ is a linear subspace if for any $\mathbf{x}, \mathbf{y} \in \mathbf{L}$ we have $\alpha\mathbf{x} + \beta\mathbf{y} \in \mathbf{L}$, $\alpha, \beta \geqslant 0$. Thus a convex combination $\alpha\mathbf{x} + (1-\alpha)\mathbf{y}$ is just a particular case and must also belong to $\mathbf{L}$, hence $\mathbf{L}$ is convex.

Example 3.5 The solution of a system of linear inequalities:

$$a_{i1}x_1 + a_{i2}x_2 + \ldots + a_{in}x_n \leqslant b_i \qquad i = 1, \ldots, m \quad \forall x_i \geqslant 0$$

form a convex set in $\mathbf{R}^n$. This can be shown as follows. Let $\mathbf{C} = \{\mathbf{x}/\mathbf{A}\mathbf{x} \leqslant \mathbf{b}, \mathbf{x} \geqslant 0\}$ and let $\mathbf{x}, \mathbf{y} \in \mathbf{C}$ then $\mathbf{A}[\alpha\mathbf{x} + (1-\alpha)\mathbf{y}] \leqslant \alpha\,\mathbf{b} + (1-\alpha)\mathbf{b} = \mathbf{b}$, i.e. $\mathbf{A}\mathbf{z} \leqslant \mathbf{b}$ where $\mathbf{z} = \alpha\mathbf{x} + (1-\alpha)\mathbf{y}$. Now $\mathbf{x} \geqslant 0$ and $\mathbf{y} \geqslant 0$, hence for $0 \leqslant \alpha \leqslant 1$ we have $\mathbf{z} \geqslant 0$. Therefore $\mathbf{z} \in \mathbf{C}$, hence the solution set is convex.

Example 3.6 The commodity space $\mathbf{X} = \{\mathbf{x} \mid x_i \geqslant 0 \, \forall i\}$ is a convex set.

Theorem 3.7 If $\mathbf{A}$ is convex it is connected.

Additional properties of convex sets will be introduced in later chapters as they are required.

3.5 (ii) Convex and Concave Functions

Definition 3.10 (i)

A real valued function $f(\mathbf{x})$ defined on a convex set $\mathbf{X}$ is concave if and only if

$$\forall\, \mathbf{x}^1, \mathbf{x}^2 \in \mathbf{X} \quad f[\alpha\mathbf{x}^1 + (1-\alpha)\mathbf{x}^2] \geqslant \alpha f(\mathbf{x}^1) + (1-\alpha)f(\mathbf{x}^2) \qquad 0 \leqslant \alpha \leqslant 1.$$

$f(\mathbf{x})$ is strictly concave if and only if the strict inequality holds. A strictly concave function in two-dimensional space is illustrated in Fig. 3.15 (*a*). A function $f(\mathbf{x})$ is convex if $-f(\mathbf{x})$ is concave, and strictly convex if and only if $-f(\mathbf{x})$ is strictly concave. A strictly convex function is illustrated in Fig. 3.15 (*b*).

If $f(\mathbf{x})$ is also differentiable an alternative definition is:

Definition 3.10 (ii)

A real valued differentiable function $f(\mathbf{x})$ defined over a convex set $\mathbf{X}$ is concave if and only if[8]

$$\forall \mathbf{x} \in \mathbf{X} \qquad f(\mathbf{x}) \leqslant f(\mathbf{x}^0) + (\mathbf{x} - \mathbf{x}^0)' \frac{\partial f(\mathbf{x}^0)}{\partial \mathbf{x}}.$$

Conversely, $f(\mathbf{x})$ is convex if $-f(\mathbf{x})$ is concave. Strict concavity and convexity hold when the strict inequality holds. This is illustrated in Fig. 3.16.

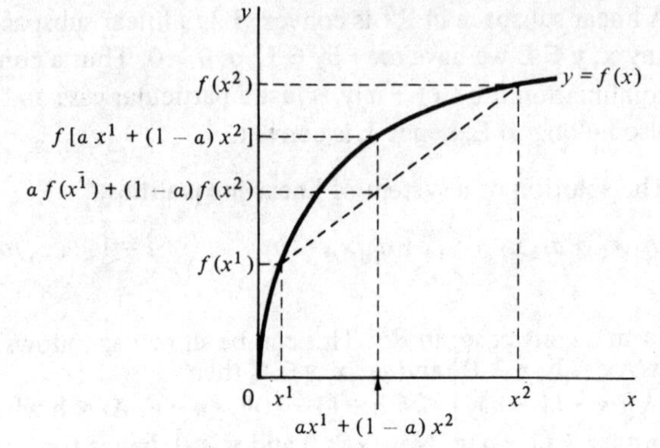

(a) Strictly concave

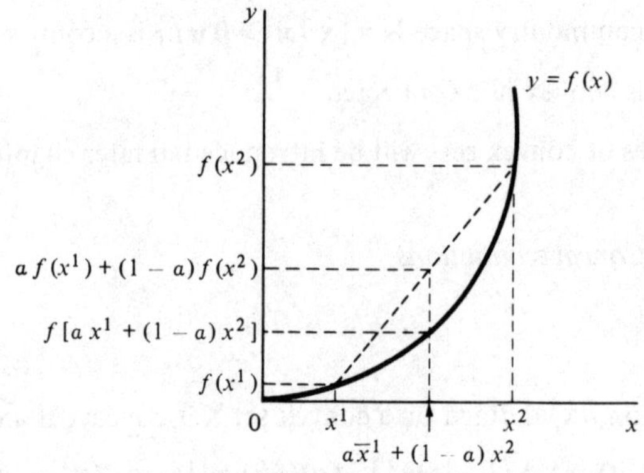

(b) Strictly convex

Fig. 3.15

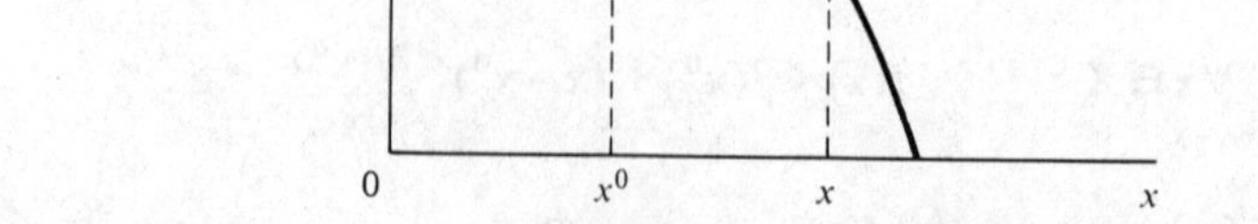

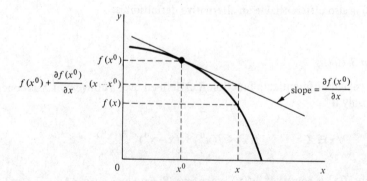

Fig. 3.16

3.5 (iii) Quasiconcave and Quasiconvex Functions

A quasiconcave function is a generalisation of a concave function, and similarly for quasiconvexity. There are three alternative ways of defining a quasiconcave function, all of which have been employed in the economic literature.

Definition 3.11 (i)

A function $f(\mathbf{x})$ defined on a convex set $\mathbf{X}$ is quasiconcave if and only if

$$\mathbf{x}^1, \mathbf{x}^2 \in \mathbf{X} \qquad (\mathbf{x}^1 \neq \mathbf{x}^2) \qquad f[a\mathbf{x}^1 + (1-a)\mathbf{x}^2] \geqslant \min\,[f(\mathbf{x}^1), f(\mathbf{x}^2)] \quad 0 < a < 1$$

For a quasiconvex function we have the condition $f[a\mathbf{x}^1 + (1-a)\mathbf{x}^2] \leqslant \max [f(\mathbf{x}^1), f(\mathbf{x}^2)]$. Strict quasiconcavity and strict quasiconvexity hold when the strict inequality is operative.

Definition 3.11 (ii)

If for each real number c, and a real valued function $f(\mathbf{x})$ defined on a convex set $\mathbf{X}$, $f(\mathbf{x})$ is quasiconcave if the set $\{\mathbf{x}/f(\mathbf{x}) \geqslant c\}$ is a convex set.

A quasiconvex function is one for which the set $\{\mathbf{x}/f(\mathbf{x}) \leqslant c\}$ is a convex set.

Definition 3.11 (iii)

If $f(\mathbf{x})$ is also differentiable then it is quasiconcave if

$$f(\mathbf{x}) \geqslant f(\mathbf{x}^0) \Rightarrow (\mathbf{x} - \mathbf{x}^0)' \frac{\partial f(\mathbf{x}^0)}{\partial \mathbf{x}}.$$

Some points are worth noting. All concave functions must be quasiconcave. This is clear because $af(\mathbf{x}^1) + (1-a)f(\mathbf{x}^2) \geqslant \min\,[f(\mathbf{x}^1), f(\mathbf{x}^2)]$; however, the converse is not true. This can be appreciated when one realises that in the case of a single variable a convex function is also quasiconcave. Also, for a quasiconcave function, if $\partial f(\mathbf{x})/\partial\,\mathbf{x} \geqslant 0$ and $\mathbf{x} \geqslant 0$ then the isovalue curves $f(\mathbf{x}) = c$ must be convex to the origin. If, on the other hand, $\partial f(\mathbf{x})/\partial\,\mathbf{x} \leqslant 0$ and $\mathbf{x} \geqslant 0$ then the isovalue curves must be concave to the origin.

3.6 The Axiom of Convexity

Consider any point $\mathbf{x}^0$ in Euclidean 2-space contained in the non-negative orthant, as in Fig. 3.17. Further consider the set of all commodity bundles which are no worse than $\mathbf{x}^0$. Let this be called the 'better set' associated with $\mathbf{x}^0$, and denoted $\mathbf{B}^0$. Defined more rigorously:

Definition 3.12

$$\forall\, \mathbf{x}^0, \mathbf{x}^1 \in \mathbf{X} \qquad (\mathbf{x}^1 \in \mathbf{B}^0 \Leftrightarrow \mathbf{x}^1 P \mathbf{x}^0 \text{ or } \mathbf{x}^1 I \mathbf{x}^0).$$

This set is shown in Fig. 3.17 (*a*). We shall use the term 'worse set' associated with $\mathbf{x}^0$, written $\mathbf{W}^0$, to denote all commodity bundles which are no better than $\mathbf{x}^0$, i.e.

Definition 3.13

$$\forall \mathbf{x}^0, \mathbf{x}^1 \in \mathbf{X} \qquad (\mathbf{x}^1 \in \mathbf{W}^0 \Leftrightarrow \mathbf{x}^0 P \mathbf{x}^1 \text{ or } \mathbf{x}^0 I \mathbf{x}^1).$$

The worse set is illustrated in Fig. 3.17 (*b*).

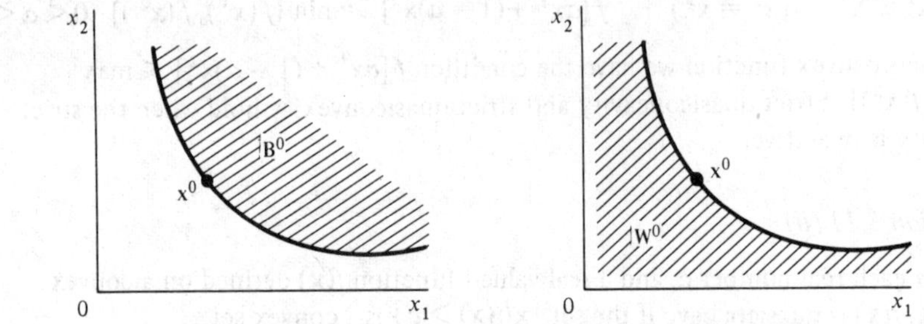

(*a*) The 'better set' (*b*) The 'worse set'

Fig. 3.17

One may ask the question whether the sets $\mathbf{B}^0$ and $\mathbf{W}^0$ divide the set $\mathbf{X}$ into two disjoint sets? The set $\mathbf{X}$ would be *partitioned* if each element of $\mathbf{X}$ belongs to one of the subsets, and if the subsets of $\mathbf{X}$ are pair-wise disjoint. In the present situation this requires that any $\mathbf{x} \in \mathbf{X}$ belongs to either $\mathbf{B}^0$ or $\mathbf{W}^0$, or alternatively $\mathbf{B}^0 \cup \mathbf{W}^0 = \mathbf{X}$; and secondly that $\mathbf{B}^0 \cap \mathbf{W}^0 = \emptyset$. It is clear that $\mathbf{B}^0$ and $\mathbf{W}^0$ do not partition $\mathbf{X}$, but it is true that $\mathbf{B}^0 \cup \mathbf{W}^0 = \mathbf{X}$. We must yet establish what is contained in the set $\mathbf{B}^0 \cap \mathbf{W}^0$, in particular, whether $\mathbf{B}^0 \cap \mathbf{W}^0 = \{\mathbf{x}^0\}$.

A look at Fig. 3.17 will suggest that the set $\mathbf{B}^0$ is convex whilst $\mathbf{W}^0$ is not. The convexity of preferences is vital to neoclassical consumer theory and so we shall make this condition most explicit in terms of Axiom 10:

Axiom 10 (Convexity) $\mathbf{B}^0$ is a convex set.

Axiom 10, along with Theorem 3.7 (p. 59) ensures that the set $\mathbf{B}^0$ has a continuous boundary. The 'boundary' to the set $\mathbf{B}^0$ is an equivalence class and is denoted $\mathbf{I}^0$. The set $\mathbf{I}^0$ consists of all the commodity bundles which are indifferent to $\mathbf{x}^0$. But to ensure that $\mathbf{I}^0$ is an indifference *curve*, as employed in neoclassical consumer theory, we must establish that this boundary set contains no interior points. Fig. 3.18 illustrates this problem. Although $\mathbf{I}^0$ is the 'boundary' of the set $\mathbf{B}^0$ there is no reason to suppose it is not as shown. The point $\mathbf{x}^1$ is an interior point of $\mathbf{I}^0$ since $N_\epsilon(\mathbf{x}^1) \subset \mathbf{I}^0$. We eliminate this possibility by the following axiom:

Axiom 11 $\quad \forall \mathbf{x}^1 \in \mathbf{B}^0 \cap \mathbf{W}^0 \qquad N_\epsilon(\mathbf{x}^1) \notin \mathbf{B}^0 \cap \mathbf{W}^0.$

In other words, the set $\mathbf{I}^0 = \mathbf{B}^0 \cap \mathbf{W}^0$ contains no interior points, and consists only of boundary points, i.e. $B(\mathbf{B}^0) = \mathbf{I}^0$ (or $B(\mathbf{W}^0) = \mathbf{I}^0$).

It is the axiom of convexity and the axiom of no interior points which ensures that the indifference sets are as normally portrayed, e.g. Hicks in his *Value and Capital* [52]. However, the neoclassical treatment is stronger still in requiring that

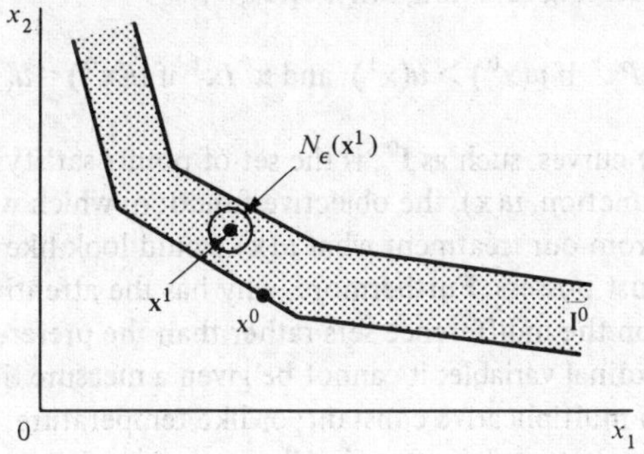

Fig. 3.18

the better set be strictly convex. Let us reflect on the significance of this. If an indifference curve cuts the axis then the better set will be weakly convex when we remember only the non-negative orthant is relevant, as illustrated in Fig. 3.19. Given a linear budget line, therefore, and a strictly convex better set, the optimal point for the consumer must be such that some of every good is consumed as

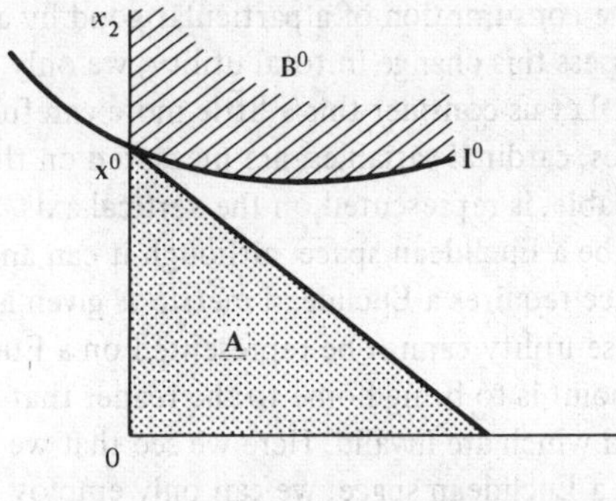

Fig. 3.19. Corner solution

illustrated in Fig. 3.12 (*c*). A corner solution is only possible if we allow $\mathbf{B}^0$ to be weakly convex. As we shall see in Chapter 4, it is possible to deal with corner solutions, and we shall therefore retain our Axiom 10 in this more general form, allowing $\mathbf{B}^0$ to be either weakly or strictly convex as the situation requires.

3.7 The Utility Function

In many ways the concentration on indifference curves is misleading to the extent that what they are showing is a projected view, in a two-dimensional space, of the utility function. This function as we have said will allow us to obtain indifference sets and preferences. What the above axioms have allowed us to do is to define a real-valued order-preserving function, $u(\mathbf{x})$. Thus,

$$\mathbf{x}^0 P \mathbf{x}^1 \text{ if } u(\mathbf{x}^0) > u(\mathbf{x}^1), \text{ and } \mathbf{x}^0 I \mathbf{x}^1 \text{ if } u(\mathbf{x}^0) = u(\mathbf{x}^1).$$

Also the indifference curves, such as $\mathbf{I}^0$, is the set of points satisfying $u(\mathbf{x}^0)$ = constant. But it is the utility function, $u(\mathbf{x})$, the objective function, which we must maximise. It is not at all clear from our treatment what $u(\mathbf{x})$ would look like or, more generally, what properties it must possess. Furthermore, why has the attention of neoclassical economists centred on the indifference sets rather than the preference function?

Utility is not a cardinal variable; it cannot be given a measure like weight, which is measurable up to a multiplicative constant; or like temperature, which is measurable up to a linear transformation.[9] All we require of our measure is that it ranks preferences consistently, hence any monotonically increasing transformation of our measure is equally acceptable. It is important, however, to bear in mind the following. A linear transformation of the form $u^* = a + bu$, $b > 0$ is a monotonically increasing function which in fact preserves ratios; if, from the class of all monotonically increasing functions, we apply such a transformation then we cannot attach any significance whatsoever to the ratios, even though they are preserved.

This analysis means that we cannot measure, in a cardinal sense, total utility as represented by the utility function. This also means that we cannot measure marginal utility because marginal utility is the change in total utility arising from increasing or decreasing the consumption of a particular good by an infinitesimal amount, and we cannot assess this change in total utility; we only know it is either positive, negative, or zero. Let us consider this a little more carefully by considering Fig. 3.20. The commodities, cardinal variables, are measured on the axes x_1 and x_2; and utility, an ordinal variable, is represented on the vertical axis. This three-dimensional space cannot be a Euclidean space, although it can and is a real space, $\mathbf{R}^3$. To be a Euclidean space requires a Euclidean metric as given above on p. 47, but this we do not have because utility cannot be represented on a Euclidean line. Why we have emphasised this point is to bring home to the reader that so often mathematical properties are used which are invalid. Here we see that we cannot employ any theorems that require a Euclidean space; we can only employ theorems defined on the real space.

Let us now see what restrictions the above axioms impose on the utility function. We shall list them first and then discuss each in turn.

(i) u is monotonically increasing,
(ii) u is quasiconcave,
(iii) u is continuous and twice differentiable.

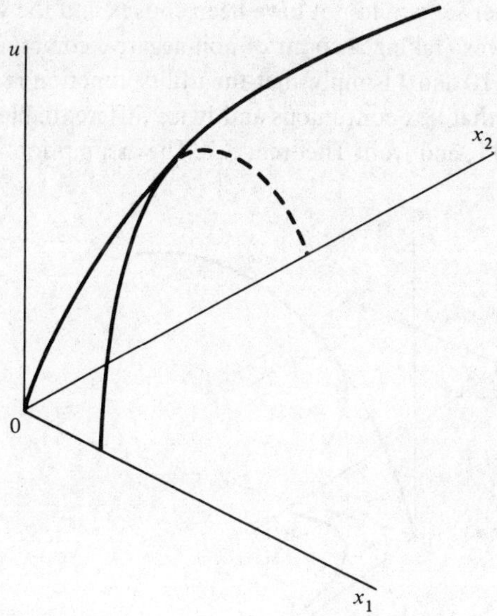

Fig. 3.20. A utility function $u(x_1, x_2)$

(i) We have already accounted for this condition that must be placed on u, and it arises from Axiom 9, the axiom of insatiability. If a point of satiation arose, as in Figs. 3.12 (*a*) and (*b*), then this implies u is, in a three-dimensional space, a hill which has a maximum.

(ii) Axiom 10 requires that the better set is convex but neoclassical demand is somewhat stronger in requiring that the better set is *strictly* convex. Also, Axiom 11 implies that the indifference set is a curve and as such contains no interior points. However, an indifference curve is the commodity combinations for which utility is constant, i.e. it is the set

$$\mathbf{I}^0 = \{\mathbf{x} \mid u(\mathbf{x}) = u^0, \mathbf{x} \in \mathbf{X}\}.$$

Now we know that the commodity space $\mathbf{X}$ is a convex set. Furthermore, we have stipulated that u is such that the better set, which may now be expressed $\{\mathbf{x} \mid u(\mathbf{x}) \geqslant u^0, \mathbf{x} \in \mathbf{X}\}$, is strictly convex. But this is the very condition which results from $u(\mathbf{x})$ being strictly quasiconcave (see Definition 3.11 (ii), p. 61). Some economists in the past have stipulated that u is concave, but all concave functions are quasiconcave, but not conversely. Since it is the convexity of the better set which is the important condition, then to assume only concavity rules out certain utility functions which satisfy this convexity requirement on the better set and are accordingly well behaved.

Fig. 3.21 compares a quasiconcave and a concave utility function. The indifference set satisfies $u(\mathbf{x}) = u^0$ and the better set is $\{\mathbf{x} \mid u(\mathbf{x}) \geqslant u^0, \mathbf{x} \in \mathbf{X}\}$ which in both cases is strictly convex. It should now be clear that had we drawn a convex utility function then the better set would not have been convex and the worse set would have been weakly convex (taking account of non-negative commodities). Thus at the very least Axioms 10 and 11 imply that the utility function is quasiconcave.

(iii) The condition that u is continuous and twice differentiable partly arises from Axioms 10 and 11, and from Theorem 3.7. The assumption of differentiability,

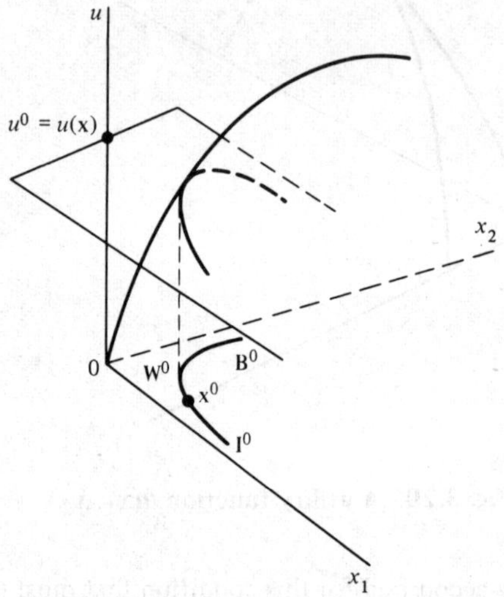

(*a*) A strictly concave utility function

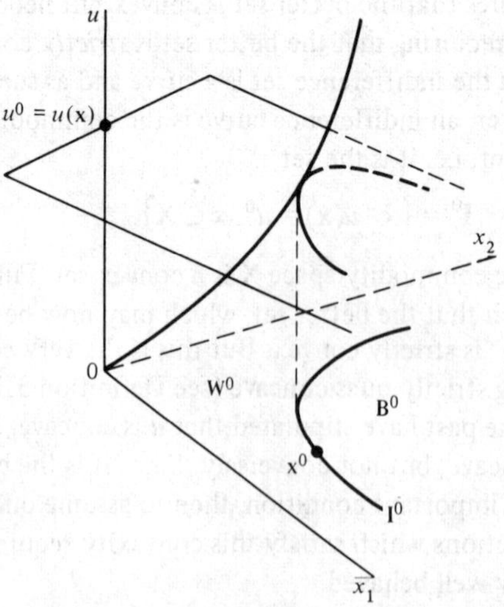

(*b*) A quasiconcave utility function

Fig. 3.21

we would argue, belongs to the class P_γ (see Section 1.3). It is purported to be a simplifying assumption in the sense used in Chapter 1. This assumption has the obvious implication that the techniques of the differential calculus can be used. However, it does rule out the consideration of indivisible commodities for which **X** is not connected.

It is important to realise that consumer theory can either be considered in terms of the preference relation or in terms of the preference function, i.e. the utility function. The axioms we have listed in this chapter are in terms of preferences. The preference approach is the modern approach whilst the utility version is the more traditional. To highlight the equivalence between the two approaches we list in Table 3.1 the neoclassical assumptions in terms of both preferences and utility.

TABLE 3.1 Neoclassical Assumptions of Consumer Theory

Traditional (utility)	*Modern (preference)*
1. u is monotonically non-decreasing	1. There exists no point of satiation
2. u is strictly quasiconcave	2. The better set is strictly convex
3. u is continuous and twice differentiable	3. The relation P on **X** is continuous, the better set is strictly convex, and the indifference set contains no interior points
4. Some of every good is consumed	4. **X** = **K**

3.8 Some Deductions from Neoclassical Utility Theory

We have established that a concave or quasiconcave utility function gives us convex indifference sets and convex better sets. This readily follows if the utility function is strictly concave or strictly quasiconcave. Axioms 10 and 11, along with Theorem 3.7, ensures that the indifference curve is continuous, and with strict convexity it must be convex to the origin (to phrase it in its more usual form). The slope of any particular indifference curve for the two-commodity model is readily obtained. If $u^0 = u(x_1, x_2)$ then if we remain on the same indifference curve:

$$du^0 = \frac{\partial u}{\partial x_1}\, dx_1 + \frac{\partial u}{\partial x_2}\, dx_2 = 0,$$

$$\text{i.e.}\quad \frac{dx_2}{dx_1} = -\frac{\partial u/\partial x_1}{\partial u/\partial x_2} = -\frac{u_1}{u_2}.$$

This Hicks christened the marginal rate of substitution (MRS) in consumption [52]. Let us make a note of some characteristics of this result. First, it is measuring the marginal rate of substitution of good 2 for good 1; this is clear from the direction in which the limit is taken: this indicates good 1 is being given up for good 2. It also follows that the marginal rate of substitution of good 1 for good 2 is the reciprocal of this expression. Second, even though we cannot measure utility there is no reason to abandon the useful term of 'marginal utility'. Since this is, by definition, the change in total utility from increasing (or decreasing) consumption by an infinitesimal amount, holding the other goods constant, we have the marginal utility of the first good, $\partial u/\partial x_1$; and of the second good, $\partial u/\partial x_2$. Since the MRS is the ratio of two marginal utilities it is a pure number, i.e. it is free of any units (it has a dimension of zero). Third, for any utility function which is a monotonic increasing function of another, the MRS remains invariant. Let $u^* = F(u)$, where $F'(u) > 0$. Then

$$\partial u^*/\partial x_1 = F'(u).\partial u/\partial x_1 \text{ and } \partial u^*/\partial x_2 = F'(u).\partial u/\partial x_2$$

from which it follows

$$\text{MRS} = (\partial u^*/\partial \underline{x}_1)/(\partial u^*/\partial \underline{x}_2) = (\partial u/\partial x_1)/(\partial u/\partial \underline{x}_2)$$

and hence is invariant to a change in utility function. Fourth, if the indifference curve is *strictly* convex, the MRS must diminish at every point as one moves from left to right in Fig. 3.22. The reader should satisfy himself which of these results depend upon the indifference set being strictly convex, and what would happen if it was weakly convex.

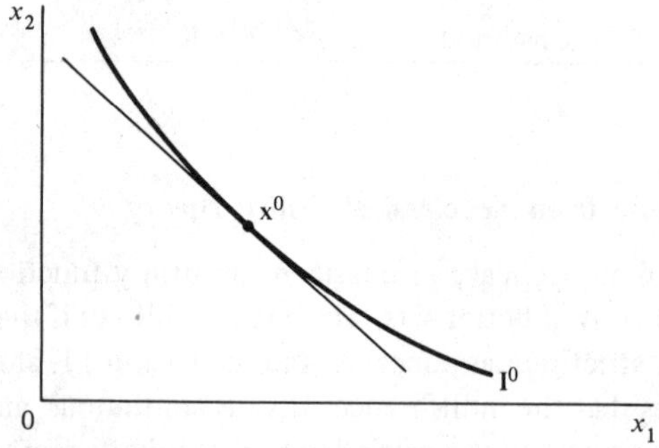

Fig. 3.22

Another consideration is that strict convexity of the indifference curve does not imply, and is not implied by, the condition of diminishing marginal utility. This latter condition is that $\partial(\partial u/\partial x_i)\partial x_i = \partial^2 u/\partial x_i^2 < 0$. But this should be apparent since the strict convexity is a relationship existing between *both* x_1 and x_2 whilst diminishing marginal utility refers only to a single good; furthermore, in that diminishing marginal utility uses partial derivatives, x_2 is held constant but in considering the convexity property both x_1 and x_2 are changing. The condition for convexity is that

$$(u_{11}u_2^2 - 2u_1u_2u_{12} + u_{22}u_1^2) < 0,$$ [10]

which is not necessarily satisfied if $u_{ii} < 0$ $(i = 1, 2)$.

3.9 Separability of the Utility Function and Some Extensions

Historically, the utility function took the form:[11]

$$u(x_1, \ldots, x_n) = h_1(x_1) + h_2(x_2) + \ldots + h_n(x_n)$$

and has recently been given attention by Houthakker [57]. This (direct) additive formulation has a number of implications.[12] First, the marginal utility of a commodity does not depend upon the level of any other commodity. This means $u_{ij} = 0\ (i \neq j)$. Second, if each commodity exhibits diminishing marginal utility, in the present case this is necessary and sufficient for a strictly convex indifference curve. In the two-commodity situation, since $u_{12} = 0$ and $u_{11} < 0, u_{22} < 0$, it necessarily follows that

$$u_{11}u_2^2 + u_{22}u_1^2 < 0.$$

Third, since the marginal utilities of commodities i and j depend only on commodities i and j respectively, it follows then that the MRS between commodities i and j is independent of any other commodity.

In the history of economic analysis the utility function is not the only function to be expressed in additive form. In Appendix 2B we discussed the social welfare function $\emptyset$. Such a function was expressed in terms of the relations R_i. However, like the consumer, we can express this in terms of the utilities of the individuals. If u^k denotes the utility function of the kth individual, then we can write the social welfare function as:

$$W(u^1, \ldots, u^m).$$

Some writers have assumed that we can write W in additive form and we obtain, what is called by de Graaff [46], an elementary Paretian welfare function:

$$W(u^1, \ldots, u^m) = u^1 + u^2 + \ldots + u^m.$$

This issue of an additive welfare function will be taken up later when we discuss welfare economics.

The additive utility function discussed above can be considered as an extreme case of a *separable utility function.* To see this, suppose consumers make decisions in two stages. First they attach utility to individual goods of a 'similar' type. Suppose we divide all goods into three groups: food, clothing and the rest. We have a function, say v_1, which indicates the consumer's preferences for food in terms of a utility function. We then have another function, u say, which determines the utilities of the various groups. Consider the following schema which allocates the various goods to the three groups just mentioned. The vector $\mathbf{x} = (x_1, \ldots, x_n)$ can be written $\mathbf{x} = (\mathbf{x}^1, \mathbf{x}^2, \mathbf{x}^3)$

$$\underbrace{x_1, x_2,}_{\substack{\mathbf{x}^1 \\ \text{food}}}\ \underbrace{x_3, x_4, x_5,}_{\substack{\mathbf{x}^2 \\ \text{clothing}}}\ \underbrace{x_6, x_7, \ldots, x_n}_{\substack{\mathbf{x}^3 \\ \text{other goods}}}$$

Now let $v_g(\mathbf{x}^g)$ denote the utility of the gth group, in this instance $g = 1, 2, 3$. $v_1(\mathbf{x}^1)$, for example, considers the utility function of food, $v_2(\mathbf{x}^2)$ that for clothing, etc. Each function $v_g(\mathbf{x}^g)$ indicates the consumer's ranking of goods within that group and making no reference to the ranking in other groups. However, when choices are being made between food and clothing then the overall utility function u is what matters, i.e.

$$u(\mathbf{x}) = u\,[v_1(\mathbf{x}^1), v_2(\mathbf{x}^2)\, v_3(\mathbf{x}^3)]\,.$$

If the marginal rate of substitution between two goods, for instance x_1 and x_2, and another good, for example x_4, is independent, i.e. has a value zero, then we say x_1 and x_2 are separable in u. Put mathematically, if

$$\frac{\partial}{\partial x_4}\left(\frac{\partial u/\partial x_1}{\partial u/\partial x_2}\right) = \frac{u_{14}u_2 - u_{24}u_1}{u_2^2} = 0$$

then goods x_1 and x_2 are said to be separable from x_4.

In order that we can state various forms of separability it will be helpful if we generalise the problem. Suppose the commodities $x_1, \ldots, x_n$ can be divided into G subgroups such that the gth group has G_g commodities and where

$$\sum_{g=1}^{G} G_g = n.$$

We have then the following representative vectors for the 1st, g^{th} and G^{th} groups:

$$\mathbf{x}^1 = \begin{pmatrix} x_1^1 \\ \cdot \\ \cdot \\ \cdot \\ x_{G_1}^1 \end{pmatrix}, \quad \mathbf{x}^g = \begin{pmatrix} x_1^g \\ \cdot \\ \cdot \\ \cdot \\ x_{G_g}^g \end{pmatrix}, \quad \mathbf{x}^G = \begin{pmatrix} x_1^G \\ \cdot \\ \cdot \\ \cdot \\ x_{G_G}^G \end{pmatrix}.$$

It follows that $\mathbf{x} = (x_1, \ldots, x_n) = (\mathbf{x}^1, \ldots, \mathbf{x}^G)$. We can now define three types of separability.

Definition 3.14

A utility function $u(\mathbf{x})$ is said to be *weakly separable* if

$$u(\mathbf{x}) = u\,[v_1(\mathbf{x}^1), \ldots, v_g(\mathbf{x}^g), \ldots, v_G(\mathbf{x}^G)]\,.$$

Strongly separable if

$$u(\mathbf{x}) = u\left[\sum_{g=1}^{G} v_g(\mathbf{x}^g)\right].$$

Additively separable (or completely additively separable) if

$$u(\mathbf{x}) = \sum_{i=1}^{n} h_i(x_i).$$

Given these definitions of separability it follows that the marginal rate of substitution between any two goods in a group is independent of a good not in that group. One important implication of this definition of separability is that, for any monotonically increasing transformation of the utility function, a group formerly separable remains so after such a transformation, i.e. separability, as defined here, is independent of the utility function chosen. This can readily be shown. Suppose i and j are separable from k then we have

$$\frac{\partial}{\partial x_k}\left(\frac{\partial u/\partial x_i}{\partial u/\partial x_j}\right) = 0.$$

Now consider $F[u(\mathbf{x})]$ where $F'(u) > 0$. Then it follows

$$\frac{\partial}{\partial x_k}\left(\frac{\partial F/\partial x_i}{\partial F/\partial x_j}\right) = \frac{\partial}{\partial x_k}\left(\frac{F'\partial u/\partial x_i}{F'\partial u/\partial x_j}\right) = \frac{\partial}{\partial x_k}\left(\frac{\partial u/\partial x_i}{\partial u/\partial x_j}\right) = 0.$$

Hence separability is independent of the *level* of utility.

Earlier in the chapter we showed a correspondence between the preference approach and that of utility. We may now ask, therefore, what is the connection between a separable utility function and the preference structure on which it is based? We shall deal with this only briefly here; an extended discussion will be found in Simmons [115]. Put succinctly, for u to be separable then it is necessary that the ordering relation R, at least preferred to, is also separable. Let R_g denote the gth subordering of R in the sense

$$\mathbf{x}^g R_g \mathbf{y}^g \Leftrightarrow v_g(\mathbf{x}^g) \geqslant v_g(\mathbf{y}^g)$$

where $\mathbf{x}^g$ and $\mathbf{y}^g$ are two commodity vectors of the gth group. The relation between R_g and R can be made a little clearer as follows. Let $\mathbf{x}^{\bar{g}}$ denote all commodities excluding $\mathbf{x}^g$, i.e. the complement set of commodities to $\mathbf{x}^g$ in $\mathbf{x}$. Two commodity bundles which differ only with respect to the gth group can therefore be denoted $(\mathbf{x}^g, \mathbf{x}^{\bar{g}})$ and $(\mathbf{y}^g, \mathbf{x}^{\bar{g}})$. Then,

$$\mathbf{x}^g R_g \mathbf{y}^g \Leftrightarrow (\mathbf{x}^g, \mathbf{x}^{\bar{g}}) R (\mathbf{y}^g, \mathbf{x}^{\bar{g}}) \quad \forall g.$$

It is to be noted that the separability of R must be with respect to a particular grouping of goods.

Before discussing the implications of separability we shall first discuss some proposed extensions to the utility function since these have a bearing on the relevance of separability. Such extensions take many forms but we shall discuss only two. (1) The introduction of prices into the utility function, and (2) the inclusion of money and bonds into the utility function. The introduction of prices into the utility function arises from attempts to deal with quality, the argument being that price reflects quality – this does seem to be so for certain types of machine tools. Let $\mathbf{p} = (p_1, \ldots, p_n)$ denote a vector of prices corresponding to

$\mathbf{x} = (x_1, \ldots, x_n)$; then if we can assume the same properties of u listed in Table 1.1 also apply to this extended utility function we can write $u = u(\mathbf{x}, \mathbf{p})$. Under these conditions a change in price will alter the indifference map since the latter is constructed in the commodity space for a given set of prices. A number of implications for consumer demand result from this extension and we shall return to these in the next chapter.

A second extension has been one which has attempted to bridge the gap between value theory and monetary theory. In its most simple form real balances, nominal money stock M_0 deflated by a general price index π, is introduced into the utility function. Thus $u = u(\mathbf{x}, M_0/\pi)$. Patinkin in his *Money, Interest, and Prices* makes it quite explicit in what sense he considers real balances can give utility; he argues that utility is derived from the *holding* of and not with the *spending* of real balances [96, p. 79]. It is generally assumed that $\partial u/\partial(M_0/\pi) > 0$. More generally we may consider

$$u = u\left(\mathbf{x}_1, \ldots, x_n; \frac{M_0}{\pi}, \frac{B_0}{\pi}, r\right)$$

where B_0 is bonds and r the rate of interest used in discounting future wealth.

Suppose u is separable in the following manner.

$$u = u\left[v_1\left(x_1, \ldots, x_n\right), v_2\left(\frac{M_0}{\pi}, \frac{B_0}{\pi}, r\right)\right]$$

where we have implicitly assumed that the real side and money side of exchange, although not independent, are weakly separable. It is now possible to discern three approaches to utility maximisation:

(1) Classical case $\quad \text{Max } v_1(x_1, \ldots, x_n)$

$$\text{s.t. } \mathbf{p}'\mathbf{x} = y$$

(2) Monetary case $\quad \text{Max } v_2\left(\frac{M_0}{\pi}, \frac{B_0}{\pi}, r\right)$

$$\text{s.t. } \frac{M_0}{\pi} + \frac{B_0}{\pi} = A$$

(3) General case $\quad \text{Max } u\left[v_1(x_1, \ldots, x_n), v_2\left(\frac{M_0}{\pi}, \frac{B_0}{\pi}, r\right)\right]$

$$\text{s.t. } \mathbf{p}'\mathbf{x} + \frac{M_0}{\pi} + \frac{B_0}{\pi} = y + A$$

where y is income and A is wealth from real balances and bonds. It would appear from (3) that the bridge between value theory (1) and monetary theory (2) will in part at least depend upon the form of the utility function. In the general case, which was first outlined by Morishima [86], we have assumed weak separability. The links between the two sides are more tenuous if the utility function is strongly separable and more so if the utility function is completely additively separable.

3.10 Revealed Preference Theory

Throughout a number of the earlier sections our attention has centred on the utility function. However, in many economists' eyes there is something unsatisfactory about a theory of demand based on the introspection of ordinal utility. Why this is so is that theories deduced from it tend to be non-operational (see p. 6). It was considered by Samuelson that if one considered a consumer's actual choices which he makes in the market then a consistent and rational person would reveal his preferences by his market behaviour and there would be no necessity to resort to introspection.

Revealed preference theory has grown largely from the work of Samuelson [107], and has been extended by Houthakker [56] and Uzawa [121]. The importance of this alternative approach to consumer behaviour is that it is based solely on behaviour and can therefore be tested. More startling is the fact that it requires only two axioms.

In this section we shall be concerned only with the relation properties of revealed preference theory, leaving discussions about demand to the next chapter.

Throughout this section $\mathbf{p}^0\mathbf{x}^0 = \sum_{i=1}^{n} p_i^0 x_i^0$, where we have suppressed the transpose on the price vector.

Axiom RP.1 $\quad \forall\, \mathbf{x}^0, \mathbf{x}^1 \in \mathbf{X}$ either $C\mathbf{x}^0$ or $C\mathbf{x}^1$,

i.e. given any set of alternative commodity bundles the consumer will always choose one. This is not the same as the completeness axiom (Axiom 1) which says the consumer either prefers one collection over the other or he is indifferent between them. No assumption is made concerning preferences; all that is required is that the consumer must make a choice.

Let $\mathbf{p}^0$ and $\mathbf{x}^0$ denote price and quantity vectors. The consumer's expenditure on $\mathbf{x}^0$ is $\mathbf{p}^0\mathbf{x}^0$. Consider now an alternative vector of goods $\mathbf{x}^1$ which the consumer could have purchased but chose not to do so. The total cost of the collection $\mathbf{x}^1$ must not exceed that of the bundle actually chosen, i.e. $\mathbf{p}^0\mathbf{x}^1 \leqslant \mathbf{p}^0\mathbf{x}^0$. If $\mathbf{x}^0$ is at least as expensive as $\mathbf{x}^1$ and if at the same set of prices the consumer chooses $\mathbf{x}^0$ with $\mathbf{x}^1$ available to him then we say '$\mathbf{x}^0$ is revealed preferred to $\mathbf{x}^1$'. We shall write this binary relation as $\mathbf{x}^0 RP \mathbf{x}^1$, where RP is the relation 'revealed preferred'.

The second axiom can now be stated;

Axiom RP.2 (Weak axiom of Revealed Preference Theory)

$$\mathbf{x}^0, \mathbf{x}^1 \in \mathbf{X}, \mathbf{x}^0 \neq \mathbf{x}^1, \mathbf{x}^0 RP \mathbf{x}^1 \Rightarrow \sim(\mathbf{x}^1 RP \mathbf{x}^0),$$

i.e. given any two commodity bundles open to the consumer, if the consumer chooses $\mathbf{x}^0$ over $\mathbf{x}^1$ showing he reveal prefers $\mathbf{x}^0$ to $\mathbf{x}^1$ then he can never, at the same set of prices, reveal prefer $\mathbf{x}^1$ over $\mathbf{x}^0$.

If $\mathbf{x}^1 RP \mathbf{x}^0$ this can only be true at a new price set, say $\mathbf{p}^1$, and this would mean $\mathbf{p}^1\mathbf{x}^0 \leqslant \mathbf{p}^1\mathbf{x}^1$. The condition in Axiom RP.2 can therefore be written in terms of expenditures:

$$\mathbf{p}^0\mathbf{x}^1 \leqslant \mathbf{p}^0\mathbf{x}^0 \Rightarrow \mathbf{p}^1\mathbf{x}^0 > \mathbf{p}^1\mathbf{x}^1.$$

In listing the axioms of consumer demand importance was placed on the transitivity of preferences. However, to discuss transitivity we must compare at least three bundles and neither Axiom RP.1 nor RP.2 involves a third bundle. It might be asked, therefore, whether this approach allows intransitivity. This issue of transitivity of revealed preference has, in the literature, been closely associated with the concern to reconcile this theory with utility theory. Houthakker thus shows that Axiom RP.2 is too weak, hence the title 'weak axiom of revealed preference theory' [56]. The strong axiom introduced by Houthakker states:

Axiom RP.2′ (Strong axiom of Revealed Preference Theory)

$$\forall \mathbf{x}^0 \mathbf{x}^1, \ldots, \mathbf{x}^S \in \mathbf{X}, \mathbf{x}^0 RP \mathbf{x}^1 \ \& \ \mathbf{x}^1 RP \mathbf{x}^2, \ldots, \& \ \mathbf{x}^{S-1} RP \mathbf{x}^S \Rightarrow \sim (\mathbf{x}^S RP \mathbf{x}^0),$$

i.e. if there is a sequence of bundles, where each is revealed preferred to its successor, then the last bundle in the sequence must not be revealed to be preferred to the first.

Recently, however, Sen has argued that Samuelson's weak axiom does in fact imply transitivity and that Houthakker's strong axiom is unnecessary. He does add that it all depends upon the interpretation of revealed preference theory. His argument rests on the consideration of the *whole set of observed choices.* If in this set, taking two at a time, $\mathbf{x}RP\mathbf{y}$ and $\mathbf{y}RP\mathbf{z}$, then, when faced with a choice between $\mathbf{x}$ and $\mathbf{z}$, Axiom 2 must require $\mathbf{x}RP\mathbf{z}$. 'The weak axiom not only guarantees two term consistency, it also prevents the violation of transitivity. The fact that the Axiom applies to two choices at a time does not rule out its repeated use to get the result of transitivity.' [112, p. 245].

One result is to be noted. If we have enough observations on a person's behaviour it is, in principle, possible to construct his indifference map. It has been argued by Houthakker that in order to satisfy the integrability condition, i.e. to be able to derive a utility function from an indifference surface, then the strong axiom of revealed preference theory is required. However, if we accept Sen's interpretation then integrability is implied by Samuelson's weak axiom.

We must now turn to consider consumer demand by bringing together the constraint set and the utility function. This we shall do in the next chapter.

EXERCISES

1. Prove:

$$\forall\ \mathbf{x}^0, \mathbf{x}^1 \in \mathbf{X} \qquad \mathbf{x}^0 I \mathbf{x}^1 \Rightarrow [\sim(\mathbf{x}^0 \geqslant \mathbf{x}^1) \text{ or} \sim (\mathbf{x}^1 \geqslant \mathbf{x}^0)].$$

2. To what extent is the axiom of non-satiation necessary in discussing the convexity of preferences? If satiation is allowed prove that:

$$\mathbf{x}^0 P \mathbf{x}^1 \nRightarrow \mathbf{x}^0 \geqslant \mathbf{x}^1$$

3. Suppose there exists an $\mathbf{x}^0 \in \mathbf{B}^0 \cap \mathbf{W}^0$ such that $N\epsilon\ (\mathbf{x}^0) \subset \mathbf{I}^0\ (= \mathbf{B}^0 \cap \mathbf{W}^0)$. Does it follow that if $\mathbf{x}^0, \mathbf{x}^1 \in \mathbf{I}^0$ that $\mathbf{x}^2 = a\mathbf{x}^0 + (1-a)\mathbf{x}^1 \notin \mathbf{I}^0$ and that $\mathbf{x}^2 P \mathbf{x}^0$ & $\mathbf{x}^2 P \mathbf{x}^1$?

4. Show that a quasiconcave utility function has a marginal utility of expenditure which is increasing or decreasing for different regions of the commodity space. Is this true for a strictly concave utility function?

5. Which of the following utility functions are (*a*) concave, (*b*) convex, (*c*) quasiconcave, and (*d*) quasiconvex?

(i) $u = a_0 x_1^{a_1} x_2^{a_2} \qquad a_1 + a_2 < 1$

(ii) $u = a_0 x_1^{a_1} x_2^{a_2} \qquad a_1 + a_2 = 1$

(iii) $u = a_0 x_1^{a_1} x_2^{a_2} \qquad a_1 + a_2 > 1$

(iv) $u = a_0\ [a_1 x_1^{-\rho} + a_2 x_2^{-\rho}]^{-\nu/\rho} \qquad a_0, a_1, a_2 > 0 \qquad \nu > 0 \qquad \rho \geqslant -1$

(v) $u = a_1 \log(x_1 - \gamma_1) + a_2 \log(x_2 - \gamma_2) \qquad a_1 + a_2 = 1 \qquad \gamma_1, \gamma_2 \geqslant 0$

6. Write the non-satiation axiom in terms of the utility function. What does this axiom imply about marginal utilities?

7. Under what conditions does diminishing marginal utility for both goods imply a convex indifference curve?

8. Show that continuity implies that if $\mathbf{x}^1 P \mathbf{x}^2 P \mathbf{x}^3$ then any continuous curve connecting $\mathbf{x}^1$ and $\mathbf{x}^3$ passes through a point $\mathbf{x}^4$ such that $\mathbf{x}^4 I \mathbf{x}^2$.

9. Which of the following sets are convex, stating whether they are strict or weak?

(i) $\mathbf{S} = \{(x_1, x_2)/p_1 x_1 + p_2 x_2 \leqslant y;\ \ x_1 \geqslant 0, x_2 \geqslant 0\}$

(ii) $\mathbf{S} = \{(x, y)/x^2 - y^2 < 1\}$

(iii) $S = \{(x, y)/x^2 + y^2 < 4\}$

(iv) $N_\epsilon(\mathbf{x}) = \{\mathbf{y} \in \mathbf{X}/d(\mathbf{x}, \mathbf{y}) < \epsilon\}$

(v) $S = \{\mathbf{x}/\mathbf{x} \in B(\mathbf{x}^0), \mathbf{x}^0 \in \mathbf{I}^0\}$

(vi) $S = \{\mathbf{x}/\mathbf{x} \in W(\mathbf{x}^0), \mathbf{x}^0 \in \mathbf{I}^0\}$

(vii) $S = S_1 \cap S_2$, where $S_1 = \{(x, y)/x^2 + y^2 < 9; x > 0, y > 0\}$ and
$S_2 = \{(x, y)/x^2/16 + y^2/4 = 1; x \geqslant 0, y \geqslant 0\}$

10. Prove that the set of non-negative solutions to a system of linear equations is a convex set.

11. Consider the utility function:

$$u(x_1, x_2) = (\tfrac{1}{4}) \log(x_1 - 2) + (\tfrac{3}{4}) \log(x_2 - 4).$$

(i) What does this imply about the preference relation over the set:

$S = \{\mathbf{x} \in \mathbf{X}/0 \leqslant x_1 \leqslant 2, 0 \leqslant x_2 \leqslant 4\}$?

(ii) Show that the marginal utilities are positive and independent of each other.

(iii) Demonstrate that this function is strictly concave, and hence show that the Hessian is negative definite. Over what domain of the commodity space is the Hessian negative definite?

(iv) If $u^0 = 0{\cdot}6931$, show that the indifference curve is given by

$$x_1 = \frac{16}{(x_2 + 4)^3} + 2$$

and also show that this is convex to the origin. Draw this curve.

(v) Indicate the relations (preference and indifference) between the following points:

(*a*) (2¼, 8) and (4, 6)

(*b*) (83, 5) and (18, 5)

12. Let A_1 and A_2 represent the attainable sets of two consumers, where

$$A_1 = \{(x_1, x_2)/p_1x_1 + p_2x_2 \leqslant 10; x_1 \geqslant 0, x_2 \geqslant 0\}$$

$$A_2 = \{(x_1, x_2)/p_1x_1 + p_2x_2 \leqslant 15; x_1 \geqslant 0, x_2 \geqslant 0\}$$

If the society is composed only of these two individuals, and prices are the same for both with $p_1 = 1$ and $p_2 = 2$, obtain the community's attainable set, i.e. obtain $A_1 + A_2$ and draw all three attainable sets on the one diagram.

13. Prove that a convex set is a connected set.

14. Consider the following three measures of distance between two vector (points) x and y.

(*a*) $d_1(\mathbf{x}, \mathbf{y}) = |\mathbf{x} - \mathbf{y}| = \left[\sum (x_i - y_i)^2\right]^{1/2}$

(*b*) $d_2(\mathbf{x}, \mathbf{y}) = \left| \dfrac{\mathbf{x}}{\sum x_i} - \dfrac{\mathbf{y}}{\sum y_i} \right| = \left[\sum_{i=1}^{n} \left(\dfrac{x_i}{\sum x_i} - \dfrac{y_i}{\sum y_i} \right)^2 \right]^{1/2}$

(*c*) $d_3(\mathbf{x}, \mathbf{y}) = \left| \dfrac{\mathbf{x}}{\|\mathbf{x}\|} - \dfrac{\mathbf{y}}{\|\mathbf{y}\|} \right| = \left[\sum_{i=1}^{n} \left(\dfrac{x_i}{\sum x_i^2} - \dfrac{y_i}{\sum y_i^2} \right)^2 \right]^{1/2}$

(i) Draw these three alternative measures on the one diagram for the vectors $\mathbf{x} = (1, 1)$ and $\mathbf{y} = (2, 3)$.

(ii) Let $\mathbf{S}_1$, $\mathbf{S}_2$ and $\mathbf{S}_3$ represent the set of points defined for each distance function respectively. Are these sets homomorphic?

15. If $u(\mathbf{x})$ is completely additively separable show that $\mathbf{U} = [u_{ij}]$ is a diagonal matrix. Also show that in this instance

$$d^2u = \mathbf{dx}'\mathbf{U}\,\mathbf{dx}$$

is negative definite if diminishing marginal utility holds for all goods.

4

NEOCLASSICAL AND MODERN CONSUMER CHOICE COMPARED

4.1 Neoclassical Optimisation

We have seen that if the axioms of choice theory are specified such that some of every good is consumed then the consumer spends all his income, and that the indifference curves are continuous and strictly convex to the origin, then we are dealing with the neoclassical theory of consumer behaviour. Although it must be apparent that this is an extreme interpretation, it is the theory which has dominated demand analysis and for this reason alone we must consider some of the results which have been investigated. We shall undertake this with one major difference. Consumer demand has not until the 1960s been analysed in terms of matrix algebra, but this more recent formulation has much to commend it and so we shall follow this treatment of Barten [11], Theil [119] and Goldberger [44].

Let x_i denote the quantity of the ith good ($i = 1, \ldots, n$), p_i its price, and y income. All variables are assumed non-negative. We define two vectors, each $n \times 1$.

$$\mathbf{x} = \begin{bmatrix} x_1 \\ \cdot \\ \cdot \\ \cdot \\ x_n \end{bmatrix} \qquad \mathbf{p} = \begin{bmatrix} p_1 \\ \cdot \\ \cdot \\ \cdot \\ p_n \end{bmatrix}.$$

Given the vector of prices, p, and income, y, the consumer chooses that quantity which maximises the value of his utility function:

$$u(\mathbf{x}) = u(x_1, \ldots, x_n)$$

subject to his budget constraint: $\mathbf{p}'\mathbf{x} = y$ or $\sum_{i=1}^{n} p_2 x_2 = \mathrm{y}$. The optimisation problem becomes therefore:

$$\begin{aligned} & \max u(\mathbf{x}) \\ & \mathbf{x} \in \mathbf{X} \\ \text{s.t.} \quad & \mathbf{p}'\mathbf{x} = y \\ & \mathbf{x} \geqslant 0. \end{aligned}$$

Let $u_i = \dfrac{\partial u}{\partial x_i}$ and $u_{ij} = \dfrac{\partial^2 u}{\partial x_i \partial x_j}$, and denote the vector of $n \times 1$ marginal utilities

$\mathbf{u}_x$ by:

$$\mathbf{u}_x = \frac{\partial u}{\partial \mathbf{x}} = \begin{bmatrix} u_1 \\ \cdot \\ \cdot \\ \cdot \\ u_n \end{bmatrix}$$

and denote the $n \times n$ second-order matrix $\mathbf{U}$ by:[1]

$$\mathbf{U} = \frac{\partial \mathbf{u}_x}{\partial \mathbf{x}'} = \begin{bmatrix} u_{11} & \ldots & u_{1n} \\ \cdot & & \cdot \\ \cdot & & \cdot \\ \cdot & & \cdot \\ u_{n1} & \ldots & u_{nn} \end{bmatrix}.$$

The maximisation condition can therefore be written:

$$L(\mathbf{x}, \lambda) = u(\mathbf{x}) - \lambda(\mathbf{p}'\mathbf{x} - y)$$

where λ is the Lagrangian multiplier. The necessary conditions for a maximum are:

$$\mathbf{L}_x = \mathbf{u}_x - \lambda \mathbf{p} = 0$$

$$L_\lambda = -(\mathbf{p}'\mathbf{x} - y) = 0. \tag{4.1}$$

These comprise $n + 1$ equations in $n + 1$ unknowns. If $\mathbf{U}$ is negative definite then a maximum rather than a minimum is assured,[2] and we can solve the Equations (4.1) uniquely in terms of $\mathbf{p}$ and y. We can denote these solutions:

$$\mathbf{x} = \mathbf{x}(\mathbf{p}, y) \qquad \text{and} \qquad \lambda = \lambda(\mathbf{p}, y)$$

where $\mathbf{x} = \mathbf{x}(\mathbf{p}, y)$ is a vector of n-demand equations:

$$x_i = x_i(p_1, \ldots, p_n, y) \qquad i = 1, \ldots, n.$$

Let us first take note of some important results. We have from (4.1) for the goods i and j:

$$\frac{u_i}{u_j} = \frac{p_i}{p_j} \qquad \forall i \text{ and } j.$$

But we know from Chapter 3.8 that the slope of the indifference curve for goods i and j is $dx_j/dx_i = u_i/u_j$, hence

$$\text{MRS}_{ij} = \frac{dx_j}{dx_i} = \frac{u_i}{u_j} = \frac{p_i}{p_j}.$$

We can interpret this by saying that the consumer is in an optimal position when the marginal utilities of any two goods taken in combination are proportional to their respective prices, or that the marginal rate of substitution of good j for good i is equal to the ratio of their prices.

Let us next give an economic interpretation to the Lagrangian multiplier, λ. From the utility function we have:

$$du = \mathbf{u}'_x\, \mathbf{dx}.$$

Substituting the first-order conditions given in (4.1) we have:

$$du = \lambda \mathbf{p}'\mathbf{dx}.$$

But $y = \mathbf{p}'\mathbf{x}$ and with prices and income held constant we must have $dy = \mathbf{p}'\mathbf{dx}$ Substituting we get:

$$\frac{du}{dy} = \lambda.$$

This means that the marginal utility of an infinitesimal change in spending is equal to λ. Furthermore, we have the condition that when the consumer is in an optimal position each good must satisfy:

$$\frac{u_i}{p_i} = \lambda = \frac{du}{dy} \qquad \forall i.$$

What this means is that if $u_i/p_i > du/dy$ then, at the going price, a consumer would prefer to hold good i rather than spend some of his income on other goods. If $u_i/p_i < du/dy$ money would be preferable and the consumer would give up good i and increase money spending elsewhere. Since all the budget must be spent the consumer will be in an optimal position only when the marginal utilities weighted by the reciprocal of their respective prices are equal everywhere.

Before leaving this discussion an important consideration must be made explicit. We have already said in Chapter 3.8 that the MRS remains invariant to a change in the utility function, so too, therefore, does the optimal solution. But there are two important differences. Consider $F(u)$ where $F'(u) > 0$ so that F is an increasing monotonic function of u. Then

$$L^* = F[u(\mathbf{x})] - \mu(\mathbf{p}'\mathbf{x} - y).$$

With first-order conditions:

$$\mathbf{L}^*_x = F'(u)\mathbf{u}_x - \mu\mathbf{p} = 0$$

$$L^*_\mu = -(\mathbf{p}'\mathbf{x} - y) = 0.$$

But since $F'(u)u_i/F'(u)u_j = u_i/u_j = p_i/p_j$ the optimal solution must be unaltered. However, compare the two following equations:

$$\mathbf{L}_x = \mathbf{u}_x - \lambda\mathbf{p} = 0$$

$$\mathbf{L}^*_x = \mathbf{u}_x - \frac{\mu\mathbf{p}}{F'(u)} = 0$$

where $\mathbf{L}^*_x$ has been made comparable with $\mathbf{L}_x$ by dividing throughout by $F'(u)$ From the first equation the marginal utility of money spending is λ and in the second it is μ. But if λ is to equal $\mu/F'(u)$, and hence the marginal utility of money spending to remain invariant to a change in the utility function, then we require $F'(u) = 1$, which will generally not be true. In other words, the marginal utility of money spending *is* dependent upon the utility function chosen. Put another way, the utility to the reader of an additional £1 cannot be ascertained without knowing his utility function exactly.

The second consideration is this: u_i is the marginal utility of the ith good, but equally $F'(u)u_i$ is also the marginal utility of the ith good, and generally these are not the same. In other words, the marginal utility of a good is dependent upon the choice of utility function and, in this case, has no strict interpretation. However, the MRS is independent of the choice of utility function and is therefore meaningful.

To illustrate the points made in this section let $u(\mathbf{x}) = a_0 x_1^{\;a_1} x_2^{\;a_2}$ for a two-good situation. The first-order conditions are:

$$L_{x_1} = \frac{a_1 u}{x_1} - \lambda p_1 = 0$$

$$L_{x_2} = \frac{a_2 u}{x_2} - \lambda p_2 = 0$$

$$L_\lambda = -(p_1 x_1 + p_2 x_2 - y) = 0.$$

This gives solutions:

$$x_1 = \frac{a_1 y}{(a_1 + a_2)p_1},\; x_2 = \frac{a_2 y}{(a_1 + a_2)p_2},\; \lambda = \frac{a_0 a_1^{\,a_1} a_2^{\,a_2} y^{a_1 + a_2 - 1}}{(a_1 + a_2)^{a_1 + a_2 - 1} p_1^{\,a_1} p_2^{\,a_2}},\; \frac{du}{dy} = \lambda.$$

Furthermore, suppose we consider $F(u) = \log u$. Then $\log u = \log a_0 x_1^{\,a_1} x_2^{\,a_2} = \log a_0 + a_1 \log x_1 + a_2 \log x_2$. This gives first-order conditions:

$$L^*_{x_1} = \frac{a_1}{x_1} - p_1 = 0$$

$$L^*_{x_2} = \frac{a_2}{x_2} - p_2 = 0$$

$$L^*_\mu = -(p_1 x_1 + p_2 x_2 - y) = 0.$$

It is readily verified that these give the same demand equations for x_1 and x_2 but that $\mu = (a_1 + a_2)/y$. It is further to be observed that if $a_1 + a_2 < 1$, then both λ and μ are inversely proportional to income, but if $a_1 + a_2 > 1$ then λ is directly proportional to income while μ remains inversely proportional. Finally, in the often-used example of $a_1 + a_2 = 1$, then for the Cobb–Douglas utility function, λ is independent of income while μ is inversely proportional to income by a factor of unity. Returning to the reader's marginal utility of an extra £1, for the Cobb–Douglas situation it is a constant whilst for the transformed function it depends upon your present level of income and furthermore, is smaller the higher your income. It is therefore impossible to know (predict) the marginal utility to you of a £1 increase in direct tax without knowing your exact utility function. Furthermore, to discuss redistribution of income and its utility effect on any individual equally requires us to know exactly what the utility function is. Only in a small number of instances can we make any predictions without this knowledge.[3] Finally, it is readily observed that the marginal utility in the first instance is $a_i(u/x_i)$ whilst in the second instance it is a_i/x_i, i.e. $a_i/x_i = F'(u) \cdot a_i(u/x_i)(i = 1, 2)$.

4.2 Restrictions on the Demand Equations

It has been argued that, historically, demand analysis has moved along two paths: one concerned with obtaining general laws and the second, more applied, has been concerned with the underlying psychological laws of preferences [19]. As the development of econometrics has grown there has been a demand for testable hypotheses. In the early period of estimation the theoretical foundations of demand rested very much on the analysis of Slutsky [116] and Hicks and Allen [53]. Our first task in this section, therefore, will be to derive the Slutsky decomposition of demand into the substitution effect and the income effect. In so far as earlier studies looked at only selected commodities the Slutsky equation was the only theoretical foundation. However, in the late 1950s and early 1960s questions have turned to the correct methodology for obtaining demand equations. For example, must an investigator obtain a whole set of demand equations rather than just an isolated demand equation? One important implication of the testing of a whole set of demand equations is that it can be considered as a method of testing the maximisation model discussed in Section 4.1. To see how one is considering the model it is important to know what restrictions are placed on the model, i.e. on the whole set of equations $\mathbf{x} = \mathbf{x}(\mathbf{p}, y)$. In fact, the optimisation process of neoclassical consumer demand places a number of restrictions on the set of demand functions, many of which have attracted a great deal of attention in the literature, e.g. Barten [11], Theil [119], Houthakker [57] and Frisch [41] to name but a few. These restrictions include aggregation across equations, the symmetry of the substitution term, homogeneity of the demand equations, and the negative semi-definiteness of the substitution matrix. We therefore elaborate on these restrictions after deriving the Slutsky equation.

The Slutsky equation is part of the comparative statics of consumer demand. We accordingly totally differentiate the first-order conditions:

$$\mathbf{u}_x - \lambda\mathbf{p} = 0$$
$$\mathbf{p}'\mathbf{x} = y$$

giving

$$\mathbf{U}\mathbf{dx} - \mathbf{p}d\lambda = \lambda\mathbf{dp}$$
$$\mathbf{p}'\mathbf{dx} = dy - \mathbf{x}'\mathbf{dp}.$$

Or in terms of matrices:

$$\begin{bmatrix} \mathbf{U} & \mathbf{p} \\ \mathbf{p}' & 0 \end{bmatrix} \begin{bmatrix} \mathbf{dx} \\ -d\lambda \end{bmatrix} = \begin{bmatrix} \lambda \mathbf{dp} \\ dy - \mathbf{x}'\mathbf{dp} \end{bmatrix}. \tag{4.2}$$

Using the result for the inverse of a partitioned matrix[4] we obtain:

$$\begin{bmatrix} \mathbf{dx} \\ -d\lambda \end{bmatrix} = (\mathbf{p}'\mathbf{U}^{-1}\mathbf{p})^{-1} \begin{bmatrix} (\mathbf{p}'\mathbf{U}^{-1}\mathbf{p})\mathbf{U}^{-1} - (\mathbf{U}^{-1}\mathbf{p})(\mathbf{U}^{-1}\mathbf{p})' & \mathbf{U}^{-1}\mathbf{p} \\ (\mathbf{U}^{-1}\mathbf{p})' & -1 \end{bmatrix} \begin{bmatrix} \lambda \mathbf{dp} \\ dy - \mathbf{x}'\mathbf{dp} \end{bmatrix}.$$

First let us obtain the effect on the quantities and λ as a result of an income change, prices held constant.

$$\frac{\partial \mathbf{x}}{\partial y} = \mathbf{x}_y = (\mathbf{p}'\mathbf{U}^{-1}\mathbf{p})^{-1}\mathbf{U}^{-1}\mathbf{p}$$

and

$$\frac{\partial \lambda}{\partial y} = \lambda_y = (\mathbf{p}'\mathbf{U}^{-1}\mathbf{p})^{-1}$$

where $\mathbf{x}_y$ is an $n \times 1$ column vector of demand responses to an income change, and λ_y is a scalar. It is worth noting that $\mathbf{x}_y$ is a vector whose n elements are the slopes of the respective Engel curves at a given level of income. Since we have shown in the previous section that $\lambda = du/dy$ it follows that $\lambda_y = d(du/dy) = d^2u/dy^2$ and this tells us whether the marginal utility of money spending is increasing, decreasing, or constant (but see Exercise 4).

Next assume income is constant but prices change, then:

$$\frac{\partial \mathbf{x}}{\partial \mathbf{p}'} = \mathbf{X}_p = \lambda(\mathbf{p}'\mathbf{U}^{-1}\mathbf{p})^{-1}(\mathbf{p}'\mathbf{U}^{-1}\mathbf{p})\mathbf{U}^{-1} - \lambda(\mathbf{p}'\mathbf{U}^{-1}\mathbf{p})^{-1}(\mathbf{U}^{-1}\mathbf{p})(\mathbf{U}^{-1}\mathbf{p})'$$

$$- (\mathbf{p}'\mathbf{U}^{-1}\mathbf{p})^{-1}\mathbf{U}^{-1}\mathbf{p}\mathbf{x}' = \lambda\mathbf{U}^{-1} - \lambda\mathbf{x}_y(\mathbf{U}^{-1}\mathbf{p})' - \mathbf{x}_y\mathbf{x}'$$

i.e.

$$\mathbf{X}_p = \lambda\mathbf{U}^{-1} - \lambda\mathbf{x}_y\mathbf{x}'_y\lambda_y^{-1} - \mathbf{x}_y\mathbf{x}' \tag{4.3}$$

and

$$\frac{\partial \lambda}{\partial \mathbf{p}} = \boldsymbol{\lambda}_p = -[\lambda(\mathbf{p}'\mathbf{U}^{-1}\mathbf{p})^{-1}(\mathbf{U}^{-1}\mathbf{p}) + (\mathbf{p}'\mathbf{U}^{-1}\mathbf{p})^{-1}\mathbf{x}]$$

$$= -[\lambda\mathbf{x}_y + \lambda_y\mathbf{x}].$$

It is to be noted that $\mathbf{X}_p$ is an $n \times n$ price response matrix; $\boldsymbol{\lambda}_p$ is an $n \times 1$ column vector denoting the effect on λ of a change in each price. Notice too that in obtaining $\boldsymbol{\lambda}_p$ the differential is with respect to a column vector but that in obtaining X_p it is with respect to a row vector. We have then:

$$\mathbf{x}_y = \begin{bmatrix} \partial x_1/\partial y \\ \cdot \\ \cdot \\ \cdot \\ \partial x_n/\partial y \end{bmatrix} \qquad \lambda_y = \frac{\partial \lambda}{\partial y} \qquad \mathbf{X}_p = \begin{bmatrix} \frac{\partial x_1}{\partial p_1} & \cdots & \frac{\partial x_1}{\partial p_n} \\ \cdot & & \cdot \\ \cdot & & \cdot \\ \cdot & & \cdot \\ \frac{\partial x_n}{\partial p_1} & \cdots & \frac{\partial x_n}{\partial p_n} \end{bmatrix}$$

or

$$\mathbf{X}_p = \begin{bmatrix} x_{11} & \cdots & x_{1n} \\ \cdot & & \cdot \\ \cdot & & \cdot \\ \cdot & & \cdot \\ x_{n1} & \cdots & x_{nn} \end{bmatrix} \quad \boldsymbol{\lambda}_p = \begin{bmatrix} \partial\lambda/\partial p_1 \\ \cdot \\ \cdot \\ \cdot \\ \partial\lambda/\partial p_n \end{bmatrix}.$$

The response vectors and matrices $\mathbf{x}_y, \lambda_y, \mathbf{X}_p$, and $\boldsymbol{\lambda}_p$ can be obtained in a slightly different way which is used by Barten [11] and Theil [119]. The equations in (4.2) can be rewritten as follows:

$$\begin{bmatrix} \mathbf{U} & \mathbf{p} \\ \mathbf{p}' & 0 \end{bmatrix} \begin{bmatrix} \mathbf{dx} \\ -d\lambda \end{bmatrix} = \begin{bmatrix} 0 & \lambda\mathbf{I} \\ 1 & -\mathbf{x}' \end{bmatrix} \begin{bmatrix} dy \\ \mathbf{dp} \end{bmatrix}. \tag{4.4}$$

This has been called by Barten the *fundamental matrix equation of the theory of consumer demand in terms of infinitesimal changes.* Now consider the equations $\mathbf{x} = \mathbf{x}(\mathbf{p}, y)$ and $\lambda = \lambda(\mathbf{p}, y)$. Totally differentiating these equations we get:

$$\mathbf{dx} = \mathbf{X}_p \mathbf{dp} + \mathbf{x}_y \, dy$$
$$d\lambda = \boldsymbol{\lambda}'_p \, \mathbf{dp} + \lambda_y \, dy.$$

More compactly:

$$\begin{bmatrix} \mathbf{dx} \\ -d\lambda \end{bmatrix} = \begin{bmatrix} \mathbf{x}_y & \mathbf{X}_p \\ -\lambda_y & -\boldsymbol{\lambda}'_p \end{bmatrix} \begin{bmatrix} dy \\ \mathbf{dp} \end{bmatrix}. \tag{4.5}$$

Since both (4.4) and (4.5) hold for arbitrary dy and $\mathbf{dp}$ it follows that:

$$\begin{bmatrix} \mathbf{U} & \mathbf{p} \\ \mathbf{p}' & 0 \end{bmatrix} \begin{bmatrix} \mathbf{x}_y & \mathbf{X}_p \\ -\lambda_y & -\boldsymbol{\lambda}'_p \end{bmatrix} = \begin{bmatrix} 0 & \lambda\mathbf{I} \\ 1 & -\mathbf{x}' \end{bmatrix}.$$

This Barten calls the *fundamental matrix equation of consumer demand theory in terms of marginal responses.* Hence:

$$\begin{bmatrix} \mathbf{x}_y & \mathbf{X}_p \\ -\lambda_y & -\boldsymbol{\lambda}'_p \end{bmatrix} = (\mathbf{p}'\mathbf{U}^{-1}\mathbf{p})^{-1} \begin{bmatrix} \mathbf{U}^{-1}\mathbf{p} & \lambda(\mathbf{p}'\mathbf{U}^{-1}\mathbf{p})\mathbf{U}^{-1} - \lambda(\mathbf{U}^{-1}\mathbf{p})(\mathbf{U}^{-1}\mathbf{p})' - \mathbf{U}^{-1}\mathbf{p}\mathbf{x}' \\ -1 & \lambda(\mathbf{U}^{-1}\mathbf{p})' + \mathbf{x}' \end{bmatrix}$$

which, with a little manipulation, gives the same results as before.

Equation (4.3) is the famous Slutsky decomposition-of-price response into substitution and income effects. The income effect is readily identifiable as $-\mathbf{x}_y\mathbf{x}'$. However, the substitution term is not so readily identifiable as the remainder. The substitution effect is the effect on a good of a price change when the consumer has been income-compensated such that he remains at the same level of utility after the price change as the level he was before the price change.

If utility is to remain constant then we must have:

$$du = \mathbf{u}'_x\,\mathbf{dx} = \lambda\mathbf{p}'\mathbf{dx} = 0.$$

But we know that $\mathbf{p}'\mathbf{dx} = dy - \mathbf{x}'\mathbf{dp}$, from which it follows $(dy - \mathbf{x}'\mathbf{dp}) = 0$ for $\lambda > 0$. With a constant level of utility, therefore, we have the compensated demand responses and income-compensated price response:

$$\begin{bmatrix} \mathbf{dx} \\ -d\lambda \end{bmatrix} = (\mathbf{p}'\mathbf{U}^{-1}\mathbf{p})^{-1} \begin{bmatrix} (\mathbf{p}'\mathbf{U}^{-1}\mathbf{p})\mathbf{U}^{-1} - (\mathbf{U}^{-1}\mathbf{p})(\mathbf{U}^{-1}\mathbf{p})' & \mathbf{U}^{-1}\mathbf{p} \\ (\mathbf{U}^{-1}\mathbf{p})' & -1 \end{bmatrix} \begin{bmatrix} \lambda\mathbf{dp} \\ 0 \end{bmatrix}.$$

Let $\mathbf{S}_p$ denote the matrix $\left.\frac{\partial\mathbf{x}}{\partial\mathbf{p}'}\right|_{u = \text{const.}}$ and $\boldsymbol{\lambda}^*_p = \left.\frac{\partial\lambda}{\partial\mathbf{p}}\right|_{u = \text{const.}}$ then we obtain

$$\mathbf{S}_p = \lambda(\mathbf{p}'\mathbf{U}^{-1}\mathbf{p})^{-1}(\mathbf{p}'\mathbf{U}^{-1}\mathbf{p})\mathbf{U}^{-1} - \lambda(\mathbf{p}'\mathbf{U}^{-1}\mathbf{p})^{-1}(\mathbf{U}^{-1}\mathbf{p})(\mathbf{U}^{-1}\mathbf{p})'$$

i.e. $\mathbf{S}_p = \lambda\mathbf{U}^{-1} - \lambda\mathbf{x}_y\mathbf{x}'_y\lambda_y^{-1}$

and $\boldsymbol{\lambda}^*_p = -\lambda(\mathbf{p}'\mathbf{U}^{-1}\mathbf{p})^{-1}(\mathbf{U}^{-1}\mathbf{p})$

i.e. $\boldsymbol{\lambda}^*_p = -\lambda\mathbf{x}_y$.

The substitution matrix, $\mathbf{S}_p$, can further be subdivided into the specific substitution matrix, $\mathbf{S}^*_p$, and the general substitution matrix, $\mathbf{S}^{**}_p$. The specific substitution matrix denotes the effect on a good of a price change assuming that the consumer's marginal utility of money spending remains constant, rather than the level of total utility. Let $\mathbf{S}^*_p = \left.\frac{\partial\mathbf{x}}{\partial\mathbf{p}'}\right|_{\lambda = \text{const.}}$ To obtain this, totally differentiate the marginal utility equation $\lambda = \lambda(\mathbf{p}, y)$, giving:

$$d\lambda = \boldsymbol{\lambda}'_p\,\mathbf{dp} + \lambda_y\,dy = 0$$

since λ is assumed to be constant. This can be rearranged, by noting that λ_y is a scalar, to $dy = \boldsymbol{\lambda}'_p\lambda_y^{-1}\mathbf{dp}$. But we have already established that $\boldsymbol{\lambda}_p = -(\lambda\mathbf{x}_y + \lambda_y\mathbf{x})$.

Substituting we obtain

$$dy = -\boldsymbol{\lambda}'_p \lambda_y^{-1}\,\mathbf{dp} = (\lambda \mathbf{x}_y + \lambda_y \mathbf{x})' \lambda_y^{-1}\,\mathbf{dp}$$

i.e.

$$dy = (\lambda \mathbf{x}'_y \lambda_y^{-1} + \mathbf{x}')\mathbf{dp}. \tag{4.6}$$

Now totally differentiating the demand equations $\mathbf{x} = \mathbf{x}(\mathbf{p}, y)$ and substituting Equation (4.6) into this we obtain:

$$\begin{aligned}\mathbf{dx} &= \mathbf{X}_p \mathbf{dp} + \mathbf{x}_y dy\\ &= \mathbf{X}_p \mathbf{dp} + (\lambda \mathbf{x}_y \mathbf{x}'_y \lambda_y^{-1} + \mathbf{x}_y \mathbf{x}')\mathbf{dp}\\ &= (\mathbf{X}_p + \lambda \mathbf{x}_y \mathbf{x}'_y \lambda_y^{-1} + \mathbf{x}_y \mathbf{x})\mathbf{dp}.\end{aligned}$$

But from Equation (4.3) $\mathbf{X}_p = \lambda \mathbf{U}^{-1} - \lambda \mathbf{x}_y \mathbf{x}'_y \lambda_y^{-1} - \mathbf{x}_y \mathbf{x}'$. It therefore follows that

$$\mathbf{S}_p^* = \left.\frac{\partial \mathbf{x}}{\partial \mathbf{p}'}\right|_{\lambda = \text{const.}} = \lambda \mathbf{U}^{-1}.$$

Hence

$$\mathbf{S}_p^{**} = \lambda \mathbf{x}_y \mathbf{x}'_y \lambda_y^{-1}.$$

To summarise, we have shown that

$$\begin{aligned}\mathbf{X}_p &= \lambda \mathbf{U}^{-1} - \lambda \mathbf{x}_y \mathbf{x}'_y \lambda_y^{-1} - \mathbf{x}_y \mathbf{x}'\\ &= \mathbf{S}_p - \mathbf{x}_y \mathbf{x}'\\ &= \mathbf{S}_p^* + \mathbf{S}_p^{**} - \mathbf{x}_y \mathbf{x}'\end{aligned}$$

where

$\mathbf{X}_p$ = total price effect

$\mathbf{S}_p$ = substitution effect

$\mathbf{S}_p^*$ = $\lambda \mathbf{U}^{-1}$ = specific substitution effect

$\mathbf{S}_p^{**}$ = $\lambda \mathbf{x}_y \mathbf{x}'_y \lambda_y^{-1}$ = general substitution effect

$-\mathbf{x}_y \mathbf{x}'$ = income effect.

We have shown that the Slutsky decomposition can be written $\mathbf{X}_p = \mathbf{S}_p - \mathbf{x}_y \mathbf{x}'$. If we let x_{ij} denote the $(i, j)^{\text{th}}$ element of $\mathbf{X}_p$, and s_{ij} the $(i, j)^{\text{th}}$ element of $\mathbf{S}_p$, then we have for good i, and a change in the price p_j, the more usual formulation:

$$x_{ij} = s_{ij} - x_j \frac{\partial x_i}{\partial y}$$

$$\frac{\partial x_i}{\partial p_j} = \left(\frac{\partial x_i}{\partial p_j}\right)_{u = \text{const.}} - x_j \frac{\partial x_i}{\partial y}.$$

In concluding our discussion of the Slutsky decomposition it is useful to note that many authors introduce into the above results the *income flexibility parameter.* The majority of authors define this in terms of the reciprocal of the income elasticity of the marginal utility of money spending. If this latter parameter is denoted $\eta_{\lambda y} = \lambda_y \lambda^{-1} y$ then the income flexibility parameter, $\emptyset$, is given by:

$$\emptyset = \lambda_y{}^{-1} \lambda y^{-1}.$$

This definition is used by Theil and Barten. However, there is no general agreement on the use of this term. Frisch discusses 'money flexibility' which he defines as $\lambda_y \lambda^{-1} y$; whilst Houthakker defines the 'income flexibility' as $\lambda_y^{-1} \lambda$.

We can therefore redefine the important equations above as follows:

(i) $\mathbf{x}_y = (\mathbf{p}'\mathbf{U}^{-1}\mathbf{p})^{-1}\mathbf{U}^{-1}\mathbf{p}$

(ii) $\lambda_y = (\mathbf{p}'\mathbf{U}^{-1}\mathbf{p})^{-1}$

(iii) $\mathbf{X}_p = \lambda\mathbf{U}^{-1} - \lambda\mathbf{x}_y\mathbf{x}_y'\lambda_y^{-1} - \mathbf{x}_y\mathbf{x}'$
$= \lambda\mathbf{U}^{-1} - y\emptyset\mathbf{x}_y\mathbf{x}_y' - \mathbf{x}_y\mathbf{x}'$

(iv) $\boldsymbol{\lambda}_p = -(\lambda\mathbf{x}_y + \lambda_y\mathbf{x})$
$= -\lambda[\mathbf{x}_y + (\emptyset y)^{-1}\mathbf{x}] = -\lambda_y[(\emptyset y)\mathbf{x}_y + \mathbf{x}]$.

Rather than set out a detailed example the reader is advised at this point to attempt Exercise 5, and obtain the Slutsky decomposition for the case $u = \boldsymbol{\alpha}' \log \mathbf{x}$ where $\boldsymbol{\iota}'\boldsymbol{\alpha} = 1$. It is to be noted, however, that in this case λ is independent of prices and is equal to the inverse of the level of income; second, that the direct substitution effect is equal to the total price effect, which implies that the indirect substitution effect is equal to the income effect; finally, that the income flexibility parameter has a value of minus unity. These very extreme results do show why this function is of little use in empirical work but it does have theoretical interest. A more empirically revealing utility function is that of the Stone–Geary utility function, which takes the form

$$u = \boldsymbol{\alpha}' \log (\mathbf{x} - \boldsymbol{\gamma}) \qquad 0 \ll \boldsymbol{\alpha} \ll \boldsymbol{\iota} \qquad \boldsymbol{\iota}'\boldsymbol{\alpha} = 1, \boldsymbol{\gamma} \geqslant 0.$$

Its most interesting feature is that it gives rise to a linear expenditure function of the form[5]

$$\mathbf{v} = \hat{\mathbf{p}}\,\mathbf{x} = y\boldsymbol{\alpha} + \mathbf{A}\mathbf{p}$$

where $\mathbf{A} = (\mathbf{I} - \boldsymbol{\alpha}\boldsymbol{\iota}')\hat{\boldsymbol{\Upsilon}}$ (see Exercise 6).

We can now turn to the restrictions on the demand curves. These are:

(i) Aggregation: (*a*) Engle aggregation; (*b*) Cournot aggregation.
(ii) Symmetry.
(iii) Homogeneity.
(iv) Negativity.

Also we shall illustrate each restriction with the demand curves derived from the Stone–Geary utility function, i.e. from the function.

$$\mathbf{x} = \boldsymbol{\gamma} + (y - \mathbf{p}'\boldsymbol{\gamma})\hat{\mathbf{p}}^{-1}\boldsymbol{\alpha}$$

where the various income and price response vectors and matrices will be found in Exercise 7.

4.2 (i) Aggregation Restrictions

(*a*) *Engel Aggregation.* This concerns the Engel curves. It says that if all the budget is spent then the value of the change in consumption must equal the change in income. Alternatively,

$$\mathbf{p}'\mathbf{x}_y = 1.$$

This is readily proved as follows:

$$\mathbf{p}'\mathbf{x}_y = \mathbf{p}'(\mathbf{p}'\mathbf{U}^{-1}\mathbf{p})^{-1}\mathbf{U}^{-1}\mathbf{p} = \lambda_y\mathbf{p}'\mathbf{U}^{-1}\mathbf{p} = \lambda_y^{-1}\lambda_y = 1.$$

For the Stone–Geary case $\mathbf{p}'\mathbf{x}_y = \mathbf{p}'\,\hat{\mathbf{p}}^{-1}\boldsymbol{\alpha} = \boldsymbol{\iota}'\boldsymbol{\alpha} = 1$.

(*b*) *Cournot Aggregation.* This says that if prices change and the budget is to be exhausted it must follow that:

$$\mathbf{X}'_p\mathbf{p} = -\mathbf{x}.$$

This is readily shown:

$$\begin{aligned}\mathbf{X}'_p\,\mathbf{p} &= (\lambda\mathbf{U}^{-1} - \lambda\lambda_y^{-1}\mathbf{x}_y\mathbf{x}'_y - \mathbf{x}\mathbf{x}'_y)\mathbf{p}\\ &= \lambda\mathbf{U}^{-1}\mathbf{p} - \lambda\lambda_y^{-1}\mathbf{x}_y\mathbf{x}'_y\mathbf{p} - \mathbf{x}\mathbf{x}'_y\mathbf{p}\\ &= \lambda\lambda_y^{-1}\mathbf{x}_y - \lambda\lambda_y^{-1}\mathbf{x}_y - \mathbf{x}\end{aligned}$$

since $\mathbf{p}'\mathbf{x}_y = \mathbf{x}'_y\mathbf{p} = 1$. Hence,

$$\mathbf{X}'_p\,\mathbf{p} = -\mathbf{x}.$$

For the Stone–Geary case,

$$\begin{aligned}\mathbf{X}'_p\mathbf{p} &= -(y - \mathbf{p}'\boldsymbol{\gamma})\,\hat{\mathbf{p}}^{-1}\hat{\boldsymbol{\alpha}}\,\hat{\mathbf{p}}^{-1}\mathbf{p} - \boldsymbol{\gamma}\boldsymbol{\alpha}'\,\hat{\mathbf{p}}^{-1}\mathbf{p}\\ &= -(y - \mathbf{p}'\boldsymbol{\gamma})\,\hat{\mathbf{p}}^{-1}\hat{\boldsymbol{\alpha}}\boldsymbol{\iota} - \boldsymbol{\gamma}\boldsymbol{\alpha}'\boldsymbol{\iota}\\ &= -\,[(y - \mathbf{p}'\boldsymbol{\gamma})\,\hat{\mathbf{p}}^{-1}\boldsymbol{\alpha} + \boldsymbol{\gamma}] = -\,\mathbf{x}.\end{aligned}$$

4.2 (ii) Symmetry

This says that the substitution matrix $\mathbf{S}_p$ is symmetric, i.e.

$$\mathbf{S}_p = \mathbf{S}'_p.$$

This can be demonstrated quite readily. $\mathbf{S}_p = \lambda\mathbf{U}^{-1} - \lambda\mathbf{x}_y\mathbf{x}'_y\lambda_y^{-1}$. We know that $\mathbf{U}$ is symmetric, then so is $\mathbf{U}^{-1}$. Also $\lambda\mathbf{x}_y\mathbf{x}'_y\lambda_y^{-1}$ is symmetric when we remember λ and λ_y^{-1} are scalars. Hence $\mathbf{S}_p = \mathbf{S}'_p$.

For the Stone–Geary case,

$$\mathbf{S}_p = -(y - \mathbf{p}'\boldsymbol{\gamma})^{-1}\,(\hat{\mathbf{x}} - \hat{\boldsymbol{\gamma}})\,\hat{\boldsymbol{\alpha}}^{-1}\,(\hat{\mathbf{x}} - \hat{\boldsymbol{\gamma}}) + (y - \mathbf{p}'\boldsymbol{\gamma})\hat{\mathbf{p}}^{-1}\,\boldsymbol{\alpha}\boldsymbol{\alpha}'\hat{\mathbf{p}}^{-1}$$

since $(y - \mathbf{p}'\boldsymbol{\gamma})$ is a scalar and the transpose of a diagonal matrix is itself, then both expressions in $\mathbf{S}_p$ are symmetric and it immediately follows that $\mathbf{S}_p = \mathbf{S}'_p$.

4.2 (iii) Homogeneity

This is the condition that the demand functions are homogeneous of degree zero in prices and income. Implied in the restrictions so far is the condition,

$$\mathbf{X}_p\mathbf{p} = -\mathbf{x}_y y.$$

This can be shown as follows. First postmultiply the matrix $\mathbf{S}_p$ by the vector $\mathbf{p}$, and use the fact that $\mathbf{S}_p = \mathbf{S}'_p$, so that

$$\begin{aligned}\mathbf{S}_p\mathbf{p} &= (\mathbf{X}_p + \mathbf{x}_y\mathbf{x}')\mathbf{p} = (\mathbf{X}'_p + \mathbf{x}\mathbf{x}'_y)\mathbf{p}\\ &= \mathbf{X}'_p\,\mathbf{p} + \mathbf{x}\mathbf{x}'_y\mathbf{p}.\end{aligned}$$

But we know from the Cournot aggregation that $\mathbf{X}'_p\mathbf{p} = -\mathbf{x}$ and from the Engel aggregation that $\mathbf{x}'_y\mathbf{p} = 1$. Hence,

$$\begin{aligned}\mathbf{S}_p\mathbf{p} &= -\mathbf{x} + \mathbf{x}\\ \therefore\ \mathbf{X}_p\mathbf{p} + \mathbf{x}_y\mathbf{x}'\mathbf{p} &= 0\end{aligned}$$

from which it follows that $\mathbf{X}_p\mathbf{p} = -\mathbf{x}_y y$. But this condition is implied by homogeneity of degree zero in $\mathbf{p}$ and y of the demand equations $\mathbf{x} = \mathbf{x}(\mathbf{p}, y)$. By Euler's theorem we have:

$$\mathbf{X}_p\mathbf{p} + \mathbf{x}_y y = 0$$

i.e.

$$\mathbf{X}_p\mathbf{p} = -\mathbf{x}_y y.$$

The homogeneity condition says that, with a proportional change in all prices and income, the optimal choice of commodities remains unchanged.

For the Stone–Geary case,

$$\begin{aligned}\mathbf{X}_p\mathbf{p} &= -(y - \mathbf{p}'\boldsymbol{\gamma})\hat{\mathbf{p}}^{-1}\hat{\boldsymbol{\alpha}}\hat{\mathbf{p}}^{-1}\mathbf{p} - \hat{\mathbf{p}}^{-1}\boldsymbol{\alpha}\boldsymbol{\gamma}'\mathbf{p}\\ &= -(y - \mathbf{p}'\boldsymbol{\gamma})\hat{\mathbf{p}}^{-1}\hat{\boldsymbol{\alpha}} - \hat{\mathbf{p}}^{-1}\boldsymbol{\alpha}\boldsymbol{\gamma}'\mathbf{p}\\ &= -y\hat{\mathbf{p}}^{-1}\boldsymbol{\alpha} + (\mathbf{p}'\boldsymbol{\gamma})\hat{\mathbf{p}}^{-1}\boldsymbol{\alpha} - \hat{\mathbf{p}}^{-1}\boldsymbol{\alpha}(\boldsymbol{\gamma}'\mathbf{p})\\ &= -y\hat{\mathbf{p}}^{-1}\boldsymbol{\alpha} = -y\mathbf{x}_y.\end{aligned}$$

The homogeneity condition has an important implication concerning the elasticities of demand. Since we will require these elasticity matrices in the future we shall define them here. Let

$$E_{ij} = \frac{\partial x_i}{\partial p_j}\,\frac{p_j}{x_i} \quad\text{and}\quad E_{iy} = \frac{\partial x_i}{\partial y}\,\frac{y}{x_i}\,.$$

Further let $\mathbf{E}_p$ denote the $n \times n$ price elasticity matrix and $\mathbf{E}_y$ the $n \times 1$ vector of income elasticities, thus

$$\mathbf{E}_p = \begin{bmatrix} E_{11} & \cdots & E_{1n}\\ \vdots & & \vdots\\ E_{n1} & \cdots & E_{nn}\end{bmatrix} \qquad \mathbf{E}_y = \begin{bmatrix} E_{1y}\\ \vdots\\ E_{ny}\end{bmatrix}$$

We shall use the convention of a circumflex above a vector to denote a diagonal matrix formed from a vector, as we have done so far. We can then employ the following definitions:

Definition 4.1

The price elasticity matrix, $\mathbf{E}_p$, and the income elasticity matrix, $\mathbf{E}_y$, are given by:

$$\mathbf{E}_p = \hat{\mathbf{x}}^{-1} \mathbf{X}_p \hat{\mathbf{p}}$$

$$\text{and} \quad \mathbf{E}_y = y \hat{\mathbf{x}}^{-1} \mathbf{x}_y .$$

From the demand functions $\mathbf{x} = \mathbf{x}(\mathbf{p}, y)$ we have:

$$\mathbf{dx} = \mathbf{X}_p \mathbf{dp} + \mathbf{x}_y dy.$$

Premultiply by $\hat{\mathbf{x}}^{-1}$ then

$$\hat{\mathbf{x}}^{-1} \mathbf{dx} = (\hat{\mathbf{x}}^{-1} \mathbf{X}_p \hat{\mathbf{p}})\, \hat{\mathbf{p}}^{-1} \mathbf{dp} + (\hat{\mathbf{x}}^{-1} \mathbf{x}_y y) y^{-1} dy.$$

If all prices and income change in the same proportion then optimal demands remain unchanged and so $\mathbf{dx} = 0$ and $\hat{\mathbf{p}}^{-1}\mathbf{dp}$ becomes the $n \times 1$ unit vector, and $y^{-1}dy$ takes the value of unity. Hence:

$$0 = \mathbf{E}_p \boldsymbol{\iota} + \mathbf{E}_y$$

i.e.

$$\mathbf{E}_p \boldsymbol{\iota} = - \mathbf{E}_y$$

or

$$\sum_{j=1}^{n} E_{ij} = - E_{iy} \qquad \forall i$$

In the Stone–Geary case it can be shown that

$$\mathbf{E}_p = \emptyset\, \hat{\mathbf{E}}_y - \mathbf{E}_y (y^{-1} \boldsymbol{\gamma}' \hat{\mathbf{p}})$$

Then,

$$\mathbf{E}_p \boldsymbol{\iota} = \emptyset\, \hat{\mathbf{E}}_y \boldsymbol{\iota} - \mathbf{E}_y (y^{-1} \boldsymbol{\gamma}' \hat{\mathbf{p}} \boldsymbol{\iota})$$

$$= \emptyset\, \mathbf{E}_y - \mathbf{E}_y y^{-1} \boldsymbol{\gamma}' \mathbf{p}.$$

But $\boldsymbol{\gamma}'\mathbf{p} = \mathbf{p}'\boldsymbol{\gamma} = y(1 + \emptyset)$ so that

$$\mathbf{E}_p \boldsymbol{\iota} = \emptyset \mathbf{E}_y - \mathbf{E}_y (1 + \emptyset) = - \mathbf{E}_y .$$

4.2 (iv) Negativity

This condition states that $\mathbf{S}_p$ is negative semidefinite, i.e.

$$\mathbf{q}' \mathbf{S}_p \mathbf{q} \leqslant 0$$

We know $\mathbf{S}_p = \lambda\, \mathbf{U}^{-1} - \lambda (\mathbf{p}' \mathbf{U}^{-1} \mathbf{p})^{-1} (\mathbf{U}^{-1} \mathbf{p})(\mathbf{U}^{-1} \mathbf{p})'.$

Let $$\mathbf{A} = \mathbf{U}^{-1} - (\mathbf{p}'\mathbf{U}^{-1}\mathbf{p})^{-1}(\mathbf{U}^{-1}\mathbf{p})(\mathbf{U}^{-1}\mathbf{p})'$$

then

$$\mathbf{q}'\mathbf{A}\mathbf{q} = (\mathbf{p}'\mathbf{U}^{-1}\mathbf{p})^{-1}\ [(\mathbf{q}'\mathbf{U}^{-1}\mathbf{q})(\mathbf{p}'\mathbf{U}^{-1}\mathbf{p}) - (\mathbf{q}'\mathbf{U}^{-1}\mathbf{p})^2].$$

If there exists a scalar c such that $\mathbf{q} = c\mathbf{p}$ then the term in brackets equals zero. Otherwise the bracketed expression is positive.[6] Therefore, given that $(\mathbf{p}'\mathbf{U}^{-1}\mathbf{p}) < 0$ since $\mathbf{U}$ is negative definite, the matrix $\mathbf{A}$, and hence $\mathbf{S}_p$, are negative semidefinite.

We can write the first three restrictions on the demand equations in elasticity form. To do this we make use of the average budget share:

Definition 4.2 If $w_i = p_i x_i / y$ then $\mathbf{w} = y^{-1}\ \hat{\mathbf{p}}\mathbf{x} = y^{-1}\ \hat{\mathbf{x}}\mathbf{p}$, where $\mathbf{w}$ is an $n \times 1$ vector.

The table below sets out the comparable results and it is left to the reader as part of the exercises (Exercise 8) to prove the elasticity equivalents.

Conditions		*Standard form*	*Elasticity form*
1. Aggregation:	Engel	$\mathbf{p}'\mathbf{x}_y = 1$	$\iota'\mathbf{w} = 1$
	Cournot	$\mathbf{X}'_p\mathbf{p} = -\mathbf{x}$	$\mathbf{E}'_p\ \mathbf{w} = -\mathbf{w}$
2. Symmetry		$\mathbf{S}_p = \mathbf{S}'_p$	$[\hat{\mathbf{w}}(\mathbf{E}_p + \mathbf{E}_y\mathbf{w}')]' = \hat{\mathbf{w}}(\mathbf{E}_p + \mathbf{E}_y\mathbf{w}')$
3. Homogeneity		$\mathbf{X}_p\mathbf{p} = -\mathbf{x}_y y$	$\mathbf{E}_p\iota = -\mathbf{E}_y$

4.3 Compensated Demand Curves

The demand curves which we have so far obtained, namely $\mathbf{x} = \mathbf{x}(\mathbf{p}, y)$, along with their properties, are sometimes called ordinary demand functions or uncompensated demand functions. If, however, following a price change we compensate a consumer for the change in income so that he remains at the same level of utility, say u, then income is no longer a parameter but rather u. The consumer will now wish to minimise his expenditure subject to $u(\mathbf{x}) = u$, i.e.

$$\min_{\mathbf{x}\in\mathbf{X}} \mathbf{p}'\mathbf{x}$$

$$\text{s.t.} \quad u(\mathbf{x}) = u$$

$$\mathbf{x} \geqslant 0.$$

The Lagrangian expression becomes:

$$V = \mathbf{p}'\mathbf{x} - \mu[u(\mathbf{x}) - u].$$

With first-order conditions:

$$V_x = \mathbf{p} - \mu \mathbf{u}_x = 0$$
$$V_\mu = -[u(\mathbf{x}) - u] = 0.$$

Solving for $\mathbf{x}^*$ and μ, where $\mathbf{x}^*$ denotes demand at which the individual's income is compensated, we get:

$$\mathbf{x}^* = \mathbf{x}^*(\mathbf{p}, u)$$
$$\mu = \mu(\mathbf{p}, u).$$

It follows immediately from our earlier analysis that:

$$\frac{\partial \mathbf{x}^*}{\partial \mathbf{p}'} = \mathbf{S}_p.$$

4.4 Groups of Commodities

Part of the interest in demand theory is in applying the results to groups of commodities. There are two broad categories. The first concerns properties possessed by a single good, i.e. in isolation, e.g. whether it is inferior or not. The second category comprises properties of goods taken together, e.g. whether two goods are substitutes or complements. The first category concerns itself with the vector $\mathbf{x}_y$ and with the diagonal elements of $\mathbf{X}_p$. The second group is largely concerned with the off-diagonal elements of $\mathbf{X}_p$ and $\mathbf{S}_p$.

The literature invariably talks of inferior goods, and sometimes, particularly in the applied field, of necessities and luxuries. These groups are formed according to which definition is used. The most common for each is the following:

Definition 4.3

A good x_i is

(*a*) an inferior good if $\dfrac{\partial x_i}{\partial y} < 0$

(*b*) a necessity if $0 < \dfrac{\partial x_i}{\partial y} < 1$

(*c*) a luxury if $\dfrac{\partial x_i}{\partial y} > 1$.

Other groups mentioned in the literature are normal goods and Giffen goods. These are classified according to the sign of the diagonal terms of $\mathbf{X}_p$.

Definition 4.4

A good x_i is

(*a*) a normal good if $x_{ii} = \partial x_i / \partial p_i < 0$

and

(*b*) a Giffen good if $x_{ii} = \partial x_i/\partial p_i > 0$.

A good is referred to as normal if it has a downward-sloping demand curve, and a Giffen good if it has an upward-sloping demand curve.

These definitions are arbitrary. Since they are each defined in terms of partial derivatives they are defined only at a point. Hence a good could be said to be inferior only if $\partial x_i/\partial y < 0$ for all $\mathbf{p}$ and y. However, we would normally expect a good to be non-inferior for some $\mathbf{p}$ and y but inferior for others. This is a shortcoming of all the groups listed in Definitions 4.3 and 4.4.

It is intuitively appealing to have two classes of goods, namely, complementary goods and substitute goods. Two questions are immediate. What is the criterion for placing a good in one category rather than the other? Second, even if the groups, as we would hope, are mutually exclusive, are they exhaustive? Can a good be neither a complement nor a substitute? It is clear that the answer to the second question depends upon the answer to the first question.

An early definition used by Pareto and Fisher was based on the shape of the indifference curve[107]. Goods i and j are, for a utility function $u(x_1, \ldots, x_n)$,

$$\text{Complements if } u_{ij} > 0$$

$$\text{Substitutes if } u_{ij} < 0.$$

Since $\mathbf{U}$ is symmetric it follows that if i is a complement (substitute) for j then j is a complement (substitute) for i. The definition only holds for utility functions defined up to a linear transformation. This is seen by considering the transformation $F(u)$. The first and second derivatives of $F(u)$ are:

$$F'(u)u_i$$

$$\text{and } F'(u)u_{ij} + F''(u)u_i u_j .$$

Only if $F''(u) = 0$ does it follow that the sign of the cross partial remains invariant to a change in the utility function. Such a transformation is $F(u) = a + bu$. Finally, u_{ij} is evaluated at a point so it is quite possible for $u_{ij}(\mathbf{x}^0) > 0$ and $u_{ij}(\mathbf{x}^1) < 0$ for $\mathbf{x}^0, \mathbf{x}^1 \in \mathbf{X}$. To obtain an unambiguous definition we would require $u_{ij}(\mathbf{x}) > 0$ $(\forall \mathbf{x} \in \mathbf{X})$ and $u_{ij}(\mathbf{x}) < 0$ $(\forall \mathbf{x} \in \mathbf{X})$ for complementarity and substitutability respectively.

Hicks later supplied an alternative measure which is based on the elements of the substitution matrix, $\mathbf{S}_p$.

Definition 4.5

(Net Complements and Substitutes)
Goods i and j are net complements and net substitutes if $s_{ij} < 0$ and $s_{ij} > 0$ respectively.

They are called *net* because they are defined in terms of the elements of $\mathbf{S}_p$; we shall see shortly that *gross* complements and substitutes have been defined in terms of the elements of $\mathbf{X}_p$. The elements s_{ij} are the partial derivatives about the points $(\mathbf{p}, y)$. Again, therefore, if we are demanding consistency we must have $s_{ij}(\mathbf{p}, y) > 0$ $(\forall \mathbf{p}, y)$ and $s_{ij}(\mathbf{p}, y) < 0$ $(\forall \mathbf{p}, y)$ for net complements and net substitutes. This measure is, however, independent of the utility function. As we have shown already $\mathbf{S}_p\mathbf{p} = 0$. If there are only two goods this means:

$$s_{11}p_1 + s_{12}p_2 = 0 \qquad \forall p_1, p_2 > 0.$$

It follows immediately that if $s_{11} < 0$ then $s_{12} > 0$. In other words, in a two-commodity model only net substitutes exist; a model must contain at least three goods in order to discuss net complementarity. It also follows in an n-commodity model that since $\sum_{j=1}^{n} s_{ij}p_j = 0$ then at least one pair of goods must be net substitutes.

Gross complements and substitutes are defined analogously.

Definition 4.6

(Gross complements and substitutes)
Goods i and j are gross complements and gross substitutes if $x_{ij} < 0$ and $x_{ij} > 0$ respectively.

This definition has an immediate implication. Since $\mathbf{S}_p = \mathbf{S}'_p$ it follows that net complementarity and substitutability between goods i and j is symmetric. However, generally $\mathbf{X}_p \neq \mathbf{X}'_p$ and so it is possible for good i to be a gross substitute for good j but not conversely. Since $x_{ij} = s_{ij} - x_j(\partial x_i/\partial y)$ then if goods i and j are net complements $(s_{ij} < 0)$ they will also be gross complements $(x_{ij} < 0)$ unless good i is strongly inferior. Notice that in saying this we are not including the inferiority of x_j, this only becomes relevant for x_{ji}. If good i is a strong inferior good and good j is a normal good then if i and j are net complements it is still possible to have $x_{ij} > 0$ but $x_{ji} < 0$.

4.5 Prices in the Utility Function

So far we have been concerned with a utility function of commodities only. In Chapter 3.9 we discussed the inclusion of prices in the utility function, i.e. $u = u(\mathbf{x}, \mathbf{p})$. It might be asked what effect this has on the comparative static results discussed in Section 4.2. It is surely no surprise to find that the results become obscure. Our problem is

$$\max_{\mathbf{x} \in \mathbf{X}} u(\mathbf{x}, \mathbf{p})$$

$$\text{s.t.} \quad \mathbf{p}'\mathbf{x} = y$$

$$\mathbf{x} \geqslant 0 \quad \mathbf{p} > 0$$

It is left to the reader as an exercise to carry out the optimisation following exactly the same procedure as in Section 4.2 (see Exercises 10–12). However, let us here take note of some of the differences. Solving the first-order conditions will give $2n + 1$ equations but not of the same form because the vector of marginal utilities $\mathbf{u}_x = \partial u(\mathbf{x}, \mathbf{p})/\partial \mathbf{x}$ is no longer the same. Second, in obtaining the comparative static results a new matrix enters the scene. Consider $\mathbf{u}_x(\mathbf{x}, \mathbf{p})$. If this is totally differentiated we get $\mathbf{U}_x \mathbf{dx} + \mathbf{U}_p \mathbf{dp}$ where

$$\mathbf{U}_x = \frac{\partial \mathbf{u}_x(\mathbf{x}, \mathbf{p})}{\partial \mathbf{x}'}, \quad \mathbf{U}_p = \frac{\partial \mathbf{u}_x(\mathbf{x}, \mathbf{p})}{\partial \mathbf{p}'}$$

both of order $n \times n$. It is the presence of the matrix $\mathbf{U}_p$ which gives rise to nearly all the changes in the comparative static results.

The vector $\mathbf{x}_y$ and the scalar λ_y remain unchanged except that now $\mathbf{U}$ is replaced by $\mathbf{U}_x$. However,

$$\mathbf{X}_p = \lambda \mathbf{U}_x^{-1} - \lambda \mathbf{x}_y \mathbf{x}_y' \lambda_y^{-1} \mathbf{x}_y \mathbf{x}' + \mathbf{U}_x^{-1} \mathbf{U}_p$$

and

$$\boldsymbol{\lambda}_p = -[\lambda \mathbf{x}_y + \lambda_y \mathbf{x}] + \mathbf{x}_y \mathbf{U}_p .$$

In deriving the substitution term we must note that the total derivative of the utility function now becomes

$$du = \mathbf{u}_x' \, \mathbf{dx} + \mathbf{u}_p' \, \mathbf{dp}$$

where $\mathbf{u}_p = \partial u/\partial \mathbf{p}$, a $n \times 1$ vector. This gives rise to a substitution matrix of the form:

$$\mathbf{S}_p = \lambda \mathbf{U}_x^{-1} - \lambda \mathbf{x}_y \mathbf{x}_y' \, \lambda_y^{-1} - \mathbf{U}_x^{-1} \mathbf{U}_p + \mathbf{x}_y \mathbf{x}_y' \lambda_y^{-1} \mathbf{U}_p - \lambda^{-1} \mathbf{U}_x^{-1} \mathbf{p} \mathbf{u}_p' .$$

Hence,

$$\mathbf{X}_p = \mathbf{S}_p - \mathbf{x}_y \mathbf{x}' + (\lambda^{-1} \mathbf{U}_x^{-1} \mathbf{p} \mathbf{u}_p' - \mathbf{x}_y \mathbf{x}_y' \lambda_y^{-1} \mathbf{U}_p)$$

where the additional effect due to the presence of prices in the utility function is the last term in brackets.

It can be demonstrated (see exercises) that in the present situation the Engel aggregation still holds but not the Cournot aggregation; that the substitution matrix is no longer symmetric; and that the demand curves are no longer homogeneous of degree zero in $\mathbf{p}$ and y.

4.6 The Kuhn–Tucker Conditions for an Optimal Solution

The analysis in this chapter so far has assumed that the consumer spends all of his income and that the optimal solution is such that some of every good is consumed. It could be argued that this is a misinterpretation of neoclassical consumer demand; however, the very discussion of the Slutsky decomposition and the comparative statics of consumer demand implicitly if not explicitly assumes some of every good is demanded at both the old and the new equilibrium. This condition in all probability arose because the mathematical techniques for exhibiting a consumer's optimal position could not take account of some of the goods not being consumed. It must be recognised, however, that at least diagrammatically corner solutions were not ruled out.

Another problem also is that we have assumed the consumer must spend all his income at the optimal solution. Even if we do not agree that there is no point of satiation it seems not unreasonable to suppose that it will in all probability lay outside his budget constraint. If this is so, then to assume all the budget is spent violates nothing and considerably simplifies the analysis. But this is true only so long as we do not constrain the consumer in any other way at the same time. Rationing, for example, either in terms of quotas or in terms of points, would add a second constraint. Suppose we consider the situation when *points rationing* is introduced.[7] For simplicity we shall assume a two-good world for which both goods are rationed. The consumer has a points budget in the sense he has a total allocation of points contained in the ration books. There is a points price which is marked on a coupon and denotes the price for a standard unit and these points give some idea of the scarcity of the goods. Notice too that there exists relative points prices which is just the ratio of the respective points for the two goods. There will exist, therefore, two constraints faced by a consumer; a money budget constraint and a points budget constraint, both of which must be satisfied at any moment of time. The situation is depicted in Fig. 4.1. As the diagram indicates, it is quite feasible for the optimal solution to lie on the points budget line but *inside the money budget line.*

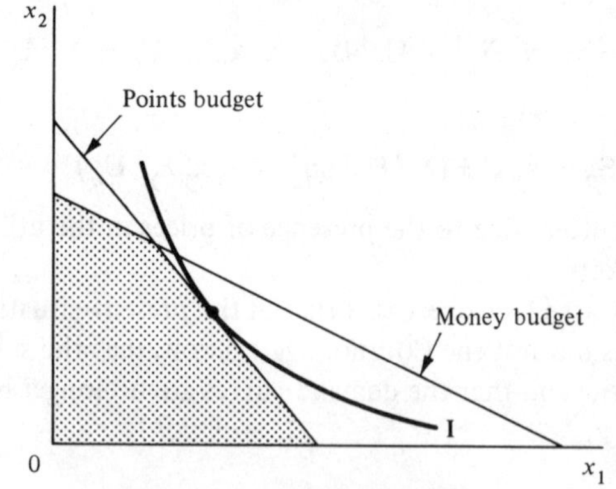

Fig. 4.1. Points rationing

In fact, this explains why it is likely that during war-time, when rationing is at its highest, hoarding of money takes place. Such accumulated income can only be accounted for by assuming that the optimal solution for a number of consumers lies on the points budget and inside the money budget line; if not, the rational consumer would have spent all his income.

The presence of corner solutions and solutions at which some or all of the constraints are not binding does mean we must reconsider the specification of the equilibrium conditions. It is necessary to do so because such situations are even more likely to occur in production theory – one only needs to think of bus and train services with peak and off-peak pricing. This problem was tackled by Kuhn and Tucker [71], and for this reason the optimal solution to be derived is often called the Kuhn–Tucker conditions for an optimal solution. Although this originated in the field of mathematical programming it soon became apparent that neoclassical theory is a form of classical programming (see Table 2.3, p. 31) and so theorems proved for the latter are relevant to the former. We use the term 'optimisation' to mean the maximisation or minimisation of an objective function. Such objective functions in economics include the utility function, the profits function, the cost function, the social welfare function, and so on.

Our procedure is as follows. We shall first illustrate the shortcomings of the Lagrangian method for obtaining economically meaningful solutions in certain cases. We shall then lay down the Kuhn–Tucker conditions for a general optimisation problem followed by an intuitive explanation. That these conditions are required for an optimal solution is given in the appendix to this chapter. Following this we give an interpretation to the role of the Lagrangian multipliers, assuming that all constraints are binding. In the next section we shall return to neoclassical optimisation in the light of the Kuhn–Tucker conditions.

The student learns very early in mathematics that for a turning-point of $y = f(x)$ the first derivative must be zero, i.e. $dy/dx = 0$. A sufficient condition for the turning-point to be a maximum is $d^2y/dx^2 < 0$, and for a minimum the requirement is $d^2y/dx^2 > 0$. A necessary and sufficient condition for a maximum at the point x^0 is that $f'(x^0) = 0$ and that $f''(x)$ changes sign from positive to negative in the neighbourhood of the point x^0. The next development a student of economics learns is that most objective functions vary over a restricted domain, i.e. the function is maximised or minimised subject to a constraint, or number of constraints. In other words, the objective function is defined over some feasible set (the domain) which limits the range of the function. However, so long as the constraint is written in the form of an equality the Lagrangian method appears the most obvious to use. The approach has two shortcomings. First, suppose the objective function has arguments which to make economic sense must be non-negative. There is no guarantee that the solutions to the Lagrangian function will give positive values. Take, for example, the consumer problem:

$$\max u(x_1, x_2) = (x_1 + 15)^2 x_2$$
$$\text{s.t.} \quad 3x_1 + 4x_2 = 20.$$

The solution values to this problem are $(x_1, x_2) = (-5/9, 5\,5/12)$, but $x_1 = -5/9$ is economically unacceptable.

The second shortcoming of the Lagrangian method concerns the constraint equations, which define the feasible set. Suppose the constraint functions take the form of inequalities rather than equalities, then the Lagrangian in its present form cannot be employed since this always presupposes the constraint to be operative.

However, there is no *a priori* reason for supposing this to be so.

The Kuhn–Tucker conditions are those conditions required for an optimal solution to the objective function given *inequality* constraints and *non-negativity* conditions on the variables.

Consider, therefore, the following general optimisation problem with inequality constraints and non-negative restrictions on the variables:

$$\begin{aligned} &\max_{\mathbf{x}\in\mathbf{S}} F(x_1,\ldots,x_n) \\ \text{s.t.}\quad & g_1(x_1,\ldots,x_n)\leqslant b_1 \\ & g_2(x_1,\ldots,x_n)\leqslant b_2 \\ & \quad\vdots \\ & g_m(x_1,\ldots,x_n)\leqslant b_m \\ & x_1\geqslant 0,\ldots,x_n\geqslant 0. \end{aligned} \tag{4.7}$$

Throughout we shall use matrix algebra. Therefore, let

$$\mathbf{x}=\begin{bmatrix} x_1\\ \cdot\\ \cdot\\ \cdot\\ x_n\end{bmatrix}\quad \mathbf{g}(\mathbf{x})=\begin{bmatrix} g_1(x_1,\ldots,x_n)\\ \cdot\\ \cdot\\ \cdot\\ g_m(x_1,\ldots,x_n)\end{bmatrix}\quad \mathbf{b}=\begin{bmatrix} b_1\\ \cdot\\ \cdot\\ \cdot\\ b_m\end{bmatrix}$$

We can then write:

$$\begin{aligned} &\max_{\mathbf{x}\in\mathbf{S}} F(\mathbf{x}) \\ \text{s.t.}\quad & \mathbf{g}(\mathbf{x})\leqslant \mathbf{b} \\ & \mathbf{x}\geqslant 0. \end{aligned}$$

The Lagrangian function is:

$$L(\mathbf{x},\boldsymbol{\lambda})=F(\mathbf{x})+\boldsymbol{\lambda}'[\mathbf{b}-\mathbf{g}(\mathbf{x})]$$

where $\boldsymbol{\lambda}$ is an $m \times 1$ vector of Lagrangian multipliers. We shall further define

$$\mathbf{F}_x=\frac{\partial F}{\partial \mathbf{x}}\qquad \mathbf{G}_x=\frac{\partial \mathbf{g}}{\partial \mathbf{x}'}=\begin{bmatrix} \partial g_1/\partial x_1 & \ldots & \partial g_1/\partial x_n\\ \cdot & & \cdot\\ \cdot & & \cdot\\ \cdot & & \cdot\\ \partial g_m/\partial x_1 & \ldots & \partial g_m/\partial x_n\end{bmatrix}$$

where $\mathbf{F}_x$ is $n \times 1$ and $\mathbf{G}_x$ is $m \times n$.

The Kuhn–Tucker conditions are then given by:

$$\begin{aligned}
\mathbf{L}_x &= (\mathbf{F}_x - \mathbf{G}'_x\,\boldsymbol{\lambda}) \leqslant 0 \\
\mathbf{x}'\mathbf{L}_x &= \mathbf{x}'(\mathbf{F}_x - \mathbf{G}'_x\,\boldsymbol{\lambda}) = 0 \\
\mathbf{x} &\geqslant 0 \\
\mathbf{L}_\lambda &= \mathbf{b} - \mathbf{g}(\mathbf{x}) \geqslant 0 \\
\boldsymbol{\lambda}'\mathbf{L}_\lambda &= \boldsymbol{\lambda}'[\mathbf{b} - \mathbf{g}(\mathbf{x})] = 0 \\
\boldsymbol{\lambda} &\geqslant 0.
\end{aligned} \tag{4.8}$$

These conditions can be written:

$$\begin{aligned}
&\left(\frac{\partial F}{\partial x_i} - \sum_{j=1}^{m} \lambda_j \frac{\partial g_j}{\partial x_i}\right) \leqslant 0 \qquad i = 1, \ldots, n \\
&\sum_{i=1}^{n}\left(\frac{\partial F}{\partial x_i} - \sum_{j=1}^{m} \lambda_j \frac{\partial g_j}{\partial x_i}\right) x_i = 0 \\
&x_1 \geqslant 0, \ldots, x_n \geqslant 0 \\
&b_j - g_j(x_1, \ldots, x_n) \geqslant 0 \qquad j = 1, \ldots, m \\
&\sum_{j=1}^{m} \lambda_j[b_j - g_j(x_1, \ldots, x_n)] = 0 \\
&\lambda_1 \geqslant 0, \ldots, \lambda_m \geqslant 0.
\end{aligned} \tag{4.9}$$

We can explain these conditions intuitively in the following way. We first note that $\mathbf{L}_x$ is not set equal to zero but set equal to or less than zero. Why should this be so? The reason is because we are allowing corner solutions. Consider Fig. 4.2. In each case the maximum value is at $x = x^0$. In Fig. 4.2 (*a*) and 4.2 (*c*) the function is maximised and satisfies $f'(x^0) = 0$. However, Fig. 4.2 (*b*) illustrates a situation in which the function is maximised with $f'(x^0) < 0$, since x is constrained to satisfy $x \geqslant 0$. Taking account of all possible situations we can say that a maximum is where $f'(x^0) \leqslant 0$, and this is just what we have done in stating $\mathbf{L}_x \leqslant 0$.

The second condition $\mathbf{x}'\mathbf{L}_x = 0$ is most important and not so easy to justify. However, Fig. 4.2 is an aid in understanding the significance of this result. Consider $f'(x^0)$, then either $f'(x^0) = 0$ or $x^0 = 0$ or both. If $x^0 > 0$, as in Fig. 4.2 (*a*), then it follows that $f'(x^0) = 0$ and $f'(x^0)x^0 = 0$. In Fig. 4.2 (*b*) we have $f'(x^0) < 0$ and $x^0 = 0$, in which case $f'(x^0)x^0 = 0$. Finally, in Fig. 4.2 (*c*) both $f'(x^0) = 0$ and $x^0 = 0$ and clearly $f'(x^0)x^0 = 0$. We conclude, therefore, that if $x^0 > 0$ then $f'(x^0) = 0$, or that if $f'(x^0) \leqslant 0$ then $x^0 = 0$. Since this holds for each term in the summation $\mathbf{x}'\mathbf{L}_x$, it must hold for the summation, hence $\mathbf{x}'\mathbf{L}_x = 0$.

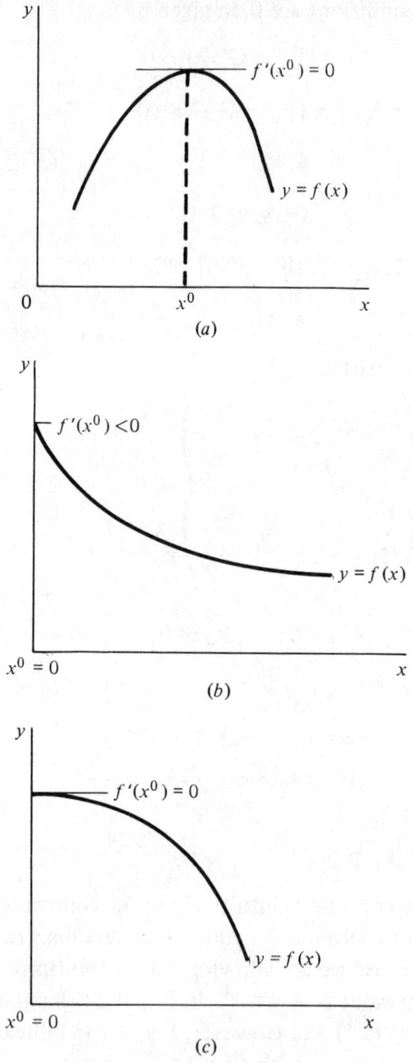

Fig. 4.2

The same reasoning holds for the constraints. For $\mathbf{L}_\lambda$ to be a minimum (remember $L(\mathbf{x}, \boldsymbol{\lambda})$ is a saddle-valued function – see Appendix) we must have $\mathbf{L}_\lambda \geqslant 0$, and in addition $\boldsymbol{\lambda}'\mathbf{L}_\lambda = 0$. If $\lambda_j > 0$ then $b_j = g_j(\mathbf{x})$ and if $\lambda_j = 0$ then $g_j(\mathbf{x}) < b_j$.

In the economic analysis of the next section, and in other parts of the book, the Lagrangian multiplier plays an important role. This role arises, however, only when $\lambda_j > 0$, which means it has significance only when the constraint is operating. It is also clear that if we alter any one of the constraints in all probability we will alter the optimal value of the objective function. If F^0 is the optimal value of the objective function we will now show that:

$$\frac{dF^0}{\mathbf{db}} = \mathbf{F}_b^0 = \boldsymbol{\lambda}.$$

Totally differentiating $F^0 = F(x_1^0, \ldots, x_n^0)$ and $\mathbf{b} = \mathbf{g}(\mathbf{x})$, where we have assumed all constraints are operating, and noting dF^0 is a scalar and $\mathbf{db}$ an $m \times 1$ vector, we get:

$$dF^0 = \mathbf{F}'_x \, \mathbf{dx}$$

and

$$\mathbf{db} = \mathbf{G}_x \, \mathbf{dx}.$$

If we premultiply the second equation by $\boldsymbol{\lambda}'$ and subtract it from the first, we have

$$dF^0 - \boldsymbol{\lambda}'\mathbf{db} = (\mathbf{F}'_x - \boldsymbol{\lambda}'\mathbf{G}_x)\mathbf{dx}.$$

Taking the derivative of dF^0 with respect to the column vector $\mathbf{db}$, and noting that $\mathbf{dx}/\mathbf{db}$ is an $m \times n$ matrix, we obtain:

$$\frac{dF^0}{\mathbf{db}} - \boldsymbol{\lambda} = \frac{\mathbf{dx}}{\mathbf{db}} (\mathbf{F}_x - \mathbf{G}'_x \boldsymbol{\lambda}).$$

But $\mathbf{F}_x - \mathbf{G}'_x\boldsymbol{\lambda} = \mathbf{0}$ with $\mathbf{0}$ of order n x 1 from the necessary condition for a maximum, hence:

$$\frac{dF^0}{\mathbf{db}} = \mathbf{F}_b^0 = \boldsymbol{\lambda}.$$

The necessary conditions for an optimum set out in (4.8) and (4.9) only describe or characterise an optimum solution. Unfortunately, they do not tell us how we can obtain such an optimal solution; such a solution is obtained by trial and error.

4.7 Neoclassical Optimisation Reconsidered

We are now in a position to re-examine the consumer optimisation problem again. The difference is that now we explicitly allow for the possibility that a consumer may have an optimal position within his budget equation; also we explicitly take account of the non-negativity of the commodities. Note that in this particular problem we have only one inequality constraint and hence one Lagrangian multiplier as far as $\mathbf{g}(\mathbf{x})$ is concerned. Thus the consumer's optimisation now becomes:

$$\max_{\mathbf{x} \in \mathbf{X}} u(\mathbf{x})$$

$$\text{s.t.} \quad \mathbf{p}'\mathbf{x} \leqslant y$$
$$\mathbf{x} \geqslant 0.$$

We have the Lagrangian expression as before:

$$L(\mathbf{x}, \lambda) = u(\mathbf{x}) - \lambda(\mathbf{p}'\mathbf{x} - y).$$

The conditions for an optimum now are:

$$\mathbf{L}_x = \mathbf{u}_x - \lambda\mathbf{p} \leqslant 0$$
$$\mathbf{x}'\mathbf{L}_x = \mathbf{x}'(\mathbf{u}_x - \lambda\mathbf{p}) = 0$$
$$\mathbf{x} \geqslant 0$$
$$y - \mathbf{p}'\mathbf{x} \geqslant 0$$
$$\lambda(y - \mathbf{p}'\mathbf{x}) = 0$$
$$\lambda \geqslant 0.$$

In the example sighted above where $u = (x_1 + 15)^2 x_2$ and with the budget constraint $3x_1 + 4x_2 \leqslant 20$ we obtain the optimal values $x_1^0 = 0, x_2^0 = 5$ and $\lambda^0 = 56\frac{1}{4}$.

We also know from our earlier analysis that λ is the marginal utility of money spending. If $\lambda > 0$, as in the above example, then the constraint takes the form of an equality $\mathbf{p}'\mathbf{x} = y$ and so the optimal position for the consumer is on his budget line. If, however, $\lambda = 0$ then $\mathbf{p}'\mathbf{x} < y$. In other words, if the marginal utility of money spending is zero the consumer would not spend all his income. This is because under such conditions the marginal utility obtained from consuming additional goods purchased from the surplus income is less than the marginal utility of holding that additional income and foregoing consumption.

A number of problems in microeconomics become more tractable when the Kuhn–Tucker conditions are used in the analysis. Consider the situation of points rationing discussed at the beginning of the previous section. The consumer is confronted with two constraints, one a money budget constraint the other a points budget constraint. Since we do not know which of these constraints will be operative at the optimal solution they must be written as inequalities. Take, for example, the following case:

$$\max_{\mathbf{x} \in \mathbf{X}} u = x_1^{1/2} x_2^{1/2}$$

$$\text{s.t.} \quad 3x_1 + 4x_2 \leqslant 20 \quad \text{money budget}$$
$$3x_1 + x_2 \leqslant 10 \quad \text{points budget}$$
$$x_1 \geqslant 0, x_2 \geqslant 0.$$

By trial and error we obtain the optimal solution:

$$x_1^0 = 2\tfrac{2}{9} \qquad \lambda_1^0 = \sqrt{2}/(12\sqrt{3})$$
$$x_2^0 = 3\tfrac{1}{3} \qquad \lambda_2^0 = \sqrt{2}/(6\sqrt{3})$$

This solution, illustrated in Fig. 4.3, shows that the optimal condition must be at the vertex **Q** since both λ_1 and λ_2 are positive. For the optimal solution to satisfy both constraints it must be where they intersect. However, it is clear that, depending on the utility function and the constraints, a solution could be on the points budget at a point inside the money budget, such as R in Fig. 4.3.

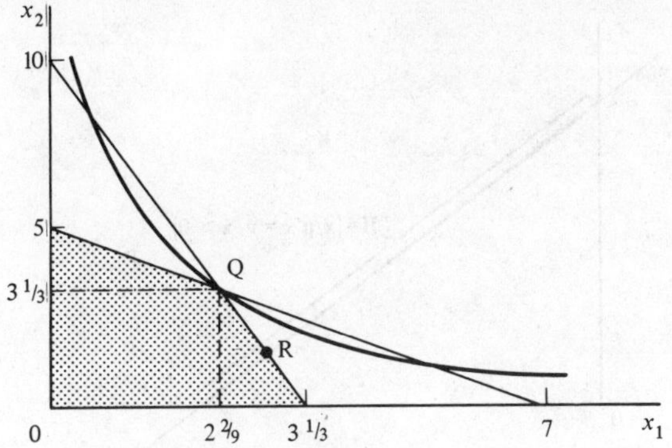

Fig. 4.3. Points rationing

4.8 A New Look at Consumer Optimality

Let us first reconsider the budget line $y = \mathbf{p}'\mathbf{x} = \sum_{i=1}^{n} p_i x_i$. This will denote a set of points in the commodity space for a given set of prices and income. If for the moment we do not restrict the quantities to be non-negative we may write this set $\mathbf{H}^* = \{\mathbf{x}/\mathbf{p}'\mathbf{x} = y\}$. In fact this defines a hyperplane in $\mathbf{E}^n$, more generally:

Definition 4.7

A hyperplane **H** in $\mathbf{E}^n$ is defined by the set of points
$\mathbf{H} = \{\mathbf{x}/\mathbf{a}'\mathbf{x} = b\}$ $\quad$ $\mathbf{a} \neq 0$ and b a constant.

The budget equation is, therefore, a particular example of a hyperplane belonging to $\mathbf{E}^n$. There will be no confusion if we define the budget hyperplane **H** to be defined over the non-negative orthant as illustrated in Fig. 4.4.

The hyperplane **H** divides the commodity space **X** into three subsets:

1 The set of points below the line **H**, i.e. $\{\mathbf{x}/\mathbf{p}'\mathbf{x} < y, \mathbf{x} \geqslant 0\}$.
2. The set of points on the line **H**, i.e. $\{\mathbf{x}/\mathbf{p}'\mathbf{x} = y, \mathbf{x} \geqslant 0\}$.
3. The set of points above the line **H**, i.e. $\{\mathbf{x}/\mathbf{p}'\mathbf{x} > y, \mathbf{x} \geqslant 0\}$.

We are in fact interested in two closed half-spaces which are defined as follows:

Definition 4.8

$$\mathbf{H}^+ = \{\mathbf{x}/\mathbf{p}'\mathbf{x} \geqslant y, \mathbf{x} \geqslant 0\} \text{ and } \mathbf{H}^- = \{\mathbf{x}/\mathbf{p}'\mathbf{x} \leqslant y, \mathbf{x} \geqslant 0\}$$

where H^+ and H^- are referred to as the positive half-space and negative halfspace respectively. The set **H**, therefore, divides the commodity space, **X**, into two closed halfspaces H^+ and H^- such that $H^+ \cap H^- = H$. It is to be noted also that the sets H, H^+, and H^- are all convex sets. Finally, since **X** is a connected set then H, H^+, and H^- are connected since they are subsets of **X**.

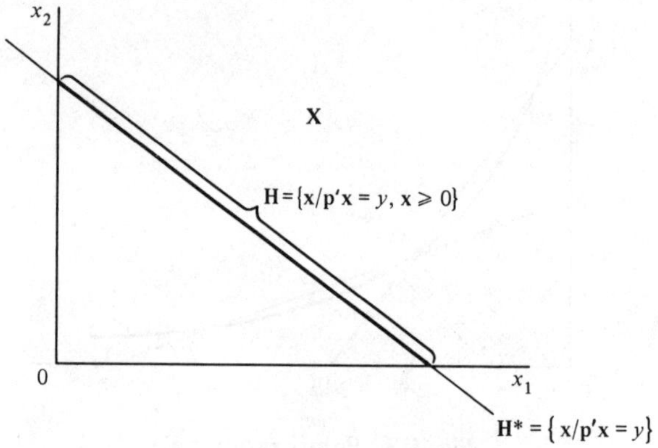

Fig. 4.4. Budget hyperplane

Hyperplanes play an important role in modern microeconomics, both in consumption theory and production theory, so that it is worth while investigating some features of hyperplanes a little further. We can consider three hyperplanes:

1. Bounding hyperplanes,
2. Supporting hyperplanes,
3. Separating hyperplanes.

We define the first two as follows:

Definition 4.9

(i) Given any convex closed set **A** in E^n and a point $y \in E^n$, if $y \notin A$ then there exists a *bounding hyperplane* $H = \{x \in E^n / a'x = b\}$ containing **y** for which all points in **A** lie in one of the closed half-spaces determined by **H**,

i.e. $\quad a'y = b$ and either $a'z \leqslant b$ or $a'z \geqslant b \qquad \forall z \in A.$

(ii) Given a boundary point **y** of a convex set **A** in E^n then $H = \{x \in E^n / a'x = b\}$ is called a *supporting hyperplane* of **y** if $a'y = b$ and if all of **A** lies in one closed half-space produced by the hyperplane, i.e.

$$a'z \geqslant b \qquad \forall z \in A \quad \text{or} \quad a'z \leqslant b \qquad \forall z \in A.$$

These two hyperplanes are illustrated in Fig. 4.5.

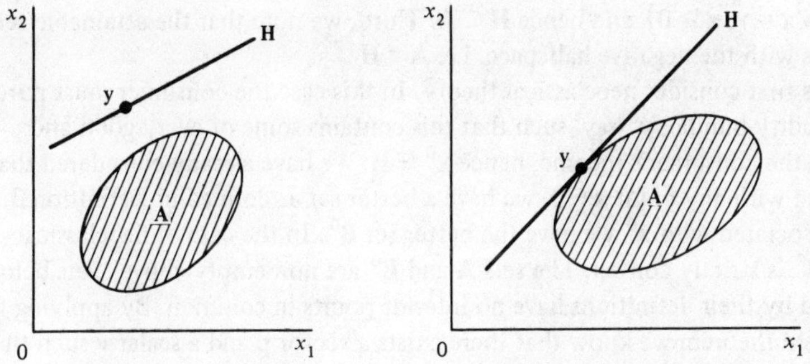

(*a*) Bounding hyperplane (*b*) Supporting hyperplane

Fig. 4.5

Separating hyperplanes are most important, and the *theorem of separating hyperplanes,* due to Minkowski, takes the form:

Theorem 4.1 Given two non-empty convex sets **A** and **B** in $\mathbf{E}^n$ where **A** and **B** have no interior points in common, then there exists a vector **a** and a scalar b such that

$$\mathbf{x} \in \mathbf{A} \Rightarrow \mathbf{a}'\mathbf{x} \leqslant b \text{ and } \mathbf{x} \in \mathbf{B} \Rightarrow \mathbf{a}'\mathbf{x} \geqslant b.$$

In other words, there exists a hyperplane which separates the two convex sets such that each lies in a closed halfspace. (The definition takes **A** to be in the negative halfspace and **B** in the positive.) The Minkowski theorem is illustrated in Fig. 4.6, where 4.6 (*a*) has **A** and **B** disjoint and both strictly convex; while 4.6 (*b*) has $\mathbf{A} \cap \mathbf{B}$ non-empty and both **A** and **B** are weakly convex.

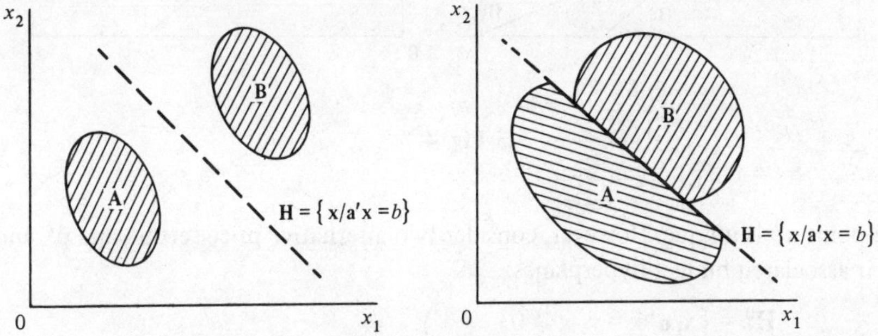

(*a*) (*b*)

Fig. 4.6. Minkowski's separating hyperplanes

We are now in a position to reconsider consumer optimality. First we note that the attainable set of the consumer is $\mathbf{A} = \{\mathbf{x}/\mathbf{p}'\mathbf{x} \leqslant y, \mathbf{x} \geqslant 0\}$ which is a closed convex set, and is both connected and compact. Second, the budget hyperplane is

$\mathbf{H} = \{\mathbf{x}/\mathbf{p}'\mathbf{x} = y, \mathbf{x} \geqslant 0\}$ and hence $\mathbf{H} \subset \mathbf{A}$. Third, we note that the attainable set coincides with the negative halfspace, i.e. $\mathbf{A} = \mathbf{H}^-$.

Let us first consider neoclassical theory. In this case the consumer must purchase a commodity bundle, $\mathbf{x}^0$ say, such that this contains some of every good and exhausts the consumer's income, hence $\mathbf{x}^0 \in \mathbf{H}$. We have already considered that associated with any point $\mathbf{x} \in \mathbf{X}$ we have a better set as defined in Definition 3.12; hence associated with $\mathbf{x}^0$ we have the better set $\mathbf{B}^0$. In the case of neoclassical theory $\mathbf{B}^0$ is strictly convex. The sets $\mathbf{A}$ and $\mathbf{B}^0$ are non-empty convex sets belonging to $\mathbf{X}$, and by their definitions have no interior points in common. By applying the Minkowski theorem we know that there exists a vector $\mathbf{p}$ and a scalar y such that:

$$\mathbf{x}^0 \in \mathbf{A} \Rightarrow \mathbf{p}'\mathbf{x}^0 \leqslant y \text{ and } \mathbf{x}^0 \in \mathbf{B}^0 \Rightarrow \mathbf{p}'\mathbf{x}^0 \geqslant y.$$

Since $\mathbf{B}^0$ is strictly convex it follows that because $\mathbf{x}^0 \in \mathbf{A}$ and to $\mathbf{B}^0$ it belongs to the hyperplane and is a unique point, i.e. $\mathbf{H}^0 = \{\mathbf{x}/\mathbf{p}'\mathbf{x} = y, \mathbf{x} \geqslant 0\}$ is a supporting hyperplane to $\mathbf{B}^0$ at the point $\mathbf{x}^0$ and so the consumer's utility is maximised.

There is, however, no reason to restrict the analysis to strictly convex better sets. From Axiom 10 we need state only that $\mathbf{B}^0$ is convex, either strictly or weakly. Two possibilities of interest arise which are illustrated in Fig. 4.7. In Fig. 4.7 (*a*)

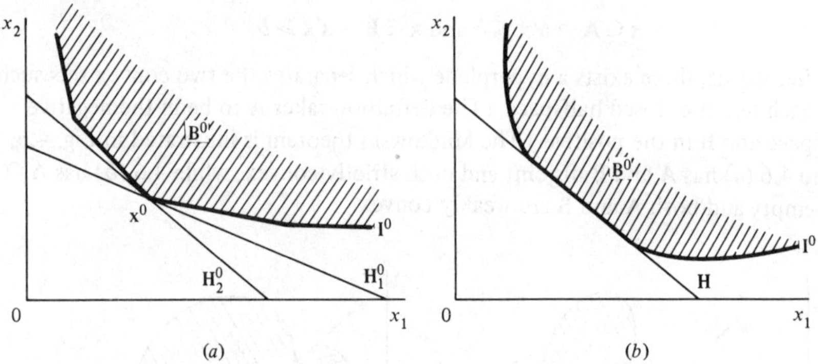

Fig. 4.7

the point $\mathbf{x}^0$ is unique. However, consider two alternative price sets $\mathbf{p}^1$ and $\mathbf{p}^2$ and their associated budget hyperplanes:

$$\left.\begin{aligned} \mathbf{H}_1^0 &= \{\mathbf{x}/\mathbf{p}^1\mathbf{x} = y, \mathbf{x} \geqslant 0\} \\ \mathbf{H}_2^0 &= \{\mathbf{x}/\mathbf{p}^2\mathbf{x} = y, \mathbf{x} \geqslant 0\} \end{aligned}\right\} \mathbf{p}^1\mathbf{x}^0 = \mathbf{p}^2\mathbf{x}^0 = y$$

Since both $\mathbf{H}_1^0$ and $\mathbf{H}_2^0$ are supporting hyperplanes to $\mathbf{B}^0$ the consumer's optimal position is the same for a *set* of price vectors. Let $\mathbf{P} = \{\mathbf{p}/C\mathbf{x}^0\ \forall \mathbf{p}\}$ then we have a set-to-point mapping f: $\mathbf{P} \to \mathbf{x}$. Alternatively, in Fig. 4.7 (*b*) for a given price vector the supporting hyperplane gives a whole set of commodity bundles each of which is a possible optimal bundle. Let $\widetilde{\mathbf{Q}} = \{\mathbf{x}/C\mathbf{x} \text{ given } \mathbf{p}\}$ then we have a point-to-set mapping $g: \mathbf{p} \to \widetilde{\mathbf{Q}}$. Which $\mathbf{x} \in \widetilde{\mathbf{Q}}$ will be chosen is purely a random event. What are some of the implications of these possibilities? Which restrictions on the demand curves, for example, remain? We shall return to these issues in Chapter 8. What we can say is that continuously diminishing MRS is now ruled out.

Finally, notice that it is not necessary for the consumer to be consuming some of every good. If $\mathbf{X}$ is $\mathbf{E}^n \subset \mathbf{E}^k$ with $n < k$ then the budget hyperplane is $(n-1)$-dimensional and the sets $\mathbf{B}^0$ and $\mathbf{A}$ reduce to n-dimensional sets.

4.9 The Generalised Substitution Theorem

We have already noted that:

$$x_{ii} = s_{ii} - x_i\,(\partial x_i/\partial y).$$

If, therefore, good i is not an inferior good and, because $\mathbf{S}_p$ is negative semidefinite, it follows immediately that $x_{ii} \leqslant 0$. It is observed therefore that the downward-sloping demand curve is very dependent upon the non-positive sign of s_{ii}. It is important to note that the non-positiveness of s_{ii} is being established on *a priori* grounds and is a deduction from the premises we have laid down. However, whether the good is inferior or not can only be established from empirical work.

The generalised substitution theorem is an alternative to stating that $\mathbf{S}_p$ is negative semidefinite.

Theorem 4.2 (Generalised Substitution Theorem) Let $\mathbf{dp}$ denote a vector of price changes and $\mathbf{dx}$ a vector of quantity changes, given that the consumer has been income-compensated then

$$\mathbf{dp'dx} \leqslant 0.$$

Why it is desirable to have an alternative proof of this non-positive substitution effect is because in the present case we do not require differentiability. It will be recalled that the matrix $\mathbf{S}_p$ is composed of partial derivatives of substitution terms.

Proof Let the set $\mathbf{B}^0$ be strictly convex. As an aid to understanding this theorem we shall diagram the case for two goods but the derivation applies to any number of goods. For a given commodity bundle $\mathbf{x}^0$ and a given set of prices $\mathbf{p}^0$ and fixed income y, the consumer's indifference set is $\mathbf{I}^0$ associated with $\mathbf{x}^0$. Prices now change to $\mathbf{p}^1$. Since we are only concerned about the substitution effect we eliminate the income effect by compensating the consumer so that he remains at the set $\mathbf{I}^0$. Thus we find a commodity bundle $\mathbf{x}^1 \in \mathbf{I}^0$ which is chosen when the prices are $\mathbf{p}^1$. This is illustrated in Fig. 4.8, where $\mathbf{H}_0 = \{\mathbf{x}/\mathbf{p}^0\mathbf{x} = y^0, \mathbf{x} \geqslant 0\}$ and $\mathbf{H}_1 = \{\mathbf{x}/\mathbf{p}^1\mathbf{x} = y^1, \mathbf{x} \geqslant 0\}$ and y^1 is the level of income when the consumer has been compensated.

The choice criterion is that of choosing $\mathbf{x}^0, \mathbf{x}^1$ so as to minimise the income spent, i.e. we wish to find the minimum between $\mathbf{p}^0\mathbf{x}$ and $\mathbf{p}^1\mathbf{x}$, for all $\mathbf{x} \in \mathbf{B}^0$. Let

$y^0 = \mathbf{p}^0\mathbf{x}^0$ and $y^1 = \mathbf{p}^1\mathbf{x}^1$ and consider the hyperplane $\mathbf{H}^0$. This will define two halfspaces $\mathbf{H}_0^+ = \{\mathbf{x}/\mathbf{p}^0\mathbf{x} \geqslant y^0, \mathbf{x} \geqslant 0\}$ and $\mathbf{H}_0^- = \{\mathbf{x}/\mathbf{p}^0\mathbf{x} \leqslant y^0, \mathbf{x} \geqslant 0\}$ where $\mathbf{x} \in \mathbf{X}$ and is not necessarily in $\mathbf{B}^0$.

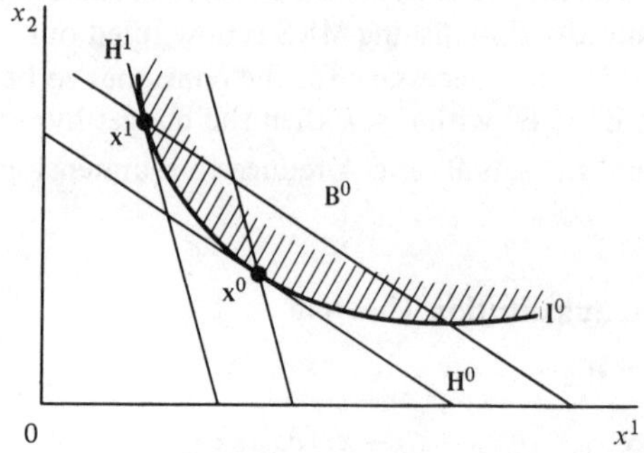

Fig. 4.8

Our procedure is as follows. We establish that $\mathbf{H}^0$ is a supporting hyperplane to $\mathbf{B}^0$. Since $\mathbf{B}^0$ is strictly convex $\mathbf{x}^1$ coincides with $\mathbf{x}^0$ or is different from $\mathbf{x}^0$. If $\mathbf{x}^0 \neq \mathbf{x}^1$ then we shall show that $\mathbf{p}^0\mathbf{x}^1 > \mathbf{p}^0\mathbf{x}^0$. In the same way we shall show that $\mathbf{p}^1\mathbf{x}^0 > \mathbf{p}^1\mathbf{x}^1$ from which the result of the theorem follows.

We first establish that no point in $\mathbf{B}^0$ is in the interior of $\mathbf{H}_0^-$ and we do this by contradiction. Suppose there is a point $\mathbf{z} \in \mathbf{B}^0$ which is also contained in the interior of $\mathbf{H}_0^-$, i.e. $N_\epsilon(\mathbf{z}) \subset \{\mathbf{x}/\mathbf{p}^0\mathbf{x} \leqslant y^0\}$. If $\mathbf{z}$ is interior then $\mathbf{p}^0\mathbf{z} < y$, that is we can find a $y < y^0$. But if $\mathbf{z} \in \mathbf{B}^0$ then either $\mathbf{z}P\mathbf{x}^0$ or $\mathbf{z}I\mathbf{x}^0$. This means we could have chosen a commodity bundle $\mathbf{z}$ at a lower income than $\mathbf{x}^0$ which was at least preferred to $\mathbf{x}^0$. This is a contradiction of the axioms of rationality. Therefore, the only points of $\mathbf{B}^0$ in $\mathbf{H}_0^-$ are those actually belonging to $\mathbf{H}_0$. Hence, $\mathbf{B}^0$ lies wholly in $\mathbf{H}_0^+$, and $\mathbf{H}_0$ is the supporting hyperplane of the strictly convex set $\mathbf{B}^0$ at the point $\mathbf{x}^0$.

Consider the commodity bundle $\mathbf{x}^1$. Since $\mathbf{x}^1 \in \mathbf{I}^0$ then $\mathbf{x}^1 \in \mathbf{B}^0$. But we know $\mathbf{B}^0$ is contained in the positive halfspace, $\mathbf{B}^0 \subset \mathbf{H}_0^+$. Two possibilities are open. Either $\mathbf{x}^1 = \mathbf{x}^0$ in which case $\mathbf{x}^1 \in B(\mathbf{H}_0^+)$, or else $\mathbf{x}^1$ is in the interior of $\mathbf{H}_0^+$, which is the situation in Fig. 4.8. If $\mathbf{x}^1 = \mathbf{x}^0$ then we have $\mathbf{p}^0\mathbf{x}^0 = \mathbf{p}^1\mathbf{x}^1 = y^0$; if $\mathbf{x}^1 \in I(\mathbf{H}_0^+)$ then $\mathbf{p}^0\mathbf{x}^1 > \mathbf{p}^0\mathbf{x}^0$. To summarise:

Either $$\mathbf{x}^1 = \mathbf{x}^0 \text{ or } \mathbf{p}^0\mathbf{x}^1 > \mathbf{p}^0\mathbf{x}^0.$$

Now define another hyperplane $\mathbf{H}_1 = \{\mathbf{x}/\mathbf{p}^1\mathbf{x} = y^1, \mathbf{x} \geqslant 0\}$. Since $y^1 = \mathbf{p}^1\mathbf{x}^1$ then $\mathbf{H}_1$ must be a supporting hyperplane to $\mathbf{B}^0$ at the point $\mathbf{x}^1$ since $\mathbf{x}^1 \in B(\mathbf{B}^0)$. It follows, as in the case above, that $\mathbf{B}^0 \subset \mathbf{H}_1^+$ and we have:

Either $$\mathbf{x}^1 = \mathbf{x}^0 \text{ or } \mathbf{p}^1\mathbf{x}^0 > \mathbf{p}^1\mathbf{x}^1.$$

Let us consider first the situation of $\mathbf{x}^1 = \mathbf{x}^0$. A strictly convex set can have more than one supporting hyperplane through any one point. In other words, if

$\mathbf{a'x} = b$ is a hyperplane through $\mathbf{x}^0$ then $\lambda\mathbf{a'x} = \lambda b$ is also a hyperplane through $\mathbf{x}^0$. This, of course, is no more than our homogeneity condition, if all prices and income are increased by a proportion λ with $\mathbf{p}^1 = \lambda\mathbf{p}^0$ and $y^1 = \lambda y^0$ then our budget hyperplane remains unaltered and $\mathbf{x}^1 = \mathbf{x}^0$. When prices change in different proportions, however, we have:

$$\mathbf{p}^0\mathbf{x}^0 - \mathbf{p}^0\mathbf{x}^1 < 0$$

and
$$-\mathbf{p}^1\mathbf{x}^0 + \mathbf{p}^1\mathbf{x}^1 < 0.$$

Adding these two equations we get:

$$\mathbf{p}^1(\mathbf{x}^0 - \mathbf{x}^1) - \mathbf{p}^1(\mathbf{x}^0 - \mathbf{x}^1) < 0$$
$$(\mathbf{p}^0 - \mathbf{p}^1)(\mathbf{x}^0 - \mathbf{x}^1) < 0$$
$$\mathbf{dp'dx} < 0.$$

Taking both cases into account, then:

$$\mathbf{dp'dx} \leqslant 0. \qquad \textit{Q.E.D.}$$

If only the ith price changes, all other prices constant, then we have:

$$dp_i dx_i < 0$$

which, if we have all functions differentiable, corresponds to $s_{ii} < 0$.

In the proof we stipulated $\mathbf{B}^0$ to be strictly convex. What happens, therefore, when $\mathbf{B}^0$ is weakly convex, as in Fig. 4.7? In the case of Fig. 4.7 (*a*) it is possible that even though $\mathbf{p}^1 \neq \mathbf{p}^0$ we have $\mathbf{x}^1 = \mathbf{x}^0$ so that $\mathbf{dp'dx} = 0$. Furthermore, along a straight-line segment, as in Fig. 4.7 (*a*) and (*b*), it is possible for $\mathbf{p}^0 = \mathbf{p}^1$ but $\mathbf{x}^0 \neq \mathbf{x}^1$ and so we can have $\mathbf{dp'dx} = 0$. Although in both cases the term $\mathbf{dp'dx} = 0$ the two situations are different. In the former $\mathbf{dx} = 0$, in the latter it is $\mathbf{dp} = 0$. Hence even in the situation of $\mathbf{B}^0$ being weakly convex we have:

$$\mathbf{dp'dx} \leqslant 0,$$

the equality occurring for a greater price set. Although we can relax strict convexity of $\mathbf{B}^0$ it must still have a continuous boundary; it is only differentiability which has been relaxed.

4.10 Revealed Preference Theory Revisited

In Section 3.10 we set down the axioms of revealed preference theory. Basically there were only two and it is surprising that with just these two axioms the usual results of demand theory, such as the existence of demand functions, the homogeneity of degree zero in **p** and y for these demand functions and the fact that the substitution effect is non-positive, can be demonstrated. A most thorough treatment of these is given in Uzawa [121].

In Chapter 1 we argued that as a method of procedure we should lay down the minimum number of axioms on which to build our theories. Utility theory of consumer behaviour required eleven axioms to derive the results of the present chapter and yet revealed preference theory has only two! Have we, therefore, been unnecessarily roundabout? The answer lies in where we go after these results. If consumer demand comprised only what we have discussed so far it would be more expeditious to present the theory in terms of revealed preference. However, many other problems in microeconomics, particularly of an applied nature, have been tackled through the medium of neoclassical utility theory, while revealed preference theory appears not to aid or further our understanding. Problems involving risk and time or those closely allied with welfare, such as cost–benefit analysis, have utilised neoclassical utility theory. The contribution of utility in these areas is in establishing the logic of the issues and to some degree the predictions arising from it. However, its major limitation is that a number of these predictions are non-operational and cannot be formulated in such a way that they can be put to empirical test.

There is no doubt that the changes which will take place in this area of economics in the future will be towards greater empirical refutability of hypotheses.

Appendix 4A

THE KUHN–TUCKER THEOREMS

4A.1 Two Theorems on Saddle Points

The Lagrangian function, as we outlined in Section 4.5, is a saddle-valued function. These functions play an important role in the Kuhn—Tucker theorems and we shall therefore preface the latter with two theorems on saddle points. First we shall define a saddle-valued function.

Definition 4A.1

A differentiable function $\phi(\mathbf{x}, \boldsymbol{\lambda})$ is a saddle-valued function if and only if

$$\phi(\mathbf{x}, \boldsymbol{\lambda}^0) \leqslant \phi(\mathbf{x}^0, \boldsymbol{\lambda}^0) \leqslant \phi(\mathbf{x}^0, \boldsymbol{\lambda}) \qquad \forall \mathbf{x} \geqslant 0, \boldsymbol{\lambda} \geqslant 0.$$

The point $\phi(\mathbf{x}^0, \boldsymbol{\lambda}^0)$ is called a saddle point.

Theorem 4A.1 If $\phi(\mathbf{x}^0, \boldsymbol{\lambda}^0)$ is a saddle point, then

$$(1) \quad \boldsymbol{\phi}_x \leqslant 0 \text{ and } (\mathbf{x}^0)'\boldsymbol{\phi}_x = 0 \qquad \forall \mathbf{x}^0 \geqslant 0$$

$$(2) \quad \boldsymbol{\phi}_\lambda \geqslant 0 \text{ and } (\boldsymbol{\lambda}^0)'\boldsymbol{\phi}_\lambda = 0 \qquad \forall \boldsymbol{\lambda}^0 \geqslant 0$$

Proof Suppose $\partial\phi(\mathbf{x}^0, \boldsymbol{\lambda}^0)/\partial x_i > 0$ for some i and $\partial\phi(\mathbf{x}^0, \boldsymbol{\lambda}^0)/\partial x_j = 0 \ (j \neq i)$ then it follows $\boldsymbol{\phi}_x \geqslant 0$. If this is true then $\phi(x_1^0, \ldots, x_i^0 + \delta x_i, \ldots, x_n^0; \boldsymbol{\lambda}^0) > \phi(\mathbf{x}^0, \boldsymbol{\lambda}^0)$ which means $\phi(\mathbf{x}^0, \boldsymbol{\lambda}^0)$ cannot be a saddle point, for if it were a maximum over $\phi(\mathbf{x}, \boldsymbol{\lambda}^0)$ at $\mathbf{x}^0$ then the L.H.S. should be less than $\phi(\mathbf{x}^0, \boldsymbol{\lambda}^0)$.

Suppose $\partial\phi(\mathbf{x}^0, \boldsymbol{\lambda}^0)/\partial x_i < 0$ where $x_i^0 > 0$. Then

$$\phi(x_1^0, \ldots, x_i^0 - \delta x_i, \ldots, x_n^0; \boldsymbol{\lambda}^0) > \phi(\mathbf{x}^0, \boldsymbol{\lambda}^0)$$

since if x_i^0 is decreased $\phi(\mathbf{x}^0, \boldsymbol{\lambda}^0)$ is increased by supposition. Hence $\phi(\mathbf{x}^0, \boldsymbol{\lambda}^0)$ is not a saddle point, i.e. to be a saddle point we must have:

$$\boldsymbol{\phi}_x \leqslant 0 \text{ and } (\mathbf{x}^0)'\boldsymbol{\phi}_x = 0 \qquad \forall \mathbf{x}^0 \geqslant 0.$$

The same argument holds for (2) of the theorem.

Q.E.D.

Theorem 4A.1 says that if ϕ is a saddle-valued function then at the point $\phi(\mathbf{x}^0, \boldsymbol{\lambda}^0)$ if $x_i > 0$ (i.e. $\mathbf{x}^0 > 0$) then $\partial\phi(\mathbf{x}^0, \boldsymbol{\lambda}^0)/\partial x_i = 0$ and if $x_i = 0$ at the saddle point then $\partial\phi(\mathbf{x}^0, \boldsymbol{\lambda}^0)/\partial x_i \leqslant 0$. Similarly for $\boldsymbol{\lambda}$. Notice, however, that it must be true that both $(\mathbf{x}^0)'\boldsymbol{\phi}_x$ and $(\lambda^0)'\boldsymbol{\phi}_\lambda$ equal zero.

Theorem 4A.1 gives only the necessary conditions for a saddle point since it deals only with neighbourhoods of $(\mathbf{x}^0, \boldsymbol{\lambda}^0)$. Theorem 4A.2 supplies the sufficient conditions.

Theorem 4A.2 If conditions (1) and (2) of Theorem 4A.1 hold and also

$$(3) \quad \phi(\mathbf{x}, \boldsymbol{\lambda}^0) \leqslant \phi(\mathbf{x}^0, \boldsymbol{\lambda}^0) + (\mathbf{x} - \mathbf{x}^0)'\boldsymbol{\phi}_x \qquad \forall \mathbf{x} \geqslant 0$$

$$\text{and} \quad (4) \quad \phi(\mathbf{x}^0, \boldsymbol{\lambda}) \geqslant \phi(\mathbf{x}^0, \boldsymbol{\lambda}^0) + (\boldsymbol{\lambda} - \boldsymbol{\lambda}^0)'\boldsymbol{\phi}_\lambda \qquad \forall \lambda \geqslant 0$$

then $\phi(\mathbf{x}^0, \boldsymbol{\lambda}^0)$ is a saddle point.

Proof From (1) we have $\boldsymbol{\phi}_x \leqslant 0$ and $(\mathbf{x}^0)'\boldsymbol{\phi}_x = 0$. From (3), since $\mathbf{x}'\boldsymbol{\phi}_x \leqslant 0$ and $(\mathbf{x}^0)'\boldsymbol{\phi}_x = 0$, it follows $\phi(\mathbf{x}, \boldsymbol{\lambda}^0) \leqslant \phi(\mathbf{x}^0, \boldsymbol{\lambda}^0)$. Similarly from (2) we have $\boldsymbol{\phi}_\lambda \geqslant 0$ and $(\boldsymbol{\lambda}^0)'\boldsymbol{\phi}_\lambda = 0$, it follows $\phi(\mathbf{x}^0, \boldsymbol{\lambda}) \geqslant \phi(\mathbf{x}^0, \boldsymbol{\lambda}^0)$. Combining we obtain:

$$\phi(\mathbf{x}, \boldsymbol{\lambda}^0) \leqslant \phi(\mathbf{x}^0, \boldsymbol{\lambda}^0) \leqslant \phi(\mathbf{x}^0, \boldsymbol{\lambda})$$

hence $\phi(\mathbf{x}^0, \boldsymbol{\lambda}^0)$ is a saddle point. *Q.E.D.*

4A.2 The Kuhn–Tucker Constraint Qualification

The Kuhn–Tucker constraint qualification says that at the optimal point $\mathbf{x}^0$ contained in the constraint set, at which there is a tangent, there exists an arc contained totally in the constraint set. This is shown in Fig. 4A.1. A violation of this qualification is illustrated in Fig. 4A.2, which shows a 'cusp' in the constraint set.

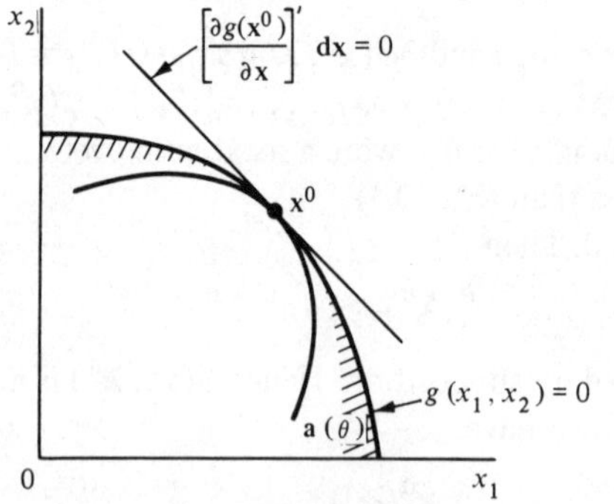

Fig. 4A.1
Constraint qualification satisfied

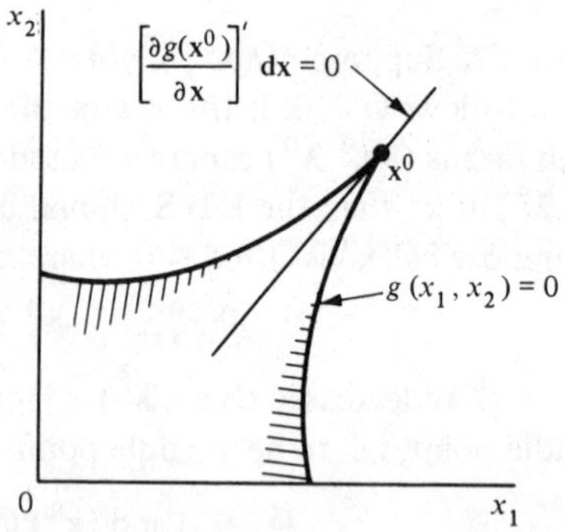

Fig. 4A.2
Constraint qualification violated

Consider a set of constraints $g_1(\mathbf{x}) \geqslant 0, \ldots, g_m(\mathbf{x}) \geqslant 0$ and any $\mathbf{x}^0$ on the boundary of the constraint set. Let

$$\mathbf{G}_1(\mathbf{x}^0) = \begin{cases} g_1(\mathbf{x}^0) = 0 \\ \cdot \\ \cdot \\ \cdot \\ g_r(\mathbf{x}^0) = 0 \end{cases} \quad \mathbf{G}_2(\mathbf{x}^0) = \begin{cases} g_{r+1}(\mathbf{x}^0) > 0 \\ \cdot \\ \cdot \\ \cdot \\ g_m(\mathbf{x}^0) > 0 \end{cases} \quad \mathbf{G}(\mathbf{x}) = \begin{bmatrix} \mathbf{G}_1(\mathbf{x}^0) \\ \mathbf{G}_2(\mathbf{x}^0) \end{bmatrix}.$$

Let **I** be the identity matrix which is partitioned $\mathbf{I} = \begin{bmatrix} \mathbf{I}_1 \\ \mathbf{I}_2 \end{bmatrix}$ where $\mathbf{I}_1$ corresponds to all $x_i^0 = 0$ and $\mathbf{I}_2$ to all $x_i^0 > 0$. Hence:

$$\mathbf{G}_1(\mathbf{x}^0) = 0 \qquad \mathbf{G}_2(\mathbf{x}^0) > 0$$

$$\mathbf{I}_1(\mathbf{x}^0) = 0 \qquad \mathbf{I}_2(\mathbf{x}^0) > 0.$$

The constraint qualification is that for each $\mathbf{x}^0$ on the boundary of the constraint set for any **dx** such that

$$\left[\frac{\partial \mathbf{G}_1(\mathbf{x}^0)}{\partial \mathbf{x}}\right]' \mathbf{dx} \geqslant 0$$

$$\mathbf{I}_1 \mathbf{dx} \geqslant 0$$

then $[\partial \mathbf{G}(\mathbf{x}^0)/\partial \mathbf{x}]'\mathbf{dx}$ is tangent to an arc $\mathbf{a}(\theta)$ contained in the constraint set, where $0 \leqslant \theta \leqslant 1$, and $\mathbf{a}(0) = \mathbf{x}^0$.

4A.3 The Kuhn–Tucker Theorems

In proving the Kuhn–Tucker theorems it will be helpful to define the following sets:

I = set of all integers for which $x_i = 0$
J = set of all integers for which $x_j > 0$
K = set of all integers for which $g_j(\mathbf{x}) = 0$
L = set of all integers for which $g_j(\mathbf{x}) > 0$
M = set of all integers for which $\lambda_i > 0$
N = set of all integers for which $\lambda_j = 0$.

Theorem 4A.3 (Kuhn–Tucker's First Theorem)
If $\mathbf{x}^0$ is a solution to a vector maximum problem:

$$\max f(\mathbf{x})$$
$$\text{s.t.} \quad \mathbf{g}(\mathbf{x}) \geqslant 0$$
$$\mathbf{x} \geqslant 0$$

and if the constraint qualification holds, then $\mathbf{x}^0$ and $\boldsymbol{\lambda}^0$ must satisfy:

$$\boldsymbol{\phi}_x \leqslant 0 \qquad (\mathbf{x}^0)'\boldsymbol{\phi}_x = 0 \text{ for } \mathbf{x}^0 \geqslant 0$$

$$\boldsymbol{\phi}_\lambda \geqslant 0 \qquad (\lambda^0)'\boldsymbol{\phi}_\lambda = 0 \text{ for } \boldsymbol{\lambda}^0 \geqslant 0$$

where $\phi(\mathbf{x}, \boldsymbol{\lambda}) = f(\mathbf{x}) + \boldsymbol{\lambda}'\mathbf{g}(\mathbf{x})$.

Proof Let $\mathbf{x}^0$ be a solution. Since $f(\mathbf{x})$ is concave then $f(\mathbf{x}^0)$ is a curve through $\mathbf{x}^0$ which is convex to the origin. Hence $\partial f(\mathbf{x}^0)/\partial x_i < 0$. But from the constraint qualification we have $dx_i \geqslant 0$, hence

$$\frac{\partial f(\mathbf{x}^0)}{\partial x_i}\, dx_i \leqslant 0 \qquad \forall dx_i$$

$$\sum_{i=1}^{n} \frac{\partial f(\mathbf{x}^0)}{\partial x_i}\, dx_i \leqslant 0.$$

Consider now the differential of $\phi(\mathbf{x}^0, \boldsymbol{\lambda}^0)$ w.r.t. x_i:

$$\frac{\partial \phi(\mathbf{x}^0, \boldsymbol{\lambda}^0)}{\partial x_i} = \frac{\partial f(\mathbf{x}^0)}{\partial x_i} + \sum_{j=1}^{m} \lambda_j^0 \frac{\partial g_j(\mathbf{x}^0)}{\partial x_i}.$$

Now this is true only for $\lambda_j^0 > 0$ and $x_i = 0$. If we take account of $\lambda_j = 0$ for $j \in \mathbf{N}$ we have:

$$\frac{\partial \phi(\mathbf{x}^0, \boldsymbol{\lambda}^0)}{\partial x_i} = \frac{\partial f(\mathbf{x}^0)}{\partial x_i} + \sum_{j=1}^{m} \lambda_j^0 \frac{\partial g_j(\mathbf{x}^0)}{\partial x_i} \qquad \forall j \in \mathbf{M}$$

Suppose we include $\mathbf{x} \geqslant 0$ explicitly as a set of constraints with Lagrangian coefficients μ_i, then if $x_j^0 = 0$, $\mu_j^0 > 0$ and if $x_j^0 > 0$ then $\mu_j^0 = 0$. Hence

$$\frac{\partial \phi(\mathbf{x}^0, \boldsymbol{\lambda}^0)}{\partial x_i} = \frac{\partial f(\mathbf{x}^0)}{\partial x_i} + \sum_{j=1}^{m} \lambda_j^0 \frac{\partial g_j(\mathbf{x}^0)}{\partial x_i} + \mu_i^0 \qquad \forall i \in \mathbf{I}, j \in \mathbf{M}.$$

But by Farkas's Lemma we have:

$$-\frac{\partial f(\mathbf{x}^0)}{\partial x_i} = \sum_{j=1}^{m} \lambda_j^0 \frac{\partial g_j(\mathbf{x}^0)}{\partial x_i} + \mu_i^0 \qquad \forall i \in \mathbf{I}, j \in \mathbf{M}; \lambda^0 \geqslant 0, \mu^0 \geqslant 0.$$

Adding the zero elements to the λ's and μ's we have:

$$-\frac{\partial f(\mathbf{x}^0)}{\partial x_i} = \sum_{j=1}^{m} \lambda_j^0 \frac{\partial g_j(\mathbf{x}^0)}{\partial x_i} + \mu_i^0 \qquad \forall i \in \mathbf{I} + \mathbf{J}, j \in \mathbf{M} + \mathbf{N}$$

i.e.

$$\frac{\partial f(\mathbf{x}^0)}{\partial x_i} + \sum_{j=1}^{m} \lambda_j^0 \frac{\partial g_j(\mathbf{x}^0)}{\partial x_i} + \mu_i^0 = 0.$$

From Farkas's Lemma we know $\mu_i^0 \geqslant 0\ \forall i$, it therefore follows that

$$\frac{\partial \phi(\mathbf{x}^0, \boldsymbol{\lambda}^0)}{\partial x_i} = \frac{\partial f(\mathbf{x}^0)}{\partial x_i} + \sum_{j=1}^{m} \lambda_j^0 \frac{g_j(\mathbf{x}^0)}{\partial x_i} \leqslant 0 \qquad \forall i \in \mathbf{I} + \mathbf{J}$$

which proves the first part of the condition.

Now

$$\sum_{i=1}^{n} \frac{\partial f(\mathbf{x}^0)}{\partial x_i} x_i^0 + \sum_{i=1}^{n} \sum_{j=1}^{m} \lambda_j^0 \frac{\partial g_j(\mathbf{x}^0)}{\partial x_i} x_i^0 + \sum_{i=1}^{n} \mu_i^0 x_i = 0.$$

But $\sum_{i=1}^{n} \mu_i^0 x_i^0 = 0$ because either $x_i^0 = 0$ or else $\mu_i^0 = 0$. Therefore

$$\sum_{i=1}^{n} \frac{\partial f(\mathbf{x}^0)}{\partial x_i} x_i^0 + \sum_{i=1}^{n} \sum_{j=1}^{m} \lambda_j^0 \frac{\partial g_j(\mathbf{x}^0)}{\partial x_i} x_i^0 = 0.$$

Hence,

$$\sum_{i=1}^{n} \frac{\partial \phi(\mathbf{x}^0, \boldsymbol{\lambda}^0)}{\partial x_i} x_i^0 = \sum_{i=1}^{n} \frac{\partial f(\mathbf{x}^0)}{\partial x_i} x_i^0 + \sum_{i=1}^{n} \sum_{j=1}^{m} \lambda_j^0 \frac{\partial g_j(\mathbf{x}^0)}{\partial x_i} x_i^0 = 0$$

i.e.

$$(\mathbf{x}^0)' \phi_x = 0$$

which proves part two of the first condition.

We have by definition

$$\frac{\partial \phi(\mathbf{x}^0, \boldsymbol{\lambda}^0)}{\partial \lambda_j} = g_j(\mathbf{x}^0) \geqslant 0 \quad \text{the first part of condition two,}$$

$$\therefore \quad \sum_{j=1}^{m} \frac{\partial \phi(\mathbf{x}^0, \boldsymbol{\lambda}^0)}{\partial \lambda_j} \lambda_j^0 = \sum_{j=1}^{m} \lambda_j^0 g_j(\mathbf{x}^0) \geqslant 0 \quad \text{since } \lambda_j^0 \geqslant 0.$$

But $g_j(\mathbf{x}^0) = 0 \quad \forall j \in \mathbf{K}$ and $\lambda_j = 0 \quad \forall j \in \mathbf{N}$. Therefore

$$\sum_{j=1}^{m} \frac{\partial \phi(\mathbf{x}^0, \boldsymbol{\lambda}^0)}{\partial \lambda_j} \lambda_j^0 = \sum_{j=1}^{m} \lambda_j^0 g_j(\mathbf{x}^0) = 0$$

i.e.

$$(\boldsymbol{\lambda}^0)' \phi_\lambda = 0$$

which proves part two.

Q.E.D.

Theorem 4A.4 (Kuhn–Tucker's Second Theorem)
If $\mathbf{x}^0$ and $\boldsymbol{\lambda}^0$ satisfy:

(1) $\phi_x \leqslant 0$ and $(\mathbf{x}^0)'\phi_x = 0 \qquad \forall \mathbf{x}^0 \geqslant 0$

(2) $\phi_\lambda \geqslant 0$ and $(\boldsymbol{\lambda}^0)'\phi_\lambda = 0 \qquad \forall \boldsymbol{\lambda}^0 \geqslant 0$

(3) $\phi(\mathbf{x}, \boldsymbol{\lambda}^0) \leqslant \phi(\mathbf{x}^0, \boldsymbol{\lambda}^0) + (\mathbf{x} - \mathbf{x}^0)'\boldsymbol{\phi}_x \qquad \forall \mathbf{x} \geqslant 0$

for $\phi(\mathbf{x}, \boldsymbol{\lambda}) = f(\mathbf{x}) + \boldsymbol{\lambda}'\mathbf{g}(\mathbf{x})$, then $\mathbf{x}^0$ is an optimal solution of

$$\max f(\mathbf{x})$$
$$\text{s.t.} \quad \mathbf{g}(\mathbf{x}) \geqslant 0$$
$$\mathbf{x} \geqslant 0.$$

Proof From (3) we have:

$$f(\mathbf{x}) + (\boldsymbol{\lambda}^0)'\mathbf{g}(\mathbf{x}) = \phi(\mathbf{x}, \boldsymbol{\lambda}^0) \leqslant \phi(\mathbf{x}^0, \boldsymbol{\lambda}^0) + (\mathbf{x} - \mathbf{x}^0)'\boldsymbol{\phi}_x.$$

But $\mathbf{x}'\boldsymbol{\phi}_x \leqslant 0$ if $\phi(\mathbf{x}^0, \boldsymbol{\lambda}^0)$ is a saddle point and we know from condition (1) that $(\mathbf{x}^0)'\boldsymbol{\phi}_x = 0$, hence

$$f(\mathbf{x}) + (\boldsymbol{\lambda}^0)'\mathbf{g}(\mathbf{x}) \leqslant \phi(\mathbf{x}^0, \boldsymbol{\lambda}^0).$$

But by Theorem 4A.3 we have $(\boldsymbol{\lambda}^0)'\mathbf{g}(\mathbf{x}) = 0$. Thus

$$\phi(\mathbf{x}^0, \boldsymbol{\lambda}^0) = f(\mathbf{x}^0) + (\boldsymbol{\lambda}^0)'\mathbf{g}(\mathbf{x}^0) = f(\mathbf{x}^0).$$

Therefore

$$f(\mathbf{x}) \leqslant f(\mathbf{x}^0).$$

Q.E.D.

These Kuhn–Tucker theorems will be applied in various sections of the book when we come to relax neoclassical analysis, in both the areas of consumption theory and production theory.

EXERCISES

1. Obtain uncompensated and compensated demand functions for the following utility functions:

(i) $u = a_0 x_1^{a_1} x_2^{a_2}$

(ii) $u = a_0 [a_1 x_1^{-\rho} + a_2 x_2^{-\rho}]^{-\nu/\rho}$

(iii) $u = a_1 \log(x_1 - \gamma_1) + a_2 \log(x_2 - \gamma_2)$.

Compare your results.

2. For each of the utility functions in question 1 obtain the marginal utility of expenditure in terms of p_1, p_2, and y. Are these functions homogeneous, and if so of what degree? What significance can be attached to a homogeneity of degree different from zero for these functions?

3. Show that if $u = a_0 x_1^{a_1} x_2^{a_2}$ then $v = \log u$ has the same demand functions but not the same Lagrangian multipliers. Further show that the Lagrangian associated with u is equal to that associated with v multiplied by u. Is this result true for the utility function $u = a_0 [a_1 x_1^{-\rho} + a_2 x_2^{-\rho}]^{-\nu/\rho}$?

4. On p. 83 we have that $\lambda_y = (\mathbf{p}'\mathbf{U}^{-1}\mathbf{p})^{-1}$. Consider now the following monotonic transformation $F(u) = \log u$. Obtain the response μ_y where μ_y is the Lagrangian multiplier for this new utility function and further show that $\mu_y \neq \lambda_y$.

5. For the utility function

$$u = \boldsymbol{\alpha}' \log \mathbf{x} \qquad \boldsymbol{\iota}'\boldsymbol{\alpha} = 1$$

obtain the results in the following table:

Income responses	*Price responses*
1. $\mathbf{x}_y = \hat{\mathbf{p}}^{-1} \boldsymbol{\alpha}$	1. $\mathbf{X}_p = y\, \hat{\mathbf{p}}^{-1} \boldsymbol{\alpha} \hat{\mathbf{p}}^{-1}$
2. $\lambda_y = -y^{-2}$	2. $\mathbf{S}_p = y^{-1} \hat{\mathbf{x}} \hat{\boldsymbol{\alpha}}^{-1} \mathbf{x} + y\, \mathbf{p}^{-1} \boldsymbol{\alpha}\boldsymbol{\alpha}' \mathbf{p}^{-1}$
	$\mathbf{S}_p^* = \mathbf{X}_p$
	$\mathbf{S}_p^{**} = \mathbf{x}_y \mathbf{x}'$
3. $\phi = \eta_{\lambda y} = -1$	3. $\boldsymbol{\lambda}_p = 0$

6. Given the Stone–Geary utility function

$$u = \boldsymbol{\alpha}' \log(\mathbf{x} - \boldsymbol{\gamma}) \qquad \boldsymbol{\iota}'\boldsymbol{\alpha} = 1, 0 \ll \boldsymbol{\alpha} \ll \boldsymbol{\iota}, \qquad \boldsymbol{\gamma} \geqslant 0.$$

Show that

$$\mathbf{x} = \boldsymbol{\gamma} + (y - \mathbf{p}'\boldsymbol{\gamma})\hat{\mathbf{p}}^{-1}\boldsymbol{\alpha}.$$

Further show that the expenditure functions $\mathbf{v} = \hat{\mathbf{p}}\mathbf{x}$ can be written in the linear form:

$$\mathbf{v} = \hat{\mathbf{p}}\mathbf{x} = y\boldsymbol{\alpha} + \mathbf{A}\mathbf{p}.$$

7. For the Stone–Geary utility function derive the following comparative static results:

$$\mathbf{X}_p = -(y - \mathbf{p}'\boldsymbol{\gamma})\,\hat{\mathbf{p}}^{-1}\,\hat{\boldsymbol{\alpha}}\,\hat{\mathbf{p}}^{-1} - \hat{\mathbf{p}}^{-1}\,\boldsymbol{\alpha}\boldsymbol{\gamma}'$$

$$\mathbf{S}_p = -(y - \mathbf{p}'\boldsymbol{\gamma})^{-1}\,(\hat{\mathbf{x}} - \hat{\boldsymbol{\gamma}})\,\hat{\boldsymbol{\alpha}}^{-1}\,(\hat{\mathbf{x}} - \hat{\boldsymbol{\gamma}}) + (y - \mathbf{p}'\boldsymbol{\gamma})\,\hat{\mathbf{p}}^{-1}\,\boldsymbol{\alpha}\boldsymbol{\alpha}'\,\hat{\mathbf{p}}^{-1}$$

$$\mathbf{x}_y = \hat{\mathbf{p}}^{-1}\,\boldsymbol{\alpha}$$

$$\lambda_y = -(y - \mathbf{p}'\boldsymbol{\gamma})^{-2}$$

$$\boldsymbol{\lambda}_p = (y - \mathbf{p}'\boldsymbol{\gamma})^{-2}\,\boldsymbol{\gamma}$$

$$\boldsymbol{\phi} = -y^{-1}\,(y - \mathbf{p}'\boldsymbol{\gamma}).$$

8. Prove the elasticity forms of the demand restrictions.

9. (*a*) If good *i* is a Giffen good does it follow that it is also an inferior good?
(*b*) Are all inferior goods Giffen goods?
(*c*) If goods *i* and *j* are net complements under what conditions will they also be gross substitutes?

10. For the optimisation problem discussed in Section 4.5 derive the Slutsky decomposition of $\mathbf{X}_p$ into the three effects: substitution, income and additional.

11. Show that for the optimisation problem discussed in Section 4.5 the Engel aggregation is satisfied but not the Cournot aggregation since

$$\mathbf{X}_p'\,\mathbf{p} = -\mathbf{x} + \mathbf{u}_p'\,\mathbf{x}_y\,\lambda_y^{-1}.$$

12. Show that

$$\mathbf{X}_p\,\mathbf{p} = -\mathbf{x}_y\,y + \mathbf{U}_x^{-1}\,\mathbf{U}_p\,\mathbf{p}$$

and hence explain why, in this case, demand curves are not homogeneous of degree zero in **p** and *y*.

13. Consider the hyperplane $\mathbf{H} = \{(x_1, x_2)/\ 6x_1 + 3x_2 = 4\}$. Show that the vector $\mathbf{a} = (6, 3)$ is a normal to this hyperplane, and that the unit normal is the vector $\mathbf{b} = (2\sqrt{5}, 1/\sqrt{5})$. Further show that the distance of the hyperplane from the origin is ${}^4/_3\sqrt{5}$ and that the vector $\mathbf{c} = ({}^1/_6, 1)$ has the same length, and hence that c lies in the set **H**. Draw all these results on a diagram.

14. Given $u = (¼)\log x_1 + (¾)\log x_2$
(a) If $u^0 = 0{\cdot}6931$ show that the better set is given by
$$\mathbf{B} = \{(x_1, x_2)/\ x_1 \geqslant 16/x_2^3,\ x_1 \geqslant 0, x_2 \geqslant 0\}.$$
(*b*) Which of the following hyperplanes are bounding and which supporting to the better set in part (*a*):

$$\mathbf{H}_1 = \{(x_1, x_2)\,/\,4x_1 + 3x_2 = 10\}$$
$$\mathbf{H}_2 = \{(x_1, x_2)\,/\,4x_1 + 3x_2 = 14\}$$
$$\mathbf{H}_3 = \{(x_1, x_2)\,/\,x_1 + 48x_2 = 64\}$$
$$\mathbf{H}_4 = \{(x_1, x_2)\,/\,x_1 + 48x_2 = 30\}.$$

15. Prove that a hyperplane is a convex set.

16. Demonstrate that when there are only two goods that the cross substitution term s_{12} must be positive and hence that no net complementarity is possible. Is this result true for gross complementarity? What is the extent of net complementarity when there are three goods?

17. Suppose a consumer with utility function $u(x_1, x_2)$ is faced with the rationing $x_1 \leqslant b_1$ and $x_2 \leqslant b_2$, where b_i represents the maximum quota of the ith commodity. If the consumer has the budget constraint $p_1x_1 + p_2x_2 \leqslant y$, obtain the equilibrium conditions. Show that if the consumer is not using the whole of quota 1 then $\lambda_1 = 0$ and $s_1 > 0$, where λ_1 is the marginal utility of the ration b_1 and s_1 is the amount of the quota not taken up. Also show that it is possible for both rations to be operative, i.e. that $\lambda_1 > 0$, $s_1 = 0$ and $\lambda_2 > 0$, $s_2 = 0$, but that this will generally mean that not all income is spent.

18. For the optimisation problem:

$$\max u = x_1^{1/2} x_2^{1/2}$$

$$\text{s.t. } 3x_1 + 4x_2 \leqslant 20$$

$$0 \leqslant x_1 \leqslant 5, x_2 \geqslant 0.$$

Show that the optimal solution is given by:

$$x_1^0 = 3\tfrac{1}{3} \qquad \lambda_1^0 = \sqrt{3}/12$$

$$x_2^0 = 2\tfrac{1}{2} \qquad \lambda_2^0 = 0$$

Diagram this result.

19. Using the same utility function and budget constraint as in question 18, but $0 \leqslant x_1 \leqslant 3$ and $x_2 \geqslant 0$, show that the optimal solution is:

$$x_1^0 = 3 \qquad \lambda_1^0 = \sqrt{33}/44$$

$$x_2^0 = 2\tfrac{3}{4} \qquad \lambda_2^0 = \sqrt{33}/66$$

Now let $0 \leqslant x_2 \leqslant 2$ and show that the consumer will consume all of both quotas. What are the marginal utilities of each ration? Explain why the marginal utility of the first ration is different in both these cases.

Part III
PRODUCTION THEORY

Chapters 5–7 are concerned with the theory of production. Once again we begin by laying the axiomatic base on which we aim to discuss production. This approach does depart from the more traditional in that we have not made the production function our central point. In fact, the production function is discussed fully only in Chapter 7 when we turn to neoclassical production theory. The central concept is that of 'transformation', which we take to be a primitive of production theory. By means of this primitive we establish the production set and then we elaborate on certain of its features, e.g. whether it is convex, whether the origin is contained in the set and what this means in economic terms. The central question is: In what way are producers' choices constrained by production technology?

It becomes apparent very early in the discussion that one of the main distinguishing features of the various production theories is the assumption about activities. For instance, the assumption that there is only one activity for the firm in a Leontief production model; that an activity approach has at least two activities, but which are finite; whilst in neoclassical production theory the number of activities are infinite. As far as each theory is concerned what is assumed about activities is vital and there is no doubt that such an assumption belongs to the set P_a of fundamental propositions discussed in Chapter 1. Furthermore, it is also clear that these alternative assumptions are by no means self-evident and are merely a means of limiting the domain of study. Part of our task, therefore, is to highlight the implications of the alternative approaches to production theory.

In so far as linear theories of the firm, and the economy, are exhibited in terms of convex cones it is desirable that the properties of these are understood. Therefore, in Section 5.3 we discuss the mathematical properties of convex cones. In Section 5.4 we attempt to bring the firm and the economy together. This process is carried through in Chapter 6 on linear production theory but not in Chapter 7 on non-linear production theory, since the latter does not allow analysis to go from the firm to the economy so readily. A particular question being asked is: To what extent can a theory of production at the firm level be aggregated to obtain a theory of production at the economy level? It is in this regard that we see how vital a number of the axioms become.

Also in Chapter 5 we discuss two mathematical concepts which are used throughout production theory and general equilibrium (Part IV). The first is the distinction between a function and a correspondence; whilst the second is concerned with continuity and semi-continuity of functions and correspondences. The reader is reminded that these are meant to be for reference purposes since they are used also in Part IV. However, without a knowledge of these concepts it is not at all clear why, for example, a supply correspondence is upper semi-continuous whilst profits is a continuous function.

For convenience production theory is divided into linear and non-linear versions. Under the former we discuss three types. (1) A Ricardian theory of production; (2) A Leontief model; (3) An activity model. It seems natural to discuss a Ricardian model for two reasons. First, it is by far the simplest and leads quite naturally into the Leontief model and consists solely of a single basic input, viz. labour. A second reason is that the Ricardian model forms the basis for discussions of comparative advantage and also J. S. Mill's approach to international trade. For the Leontief model we discuss two types. The *closed* version, which assumes that all production is used by the industries in that system and there is no input from outside the system (such as labour) and no final demand. Although this is unrealistic it does have some insights and sets the scene for the *open* Leontief model which allows for basic inputs (such as labour and raw materials) and also allows production to be lost from the system in terms of final consumption. In Section 6.4 we have singled out two formal problems: decomposability of matrices and the Perron–Frobenius theorem. The reason for this is because these mathematical results have direct application to linear production theory. Part of the aim of Chapters 5 and 6 is to lead the reader into some of the recent advances in production theory. These advances are highly mathematical and so we have here given only an introductory treatment.

The final chapter of Part III is concerned with neoclassical production theory. The discussion has been kept brief largely because there are many excellent texts on this area, e.g. Ferguson [38]. Stress has therefore been placed on the role of production and profits functions and in what way neoclassical production theory is extreme in its assumptions. For this reason, however, the neoclassical theory is fruitful at the firm level but not so successful at the economy level.

It is to be stressed that Part III is about production theory and *not* directly with theories of the firm. Part of the reason for this emphasis is so that we can establish results which will be useful when we come to discuss general equilibrium theory in Part IV.

5

THE THEORY OF PRODUCTION

5.1 Introduction

Production, in its widest sense, is concerned with the transformation of one thing into something else. The decision unit that carries out this transformation is the *firm*, which we take to be a theoretical construct and which satisfies the axioms of production to be presented below. This theoretical construct should not be taken to mean a typical firm in the real world. It is an abstraction, an analogue, of the decision-making processes and the technological processes under which we consider most firms operate.

We shall be concerned in this chapter, and later chapters, with production; but production on two levels. First, we shall be concerned with the production of an individual decision unit, namely, the firm. Second, we shall also be concerned with the production of an economy as a whole. Why we consider an economy's production is an important question. The reason lies in our ultimate concern with how, and in what way, community's preferences interact with producers' preferences. This interaction leads us into such problems as the theory of exchange, resource allocation and welfare. In considering an economy, as distinct from an individual unit, we must be careful not to engage in the fallacy of composition: of assuming that what holds for the production of a firm also holds for the production of an economy. As we shall see, the production set of a firm is convex; can we therefore conclude that the production set of an economy is convex?

Before we can consider how consumer and producer units combine we must build up a theory of the production process. As in the theory of choice, we must be clear as to the primitives of our theory. With the use of these primitives we shall establish a set of production axioms on which the theory of the firm and the production set of an economy is based. In establishing these axioms the reader should bear in mind whether they are essential, i.e. whether they belong to the set P_α, or whether they are introduced as a means of taking the analysis a stage further, i.e. whether they belong to the set P_γ. Production theory, even more so than consumer theory, has many alternative formulations. These alternatives must arise from the rejection of certain axioms in preference to others. Part of our job, therefore, is to establish as clearly as possible which of the axioms are being replaced in the various alternative formulations.

5.2 Axioms of Production[1]

Production, like preference, is a binary relation. It is a relation between something we shall denote as $\mathbf{x}$, a vector which may have only one element, which is to be transformed into something else, which we denote as **y**, a vector which may have only one element. In order to discuss this relation, or transformation, we introduce a primitive *T* for transformation. Thus **x***T***y** means that '**x** is transformed into **y**'. In one sense this is a broader concept than it first appears. As a consumer, if an individual has a commodity, say money, which he gives up for another commodity, say apples, there is no loss if we say that money has been transformed into apples: the process which carries out this transformation is the exchange system. We shall, however, consider only the production process here, although the axioms equally apply to this pure exchange system. Furthermore, the transformation applies equally to the producer as to the economy; in the case of the economy, however, we require a greater specification as to how the individual producers react together.

The first axiom of production ensures that the set of all possible transformations is non-empty.

Axiom 12 $\exists \mathbf{x}, \mathbf{y} \quad (A\mathbf{x} \,\&\, \mathbf{x}T\mathbf{y})$.

In other words, there exists at least an element **x** in the attainable set which may be transformed into **y**. Implicit in Axiom 12 is the definition of an 'input' and an 'output'. To say that there is an **x** (a vector which may have only a single element) which can be transformed into **y** (a vector which may have only a single element) is to say that **y** is a vector of outputs of the transformation. With the help of this axiom we can define the production set. There is, however, a problem of notation here. In stating the axioms we shall take inputs as **x** and outputs as **y**. However, because of convention and certainly because it simplifies the mathematical exposition, *both* inputs and outputs are denoted by **y** with the difference that inputs have negative signs and outputs positive signs. Thus, in terms of the axioms to follow the *production set* is the set of all input–output combinations which are feasible, i.e. satisfy the relation *T*. In terms of the convention about signs the production set, denoted **Y**, is the set of all **y**(*both* inputs and outputs). The reader is warned that it is only from the context will it be clear which alternative is being employed.

We now turn to the axiom which Walsh has called the *neutrality of transformations.*[2]

Axiom 13 If $\mathbf{x}^0 \, T_1 \mathbf{y}^0$ and $\mathbf{x}^1 T_2 \mathbf{y}^1$

$$\mathrm{T}_1 I \mathrm{T}_2 \Leftrightarrow (\mathbf{x}^0 I \mathbf{x}^1 \ \& \ \mathbf{y}^0 I \mathbf{y}^1),$$

i.e. transformations are judged solely by their inputs and outputs and not on anything else such as the social consequences of operating such transformations. In other words, activities do not give rise to preferences. To illustrate this suppose a commodity can be produced with much labour and little capital or by little labour and much capital, each combination being treated indifferently, and that the same output is produced under each alternative. The axiom requires that these two transformations are indifferent. A situation where the second process, in using less labour than the first, gives rise to unemployment which is socially unacceptable is ruled out by Axiom 13. In this regard the transformation process is independent of the types of constraint the firm or the economy may be operating under. It also means that production decisions are independent of consumption decisions.

We see in Axiom 13 a point of difference. All production theory to date is crucially dependent upon it. However, the followers of Galbraith, and particularly those of the American New Left, would argue that production decisions are not independent of consumption decisions. To the extent that advertising can, besides expanding a market, create a market, then consumption can to varying degrees be linked to the production process. But even if one accepts such notions the theorist must replace Axiom 13 with some alternative, and it is not at all clear what can be put in its place.

It is important to remember that since production is a problem of choice then Axioms 1–7 are relevant. Axiom 2 says that decisions (preferences) are transitive. It would be desirable for production decisions to exhibit transitivity and we shall do this explicitly in the form of Axiom 14:

Axiom 14 $\mathbf{x}T\mathbf{y} \;\&\; \mathbf{y}T\mathbf{z} \Rightarrow \mathbf{x}T\mathbf{z}$.

We can in this instance think of $\mathbf{y}$ as an 'intermediate good'. Such a good is an output of one transformation and an input of another transformation. With Axiom 14 consideration need only be given to inputs and outputs without considering intermediate goods. However, for certain problems we shall be interested in intermediate production.

The next axiom is most important because it has far-reaching implications which are not obvious on a first consideration.

Axiom 15 $\mathbf{x}^0 T\mathbf{y}^0 \;\&\; \mathbf{x}^1 T\mathbf{y}^1 \Rightarrow (\mathbf{x}^0 + \mathbf{x}^1)\, T(\mathbf{y}^0 + \mathbf{y}^1)$.

This axiom says that if a firm or an economy combines two possible inputs then the output is the addition of each. Suppose, for example, that a firm uses labour and capital, $\mathbf{x}^0$, to produce cars and bicycles, $\mathbf{y}^0$. Also it may use different amounts of labour and capital, $\mathbf{x}^1$, to produce a different amount of cars and bicycles, $\mathbf{y}^1$. If it has available labour and capital of $\mathbf{x}^0 + \mathbf{x}^1$ then Axiom 15 says that the firm can produce the addition of cars and bicycles that it would have obtained from each transformation separately, i.e. with input $\mathbf{x}^0 + \mathbf{x}^1$ it can produce $\mathbf{y}^0 + \mathbf{y}^1$, and no more than this sum. Not only does this apply to the firm, it applies for any transformation process; in particular, it applies to the economy. What this axiom implies, therefore, is that there is no interaction between production processes or between firms.

Axiom 15, like that of Axiom 13, is specifically introduced not because it is obviously true but rather to delimit the domain of study. As Koopmans points out, 'Economic literature abounds with examples of interaction, such as water or air pollution, drawing on subsoil water or oil, effect of deforestation on water runoff, etc.' [69, p. 75]. Consequently the interest in social cost is ruled out by Axiom 15. Any consideration of externalities and the phenomenon of social cost must replace Axiom 15 (and Axiom 16 to follow) with an alternative. Unfortunately, economists have not yet devised any suitable axiom. Even though we cannot deal with externalities, at this level of abstraction, Axiom 15 does allow us to arrive at some understanding of production theory. All we can do at this stage is to see what implications follow from introducing Axiom 15 into our axiom set.

If $\mathbf{x}^1 = \mathbf{x}^0$ we have $(2\mathbf{x}^0)T(2\mathbf{y}^0)$, and so on for any integer. We see, therefore, that Axiom 15 applies to indivisible inputs and outputs. It is to be distinguished from the following constant-returns-to-scale axiom which holds for any real $\lambda \geqslant 0$.

Axiom 16 $\mathbf{x}T\mathbf{y} \quad \& \quad \lambda \geqslant 0 \qquad (\lambda\mathbf{x})T(\lambda\mathbf{y})$.

Axiom 16 asserts that if $\mathbf{x}T\mathbf{y}$ is a possible transformation then so is $(\lambda\mathbf{x})T(\lambda\mathbf{y})$. If we are to consider divisible commodities then Axiom 15 is insufficient. A divisible commodity is one for which, if y is feasible then for any $0 < a < 1$, $a\mathbf{y}$ is also feasible. However, additivity plus divisibility implies Axiom 16. In place of introducing a continuity axiom we have the constant-returns-to-scale axiom which gives meaning to *any* level of input and output. This is a very strong assumption and the most recent literature is attempting to replace it. But its introduction is crucial in understanding the theories of linear programming, input–output analysis, and activity analysis.

To arrive at a consistent set of axioms, we must allow for the situation of a firm or an economy not producing at all. This decision is embodied in Axiom 17.

Axiom 17 $\exists \mathbf{x} \qquad \mathbf{x}T0$.

In other words, anything may be transformed into nothing. From this axiom we immediately have $0T0$, i.e. nothing can be transformed into nothing. The decision of not to produce at all means that there exists a $\mathbf{y} = 0$ which belongs to the production set (i.e. $\exists \mathbf{y} = 0 \; \mathbf{y} \in \mathbf{Y}$). A stronger form of this axiom, which was employed by Debreu [30], is that we allow free disposal. If we consider a negative output as disposing of a good, and since inputs are denoted as negative terms, then it follows that the production set contains the negative orthant, $-\Omega$.[3] Hence

Axiom 17′ $(-\Omega) \subset \mathbf{Y}$.

Since $0 \in -\Omega$ then it immediately follows that there exists an input combination which can be transformed into nothing and also that nothing can be transformed into nothing. Thus Axiom 17′ implies Axiom 17 but not conversely.

Although we have $0T0$, we have not ruled out the possibility that $0T\mathbf{y}$ exists for $\mathbf{y} \neq 0$. Clearly, to produce an output with no input is unreasonable, and in order to eliminate such free production we include in our axiom set:

Axiom 18 $0T\mathbf{y} \Rightarrow \mathbf{y} = 0$

Axioms 12–18 apply to any transformation relation T, whether it is for a firm or an economy. We must now turn to axioms which apply specifically to the firm. Throughout we shall consider firm j. Thus, when we are considering the production set, this is the production set of the jth firm and we shall denote it $\mathbf{Y}_j$. The production axioms so far presented place restrictions on the production set $\mathbf{Y}_j$ of the

j^{th} producer. But what are these restrictions? Axiom 16, the constant-returns-to-scale axiom, implies that the production set $\mathbf{Y}_j$ is weakly convex. This is clear from Fig. 5.1, where output is taken as positive and input as negative. (It is also assumed that firm j uses input x to produce output y and does not use 'input' y to produce 'output' x, and that Axiom 17 rather than 17′ applies.) The production set $\mathbf{Y}_j$ is clearly a weakly convex set.

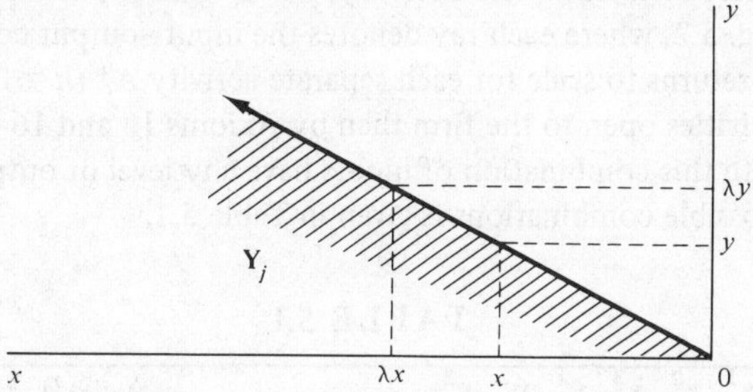

Fig. 5.1. A production set with constant returns to scale.

The condition of convexity is so important to all the various theories of production that it is worth stating it explicitly:

Axiom 19 $\mathbf{Y}_j$ is a convex set.

This axiom has been stated in the form: '$\mathbf{Y}_j$ is a convex set', without stating whether it is weakly or strictly convex in order to highlight the alternative theories of production. A production process which exhibits decreasing returns to scale violates Axiom 16 but does not violate Axiom 19, because the production set $\mathbf{Y}_j$ under these conditions is a strictly convex set. What Axiom 19 does rule out is increasing returns to scale. If this were not ruled out then the production set $\mathbf{Y}_j$ would be non-convex. It must be remembered that linear production theory rests on the condition that $\mathbf{Y}_j$ is weakly convex, whilst neoclassical production theory, along with other non-linear production models, rests on the condition that $\mathbf{Y}_j$ is strictly convex. It is also to be noted that additivity plus divisibility implies convexity. We also noted earlier that additivity plus divisibility implies the constant-return-to-scale axiom (Axiom 16); however, it is true that convexity implies divisibility but it does not imply additivity.

We have in discussing the axioms of production referred to processes or activities. We shall denote these by $\mathbf{A}^h$ for the hth activity. Besides the convexity axiom, it is also with regard to activities that differences arise in alternative theories of production. In neoclassical production theory the number of activities is infinite; in Leontief input–output analysis there is only one activity; whilst in activity analysis there are many activities but they are finite in number. Until we come to discuss neoclassical production theory we shall assume there are a finite set of activities – which includes the Leontief case:

Axiom 20 The set of activities is finite: $\mathbf{A} = \{\mathbf{A}^1, \ldots, \mathbf{A}^g\}$.

Let us consider the implications of Axiom 20 and some of the earlier axioms of production. Consider a firm (firm j) which uses two inputs, x_1 and x_2, to produce a single output, y; so that $\mathbf{x}$ has two elements and $\mathbf{y}$ has a single element in the transformation $\mathbf{x}T\mathbf{y}$. By Axiom 16 we have $(\lambda\mathbf{x})T(\lambda\mathbf{y})$ is feasible if $\mathbf{x}T\mathbf{y}$ is feasible. If we draw this for a given activity, i.e. a given input–output technique, we obtain a ray through the origin analogous to that in Fig. 5.1, but now drawn in a three-dimensional space. With three activities, say, we have three possible rays as illustrated in Fig. 5.2, where each ray denotes the input–output combinations under constant returns to scale for each separate activity $\mathbf{A}_j^h$ $(h = 1, 2, 3)$. If these are the only activities open to the firm then by Axioms 15 and 16 we can combine any two and with this combination of inputs have any level of output along its ray. The set of all possible combinations is given in Table 5.1.

TABLE 5.1

Activities	$\mathbf{x}^1, \mathbf{x}^2, \mathbf{x}^3, \mathbf{y}^1, \mathbf{y}^2, \mathbf{y}^3$	$\lambda_1 \geqslant 0, \lambda_2 \geqslant 0, \lambda_3 \geqslant 0$
$\mathbf{A}_j^1$ and $\mathbf{A}_j^2$	$\mathbf{x}^1 T\mathbf{y}^1$ & $\mathbf{x}^2 T\mathbf{y}^2 \Rightarrow (\mathbf{x}^1 + \mathbf{x}^2)T(\mathbf{y}^1 + \mathbf{y}^2)$	$(\lambda_1\mathbf{x}^1 + \lambda_2\mathbf{x}^2)T(\lambda_1\mathbf{y}^1 + \lambda_2\mathbf{y}^2)$
$\mathbf{A}_j^1$ and $\mathbf{A}_j^3$	$\mathbf{x}^1 T\mathbf{y}^1$ & $\mathbf{x}^3 T\mathbf{y}^3 \Rightarrow (\mathbf{x}^1 + \mathbf{x}^3)T(\mathbf{y}^1 + \mathbf{y}^3)$	$(\lambda_1\mathbf{x}^1 + \lambda_3\mathbf{x}^3)T(\lambda_1\mathbf{y}^1 + \lambda_3\mathbf{y}^3)$
$\mathbf{A}_j^2$ and $\mathbf{A}_j^3$	$\mathbf{x}^2 T\mathbf{y}^2$ & $\mathbf{x}^3 T\mathbf{y}^3 \Rightarrow (\mathbf{x}^2 + \mathbf{x}^3)T(\mathbf{y}^2 + \mathbf{y}^3)$	$(\lambda_2\mathbf{x}^2 + \lambda_3\mathbf{x}^3)T(\lambda_2\mathbf{y}^2 + \lambda_3\mathbf{y}^3)$

What this table reveals is that the production set for this firm is the shaded cone formed from the faces $\mathbf{A}_j^1\mathbf{A}_j^2$, $\mathbf{A}_j^1\ \mathbf{A}_j^3$ and $\mathbf{A}_j^2\mathbf{A}_j^3$ and including the area within these faces. It is also clear that implied in the axioms is that $\mathbf{Y}_j$ is convex, in the present case being weakly convex. Note also that an implication of Axiom 17 is that the convex cone $\mathbf{Y}_j$ in Fig. 5.2 contains the origin.[4]

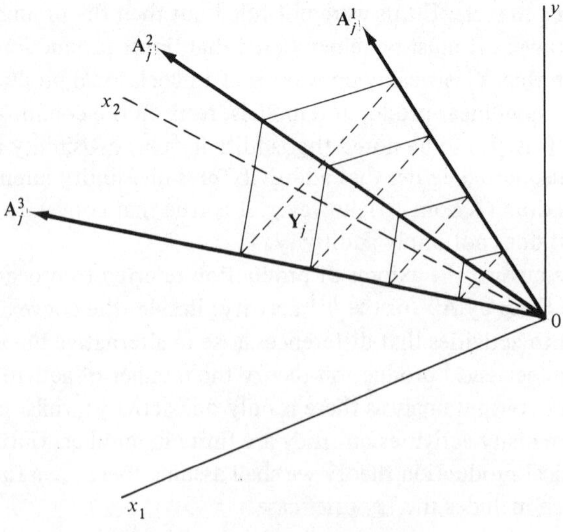

Fig. 5.2. A typical production set

Having obtained the production set we must distinguish the efficient from the inefficient productive processes. Efficiency is defined as:

Definition 5.1

An element $\mathbf{y} \in \mathbf{Y}$ is efficient if and only if there is no other element $\mathbf{y}' \in \mathbf{Y}$ such that $\mathbf{y}' > \mathbf{y}$.

i.e. a production plan, either for a firm or an economy, is efficient if and only if there is no other possible production plan which uses less of at least one input, or produces more of at least one output whilst using no more of any other input and producing no less of any other output. It will be demonstrated below that such efficient points in linear production theory constitute the flat faces or *facets* of the convex cone illustrated in Fig. 5.2.

It is useful at this point to highlight some of the features of the axioms and, in particular, the form of production sets which are excluded as well as those which are included. In Fig. 5.3 are drawn six diagrams which illustrate certain features of production theory. First note that inputs are given negative signs and outputs positive signs. In diagram (*a*) the firm uses input y_1 to produce a single output y_2. The free disposal axiom (Axiom 17′) means that $-\Omega$ is contained in the set $\mathbf{Y}_j$, as shown by the shading. In diagram (*b*) it is assumed that the firm produces both y_1 and y_2 using inputs y_2 and y_1 respectively. It is to be noted that both diagrams (*a*) and (*b*) have production sets which are convex and that neither of them satisfy the additivity axiom; as drawn they exhibit decreasing returns to scale for y_2 in diagram (*a*) and for both y_1 and y_2 in diagram (*b*). In diagram (*c*) and (*d*), however, the firm has increasing returns to scale; in diagram (*c*) this is true for both y_1 and y_2, whilst in diagram (*d*) the firm has increasing returns to scale in the production of y_2 but decreasing returns to scale in the production of y_1. In both cases the production sets are not convex. Finally, diagrams (*e*) and (*f*) show firms with constant returns to scale which in turn implies the additivity axiom is satisfied. In diagram (*e*) only one output is produced by the jth firm whilst in diagram (*f*) two outputs are produced. Both production sets are weakly convex. Notice also that in all six diagrams $0 \in \mathbf{Y}_j$ and $(-\Omega) \subset \mathbf{Y}_j$.

Consider once again the set $\mathbf{Y}_j$. We can look at this in a different way which proves to be useful. Suppose we have a situation of two outputs y_1 and y_2 and two inputs y_3 and y_4. Suppose further that we are concerned only with outputs for a specified level of inputs. Let the specified level of inputs be y_3^0 and y_4^0, then we can plot the feasible outputs y_1 and y_2 in the output space, as illustrated in Fig. 5.4 (*a*). We call this set the *production possibility set*, and whenever it is drawn it must always be for specified input levels.[5] Alternatively, for a given set of outputs such as y_1^0 and y_2^0 we can plot the feasible inputs y_3 and y_4 in the input space, as illustrated in Fig. 5.4 (*b*). We call this set the *isoproduct set*, and whenever this is drawn it must always be for specified output levels.

Now consider more carefully the isoproduct set. If we have only one output then for any specified level of this output, say $\mathbf{y}^0{}_j \in \mathbf{Y}_j$, there will be an associated indifference set I_0 which is the boundary of the isoproduct set; this is often called an *isoquant* and one is illustrated in Fig. 5.4 (*b*). For each different level of output there will be a corresponding isoquant, none of which intersect in the input space. If, however, we have more than one output then the isoproduct and the isoquant lose their usefulness because a change in either output may give rise to a new

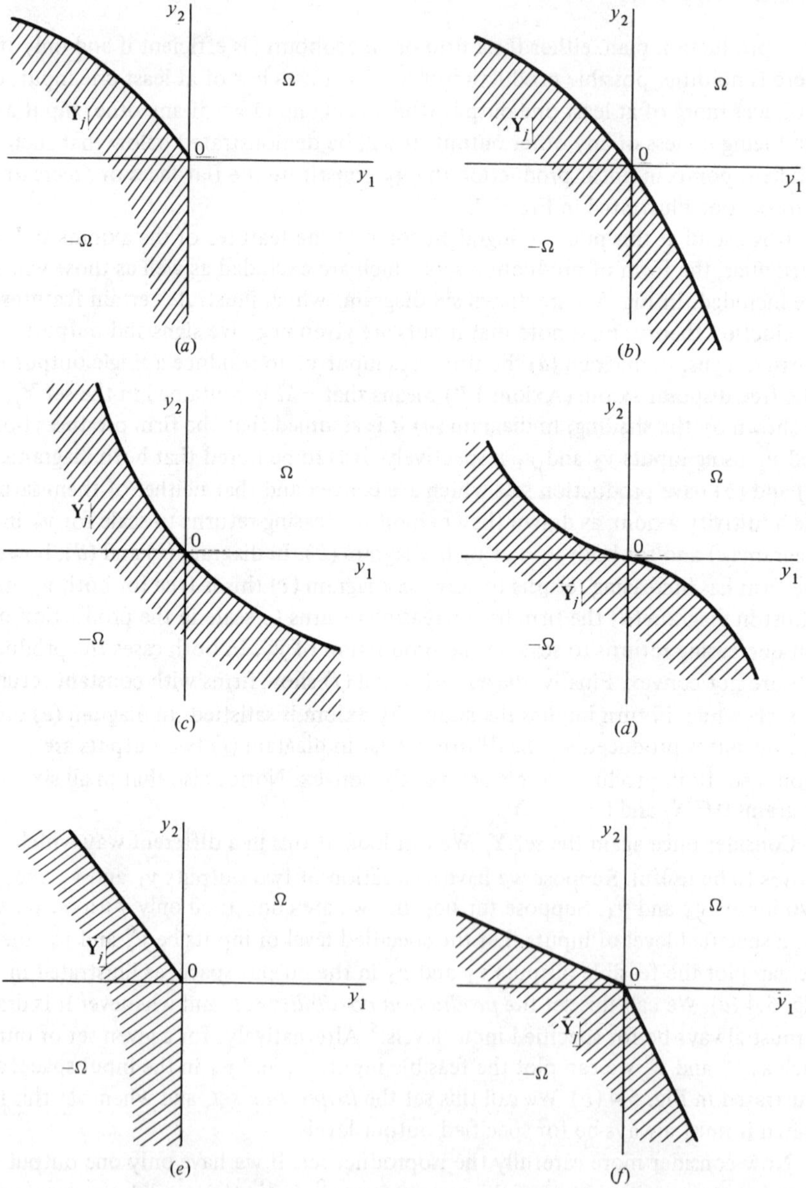

Fig. 5.3. Typical production sets

isoquant which intersects the old one. Most neoclassical theory of production is concerned with only a single output firm and so the isoquant plays a major role in its analysis. In the linear theories with multiple outputs it is barely discussed.

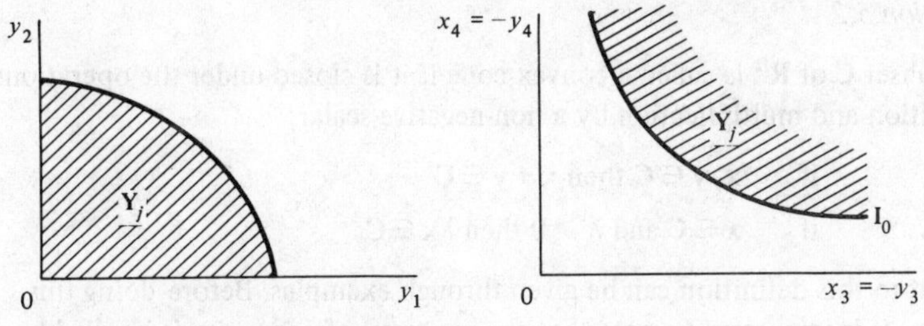

(*a*) Production possibility set (*b*) Isoproduct set

Fig. 5.4

Up to this point we have not considered any choice function which will enable the producer, or the economy, to choose between the various input–output combinations. It is in this regard that alternative models of the firm arise. Although with a single-output model it is possible to rank purely on the levels of output, this criterion breaks down in the many-commodity models. Since we are interested as much in the economy as we are in the firm it seems fruitless to consider a criterion based on a single-output model, at least at the economy level. We shall, therefore, take as our criterion the most well-known and longest established, viz. profit maximisation. Let $\mathbf{y}^0$ and $\mathbf{y}^1$ be two input–output combinations belonging to the production set $\mathbf{Y}$ (they can equally be taken to belong to $\mathbf{Y}_j$). Then if the profits associated with $\mathbf{y}^0$ are greater than those associated with $\mathbf{y}^1$ we can say that $\mathbf{y}^0$ is preferred to $\mathbf{y}^1$. It is to be emphasised that this rule applies equally to the firm as it does to the economy stated symbolically.

Axiom 21 $\forall \mathbf{y}^0, \mathbf{y}^1 \in \mathbf{Y}\ \mathbf{y}^0 P \mathbf{y}^1 \Leftrightarrow \pi(\mathbf{y}^0) > \pi(\mathbf{y}^1)$

The technology is now complete. Production activities have been defined and the production set has been obtained. Efficient production has been distinguished, and a criterion of choice has been presented. It must be possible therefore to establish the equilibrium of a firm. This we shall consider in the next chapter. For the present it must be apparent that production theory in its linear form involves properties of convex cones. In fact, much of the advanced theory of linear production is concerned with their properties; so if we are to appreciate linear production theory it is necessary to become familiar with the properties of convex cones. The next section, therefore, gives an outline of the *mathematical* properties of convex cones, leaving Chapter 6 to bring out the *economic* properties of such cones.

5.3 Convex Cones

In establishing the mathematical properties of convex cones the reader will be aided by a knowledge of vector spaces.[6] We first define a convex cone:

Definition 5.2

A subset **C** of $\mathbf{R}^n$ is called a convex cone if it is closed under the operations of addition and multiplication by a non-negative scalar,

i.e. if $\mathbf{x}, \mathbf{y} \in \mathbf{C}$ then $\mathbf{x} + \mathbf{y} \in \mathbf{C}$

if $\mathbf{x} \in \mathbf{C}$ and $\lambda \geqslant 0$ then $\lambda\mathbf{x} \in \mathbf{C}$.

Content to this definition can be given through examples. Before doing this, however, it is important to note that the property of convexity is implied by this definition. If $\lambda \geqslant 0$ then we consider a convex combination of $\mathbf{x}, \mathbf{y} \in \mathbf{C}$ such that $\lambda\mathbf{x} + (1-\lambda)\,\mathbf{y} \in \mathbf{C}$; hence **C** is convex.

Example 5.1 A subspace **L** of a vector space **V** is linear if it is closed under addition and scalar multiplication, i.e. if $\mathbf{x}, \mathbf{y} \in \mathbf{L}$ then $\mathbf{x} + \mathbf{y} \in \mathbf{L}$ and if $\mathbf{x} \in \mathbf{L}$ and λ is a scalar $\lambda\mathbf{x} \in \mathbf{L}$. Hence, any *linear* subspace is a convex cone.

Example 5.2 Let $\mathbf{x}_i \geqslant 0$ be a non-negative vector in $\mathbf{R}^n$. Then the set of all such vectors of $\mathbf{R}^n$ is a convex cone, and is referred to as the *non-negative orthant* of $\mathbf{R}^n$ i.e. $\Omega = \{\mathbf{x}_i \geqslant 0, i = 1, \ldots, n\}$ denotes the non-negative orthant. We shall use this symbol throughout.

Example 5.3 For any vector $\mathbf{a} \in \mathbf{R}^n$, the set of vectors of the form $\lambda\mathbf{a}\ \lambda \geqslant 0$, is a convex cone, and $\mathbf{L} = \{\mathbf{x}/\mathbf{x} = \lambda\mathbf{a}, \lambda \geqslant 0\}$ is called a *half-line.* Two typical half-lines are illustrated in Fig. 5.5.

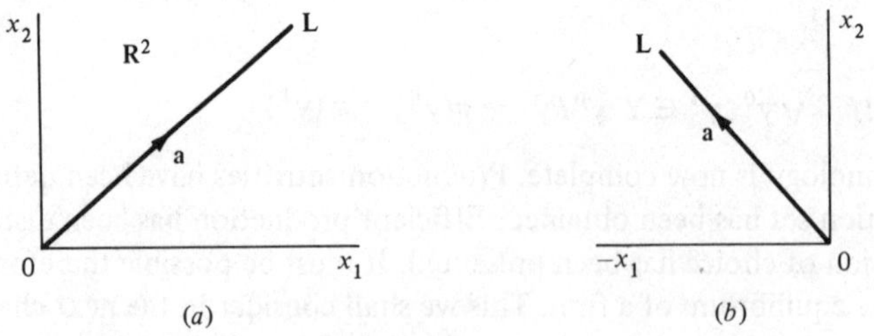

Fig. 5.5. Half-lines

Example 5.4 The set of all solutions to $\mathbf{Ax} \leqslant 0$ is a convex cone, and is called a *half-space.* This follows because if **x** is a solution then so is **z** where $\mathbf{Az} = \mathbf{A}(\mathbf{x}_1 + \mathbf{x}_2) \leqslant 0$. Also, if **x** is a solution so is $\mathbf{y} = \lambda\mathbf{x}$ and thus $\mathbf{Ay} \leqslant 0$.

The next step in the analysis is to consider three important operations on convex cones: addition, intersection, and duality.

1. *Addition.* If $\mathbf{C}_1$ and $\mathbf{C}_2$ are convex cones, their sum $\mathbf{C}_1 + \mathbf{C}_2$, defined by

$$\mathbf{C}_1 + \mathbf{C}_2 = \{\mathbf{x}/\mathbf{x} = \mathbf{x}_1 + \mathbf{x}_2, \mathbf{x}_1 \in \mathbf{C}_1 \;\&\; \mathbf{x}_2 \in \mathbf{C}_2\},$$

is also a convex cone. This is illustrated in Fig. 5.6. The operation of addition is most important for production theory because it means that if each firm operates under a convex cone, the economy, if we can take it to be the sum of the firms, also operates under a convex cone by the addition property.

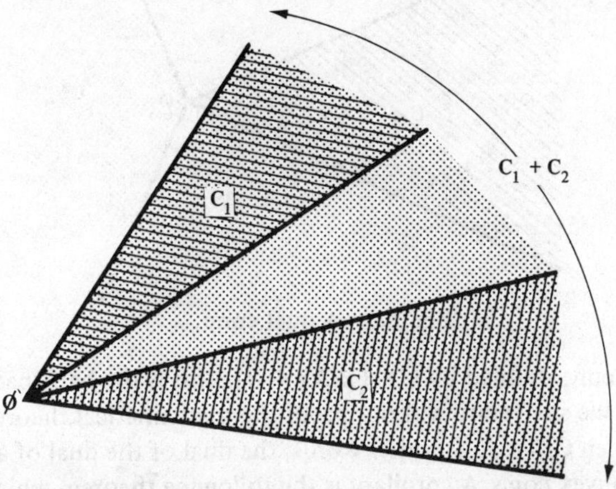

Fig. 5.6. The addition of convex cones is a convex cone

2. *Intersection.* If $\mathbf{C}_1$ and $\mathbf{C}_2$ are convex cones then their intersection $\mathbf{C}_1 \cap \mathbf{C}_2$ is also a convex cone. This is illustrated in Fig. 5.7.

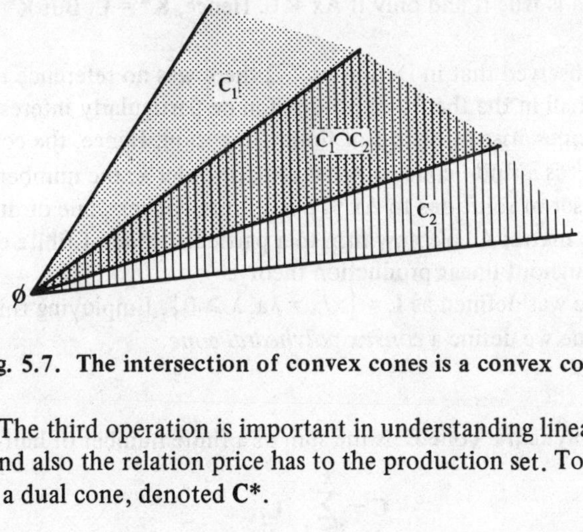

Fig. 5.7. The intersection of convex cones is a convex cone

3. *Duality.* The third operation is important in understanding linear programming and also the relation price has to the production set. To any cone $\mathbf{C}$ there will exist a dual cone, denoted $\mathbf{C}^*$.

Definition 5.3

(Dual cone) If **C** is a convex cone, the dual cone, denoted $\mathbf{C}^*$, is given by

$$\mathbf{C}^* = \{\mathbf{y}/\ \mathbf{x}'\mathbf{y} \leqslant 0,\ \forall \mathbf{x} \in \mathbf{C}\}.$$

The dual of a cone **C** is a cone whose vectors make a non-acute angle with all vectors in **C**. Fig. 5.8 gives a more general representation of a dual cone.

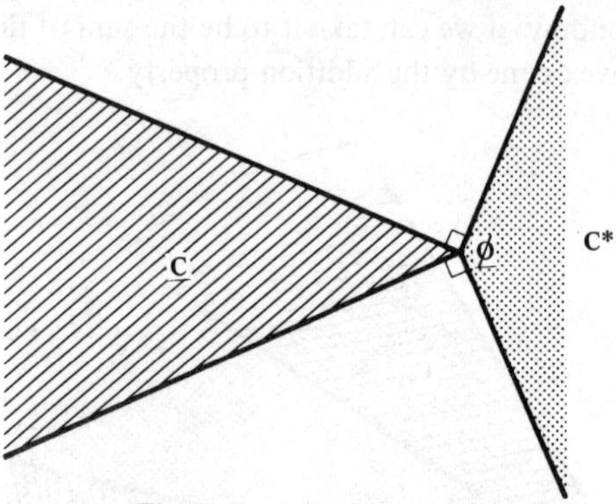

Fig. 5.8. A dual cone

Consider the cone defined by $\mathbf{C} = \{\mathbf{x}/\mathbf{Ax} \leqslant 0\}$, this is the half-space referred to in Example 5.4. We shall state without proof the mathematical theorem that if **C** is a convex cone then $\mathbf{C}^{**} = \mathbf{C}$. In other words, the dual of the dual of a convex cone is the original convex cone. A corollary is the following theorem which we shall use in our economic analysis:

Theorem 5.1 If $\mathbf{C} = \{\mathbf{x}/\mathbf{Ax} \leqslant 0\}$ then $\mathbf{C}^* = \{\mathbf{x}/\mathbf{x} = \mathbf{yA},\ \mathbf{y} \geqslant 0\}$.

Proof Let $\mathbf{K} = \{\mathbf{x}/\mathbf{x} = \mathbf{yA},\ \mathbf{y} \geqslant 0\}$. We must prove that $\mathbf{K} = \mathbf{C}^*$. By Definition 5.3 of dual cones $\mathbf{K}^* = \{\mathbf{x}/\mathbf{Ax} \leqslant 0,\ \mathbf{x} \in \mathbf{K}\}$. But $\mathbf{x} \in \mathbf{K}^*$ if and only if $\mathbf{yAx} \leqslant 0$ for all $\mathbf{y} \geqslant 0$, which is true if and only if $\mathbf{Ax} \leqslant 0$. Hence, $\mathbf{K}^* = \mathbf{C}$. But $\mathbf{K}^{**} = \mathbf{C}^* = \mathbf{K}$. *Q.E.D.*

It is to be observed that in Definition 5.2 there was no reference to a finite space. However, we shall in the theory of production be particularly interested in finite cones. These cones arise in spaces of finite dimension. Hence, the convex cone belonging to $\mathbf{R}^n$ is a finite cone. If **A** has rank of order k, the number of columns of **A**, then the set of solutions to $\mathbf{Ax} \leqslant 0$ is a finite convex cone of dimension the columns of the matrix **A**. We now turn to a particular kind of finite cone which is employed throughout linear production theory.

The half-line was defined as $\mathbf{L} = \{\mathbf{x}/\mathbf{x} = \lambda\mathbf{a},\ \lambda \geqslant 0\}$. Employing this along with that of a convex cone we define a *convex polyhedral cone*:

Definition 5.4

A convex polyhedral cone **C** is the sum of a finite number of half-lines:

$$\mathbf{C} = \sum_{i=1}^{k} \mathbf{L}_i.$$

Since $\mathbf{L}_i$ is a convex cone, and since by the operation of addition, the sum is also a convex cone, then $\sum_{i=1}^{k} \mathbf{L}_i$ is a convex cone. The convex polyhedral cone can be illustrated by considering three vectors $\mathbf{a}_1$, $\mathbf{a}_2$, and $\mathbf{a}_3$ in $\mathbf{E}^3$. Then

$$\mathbf{L}_1 = \{\mathbf{x}/\mathbf{x} = \lambda \mathbf{a}_1, \lambda \geqslant 0\}$$
$$\mathbf{L}_2 = \{\mathbf{x}/\mathbf{x} = \lambda \mathbf{a}_2, \lambda \geqslant 0\}$$
$$\mathbf{L}_3 = \{\mathbf{x}/\mathbf{x} = \lambda \mathbf{a}_3, \lambda \geqslant 0\}.$$

The cone C generated by these three half-lines is a convex polyhedral cone, as illustrated in Fig. 5.9. This figure should be compared with Fig. 5.3, which will show the immediate application to linear production theory.

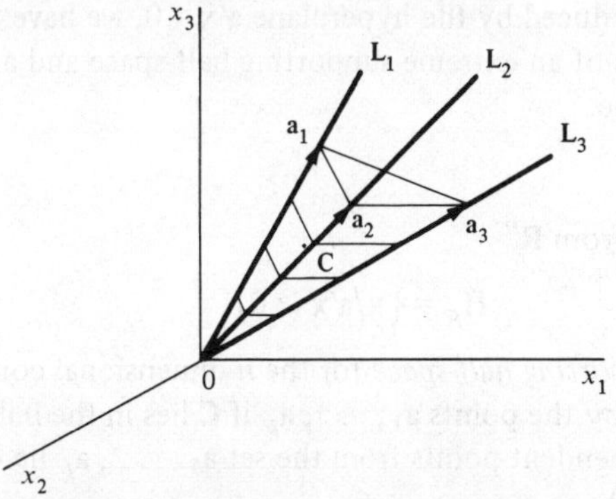

Fig. 5.9. A convex polyhedral cone

We can readily generalise the result. Let $\mathbf{A}$ be an $n \times k$ matrix, $\mathbf{A} = (\mathbf{a}_1, \ldots, \mathbf{a}_k)$ where each column vector is composed of n elements. Then the set $\mathbf{C} = \{\mathbf{y}\}$ of points

$$\mathbf{y} = \mathbf{A}\mathbf{x} = \sum_{i=1}^{k} x_i \mathbf{a}_i \qquad \forall \mathbf{x} \geqslant 0$$

is a convex polyhedral cone in $\mathbf{E}^n$. This follows from the fact that if the point $\mathbf{a}_i$ generates a half-line $\mathbf{L}_i$ then $\mathbf{C} = \sum_{i=1}^{k} \mathbf{L}_i = \sum_{i=1}^{k} x_i \mathbf{a}_i$ is the sum of a finite number of half-lines and by Definition 5.4 constitutes a convex polyhedral cone. Let us use this result to prove the following theorem:

Theorem 5.2 If $\mathbf{A}\mathbf{x} = \mathbf{b}$ then there exists a non-negative solution $\mathbf{x} \geqslant 0$ if and only if $\mathbf{b}$ is an element of the convex polyhedral cone generated by the columns of the matrix $\mathbf{A}$.

Proof We have already shown that the set $\mathbf{C} = \{\mathbf{b}\}$ of all points

$\mathbf{b} = \mathbf{A}\mathbf{x} = \sum_{i=1}^{k} x_i \mathbf{a}_i$, $\forall \mathbf{x} \geqslant 0$ is a convex polyhedral cone. Hence if

$\mathbf{b} \in \mathbf{C}$ then $\mathbf{b}$ is a solution to $\mathbf{A}\mathbf{x} = \mathbf{b}$ and $\mathbf{x} \geqslant 0$.[7]

Q.E.D.

We turn now to some features of the convex cone which will be of considerable importance when we come to discuss linear production theory. In Chapter 4 we defined a bounding hyperplane (Definition 4.9 (i), p. 104) and following this definition is that of supporting and separating hyperplanes. It will become important to know whether the convex polyhedral cone has a supporting hyperplane or not. It may not be true that all of the cone **C** will lie in one of the closed half-spaces $\mathbf{a}'\mathbf{x} \geqslant 0$ or $\mathbf{a}'\mathbf{x} \leqslant 0$ for any vector **a**. If **C** does lie in one of the closed half-spaces produced by the hyperplane $\mathbf{a}'\mathbf{x} = 0$, we have the following important definitions of an extreme supporting half-space and an extreme supporting hyperplane.

Definition 5.5

The set of points from $\mathbf{R}^n$

$$\mathbf{H}_F = \{\mathbf{x}/\mathbf{a}'\mathbf{x} \geqslant 0\}$$

is an *extreme supporting half-space* for the *n*-dimensional convex polyhedral cone **C** generated by the points $\mathbf{a}_1, \ldots, \mathbf{a}_k$ if **C** lies in the half-space $\mathbf{H}_F$ and $k-1$ linearly independent points from the set $\mathbf{a}_1, \ldots, \mathbf{a}_k$ lie on the hyperplane $\mathbf{a}'\mathbf{x} = 0$.

Definition 5.6

The hyperplane $\mathbf{a}'\mathbf{x} = 0$, which forms the boundary of the extreme supporting half-space, is called an *extreme supporting hyperplane* for the convex polyhedral cone **C**.

Fig. 5.10 illustrates an extreme supporting half-space with a supporting hyperplane; whilst Fig. 5.11 shows an extreme supporting half-space with an extreme supporting hyperplane.

To see the significance of extreme supporting hyperplanes consider the convex polyhedral cone **C** formed from three linearly independent vectors $\mathbf{a}_1$, $\mathbf{a}_2$, and $\mathbf{a}_3$ as illustrated in Fig. 5.12. Any two of the vectors from $\mathbf{a}_1$, $\mathbf{a}_2$, and $\mathbf{a}_3$ uniquely determines a plane through the origin such that the cone **C** is contained in one half-space produced by this plane. Since any such pair are linearly independent the resulting hyperplane must be an extreme supporting hyperplane. It follows that the intersection of **C** with any one of these three possible extreme supporting hyperplanes yields a face or *facet* of the cone **C**. This facet is also a convex cone because the extreme supporting hyperplane is a convex cone and **C** is a convex cone; hence by the property of intersection, their intersection is also a convex cone. The

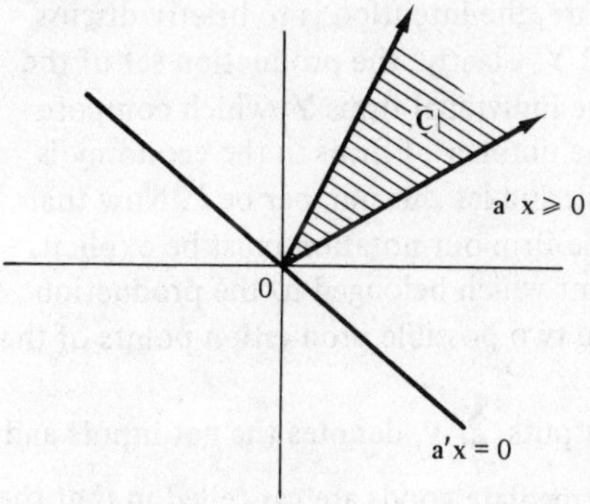

Fig. 5.10. Supporting hyperplane to C

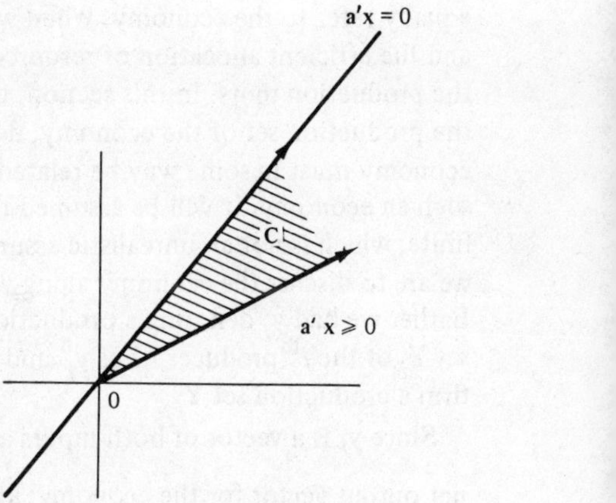

Fig. 5.11. Extreme supporting hyperplane to C

facet, which is itself a convex cone, we shall label **F**. Consider, for example, the convex polyhedral cone **C** in Fig. 5.12. The facet formed by $\mathbf{a}_1$ and $\mathbf{a}_2$ is given by

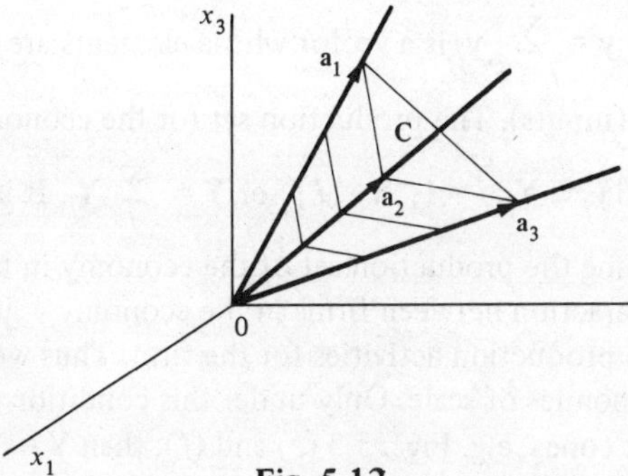

Fig. 5.12

$\mathbf{x} = \mathbf{F}\lambda$, $\lambda \geqslant 0$ where $\mathbf{F} = (\mathbf{a}_1, \mathbf{a}_2)$, each vector $\mathbf{a}_i$ having three elements. More generally:

Definition 5.7

An $(n-1)$-dimensional convex polyhedral cone **F** is the intersection of an n-dimensional polyhedral cone **C** in $\mathbf{R}^n$ with an extreme supporting hyperplane, and is called a *facet* of the cone **C**.

5.4 The Production Set of the Economy

So far in this chapter we have laid the foundations of the technology of a single producer, i.e. the properties possessed by $\mathbf{Y}_j$; however, a number of the axioms equally refer to the economy. When we come to discuss the theory of exchange and the efficient allocation of resources we must inevitably be concerned with all the production units. In this section, therefore, the intention is to briefly discuss the production set of the economy, denoted **Y**. Clearly, the production set of the economy must in some way be related to the individual firms $\mathbf{Y}_j$ which compose such an economy. It will be assumed that the number of firms in the economy is finite, which is not an unrealistic assumption, and let this number be l. Now that we are to discuss the economy along with the firm our notation must be explicit. Earlier we had $\mathbf{y}_j$ denoting a production point which belonged to the production set $\mathbf{Y}_j$ of the jth producer, thus $\mathbf{y}_j^0$ and $\mathbf{y}_j^1$ are two possible production points of the firm's production set $\mathbf{Y}_j$.

Since $\mathbf{y}_j$ is a vector of both inputs and outputs $\sum_j \mathbf{y}_j$ denotes the net inputs and net output vector for the economy; all intermediate goods are cancelled in that they appear as both negative and positive values of exactly the same magnitude. Notice, however, that if y_{1j} is an output of good 1 by firm j and y_{1k}, equalling $\frac{1}{2}y_{1j}$ say, is the input of this commodity into firm k then, assuming these are the only two firms in the economy, firm 1 contributes $\frac{1}{2}y_1$ to total production. If firm k produces no y_1 then $\frac{1}{2}y_1$ is the net output for the economy. A similar argument holds for inputs. Thus the vector $\mathbf{y} = \sum_{j=1}^{l} \mathbf{y}_j$ is a vector whose elements are both positive (outputs) and negative (inputs). The production set for the economy is the set of all $\mathbf{y}$, i.e. $\mathbf{Y} = \{\mathbf{y} = \sum_{j=1}^{l} \mathbf{y}_j \mid \mathbf{y}_j \in \mathbf{Y}_j, j = 1, \ldots, l\}$ or $\mathbf{Y} = \sum_j \mathbf{Y}_j$. It is important to remember that in defining the production set of the economy in this additive way we are assuming no interaction between firms in the economy – just as we assumed no interaction between production activities for the firm. Thus we are explicitly ruling out external economies of scale. Only under this condition can we say that if $\mathbf{Y}_1, \ldots, \mathbf{Y}_l$ are convex cones, e.g. Figs. 5.3 (*e*) and (*f*), then $\mathbf{Y} = \sum_j \mathbf{Y}_j$ is also a convex cone by the rule of additivity of convex cones (p. 133). Furthermore, if each $\mathbf{Y}_j$ is strictly convex but not a convex cone, such as the firm in Fig. 5.3 (*b*), then by the addition rule of convex sets, $\mathbf{Y} = \sum_j \mathbf{Y}_j$ is also convex and will show similar features of decreasing returns to scale. Clearly, if any of the $\mathbf{Y}_j$ are not convex, e.g. the firm in Fig. 5.3 (*c*), then **Y** will not itself be convex.

Let us take a simple case to highlight the relationship between the production sets of the firms and that of the economy.[8] Suppose we have two firms with production sets $\mathbf{Y}_1$ and $\mathbf{Y}_2$. We shall assume a very simple case of only a single activity for each firm. Firm 1 produces commodity 3 by means of commodity 1 while firm 2, who also produces commodity 3, uses as input commodity 2. Both firms use their respective inputs in fixed proportions. The production sets are represented by the half-lines $\mathbf{Y}_1$ and $\mathbf{Y}_2$ in Fig. 5.13. Consider now two representative points $\mathbf{y}_1^0 \in \mathbf{Y}_1$ and $\mathbf{y}_2^0 \in \mathbf{Y}_2$. Then the vector $\mathbf{y}^0 = \mathbf{y}_1^0 + \mathbf{y}_2^0$ is the vector formed from the vertex of the parallelogram constructed from Oy_1^0 and Oy_2^0, and must from the assumption of additivity be feasible for the economy. All such points are the set $\mathbf{Y} = \sum_j \mathbf{Y}_j$ and is shown by the shaded region in Fig. 5.13.

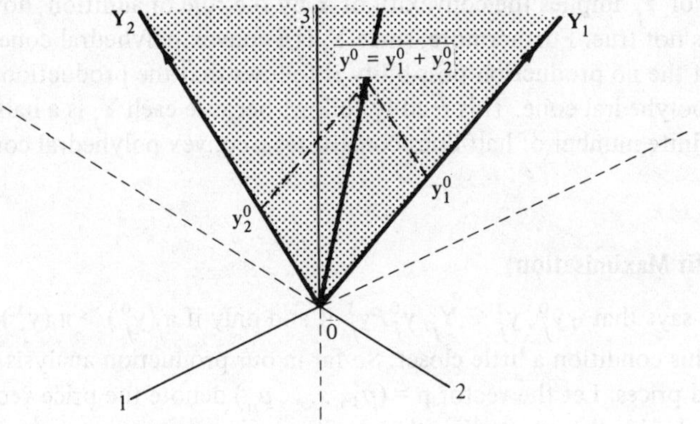

Fig. 5.13. Economy production set

There is, as we have pointed out, a connection between $\mathbf{Y}_j$ and $\mathbf{Y}$. The axioms so far laid down concerning $\mathbf{Y}_j$ will to some extent circumscribe the form of the production set $\mathbf{Y}$. However, for ease of reference we shall list as a set of separate axioms those referring explicitly to the production set of the economy. In these axioms the symbol Ω refers to the non-negative orthant, and $-\Omega$ to the non-positive orthant.[9]

Axioms of the Production Set **Y**

1. $\mathbf{Y}$ is closed
2. $0 \in \mathbf{Y}$ No production possibility
3. $\mathbf{Y} \cap \Omega = \{0\}$ No free production
4. $\mathbf{Y} \cap (-\mathbf{Y}) = \{0\}$ No reversibility
5. $\mathbf{Y}$ is convex
6. $(-\Omega) \subset \mathbf{Y}$ Free disposal
7. $(\mathbf{Y} - \Omega) \subset \mathbf{Y}$

The closedness axiom says that if we have a technologically feasible output **y** then any sequence of production points tending to **y** must also be technologically feasible. The second axiom allows the economy to produce nothing at all. The meaning of axiom three is that to produce an output at least one input (a negative element) is required, so that the production set **Y** cannot be contained in the non-negative orthant and that the only common element is the origin. It follows from this that there exists a supporting hyperplane of **Y** which passes through the origin. Axiom 4 states that if **y** is feasible then $-\mathbf{y}$ is not, given $\mathbf{y} \neq 0$. If a production process uses a basic input such as labour then no process is reversible since such a reversal will always require additional amounts of the basic input. The condition of no free production along with that of no reversibility means that the production set **Y** is contained in a half-space and that there exists a separating hyperplane to the sets **Y** and Ω, which has only the origin in common. The convexity of $\mathbf{Y}_j$ implies the convexity of **Y** by the rule of addition; however, the converse is not true. Furthermore, since $\mathbf{Y}_j$ is a convex polyhedral cone then taking account of the no production possibility it follows that the production set **Y** is also a convex polyhedral cone. This readily follows because each $\mathbf{Y}_j$ is a half-line and the sum of a finite number of half-lines constitutes a convex polyhedral cone.

5.5 Profit Maximisation

Axiom 21 says that $\forall \mathbf{y}_j^0, \mathbf{y}_j^1 \in \mathbf{Y}_j, \mathbf{y}_j^0 P \mathbf{y}_j^1$ if and only if $\pi_j(\mathbf{y}_j^0) > \pi_j(\mathbf{y}_j^1)$. Let us consider this condition a little closer. So far in our production analysis we have not introduced prices. Let the vector $\mathbf{p} = (p_1, \ldots, p_n)$ denote the price vector. Since we are employing the convention that positive **y** denotes output and negative **y** denotes input, then $\mathbf{p}'\mathbf{y}_j$ will denote revenue minus costs for the jth producer. Using the usual convention, therefore, we define profits for the jth firm, given a fixed price vector **p**, as $\pi_j = \mathbf{p}'\mathbf{y}_j$. The profit function is then defined as:

Definition 5.8

The profit function for the jth firm is $\pi_j(\mathbf{p}) = \max\limits_{\mathbf{y}_j \in \mathbf{Y}_j} \mathbf{p}'\mathbf{y}_j$

Strictly this definition holds only if the set $\mathbf{Y}_j$ is bounded above, i.e. in the input–output space the set $\mathbf{Y}_j$ has a maximum $\pi_j = \mathbf{p}'\mathbf{y}_j$ at which any greater profit gives rise to an output which is non-feasible. In terms of Fig. 5.14 profits π_j^2 forms a bounding hyperplane (see Definition 4.9 (i)) to the set $\mathbf{Y}_j$. This is an important consideration because under constant returns to scale the production set is a convex polyhedral cone for which $\mathbf{Y}_j$ is not bounded from above,[10] in the sense that there can always be found a profit level π_j which can be exceeded, for a given price vector **p**, as a look at Fig. 5.3 (*e*) reveals. This result would also follow if the set $\mathbf{Y}_j$ was not convex, as in Fig. 5.3 (*c*), i.e. if increasing returns to scale were allowed then profits could increase indefinitely.[11]

As an aid to understanding the profit function and the supply correspondence, to be discussed below, consider Fig. 5.14. Given the assumption of constant input and output prices then the isoprofit curves (i.e. curves which give the same level of profits) are hyperplanes:

$$\pi_j = \{\mathbf{y}_j / \mathbf{p}'\mathbf{y}_j = \pi_j\}.$$

For example, the hyperplane through the origin in Fig. 5.14 is the set $\pi_j^0 = \{\mathbf{y}_j/\mathbf{p}'\mathbf{y}_j = 0\}$. The hyperplanes π_j^1 and π_j^2 are obtained for positive profits. Those below π_j^0 (not shown) denote negative profits. It is a well-known condition of vector algebra that two vectors **a** and **b** say, are orthogonal (geometrically, are at right angles) if their inner product is zero, i.e. if $\mathbf{a'b} = 0$. Considering the hyperplane $\pi_j^0 = \{\mathbf{y}_j / \mathbf{p'y}_j = 0\}$ therefore reveals that the price vector $\mathbf{p}$ is at right angles to all isoprofit planes. Turning this around, we can say that for any given price vector $\mathbf{p}$ there are a well-defined set of isoprofit planes; if $\mathbf{p}^1 = \lambda\mathbf{p}^0$ the profit planes coincide, and if $\mathbf{p}^1 \neq \lambda\mathbf{p}^0$ then the profit planes are different. Given a strictly convex set $\mathbf{Y}_j$, as illustrated in Fig. 5.14, and given that the firm wishes to maximise profits, it will

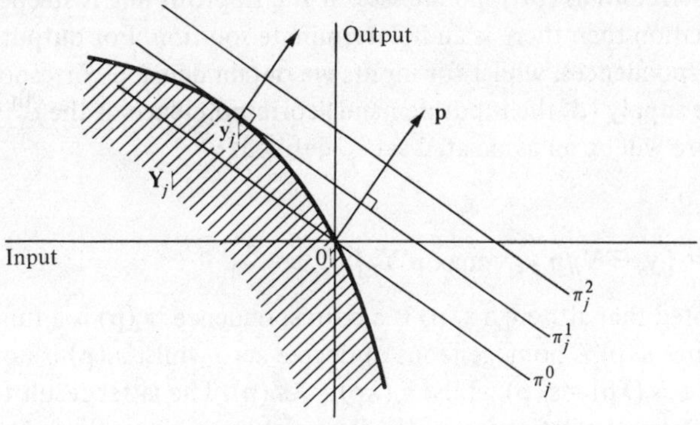

Fig. 5.14. Isoprofit lines

choose that input–output combination at which the isoprofit plane is a supporting hyperplane to the production set $\mathbf{Y}_j$, such as point $\mathbf{y}_j$ in the figure. If $\mathbf{Y}_j$ is strictly convex then for a given price vector $\mathbf{p}$ there is only one $\mathbf{y}_j$ which maximises $\mathbf{p'y}_j$. For a different price vector we establish another unique $\mathbf{y}_j$. In this particular instance there is a one-to-one correspondence between price and output $\mathbf{y}_j$ – or demand if the $\mathbf{y}_j$ is a negative input.

Consider now the situation of constant returns to scale. The production sets are as shown in Fig. 5.15 and 5.16. In both cases the production sets are convex polyhedral cones with vertices at the origin. In the situation depicted in Fig. 5.15

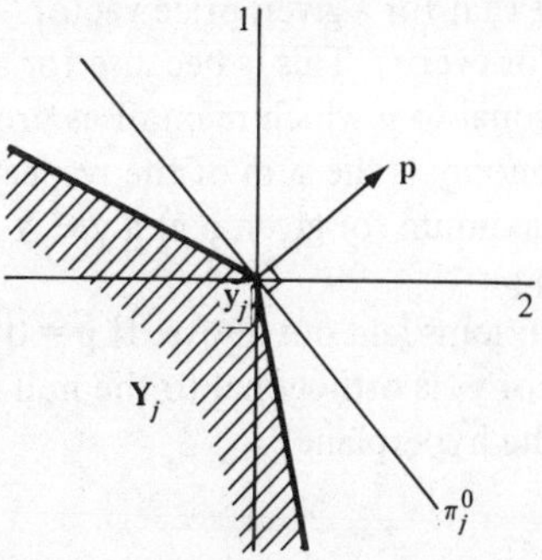

Fig. 5.15. Zero profit and no output

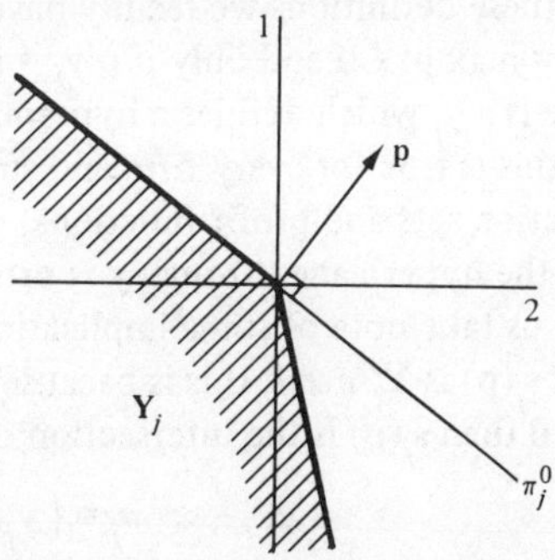

Fig. 5.16. Zero profit but output indeterminate

so long as the isoprofit plane is steeper than the rate of transformation profits will be either negative or zero, and will be therefore maximised if the firm does not undertake to produce at all. From the point of view of Fig. 5.16 the isoprofit plane is as steep as the boundary of the production set and *any* input–output combination will maximise profits at a zero level. In the first instance we have a set-to-point mapping and in the second instance we have a point-to-set mapping. These are referred to as *correspondences.* If the isoprofit line is steeper than the rate of transformation then there is an indeterminate solution. For outputs we obtain supply correspondences, whilst for inputs we obtain demand correspondences. Let $\mathbf{s}_j$ denote the supply ($\mathbf{d}_j$ the input demand) correspondence of the jth producer. For a given $\mathbf{p}$ there will be an associated set $\mathbf{s}_j$, defined:

Definition 5.9

$$\mathbf{s}_j = \mathbf{s}_j(\mathbf{p}) = \{\mathbf{y}_j \in \mathbf{Y}_j / \mathbf{p}'\mathbf{y}_j = \max \mathbf{p}'\mathbf{Y}_j\}.$$

It is to be noted that although $\mathbf{s}_j(\mathbf{p})$ is a correspondence $\pi_j(\mathbf{p})$ is a function. The correspondence $\mathbf{s}_j(\mathbf{p})$ is homogeneous of degree zero whilst $\pi_j(\mathbf{p})$ is homogeneous of degree one, i.e. $\mathbf{s}_j(\lambda\mathbf{p}) = \mathbf{s}_j(\mathbf{p})$ whilst $\pi_j(\lambda\mathbf{p}) = \lambda\pi_j(\mathbf{p})$. The latter result follows immediately from the definition of the isoprofit hyperplane. Since for all $\mathbf{p}^1 = \lambda\mathbf{p}^0$ the profit hyperplanes coincide the supplies (demands) associated with such prices remain the same, which is clear from Fig. 5.14, and is no more than saying $\mathbf{s}_j(\lambda\mathbf{p}) = \mathbf{s}_j(\mathbf{p})$.

Thus far we have established a profit function $\pi_j(\mathbf{p})$ and a supply correspondence $\mathbf{s}_j(\mathbf{p})$ for firm j. Similarly, we can obtain a total profit function $\pi(\mathbf{p})$ and a total supply correspondence $\mathbf{s}(\mathbf{p})$ for the economy as a whole.

Definition 5.10

The total profit function is $\pi(\mathbf{p}) = \sum_{j=1}^{l} \pi_j(\mathbf{p})$.

The total supply correspondence is $\mathbf{s}(\mathbf{p}) = \sum_{j=1}^{l} \mathbf{s}_j(\mathbf{p})$.

From these definitions we readily have the result that for a given price vector $\mathbf{p}$, $\mathbf{p}'\mathbf{y} = \max \mathbf{p}'\mathbf{Y}$ if and only if $\mathbf{p}'\mathbf{y}_j = \max \mathbf{p}'\mathbf{Y}_j$ for every j. This is because for a given $\mathbf{p}$ there is a $\mathbf{y}_j$ which defines a hyperplane orthogonal to $\mathbf{p}$ which maximises profits. Since this is true for every firm and since the economy is the sum of the respective production sets and profit functions, $\pi(\mathbf{p})$ is a maximum for given $\mathbf{p}$ at a $\mathbf{y} \in \mathbf{Y}$ where the hyperplane through $\mathbf{y}$ is orthogonal to $\mathbf{p}$.

Let us take note of some implications of the axioms laid out above. If $\mathbf{p} = 0$ then the set $\mathbf{s}_j(\mathbf{p})$ is $\mathbf{Y}_j$ itself; this is because every vector $\mathbf{y}_j$ is orthogonal to the null set. If $\mathbf{p} \neq 0$ then $\mathbf{s}_j(\mathbf{p})$ is the intersection of $\mathbf{Y}_j$ and the hyperplane

$$\pi_j = \{\mathbf{y}_j / \mathbf{p}'\mathbf{y}_j = \pi_j\}.$$

Since both $\mathbf{Y}_j$ and π_j are convex sets, then from the property of intersection, $\mathbf{s}_j(\mathbf{p})$ is a convex set $\mathbf{s}_j = \mathbf{Y}_j \cap \pi_j$. Furthermore, from the property of addition it follows that $\mathbf{s}(\mathbf{p})$ being the addition of all $\mathbf{s}_j(\mathbf{p})$, must itself be a convex set. This is also true of $\pi(\mathbf{p})$.

If $\mathbf{Y}_j$ is a weakly convex set we are in the realm of constant returns to scale, and the production set is a convex polyhedral cone with vertex at 0, e.g. Fig. 5.15 and 5.16. Using the concept of a dual cone we can establish that the price set is the dual cone to $\mathbf{Y}_j$, namely $\mathbf{Y}_j^*$, and that the set $\mathbf{s}_j(\mathbf{p})$ is a cone with vertex 0. Using Definition 5.3 (p. 134) we can say that if $\mathbf{Y}_j^*$is a convex cone then

$$\mathbf{Y}_j^* = \{\mathbf{p}/\mathbf{p}'\mathbf{y}_j \leqslant 0, \forall \mathbf{y}_j \in \mathbf{Y}_j\}.$$

Since $\mathbf{Y}_j^*$ consists of all the vectors which make a non-acute angle with all the vectors in $\mathbf{Y}_j$ it follows $\mathbf{Y}_j$ is a convex cone with vertex 0; as illustrated in Fig. 5.17.

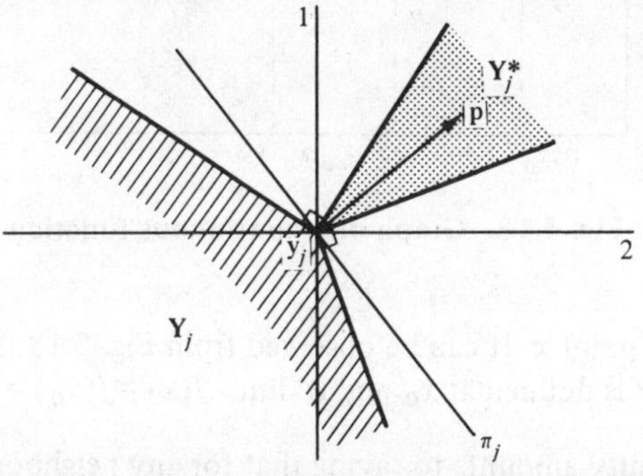

Fig. 5.17. The production set and its dual price set

If $\mathbf{p} \notin \mathbf{Y}_j^*$ the function $\pi_j(\mathbf{p})$ and the correspondence $\mathbf{s}_j(\mathbf{p})$ are either zero or not defined. If $\mathbf{p}$ is in the interior of $\mathbf{Y}_j$ the hyperplane orthogonal to $\mathbf{p}$ has the output $\mathbf{y}_j$ at the origin, and this will be a profit-maximising output. If $\mathbf{p}$ is on the boundary of $\mathbf{Y}_j^*$ profits will be maximised at the zero level and any $\mathbf{y}_j$ is consistent with this price. Finally, if $\mathbf{p} = 0$ we have already said that $\mathbf{s}_j(\mathbf{p})$ is the set $\mathbf{Y}_j$; if $\mathbf{p}$ is in the interior of $\mathbf{Y}_j^*$ then $\mathbf{s}_j(\mathbf{p})$ is the origin; and if $\mathbf{p}$ is on the boundary of $\mathbf{Y}_j^*$, $\mathbf{s}_j(\mathbf{p})$ is the boundary of $\mathbf{Y}_j$. In all cases $\mathbf{s}_j(\mathbf{p})$ is a convex cone with the origin as its vertex. From our analysis it follows that the feasible price set is the dual cone to $\mathbf{Y}_j$, namely $\mathbf{Y}_j^*$, and that the set $\mathbf{s}_j(\mathbf{p})$ is a cone with vertex at the origin.

5.6 Continuity and Semi-continuity of Functions and Correspondences

The distinction between functions and correspondences, alluded to in the last section, has particular significance for the concept of continuity. A clear understanding of continuity is essential because firstly the concept will be used repeatedly in the remainder of this book; and secondly, the literature of economics abounds with reference to it without explanation. We begin with the definition of the continuity of a function.

Definition 5.11

A function f is continuous at x_0 if for every $\epsilon > 0$ there is a $\delta > 0$ such that $|f(x) - f(x)| < \epsilon$ whenever $|x - x_0| < \delta$.

The idea of continuity is illustrated in Fig. 5.18. A function f is continuous if it is

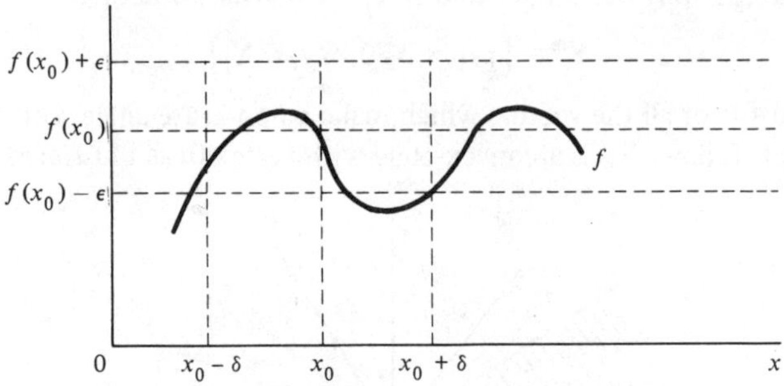

Fig. 5.18. Graph of a continuous function

continuous at every point x. It can be observed from Fig. 5.18 that a function is continuous at x_0 if f is defined at x_0 and if $\lim_{x \to x_0} f(x) = f(x_0) = \lim_{x_0 \leftarrow x} f(x)$. This definition of continuity amounts to saying that for any neighbourhood of x_0, i.e. the open interval $(x_0 - \delta, x_0 + \delta)$ if we take any sequence x belonging to this neighbourhood which approaches x_0 then the sequence $f(x)$ approaches $f(x_0)$. In other words, we do not wish to have any jumps in the function.

We shall state without proof the following mathematical theorem concerning continuous functions:

Theorem 5.3 Let f and g be continuous functions at x_0. Then $f \pm g$, and the product $f \cdot g$ are continuous at x_0. The quotient f/g is continuous at x_0 if $g(x_0) \neq 0$.

Even though a function is claimed to be discontinuous when a jump occurs in its graph, there does remain an element of confusion. This arises when we consider a weaker type of continuity, called *semi-continuity.*[12] It is possible to approach semi-continuity of a function by considering Definition 5.11 more closely. It is possible to express this definition in terms of two separate conditions. For all $|x - x_0| < \delta$ we require:

(1) $f(x) - f(x_0) < \epsilon$

(2) $f(x) - f(x_0) > -\epsilon.$

Now given that the point $f(x_0)$ is defined, it is still possible that at a point x_0 only one of these conditions is met. If (1) is met, the function is said to be upper semi-continuous at x_0; if (2) is met, it is lower semi-continuous. If for every x in the domain each point is upper (lower) semi-continuous then the function is upper (lower) semi-continuous. Consider, for example, the illustrations in Fig. 5.19. In each case the domain is (a, b). In Fig. 5.19 (a) x' and x'' are both upper

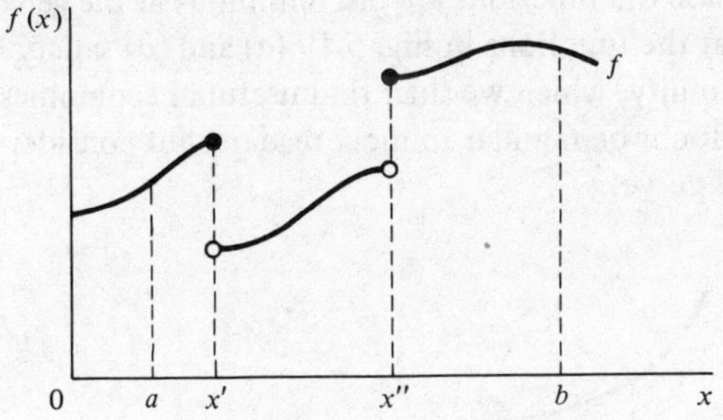

(a)

f is upper semi-continuous

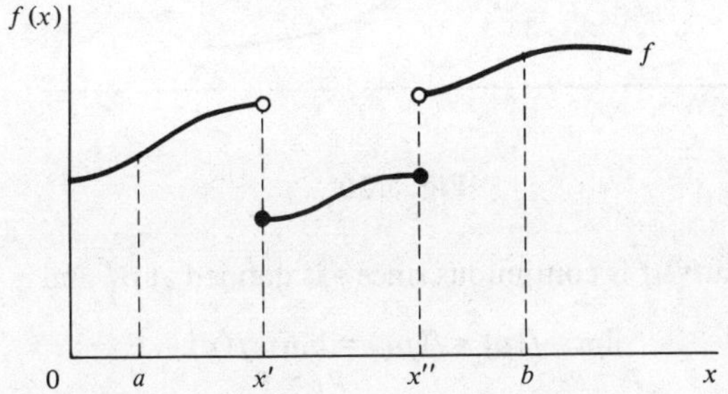

(b)

f is lower semi-continuous

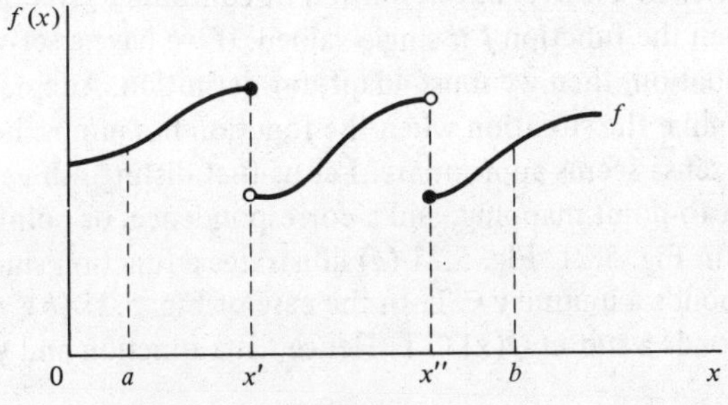

(c)

f is neither upper nor lower semi-continuous

Fig. 5.19

semi-continuous and f is continuous at every other point; hence f is upper semi-continuous. In Fig. 5.19 (*b*) x' and x'' are both lower semi-continuous and f is continuous at every other point in the domain, hence f is lower semi-continuous. On the other hand, Fig. 5.19 (*c*) has x' upper semi-continuous and x'' lower semi-continuous, therefore f is neither continuous nor semi-continuous. It is to be observed that in each case the functions are discontinuous in the generally accepted sense, but that the functions in Fig. 5.19 (*a*) and (*b*) satisfy the weaker condition of semi-continuity, which we shall find useful in economics.

Continuity will no doubt be familiar to most readers, but consider the following not so unusual demand curve:

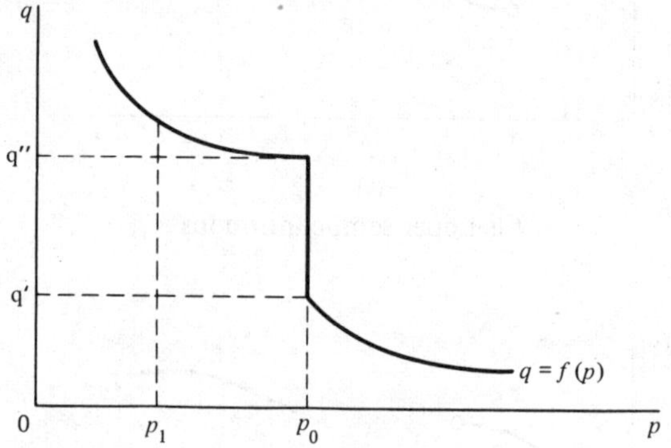

Fig. 5.20

At p_1 the demand curve f is continuous since f is defined at p_1 and

$$\lim_{p \to p_1} f(p) = f(p_1) = \lim_{p_1 \leftarrow p} f(p).$$

But can this be said of $f(p_0)$? There is a whole set corresponding to p_0, namely the interval $q'q''$! Can one say that as $p \to p_0, q \to q'$ or that $q \to q''$ or some other value between these two? Clearly, our definition of continuity given in Definition 5.11 only holds when the function f is single-valued. If we have a set-valued mapping, as in the present situation, then we must adapt our definition. Adaptation is appropriate here, unlike the situation when the function has jumps, because continuity in some sense seems appropriate. Let us first distinguish generally a function, or a point-to-point mapping, and a correspondence, or point-to-set mapping, as shown in Fig. 5.21. Fig. 5.21 (*a*) illustrates a function since for each $\mathbf{x} \in \mathbf{S}$ there corresponds a unique $\mathbf{y} \in \mathbf{T}$. In the case of Fig. 5.21 (*b*), to each $\mathbf{x} \in \mathbf{S}$ there corresponds a subset $\boldsymbol{\phi}(\mathbf{x}) \subset \mathbf{T}$. Hence f is a function and $\boldsymbol{\phi}$ is a correspondence

So far we have discussed continuity and semi-continuity of functions, but we require the same concepts in discussing correspondences. We shall first look at the semi-continuity of correspondences and then define continuity in terms of

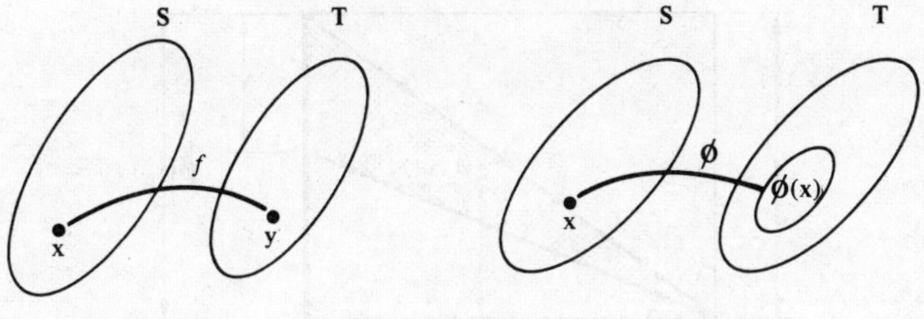

(a) f is a function

(b) ø is a correspondence

Fig. 5.21

semi-continuity. Let **S** denote the domain and **T** the range, $\{x^0\}$ a sequence of points of **S** and $\{y^\nu\}$ a sequence of points of **T**, and ϕ a correspondence of **S** into **T**.

Definition 5.12

The correspondence ϕ is upper semi-continuous at the point x_0 if

$$x^\nu \to x_0,\ y^\nu \in \phi(x^\nu),\ y^\nu \to y_0 \Rightarrow y_0 \in \phi(x_0).$$

In other words, if every sequence x^ν tends to x_0 and has limit points then this set of limit points, **Y**, lies in the image set of x_0.

Definition 5.13

The correspondence ϕ is lower semi-continuous at the point x_0 if

$$x^\nu \to x_0,\ y_0 \in \phi(x_0) \Rightarrow \exists \{y^\nu\},\ y^\nu \in \phi(x^\nu),\ y^\nu \to y_0.$$

In other words, if x^ν tends to x_0 and if y_0 belongs to the image set of x_0, then each y^ν lies in the image set of its associated x^ν, i.e. the limit set, **Y**, contains the image set $\phi(x_0)$.

Definition 5.14

A correspondence ϕ is continuous at a point x_0 if it is both upper and lower semi-continuous at this point.

This of course requires that the set of limit points, **Y**, is equal to the image set of x_0, i.e. $Y = \phi(x_0)$. The three definitions are illustrated in Fig. 5.22. **S** and **T** are two compact real intervals, where **S** is the domain and **T** the range. The graph ϕ is the shaded region, where the heavy boundary is also included. **Y** denotes the limit points of $x \to x_0$, while $\phi(x_0)$ is the image set at the point x_0. Hence, Fig. 5.22 (*a*) illustrates upper semi-continuity of ϕ at x_0; Fig. 5.22 (*b*) lower semi-continuity of ϕ at x_0; and Fig. 5.22 (*c*) continuity of ϕ at x_0.

A correspondence ϕ is upper (lower) semi-continuous if it is upper (lower) semi-continuous for all points in the domain **S**.

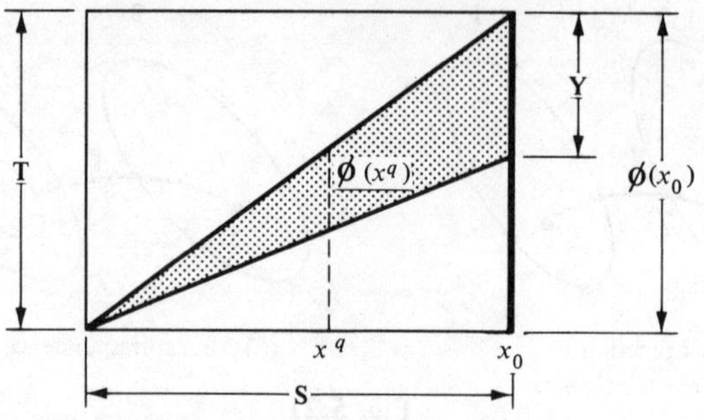

(*a*)

ϕ is upper semi-continuous at x_0

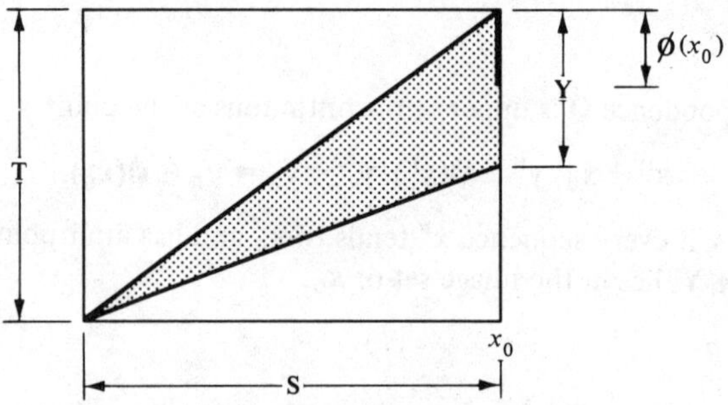

(*b*)

ϕ is lower semi-continuous at x_0

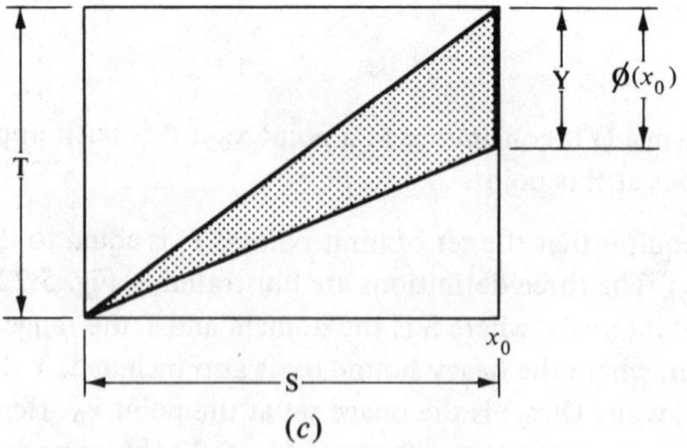

(*c*)

ϕ is continuous at x_0

Fig. 5.22

A theorem which will be useful in discussing multimarket equilibrium is the following, which will not be proved:

Theorem 5.4 If ϕ_1 and ϕ_2 are two upper (lower) semi-continuous correspondences, defined over the same domain, then $\phi_1 + \phi_2$ is upper (lower) semi-continuous, furthermore $\phi_1\phi_2$ is upper (lower) semi-continuous.

This theorem, although stated for correspondences, equally holds for functions. Finally, we shall state another mathematical theorem without proof. Let f be a real valued function defined on $\mathbf{S}\times\mathbf{T}$, i.e. $f(\mathbf{x}, \mathbf{y})$ where $\mathbf{x} \in \mathbf{S}$ and $\mathbf{y} \in \mathbf{T}$. If $\mathbf{x}$ is given, we have an image set $\phi(\mathbf{x})$. Now with $\mathbf{x}$ given we have f in terms of $\mathbf{y}$ only. Let $\mu(\mathbf{x})$ denote the subset of $\phi(\mathbf{x})$ for which f, for given $\mathbf{x}$, is a maximum. Fig. 5.23 may be helpful in visualising these conditions. Finally, let $g(\mathbf{x})$ denote the maximum value of f on $\phi(\mathbf{x})$ for given $\mathbf{x}$.

Theorem 5.5 If f is continuous on $\mathbf{S}\times\mathbf{T}$, and if ϕ is continuous at $\mathbf{x} \in \mathbf{S}$, then μ is upper semi-continuous at $\mathbf{x}$, and g is continuous at $\mathbf{x}$.

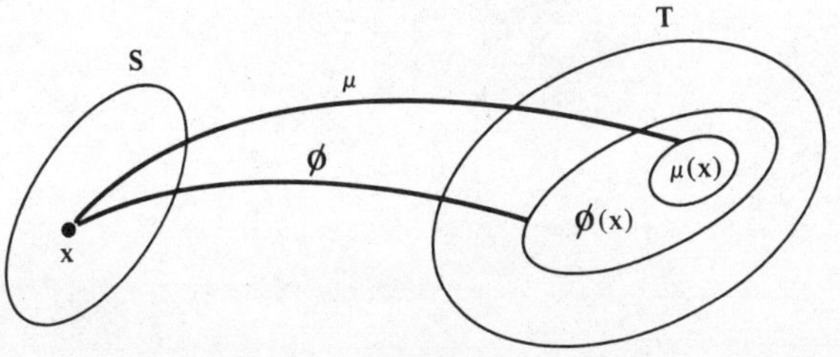

Fig. 5.23

Upper semi-continuity plays an important role in establishing the existence of a competitive equilibrium and has applications in the theory of economic growth.

Even so, the concept of semi-continuity is becoming increasingly used in economics and it is an aspect the mathematicians rarely discuss. It is for these reasons that we have taken great pains to discuss at some length this important mathematical concept.

In concluding this section let us return to the profit-maximising firm and attempt to apply Theorem 5.5. The profit for the jth firm is $\mathbf{p}'\mathbf{y}_j$. Now $\mathbf{p}$ is an n-dimensional vector, hence $\mathbf{p} \in \mathbf{R}^n$ whilst $\mathbf{y}_j \in \mathbf{Y}_j$. We know profits are continuous because prices are arbitrary, hence we have a continuous function of $(\mathbf{p}, \mathbf{y}_j)$ on $\mathbf{R}^n\times\mathbf{Y}_j$. Hence, for given $\mathbf{p}$ the image set $\phi(\mathbf{p})$ from $\mathbf{R}^n$ to $\mathbf{Y}_j$ is $\mathbf{Y}_j$ itself for every $\mathbf{p} \in \mathbf{R}^n$, i.e. $\phi(\mathbf{p}) = \mathbf{Y}_j, \forall \mathbf{p} \in \mathbf{R}^n$; this is so because whatever the price vector the set of all $\mathbf{y}_j$ remains the same (see Fig. 5.14). Since $\phi(\mathbf{p}) = \mathbf{Y}_j$ and $\mathbf{Y}_j$ remains constant it is trivially true that ϕ is continuous. We have already established that $\mathbf{s}_j(\mathbf{p})$ is the subset of $\mathbf{Y}_j$ for which $(\mathbf{p}, \mathbf{y}_j)$ is a maximum and that $\pi_j(\mathbf{p})$ is the maximum value of the profit function for given $\mathbf{p}$; hence by Theorem 5.5 $\mathbf{s}_j(\mathbf{p})$ is upper semi-continuous and $\pi_j(\mathbf{p})$ is continuous. The important stipulation for this result to hold is that

$\mathbf{Y}_j$ is a compact set, and this we assume to be so. Finally, if all $\mathbf{Y}_j$ are compact and because $\mathbf{s}(\mathbf{p}) = \sum_{j=1}^{l} \mathbf{s}_j(\mathbf{p})$ then by Theorem 5.4 the total supply correspondence $\mathbf{s}(\mathbf{p})$ is upper semi-continuous, and the total profit function $\pi(\mathbf{p}) = \sum_{j=1}^{l} \pi_j(\mathbf{p})$ is continuous.

EXERCISES

1. Show that if **x** is a point in the Edgeworth–Bowley box which exhibits the allocation of two goods between two consumers then a movement to another point, **y**, is a transformation. Does it follow that the efficiency locus is a set of points which constitutes a subset of all possible transactions? Take a point **x** off the efficiency locus. Show those transactions which make at least one person better off. Is this set equivalent to the contract curve?

2. Consider the following axiom due to Afriat [1]:

Axiom of Separation $\mathbf{x}T\mathbf{y}\ \&\ \mathbf{z} \geqslant 0 \Rightarrow (\mathbf{x}+\mathbf{z})T(\mathbf{y}+\mathbf{z})$.

Explain what this axiom means. Suppose a firm divides its allocation of goods into two parts and that it transforms one part during production leaving the other unchanged. Is this consistent with the axiom of separation? Show that the axiom of additivity, Axiom 15, can be derived from the axiom of separation and the axiom of transitivity, Axiom 14.

3. Which of the following is true, explaining how you come to your result:

(*a*) T is reflexive.
(*b*) T is anti-symmetric.
(*c*) T is complete.
(*d*) T is asymmetric.
(*e*) T is symmetric.

4. Consider the following axiom due to Afriat:

Axiom of Economy $\mathbf{x} \leqslant \mathbf{y} \Rightarrow \sim(\mathbf{x}T\mathbf{y})$.

Show that if this is not true then it would be inconsistent with Axiom 17.

5. In what way are Baumol's revenue-maximisation and Simon's satisficing behaviour replacements of Axiom 21? Write out in terms of an axiom to replace Axiom 21,

(*a*) a revenue-maximisation axiom,
and (*b*) a satisficing axiom.

6. Show that if $\mathbf{C}_1 \subset \mathbf{C}_2$ then $\mathbf{C}_2^* \subset \mathbf{C}_1^*$.

7. Prove that $(\mathbf{C}_1 + \mathbf{C}_2)^* = \mathbf{C}_1^* \cap \mathbf{C}_2^*$.

8. Let $\mathbf{a}_1 = \begin{bmatrix} 2 \\ 2 \\ -1 \end{bmatrix}$ $\mathbf{a}_2 = \begin{bmatrix} 3 \\ 0 \\ -1 \end{bmatrix}$ $\mathbf{a}_3 = \begin{bmatrix} 1 \\ 3 \\ -1 \end{bmatrix}$. Draw the convex cone defined by these vectors. Obtain the three facets of this cone, and demonstrate that each is a convex cone.

9. Explain in what way the irreversibility axiom is dependent upon the presence of a *basic* input. Sketch a production set which illustrates reversibility. Also sketch a convex cone which violates Axiom 3 of the production set **Y**.

10. Define a reversible transformation relation RT by:

$$\mathbf{x}RT\mathbf{y} \Leftrightarrow \mathbf{x}T\mathbf{y}\ \&\ \mathbf{y}T\mathbf{x}.$$

(i) What properties does the relation RT possess?
(ii) Does RT order the input–output set $\mathbf{Y}_j$ into equivalence classes?
(iii) What does this relation imply about the reversibility or irreversibility of T?

11. Discuss the continuity of

$$f(x) = \frac{x}{(x-3)} \qquad -\infty < x < \infty$$

Is it possible to redefine $f(3)$ such that $f(x)$ is continuous over the whole domain? Draw the graph of this function.

12. Draw the graph of

$$f(x) = \frac{x}{x} \qquad x \neq 0.$$

Show that at $x = 0$ there is a 'jump discontinuity'. Can this be eliminated by redefining $f(0)$? In what way is this different from the function in Exercise 11?

6

LINEAR THEORIES OF PRODUCTION

6.1 Introduction

In this chapter we shall use the concepts of production discussed in the previous chapter to elaborate on three linear approaches to the firm and the economy. This will be done in two stages. First, we shall concentrate on the firm and consider what light we can shed on a firm's behaviour. Second, we shall consider the input–output behaviour of the economy as a whole. The three models are the Ricardian model, the input–output model (or Leontief model), and the activity model. The essential difference between these three models is a matter of degree only, and rests on the interpretation of Axiom 20, i.e. on the finite set of activities. The Ricardian and input–output model have only one activity whilst the activity model has at least two, but still finite number of, activities.

The research into linear models is relatively new in comparison to the neoclassical theory of the firm, which we shall investigate in the following chapter. However, as will be shown in this chapter, it is possible to consider a number of problems about production in the context of linear models which will be found to be excluded in non-linear production models. On the other hand, linear production models have restrictions of their own, of which linearity is an obvious case in point. There is no one theory of production and costs but a set of theories. None are wholly correct or adequate in answering all our questions concerning production, and each has something to offer to our understanding of the production process. Part of our job is to see the merits and limitations of each approach, and never pre-suppose that there can be only one 'true' theory of production and cost.

6.2 Ricardian Model[1]

Consider a firm which uses one basic resource input, denoted r_1, which we can think of as labour. This input is used to produce a single output, which for this firm (firm 1), we shall label y_1. We shall employ the convention of the last chapter of denoting inputs negative and outputs positive, i.e. $y_1 \geqslant 0$ and $r_1 \leqslant 0$. In the Ricardian tradition, we shall suppose that the input requirement is proportional to the output, i.e.

$$r_{11} = -b_{11}y_1 \qquad b_{11} > 0 \text{ and } y_1 \geqslant 0$$

where b_{ik} ($i = k = 1$ in this case) denotes the amount of the ith *basic* factor required to produce one unit of the kth output, and r_{ik} is the amount of the ith basic input used in the production of the kth output (again $i = k$).[2] This equation can be considered as a typical Ricardian production function where $1/b_{11}$ denotes the scale of operation. Fig. 6.1 gives a helpful representation.

Consider more closely the above equation. We can rewrite this equation in the following way:

$$r_{11} + b_{11}y_1 = [r_{11}, y_1]\begin{bmatrix}1\\ b_{11}\end{bmatrix} = 0.$$

Now the vector $[r_{11}, y_1]$ represents the co-ordinates of any arbitrary point on the ray denoted $\mathbf{Y}_1$, i.e. $\mathbf{Y}_1$ is the ray satisfying all points $[\lambda r_{11}, \lambda y_1]$ for all $\lambda \geqslant 0$.

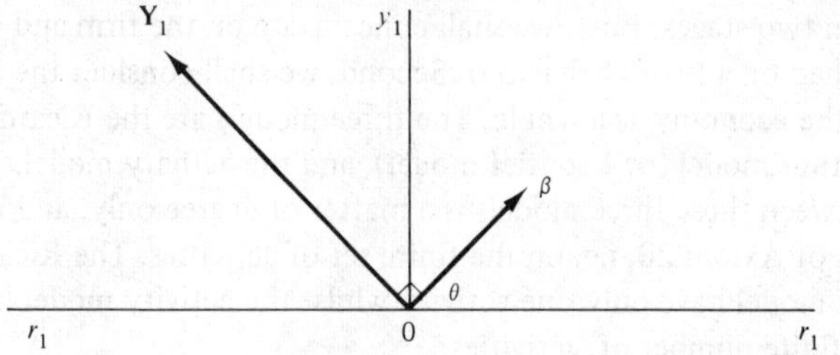

Fig. 6.1

Hence, $\mathbf{Y}_1$ denotes the production set of firm 1. Notice also that $\mathbf{Y}_1$ is a half-line, a fact we shall be making use of below. Let $\boldsymbol{\beta} = \begin{bmatrix}1\\ b_{11}\end{bmatrix}$. We know, however, that if the inner product of two vectors is zero then these vectors are orthogonal, i.e. the vectors are at right angles. Hence, the vector $\boldsymbol{\beta}$ is drawn at right angles to the ray $\mathbf{Y}_1$ in Fig. 6.1. We further note that the co-ordinates of $\boldsymbol{\beta}$ are $[1, b_{11}]$ and consequently the slope of this vector is b_{11}, i.e. $\tan\theta = b_{11}$.

Although the firm is here considered in isolation we must, if we are to introduce product and factor prices, make some assumption of the type of market the firm belongs. We therefore make the following assumption:

Assumption All firms operate in perfectly competitive product and factor markets.

It is to be noted that under this assumption all prices are given as far as the firm is concerned. Our aim, therefore, is to investigate the firm's behaviour in this simple existence and satisying the proportionality requirment of its single basic input.

Let p_1 and w_1 denote the commodity price and factor price respectively. Then the profit for this firm is:

$$\pi_1(p, w) = p_1y_1 + w_1r_{11}$$
$$= (p_1 - b_{11}\, w_1)y_1.$$

It is assumed that the firm wishes to maximise profits – Axiom 21 of Chapter 5.2. It follows immediately that if $p_1 < b_{11}w_1$ and $y_1 > 0$ then profits will be negative;

if $y_1 = 0$ profits will be zero. The profit-maximising decision, therefore, when $p_1 < b_{11}w_1$ is to set $y_1 = 0$. In so doing $r_{11} = 0$, which means the firm does not engage in production. This, of course, is consistent with Axiom 17. If $p_1 = b_{11}w_1$ then profits are zero regardless of the level of output y_1. This situation can be considered in the following way. At any level of output y_1, so long as the input is consistently chosen, any level is a profit-maximising output. Lastly, if $p_1 > b_{11}w_1$ an increase in output will increase profits indefinitely: there is no profit-maximising output. In other words, $\pi_1(p, w)$ is unbounded because the production set is unbounded, hence the supply correspondence is undefined under these conditions. In saying this we have not taken account of any resource limitations, which will be discussed below.

Let us look a little closer into the supply correspondence and the profit function obtained under these conditions. Consider a price vector, which we shall denote **p**, so that $\mathbf{p} = (w_1, p_1)$. The slope of this vector is p_1/w_1. Two typical vectors **p** and $\boldsymbol{\beta}$ are drawn in Fig. 6.2 (*a*). A price vector with slope less than $\boldsymbol{\beta}$ has the condition that $p_1/w_1 < b_{11}$, i.e. $p_1 - b_{11}w_1 < 0$. In this case the optimal output is $y_1 = 0$ with $\pi_1(\mathbf{p}) = 0$. If the price vector coincides with $\boldsymbol{\beta}$ then $p_1/w_1 = b_{11}$, i.e. $p_1 - b_{11}w_1 = 0$. In this situation the supply correspondence is a vertical line as shown in Fig. 6.2 (*b*); in other words the supply is infinitely elastic at this price set. Furthermore, regardless of the output the profit is maximised at $\pi(\mathbf{p} = \boldsymbol{\beta}) = 0$. For a price vector with a slope greater than that of $\boldsymbol{\beta}$, the supply curve is undefined and the profit function rises continuously as output increases. It is possible to summarise the conditions for firm 1 as follows:

$$p_1 - b_{11}w_1 \leqslant 0 \text{ for } y_1 \geqslant 0 \text{ giving } \pi_1(\mathbf{p}) = 0. \tag{6.1}$$

Before leaving this topic let us see in what way Section 5.5 has a bearing. In Chapter 5.5 we established that the price set belongs to the dual of $\mathbf{Y}_j$. Since we have only a single input and a single output the dual to $\mathbf{Y}_1$ is the set of all vectors which make a non-acute angle with $\mathbf{Y}_1$, which is the shaded region in Fig. 6.2 (*a*). We further established previously that when the price vector belonged to the boundary of the dual set then profits would be maximised at the zero level for any

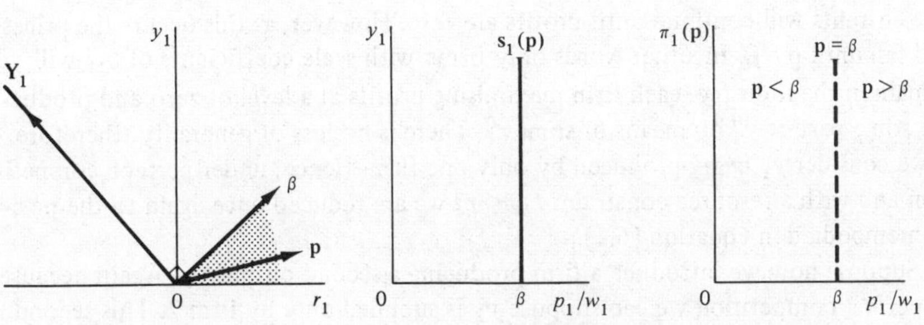

(*a*) Ricardian model (*b*) Supply correspondence (*c*) Profit function

Fig. 6.2

output. This is consistent with our present analysis since the boundary of the dual set is the vector **β**. This duality consideration will constantly reoccur throughout our discussion of linear production theory.

Thus far we have not assumed any resource limitations. Suppose the economy in which this firm operates has a total endowment of the first resource given by r_1^0. If firm 1 uses all of the economy's basic resource input then the maximum output it can produce is $y_1^0 = (-1/b_{11})r_1^0$, where $r_{11} = r_1^0$. This gives rise to a somewhat different picture. If the price vector is less steep than that of **β** then $y_1 = 0$ and $\pi_1(\mathbf{p}) = 0$ as before. If the price vector coincides with **β**, i.e. belongs to the boundary of the dual of $\mathbf{Y}_1$, then the supply will be infinitely elastic up to the level y_1^0 and thereafter infinitely inelastic; also at this price $\pi_1(\mathbf{p}) = 0$. However, if the slope of **p** exceeds that of **β** profits will be positive and output will rise up to the maximum y_1^0. Thus $\pi_1^0(\mathbf{p}) = p_1 y_1^0 + w_1 r_1^0 = (p_1 - b_{11} w_1) y_1^0$. This must be the case because although we have constant returns to scale the set $\mathbf{Y}_1$ is now bounded, and so also is $\pi_1(\mathbf{p})$. The situation is illustrated in Fig. 6.3.

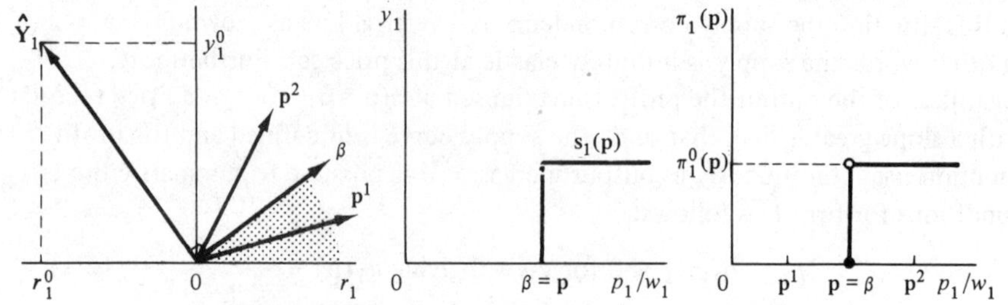

(*a*) Ricardian model with resource constraint (*b*) Supply correspondence (*c*) Profit function

Fig. 6.3

In a situation of perfect competition if the price vector was $\mathbf{p}^2$ say, as in Fig. 6.3 (*a*), then another less efficient firm can enter the industry and produce y_1. The entrants will continue until profits are zero. However, as this occurs the prices will fall until $\mathbf{p} = \boldsymbol{\beta}$. In other words only firms with scale coefficients of b_{11} will remain in the industry, each firm maximising profits at a level of zero and producing some part of y_1^0 by means of some r_1^0. There is no loss of generality, therefore, if we consider y_1 being produced by only one firm. Hence, under perfect competition and with a resource constraint $r_{11} < r_1^0$ we are reduced once again to the position embodied in equation (6.1).

Suppose now we introduce a firm producing a second output y_2. Again because of perfect competition we can suppose y_2 is supplied only by firm 2. This second firm also uses the basic input r_1, so we have for firm 2

$$r_{12} = -b_{12} y_2$$

and profit function:

$$\pi_2(p, w) = p_2 y_2 + w_1 r_{12}$$
$$= (p_2 - b_{12} w_1) y_2.$$

The production set for each firm is therefore $\mathbf{Y}_1$ and $\mathbf{Y}_2$ which constitutes the half-lines in Fig. 6.4. The scale vectors are $\boldsymbol{\beta}_1$ and $\boldsymbol{\beta}_2$ for firms 1 and 2 and are orthogonal to $\mathbf{Y}_1$ and $\mathbf{Y}_2$ respectively. The economy's production set is the sum of

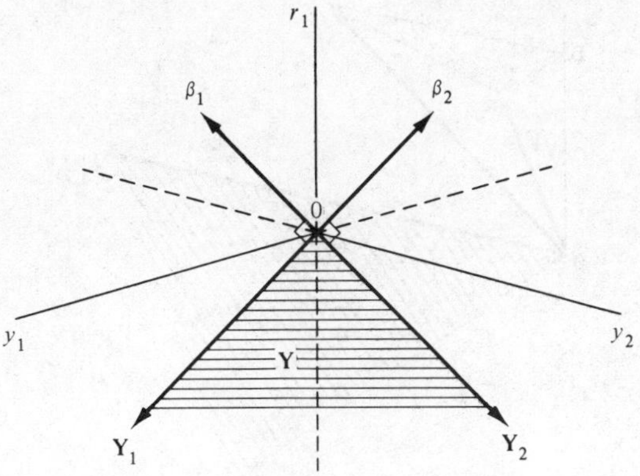

Fig. 6.4

all productions of firms 1 and 2, i.e.

$$\mathbf{Y} = \sum_{j=1}^{2} \mathbf{Y}_j.$$

But since $\mathbf{Y}_j$ are half-lines, by Definition 5.4 the sum of a finite set of half-lines constitutes a convex polyhedral cone, which is shown by the shaded region in Fig. 6.4. The profit for the whole economy also readily follows:

$$\pi(p, w) = \sum_j \pi_j(p, w) = \sum_j p_j y_j + \sum_j w_1 r_{1j}$$
$$= p_1 y_1 + p_2 y_2 + w_1 r_{11} + w_1 r_{12}$$
$$= (p_1 - b_{11} w_1) y_1 + (p_2 - b_{12} w_1) y_2.$$

In order to understand the situation for the economy as a whole it is worth while contemplating Fig. 6.5 for a few minutes. This is an elaboration of the positive quadrant of Fig. 6.4 and the two figures are intricately connected. The vectors $\boldsymbol{\beta}_1$ and $\boldsymbol{\beta}_2$ are the same in both figures (only the axes have been 'turned' for a clearer picture). $\boldsymbol{\beta}_1$ lies in the $r_1 - y_1$ plane, whilst $\boldsymbol{\beta}_2$ lies in the $r_1 - y_2$ plane because of the positions of the half-lines $\mathbf{Y}_1$ and $\mathbf{Y}_2$. The dual cone to $\mathbf{Y}$ is shown in Fig. 6.4 by $0\boldsymbol{\beta}_1\boldsymbol{\beta}_2\mathbf{D}$ and as earlier is denoted $\mathbf{Y}^*$. Since we are interested in the outputs we need the projection of $\mathbf{Y}$ in the $y_1 - y_2$ plane and in the present case this corresponds to the non-negative plane $y_1 - y_2$. We shall denote this Pro (**Y**). We further note other cones of interest. The cone $0\boldsymbol{\beta}_1 D$ is the dual cone for firm 1, i.e. $0\boldsymbol{\beta}_1 D = \mathbf{Y}_1^*$. Similarly, $0\boldsymbol{\beta}_2 D = \mathbf{Y}_2^*$, the dual cone of $\mathbf{Y}_2$. Finally, as a matter of notation we shall denote all interior points of a cone by Int $(\mathbf{Y}_j)$ or Int $(\mathbf{Y}_j^*)$.

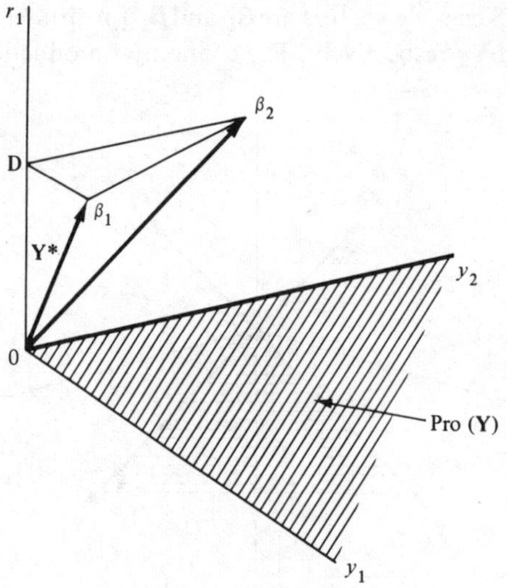

Fig. 6.5. A dual cone to Y

Any vector in the interior of $\mathbf{Y}_1^*$ has a slope (relative to the r_1 axis) smaller than the slope $\boldsymbol{\beta}_1$. Similarly, any vector in the interior of $\mathbf{Y}_2^*$ has a slope smaller than that of $\boldsymbol{\beta}_2$. Consider a given price vector $\mathbf{p} = (w_1, p_1, p_2)$. A number of possibilities arise. If $\mathbf{p} \in$ Int $(\mathbf{Y}_1^*)$ then the optimal strategy for firm 1 is $y_1 = 0$. On the other hand, firm 2 will produce y_2 at a zero profit. Hence, the economy specialises in the production of y_2. If, however, $\mathbf{p} \in$ Int$(\mathbf{Y}_2^*)$ then the economy specialises in the production of y_1 at a zero rate of profit. If $\mathbf{p} \in \boldsymbol{\beta}_1 0 \boldsymbol{\beta}_2$, i.e. $\mathbf{p} \in$ Int $(\mathbf{Y}^\perp)$ the interior of the orthogonal dual to **Y**, both y_1 and y_2 will be produced. For a given $\mathbf{p} \in \mathbf{Y}^\perp$ there is a unique **y** (up to a multiplicative constant) which is the projection of **p** on to the $y_1 - y_2$ plane. If **p** lies 'below' $\mathbf{Y}^\perp$ (i.e. a slope relative to r_1 greater than $\mathbf{Y}^\perp$) then profits are negative in *both* industries because this situation implies $p_1 - b_{11} w_1 < 0$ and $p_2 - b_{12} w_1 < 0$, and hence neither y_1 nor y_2 will be produced. If $\mathbf{p} \in$ Int $(\mathbf{Y}^*)$ then profits are positive and firms will enter the industry until **p** belongs to $\mathbf{Y}_1^*$, or $\mathbf{Y}_2^*$ or $\mathbf{Y}^\perp$. Hence, the dual cone of **Y** is that cone bounded by the faces $\mathbf{Y}_1^*$, $\mathbf{Y}_2^*$ and $\mathbf{Y}^\perp$.

For the supply correspondence to be defined with $\mathbf{y} \geqslant 0$ we must have $\mathbf{p} \in \mathbf{Y}^*$ and if both firms are to produce at all with zero profits it is necessary that $\mathbf{p} \in$ Int $(\mathbf{Y}^\perp)$ and hence $\mathbf{p}'\mathbf{y} = 0$ for $\mathbf{y} \geqslant 0$. Taking all situations into account, if $\mathbf{p} \in \mathbf{Y}^*$ then $\mathbf{p}'\mathbf{y} \leqslant 0$ for $\mathbf{y} \geqslant 0$.

For this economy, therefore, to have a non-negative output vector the following requirement must be met:

$$p_1 - b_{11} w_1 \leqslant 0 \qquad y_1 \geqslant 0$$

$$p_2 - b_{12} w_1 \leqslant 0 \qquad y_2 \geqslant 0.$$

Or in matrix notation

$$\mathbf{p}' \leqslant w_1 \mathbf{b}_1' \qquad \mathbf{y} \geqslant 0.$$

Let us extend the model slightly by considering a resource limitation $r_1 = r_1^0$. In our two-output version, if all the input is used in the production of the first commodity then $y_1^0 = (-1/b_{11})r_1^0$; if all of the input is used in the production of the second commodity we have $y_2^0 = (-1/b_{12})r_1^0$. It therefore follows that the production set for the economy as a whole takes the form of a truncated cone, A0B in Fig. 6.6. We shall adopt the convention of using a circumflex above a production set to indicate that it is a truncated cone. Hence $\hat{\mathbf{Y}}_1$, $\hat{\mathbf{Y}}_2$ and $\hat{\mathbf{Y}}$ denote the truncated cone 0A, 0B and 0AB respectively. Furthermore, the projection of $\hat{\mathbf{Y}}$ into the $y_1 - y_2$ plane is given by Pro $(\hat{\mathbf{Y}})$ in Fig. 6.6.

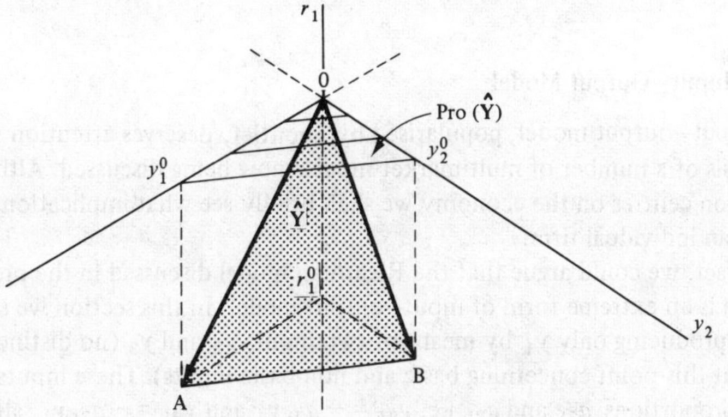

Fig. 6.6. A truncated production set

Of course the economy must have a solution to its optimisation problem for which the aggregate demand for the basic resource does not exceed the given supply. We require to impose the following constraint therefore,

$$r_1^0 \geqslant r_{11} + r_{12} = b_{11}\, y_1 + b_{12}\, y_2 = \mathbf{b}_1'\, \mathbf{y}.$$

The problem remains basically the same: we require $\mathbf{p} \in \hat{\mathbf{Y}}^*$ such that $\mathbf{p}'\mathbf{y} \leqslant 0$, $\mathbf{y} \geqslant 0$ and $\mathbf{y} \in \hat{\mathbf{Y}}$.

The Ricardian model can very easily be generalised with regard to the number of inputs. Let the number of inputs be s and each firm (industry!) produces only a single output so there are n commodities. With no resource constraint a solution requires that

$$p_i - \sum_{\nu=1}^{s} b_{\nu i} w_i \leqslant 0 \qquad y_i \geqslant 0 \qquad i = 1, \ldots, n$$

or

$$\mathbf{p}' \leqslant \mathbf{w}' \mathbf{B} \qquad \mathbf{y} \geqslant 0$$

where **B** is $s \times n$, and **w** is $s \times 1$ and **p** is $n \times 1$. This condition maximises profits $\pi(\mathbf{p}, \mathbf{w})$ at the zero level. If there exists a resource constraint of $\mathbf{r}^0$ then

$$r_\nu^0 \geqslant \sum_{i=1}^{n} r_{\nu i} = \sum_{i=1}^{n} b_{\nu i} y_i \qquad \nu = 1, \ldots, s$$

i.e.

$$\mathbf{r}^0 \geqslant \mathbf{B}\mathbf{y}$$

where, as before, **B** is an $s \times n$ matrix, $\mathbf{r}^0$ an $s \times 1$ vector of given resource endowments and **y** an $n \times 1$ output vector. Hence, for given factor endowment $\mathbf{r}^0$ we can find a non-negative output vector $\mathbf{y} \geqslant 0$ which maximises π (**p**, **w**) at the zero level if

$$\mathbf{p}' \leqslant \mathbf{w}'\mathbf{B}$$

and

$$\mathbf{r}^0 \geqslant \mathbf{B}\mathbf{y}.$$

6.3 Input–Output Model

The input–output model, popularised by Leontief, deserves attention because it is the basis of a number of multimarket models now being discussed. Although attention centres on the economy we shall briefly see what implications there are about an individual firm.

In fact, we could argue that the Ricardian model discussed in the previous section is an extreme form of input–output model. In this section we shall consider a firm producing only y_1 by means of two inputs y_2 and y_3 (no distinction will be made at this point concerning basic and non-basic inputs). These inputs are used in fixed proportions, a_{21} and a_{31} i.e. $y_{21} = -a_{21} y_1$ and $y_{31} = -a_{31} y_1$, all a's being non-negative. The production set of the firm consists of the half-line $\mathbf{Y}_1$ in Fig. 6.7.

The only difference here from the model in the previous section is in the introduction of an additional input. The vector $\boldsymbol{\beta} = (1, a_{21}, a_{31})$, where the first element reveals we are discussing a unit of output y_1, is orthogonal to $\mathbf{Y}_1$. Consider a price vector $\mathbf{p} = (p_1, p_2, p_3)$ incorporating both commodity and factor prices. The profit function for the firm is:

$$\begin{aligned}\pi_1(\mathbf{p}) &= p_1 y_1 + p_2 y_{21} + p_3 y_{31}\\ &= (p_1 - a_{21} p_2 - a_{31} p_3) y_1.\end{aligned}$$

Fig. 6.8 is useful in understanding the profit function. The angle θ is the angle of $\boldsymbol{\beta}$ with its projection on to the p_2–p_3 plane. If **p** coincides with $\boldsymbol{\beta}$ we have immediately that $p_1 - a_{21} p_2 - a_{31} p_3 = 0$. In this case $\pi_1(\mathbf{p}) = 0$ and supply is infinitely elastic. Allowing only the commodity price to vary if **p** lies below **β** in the shaded region, i.e. the slope of **p** is less than θ, then $p_1 - a_{21}p_2 - a_{31}p_3 < 0$ and profits will be maximised at $y_1 = 0$. If **p** lies outside the shaded region then $p_1 - a_{21}p_2 - a_{31}p_3 > 0$ and the supply correspondence is undefined. Hence, the

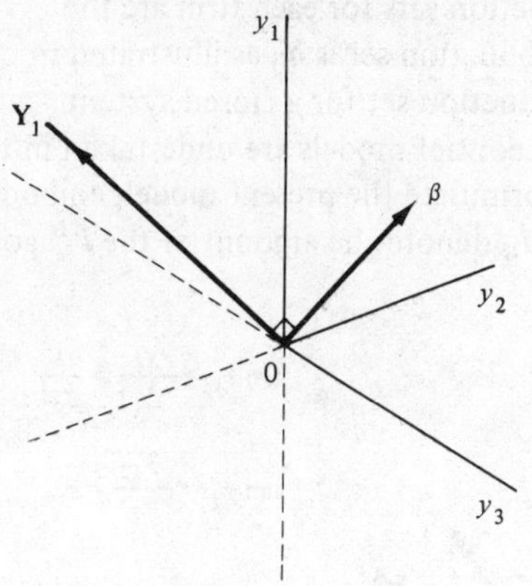

Fig. 6.7

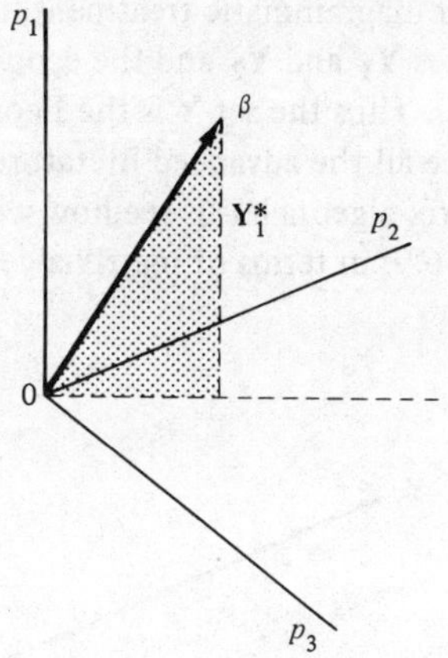

Fig. 6.8

supply correspondence and the profit function are exactly the same as those in Fig. 6.2 (*b*); again we have demonstrated that if $\mathbf{p} \in \mathbf{Y}_1^*$ then

$$p_1 - a_{21}p_2 - a_{31}p_3 \leqslant 0 \text{ and } y_1 \geqslant 0.$$

It is to be noticed that even if we increase the number of inputs so long as we retain a single output the conclusion remains the same. The close association between the Ricardian model and the present model is now obvious. However, the input–output model has far greater generality as we distinguish non-basic and basic factors of production. This distinction has no implications at the firm level: it makes little difference whether y_2 is basic while y_3 is non-basic. We shall therefore continue our discussion at the economy level.

In discussing the input–output model at the economy level two systems have been distinguished in the literature, and are referred to as:

(i) the closed Leontief model, and
(ii) the open Leontief model.

In the closed systems, all inputs to firms are outputs of other firms. This is not, of course, very realistic because it implies that production is carried on for its own sake, that production is perpetual and self-generating – the most extreme form of the capitalist process. More to the point, it means that no supply is lost from the system; in other words, no goods are consumed by anyone outside the system. Even though such a system is unrealistic many insights into the open system can be gleaned from first considering this simpler closed Leontief model.

6.3 (i) Closed Leontief Model

A system is *closed* if the commodities appearing as inputs at least once in the system are solely obtained from outputs of that system. If we have just two firms (industries!), firm 1 producing y_1 and using y_2 as input; firm 2 producing y_2 and using y_1 as input then the output set is the same as the input set. In our now familiar diagrammatic treatment, the production sets for each firm are the half-lines $\mathbf{Y}_1$ and $\mathbf{Y}_2$ and the economy's production set is $\mathbf{Y}$, as illustrated in Fig. 6.9. Thus the set $\mathbf{Y}$ is the Leontief production set for a closed system.

Since all the advanced literature of the Leontief models are undertaken in terms of matrix algebra let us see how we can reformulate the present model, embodied in Fig. 6.9, in terms of matrix algebra. Let a_{ij} denote the amount of the ith good

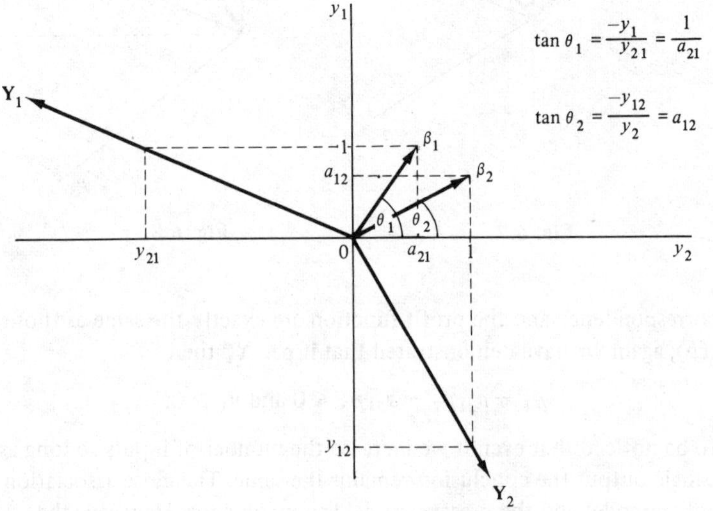

Fig. 6.9

required to produce one unit of the jth good, $a_{ij} \geqslant 0$. In the present two-commodity example there is a requirement of $a_{12}y_2$ of commodity 1 and $a_{21}y_1$ of commodity 2 – remembering that the input is proportional to the output, and letting $y_i \geqslant 0$. Let us define an *input matrix* (in *net* terms so that $a_{ii} = 0$)[3] by:

Definition 6.1

An input matrix of order $n \times n$ is given by:

$$\mathbf{A} = \begin{bmatrix} 0 & a_{12} & a_{13} & \dots & a_{1n} \\ a_{21} & 0 & a_{23} & \dots & a_{2n} \\ \cdot & & & & \cdot \\ \cdot & & & & \cdot \\ \cdot & & & & \cdot \\ a_{n1} & a_{n2} & a_{n3} & \dots & 0 \end{bmatrix}.$$

In our present example $\mathbf{A} = \begin{bmatrix} 0 & a_{12} \\ a_{21} & 0 \end{bmatrix}$. It immediately follows that we can express the input requirement as $y_{12} = -a_{12}y_2$ and $y_{21} = -a_{21}y_1$, i.e.

$$\begin{bmatrix} y_{12} \\ y_{21} \end{bmatrix} = -\mathbf{Ay} = \begin{bmatrix} 0 & -a_{12} \\ -a_{21} & 0 \end{bmatrix} \begin{bmatrix} y_1 \\ y_2 \end{bmatrix} = \begin{bmatrix} -a_{12}y_2 \\ -a_{21}y_1 \end{bmatrix}.$$

If we made the rash assumption that the output from each firm is just sufficient to satisfy the input requirement, then we have the condition $-\mathbf{y} = -\mathbf{Ay}$ or

$$\mathbf{y} = \mathbf{Ay}$$

i.e.

$$\mathbf{y} - \mathbf{Ay} = (\mathbf{I} - \mathbf{A})\,\mathbf{y} = 0$$

Definition 6.2

Given an input matrix **A** or order $n \times n$ we define a *transactions matrix* of order $n \times n$ as

$$(\mathbf{I} - \mathbf{A}) = \begin{bmatrix} 1 & -a_{12} \ldots & -a_{1n} \\ -a_{21} & 1 & -a_{2n} \\ \cdot & & \cdot \\ \cdot & & \cdot \\ \cdot & & \cdot \\ -a_{n1} & -a_{n2} \ldots & 1 \end{bmatrix}.$$

In the present example $(\mathbf{I} - \mathbf{A}) = \begin{bmatrix} 1 & -a_{12} \\ -a_{21} & 1 \end{bmatrix}$. Positive signs refer to outputs, unit outputs in the present case, and negative signs denote inputs.

Now let us consider the meaning of $(\mathbf{I} - \mathbf{A})\mathbf{y} = 0$.

$$\begin{bmatrix} 1 & -a_{12} \\ -a_{21} & 1 \end{bmatrix} \begin{bmatrix} y_1 \\ y_2 \end{bmatrix} = 0$$

i.e.

$$y_1 = a_{12}y_2,$$
$$y_2 = a_{21}y_1.$$

In other words, the input requirement is just satisfied by the output of the system. The net output of firm 1 is just the required input for firm 2 and the net output of firm 2 is just the required input for firm 1.

For the closed system to have a non-negative solution, therefore, we require $(\mathbf{I} - \mathbf{A})\mathbf{y} = 0$. Ignoring the trivial solution of all $y_i = 0$, for a non-trivial solution to this homogeneous linear equation we require:[4]

$$|\mathbf{I}-\mathbf{A}|=0 \text{ or } \begin{vmatrix} 1 & -a_{12} \\ -a_{21} & 1 \end{vmatrix} = 0$$

i.e. $$a_{12}a_{21} = 1.$$

So far consideration has been given only to the production set, or the restrictions placed on the transactions matrix $(\mathbf{I}-\mathbf{A})$. But we have already seen in the Ricardian model of the firm that for a solution to be viable, i.e. for the decisions of the firm to be such that production will take place at a non-negative level, we require a consistent price vector. Let us therefore write out the profit functions for each firm and the economy.

$$\begin{aligned}\pi_1(\mathbf{p}) &= p_1y_1 + p_2y_{21} = (p_1 - a_{21}p_2)y_1 \\ \pi_2(\mathbf{p}) &= p_2y_2 + p_1y_{12} = (p_2 - a_{12}p_1)y_2 \\ \pi(\mathbf{p}) &= \pi_1(\mathbf{p}) + \pi_2(\mathbf{p}) \\ &= (p_1 - a_{21}p_2)y_1 + (p_2 - a_{21}p_1)y_2.\end{aligned}$$

Thus the economy's profits will be maximised at the zero level if

$$p_1 - a_{21}p_2 = 0$$

$$p_2 - a_{12}p_2 = 0$$

or $$\mathbf{p}'(\mathbf{I}-\mathbf{A}) = 0.$$

Once again we have a set of linear homogeneous equations and a non-trivial solution exists for $\mathbf{p} > 0$ if $|\mathbf{I}-\mathbf{A}| = 0$ as before. This implies

$$\frac{p_1}{p_2} = a_{21} \quad \text{and} \quad \frac{p_2}{p_1} = a_{12}.$$

However, in Fig. 6.9 the angle of $\boldsymbol{\beta}_1$ with respect to the y_2 axis is $1/a_{21}$ whilst the angle of $\boldsymbol{\beta}_2$ with respect to the y_2 axis is a_{12}. If we are to satisfy the conditions for a non-negative solution we must have the angles of $\boldsymbol{\beta}_1$ and $\boldsymbol{\beta}_2$ the same. What is implied, therefore, is that a viable solution exists if and only if the price vector coincides with this *single* vector $\boldsymbol{\beta}$ $(\boldsymbol{\beta}_1 = \boldsymbol{\beta}_2)$. In this instance $\mathbf{Y}_1$ and $\mathbf{Y}_2$ form a straight line through the origin, and $\mathbf{p} = \boldsymbol{\beta}$ is the normal to this line. In this instance also the projection of $\mathbf{Y}$ in the y_1–y_2 plane is the whole non-negative orthant and any level of y_1 and y_2 can be produced since the production possibility set is unbounded from above. In the case of the production set $\mathbf{Y}$ in Fig. 6.9 the projection in the y_1–y_2 plane covers all the non-negative orthant and is illustrated in Fig. 6.10. It is to be noticed that it is the mirror image of $\mathbf{Y}$.

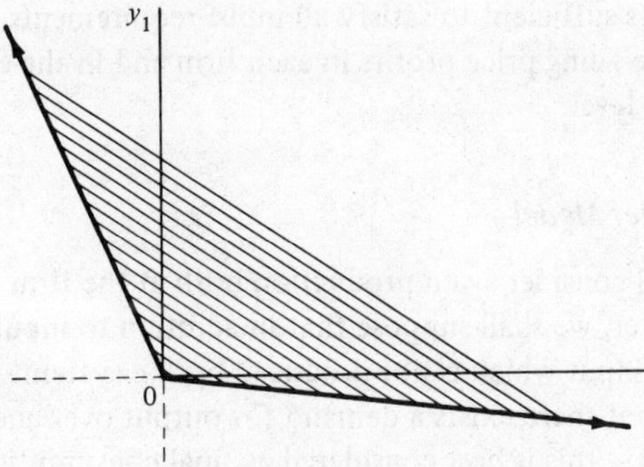

Fig. 6.10

The generalisation to the n commodity case is immediate. Both the input matrix and the transactions matrix are of order $n \times n$. The output and input vector **y** is of order $n \times 1$, and the price vector **p** is of order $n \times 1$. We can find a non-negative **y** and **p** satisfying

$$\begin{aligned} (\mathbf{I} - \mathbf{A})\,\mathbf{y} &= 0 \\ \mathbf{p}'(\mathbf{I} - \mathbf{A}) &= 0 \qquad (6.2) \end{aligned}$$

if $$|\mathbf{I} - \mathbf{A}| = 0.$$

Notice, however, that Equations (6.2) only establish the strucutre of the economy as embodied in the transactions matrix. The *scale* of the economy is indeterminate. This readily follows from Equation (6.2) since for any **p** and **y** satisfying (6.2) then $\lambda\mathbf{p}$ and $\lambda\mathbf{y}$, $\lambda > 0$ will also satisfy these equations. If the rank of **A** is $n-1$, then it is the ratios of outputs and prices which are determined by Equations (6.2). The scale of **y** and **p** is fixed only when we fix one output and one price, e.g. the labour supply and the wage rate. But then we have an open system because the exogeneous labour supply is not an output of the system.

Leontief systems are readily solved if we know the numerical values of a_{ij}. However, these in theoretical work are not known and it would be helpful therefore if we had some way of establishing whether a viable solution exists without such a knowledge. Investigations have shown that this can be done in terms of the characteristic roots of the **A** matrix.[5] Consider the simple example outlined above which, although unrealistic, does ease the understanding of the open Leontief model. The characteristic equation is

$$|\kappa\mathbf{I} - \mathbf{A}| = 0$$

if $\mathbf{A} = \begin{bmatrix} 0 & a_{12} \\ a_{21} & 0 \end{bmatrix}$ then the characteristic roots are $\lambda_1 = a_{12}a_{21}$ and $\lambda_2 = -a_{12}a_{21}$.

If we let λ^* denote the maximal characteristic root then if we are to have a viable solution $\lambda^* = a_{12}a_{21} = 1$. In other words, in a closed Leontiěf model, if the matrix **A** is such that its maximal characteristic root is equal to unity then the system will produce all net outputs sufficient to satisfy all input requirements and the situation will be such that at the going price profits in each firm and in the economy will be maximised at the zero level.

6.3 (ii) Open Leontief Model

In this section we shall consider again production both at the firm level and the economy level. However, we shall suppose that in addition to inputs produced by the system there is an input which is not produced by the system – best considered as labour – and also that there exists a demand for output over and above the demand by the system – this is best considered as final consumption demand. Labour need not be the only *basic* input; raw materials would be another example of an input which is not produced within the system. The introduction of final demand is an essential realism; for after all production is only a means to an end and that end is consumption.

First let us consider a firm which produces y_1 using an input y_2 produced elsewhere in the system and a basic resource r_1. For this firm we have:

$$y_{21} = -a_{21}y_1$$
$$r_{11} = -b_{11}y_1$$

where r_{ij} denotes the ith basic input employed by firm j, also a_{ij} and b_{ij} are defined as before. Let the prices of the commodities produced within the system be denoted p_1 and p_2, whilst the price of the basic input w_1. Then the profit function for firm 1 is

$$\pi_1(\mathbf{p}, \mathbf{w}) = p_1y_1 + p_2y_{21} + w_1r_{11}$$
$$= (p_1 - a_{21}p_2 - b_{11}w_1)y_1.$$

We see immediately that this is the situation discussed at the beginning of Section 6.3. A non-negative output will be produced if $p_1 - a_{21}p_2 - b_{11}w_1 \leqslant 0$, i.e. if and only if the price vector lies in the dual cone $\mathbf{Y}_1^*$, as illustrated in Fig. 6.8. Notice that the situation is undefined for $p_1 - a_{21}p_2 - b_{11}w_1 > 0$.

In this *partial* analysis it must be assumed that the solution for firm 1 is sufficient to cater for both the inter-sectoral demand for y_1 and the final demand for y_1. We cannot at the partial level establish whether this is so; we can only do this at the economy level.

Consider an economy composed of two firms. The inter-sectoral demand requirements are:

Firm 1	$y_{21} = -a_{21}y_1$	Firm 2	$y_{12} = -a_{12}y_2$
	$r_{11} = -b_{11}y_1$		$r_{12} = -b_{12}y_2.$

We can express the input requirements in matrix form. The inter-industry input requirement is

$$\begin{bmatrix} y_{12} \\ y_{21} \end{bmatrix} = \begin{bmatrix} -a_{12}y_2 \\ -a_{21}y_1 \end{bmatrix} = \begin{bmatrix} 0 & -a_{12} \\ -a_{21} & 0 \end{bmatrix} \begin{bmatrix} y_1 \\ y_2 \end{bmatrix} = -\mathbf{Ay}$$

while the basic input requirement is:

$$r_{11} + r_{12} = -(b_{11}y_1 + b_{12}y_2) = -[b_{11}, b_{12}] \begin{bmatrix} y_1 \\ y_2 \end{bmatrix} = -\mathbf{b}_1'\mathbf{y}.$$

For the economy as a whole we wish to find a vector **y** such that the output is sufficient to supply inter-industry demand, **Ay**, and a given total final demand, which we shall label $\mathbf{c}^0$; hence in the present example $\mathbf{c}^0 = (c_1^0, c_2^0)$. We also require that the total demand for the basic factor, $\mathbf{b}_1'\mathbf{y}$, does not exceed the given supply, r_1^0. We require, therefore,

$$\begin{aligned} \mathbf{y} &\geqslant \mathbf{Ay} + \mathbf{c}^0 & & (\mathbf{I} - \mathbf{A})\mathbf{y} \geqslant \mathbf{c}^0 \\ \mathbf{b}_1'\mathbf{y} &\leqslant r_1^0 & \text{or} \quad & \mathbf{b}_1'\mathbf{y} \leqslant r_1^0. \end{aligned} \tag{6.3}$$

The significance of Equations (6.3) can be aided by considering Fig. 6.11 and 6.12. Since there is a given resource endowment we have a truncated production cone $\hat{\mathbf{Y}}$, which has been derived from $\hat{\mathbf{Y}}_1$ and $\hat{\mathbf{Y}}_2$. The final consumption vector $\mathbf{c}^0$ is in the y_1–y_2 plane. Our problem is to find a $\mathbf{y} \geqslant 0$ which satisfies inter-industry demands and final demands. Consider now the profit function for the economy:

$$\begin{aligned} \pi(\mathbf{p}, \mathbf{w}) &= \pi_1(\mathbf{p}, \mathbf{w}) + \pi_2(\mathbf{p}, \mathbf{w}) \\ &= (p_1 - a_{21}p_2 - b_{11}w_1)y_1 + (p_2 - a_{12}p_1 - b_{12}w_1)y_2. \end{aligned}$$

For a viable solution we require each term in brackets to be non-positive since then $y_1, y_2 \geqslant 0$, i.e. we require:

$$\begin{aligned} & p_1 - a_{21}p_2 \leqslant b_{11}w_1 \quad \text{or} \quad [p_1, p_2] \begin{bmatrix} 1 & -a_{12} \\ -a_{21} & 1 \end{bmatrix} \leqslant w_1 \; [b_{11}, b_{12}] \\ & -a_{12}p_1 + p_2 \leqslant b_{12}w_1. \end{aligned}$$

In matrix notation:

$$\mathbf{p}'(\mathbf{I} - \mathbf{A}) \leqslant w_1\mathbf{b}_1'.$$

But we know that such a condition is met if $\mathbf{p} \in \hat{\mathbf{Y}}^*$ where $\mathbf{p} = (w_1, p_1, p_2)$, i.e. the dual cone to $\hat{\mathbf{Y}}$. But is this sufficient, will any $\mathbf{p} \in \hat{\mathbf{Y}}^*$ be such that the corresponding vector $\mathbf{y} \in \hat{\mathbf{Y}}$ will satisfy both inter-industry demand *and* final demand? Let us suppose that $\mathbf{c}^0 = (c_1^0, c_2^0)$ has strictly positive elements as illustrated in Fig. 6.12.

The set $\hat{\mathbf{Y}}_1$, in Fig. 6.11, denotes output of y_1 possible with input of y_2 and r_1 (up to $r_{11} = r_1^0$). Similarly, $\hat{\mathbf{Y}}_2$ denotes output of y_2 using inputs y_1 and r_1 (up to $r_{21} = r_1^0$). $\hat{\mathbf{Y}}$ denotes the economy's truncated production set. The set $\hat{\mathbf{Y}}$ lies below the horizontal plane $y_1 - y_2$. If this set is projected on to the $y_1 - y_2$ plane we obtain Pro $(\hat{\mathbf{Y}})$, as illustrated in Fig. 6.12. The dual cone to $\hat{\mathbf{Y}}$ is the cone $0D\boldsymbol{\beta}_1\boldsymbol{\beta}_2E$ in Fig. 6.12. The line 0D lies in the plane $y_2 - r_1$ and the cone $0D\boldsymbol{\beta}_1$ is the projection of $\boldsymbol{\beta}_1$ on to the $y_2 - r_1$ plane parallel to y_1 (compare Fig. 6.8).

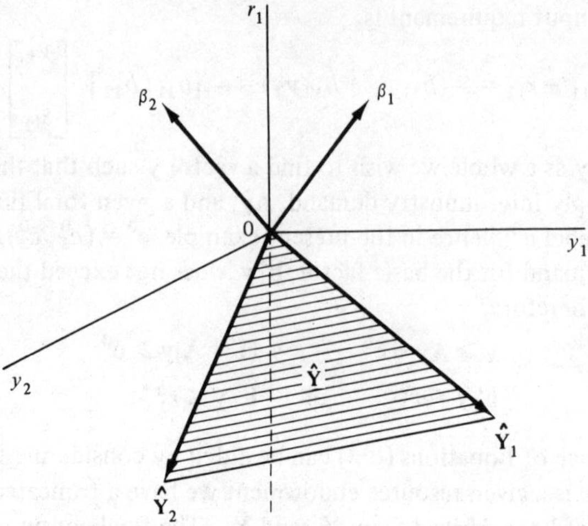

Fig. 6.11

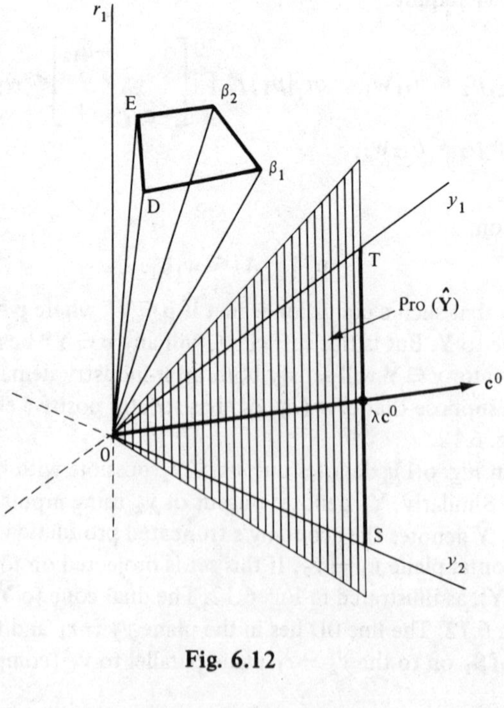

Fig. 6.12

Similarly, 0E lies in the plane $y_1 - r_1$ and the cone $0E\boldsymbol{\beta}_2$ is the projection of $\boldsymbol{\beta}$ on to the plane $y_1 - r_1$ parallel to y_2. Thus the cone $0D\boldsymbol{\beta}_1$ is $\hat{\mathbf{Y}}_1^*$ and $0E\boldsymbol{\beta}_2$ is $\hat{\mathbf{Y}}_2^*$. Finally, the cone $0D\boldsymbol{\beta}_1\boldsymbol{\beta}_2E$ is the cone $\hat{\mathbf{Y}}^*$, the dual cone of $\hat{\mathbf{Y}}$.

Now $\mathbf{p}$ will lie in the non-negative orthant. If $\mathbf{p} \in \hat{\mathbf{Y}}_1^*$ we know that $y_1 = 0$ and $y_2 > 0$, hence $\mathbf{y}$ lies on the $0y_2$ axis. If $\mathbf{p} \in \hat{\mathbf{Y}}_2^*$ then $y_2 = 0$ and $y_1 > 0$ so that y lies on the $0y_1$ axis. If $\mathbf{p} \in \text{Int}\ (\hat{\mathbf{Y}}^*)$ then both $y_1 = y_2 = 0$ and y is the origin. If $\mathbf{p} \in \text{Int}\ (\hat{\mathbf{Y}}^{\perp})$, the interior of the cone $\boldsymbol{\beta}_1\ 0\boldsymbol{\beta}_2$, then both y_1 and y_2 are positive and consequently y lies in the positive $y_1 - y_2$ plane. Given $\mathbf{c}^0$, which we scale down in the case illustrated in Fig. 6.12 to $\lambda\mathbf{c}^0$ so that it lies on the boundary of Pro $(\hat{\mathbf{Y}})$, then for inter-industry and $\lambda\mathbf{c}^0$ to be satisfied $\mathbf{p}$ must belong to Int $(\hat{\mathbf{Y}}^{\perp})$ such that its projection on to the $y_1 - y_2$ plane coincides with $\mathbf{c}^0$.

A number of features are exhibited by Fig. 6.12. First, the set 0ST denotes the production possibility set (see p. 131) and ST denotes the production possibility boundary. Second, for equilibrium we require all inter-industry demand and final demands to be met such that all the scarce basic factor is fully used; hence the solution must lie on ST. Third, if the price vector is unique then so is the solution. Finally, it is the introduction of prices which allows us to discard that part of Pro $(\hat{\mathbf{Y}})$ that is not in the non-negative orthant.

To summarise, for a given resource r_1^0 and a non-negative final demand vector $\mathbf{c}^0$ of order $n \times 1$ we can find a non-negative output vector $\mathbf{y} \geqslant 0$ of order $n \times 1$ which maximises $\pi\ (\mathbf{p}, w_1)$ at the zero level if

$$(\mathbf{I} - \mathbf{A})\mathbf{y} \geqslant \mathbf{c}^0 \quad \text{subject to} \quad \mathbf{b}_1'\mathbf{y} \leqslant r_1^0$$

and

$$\mathbf{p}'(\mathbf{I} - \mathbf{A}) \leqslant w_1\ \mathbf{b}_1'$$

where $\mathbf{A}$ is $n \times n$ and $\mathbf{b}_1'$ is $1 \times n$, the vector $\mathbf{p}$ being $n \times 1$ and w_1 the price of factor r_1. In other words, if $\mathbf{p} \in \hat{\mathbf{Y}}^*$ then a solution exists for non-negative $\mathbf{c}^0$. If $\mathbf{c}^0$ is strictly positive then we require $\mathbf{p} \in \text{Int}\ (\hat{\mathbf{Y}}^{\perp})$ if both inter-industry and final demands are to be met.

Also, we can immediately generalise to the s basic factor case by introducing once again the basic input matrix $\mathbf{B}$ of order $s \times n$. We have then to satisfy

$$(\mathbf{I} - \mathbf{A})\ \mathbf{y} \geqslant \mathbf{c}^0 \quad \text{subject to} \ \mathbf{By} \leqslant \mathbf{r}^0$$

$$\mathbf{p}'\ (\mathbf{I} - \mathbf{A}) \leqslant \mathbf{w}'\mathbf{B}$$

where now $\mathbf{w}$ is an $s \times 1$ vector of rentals and $\mathbf{r}^0$ is an $s \times 1$ vector of given basic factor endowments.

Implied in the above analysis are restrictions on the technology matrix $(\mathbf{I} - \mathbf{A})$ or, alternatively, on the input–output matrix $\mathbf{A}$. If $\mathbf{c}^0$ is given, and we shall suppose it has been scaled to lie on the production possibility boundary, then $(\mathbf{I} - \mathbf{A})\mathbf{y} = \mathbf{c}^0$ and if $(\mathbf{I} - \mathbf{A})$ is non-singular we have $\mathbf{y} = (\mathbf{I} - \mathbf{A})^{-1}\ \mathbf{c}^0$. However, even if $(\mathbf{I} - \mathbf{A})$ is non-singular this does not guarantee that $\mathbf{y} \geqslant 0$. Our problem amounts to finding under what conditions $(\mathbf{I} - \mathbf{A})^{-1} \geqslant 0$ so that $(\mathbf{I} - \mathbf{A})^{-1}\ \mathbf{c}^0 \geqslant 0$ if $\mathbf{c}^0 \geqslant 0$. The earliest statement of these conditions was that proposed by Hawkins and Simon and are referred to as the *Hawkins–Simon Conditions* [49].

Theorem 6.1 (Hawkins–Simon Conditions). If all the principal minors of $(\mathbf{I}-\mathbf{A})$ are positive then there exists a $\mathbf{y} \geqslant 0$ satisfying $(\mathbf{I}-\mathbf{A})\mathbf{y} \geqslant \mathbf{c}^0$, i.e. if

$$\begin{vmatrix} 1 & -a_{12} \\ -a_{21} & 1 \end{vmatrix} > 0, \ldots, \begin{vmatrix} 1 & -a_{12} & \cdots & -a_n \\ -a_{21} & 1 & \cdots & -a_{2n} \\ \vdots & & & \\ -a_{n1} & -a_{n2} & \cdots & 1 \end{vmatrix} > 0$$

then $\exists\ \mathbf{y} \geqslant 0$ satisfying $(\mathbf{I}-\mathbf{A})\mathbf{y} \geqslant \mathbf{c}^0$.

It is more usual now to formulate the conditions in terms of properties of the matrix **A** and its associated characteristic roots. We shall therefore return to these in the next section. Also another formulation has been proposed by Lionel McKenzie which is based on matrices with dominant diagonal elements. The reader interested in these formal properties will find discussions in Lancaster [73, p.7]; Nikaido [92, ch. 2.6]; and L. McKenzie [79].

One important implication of the Hawkins–Simon Conditions is that

$$\lim_{\nu \to \infty} \mathbf{A}^\nu = 0$$

and

$$(\mathbf{I}-\mathbf{A})^{-1} = \mathbf{I} + \mathbf{A} + \mathbf{A}^2 + \ldots$$

This result, as we shall see in the next section, holds if every characteristic root of **A** has modulus less than unity.[6] If this holds then we can express the output vector in the form

$$\mathbf{y} = \mathbf{c}^0 + \mathbf{A}\mathbf{c}^0 + \mathbf{A}^2\mathbf{c}^0 + \ldots + \mathbf{A}^\nu\mathbf{c}^0 + \ldots$$

This can be interpreted as follows. To obtain a net output $\mathbf{c}^0$ for final consumption the system requires $\mathbf{A}\mathbf{c}^0$ as input. But to produce $\mathbf{A}\mathbf{c}^0$ within the system a further $\mathbf{A}^2\mathbf{c}^0$ as input is required, and so on. Hence, the sum of $\mathbf{c}^0$ plus all inter-industry demands equals the output vector **y**.

The input–output model so far presented deals only with the production side of an economy. A more complete model would also take account of the demand for resources and the demand for final consumption goods. Whether an equilibrium exists in such a general model will be discussed in Chapter 9.5.

6.4 Decomposability and the Perron–Frobenius Theorem

Many commodities are outputs of one industry but not inputs into another. The output of canned fish, for example, is not an input into the production of coal. We see from the transactions matrix of 1968 for the United Kingdom that the 'output' of drink and tobacco is only an 'input' into agriculture, food, chemicals, etc., and miscellaneous services.[7] Consequently, many of the elements of **A** are in fact zero. The dependence or not of one industry on another can be discussed in terms of the *structure of the* **A**-*matrix.* The structure of concern to us is that of *decomposability.*

Definition 6.3

The matrix **A** is decomposable if we can find a permutation matrix Π such that

$$\Pi^{-1}\mathbf{A}\Pi = \begin{bmatrix} \mathbf{B}_{11} & \mathbf{B}_{12} \\ 0 & \mathbf{B}_{22} \end{bmatrix}$$

otherwise **A** is said to be indecomposable.

If **A** is $n \times n$ then $\mathbf{B}_{11}$ and $\mathbf{B}_{22}$ must be square; suppose $\mathbf{B}_{11}$ is $k \times k$ then $\mathbf{B}_{22}$ is $(n-k)\times(n-k)$ whilst $\mathbf{B}_{12}$ is $k \times (n-k)$, and 0 is a null matrix of order $(n-k) \times k$.

Decomposability means that a subset of equations can be considered independently of the complement subset, and is self-contained. This can be seen by considering the equation:

$$\mathbf{A}\mathbf{x} = \mu\mathbf{x}.$$

Suppose **A** is decomposable, as in Definition 6.3, then if we partition the vector **x** into $\mathbf{x}_1$ and $\mathbf{x}_2$ with elements k and n–k respectively, we can write the above equation as:

$$\begin{bmatrix} \mathbf{B}_{11} & \mathbf{B}_{12} \\ 0 & \mathbf{B}_{22} \end{bmatrix} \begin{bmatrix} \mathbf{x}_1 \\ \mathbf{x}_2 \end{bmatrix} = \mu \begin{bmatrix} \mathbf{x}_1 \\ \mathbf{x}_2 \end{bmatrix}.$$

Or in the form:

$$\begin{aligned} \mathbf{B}_{11}\mathbf{x}_1 + \mathbf{B}_{12}\mathbf{x}_2 &= \mu\mathbf{x}_1 \\ \mathbf{B}_{22}\mathbf{x}_2 &= u\mathbf{x}_2. \end{aligned}$$

Thus we can solve for $\mathbf{x}_2$ from $\mathbf{B}_{22}\mathbf{x}_2 = \mu\mathbf{x}_2$ independently of $\mathbf{x}_1$. However, to solve for $\mathbf{x}_1$ we require to know $\mathbf{x}_2$. Hence $\mathbf{x}_1$ depends on $\mathbf{x}_2$ but not conversely. Two-way independence would occur if $\mathbf{B}_{12} = 0$, and in this instance the **A** matrix, by suitable permutation, is block diagonal. This is sometimes referred to as *complete decomposability.* It is clear, therefore, that an indecomposable matrix implies that there are no subgroups of the system which are independent of the rest.

In relation to our input–output model, if **A** is decomposable into subgroups then for self-sufficient subgroups no inputs are required from industries outside that group. Furthermore, the output levels of industries not in the self-sufficient groups are independent of the output levels and final consumption levels of industries within the self-sufficient groups. This is readily verified as follows. If **A** is decomposable, as in Definition 6.3 then $(\mathbf{I}-\mathbf{A})\mathbf{y} = \mathbf{c}^0$ may be written:

$$\begin{bmatrix} (\mathbf{I}_1 - \mathbf{B}_{11}) & -\mathbf{B}_{12} \\ 0 & (\mathbf{I}_2 - \mathbf{B}_{22}) \end{bmatrix} \begin{bmatrix} \mathbf{y}_1 \\ \mathbf{y}_2 \end{bmatrix} = \begin{bmatrix} \mathbf{c}_1^0 \\ \mathbf{c}_2^0 \end{bmatrix} \tag{6.4}$$

where $\Pi^{-1}\mathbf{I}\Pi = \begin{bmatrix} \mathbf{I}_1 & 0 \\ 0 & \mathbf{I}_2 \end{bmatrix}$ and $\mathbf{y}$ and $\mathbf{c}$ have been broken down into conformable sub-vectors.

Taking the inverse of the left-hand matrix we get:

$$\begin{bmatrix} \mathbf{y}_1 \\ \mathbf{y}_2 \end{bmatrix} = \begin{bmatrix} (\mathbf{I}_1 - \mathbf{B}_{11})^{-1} & (\mathbf{I}_1 - \mathbf{B}_{11})^{-1}\,\mathbf{B}_{12}\,(\mathbf{I}_2 - \mathbf{B}_{22})^{-1} \\ 0 & (\mathbf{I}_2 - \mathbf{B}_{22})^{-1} \end{bmatrix} \begin{bmatrix} \mathbf{c}_1^0 \\ \mathbf{c}_2^0 \end{bmatrix}$$

i.e.

$$\begin{aligned} \mathbf{y}_1 &= (\mathbf{I}_1 - \mathbf{B}_{11})^{-1}\,\mathbf{c}_1^0 + (\mathbf{I}_1 - \mathbf{B}_{11})^{-1}\,\mathbf{B}_{12}(\mathbf{I}_2 - \mathbf{B}_{22})^{-1}\,\mathbf{c}_2^0 \\ \mathbf{y}_2 &= (\mathbf{I}_2 - \mathbf{B}_{22})^{-1}\,\mathbf{c}_2^0. \end{aligned} \tag{6.5}$$

Now the self-sufficient group of industries are the first k, as can be observed in the partitioned matrix of (6.4), with outputs $\mathbf{y}_1$ and final consumption levels of $\mathbf{c}_1^0$. The industries not in the self-sufficient group are the remaining $(n-k)$, and these have outputs $\mathbf{y}_2$ and final consumption levels of $\mathbf{c}_2^0$. Clearly, $\mathbf{y}_2$ is independent of $\mathbf{y}_1$ and $\mathbf{c}_1^0$. It is also immediate from equations (6.5) that if $\mathbf{B}_{12} = 0$ then both subgroups would be independent and outputs in each subgroup would depend only upon the final consumption level of that group.

Many of the properties of an industrial structure depend upon whether the input–output matrix $\mathbf{A}$ is indecomposable. In establishing exactly which properties, use is made of the Perron–Frobenius theorem. This theorem only refers to non-negative square matrices, and for such a matrix all elements $a_{ij} \geqslant 0$.

A matrix $\mathbf{A}$ is said to be non-negative if all $a_{ij} \geqslant 0$ and we can say $\mathbf{A} \geqslant 0$. If $\mathbf{A}$ is also square we talk of a non-negative square matrix. Now consider the very general equation.

$$\mathbf{A}\mathbf{x} = \rho\mathbf{x} + \mathbf{c}$$

or

$$(\rho\mathbf{I} - \mathbf{A})\,\mathbf{x} = \mathbf{c}$$

and notice that if $\rho = 1$ we have the Leontief situation. If $\mathbf{c} = 0$ then the characteristic equation of the matrix $\mathbf{A}$ is

$$\phi(\rho) = |\,\rho\mathbf{I} - \mathbf{A}\,| = 0$$

where $\phi(\rho)$ is a polynomial in terms of ρ of order the same as that of $\mathbf{A}$. Thus if $\mathbf{A}$ is $n \times n$ then $\phi(\rho)$ is of order n and consequently there are n characteristic roots or eigenvalues to this equation. Let $\{\lambda_i\}$ denote the set of n characteristic roots of $\mathbf{A}$ and let λ^* denote the characteristic root with the largest value. Also let $\mathbf{x}^*$ denote the characteristic vector associated with the characteristic root λ^*. The Perron–Frobenius theorem then states:

Theorem 6.2 (Perron–Frobenius Theorem). If $\mathbf{A} \geqslant 0$ and square then

(i) $\lambda^* \geqslant 0$ and $\mathbf{x}^* \geqslant 0$.

(ii) $(\rho\mathbf{I} - \mathbf{A})^{-1} \geqslant 0$ iff $\rho > \lambda^*$.

(iii) $\lambda^* \geqslant |\lambda_i| \ \forall i$.

(iv) If $\mathbf{Ax} \leqslant \rho\mathbf{x}$ for any real $\rho \geqslant 0$ and $\mathbf{x} \geqslant 0$ then $\lambda^* \leqslant \rho$.

Taking account of indecomposability strengthens some of the statements as follows:

Theorem 6.3 If $\mathbf{A} \geqslant 0$, square and indecomposable then

(i) $\lambda^* > 0$ and $\mathbf{x}^* \gg 0$.

(ii) $(\rho\mathbf{I} - \mathbf{A})^{-1} \gg 0$.

(iii) $\mathbf{x}^*$ is unique up to a scalar multiple.

Consider once again the closed Leontief model with $\mathbf{Ay} \leqslant \mathbf{y}$. In this instance $\rho = 1$ and by Theorem 6.2 (iv) $\lambda^* \leqslant 1$. Suppose $\lambda^* < 1$ then $\mathbf{Ay}^* = \lambda^*\mathbf{y}^* \ll \mathbf{y}^*$. But if $\mathbf{Ay}^* \ll \mathbf{y}^*$ this means the input requirement is less than the output from the system and there would therefore exist surplus commodities. To have an equilibrium with no surplus commodities we must have $\lambda^* = 1$ hence $\mathbf{Ay}^* = \mathbf{y}^*$. But we have already demonstrated that the Hawkins–Simon Conditions imply $\lambda^* = 1$ and this is where $\mathbf{p} = \boldsymbol{\beta}$ (i.e. $\mathbf{p}$ belongs to the dual of $\mathbf{Y}$).

In the open Leontief model if $\mathbf{c}^0 \geqslant 0$ then $(\mathbf{I} - \mathbf{A})^{-1}\mathbf{c}^0$ is always non-negative if $(\mathbf{I} - \mathbf{A})^{-1} \geqslant 0$. From Theorem 6.2 (ii) we know this is true if and only if $\lambda^* < 1$ (since again $\rho = 1$). If $\mathbf{A}$ is also indecomposable then $0 < \lambda^* < 1$ and by Theorem 6.3 (i) we have under this condition that $(\mathbf{I} - \mathbf{A})^{-1} \gg 0$ and also that $\mathbf{y}^* \gg 0$.

As an example consider the following square non-negative indecomposable matrix

$$\mathbf{A} = \begin{bmatrix} 0 & 0{\cdot}4 & 0{\cdot}6 \\ 0{\cdot}2 & 0 & 0{\cdot}8 \\ 0{\cdot}6 & 0{\cdot}3 & 0 \end{bmatrix} \quad \text{then } (\mathbf{I} - \mathbf{A})^{-1} = \frac{1}{0{\cdot}092} \begin{bmatrix} 0{\cdot}76 & 0{\cdot}58 & 0{\cdot}92 \\ 0{\cdot}68 & 0{\cdot}64 & 0{\cdot}92 \\ 0{\cdot}66 & 0{\cdot}54 & 0{\cdot}92 \end{bmatrix}$$

It is clear that $(\mathbf{I} - \mathbf{A})^{-1} \gg 0$ and that so long as $\mathbf{c}^0 \gg 0$ then $\mathbf{y} \gg 0$. As a second example take the *gross* input–output matrix

$$\mathbf{A}^* = \begin{bmatrix} 0{\cdot}2 & 0{\cdot}4 \\ 0{\cdot}3 & 0{\cdot}5 \end{bmatrix} \quad \text{then } (\mathbf{I} - \mathbf{A}^*)^{-1} = \frac{1}{0{\cdot}28} \begin{bmatrix} 0{\cdot}5 & 0{\cdot}4 \\ 0{\cdot}3 & 0{\cdot}8 \end{bmatrix}$$

and hence $(\mathbf{I} - \mathbf{A}^*)^{-1} \gg 0$. Also the characteristic roots are $0{\cdot}7375$ and $-0{\cdot}0375$, hence $0 < \lambda^* < 1$ and $\lambda^* > |\lambda|$ where $\lambda^* = 0{\cdot}7375$ and $\lambda = -0{\cdot}0375$. Finally, it can readily be shown that the characteristic vector of unit length is strictly positive (see Exercise 10).

The analysis in this section only barely hints at the interpretation of input–output analysis in terms of the properties of non-negative square matrices and the implications of indecomposability. But it is hoped that the earlier diagrammatic treatment gives the reader a feel for these abstract ways of specifying the viability of production in an input–output framework.

6.5 Activity Analysis

At the firm level activity analysis has much more to offer than the input–output model, and it can be considered as a compromise between the input–output model, which allows no substitution between inputs, and the neoclassical model – to be discussed in the next chapter – which allows an infinite degree of substitution between inputs. In this section, therefore, we shall pay particular attention to the firm rather than the economy.

Activity analysis is characterised by having at least two, but finite, number of processes or activities. To illustrate the features of activity analysis we shall consider a firm producing a single output, y_1, by means of three possible processes, each process employing two inputs y_2 and y_3. Let a_{vh} denote the vth input used in employing the hth technique to produce one unit of output, hence $v = 2, 3$ and $h = 1, 2, 3$. We once again assume that the input requirement is proportional to output but that this proportionality factor differs for each activity. Thus the input requirement of y_2 and y_3 by means of the first activity is $y_{21} = -a_{21}y_1$ and $y_{31} = -a_{31}y_1$ respectively. All input requirements for each activity are displayed as follows:

	Activity 1	*Activity 2*	*Activity 3*
Output	$y_1 = 1$	$y_1 = 1$	$y_1 = 1$
Input 2	$-a_{21}y_1$	$-a_{22}y_1$	$-a_{23}y_1$
Input 3	$-a_{31}y_1$	$-a_{32}y_1$	$-a_{33}y_1$

Let $\mathbf{A}^h = (1, y_{2h}, y_{3h}) = (1, -a_{2h}, -a_{3h})$ then $\mathbf{A}^h$ represents the ray which gives the input requirements of y_2 and y_3 required to produce one unit of y_1 by means of the hth activity. The rays $\mathbf{A}^h$ in Fig. 6.13 satisfy all points on $(\lambda, \lambda y_{2h}, \lambda y_{3h})$ $h = 1, 2, 3$. Hence, the production set for firm 1, $\mathbf{Y}_1$, is the convex polyhedral cone formed by the activity rays $\mathbf{A}^h$ with the vertex at the origin. This convex cone follows from the axioms of proportionality and additivity along with Axiom 18, the feasibility of no free production. It can also be demonstrated as follows. Consider a linear combination of the set of activities

$$\sum_h \beta_h \mathbf{A}^h = \sum_h \beta_h \, a_{vh} \qquad \beta_h \geqslant 0, v = 1, 2, 3$$

where $a_{11} = 1$. But $\beta_h \mathbf{A}^h$ constitutes the ray $\mathbf{A}^h$ in Fig. 6.13, and this is a half-line. Consequently this equation denotes the sum of three half-lines and by Definition 5.4 constitutes a convex polyhedral cone.

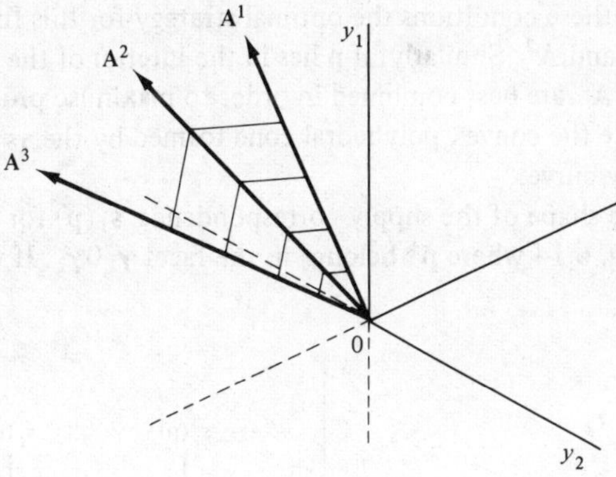

Fig. 6.13. Production set for a firm in activity analysis

Consider now the profit function for this firm:

$$\pi_1(\mathbf{p}) = p_1 y_1 + p_2 y_{21} + p_3 y_{31}$$

Let π_1^h denote the profit for firm 1 employing the hth activity, then

$$\pi_1^1(\mathbf{p}) = (p_1 - a_{21}p_2 - a_{31}p_3)y_1$$
$$\pi_1^2(\mathbf{p}) = (p_1 - a_{22}p_2 - a_{32}p_3)y_1$$
$$\pi_1^3(\mathbf{p}) = (p_1 - a_{23}p_2 - a_{33}p_3)y_1.$$

Similar to the analysis at the beginning of Section 6.3, let $\boldsymbol{\gamma}_h = (1, a_{2h}, a_{3h})$ $h = 1, 2, 3$ denote the orthogonal vectors to $\mathbf{A}^h$ as drawn in Fig. 6.13. The cone formed by the rays $\boldsymbol{\gamma}_h$ is a convex polyhedral cone. It also follows from construction that the facets $\mathbf{A}^1 0 \mathbf{A}^2$ and $\boldsymbol{\gamma}_1 0 \boldsymbol{\gamma}_2$ are orthogonal; and similarly for the remaining two facets of each of the cones.

For any given price vector $\mathbf{p} = (p_1, p_2, p_3)$ a number of possibilities are available. If $\mathbf{p}$ coincides with $\boldsymbol{\gamma}_1$ then activity 1 will be used and it follows from construction that $\mathbf{p}$ will be less than the slopes of $\boldsymbol{\gamma}_2$ and $\boldsymbol{\gamma}_3$. This means

$$\pi_1^1(\mathbf{p}) = 0, \pi_1^2(\mathbf{p}) < 0 \text{ and } \pi_1^3(\mathbf{p}) < 0$$

so that activities $\mathbf{A}^2$ and $\mathbf{A}^3$ will not be employed. Similarly, if $\mathbf{p}$ coincides with $\boldsymbol{\gamma}_2$, the optimal strategy for the firm is to supply all of y_1 by means of activity $\mathbf{A}^2$. And the same holds for $\mathbf{p}$ coinciding with $\boldsymbol{\gamma}_3$. If $\mathbf{p}$ lies in the interior of the cone formed by the $\boldsymbol{\gamma}$'s then $\pi_1^h(\mathbf{p}) < 0$, for all h. This means under such conditions the optimal strategy is not to produce at all. In other words, production is inefficient. If **p** lies in the interior of the facet $\gamma_1 0 \gamma_2$ it follows

$$\pi_1^1(\mathbf{p}) = 0, \pi_1^2(\mathbf{p}) = 0 \text{ and } \pi_1^3(\mathbf{p}) < 0.$$

In other words, under these conditions the optimal strategy for this firm is to combine activities $\mathbf{A}^1$ and $\mathbf{A}^2$. Similarly, if **p** lies in the interior of the facet $\gamma_2 0 \gamma_3$ then activities $\mathbf{A}^2$ and $\mathbf{A}^3$ are best combined in order to maximise profits. And so on. Any **p** lying outside the convex polyhedral cone formed by the γs will give rise to an undefined supply curve.

Let us look into the shape of the supply correspondence, $\mathbf{s}_1(\mathbf{p})$ for such a producer. Consider Fig. 6.14 where $\mathbf{p}^*$ belongs to the facet $\gamma_1 0 \gamma_2$. If we think of

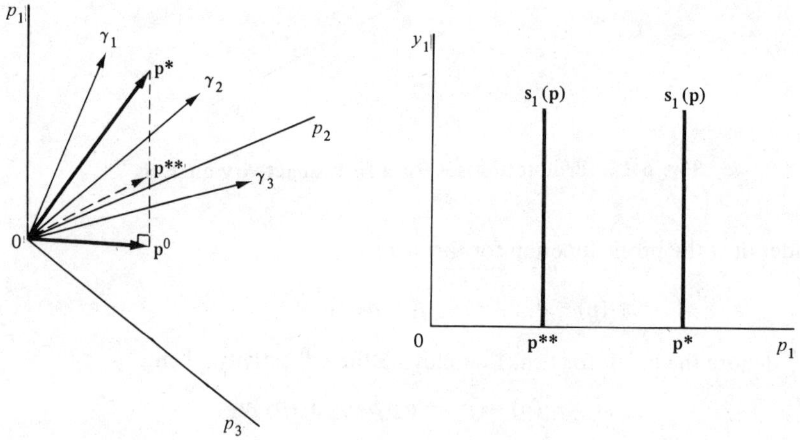

Fig. 6.14

p projected orthogonally on to the $p_2 - p_3$ plane then any **p** belonging to the projection plane $\mathbf{p}^* 0 \mathbf{p}^0$ denotes a varying p_1 with p_2 and p_3 held constant. If $\mathbf{p} = \mathbf{p}^*$ then y_1 is produced by a combination of activities $\mathbf{A}^1$ and $\mathbf{A}^2$, i.e. $\mathbf{s}_1(\mathbf{p})$ is infinitely elastic at $\mathbf{p}^*$ and the processes used are $\mathbf{A}^1$ and $\mathbf{A}^2$. As p_1 falls (hence **p** moves between $\mathbf{p}^*$ and $\mathbf{p}^0$) the vector **p** will almost certainly become interior to the cone formed by the γs. In this case no production is undertaken since $\pi_1^h(\mathbf{p}) < 0$, for all h. However, there will come a price p_1 at which **p** will intersect one of the remaining facets either at its interior, as shown by $\mathbf{p}^{**}$ which is interior to $\gamma_2 0 \gamma_3$, or in one of the rays. In either case an infinite supply is forthcoming, except that now it is by means of a different technique.

The above analysis shows only the effect of a change in the product price. To obtain the effect of a change in the factor prices it is helpful to consider the problem in the input space. In Fig. 6.13 imagine a plane, parallel to the $y_2 - y_3$ plane, which cuts the convex cone $\mathbf{Y}_1$ at $y_1 = 1$. The set formed by the intersection is the isoproduct set corresponding to a unit output of commodity 1. Alternatively, we can imagine the activity rays $\mathbf{A}^h$ projected into the input plane, $y_2 - y_3$ as illustrated in Fig. 6.15, and BCD to be the projection of the isoproduct set in the input plane – this representation of activity analysis being the most familiar. Furthermore, for efficient production only activities $\mathbf{A}^1\mathbf{A}^2$ and $\mathbf{A}^2\mathbf{A}^3$ will be combined since any point on the line segment BD can be replaced by a point either on **BC** or on **CD** and so the same output can be attained by less inputs.

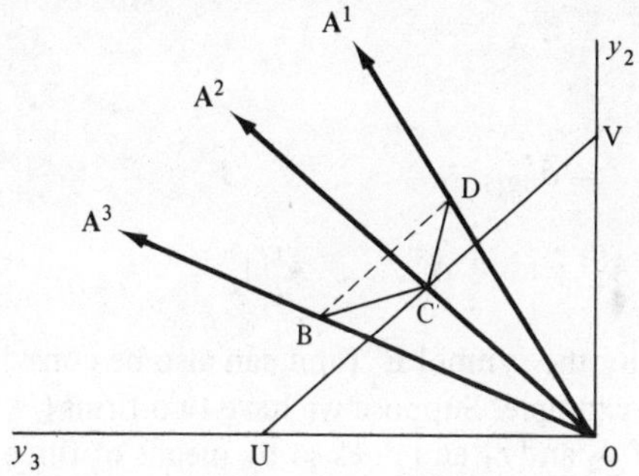

Fig. 6.15. Isoproduct set in input space

Consider now the isocost line for firm 1 given by $c_1^h = p_2 y_{21} + p_3 y_{31}$ where c_1^h is the cost associated with activity h. If the product and factor prices are given then the minimisation of $c_1^h = -a_{2h}p_2 - a_{3h}p_3$ must be equivalent to the maximisation of $\pi_1^h(\mathbf{p}) = (p_1 - a_{2h}p_2 - a_{3h}p_3)y_1$. If we concentrate solely on the input prices p_2 and p_3 the isocost line c_1^h will determine the activity h which will be operated as illustrated by activity $\mathbf{A}^2$ determined by UV in Fig. 6.15. A change in the product prices such that UV coincides with, say, BC will mean the firm undertakes a change in the technique of production, viz. from that represented by $\mathbf{A}^2$ to one which combines activities $\mathbf{A}^2$ and $\mathbf{A}^3$. For the firm in activity analysis, therefore, *substitution up to a degree is present.* Also revealing in the present analysis is that a change in the relative factor prices does not necessarily bring about a change in technique; the change in factor prices may have to be considerable before such a change takes place. It is this feature which is one of the most important predictions of activity analysis at the firm level and it is this which largely distinguishes it from Leontief input–output and neoclassical analysis. It is also to be noted how crucial this prediction arises out of the condition that the production set is a convex polyhedral cone which in turn rests on the additivity and proportionality axioms among others.

Let us now turn to the economy. Let $a_{\nu hj}$ denotes the ν^{th}input used by means of the hth activity to produce one unit of output by the jth firm. Hence, $\mathbf{A}_j^h$ denotes the hth activity ray for the jth firm. We can exhibit the various techniques by the l firms in terms of the following matrix, where we assume the jth firm has g_j activities $\sum_{j=1}^{l} g_j = g$ and so the matrix is of order $n \times lg$.

$$
n\left\{\begin{bmatrix}
\overbrace{1 & \cdots & 1}^{l} & \cdots & \overbrace{-a_{11l} & \cdots & -a_{1g_l l}}^{l} \\
-a_{211} & \cdots & -a_{2g_1 1} & & -a_{21l} & \cdots & -a_{2g_l l} \\
-a_{311} & \cdots & -a_{3g_1 1} & & -a_{31l} & \cdots & -a_{3g_l l} \\
\cdot & & \cdot & & \cdot & & \cdot \\
\cdot & & \cdot & & \cdot & & \cdot \\
\cdot & & \cdot & & \cdot & & \cdot \\
-a_{n11} & \cdots & -a_{ng_1 1} & \cdots & 1 & \cdots & 1
\end{bmatrix}\right.
$$

$$= [\mathbf{A}_1^1, \ldots, \mathbf{A}_1^{g_1} \vdots \ldots \vdots \mathbf{A}_l^1, \ldots, \mathbf{A}_l^{g_l}].$$

We shall denote this by the symbol $\bar{\mathbf{E}}_a$ (and can also be considered as $\bar{\mathbf{E}}_a = (\mathbf{I} - \mathbf{E}_a)$).

To take a specific example. Suppose we have two firms ($j = 1, 2$). Firm 1 produces y_1 by means of y_2 and r_1 and does so by means of three possible activities whilst firm 2 produces y_2 by means of y_1 and r_1 and does so by means of four activities. We then have

$$
\bar{\mathbf{E}}_a = \left[\begin{array}{ccc|cccc}
1 & 1 & 1 & -a_{112} & -a_{122} & -a_{132} & -a_{142} \\
-a_{211} & -a_{221} & -a_{231} & 1 & 1 & 1 & 1
\end{array}\right]
$$

and this is subject to the fact that for any activities, say h and k, used by firm 1 and 2 respectively we must have

$$\beta_{1h1} y_1 + \beta_{1k2} y_2 \leqslant r_1^0$$

where β_{1hj} is the labour input (basic resource r_1) required in the hth activity to produce one unit of the jth firm's output.

However, for a given price vector only one activity, or linear combination of two adjacent activities, will be profit maximising for the jth firm and so only $l(=n)$ columns of $\bar{\mathbf{E}}_a$ will be relevant (some of these l being formed from a linear combination of two columns of $\bar{\mathbf{E}}_a$). Let this matrix be denoted $\bar{\mathbf{A}}$. Thus $\bar{\mathbf{A}}$ has each column representing the profit-maximising activity for each firm. We can, therefore, suppress the activity subscript and let

$$
\bar{\mathbf{A}} = \begin{bmatrix}
1 & -a_{12} & \cdots & -a_{1n} \\
-a_{21} & 1 & & -a_{2n} \\
\cdot & \cdot & & \cdot \\
\cdot & \cdot & & \cdot \\
\cdot & \cdot & & \cdot \\
-a_{n1} & -a_{n2} & \cdots & 1
\end{bmatrix}
$$

$l = n$ since we are assuming that each firm produces only one output as in the Leontief model. The difference is that now $\bar{\mathbf{A}}$ refers to the activities which are profit maximising for each firm, whilst in the Leontief model $\bar{\mathbf{A}}$ could only take one form: the a_{ij} were given for each firm.

Does it follow that such an economy allows substitution because as product and factor prices change the columns of the $\bar{\mathbf{A}}$ matrix, derived from $\bar{\mathbf{E}}_a$, change? The answer to this question rests on the number of basic factors contained in the model. Suppose there is only *one* basic factor which is fixed in supply, best considered as labour (r_1^0). Under these circumstances the convex polyhedral cones for each firm in the economy are truncated. Now project the set which denotes the maximum that can be produced by the different techniques into the input space and then project this into the output space. For example, if once again we have firm 1 producing y_1 by means of y_2 and r_1 and it can do so by means of three activities; while firm 2 produces y_2 by means of y_1 and r_1 and can do so by means of four activities; the situation after *both* transformations is illustrated in Fig. 6.16. As drawn only activity $\mathbf{A}_1^1$ is used by firm 1 and only $\mathbf{A}_2^4$ by firm 2. Regardless of final demand, therefore, this result will always be true in the present model, final demand merely positioning itself along the production possibility boundary ST.

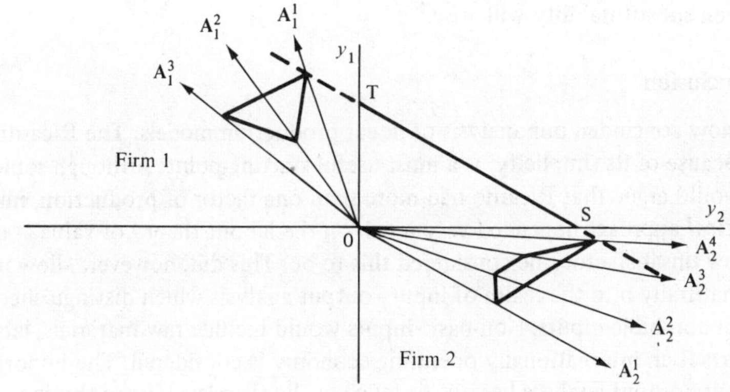

Fig. 6.16

It is possible that two activities are combined in this optimal state but once they have been a single activity represents each firm. The reason for this lies in the fact that with a single basic factor only one (or combination of adjacent two) activities can be labour saving. If all labour is used we have

$$\mathbf{p}'(\mathbf{I}-\mathbf{A}) = w_1\mathbf{b}_1' \quad \text{or} \quad \left(\frac{\mathbf{p}}{w_1}\right)' = \mathbf{b}_1'\,(\mathbf{I}-\mathbf{A})^{-1}$$

so that if w_1 increases by an amount λ then relative prices will remain unchanged and they depend solely on the direct and indirect labour content used in the production of $y_1, \ldots, y_n$. The matrix $\bar{\mathbf{E}}_a$ of the above example was given earlier and the matrix $\bar{\mathbf{A}}$ corresponding to the situation displayed in Fig. 6.16 is

$$\bar{\mathbf{A}} = \begin{bmatrix} 1 & -a_{12} \\ -a_{21} & 1 \end{bmatrix}$$

and

$$b_{11}y_1 + b_{12}y_2 = r_1^0$$

where activity 1 and 4 for firms 1 and 2 have been suppressed.

The conclusion drawn from this analysis is that with a single basic input, and whether each firm has more than one possible process, there will only be one process observable for a given technology. This is Samuelson's *substitution theorem*[8].

If, however, there were more than one basic input which was also limited in supply, e.g. capital, then the production possibility boundary would have a variety of vertices and substitution would take place. For one set of prices it may be that a labour-saving technique is most appropriate whilst at another set of prices it is a capital-saving technique which is employed. Although at any one time only a single $\bar{\mathbf{A}}$ can be observed from $\bar{\mathbf{E}}_a$, with more than one basic input and given technology more than one $\bar{\mathbf{A}}$ can be derived from $\bar{\mathbf{E}}_a$ and which depends upon the prices of factors and commodities. Finally, it is to be noted that we have throughout assumed no joint production. Even with a single basic output if joint production is present then substitutability will arise.[9]

6.6 Conclusion

We have now concluded our analysis of linear production models. The Ricardian model, because of its simplicity, is a most useful starting-point. Although some authors would argue that Ricardo had more than one factor of production, much of his *analytical* approach depended very much on the labour theory of value – no matter how unsatisfactory he considered this to be. This did, however, allow us to progress naturally into the realm of input–output analysis which distinguished basic from non-basic inputs. Non-basic inputs would include raw materials, labour, and imports if an internationally operating economy is considered. The importance of the input–output analysis lies not so much at the firm level, since this is not really any further developed than the Ricardian interpretation, but rather at the economy level where a general equilibrium analysis can be pursued. Finally, we find the generalisation allowed us by activity analysis is that each firm supplies indeterminate amounts but it can be supplied by a variety of different techniques depending upon the given price set. The most important prediction from activity analysis, at least at the firm level, is that substitution can take place but may require considerable changes in factor prices before this is carried out. At the economy level Samuelson has shown that if there is only one basic factor limited in supply then only one technique will be observed for each firm and no substitution will take place for a given technology. If, however, there is more than one basic input or if there is joint production then this non-substitution no longer holds.

EXERCISES

1. Construct the total cost, average cost and marginal cost curves corresponding to the Ricardian model of production.

2. In the Ricardian model with resource limitations is the profit function continuous? Is it semi-continuous? Is the supply correspondence continuous?

3. In the Ricardian model of production let $b_{11} = 5$. Draw the production set $\mathbf{Y}_1$ and its dual. Which of the following price sets will give rise to production?

(i) $\mathbf{p}^1 = (4, 2)$ (ii) $\mathbf{p}^2 = (2, 10)$ (iii) $\mathbf{p}^3 = (2, 15)$.

Suppose $r_1^0 = 100$. At that price set which gives rise to production obtain the maximum profit $\pi_1^0(\mathbf{p})$.

4. Suppose a second firm is present in the Ricardian model with $b_{12} = 10$. Draw a figure showing $\mathbf{Y}_1$, $\mathbf{Y}_2$ and $\mathbf{Y}$. Discuss the production situation of the economy for each of the following price sets, where $\mathbf{p} = (w_1, p_1, p_2)$.

(i) $\mathbf{p}^1 = (4, 2, 6)$ (iii) $\mathbf{p}^3 = (1, 5, 10)$

(ii) $\mathbf{p}^2 = (2, 10, 15)$ (iv) $\mathbf{p}^4 = (2, 15, 25)$.

5. Let

$$\text{(i)}\quad \mathbf{A} = \begin{bmatrix} 0 & 0{\cdot}2 \\ 0{\cdot}5 & 0 \end{bmatrix} \qquad \text{(ii)}\quad \mathbf{A} = \begin{bmatrix} 0 & 0{\cdot}4 \\ 2{\cdot}5 & 0 \end{bmatrix} \qquad \text{(iii)}\quad \mathbf{A} = \begin{bmatrix} 0 & 2{\cdot}4 \\ 1{\cdot}0 & 0 \end{bmatrix}.$$

In each case establish whether a non-trivial solution exists for the economy. Show that the two characteristic roots are the same and are less than unity, equal to unity and greater than unity respectively.

6. Let

$$\mathbf{A} = \begin{bmatrix} 0 & 0{\cdot}2 \\ 0{\cdot}5 & 0 \end{bmatrix}.$$

Given $(b_{11}, b_{12}) = (5, 10)$ establish for each of the following price sets, where $\mathbf{p} = (w_1, p_1, p_2)$, whether $\mathbf{p}'(\mathbf{I} - \mathbf{A}) \leqslant w_1 \mathbf{b}_1'$.

(i) $\mathbf{p}^1 = (4, 2, 6)$.
(ii) $\mathbf{p}^2 = (1, 7, 4)$.
(iii) $\mathbf{p}^3 = (1, 100/9, 110/9)$.

7. Carry out the same tests as in Exercise 6 given that

$$\mathbf{A} = \begin{bmatrix} 0 & 0{\cdot}4 \\ 2{\cdot}5 & 0 \end{bmatrix}.$$

Show that there is no $\mathbf{y} \geqslant 0$ for this economy.

8. Given
$$A = \begin{bmatrix} 0 & 0{\cdot}2 \\ 0{\cdot}5 & 0 \end{bmatrix}$$
show that $|\mathbf{I}-\mathbf{A}| = 0{\cdot}9$, and obtain $(\mathbf{I}-\mathbf{A})^{-1}$. Given $\mathbf{c}^0 = (10, 20)$ obtain $\mathbf{y}$.

9. Establish which of the following matrices are decomposable:

(i) $\mathbf{A} = \begin{bmatrix} 0 & 3 & 2 \\ 0 & 2 & 0 \\ 4 & 6 & 4 \end{bmatrix}$ (ii) $\mathbf{A} = \begin{bmatrix} 1 & 3 & 0 \\ 1 & 3 & 4 \\ 2 & 2 & 2 \end{bmatrix}$ (iii) $\mathbf{A} = \begin{bmatrix} 2 & 1 & 0 \\ 0 & 2 & 0 \\ 3 & 4 & 6 \end{bmatrix}$.

10. For the *gross* output case $\mathbf{A}^* = \begin{bmatrix} 0{\cdot}2 & 0{\cdot}4 \\ 0{\cdot}3 & 0{\cdot}5 \end{bmatrix}$ show that $\lambda^* = 0{\cdot}7375$ and that $\lambda^* > |\lambda|$ where λ is the remaining characteristic root. Also show that the characteristic vector of unit length $\mathbf{y}^* = (0{\cdot}5970, 0{\cdot}8022)$ is a strictly positive vector. Furthermore, demonstrate $(\mathbf{I}-\mathbf{A}^*)^{-1} \gg 0$.

11. Given $\mathbf{A} = \begin{bmatrix} 2 & 9 \\ 1 & 2 \end{bmatrix}$

(i) Show that $\mathbf{A} \geqslant 0$.
(ii) Is $\mathbf{A}$ indecomposable?
(iii) Show that λ^*, the characteristic root with the largest absolute value, is $\lambda^* = 5$.
(iv) Obtain the characteristic vector associated with λ^* and establish whether it has positive elements.

12. Explain why the isoproduct set in activity analysis must be a convex set, paying particular attention to the conditions which must be met for efficient production.

13. Obtain the total cost, average cost and marginal cost curves for a firm under activity analysis.

7

NON-LINEAR PRODUCTION THEORY

7.1 Introduction

Non-linear theories of the firm stem very much from the work of the neoclassicists. Its very non-linearity is both a gain and a limitation. It is a gain in the sense that it introduces a greater realism at the firm level, but it is a limitation in the sense that it is almost impossible to generalise to the economy level. The non-linear approach rests almost wholly on the differential calculus as its tool of analysis. This is not hard to understand when one realises that the *margin* is no more than the first derivative of a function. We have already seen in the theory of consumer behaviour that the margin was central in discussions of marginal utility and the marginal rate of substitution. In the theory of the firm also the margin plays a central role in marginal product, marginal rate of technical substitution, and marginal cost.

The central character in the non-linear theory of production is the *production function,* which we shall discuss in the next section. It is worthy of attention in its own right because so much of the literature is either directly or indirectly concerned with it. For example, the cost functions follow on from and are not independent of the form of the production function.

7.2 The Production Function

A production function denotes the maximum output that can be obtained from a set of inputs. It is a function in the mathematical sense because it is assumed that to each set of inputs there is a unique maximum output. Hence, a production function is a mapping from the input space, **X**, into the output space, which we shall denote $\overline{Q}$. Let $\mathbf{x} = (x_1, \ldots, x_s)$ denote a vector of inputs $\mathbf{x} \geqslant 0, \mathbf{x} \in \mathbf{X}$, and let $q \in \overline{Q}$ denote the quantity of output. We shall assume there is a single output. For any $\mathbf{x} \in \mathbf{X}$ there is a unique $q \in \overline{Q}$ which is the maximum.

Definition 7.1

If $\mathbf{X}$ is the input space and $\bar{Q}$ the output space, a production function is a mapping of the form:

$$f\colon \mathbf{X} \to \bar{Q} \quad \text{or} \quad q = f(x_1, \ldots, x_s).$$

In the present section we shall be concerned with the properties of f and the various forms it has taken in the literature. Two commonly used production functions, chosen for their mathematical properties and possibility of being empirically estimated, are:

(*a*) The Cobb–Douglas production function, which for the two-input case takes the form

$$q = a_0 x_1^{a_1} x_2^{a_2} \qquad a_0, a_1 a_2 > 0$$

or more generally,

$$q = a_0 \prod_{i=1}^{s} x_i^{a_i} \qquad a_i > 0 \ \forall\, i.$$

(*b*) The Constant Elasticity of Substitution production function, which for the two-input case takes the form

$$q = a_0 \, [a_1 x_1^{-\rho} + a_2 x_2^{-\rho}]^{-\nu/\rho} \qquad a_0, a_1, a_2 > 0, \nu > 0, \rho \geqslant -1$$

or more generally,

$$q = a_0 \left[\sum_{i=1}^{s} a_i x_i^{-\rho} \right]^{-\nu/\rho} \qquad a_i > 0 \ \forall i, \nu > 0, \rho \geqslant -1.$$

In this section we shall consider only the continuous forms of f.

What makes f continuous? If the inputs are continuously divisible then the input space, $\mathbf{X}$, is connected. Even if this requirement is met, however, we cannot establish the continuity of the production function: we can only assume it to be continuous, and then derive the implications of such an assumption.

Assumption The production function $f\colon \mathbf{X} \to \bar{Q}$ is continuous.

Even if f is continuous it may not be differentiable at every point $\mathbf{x} \in \mathbf{X}$. If f is differentiable at least up to the second order then by assumption $f_i = \partial q/\partial x_i$ and $f_{ij} = \partial^2 q/\partial x_i \, \partial x_j$ exists for all $i, j = 1, \ldots, s$; and are themselves continuous. Let $\mathbf{q}_x$ denote the column vector of all first derivatives, and $\mathbf{Q}$ the matrix of all second-order derivatives, i.e.

$$\mathbf{q}_x = \frac{\partial q}{\partial \mathbf{x}} = \begin{bmatrix} f_1 \\ f_2 \\ \cdot \\ \cdot \\ \cdot \\ f_s \end{bmatrix} \qquad \mathbf{Q} = \frac{\partial \mathbf{q}_x}{\partial \mathbf{x}'} = \begin{bmatrix} f_{11} & f_{12} & \cdots & f_{1s} \\ f_{21} & f_{22} & & f_{2s} \\ \cdot & & & \cdot \\ \cdot & & & \cdot \\ \cdot & & & \cdot \\ f_{s1} & f_{s2} & \cdots & f_{ss} \end{bmatrix}.$$

From elementary economics we know that the marginal product of the ith input is the amount by which q changes due to an infinitesimal change in x_i, all other inputs held constant. Hence, $f_i = \partial q/\partial x_i$ denotes the marginal product of the ith input. The fact that the marginal product is increasing, constant, or decreasing depends upon whether f_{ii} is greater than, equal to, or less than zero. Notice that both f_i and f_{ij} are functions of $x_1, \ldots, x_s$. f_{ii} denotes the slope of the marginal product function and f_{ij} $(i \neq j)$ denotes the shift in the marginal product curve due to an exogenous change in x_j. If $f_{ii} < 0$ we have a situation of *diminishing returns.*

We can illustrate most of the points just raised by considering the simple case $q = f(x_1, x_2)$ sketched in Fig. 7.1. First we shall hold x_2 fixed at x_2^0. Then $q = f(x_1, x_2^0)$ denotes the *total* product curve of x_1, and $f_1 = f_1(x_1, x_2^0)$ is the *marginal* product curve of x_1. Similar relationships hold for x_2. Another relationship of interest is the *average* product curve. This is the total output divided by the input of the factor we are interested in.

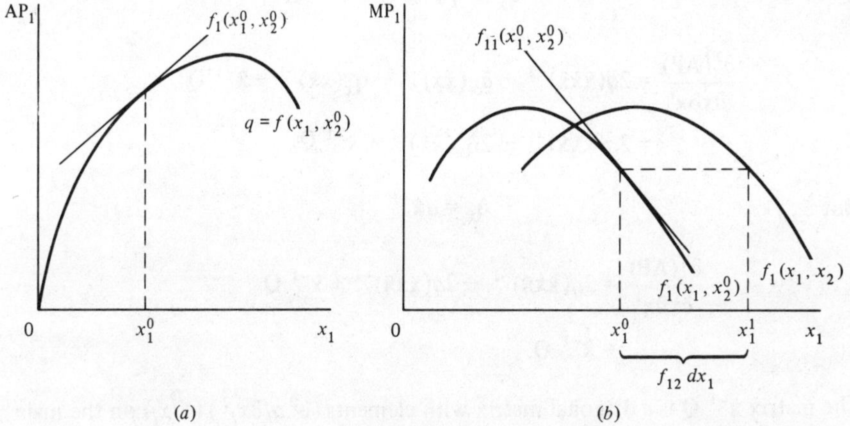

Fig. 7.1

Definition 7.2

Given a production function $q = f(\mathbf{x})$ we have for the ith input

$$\text{MP}_i = \frac{\partial q}{\partial x_i} = \frac{\partial f(\mathbf{x})}{\partial x_i} \text{ and } \text{AP}_i = \frac{q}{x_i} = \frac{f(\mathbf{x})}{x_i} \qquad x_i \neq 0, i = 1, \ldots, s$$

and the vectors of marginal and average products are

$$\text{MP} = \mathbf{q}_x \text{ and } \text{AP} = q\hat{\mathbf{x}}^{-1}\boldsymbol{\iota}$$

where $\hat{\mathbf{x}}$ is a diagonal matrix of the s inputs and $\boldsymbol{\iota}$ is a column vector $s \times 1$ of elements all unity.

We can now demonstrate our first simple proposition.

Proposition 7.1 If $q = f(\mathbf{x})$ exhibits diminishing returns for every input then the marginal product of every input equals the average product at the point of maximum average product.

Proof $\text{AP} = q\hat{\mathbf{x}}^{-1}\boldsymbol{\iota}$

$$\frac{\partial(\text{AP})}{\partial \mathbf{x}} = [-q(\hat{\mathbf{x}}\,\hat{\mathbf{x}})^{-1} + \mathbf{q}_x\,\hat{\mathbf{x}}^{-1}]\,\boldsymbol{\iota} = 0$$

$$\hat{\mathbf{q}}_x\hat{\mathbf{x}}^{-1}\boldsymbol{\iota} = q(\hat{\mathbf{x}}\,\hat{\mathbf{x}})^{-1}\boldsymbol{\iota}$$

$$\hat{\mathbf{x}}^{-1}\hat{\mathbf{q}}_x\boldsymbol{\iota} = q(\hat{\mathbf{x}}\hat{\mathbf{x}})^{-1}\boldsymbol{\iota}.$$

$$\hat{\mathbf{q}}_x\boldsymbol{\iota} = q\hat{\mathbf{x}}(\hat{\mathbf{x}}\hat{\mathbf{x}})^{-1}\boldsymbol{\iota},$$

i.e. $$\mathbf{q}_x = q\hat{\mathbf{x}}^{-1}\boldsymbol{\iota} \text{ or MP} = \text{AP}$$

$$\frac{\partial^2(\text{AP})}{\partial \mathbf{x}\partial \mathbf{x}'} = 2q(\hat{\mathbf{x}}\hat{\mathbf{x}}\hat{\mathbf{x}})^{-1} - \hat{\mathbf{q}}_x(\hat{\mathbf{x}}\hat{\mathbf{x}})^{-1} - \mathbf{q}_x(\hat{\mathbf{x}}\hat{\mathbf{x}})^{-1} + \hat{\mathbf{x}}^{-1}\,\mathbf{Q}$$

$$= 2q(\hat{\mathbf{x}}\hat{\mathbf{x}}\hat{\mathbf{x}})^{-1} - 2\hat{\mathbf{q}}_x(\hat{\mathbf{x}}\hat{\mathbf{x}})^{-1} + \hat{\mathbf{x}}^{-1}\,\mathbf{Q}.$$

But $$\hat{\mathbf{q}}_x = q\hat{\mathbf{x}}^{-1}$$

$$\frac{\partial^2(\text{AP})}{\partial \mathbf{x}\partial \mathbf{x}'} = 2q(\hat{\mathbf{x}}\hat{\mathbf{x}}\hat{\mathbf{x}})^{-1} - 2q(\hat{\mathbf{x}}\hat{\mathbf{x}}\hat{\mathbf{x}})^{-1} + \hat{\mathbf{x}}^{-1}\,\mathbf{Q}$$

$$= \hat{\mathbf{x}}^{-1}\,\mathbf{Q}.$$

The matrix $\hat{\mathbf{x}}^{-1}\,\mathbf{Q}$ is a diagonal matrix with elements $(\partial^2 q/\partial x_i^{\,2})\,(1/x_i)$ on the main diagonal. If marginal product is minimising then $\partial^2 q/\partial x_i^2 < 0$; hence if this is true for all products $\partial^2(\text{AP})/\partial\mathbf{x}\partial\mathbf{x}' < 0$ and consequently AP = MP at the maximum point of AP. *Q.E.D.*

In fact, already we have imposed certain limitations on the form which f can take. There are two important assumptions on f.

Assumption 7.2 $\exists\, \mathbf{x}^0, \mathbf{x}^1 \in \mathbf{X} \qquad \mathbf{x}^1 \geqslant \mathbf{x}^0 \Rightarrow f(\mathbf{x}^1) > f(\mathbf{x}^0)$.

In other words, there exists an *economic region,* which we shall denote **E**, in which for all $\mathbf{x} \in \mathbf{E}$ if $\mathbf{x}^1 \geqslant \mathbf{x}^0$ then $f(\mathbf{x}^1) \geqslant f(\mathbf{x}^0)$; i.e. for any movement in this region if we increase one input without decreasing any other the value of f either remains unchanged or increases. This means the region **E** is that region where all marginal products are non-negative. Thus:

$$\mathbf{E} = \{\mathbf{x} \in \mathbf{X}/\mathbf{q}_x \geqslant 0\}$$

and $\mathbf{E} \subset \mathbf{X}$.

Assumption 7.3 For all $\mathbf{x}$ in the relevant region, denoted $\mathbf{R}$, the Hessian matrix $\mathbf{Q}$ is negative definite.

Assumptions 7.2 and 7.3 together imply that the production function f is a concave function. However, this is no surprise because this follows immediately from Axiom 19, which states that the production set is convex. To demonstrate the concavity of f implied by the above assumptions consider $q = f(x_1, x_2)$. If $q = q^0$ we have the following equivalence class:

$$\mathbf{I}^0 = \{(x_1, x_2)/q^0 = f(x_1, x_2), x_1, x_2 \in \mathbf{X}, q^0 \in \bar{Q}\}.$$

This set denotes all the combinations of x_1 and x_2 which give rise to the same output q^0, and this equivalence class is referred to as an isoquant or isoproduct set, as it was referred to in Chapter 5.2. It is clear $\mathbf{I}^0 \subset \mathbf{X}$. By means of $\mathbf{I}^0$ we can divide the input space into two parts. Let

$$\mathbf{G}^0 = \{(x_1, x_2) \in \mathbf{X}/f(x_1, x_2) \geqslant q^0, q^0 \in \bar{Q}\}$$
$$\mathbf{L}^0 = \{(x_1, x_2) \in \mathbf{X}/f(x_1, x_2) \leqslant q^0, q^0 \in \bar{Q}\}.$$

Then $\mathbf{G}^0$ is the set of all input combinations which give rise to at least as great an output as that corresponding to $\mathbf{I}^0$; and $\mathbf{L}^0$ is the set of all input combinations which have less or the same output as q^0. Obviously, $\mathbf{G}^0 \cap \mathbf{L}^0 = \mathbf{I}^0$. What we must show is that Assumptions 7.2 and 7.3 imply that $\mathbf{G}^0$ is a strictly convex set. The analysis will be aided by considering Fig. 7.2.

Consider first Assumption 7.2. We have drawn in Fig. 7.2 a typical isoquant $\mathbf{I}^0$ for which $q^0 = f(x_1, x_2)$. Since $q = q^0$ for any $\mathbf{x} \in \mathbf{I}^0$ we have:

$$dq^0 = \frac{\partial f}{\partial x_1} dx_1 + \frac{\partial f}{\partial x_2} dx_2$$

i.e.

$$\frac{dx_2}{dx_1} = -\frac{f_1}{f_2} = -\frac{\mathrm{MP}_1}{\mathrm{MP}_2}.$$

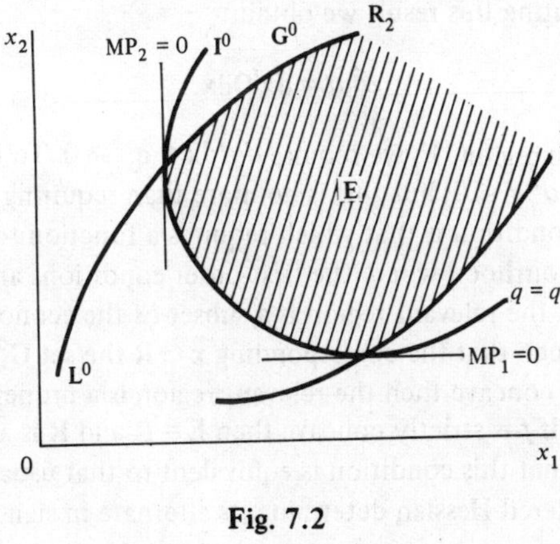

Fig. 7.2

The horizontal line in Fig. 7.2 has zero slope, i.e. $dx_2/dx_1 = 0$, which is true when $MP_1 = 0$. The vertical line has an infinite slope, i.e. $dx_2/dx_1 = -\infty$ which is true when $MP_2 = 0$. The line $\mathbf{R}_1$ represents the locus of all input combinations for various levels of output for which $MP_1 = 0$; similarly, $\mathbf{R}_2$ is the locus of all input combinations for various levels of output for which $MP_2 = 0$. For any input combination lying between these *ridge lines* we must have $-\infty < -dx_2/dx_1 < 0$ from which it follows both $MP_1 > 0$ and $MP_2 > 0$. Therefore the area subtended between these ridge lines, the lines included, is the set **E**.

The importance of Assumption 7.3 is not so obvious and so we shall consider it by means of an example. Suppose

$$q = -a_1x_1^3 + \bar{a}_2x_1^2\,x_2^2 \qquad a_1, \bar{a}_2 > 0 \text{ and } x_1 \geqslant 0.$$

Assume x_2 is held at $\bar{x}_2 \geqslant 0$, and is subsumed under $a_2 = \bar{a}_2\,\bar{x}_2^2$ thus, $q = f(x_1, \bar{x}_2) = -a_1x_1^3 + a_2\,x_1^2$. By elementary calculus the following results are readily established (Exercise 3):

(i) The total product of x_1 is a minimum at the origin and a maximum at $x_1 = 2a_2/3a_1$ where $MP_1 = 0$.
(ii) There is a point of inflexion at $x_1 = a_2/3a_1$ at which MP_1 is a maximum.
(iii) AP_1 is a maximum at $x_1 = a_2/2a_1$ and at this value $AP_1 = MP_1$.

These results are illustrated in Fig. 7.3. From Fig. 7.3 (*b*) it is clear that for $x_1 \in \mathbf{E}$ then x_1 must lie in the interval $0 \leqslant x_1 \leqslant 2a_2/3a_1$. A similar result could be established for x_2. But for many propositions concerning production we must *also* have diminishing returns. For a point to be contained in the relevant region we require $d^2q/dx_1^2 < 0$, i.e. if $x_1 \in \mathbf{R}$ then x_1 must lie in the interval $a_2/3a_1 \leqslant x_1 \leqslant 2a_2/3a_1$; with a similar requirement on x_2.

The generalisation can now be undertaken. If $q = f(\mathbf{x}) = f(x_1, \ldots, x_s)$ we can, by totally differentiating, get:

$$dq = \mathbf{q}'_x\ \mathbf{dx}$$

and totally differentiating this result we obtain:

$$d^2q = \mathbf{dx}'\mathbf{Q}\mathbf{dx}.$$

To be in the economic region, **E**, we require $dq/\mathbf{dx} = \mathbf{q}_x \geqslant 0$. To be in the relevant region, **R**, we require $d^2q < 0$; but this is no more than requiring **Q** to be negative definite. But such a condition is that which requires a function to be strictly concave in the neighbourhood where the first-order conditions are satisfied. It follows therefore that the relevant region is a subset of the economic region and that for any $q^0 \in \bar{Q}$ such that the corresponding $\mathbf{x} \in \mathbf{R}$ the set $\mathbf{G}^0$ must be strictly convex. If f is weakly concave then the relevant region is a proper convex subset of the economic region; if f is strictly concave then $\mathbf{E} = \mathbf{R}$ and **R** is a strictly convex set. It is to be noted that this condition is equivalent to that usually stated, which is that the relevant bordered Hessian determinants alternate in sign.[1]

7.3 Homogeneous and Homothetic Production Functions

Homogeneity has played a very important role in neoclassical production theory and an understanding of its implications is vital.

Definition 7.3 A function $\emptyset$ is homogeneous of degree k if

$$\emptyset(\lambda x_1, \ldots, \lambda x_s) = \lambda^k \emptyset(x_1, \ldots, x_s)$$

where k is a constant and λ any positive real number.

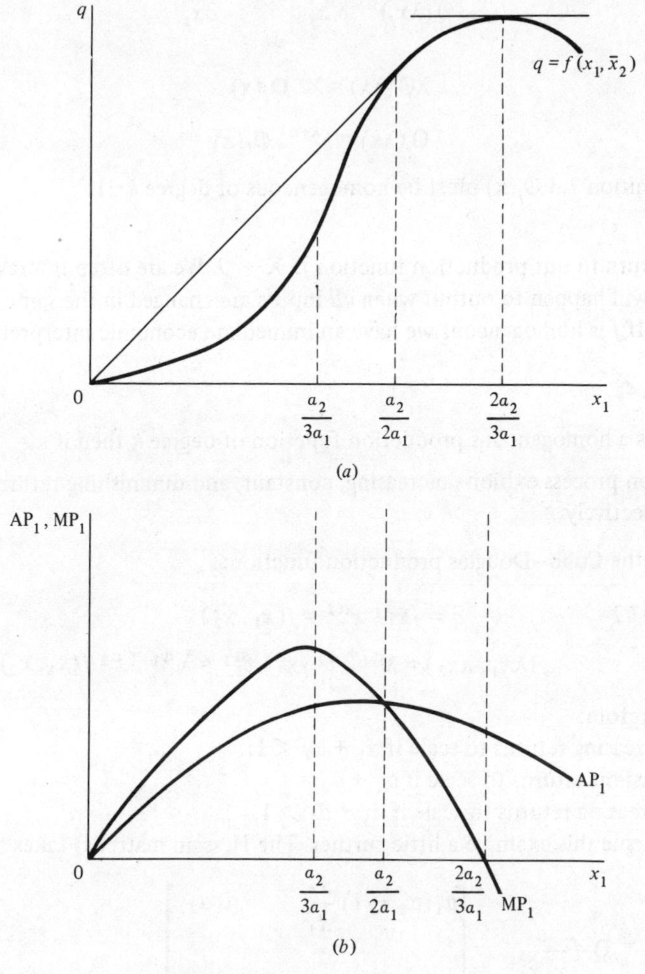

Fig. 7.3. $q = -a_1x_1^3 + a_2x_1^2$

If $k = 1$, $\emptyset$ is said to be linearly homogeneous, and consequently linear homogeneous functions form a subset of all homogeneous functions.

Proposition 7.2 If ϕ is homogeneous of degree k then the partial derivative with respect to the ith argument is homogeneous of degree $k-1$.

Proof If ϕ is homogeneous of degree k then

$$\phi(\lambda \mathbf{x}) = \lambda^k \phi(\mathbf{x}).$$

Differentiating throughout with respect to x_i we get:

$$\frac{\partial \phi(\lambda \mathbf{x})}{\partial (\lambda x_i)} \frac{\partial (\lambda x_i)}{\partial x_i} = \lambda^k \frac{\partial \phi(\mathbf{x})}{\partial x_i}$$

i.e.

$$\lambda \phi_i(\lambda \mathbf{x}) = \lambda^k \phi_i(\mathbf{x})$$

or

$$\phi_i(\lambda \mathbf{x}) = \lambda^{k-1} \phi_i(\mathbf{x}).$$

But by Definition 7.3 $\phi_i(\mathbf{x})$ must be homogeneous of degree $k-1$.

Q.E.D.

Let us return to our production function $f: \mathbf{X} \to \bar{Q}$. We are often interested to know what will happen to output when *all* inputs are changed in the same proportion. If f is homogeneous we have an immediate economic interpretation.

Definition 7.4

Given f is a homogeneous production function of degree k then if $k \gtreqless 1$ the production process exhibits increasing, constant, and diminishing returns to scale respectively.

Consider the Cobb–Douglas production function:

Example 7.1

$$q = \gamma x_1^{a_1} x_2^{a_2} = f(x_1, x_2)$$

$$f(\lambda x_1, \lambda x_2) = \lambda^{a_1 + a_2} \gamma x_1^{a_1} x_2^{a_2} = \lambda^{a_1 + a_2} f(x_1, x_2).$$

We have therefore:

(1) decreasing returns to scale if $a_1 + a_2 < 1$;
(2) constant returns to scale if $a_1 + a_2 = 1$;
(3) increasing returns to scale if $a_1 + a_2 > 1$.

Let us pursue this example a little further. The Hessian matrix $\mathbf{Q}$ takes the form:

$$\mathbf{Q} = \frac{q}{x_1 x_2} \begin{bmatrix} a_1(a_1 - 1)\dfrac{x_2}{x_1} & a_1 a_2 \\ a_1 a_2 & a_2(a_2 - 1)\dfrac{x_1}{x_2} \end{bmatrix}.$$

If we require $\mathbf{Q}$ to be negative definite then all the principle minors of $\mathbf{Q}$ must alternate in sign beginning with a negative, i.e.

$$-\frac{q}{x_1^2}a_1(a_1-1)<0 \text{ and} \left(\frac{q}{x_1x_2}\right)^2 \begin{vmatrix} a_1(a_1-1)\dfrac{x_2}{x_1} & a_1a_2 \\ a_1a_2 & a_2(a_2-1)\dfrac{x_1}{x_2} \end{vmatrix} >0.$$

Thus for $\mathbf{x} \in \mathbf{R}$ we require $a_1 < 1$ (also $a_2 < 1$) and $a_1 + a_2 < 1$. In other words, to be in the relevant region the Cobb–Douglas production function must exhibit decreasing returns to scale. If $\mathbf{Q}$ is non-positive definite then we can also have constant returns to scale since it is possible for $|\mathbf{Q}| = 0$, which means $a_1 + a_2 = 1$.

Example 7.2 The CES Production Function. Consider

$$q = \gamma\,[a_1x_1^{-\rho} + a_2x_2^{-\rho}]^{-\nu/\rho} = f(x_1, x_2) \qquad \gamma, a_1, a_2 > 0, \nu > 0,$$
$$\text{and } \rho \geqslant -1.$$

$$f(\lambda x_1, \lambda x_2) = (\lambda^{-\rho})^{-\nu/\rho}\,\gamma[a_1x_1^{-\rho} + a_2x_2^{-\rho}]^{-\nu/\rho} = \lambda^\nu f(x_1, x_2).$$

We have, therefore:

(1) decreasing returns to scale if $\nu < 1$;
(2) constant returns to scale if $\nu = 1$;
(3) increasing returns to scale if $\nu > 1$.

It is left as an exercise to see under what conditions $\mathbf{Q}$ is negative definite for the CES production function (Exercise 4).

Although the form of production function determines the type of isoquant, and in particular whether it is convex, a more explicit local measure of such convexity is the *elasticity of substitution.* This is a measure of the response in the ratio x_1/x_2 as we move around the isoquant, i.e. as the marginal rate of technical substitution changes. It is defined for two inputs only, say i and j.

Definition 7.5

The elasticity of substitution σ_{ij} between inputs i and j is given by:

$$\sigma_{ij} = \frac{\text{percentage change in } (x_i/x_j)}{\text{percentage change in } (f_i/f_j)} = \frac{\partial \log (x_i/x_j)}{\partial \log (f_i/f_j)}.$$

The elasticity of substitution in Example 7.1 is $\sigma = 1$ while for that of Example 7.2 it is $\sigma = 1/(1 + \rho)$ (see Exercise 1 (i) and (ii)).

The literature on production theory has also been concerned with homothetic production functions. Homotheticity refers to the property that any two level surfaces, isoquants in production theory, are related by a similarity transformation which preserves both angles and ratios of distances. If isoquants are related by such a homothetic transformation then each isoquant is a radial 'blow-up' of the unit isoquant. A strict definition of a homothetic function is:[2]

Definition 7.6

A function ϕ is homothetic if for any two points $\mathbf{x}^0, \mathbf{x}^1 \in \mathbf{X}$ such that $\phi(\mathbf{x}^0) = \phi(\mathbf{x}^1)$ then

$$\phi(\lambda\mathbf{x}^0) = \phi(\lambda\mathbf{x}^1)$$

for any positive real number λ.

As Whitaker and McCallum point out [126], Lancaster's definition of homothetic functions is inadequate. Let us state this as a proposition.

Proposition 7.3 If $\phi(\lambda\mathbf{x}) = \psi(\lambda)\,\phi(\mathbf{x})$ then $\psi(\lambda) = \lambda^k$.

Lancaster defines homotheticity as that function which satisfies $\phi(\lambda\mathbf{x}) = \psi(\lambda)\phi(\mathbf{x})$. This appears intuitively appealing since it seems just a more general statement than homogeneity. However, if the only interpretation that can be given to $\psi(\lambda)$ is $\psi(\lambda) = \lambda^k$ then we are no better off. Thus we must prove that $\psi(\lambda) = \lambda^k$.

Proof If $\phi(\lambda\mathbf{x}) = \psi(\lambda)\phi(\mathbf{x})$ then $\phi(\mu\lambda\mathbf{x}) = \psi(\mu\lambda)\phi(\mathbf{x})$. But $\phi(\mu\lambda\mathbf{x}) = \psi(\mu)\phi(\lambda\mathbf{x}) = \psi(\mu)\psi(\lambda)\phi(\mathbf{x})$. Consequently $\psi(\mu\lambda) = \psi(\mu)\,\psi(\lambda)$ or $\psi(\mu\lambda)/\psi(\lambda) = \psi(\mu)$. Now partially differentiating this last expression with respect to λ, then:

$$\psi(\lambda) \cdot \frac{\partial\psi(\mu\lambda)}{\partial\lambda} - \psi(\mu\lambda) \cdot \frac{\partial\psi(\lambda)}{\partial\lambda} = 0.$$

Multiplying through by λ and rearranging we obtain:

$$\frac{\partial\psi(\mu\lambda)}{\partial\lambda} \cdot \frac{\lambda}{\psi(\mu\lambda)} = \frac{\partial\psi(\lambda)}{\partial\lambda} \cdot \frac{\lambda}{\psi(\lambda)}.$$

The expression on the left-hand side is the elasticity of ψ with respect to λ at the point $\mu\lambda$, whilst the expression on the right-hand side is the elasticity of ψ with respect to λ at the point λ. Since these elasticities must be equal for all permissible λ and μ then it follows ψ must be a function with a constant elasticity. Such a function is readily found to be $\psi(\lambda) = c\lambda^k$ (Exercise 5). However, from Lancaster's definition if we let $\lambda = 1$ we get $\phi(\mathbf{x}) = \psi(1)\phi(\mathbf{x})$, which implies $\psi(1) = 1$. From our previous result we have $\psi(1) = c$; hence $c = 1$. Consequently $\psi(\lambda) = \lambda^k$.

Q.E.D.

Even though Lancaster's definition is inadequate it remains true that homogeneous functions constitute a subset of homothetic functions. But the question that may be asked is why consider homothetic functions at all? In the case of the Cobb–Douglas production function $\sigma = 1$ and in the CES case it is $\sigma = 1/(1 + \rho)$. In the former case the elasticity of substitution is constant for all points along the isoquant and is a special case. The latter has a different elasticity of substitution at different points along the isoquant, but it is constant for movements along a ray through the origin, hence the term CES. The next question is whether this constancy in the elasticity of substitution is restricted to homogeneous functions?

The answer is no! By definition of homotheticity such a function also possesses this property. The importance is that a homogeneous function is homothetic, but homothetic functions are not necessarily homogeneous. The inclusion of homothetic functions allows greater generality.[3]

What can we conclude from Sections 7.2 and 7.3? The production function is assumed continuous and twice differentiable. It is a concave function, and strictly concave under Assumption 7.3. However, if we allow **Q** to be non-positive definite we allow the production function to exhibit constant returns to scale besides decreasing returns to scale. In both cases – weak and strong concavity of the production function – the isoquants are convex and the set $\mathbf{G}^0 = \{\mathbf{x}/f(\mathbf{x}) \geqslant q^0, q^0 \in \bar{Q}\}$ is a convex set. To keep within meaningful economics, Assumption 7.2 restricts the analysis to a subset of the input space, referred to as the *economic region,* and this region is bounded by the ridge lines. The relevant region is a convex subset of the economic region, and this region satisfies both Assumptions 7.2 and 7.3. The concavity and convexity conditions imply restrictions on the type of functions that can be used. Important features which have economic significance refer to homogeneous functions. Such functions play an important role in neoclassical production (and distribution) theory. However, all homogeneous functions are homothetic whilst the converse is not true. Homothetic functions have therefore come to play an increasing role in economic theory. Part of the reason for this interest stems from the consideration of the elasticity of substitution. The meaning of 'constant' in the 'constant elasticity of substitution' refers to points on an isoquant where any ray through the origin cuts it. Homothetic functions exhibit such a constancy. Be this as it may, interest is now turning to functions which will exhibit a *variable* elasticity of substitution.

7.4 Equilibrium of the Firm

The objective of the firm remains the maximisation of profits, π, which is equal to revenue minus costs. The maximisation of the profit function is constrained by the given production function and the fact that the optimal solution must involve non-negative inputs. We assume the firm operates in a perfectly competitive market so that the product price p is given as are the input prices $\mathbf{w} = (w_1, \ldots, w_s)$. Hence:

$$\pi = \mathbf{R} - \mathbf{C}$$

$$\mathbf{R} = pq = pf(\mathbf{x})$$

$$\mathbf{C} = \mathbf{w}'\mathbf{x}.$$

Therefore:

$$\pi(\mathbf{x}) = pf(\mathbf{x}) - \mathbf{w}'\mathbf{x}.$$

The object of the firm is then to:

$$\max_{\mathbf{x} \in \mathbf{X}} \; \pi(\mathbf{x}) = pf(\mathbf{x}) - \mathbf{w}'\mathbf{x}$$

$$\text{s.t.} \quad \mathbf{x} \geqslant 0.$$

This is a long-run situation since we are imposing no constraints on the inputs, other than being non-negative. Using the Kuhn–Tucker conditions of Chapter 4.6 we have for an optimal solution:

$$\boldsymbol{\pi}_x = p\mathbf{q}_x - \mathbf{w} \leqslant 0$$

$$\mathbf{x}'\boldsymbol{\pi}_x = \mathbf{x}'(p\mathbf{q}_x - \mathbf{w}) = 0$$

$$\mathbf{x} \geqslant 0.$$

If all inputs are employed because they have positive marginal products, $\mathbf{x} \in \mathbf{E}$, then

$$p\mathbf{q}_x = \mathbf{w},$$

i.e. the marginal revenue product equals the wage for every input. If, however, some negative marginal products occur then:

$$p\frac{\partial f}{\partial x_i} < w_i \text{ and } x_i = 0$$

in which case the input is not employed. However, this is generally ruled out in neoclassical economics.

So far only the first-order conditions have been met. For $\pi(\mathbf{x})$ to be a maximum we further require:

$$\Pi = \frac{\partial \boldsymbol{\pi}_x}{\partial \mathbf{x}'}$$

to be negative definite. But $\Pi = p\mathbf{Q}$ and since p is positive we require that $\mathbf{Q}$ is negative definite, hence $\mathbf{x} \in \mathbf{R}$ if both first- and second-order conditions are to be satisfied. Given $\mathbf{x} \in \mathbf{R}$ it is possible to solve $p\mathbf{q}_x = \mathbf{w}$ uniquely in terms of p and $\mathbf{w}$. Let us denote these solutions:

$$\mathbf{x} = \mathbf{x}(p, \mathbf{w}) = \mathbf{x}(p, w_1, \ldots, w_s).$$

We assume that these s input-demand functions are homogeneous of degree zero, i.e. $\mathbf{x}(\lambda p, \lambda \mathbf{w}) = \mathbf{x}(p, \mathbf{w})$. This says no more than that the input combination which maximises $\pi(\mathbf{x})$ also maximises $\lambda\pi(\mathbf{x})$.

It is also to be noted that the supply curve in the present theory is a function rather than a correspondence; it is a function of the output price and the input prices. This readily follows by substituting $\mathbf{x} = \mathbf{x}(p, \mathbf{w})$ into $q = f(\mathbf{x})$. Thus:

$$q = f(\mathbf{x}) = f[\mathbf{x}(p, \mathbf{w})] = \eta(p, \mathbf{w}).$$

Since $\mathbf{x} = \mathbf{x}(p, \mathbf{w})$ is homogeneous of degree zero it follows the supply function is homogeneous of degree zero, i.e. $\eta(\lambda p, \lambda \mathbf{w}) = \eta(p, \mathbf{w})$.

It is possible to consider the input demand curves from another point of view which will be found useful later. Let $q = q^0$ be given, then with fixed prices p and

w and cost **C** our problem is one of:

$$\min_{\mathbf{x} \in \mathbf{X}} \quad \mathbf{C} = \mathbf{w}'\mathbf{x}$$

$$\text{s.t.} \quad q^0 = f(\mathbf{x})$$
$$\mathbf{x} \geqslant 0.$$

We shall assume all inputs have positive marginal products. Hence form the Lagrangian expression:

$$V = \mathbf{w}'\mathbf{x} - \lambda[f(\mathbf{x}) - q^0].$$

The first-order conditions for a minimum are:

$$\mathbf{V}_x = \mathbf{w} - \lambda \mathbf{q}_x = \mathbf{0}$$
$$V_\lambda = -f(\mathbf{x}) + q^0 = 0.$$

The second-order conditions amount to $-\mathbf{Q}$ being positive definite. But if $\mathbf{Q}$ is negative definite then $-\mathbf{Q}$ is positive definite. Hence, if $\mathbf{x} \in \mathbf{R}$ the first- and second-order conditions are satisfied. Hence we can solve the $s + 1$ equations uniquely in terms of **w** and q^0, i.e.

$$\mathbf{x} = \psi(\mathbf{w}, q^0)$$
$$\lambda = \lambda(\mathbf{w}, q^0).$$

Since $\mathbf{C} = \mathbf{w}'\mathbf{x}$ we can use the previous result to argue that $\mathbf{C} = \mathbf{w}'\psi(\mathbf{w}, q^0)$; hence $\mathbf{C} = \phi(\mathbf{w}, q^0)$.

So far we have expressed two ways of stating the decision problem of the firm:

$$(1) \quad \max_{\mathbf{x} \in \mathbf{R}} \ \pi(\mathbf{x}) = pf(\mathbf{x}) - \mathbf{w}'\mathbf{x}$$

$$(2) \quad \min_{\mathbf{x} \in \mathbf{R}} \ V = \mathbf{w}'\mathbf{x} - \lambda[f(\mathbf{x}) - q^0]$$

each with the optimal conditions:

$$p\mathbf{q}_x - \mathbf{w} = 0$$
$$\mathbf{w} - \lambda \mathbf{q}_x = 0.$$

These are consistent if and only if $\lambda = p$ at the optimal solution. However, we have shown that:

$$\mathbf{C} = \mathbf{w}'\mathbf{x} = \mathbf{w}'\psi(\mathbf{w}, q^0)$$

$$\therefore \quad \frac{\partial \mathbf{C}}{\partial q^0} = \mathbf{w}' \frac{\partial \mathbf{x}}{\partial q^0}.$$

Furthermore, differentiating $q^0 = f(\mathbf{x})$ with respect to q^0 we get:

$$1 = \mathbf{q}'_x \frac{\partial \mathbf{x}}{\partial q^0}.$$

However, from the first-order conditions we have $\mathbf{w} = \lambda \mathbf{q}_x$; hence

$$\lambda = \mathbf{w}' \frac{\partial \mathbf{x}}{\partial q^0} = \frac{\partial C}{\partial q^0} = p.$$

In other words, the marginal cost equals the product price.

7.5 Comparative Statics of the Firm

In carrying out the comparative static exercise it is important to bear in mind how the dependent variables are related to the prices. Making use of $\mathbf{x} = \mathbf{x}(p, \mathbf{w})$ we can restate the equilibrium conditions as:

$$q(p, \mathbf{w}) \equiv f[\mathbf{x}(p, \mathbf{w})]$$

$$p\mathbf{q}_x[\mathbf{x}(p, \mathbf{w})] \equiv \mathbf{w}.$$

Differentiating with respect to p we get:

$$q_p = \mathbf{q}'_x \mathbf{x}_p$$

$$\mathbf{q}_x + p\mathbf{Q}\mathbf{x}_p = 0$$

where

$$q_p = \frac{\partial q}{\partial p}, \mathbf{q}_x = \frac{\partial q}{\partial \mathbf{x}} \text{ and } \mathbf{x}_p = \frac{\partial \mathbf{x}}{\partial p}.$$

In matrix notation:

$$\begin{bmatrix} -1 & \mathbf{q}'_x \\ 0 & p\mathbf{Q} \end{bmatrix} \begin{bmatrix} q_p \\ \mathbf{x}_p \end{bmatrix} = \begin{bmatrix} 0 \\ -\mathbf{q}_x \end{bmatrix}.$$

Next differentiate the equilibrium conditions with respect to the vector $\mathbf{w}$:

$$\mathbf{q}'_w = \mathbf{q}'_x \mathbf{X}_w$$

$$p\mathbf{Q}\mathbf{X}_w = \mathbf{I}$$

where $\mathbf{X}_w = \dfrac{\partial \mathbf{x}}{\partial \mathbf{w}'}$ and is a matrix of order $s \times s$; $\mathbf{q}_w = \dfrac{\partial q}{\partial \mathbf{w}}$, all other terms having been defined. In matrix notation we have:

$$\begin{bmatrix} -1 & \mathbf{q}'_x \\ 0 & p\mathbf{Q} \end{bmatrix} \begin{bmatrix} \mathbf{q}'_w \\ \mathbf{X}_w \end{bmatrix} = \begin{bmatrix} 0 \\ \mathbf{I} \end{bmatrix}.$$

The two sets of matrices can be combined to form:

$$\begin{bmatrix} -1 & \mathbf{q}'_x \\ 0 & p\mathbf{Q} \end{bmatrix} \begin{bmatrix} q_p & \mathbf{q}'_w \\ \mathbf{x}_p & \mathbf{X}_w \end{bmatrix} = \begin{bmatrix} 0 & 0 \\ -\mathbf{q}_x & \mathbf{I} \end{bmatrix}.$$

This we can call *the fundamental matrix equation of the theory of the firm in terms of marginal responses.* Hence taking the partitioned inverse we get:

$$\begin{bmatrix} q_p & \mathbf{q}'_w \\ \mathbf{x}_p & \mathbf{X}_w \end{bmatrix} = \begin{bmatrix} -1 & p^{-1}\mathbf{q}'_x\mathbf{Q}^{-1} \\ 0 & p^{-1}\mathbf{Q}^{-1} \end{bmatrix} \begin{bmatrix} 0 & 0 \\ -\mathbf{q}_x & \mathbf{I} \end{bmatrix}.$$

Carrying out the matrix multiplication we obtain:

$$q_p = -p^{-1}\mathbf{q}'_x\mathbf{Q}^{-1}\mathbf{q}_x$$
$$\mathbf{x}_p = -p^{-1}\mathbf{Q}^{-1}\mathbf{q}_x$$
$$\mathbf{q}_w = p^{-1}\mathbf{Q}^{-1}\mathbf{q}_x$$
$$\mathbf{X}_w = p^{-1}\mathbf{Q}^{-1}.$$

If $\mathbf{Q}$ is negative definite then so is $\mathbf{Q}^{-1}$, from which it follows $q_p > 0$. In other words, output increases when the output price increases – the supply function is upward-sloping. Notice how this result crucially depends upon $\mathbf{Q}^{-1}$ existing and being negative definite. However, nothing can be concluded about the signs of $\mathbf{x}_p$, $\mathbf{q}_w$, and $\mathbf{X}_w$.

Although nothing can be said about the individual elements of $\mathbf{x}_p$, since $q_p > 0$ and $\mathbf{x} \in \mathbf{R}$ it means some $\partial x_k/\partial p > 0$, i.e. an increase in the output price will increase the demand for some of the factor inputs. If $\partial x_k/\partial p < 0$ we say that input k is inferior.

Finally, we notice two things about $\mathbf{X}_w$. The matrix $\mathbf{X}_w$ is the price response for the firm and, unlike its counterpart in consumer demand, it is composed only of a substitution element: there is no income response. Second, since $\mathbf{Q}$ is symmetric and negative definite, so is $\mathbf{Q}^{-1}$ and hence so also is $\mathbf{X}_w$. Because $\mathbf{X}_w$ is negative definite we can say that $\partial x_i/\partial w_i < 0, i = 1, \ldots, s$; an increase in the price of an input will always lead to a reduction in the demand for that input.

7.6 A Critique of Traditional Production Theory

Traditional production theory can be criticised at two levels. One is from the point of view of a theory intending to explain a firm's behaviour as compared with alternative theories. The other, which is not wholly independent of the first, is as a consistent theoretical framework in which to discuss production theory. In this section we shall concentrate only on the second viewpoint.

Traditional production theory, and in particular neoclassical production theory, has never been properly derived from an axiomatic base, although it is not impossible to establish such a base as we have tried to show. The reason for this appears to be because the theory has centred on the production function, just as consumer demand has centred on the utility function, on the embodiment of the production process, rather than on the production process *per se*. As with the majority of traditional theory, the relationships are single-valued, continuous, and invariably differentiable up to the second degree. However, these assumptions far from being introduced to make the theory simple, were introduced in order to invoke the differential calculus as a means of analysis. This is not to say that this should not be done, but rather having done so the limitations of the approach must be constantly kept in mind. Mathematics is but a tool in the hands of the economist, but a problem can be posed in many ways, each of which may possibly appeal to a different branch of mathematics in order to solve it.[4] The theory of production has more recently been posed in terms of sets and algebraic topology. Given our present state of knowledge we cannot as yet establish which approach is the better, all we can do is employ each, using one whenever it appears more applicable. One problem yet to be faced is to what extent topological methods will enter economics; this application is new and the future uncertain as to its full potential.

Having briefly discussed the more formal aspects of the theory, what about the economics? Traditional theory, as well as the contemporary, is based on profit maximisation as the sole objective of the firm. This is, many argue, a simplifying assumption. But is it? If we employ 'simplifying' in the sense of Chapter 1 to mean without it the theory would remain the same, then it is *not* simplifying, but rather an abstraction. This assumption belongs to the basic axiom set of production theory. Neoclassical theory does not make this clear but the axiomatic set in Chapter 5 makes this most explicit. To change such an assumption changes the whole edifice of production theory. We also note that as an axiom it is by no means self-evident. We employ this axiom in order to limit the domain of study. Whether this is the best way of approaching the problem of the firm is debatable. However, change this axiom and you change all the analysis following from it. This is important because it has constantly been said that a firm does not maximise profits but rather some other variable, such as revenue; or a set of variables, such as profits and growth. It is not just enough to say that this particular axiom is inappropriate. Neoclassical theory, for example, is a whole *system;* accordingly if it is to be replaced it must be replaced by an alternative *system.*

What writers usually intend is to replace just one axiom by an alternative leaving the rest unchanged. But this is poor analysis and smacks of the *ad hoc.* However, it must be entertained as a method of proceeding in an uncertain and complicated world. This is particularly true of the axioms. What cannot be entertained, however, is the changing of a deduction. To change a deduction means a possible inconsistency arising from the axiomatic base on which the original deduction was built. This is much the way traditional theory has developed over time, and what Leontief meant when he accused the Cambridge economists of implicit theorising [74].

Let us take an example. Neoclassical theory, as we have shown, gives rise to an upward-sloping supply curve – implying the marginal cost curve is upward-sloping also. Yet the literature abounds with discussions of U-shaped supply curves. What does this mean? Is an inconsistency present? The traditional analysis has been loosely argued and it is not easy to separate off the different issues. But our mathematical analysis is of some help. The supply curve is upward-sloping because **Q** is negative definite. If this is so we are considering only the relevant region of the economic region. In effect, it is the economic region which gives rise to a possible U-shaped supply curve, but the relevant region restricts the analysis to only the rising element of this curve above average variable cost. Consequently, in discussions concerned about capacity utilisation – in the sense of having an output less than that at minimum average cost – additional assumptions must be introduced. Such additional assumptions are typical of those which belong to the set P_γ referred to in Chapter 1. What we immediately draw from this is that for any such economic problem concerned with the downward slope of the marginal cost curve **Q** cannot be negative definite and any deductions which are dependent upon this being so no longer hold.

The economic literature is full of such propositions (P_γ) and it is too great a task to see the implications. But it should be clear from the above illustration that it is important to be aware of such analysis. One of the ways out of this dilemma is to set the theory of production on a more explicit foundation: an axiomatic foundation. We will then be in a position to alter the theories and see the various implications more precisely. Loose discussion can only lead to confused discussion, which in turn can only lead to a waste of time – a very scarce commodity.

Neoclassical theory is a consistent system and is laid on fairly sound foundations. It is the *ad hoc* treatment given to neoclassical theory in an attempt to improve it which has been its worst enemy. However, the theory which will replace it must be a well-tested and consistent *system*.

EXERCISES

1. Given the CES production function:

$$q = f(\mathbf{x}) = \gamma[a_1 x_1^{-\rho} + a_2 x_2^{-\rho}]^{-1/\rho} \qquad a_0, a_1, a_2 > 0, \rho \geqslant -1$$

(i) Prove that $\sigma = 1/(1+\rho)$.
(ii) Show that as $\sigma \to 1$, f approaches a Cobb–Douglas production function.
(iii) Show that as $\sigma \to \infty$, f approaches a linear production function of the form $q = a_1 x_1 + a_2 x_2$.
(iv) Show that as $\sigma \to 0$, f approaches an input–output production function.

2. Let ω_i denote the output elasticity of the ith input and $\boldsymbol{\omega}$ the output elasticity vector, thus

$$\omega_i = \frac{\partial q}{\partial x_i}\frac{x_i}{q} \quad \text{and} \quad \boldsymbol{\omega} = q^{-1}\hat{\mathbf{x}}q_x.$$

Prove that if $q = f(\mathbf{x})$ is a homogeneous production function of degree k then $\boldsymbol{\iota}'\boldsymbol{\omega} = k$. (Hint, use Euler's theorem.)

3. Given $q = -a_1 x_1^3 + a_2 x_1^2$ prove the results in the text.

4. For the CES production function:

$$q = \gamma[a_1 x_1^{-\rho} + a_2 x_2^{-\rho}]^{-\nu/\rho}$$

under what conditions is the matrix $\mathbf{Q}$ negative definite?

5. Prove that if the function $\psi(\lambda)$ has a constant elasticity of k then $\psi(\lambda) = c\lambda^k$, where c is an arbitrary constant.

6. Let $\boldsymbol{\theta}$ denote the input elasticity matrix with elements $\theta_{ij} = \dfrac{\partial x_i}{\partial w_j}\dfrac{w_j}{x_i}$. Then $\boldsymbol{\theta} = \hat{\mathbf{x}}^{-1}\mathbf{X}_w\hat{\mathbf{w}}$, where $\mathbf{X}_w$ is the marginal input response matrix. Let $\hat{\boldsymbol{\theta}}$ denote the diagonal matrix with diagonal elements θ_{ii}, then $\hat{\boldsymbol{\theta}} = \hat{\mathbf{x}}^{-1}\hat{\mathbf{x}}_w\hat{\mathbf{w}}$ where $\hat{\mathbf{x}}_w$ is the diagonal matrix with diagonal elements $\partial x_i/\partial w_i$. Taking account of the fact that $\hat{\boldsymbol{\theta}}^{-1} = \hat{\mathbf{w}}^{-1}\hat{\mathbf{x}}_w^{-1}\hat{\mathbf{x}} = \hat{\mathbf{w}}^{-1}\hat{\mathbf{w}}_x\hat{\mathbf{x}}$, prove that the differential of $\pi = pq - \mathbf{w}'\mathbf{x}$ with respect to output q is:

$$\pi_q = p(1 + \eta^{-1}) - \mathbf{w}'(\mathbf{I} + \hat{\boldsymbol{\theta}}^{-1})\mathbf{x}_q = 0$$

and that under perfect competition this reduces to $p = \mathbf{w}'\mathbf{x}_q$. Interpret this result.

7. Given

$$q = a_0 x_1^{a_1} x_2^{a_2}$$

and prices p, w_1, and w_2 respectively, obtain the input-demand functions $\mathbf{x} = \mathbf{x}(p, \mathbf{w})$ and the supply function $q = \eta(p, \mathbf{w})$.

8. Obtain for the Cobb–Douglas production function in Exercise 7, the output elasticity vector, $\boldsymbol{\omega}$, and show that $\boldsymbol{\iota}'\boldsymbol{\omega} = a_1 + a_2$.

Part IV

GENERAL EQUILIBRIUM THEORY

This part of the book is concerned with general equilibrium theory. So far we have been concerned largely with the individual, particularly on the side of consumption, although as far as production is concerned we have considered the economy's production set. Thus in Chapter 8 we concern ourselves with market demand and supply equations and also aggregate excess demand equations. Much of Part IV is concerned with the existence of equilibrium and to demonstrate this in the variety of models we require to go from the elementary definitions of partial equilibrium discussed in Section 8.5 to general equilibrium definitions. Consequently Chapter 8 sets the scene for the remaining discussion. In particular, attention is payed to modulate excess demand functions and normalised price sets in terms of a unit simplex. These are of particular importance in the understanding of the two fixed-point theorems which are discussed in Section 8.7. The attention of economists to the mathematical theorems of Brouwer and Kakutani which are concerned with fixed points is only recent but is central to the discussion of general equilibrium. Why? Because fixed points are no more than equilibrium points of a system. Hence, to establish a fixed point exists is to establish that an equilibrium exists for that economic system.

We next turn to a discussion of exchange. Given an economy of two individuals and an initial allocation of fixed total endowments a number of questions arise. Under what conditions will these consumers exchange? Will trade benefit both consumers or just one? Does there exist a trade which will be efficient? If a competitive equilibrium exists is it (*a*) unique, and (*b*) efficient? These and others are discussed in both Chapters 9 and 10.

In Chapter 9 we concentrate particularly on the pure exchange model, i.e. excluding production considerations, where it is demonstrated, by the use of Brouwer's fixed-point theorem, that an equilibrium exists. In Section 9.4 production as well as consumption is considered. Finally, in Section 9.5 we demonstrate the existence of an equilibrium in an open Leontief model, where in doing so use is made of Kakutani's fixed-point theorem.

The final chapter of Part IV is concerned with welfare theory. It deals with

Pareto optimality and how this is characterised in consumption and production. It also considers optimality when the better sets or the production sets are not necessarily strictly convex. It discusses the attempts which have been made to compare points which lie in the Pareto non-comparable set which include the compensation tests and the introduction of a social welfare function. Other topics dealt with include interdependent utilities, the introduction of public goods and the theory of second best. All these 'traditional' topics quite extensively use the calculus, but the problems are important and we must await developments in the set-theoretic approach to see if new insights in these areas can be obtained. A final topic, discussed only briefly, is that of the core of an economy. Analysed originally by Edgeworth, this topic is very largely a product of the 1960s and 1970s. The central question faced here is: If the number of individuals which enter into trade is large and there is no room for co-operation will the equilibrium, if one exists, be the competitive equilibrium? The interest here is that when more than two individuals trade there is room for co-operation between subsets. Consequently, new and more interesting questions can be asked of exchange models.

8

THEORY OF MARKET DEMAND AND SUPPLY

8.1 Introduction

In this chapter we shall pursue further a number of topics that we have touched on previously. Our intention is to look closer at the properties of demand and supply curves both for the individual and also for the market. Individual demand and supply is considered in Sections 8.2 and 8.3 whilst Section 8.4 is concerned with market relationships. The next section is concerned with some elementary ideas about equilibrium, in particular how equilibrium can be expressed in terms of excess demand functions. This discussion is preliminary and is a natural stepping stone to some of the more recent discussions of equilibrium. Section 8.5 lays out some recent concepts which are used in discussions of equilibrium. Two concepts are stressed, the normalised price set and the modulated excess demand function. The final section discusses the mathematics of equilibrium points, giving intuitive ideas about the fixed-point theorems of Brouwer and Kakutani. The discussion of equilibrium will be expecially relevant when we come to analyse various models in the next chapter.

Although the concepts of demand and supply date back to Adam Smith, the approach to be adopted here is relatively new and has risen largely since the Second World War. Because the economist so readily uses the tools of demand and supply it is essential that their derivation and interpretation is clearly understood. For example, implicit in our analysis so far is that we have been concerned with *flow* demand and supply, i.e. the demand for x_i per unit of time. In this sense the dimension of x_i is composed of a quantity $[Q]$, and the reciprocal of time $[T^{-1}]$ or $\dim(x_i) = [QT^{-1}]$. All variables and parameters have dimensions although some may be of zero dimension. However, flow analysis if used for discussions of price determination is not always valid. Is it, for example, new houses and new demand for houses which determines house prices? In the case of this commodity we cannot ignore the existing level of stocks. In the case of perishable goods it is true that the flow demand and supply is what determines prices. To the extent that we shall ignore stocks our analysis is only a good approximation where stocks are a very small part of the market. In order to deal with the market for goods that have a large stock element we must introduce a dynamic framework.

8.2 Derivation of Individual Demand Curves

First let us consider the neoclassical case. It has already been established in Chapter 4 that demand curves can be obtained by solving the first-order conditions for a utility maximisation, and taking it as read that the second-order conditions are satisfied. However, the demand curve when portrayed graphically is a relationship between a good and its price, all other prices and income held constant. Fig. 8.1 (*a*) gives a typical representation with two goods x_1 and x_2 and their corresponding prices p_1 and p_2. Since our concern is with partial analysis, income y, and the price of good 2 is held constant.

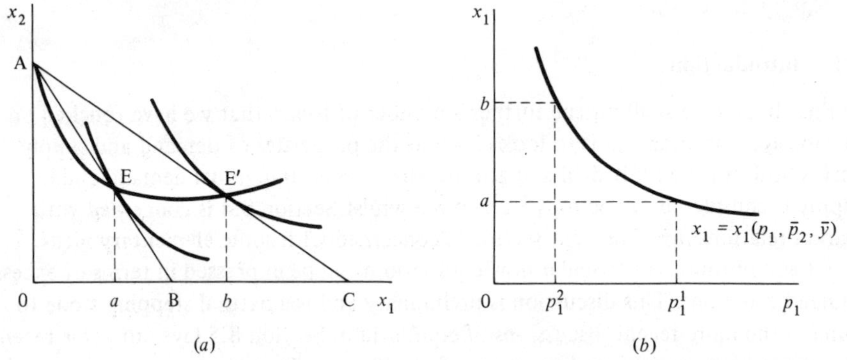

Fig. 8.1. Derivation of a demand curve

At the initial price p_1^1 and a constant $\bar{p}_2$, the bar denoting these variables are held constant, the budget is given by AB with equilibrium at E and a quantity of 0*a* demanded of x_1. When the price falls to p_1^2, as represented by the budget line AC, the new equilibrium is at E′ and a quantity of 0*b* of x_1 is now demanded. We have established in Chapter 4 that so long as x_1 is not a strongly inferior good then the quantity demanded will increase (decrease) for a fall (rise) in the price of that good, i.e. $\partial x_i/\partial p_i < 0$ so long as the income effect, $x_i\,(\partial x_i/\partial y)$, is not sufficient to swamp the substitution effect, s_{ii}. This is the case shown in Fig. 8.1. (*b*).

This analysis is familiar and so we shall just note some assumptions. First, the consumer's income is fixed and he purchases x_1 and x_2 such that his income is exhausted. Consequently, the demand curve for x_1 is dependent upon its own price, the given price $\bar{p}_2$ and given income, $\bar{y}$. Since income is exogenous, if all income is not spent then a different demand curve must be constructed. Second, the demand curve is single-valued, i.e. for a given price p_1 there is one and only one quantity of x_1 demanded. Third, the demand curve is continuous and differentiable. However, it is not necessarily defined for the whole of the price axis. This is because, in general, a given income will set a lower limit on the price corresponding to a maximum demand such that expenditure on both goods equals income, and an upper limit on price corresponding to the minimum quantity demanded where again expenditure on both goods equals income.

The three conditions just outlined are very specialised indeed. Is it not possible to have set-valued demand correspondences; demand 'curves' which are thick bands;

demand curves having discontinuities and demand curves which are not differentiable? Consider, for example, Fig. 8.2 (*a*). In this case the better sets are weakly convex which we have argued earlier is not unreasonable. If this was the case then the demand curve corresponding to such an indifference map is illustrated in Fig. 8.2 (*b*). At the price p_1^1 the consumer can choose anything in the range $0a - 0a'$, all of which are equilibrium bundles at this price. At the lower price p_1^2 only one quantity of x_1 is demanded, viz. $0b$. Even though when the price is p_1^1 one specific quantity will be chosen, this event is purely random and can be anything in the range $0a - 0a'$. We have, therefore, a correspondence, a point-to-set mapping. We have already encountered such correspondences in Chapters 5 and 6. Clearly, the more kinks there are in the indifference curves the more straight line segments there will be in the demand curve.

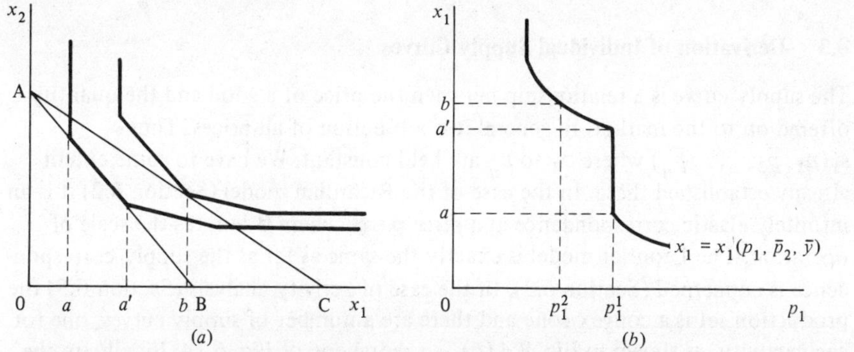

Fig. 8.2. Demand correspondence

Before leaving set-valued mappings it is worth noting that a set-to-point mapping arises with traditionally-shaped indifference curves. The condition under which they arise is easily seen from Fig. 8.3, and requires that $x_{11} = 0$, i.e. $x_1(\partial x_1/\partial y) = s_{11}$ or that the income effect must equal the substitution effect. But this would be exceptional.

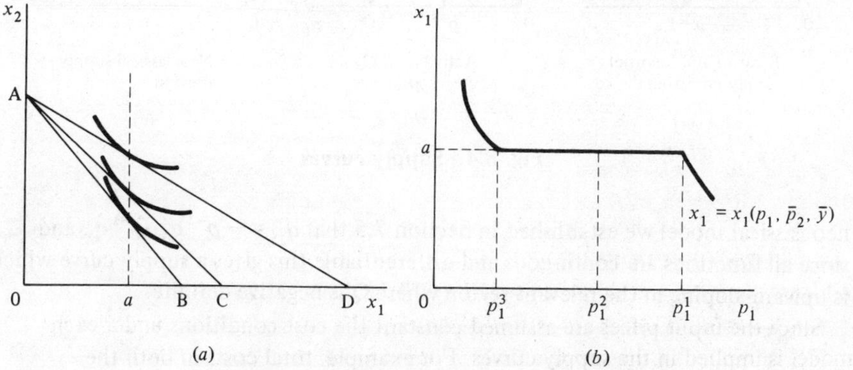

Fig. 8.3. Set-to-point demand curve

A number of other situations are possible. For example, what would be the result of excluding Axiom 11 ($\mathbf{I}^0$ contains no interior points)? The indifference sets would then contain interior points as well as boundary points. The corresponding demand curves would also contain interior points and would be drawn as thick bands. Yet another possibility arises if the commodity set **X** is not connected. This would arise if commodities took only integer values; then **X** would be a lattice. In this instance the demand curve would have jump discontinuities. All these situations are ruled out in the traditional analysis. In the eyes of traditionalists they are oddities, theoretical anomalies that can be ignored. However, the requisite tools are only just at hand and we must await the developments from recent research in order to obtain their full implications.

8.3 Derivation of Individual Supply Curves

The supply curve is a relationship between the price of a good and the quantity offered on to the market. In general it is a function of all prices. Thus $s_1 = s_1(p_1, \bar{p}_2, \ldots, \bar{p}_n)$ where p_2 to p_n are held constant. We have to some extent already established these. In the case of the Ricardian model (Section 6.2) it is an infinitely elastic correspondence at a price $\mathbf{p} = \boldsymbol{\beta}$, where $\boldsymbol{\beta}$ denotes the scale of operation. The Leontief model is exactly the same as far as the supply correspondence is concerned (Section 6.3). In the case of activity analysis (Section 6.5) the production set is a convex cone and there are a number of supply curves, one for each activity, as shown in Fig. 8.4 (*b*) – a redrawing of Fig. 6.14. Finally, in the

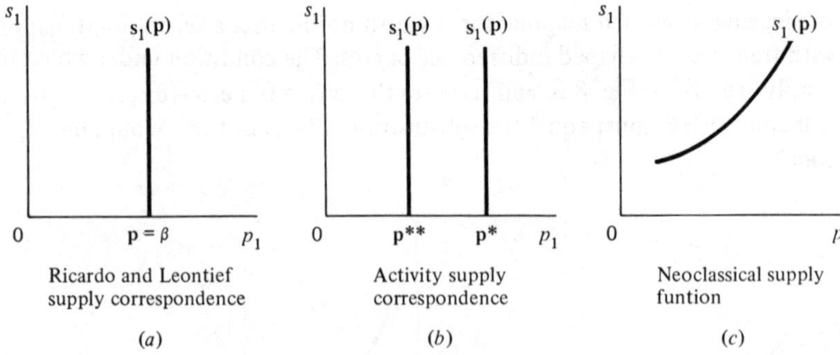

Fig. 8.4. Supply curves

neoclassical model we established in Section 7.5 that $q_p = -p^{-1}\mathbf{q}_x' \mathbf{Q}^{-1}\mathbf{q}_x$ and since all functions are continuous and differentiable this gives a supply curve which is upward-sloping in the relevant region where **Q** is negative definite.

Since the input prices are assumed constant the cost conditions under each model is implied in the supply curves. For example, total costs in both the Ricardian model and the Leontief model rise uniformly with output. In these cases, therefore, average and marginal costs are coincidental. Where a firm operates under a number of processes the total cost curve has kinks at the point where one process is given up in place of another. The marginal cost curve in this instance is a function which, although having jump discontinuities, is upper semi-continuous. The cost curves under activity analysis are illustrated in Fig. 8.5. These lie between the Ricardian/Leontief and the neoclassical cost curves. It is important to remember that the supply correspondences in all models can only be obtained from the marginal cost curves under the assumption of perfect competition.

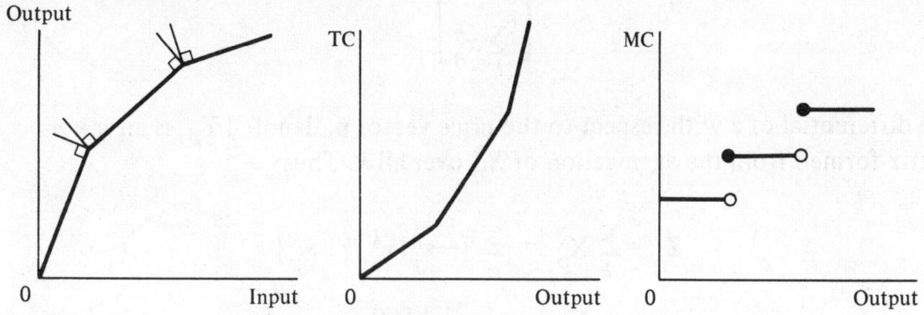

Fig. 8.5. Cost curves under activity analysis

8.4 Market Demand

We have so far neglected the somewhat difficult problem of dealing with market demand and supply. It is clear that we obtain the market curves by a direct summation over all individuals for each good. If each individual curve is continuous or semi-continuous then, by Theorems 5.3 and 5.4, their sum is continuous or semi-continuous respectively. It is tempting to argue, therefore, that the market demand curve has the same properties as the individual demand curves. This argument is common to those authors who suppose that we can think of a social welfare function whose indifference surfaces are very similar to those of the individual consumer. By altering the price of any one good we can then construct a market demand curve. Such a conclusion is true if we can conceive of a society in which all consumers have identical tastes and the same income; or alternatively, if all consumers have identical tastes and although they have different incomes the Engel curves of each consumer are coincidental and are straight lines through the origin. In the latter case the community indifference map exhibits homotheticity (see pp. 192–3). In the present context this means that if individual A transfers £10 to individual B, thus leaving aggregate income unchanged, then individual B will increase his consumption of every good by an identical amount as individual A decreases his consumption of every good. We must conclude that 'Unfortunately, attempts so far made to create a consistent theory of community demand have served only to emphasise that, in the most general case, the properties of individual demand functions do *not* hold in the aggregate and that accordingly nothing resembling the familiar indifference curve can be drawn for a group' [97, p. 101].

In so far as we must now take account of individuals the vector $\mathbf{x}$ of commodities used in Chapter 4 must be distinguished for different consumers. Let $\mathbf{x}^k$ denote the vector of commodities for the kth individual consumer. Then let the vector $\mathbf{z}$ of aggregate demands be defined

$$\mathbf{z} = \begin{bmatrix} \sum_k x_1^k \\ \cdot \\ \cdot \\ \cdot \\ \sum_k x_n^k \end{bmatrix}.$$

The differential of $\mathbf{z}$ with respect to the price vector $\mathbf{p}$, denoted $\mathbf{Z}_p$, is an $n \times n$ matrix formed from the aggregation of $\mathbf{X}_p^k$ over all k. Thus

$$\begin{aligned} \mathbf{Z}_p &= \sum_k \mathbf{X}_p^k = \sum_k [-\mathbf{x}_y^k(\mathbf{x}^k)' + \mathbf{S}_p^k] \\ &= -\sum_k \mathbf{x}^k(\mathbf{x}^k)' + \sum_k \mathbf{S}_p^k . \end{aligned}$$

Let us denote the community's price-response matrix in an analogous form to the individual, so that we can write

$$\mathbf{Z}_p = -\mathbf{z}_Y\mathbf{z}' + \mathbf{\Gamma}_p$$

where $\mathbf{\Gamma}_p$ denotes the community's substitution matrix of order $n \times n$ and $-\mathbf{z}Y\mathbf{z}'$ the community's income-response matrix. We have, therefore,

$$\mathbf{Z}_p = -\sum_k \mathbf{x}_y^k(\mathbf{x}^k)' + \sum_k \mathbf{S}_p^k = -\mathbf{z}_Y\mathbf{z}' + \mathbf{\Gamma}_p$$

and $$\mathbf{Z}_p' = -\sum_k \mathbf{x}^k(\mathbf{x}_y^k)' + \sum_k (\mathbf{S}_p^k)' = -\mathbf{z}\mathbf{z}_Y' + \mathbf{\Gamma}_p'.$$

It has been shown by Pearce [97, ch. 3] that a necessary and sufficient condition for the existence of aggregate demand curves, i.e. what are termed the integrability conditions, are that $\mathbf{\Gamma}_p \equiv \mathbf{\Gamma}_p'$. Hence, setting $\mathbf{\Gamma}_p \equiv \mathbf{\Gamma}_p'$ and noting $\mathbf{S}_p^k = (\mathbf{S}_p^k)'$ we find that

$$-\sum_k \mathbf{x}_y^k(\mathbf{x}^k)' + \mathbf{z}_Y\mathbf{z}' \equiv -\sum_k \mathbf{x}^k(\mathbf{x}_y^k)' + \mathbf{z}\mathbf{z}_Y'$$

i.e. $$[\sum_k \mathbf{x}^k(\mathbf{x}_y^k)' - \sum_k \mathbf{x}_y^k(\mathbf{x}^k)'] - [\mathbf{z}\mathbf{z}_Y' - \mathbf{z}_Y\mathbf{z}'] \equiv 0.$$

But

$$\mathbf{z} = \begin{bmatrix} \sum_k x_1^k \\ \cdot \\ \cdot \\ \cdot \\ \sum_k x_n^k \end{bmatrix} = \begin{bmatrix} m^{-1}\,\bar{x}_1 \\ \cdot \\ \cdot \\ \cdot \\ m^{-1}\,\bar{x}_n \end{bmatrix} = m^{-1}\,\bar{\mathbf{x}}.$$

Furthermore, if we differentiate z_i with respect to a unit change in aggregate income we get

$$\frac{\partial z_i}{\partial Y} = \sum_k \frac{\partial x_i^k}{\partial y^k} dy^k.$$

If we suppose that income is always shared in the existing proportion then $dy^k = y^k/Y$. However, $Y = \sum_k y^k = m^{-1}\bar{y}$. Hence, $dy^k = y^k\bar{y}^{-1}m$ and

$$\mathbf{z}_Y = \begin{bmatrix} \sum_k \frac{\partial x_1^k}{\partial y^k}\, y^k \\ \cdot \\ \cdot \\ \circ \\ \sum_k \frac{\partial x_n^k}{\partial y^k}\, y^k \end{bmatrix} \bar{y}^{-1} m = \left(\sum_k \mathbf{x}_y^k\, y^k\right) \bar{y}^{-1} m.$$

Thus

$$\mathbf{z}'_Y\mathbf{z} = (m^{-1}\,\bar{\mathbf{x}})\,(\bar{y}^{-1} m) \sum_k (\mathbf{x}_y^k)' y^k = \sum_k \bar{y}^{-1}\bar{\mathbf{x}}\,(\mathbf{x}_y^k)' y^k$$

and

$$\mathbf{z}'_Y\mathbf{z} = \sum_k \bar{y}^{-1}\,(\mathbf{x}_y^k)\bar{\mathbf{x}}' y^k.$$

Therefore the integrability conditions are

$$[\sum_k \mathbf{x}^k(\mathbf{x}_y^k)' - \sum_k \mathbf{x}_y^k(\mathbf{x}^k)'] - [\sum_k \bar{y}^{-1}\bar{\mathbf{x}}\,(\mathbf{x}_y^k)' y^k - \sum_k \bar{y}^{-1}(\mathbf{x}_y^k)\,\bar{\mathbf{x}}'\, y^k] \equiv 0.$$

i.e. $$\sum_k \{\mathbf{x}_y^k[\bar{y}^{-1}\bar{\mathbf{x}}' y^k - (\mathbf{x}^k)'] - [\bar{y}^{-1}\bar{\mathbf{x}}\, y^k - \mathbf{x}^k](\mathbf{x}_y^k)'\} \equiv 0.$$

First we note that $\sum_k [\bar{y}^{-1}\bar{\mathbf{x}}'\, y^k - (\mathbf{x}^k)'] = m^{-1}\bar{\mathbf{x}} - m^{-1}\bar{\mathbf{x}} \equiv 0$. Since $\bar{y}^{-1}\bar{\mathbf{x}}$ is independent of the summation over individuals we can therefore write:

$$\sum_k [\bar{y}^{-1}\bar{\mathbf{x}}' y^k - (\mathbf{x}^k)'] \equiv 0 \equiv \sum_k \bar{y}^{-1}\bar{\mathbf{x}}\; [\bar{y}^{-1}\bar{\mathbf{x}}' y^k - (\mathbf{x}^k)'].$$

Similarly

$$\sum_k [\bar{y}^{-1}\bar{\mathbf{x}}y^k - \mathbf{x}^k] \equiv 0 \equiv \sum_k [\bar{y}^{-1}\bar{\mathbf{x}}y^k - \mathbf{x}^k]\bar{\mathbf{x}}'\bar{y}^{-1}.$$

We have then

$$\sum_k \{\mathbf{x}_y^k[\bar{y}^{-1}\bar{\mathbf{x}}'y^k - (\mathbf{x}^k)'] - \bar{y}^{-1}\bar{\mathbf{x}}[\bar{y}^{-1}\bar{\mathbf{x}}'y^k - (\mathbf{x}^k)'] -$$

$$[\bar{y}^{-1}\bar{\mathbf{x}}\,y^k - \mathbf{x}^k]\,(\mathbf{x}^k)' + [\bar{y}^{-1}\bar{\mathbf{x}}\,y^k - \mathbf{x}^k]\bar{\mathbf{x}}'\,\bar{y}^{-1}\} \equiv 0.$$

On rearrangement this gives

$$\sum_k\{(\bar{y}^{-1}\bar{\mathbf{x}} - \mathbf{x}_y^k)\,[\bar{y}^{-1}\bar{\mathbf{x}}'\,y^k - (\mathbf{x}^k)'] - [\bar{y}^{-1}\bar{\mathbf{x}}\,y^k - \mathbf{x}^k]\,[\bar{\mathbf{x}}'\,\bar{y}^{-1} - (\mathbf{x}_y^k)']\} \equiv 0.$$

Now define $\mathbf{x}^k = \mathbf{f}^k(y) = \mathbf{f}^k$ so that $\mathbf{f}^k$ denotes the vector of Engel curves for the kth individual, then we can define the vector $\mathbf{F}^k$ by

$$\mathbf{F}^k = [\bar{y}^{-1}\bar{\mathbf{x}}y^k - \mathbf{f}^k] \text{ with } (\mathbf{F}^k)' = [\bar{y}^{-1}\bar{\mathbf{x}}'y^k - (\mathbf{f}^k)'].$$

Differentiating with respect to y we obtain

$$\mathbf{F}_y^k = [\bar{y}^{-1}\bar{\mathbf{x}} - \mathbf{x}_y^k] \quad\text{and}\quad (\mathbf{F}_y^k)' = [\bar{y}^{-1}\bar{\mathbf{x}}' - (\mathbf{x}_y^k)'].$$

The integrability condition accordingly takes the form

$$\sum_k [\mathbf{F}_y^k\,(\mathbf{F}^k)' - \mathbf{F}^k\,(\mathbf{F}_y^k)'] \equiv 0.$$

An over-sufficient condition for this to be met is that

$$\mathbf{F}_y^k\,(\mathbf{F}^k)' - \mathbf{F}^k(\mathbf{F}_y^k)' = 0 \qquad \forall k.$$

Pearce [97] has shown that an Engel curve which satisfies the integrability conditions takes the form

$$x_i^k = -\,[a_i\,(y^k)^2 - a_i(\bar{y} + a)y^k].$$

In vector notation

$$\mathbf{x}^k = -\,[\boldsymbol{\alpha}(y^k)^2 - \boldsymbol{\alpha}(\bar{y} + a)y^k].$$

Differentiating this expression with respect to income y^k we see

$$\mathbf{x}_y^k = -\,[2\boldsymbol{\alpha}y^k - \boldsymbol{\alpha}(\bar{y} + a)].$$

Hence

$$\begin{aligned}
\mathbf{x}_y^k\,(\mathbf{x}^k)' &= [2\boldsymbol{\alpha}y^k - \boldsymbol{\alpha}(\bar{y} + a)]\;[\boldsymbol{\alpha}'(y^k)^2 - \boldsymbol{\alpha}'(\bar{y} + a)y^k]\\
&= \boldsymbol{\alpha}\boldsymbol{\alpha}'[2(y^k)^3 - 3(\bar{y} + a)\,(y^k)^2 + (\bar{y} + a)y^k]\\
&= \boldsymbol{\alpha}\boldsymbol{\alpha}'\phi(y^k).
\end{aligned}$$

Let us now bring all our results together by seeing which of the restrictions on the aggregate demand curve still hold.

1. *Engel aggregation.* If this is met we must have $\mathbf{p}'\mathbf{z}_Y = 1$.

$$\mathbf{z}_Y = \sum_k \mathbf{x}_y^k\, y^k\, \bar{y}^{-1}\, m$$

$$\mathbf{p}'\mathbf{z}_Y = \sum_k \mathbf{p}'\mathbf{x}_y^k\, y^k\, \bar{y}^{-1}\, m \text{ since } \mathbf{p} \text{ is independent of } k.$$

But $\mathbf{p}'\mathbf{x}_y^k = 1$ from the Engel aggregation of individual k. Thus

$$\mathbf{p}'\mathbf{z}_Y = \sum_k y^k\, \bar{y}^{-1}\, m = 1.$$

2. *Cournot aggregation.* If this is met we must show that $\mathbf{Z}_p'\,\mathbf{p} = -\mathbf{z}$.

$$\mathbf{Z}_p' = -\sum_k \mathbf{x}^k(\mathbf{x}_y^k)' + \sum_k (\mathbf{S}_p^k)'.$$

$$\therefore \mathbf{Z}_p'\,\mathbf{p} = -\sum_k \mathbf{x}^k(\mathbf{x}_y^k)'\mathbf{p} + \sum_k (\mathbf{S}_p^k)'\mathbf{p}$$

$$= -\sum_k \mathbf{x}^k = -\mathbf{z}$$

where we have used the fact that $(\mathbf{x}_y^k)'\mathbf{p} = \mathbf{p}'(\mathbf{x}_y^k) = 1$ and $\mathbf{p}'\mathbf{S}_p^k = (\mathbf{S}_p^k)'\mathbf{p} = 0$.

3. *Symmetry.* This we have employed, by assumption, in order to satisfy the integrability conditions.

4. *Homogeneity.* If this is true we must have

(*a*) $\mathbf{Z}_p\,\mathbf{p} = -\mathbf{z}_Y Y$

and (*b*) homogeneity of $\mathbf{z}$ implying $\mathbf{Z}_p\mathbf{p} = -\mathbf{z}_Y Y$.

First consider (*a*).

$$\mathbf{\Gamma}_p\,\mathbf{p} = (\mathbf{Z}_p + \mathbf{z}_Y\,\mathbf{z}')\mathbf{p} = (\mathbf{Z}_p' + \mathbf{z}\mathbf{z}_Y')\mathbf{p}$$

$$= \mathbf{Z}_p'\,\mathbf{p} + \mathbf{z}$$

$$= -\mathbf{z} + \mathbf{z} = 0.$$

$$\therefore \mathbf{\Gamma}_p\,\mathbf{p} = 0.$$

Hence

$$\mathbf{Z}_p\,\mathbf{p} = -\mathbf{z}_Y\mathbf{z}'\mathbf{p}.$$

But

$$\mathbf{z}'\mathbf{p} = \mathbf{p}'\mathbf{z} = \sum_k y^k = Y$$

$$\therefore \mathbf{Z}_p\mathbf{p} = -\mathbf{z}_Y\, Y.$$

Now consider (*b*). Assume $\mathbf{z}$ is homogeneous of degree zero. We have

$$\mathbf{z} = \mathbf{z}(\mathbf{p}, \mathbf{y}, Y)$$

and by Euler's theorem

$$\mathbf{Z}_p\mathbf{p} + \mathbf{z}'_y\,\mathbf{y} + \mathbf{z}_Y Y = 0.$$

$$\therefore \mathbf{Z}_p\mathbf{p} = -\,\mathbf{z}_Y Y - \mathbf{z}'_y\mathbf{y}.$$

Hence homogeneity is ruled out. This is clear because we must include a distribution element when considering the change in the vector **z**, i.e.

$$\mathbf{z} = \sum_k \mathbf{x}^k = \sum_k \mathbf{x}^k(\mathbf{p}, y^k) = \mathbf{z}(\mathbf{p}, \mathbf{y}, Y)$$

$$d\mathbf{z} = \sum_k \mathbf{X}^k\, d\mathbf{p} + \left(\sum_k \mathbf{x}_y^k\, dy^k + \sum_k \mathbf{x}_y^k \frac{dy^k}{Y}\right) + \mathbf{z}_Y dY.$$

Even if total income remained fixed so that $dY = 0$ we still have to take account of the distribution vector $\sum_k \mathbf{x}^k \frac{dy^k}{Y}$. If we assume that for each individual the marginal propensity to consume any good is independent of the income which accrues to that individual from redistribution then

$$\sum_k \mathbf{x}_y^k \frac{dy^k}{Y} = \sum_k \mathbf{x}_y^k \sum_k \frac{dy^k}{Y} = 0$$

since

$$\sum_k dy^k = 0.$$

5. *Negativity.* If this were true, as for the individual, we would have $\mathbf{q}'\,\mathbf{\Gamma}_p\,\mathbf{q} \leqslant 0$, i.e. Γ_p negative semi-definite. It is this condition which ensures that the indifference surfaces for the community are convex. If we assume that we can add the better sets of consumers then $\sum_k \mathbf{B}_0^k$ will represent the better set for the community, each consuming $\mathbf{x}_0^k$. If $\mathbf{B}_0^k$ is convex for all k then $\sum_k \mathbf{B}_0^k$ is also convex since the sum of convex sets is itself convex. We can continue the present aggregate analysis to see under what conditions $\sum_k \mathbf{B}_0^k$ is a strictly convex set, given $\mathbf{B}_0^k$ is strictly convex.

We have established that

$$\mathbf{\Gamma}_p = -\sum_k \mathbf{x}_y^k(\mathbf{x}^k)' + \sum_k \mathbf{S}_p^k.$$

In what follows we shall make use of the following theorem:

Theorem 8.1 If **A** and **B** are two semi-definite matrices of the same order then **A** + **B** is a semi-definite matrix.

Since $\mathbf{S}_p^k$ is negative semi-definite then by Theorem 8.1 $\sum_k \mathbf{S}_p^k$ is a negative semi-definite matrix. It follows that $\mathbf{\Gamma}_p$ will be negative definite if $-\ {}_k\ \mathbf{x}_y^k(\mathbf{x}^k)'$

is negative semi-definite, which in turn means if $-\mathbf{x}_y^k(\mathbf{x}^k)'$ is negative semi-definite or $\mathbf{x}_y^k(\mathbf{x}^k)'$ is positive semi-definite.

Let us first take an extreme case. We have an Engel curve of the form

$$\mathbf{x}^k = -[\boldsymbol{\alpha}(y^k)^2 - \boldsymbol{\alpha}(\bar{y}+a)y^k].$$

Now if $y^k = y$, $\forall k$ and $a_i = a_j = a$, $\forall i, j$ then we have individuals with identical income and identical Engel curves. We have in this instance

$$\begin{aligned}\mathbf{x}_y^k(\mathbf{x}^k)' &= \boldsymbol{\alpha\alpha}'\emptyset(y) \\ &= (a\,\boldsymbol{\iota})(a\boldsymbol{\iota}')\emptyset(y) \\ &= a^2\boldsymbol{\iota\iota}'\emptyset(y).\end{aligned}$$

Since $\boldsymbol{\iota\iota}'$ is a positive definite matrix $a^2\boldsymbol{\iota\iota}'\emptyset(y)$ is positive semi-definite depending upon whether $\emptyset(y) \geqslant 0$, then $-\sum_k \mathbf{x}_y^k(\mathbf{x}^k)'$ is negative semi-definite.

We argued at the beginning of this section that identity of Engel curves and income is too strong a stipulation; all we require is that the preference function be homothetic. Let us see if this condition is met in the present case. The ray through the origin of an indifference diagram is the ratio of the marginal propensities to consume, say, goods i and j. We have for the kth individual

$$x_{iy}^k = 2a_i y^k - a_i(\bar{y}+a)$$

$$x_{jy}^k = 2a_j y^k - a_j(\bar{y}+a)$$

which gives

$$\frac{x_{iy}^k}{x_{jy}^k} = \frac{2a_i y^k - a_i(\bar{y}+a)}{2a_j y^k - a_j(\bar{y}+a)} = \frac{a_i}{a_j}$$

so that the ratio is independent of the level of income. Thus so long as this ratio is the same for all individuals – even with different levels of income – then $-\sum_k \mathbf{x}_y^k(\mathbf{x}^k)'$ is a negative semi-definite. Pearce [97, ch. 3.3] finds even less rigid conditions under which $-\sum_k \mathbf{x}_y^k(\mathbf{x}^k)'$ is negative semi-definite. We can conclude therefore:

Proposition 8.1 The market demand function is more likely to possess the usual properties of individual demand functions

(1) the greater the similarity of individual preferences;
(2) the smaller the correlation between the marginal propensity to consume and the accrued income;
(3) the closer the Engel curves are to linearity.

8.5 A First Introduction to Equilibrium

Equilibrium is a fundamental concept in economics and is central to both micro and macro economics. In a general sense, equilibrium refers to a balance of forces, a state where things are at rest. As Arrow points out [8], equilibrium is composed of two aspects. First, that a system to exhibit equilibrium must be sufficiently complete so as to determine the values of its variables (i.e. the endogenous variables). Second, that the system must represent a balance of forces. In order to highlight these aspects, and others to follow, let us consider a very simple example familiar to all beginning economists, namely the demand and supply model for a single good. Suppose we have the model

$$x = x(p)$$
$$s = s(p)$$
$$x = s = q.$$

First, we note that the model consists of two behavioural equations and an equilibrium condition. The system in the form $q = x(p)$ and $q = s(p)$ is composed of only two endogenous variables, i.e. variables which are to be determined by the system, and these are clearly p and q. Second, these two equations denote forces which oppose each other. Only when both equations are satisfied simultaneously will the desires of consumers, as embodied in $x(p)$, and the desires of suppliers, as embodied in $s(p)$, be balanced.

Although there are as many variables as there are equations this is not sufficient to establish an equilibrium. For example, suppose

$$\begin{aligned} q &= x(p) = a + \beta p \\ q &= s(p) = \gamma + \delta p. \end{aligned} \tag{8.1}$$

If $\beta = \delta$ then there will exist no solution if $a \neq \gamma$; graphically, the two curves never intersect. On the other hand, if $a = \gamma$ and $\beta = \delta$ then an infinity of solutions exists and every price–quantity combination satisfying either equation is an equilibrium combination.

The equilibrium price and quantity is denoted in terms of all parameters and exogenous variables of the *structural form* (Equations (8.1)); these solution values are referred to as the *reduced form.* In the present example there are only parameters in the reduced form equation, which takes the form:

$$\bar{p} = \frac{a - \gamma}{\delta - \beta}$$

$$\bar{q} = \frac{a\delta - \beta\gamma}{\delta - \beta}.$$

It is the reduced form which aids us in establishing the conditions which give us an economically meaningful equilibrium solution. If we have normal-shaped curves in the sense that the demand curve is downward-sloping ($\beta < 0$) and the supply curve upward-sloping ($\delta > 0$) then for a solution to exist such that $p \geqslant 0$ and $q \geqslant 0$ we require (i) $a \geqslant \gamma$ and (ii) $a\delta \geqslant \beta\gamma$. The model allows all possible solutions. There is no economically meaningful solution if $a < \gamma$ or if $a\delta < \beta\gamma$, the first giving a negative price, the second a negative quantity. If $a > \gamma$ and $a\delta > \beta\gamma$ then a unique solution exists in the positive quadrant, if $\beta = \delta$ then an infinity of solutions exists. In this area of economics three topics are dominant: existence, uniqueness, and stability. Our example has already illustrated the first two and we shall discuss stability in Chapter 11.

Let us return to the structural form (8.1). As written they are functions only of the price of the good concerned. Suppose this is only one of many goods in the system. Assume that all other goods are in equilibrium except for the good under discussion. Now if, at the ruling price, there is excess demand then price is assumed to rise until equilibrium is established. If this market were totally independent of the rest then the equilibrium conditions in all other markets will not be disturbed.[1] In this instance we can consider the market in isolation with no complications. If, however, the market is not independent of the rest, which is the most usual case, all other equilibrium positions will be disturbed as a result of the price adjustment in this market. If the disturbances are small and the feedbacks into this market smaller still and if we consider the market *as if* it were in isolation then there will only be a small margin of error. If the feedback effects are large, however, the consideration of a single market will give rise to a large error.

The study of one market independent of the rest is termed *partial equilibrium analysis* and where all the effects and feedbacks are taken into account we have *general equilibrium analysis.* Partial equilibrium analysis is the basic approach of the neoclassical economists and was used extensively by Marshall [83]. General equilibrium analysis, although existing prior to Leon Walras was recognised and elucidated first by him.

Consider once again our single market. Let $\bar{p}_1$ denote the equilibrium price,[2] then we have for equilibrium $x_1(\bar{p}_1) \leqslant s_1(\bar{p}_1)$, $\bar{p}_1 \geqslant 0$. If $x_1(\bar{p}_1) < s_1(\bar{p}_1)$ then $\bar{p}_1 = 0$ because all demands are satisfied at the zero price. If $x_1(p_1) > s_1(p_1)$, $\forall p_1 \geqslant 0$ then the demand and supply curves are inconsistent and no equilibrium exists. We shall find it most useful to consider many issues about equilibrium in terms of *excess demand equations.* Let $z_1(p_1) \equiv x_1(p_1) - s_1(p_1)$ denote the excess demand function or correspondence. For this market, therefore, equilibrium requires that $z_1(\bar{p}_1) \leqslant 0, \bar{p}_1 \geqslant 0$ and $\bar{p}_1 = 0$ if $z_1(p_1) < 0$. These points are illustrated in Fig. 8.6. In specifying equilibrium in terms of excess demands we first suppose $z_i(p_i)$ exists, and that it is continuous or semi-continuous. We shall make equilibrium in a single market explicit in terms of the following:

Definition 8.1

For a single good i and excess demand function $z_i(p_i) \equiv x_i(p_i) - s_i(p_i)$, p_i is an equilibrium if

$$z_i(\bar{p}_i) \leqslant 0 \qquad \forall\, \bar{p}_i \geqslant 0$$

$$\text{and} \quad z_i(\bar{p}_i) < 0 \qquad \Rightarrow \bar{p}_i = 0.$$

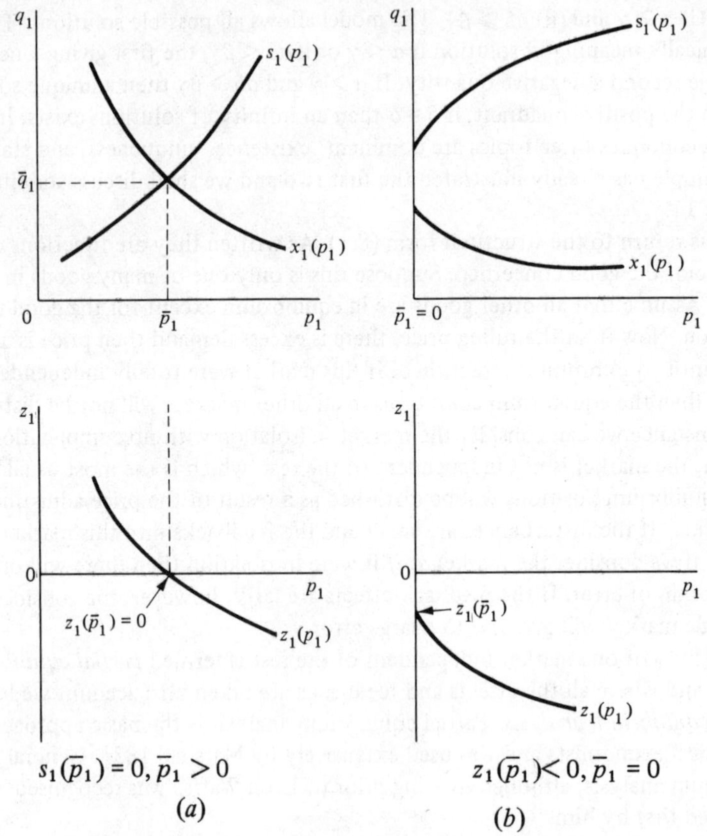

Fig. 8.6. Equilibrium in a single market

So far we have looked at the ith market in isolation. Can we specify equilibrium for a general equilibrium analysis? First we remind ourselves that in Chapter 4 we obtained, from consumer equilibrium,

$$\mathbf{x} = \mathbf{x}(\mathbf{p}, y).$$

Suppose y is the value of a consumer's existing stock of the n goods. Thus if x_i^0 denotes the stock of commodity i then $y^0 = \sum_i p_i x_i^0 = \mathbf{p}'\mathbf{x}^0$. We can therefore write $\mathbf{x}$ solely in terms of the price vector.

$$\mathbf{x} = \mathbf{g}(\mathbf{p}).$$

From Chapters 6 and 7 we know that the supply function or correspondence has only prices as its arguments, i.e.

$$\mathbf{s} = \mathbf{s}(\mathbf{p}).$$

Thus the vector of excess demands is given by:

$$\mathbf{z}(\mathbf{p}) \equiv \mathbf{g}(\mathbf{p}) - \mathbf{s}(\mathbf{p}).$$

Let $\bar{\mathbf{p}}$ denote an equilibrium price vector. We have then for general equilibrium analysis

Definition 8.2

$\bar{\mathbf{p}}$ is an equilibrium if $\mathbf{z}(\bar{\mathbf{p}}) \leqslant 0$, $\bar{\mathbf{p}} \geqslant 0$ and $z_i(\bar{\mathbf{p}}) < 0, \Rightarrow \bar{p}_i = 0$.

In other words, for $\bar{\mathbf{p}}$ to be an equilibrium price vector we require equilibrium in every market simultaneously. The first thing we note is that $\mathbf{z}(\mathbf{p})$ is homogeneous of degree zero in $\mathbf{p}$. This readily follows from the fact that $\mathbf{x} = \mathbf{x}(\mathbf{p}, y)$ is homogeneous of degree zero in $\mathbf{p}$ and y so that $\mathbf{x} = \mathbf{g}(\mathbf{p})$ is homogeneous of degree zero in $\mathbf{p}$; also we have already shown that $\mathbf{s} = \mathbf{s}(\mathbf{p})$ is homogeneous of degree zero in $\mathbf{p}$. Thus $\mathbf{z}(\lambda\mathbf{p}) = \mathbf{z}(\mathbf{p})$. This has an important consequence with respect to the numeraire as we shall see in Section 8.6 below.

As a consequence of assuming consumers operating on their budget lines it follows that the total value of sales to consumers must equal the total value of purchases by consumers $\mathbf{p}'\mathbf{x} = \mathbf{p}'\mathbf{s}$, so that $\mathbf{p}'\mathbf{z} = 0$. This is known as Walras Law.

Proposition 8.2 (Walras Law). If a consumer spends all his income then $\mathbf{p}'\mathbf{z}(\mathbf{p}) = 0$.

If consumers do not necessarily spend all their income then Walras Law does not necessarily hold. Most of the existence proofs in general equilibrium analysis depend upon the truth of Proposition 8.2, and this in turn is very much dependent upon the non-satiation axiom because it is this axiom which ensures that the optimal demands by consumers lie on their budget hyperplanes. It is also important to note that it is Proposition 8.2 which ensures that if excess demand is negative at the equilibrium price then this price is zero. This follows because if $\bar{\mathbf{p}} \geqslant 0$ and $\mathbf{z}(\bar{\mathbf{p}}) \leqslant 0$ then every element of $\bar{\mathbf{p}}'\mathbf{z}(\bar{\mathbf{p}})$ is non-positive. Suppose to the contrary that $\bar{p}_i > 0$ with $z_i(\bar{\mathbf{p}}) < 0$ then $\bar{p}_i z_i(\bar{\mathbf{p}}) < 0$ and $\bar{\mathbf{p}}'\mathbf{z}(\bar{\mathbf{p}}) < 0$ but this contradicts Walras Law, and since no price is negative it follows $\bar{p}_i = 0$.

Before leaving excess demand curves we shall in some of the proofs concerning competitive equilibrium make use of what is referred to as a *modulated excess demand function.*

Definition 8.3

If $z_i(\mathbf{p})$ is the excess demand for the ith good then the *modulated excess demand function* $M_i(\mathbf{p})$ is given by

$$M_i(\mathbf{p}) = \max\,[0, z_i\,(\mathbf{p})]\,.$$

Fig. 8.7 compares the excess and modulated excess demand functions. This figure

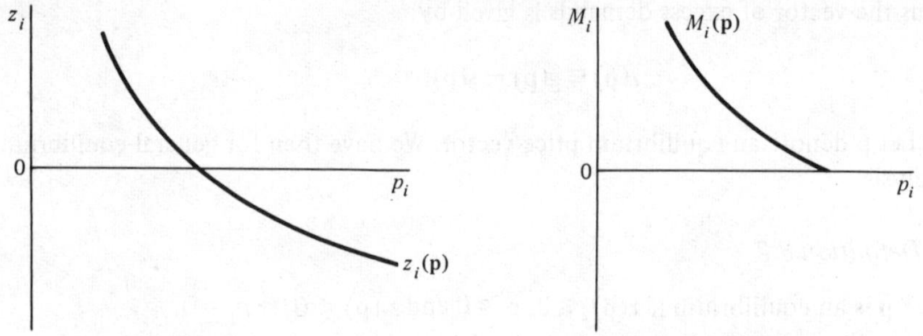

(*a*) Excess demand function (*b*) Modulated excess demand function

Fig. 8.7. Excess and modulated excess demand functions

makes clear that $M_i(\mathbf{p})$ has the properties

(1) $M_i(\mathbf{p}) > 0$ iff $z_i(\mathbf{p}) > 0$.

(2) $M_i(\mathbf{p}) = 0$ if $z_i(\mathbf{p}) = 0$.

(3) $p_i + M_i(\mathbf{p}) \geqslant 0$ $\forall i$.

8.6 Normalised Price Set

In the last section we established that $\mathbf{z}(\mathbf{p})$ is homogeneous of degree zero in prices so that $\mathbf{z}(\lambda\mathbf{p}) = \mathbf{z}(\mathbf{p})$. In other words, there exists one degree of freedom. The degree of freedom amounts to expressing all goods in terms of, say, one good. The good or goods that is (are) chosen so that all other goods are expressed in these units is called the *numeraire.* Usually one good has been taken as numeraire, e.g. Hicks in his *Value and Capital* [52], Walras in his *Elements of Pure Economics,* and more recently by Patinkin in his *Money, Interest and Prices* [96]. Marx of course took labour as the numeraire and even Keynes in his *General Theory* deflated by a labour index. If we suppose the first good is taken as numeraire, i.e. let $\lambda = 1/p_1$, then we have

$$\mathbf{z}(\mathbf{p}) = \mathbf{z}\left(1, \frac{p_2}{p_1}, \ldots, \frac{p_n}{p_1}\right).$$

However, for this to make sense we must have $p_1 \neq 0$ for if this were not so all goods would have infinite relative prices. We must conclude, therefore, that a good to be chosen as numeraire must not be a free good, i.e. command a zero price. But it is the market conditions which establish an equilibrium and which determine which good is a free good. To take a good and assume its price is strictly positive is tantamount to assuming a solution exists to the general equilibrium model, but it is this very condition we are attempting to establish.

We can overcome this difficulty by constructing a composite commodity. Make up a basket by taking one unit of every good and then total the value of the basket, which is $\iota'\mathbf{p} = \sum_i p_i$. Clearly some prices may be zero but not all goods will be free goods and hence $\iota'\mathbf{p} > 0$. Set $\iota'\mathbf{p} = 1$ so that $\lambda = 1/\iota'\mathbf{p}$ and

$$\mathbf{z}(\lambda\mathbf{p}) = \mathbf{z}\left(\frac{\mathbf{p}}{\iota'\mathbf{p}}\right) = \mathbf{z}(\mathbf{p}).$$

It is clear that each $0 \leqslant p_i/\iota'\mathbf{p} \leqslant 1$. Consequently, the normalisation $\iota'\mathbf{p} = 1$ defines a *unit simplex,* which will play an important role in our economic analysis. For this reason let us illustrate by taking the normalised price set (p_1, p_2, p_3) where $\sum_i p_i = 1$. If at least one price is non-zero then we have the following possibilities:

Either $p_1 = 0 \quad p_2 = 0 \quad p_3 = 1$ or $p_1 + p_2 = 1 \quad p_3 = 0$

$p_1 = 0 \quad p_2 = 1 \quad p_3 = 0 \qquad p_1 + p_3 = 1 \quad p_2 = 0$

$p_1 = 1 \quad p_2 = 0 \quad p_3 = 0 \qquad p_2 + p_3 = 1 \quad p_1 = 0$

giving six possibilities in all. If we sketch this it appears that the simplex $\iota'\mathbf{p} = 1$ is the triangular face denoted $\mathbf{S}_3$ in Fig. 8.8. More explicitly,

Definition 8.4.

A unit simplex $\mathbf{S}_n$ is given by the set $\mathbf{S}_n = \{\mathbf{p}/\iota'\mathbf{p} = 1, \mathbf{p} > 0\}$.

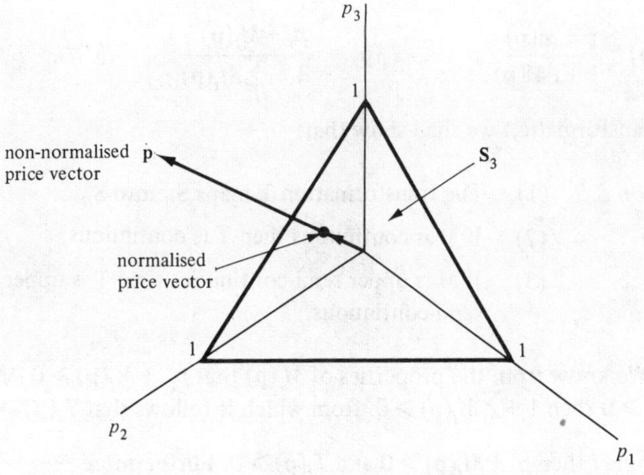

Fig. 8.8. Unit simplex $\mathbf{S}_3 = \{\mathbf{p}/\sum_i p_i = 1, \mathbf{p} > 0\}$

This simplex maps any point $\mathbf{p}$ in $\mathbf{E}^3$ into the simplex $\mathbf{S}_3$; in other words, for any non-normalised price vector the normalised price vector is the intersection of the non-normalised price vector with the set $\mathbf{S}_n$, as illustrated in Fig. 8.8. It is clear that the set $\mathbf{S}_n$ is closed, bounded and convex. Example 8.1 shows clearly how the normalised prices are obtained.

Example 8.1 Let $p_1 = \frac{1}{2}$ and $p_2 = 2$ then $\iota'\mathbf{p} = 2\frac{1}{2}$ and the normalised price set is $\mathbf{p} = (0{\cdot}2, 0{\cdot}8)$. Similarly the price set $(1, 1\frac{1}{2})$ is normalised to $(0{\cdot}4, 0{\cdot}6)$. Both these results are illustrated in Fig. 8.9.

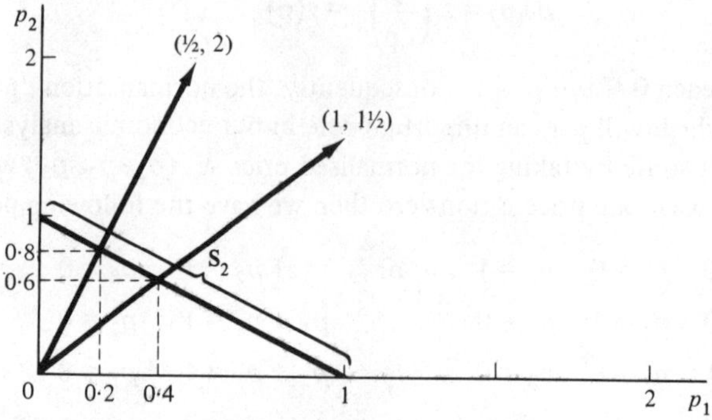

Fig. 8.9. Example 8.1

In later sections we shall make use of a transformation which maps $\mathbf{S}_n$ into itself. We shall therefore conclude this section with a discussion of the transformation concerned. Define a transformation $\mathbf{T}(\mathbf{p})$ such that

$$\mathbf{T}(\mathbf{p}) = \frac{\mathbf{p} + \mathbf{M}(\mathbf{p})}{1 + \iota'\mathbf{M}(\mathbf{p})}, \quad \text{i.e.} \quad T_i(\mathbf{p}) = \frac{p_i + M_i(\mathbf{p})}{1 + \sum_i M_i(\mathbf{p})} \qquad \forall i.$$

Using this transformation we shall show that:

Proposition 8.3 (1) The transformation $\mathbf{T}$ maps $\mathbf{S}_n$ into $\mathbf{S}_n$.

(2) If $\mathbf{M}$ is continuous then $\mathbf{T}$ is continuous.

(3) If $\mathbf{M}$ is upper semi-continuous then $\mathbf{T}$ is upper semi-continuous.

Proof We know from the properties of $M_i(\mathbf{p})$ that $p_i + M_i(\mathbf{p}) \geqslant 0 \ \forall i$, and since $M_i(\mathbf{p}) \geqslant 0$ then $1 + \sum_i M_i(\mathbf{p}) > 0$, from which it follows that $T_i(\mathbf{p}) \geqslant 0$. Assume $p_i > 0$ for some i then $p_i + M_i(\mathbf{p}) > 0$ and $T_i(\mathbf{p}) > 0$. Furthermore

$$\iota'\mathbf{T}(\mathbf{p}) = \frac{\iota'\mathbf{p} + \iota'\mathbf{M}(\mathbf{p})}{1 + \iota'\mathbf{M}(\mathbf{p})} = \frac{1 + \iota'\mathbf{M}(\mathbf{p})}{1 + \iota'\mathbf{M}(\mathbf{p})} = 1.$$

Hence, $\mathbf{T}(\mathbf{p}) \in \mathbf{S}_n$. Consequently $\mathbf{T}$ maps $\mathbf{S}_n$ into itself. The second part of the proposition readily follows. If $\mathbf{M}(\mathbf{p})$ is continuous then by Theorem 5.3 (p. 144) $\mathbf{T}(\mathbf{p})$ being the ratio of two continuous functions is itself continuous. For the same reason $\mathbf{T}(\mathbf{p})$ is upper semi-continuous because it is the ratio of two upper semi-continuous functions.

Q.E.D.

8.7 The Mathematics of Equilibrium Points

This section is concerned with two mathematical theorems which are used extensively in the literature of general equilibrium analysis. The first theorem is due to Brouwer and is referred to as Brouwer's fixed-point theorem. As we shall see, the shortcoming of Brouwer's fixed-point theorem is that it refers only to functions which are continuous. As we have seen economics has many correspondences and these are invariably upper semi-continuous. In 1944 Kakutani supplied a generalisation to the Brouwer theorem which took account of this limitation.[3]

Theorem 8.2 (Brouwer's fixed-point theorem). If f is a continuous function which maps a closed bounded convex set $\mathbf{X}$ into itself then there exists an $\bar{\mathbf{x}} \in \mathbf{X}$ such that $\bar{\mathbf{x}} = f(\bar{\mathbf{x}})$.

Let us take a very simple example to illustrate this theorem.

Example 8.2 Let $\mathbf{X} = \{x/0 \leqslant x \leqslant 1\}$ which is a closed bounded convex set. Consider a mapping f: $\mathbf{X} \rightarrow \mathbf{X}$ given by the graph $f(x) = 0{\cdot}2 + 0{\cdot}5x$. The image set $f(\mathbf{X}) = \{y/0{\cdot}2 \leqslant y \leqslant 0{\cdot}7\}$ and is clearly a subset of $\mathbf{X}$, so that f maps $\mathbf{X}$ into itself. Fig. 8.10 gives two representations of this example. In Fig. 8.10 (*a*) we have the graph of f along with the graph $f(x) = x$, which is the diagonal. Clearly where $f(x)$ cuts the diagonal we have $f(\bar{x}) = \bar{x}$, which in this example is unique with $\bar{x} = 0{\cdot}4$. In Fig. 8.10 (*b*) it is observed that only $x = 0{\cdot}4$ is vertically below showing $f(0{\cdot}4) = 0{\cdot}4$.

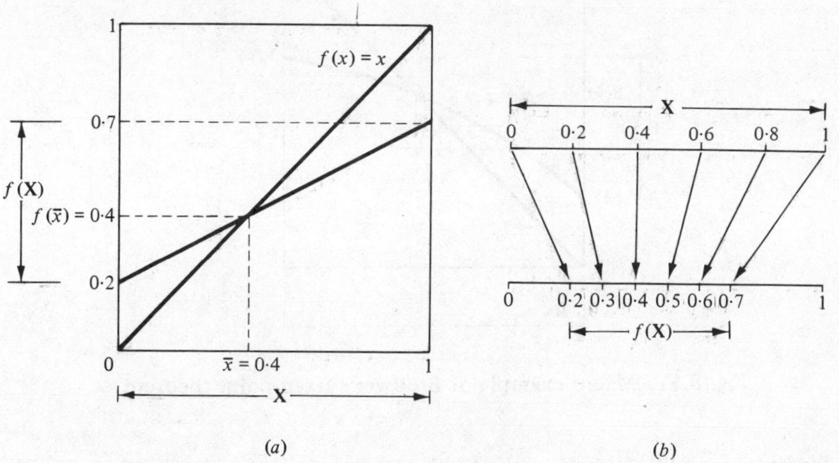

Fig. 8.10. Example of Brouwer's fixed-point theorem

Let us step outside microeconomics for a moment and consider the simplest form of the Keynesian macromodel. This will allow us to give an immediate application of Brouwer's fixed-point theorem in a situation closely associated with Example 8.2.

Example 8.3 (Keynesian Model) Let $\mathbf{Y} = \{y/0 \leqslant y \leqslant y_f\}$, i.e. the level of all incomes from zero to the full-employment level y_f. The set **Y** is closed, bounded and convex. Consider now the expenditure function $E(y) = C(y) + I(y) + G_0$, where consumption and investment are continuous functions of income, and government expenditure is treated exogenously. The expenditure function E is continuous and, as can be seen from Fig. 8.11, maps **Y** into itself. By Brouwer's fixed-point theorem there exists a $\bar{y}$ such that $\bar{y} = E(\bar{y})$. But this is no more than the equilibrium level of national income for the simple Keynesian model. Hence we see why this section is entitled 'the mathematics of equilibrium points'. This macro example clearly illuminates that fixed points are equilibrium points.

It is worth noting that Brouwer's fixed-point theorem sets out the conditions which guarantees the *existence* of a fixed point (equilibrium point). However, it does not say anything about the uniqueness of the fixed point. It is very easy to draw a function f in Example 8.2 which, even though continuous, cuts $f(x) = x$ more than once.

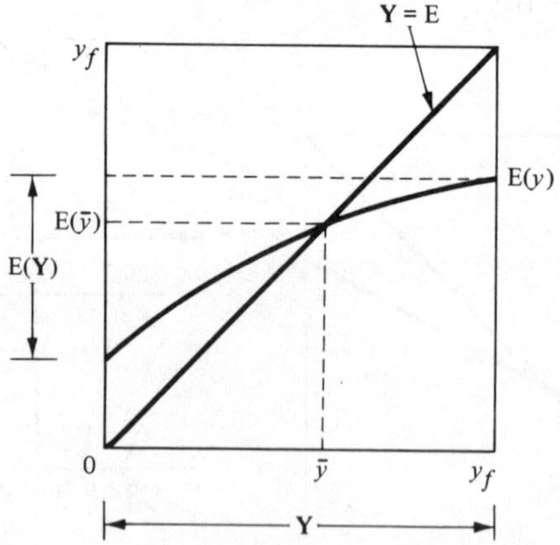

Fig. 8.11. Macro example of Brouwer's fixed-point theorem

We now turn to Kakutani's generalisation of Brouwer's fixed-point theorem. We shall, in stating this theorem, use compactness in place of closed and bounded.

Theorem 8.3 (Kakutani's fixed-point theorem) If $\boldsymbol{\psi}$ is an upper semi-continuous point-to-set mapping of a compact set $\mathbf{X}$ into itself such that each $\boldsymbol{\psi}(\mathbf{x})$ is compact and convex, then there exists a $\bar{\mathbf{x}} \in \mathbf{X}$ such that $\bar{\mathbf{x}} \in \boldsymbol{\psi}(\bar{\mathbf{x}})$.

We can shorten this with the help of the following notation, and it is often stated in this form. Let $\boldsymbol{\Phi}(\mathbf{X})$ denote all the family of closed convex subsets of $\mathbf{X}$. Then

Theorem 8.3′ If $\boldsymbol{\psi}$ is an upper semi-continuous point-to-set mapping of a compact set $\mathbf{X}$ into $\boldsymbol{\Phi}(\mathbf{X})$, then there exists a $\bar{\mathbf{x}} \in \mathbf{X}$ such that $\bar{\mathbf{x}} \in \boldsymbol{\psi}(\bar{\mathbf{x}})$.

This theorem can be pictured with the help of a Venn diagram, as in Fig. 8.12, where we have represented two subsets of $\boldsymbol{\Phi}(\mathbf{X})$, namely $\boldsymbol{\psi}(\mathbf{x})$ and $\boldsymbol{\psi}(\bar{\mathbf{x}})$.

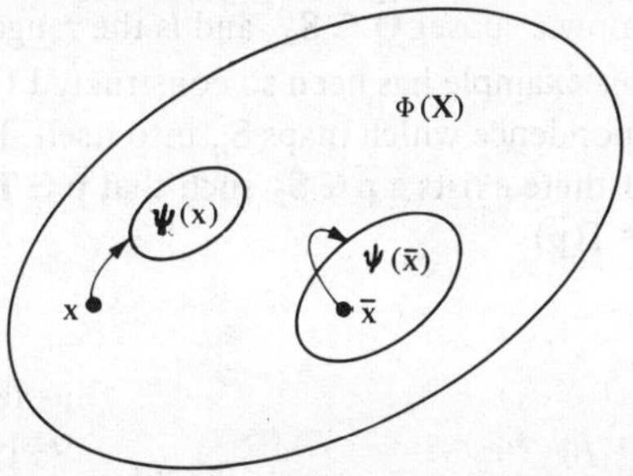

Fig. 8.12. Illustration of Kakutani's fixed-point theorem

The interpretation of this theorem can be illustrated by an example.

Example 8.4 Let there be two commodities where the excess demand for commodity 1 is a correspondence and that for commodity 2 is a function, as illustrated in Fig. 8.13. It is supposed each z_i is dependent upon both p_1 and p_2. Next consider the unit simplex $\mathbf{S}_2 = \{\mathbf{p}/p_1 + p_2 = 1, \mathbf{p} > 0\}$. Suppose at prices $p_1 = 1$ and $p_2 = 2$ we have $z_1 = 2$ and $z_2 = 1$, as shown in Fig. 8.13. In terms of the unit simplex $\mathbf{p} = (\frac{1}{3}, \frac{2}{3})$. Now define

$$\mathbf{q} = \mathbf{T}(\mathbf{p}) = \frac{\mathbf{p} + \mathbf{M}(\mathbf{p})}{1 + \iota'\mathbf{M}(\mathbf{p})} \quad \text{or} \quad q_i = \frac{p_i + M_i(\mathbf{p})}{1 + \sum_i M_i(\mathbf{p})} \qquad i = 1, 2.$$

We have already established that $\mathbf{T}$ maps $\mathbf{S}_n \to \mathbf{S}_n$ so that $q_i \in \mathbf{S}_2$ in the present example. For $\mathbf{p} = (\frac{1}{3}, \frac{2}{3})$ we obtain from this transformation the new point $\mathbf{q} = (\frac{7}{12}, \frac{5}{12})$ as illustrated in Fig. 8.14.

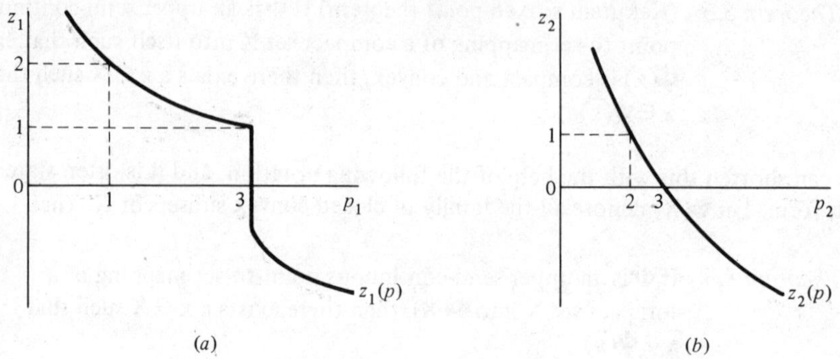

Fig. 8.13. Illustration of Example 8.4

Now consider a price vector (3, 3). The normalised form is $(\frac{1}{2}, \frac{1}{2})$ in the unit simplex. However, **q** is now a subset $\tilde{\mathbf{Q}} \subset \mathbf{S}_2$, and is the range $(\frac{3}{4}, \frac{1}{4})$ to $(\frac{1}{2}, \frac{1}{2})$. Clearly, $\mathbf{p} \in \tilde{\mathbf{Q}} \subset \mathbf{S}_2$. This example has been so constructed that $\mathbf{T(p)}$ is an upper semi-continuous correspondence which maps $\mathbf{S}_n$ into itself. Kakutani's fixed-point theorem ensures us that there exists a $\bar{\mathbf{p}} \in \mathbf{S}_2$ such that $\bar{\mathbf{p}} \in \mathbf{T}(\bar{\mathbf{p}})$ which is true for $\bar{\mathbf{p}} = (\frac{1}{2}, \frac{1}{2})$ since $\bar{\mathbf{p}} \in \tilde{\mathbf{Q}} = \mathbf{T}(\bar{\mathbf{p}})$.

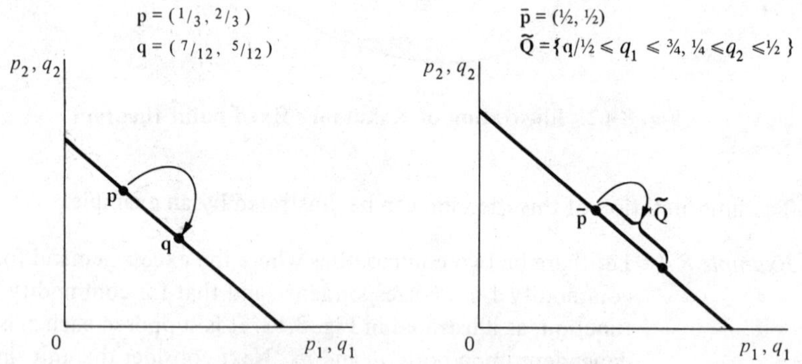

Fig. 8.14. Upper semi-continuous mapping

This analysis of fixed points and the normalised prices allows us to set the scene for the existence proofs to follow in the next chapter and sets part of the scene for welfare and for comparing competitive equilibrium with Pareto optimality.

EXERCISES

1. Show that a demand curve exhibiting the Giffen paradox for part of its range is a point-to-set mapping.

2. Show that the integrability condition for each individual is fulfilled if each x_i has an Engel curve:

$$x_i = f(y) = a_i y^2 + \beta_i y.$$

3. Explain why a demand curve exhibiting infinite elasticity can do so for only part of the price domain.

4. Show that an indifference curve possessing interior points violates the following dominance axiom:

$$\mathbf{x}^0 P \mathbf{x}^1 \text{ if } \mathbf{x}^0 \gg \mathbf{x}^1.$$

5. Will upper semi-continuous supply functions or correspondences arise in neoclassical theory? Illustrate your answer.

6. Show that if the marginal propensity to consume is independent of the accrued income for all goods and all individuals that this is a sufficient condition to satisfy the integrability condition.

7. Express the aggregate elasticity matrices $\sum_k \mathbf{E}_p^k$ and $\sum_k \mathbf{E}_y^k$ in terms of the individual matrices. What association is there between the aggregate price response matrix $\sum_k \mathbf{E}_p^k$ and the aggregate income response matrix $\sum_k \mathbf{E}_y^k$?

8. For each of the following models establish (*a*) the equilibrium price and quantity, if it exists, (*b*) the partial excess demand curves, (*c*) the partial modulated excess demand curves:

(i)	(ii)	(iii)
$x = 20 - 3p$	$x = 5 - 4p$	$x = 4 - p$
$s = -5 + 4p$	$s = 8 + 2p$	$s = 2 + 2p.$

9. Given a non-normalised price vector (6, 4) establish the normalised price vector.

Why is the non-normalised price vector (3, 2) mapped into the same normalised price vector as that of (6, 4)?

10. Let $p_1 = 3$ and $p_2 = 2$. Derive the corresponding price vector $\mathbf{p} \in \mathbf{S}_2$. Suppose $z_i(p_i)$ $i = 1, 2$ are both continuous and that at these normalised prices $z_1(p_1) = 0$ and $z_2(p_2) = 1$, show that $\mathbf{q} = [T_1(p_1), T_2(p_2)]$ is (0·3, 0·7), and hence that $\mathbf{q} \in \mathbf{S}_2$.

11. Suppose we have the following alternative definition of $\mathbf{M}(\mathbf{p})$:

$$\mathbf{M}(\mathbf{p}) = \max\,[-\mathbf{p}, \mathbf{z}(\mathbf{p})]\,, \text{ i.e. } M_i(\mathbf{p}) = \max\,[-p_i, z_i(\mathbf{p})]\,.$$

(i) Show that this satisfies the properties of $M_i(\mathbf{p})$ given in the text.

(ii) Show that the mapping $\mathbf{T}$ still maps $\mathbf{S}_n$ into $\mathbf{S}_n$.

12. Explain as clearly as you can the difference between Brouwer's fixed-point theorem and that of Kakutani.

13. Which of the following map **X** *into* itself, and specify which map **X** *onto* itself?

(1) $f(x) = 0{\cdot}4 + 0{\cdot}3x$ $\quad \mathbf{X} = \{x/0 \leqslant x \leqslant 1\}$

(2) $f(x) = 2 + 3x$ $\quad \mathbf{X} = \{x/0 \leqslant x \leqslant 1\}$

(3) $f(x) = 4 + x$ $\quad \mathbf{X} = \{x/0 \leqslant x \leqslant 5\}$

(4) $f(x) = \frac{1}{2}(x^2 + x)$ $\quad \mathbf{X} = \{x/0 \leqslant x \leqslant 1\}$

(5) $f(x) = 4x - x^2 - 2$ $\quad \mathbf{X} = \{x/0 \leqslant x \leqslant 3\}$

For each of these establish the fixed point(s). Illustrate your results.

14. Show that if $\mathbf{p} = 0$ were included in $\mathbf{S}_n$ then $\mathbf{z}(\mathbf{p})$ is not continuous at $\mathbf{p} = 0$, but continuous everywhere else. (Hint, take $\lim_{\lambda \to 0} \mathbf{z}(\lambda\mathbf{p})$ for two different price vectors.)

15. Consider the two normalisation rules:

(1) $\mathbf{S}_n = \{\mathbf{p}/\iota'\mathbf{p} = 1, \mathbf{p} > 0\}$.

(2) $\mathbf{S}'_n = \{\mathbf{p}/\mathbf{p}'\mathbf{p} = 1, \mathbf{p} > 0\}$.

Draw both of these on the one diagram. Show that for any non-normalised price vector each normalisation defines a point on the simplex where the vector intersects $\mathbf{S}_n$ and $\mathbf{S}'_n$ respectively. Show that both rules map $\mathbf{p}$ and $\lambda\mathbf{p}$ into the same point. Show also that normalisation rule (1) has a normalised vector of varying length, whilst the normalised vector under rule (2) retains unit length.

9

THEORY OF EXCHANGE AND GENERAL EQUILIBRIUM

9.1 Introduction

So far we have not brought producers and consumers together. The reason for this lies partly in the fact that we have not yet laid down any principles of exchange and allocation. Such principles are not easy because of the many variables involved and the possible variety of assumptions which can be made. The next section sets out the axioms of exchange. It deals only with pure exchange, that is to say, exchange in a system where there is no production or where production has taken place and only the exchange of such production stocks is being considered. This approach does highlight the essential features of exchange and allows us to discuss the neoclassical version of the pure exchange model in Section 9.3. A more general exchange model which incorporates production as well as consumption is included in Section 9.4. In both Section 9.2 and 9.3 attention centres on the formal properties of such exchange models and in particular discusses the existence of equilibrium in such models. The systems discussed in Sections 9.3 and 9.4 are rather general and only the minimum number of production axioms are brought into play. If we are prepared to make more rigid assumptions we can obtain more information. Thus in the final section of this chapter we consider general equilibrium in an open Leontief model.

9.2 Axioms of Exchange

The simplest exchange model considers a situation where individuals have been given allocations of goods, which can be thought of as already having been produced. The object of the system is to reallocate the goods between the individuals in some way so that at least some are better off and no one is worse off. To this end we shall consider only two consumers and two goods. The total stock of both goods, $\bar{x}_1$ and $\bar{x}_2$, held by both individuals combined is fixed. The pure exchange model has nothing to say about production decisions or how the stock of goods happened to be there and in the given allocation between the two individuals: it concerns itself only with the exchange of these goods between the two consumers. This analysis although much simplified does highlight a number of important issues.[1]

Let $\bar{x}_1$ and $\bar{x}_2$ denote the total endowments of both goods. Let $\bar{\mathbf{x}}^1 = (\bar{x}_1^1, \bar{x}_2^1)$ and $\bar{\mathbf{x}}^2 = (\bar{x}_1^2, \bar{x}_2^2)$ denote the given endowments of both commodities held by both individuals respectively, where $\bar{x}_i^1 + \bar{x}_i^2 = \bar{x}_i$ $(i = 1, 2)$. We shall denote the initial position of the consumers by t_0, as illustrated in Fig. 9.1 which gives the familiar Edgeworth–Bowley box. The further positions of the system will be denoted $t_1, t_2, t_3, \ldots$.

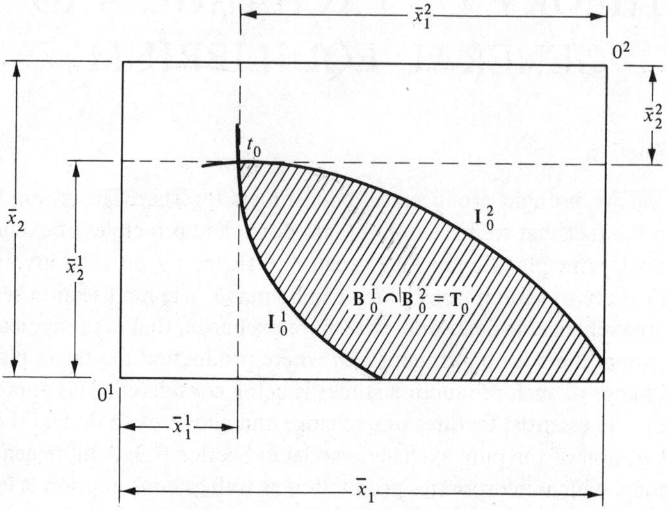

Fig. 9.1. Edgeworth–Bowley box

Consider now an indifference curve through t_0. Individual 1 will only trade if he can move to points in $\mathbf{B}_0^1$, i.e. to positions in the better set associated with $\bar{\mathbf{x}}_0^1$ – individual 1's collection of both goods at position t_0. Similarly, consumer 2 will trade only if he can move to a position in $\mathbf{B}_0^2$. The set that denotes neither party losing by a trade is $\mathbf{B}_0^1 \cap \mathbf{B}_0^2$, which will be referred to as the *trading set.* The trading set denotes all positions for which either one of the parties gain or both gain from the trade, and that such a new trading position is no worse than t_0, as seen by each individual. Let **T** denote this trading set so that $\mathbf{T} = \{t/t \in \mathbf{B}^1 \cap \mathbf{B}^2\}$. Note that the sets $\mathbf{B}_0^1$, $\mathbf{B}_0^2$ and **T** are closed convex sets; **T** is convex because it is the intersection of two convex sets.

It simplifies matters to assume away satiation. We noted in Chapter 3 that Axiom 9 of non-satiation implies that $\mathbf{x}' > \mathbf{x}''$ implies $\mathbf{x}'P\mathbf{x}''$, where $\mathbf{x}' > \mathbf{x}''$ means $\mathbf{x}'$ contains at least as much of every commodity and more of at least one commodity as $\mathbf{x}''$. Let us write this as a specific axiom of exchange theory:

Axiom 22 (Dominance) $\forall \mathbf{x}', \mathbf{x}'' \in \mathbf{X} \qquad (\mathbf{x}' > \mathbf{x}'' \Rightarrow \mathbf{x}'P\mathbf{x}'')$.

It is also to be remembered that this is true if and only if the indifference sets contain no interior points. The axiom of dominance delimits the domain of **X** over which we can say anything about a consumer's preferences. Consider a point $\mathbf{x}_0 \in \mathbf{X}$ as in Fig. 9.2. We denote the upper wedge, $\mathbf{U}_0$, associated with $\mathbf{x}_0$ by the set $\mathbf{U}_0 = \{\mathbf{x}/\mathbf{x} \geqslant \mathbf{x}_0\}$; similarly, the lower wedge, $\mathbf{L}_0$, associated with $\mathbf{x}_0$ by the set

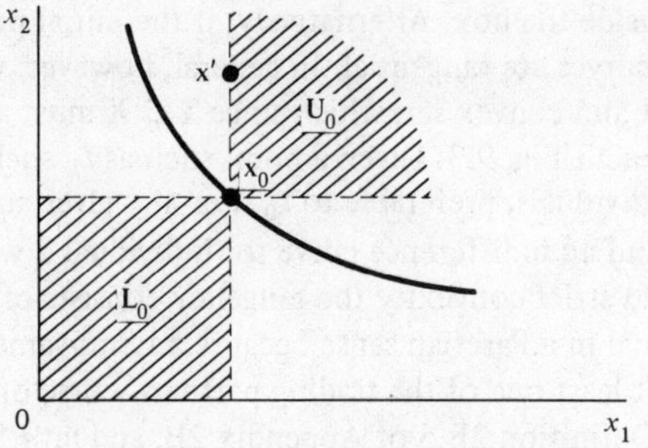

Fig. 9.2. Upper and lower wedges

$\mathbf{L_0} = \{\mathbf{x}/\mathbf{x} \leqslant \mathbf{x_0}\}$. Since $\mathbf{x_0} \in \mathbf{I_0}$ and $\mathbf{I_0}$ contains no interior points then $\mathbf{L_0} \cap \mathbf{U_0} = \{\mathbf{x_0}\}$ and $\mathbf{L_0} \subset \mathbf{W_0}$ and $\mathbf{U_0} \subset \mathbf{B_0}$. This latter condition must be so since the boundary points of $\mathbf{U_0}$ say, such as $\mathbf{x}'$, are interior points of $\mathbf{B_0}$, i.e. $N_\epsilon(\mathbf{x}') \not\subset \mathbf{U_0}$ but $N_\epsilon(\mathbf{x}') \subset \mathbf{B_0}$, and this holds for all $\mathbf{x}' \in \mathbf{U_0}$ except for $\mathbf{x_0}$ itself.

Another condition which we must take account of if we are to discuss exchange in the style of Edgeworth is that of strict convexity of the indifference set.

Axiom 23 (Strict Convexity)

$$\forall \mathbf{x}, \mathbf{x}' \in \mathbf{I_0} \qquad \exists \mathbf{x}'' = a\mathbf{x} + (1-a)\mathbf{x}' \in \mathbf{B_0} \qquad N_\epsilon(\mathbf{x}'') \subset \mathbf{B_0} \qquad 0 < a < 1.$$

In other words, $\mathbf{x}''$ is an interior point of $\mathbf{B_0}$ and so $\mathbf{I_0}$ is strictly convex.

Taking account of Axioms 22 and 23 consider once again the initial trading position t_0. Trading will be beneficial to at least one person if $\mathbf{T}$ contains elements other than t_0, i.e. any $t_j \in \mathbf{T}$ will be preferable or considered indifferent to t_0 by at least one individual given $t_j \neq t_0$. The obvious question to ask is whether there is ever a situation where $\mathbf{T}$ contains only the element t_0? This will be so in two situations. First if the initial position is such that it lies on the boundary of the Edgeworth–Bowley box and the indifference curve for individual 2 lies wholly above

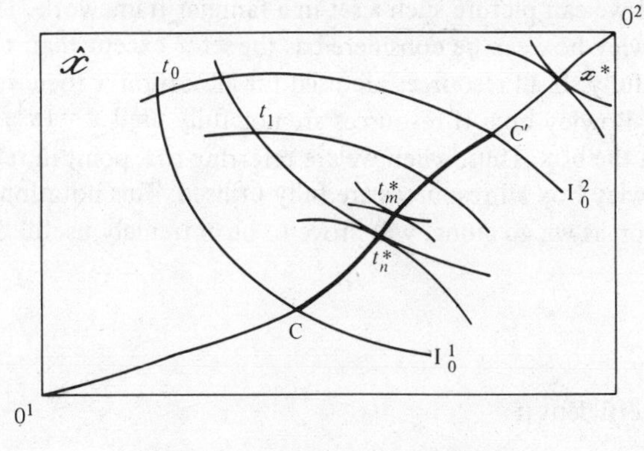

Fig. 9.3. The contract curve

that of individual 1 inside the box. Alternatively, if the initial position is such that the two indifference curves are tangential. In general, however, we can assume **T** is a non-empty compact and convex set, which since $\mathbf{T} \subset \mathbf{X}$ must also be connected.

Consider for a moment Fig. 9.3. Given a point such as t_1 such that $N_\epsilon(t_1) \subset \mathbf{T}$ then t_1 is, to *both* individuals, preferable to t_0. For any given indifference curve for individual 1 we can find an indifference curve for individual 2 which is tangential. Since we have assumed strict convexity the tangency consists of a single point. Such a point must be optimal in a Paretian sense because any movement away from this position must make at least one of the trading partners worse off. We make this explicit, in line with Definition 2B.5 of Appendix 2B, and let P^* denote society's Pareto ranking, thus

Definition 9.1 $t^* \in \mathbf{T}$ is Pareto efficient if

$$\sim \exists t \in \mathbf{T} \qquad tP^*t^*,$$

i.e. there exists no other trading position in the trading set which can make both individuals better off or at least one individual worse off.

As can be observed from Fig. 9.3 there are many points in the trading set **T** satisfying Definition 9.1, such as t_n^* and t_m^*. Notice, however, that t_1 does not satisfy the definition since both t_n^* and t_m^* are Pareto preferable to t_1. All the points satisfying Definition 9.1 lie on the curve CC′ which denotes all the points of tangency. We shall denote this efficiency set by $\mathbf{T}^*$ and the curve CC′ is usually called the *contract curve.*

It is possible to define efficiency independently of the trading set. In this case we would be considering all points in the Edgeworth–Bowley box which denotes the set of all commodity allocations open to individuals given the commodity endowments. Since $\mathbf{x}^k \in \mathbf{X}^k$ is the commodity vector of individual k we can consider a consumption allocation $\mathscr{x} = (\mathbf{x}^1, \ldots, \mathbf{x}^m)$ and $\mathscr{x} \in \mathscr{X}$ where $\mathscr{X} = \times_k \mathbf{X}^k$, the Cartesian product of k consumers' commodity sets. If we consider an economy with a given endowment set then we can represent the feasible allocation by $\hat{\mathscr{X}}$. It will be helpful if we can picture such a set in a familiar framework. The Edgeworth–Bowley box can be considered as the set $\hat{\mathscr{X}}$ except that it needs to be interpreted carefully. If all resources are used for allocation $\mathscr{x}$ then $\mathscr{x}$ is a point in the Edgeworth–Bowley box. If resources are not fully used $\mathscr{x} = (\mathbf{x}^1, \mathbf{x}^2)$ will consist of two points in the box. Thus, when we are referring to a point in relation to the Edgeworth–Bowley box all resources are fully utilised. This notation, which we shall expand upon as we go along, will prove to be extremely useful. In general, therefore,

Definition 9.2

$\mathscr{x}^* \in \mathscr{X}$ is efficient if

$$\sim \exists\ \mathscr{x} \in \hat{\mathscr{X}} \qquad \mathscr{x}P^*\mathscr{x}^*.$$

Such an allocation $\mathscr{x}^*$ is shown in Fig. 9.3. The set of all allocations satisfying Definition 9.2 we shall denote $\hat{\mathscr{X}}^*$ and is generally referred to as the *efficiency locus.*[2] Notice that $\mathbf{T}^* \subset \hat{\mathscr{X}}^*$, i.e. the efficient trading allocations is a subset of all efficient allocations. This must be so since the ranking criterion in both cases is the same, the only difference lies in the sets over which the ranking is defined.

Having established the trading set and the efficient trades we must discuss two points. First, how does exchange take consumers from a point such as t_0 to a point on the contract curve? Second, at what point, or points, will trade settle? We shall discuss in this chapter only the second, leaving to Chapter 11 a discussion of the first problem. In order to embark on a discussion of the second problem we must introduce the *exchange rate.* The straight line $t_0 t_2$ in Fig. 9.4 indicates the rate of exchange between x_1 and x_2 for individual 1. But if prices are given then this rate of exchange must also be faced by individual 2. Thus $t_0 t_2$ divides the set $\hat{\mathscr{X}}$ into two attainable sets which are half-spaces. By the axioms of dominance and strict convexity consumer 1 will optimise by moving to a point where the indifference curve is tangential to the ruling exchange rate such as t_1 and similarly for individual 2, who moves to t_2. At such a price ratio there will be an excess supply of x_1 and an excess demand for x_2.

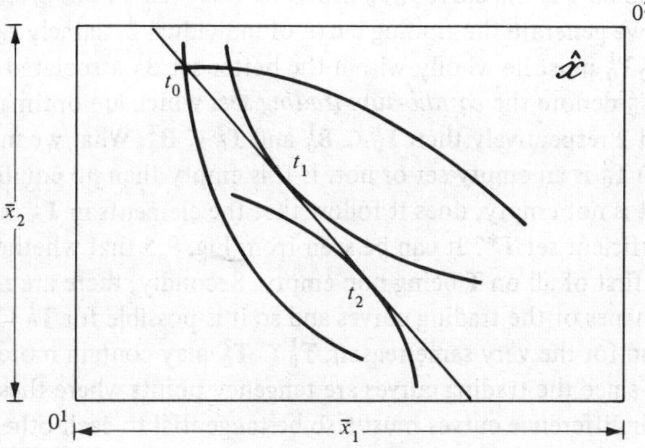

Fig. 9.4. Exchange equilibrium

We can at this stage make some observations. If we begin with an allocation t_0 then a trading set is defined. A price ratio that does not enter this trading set will not give rise to any exchange. If the exchange rate $t_0 t_2$ intersects the trade set **T** then trade can take place because some gains from trade are now possible. However, even if it intersects **T**, if the exchange rate does not intersect the set **T*** then no efficient trade is possible at this exchange rate. The set **T*** gives rise to two limits on the exchange rate which will allow (*a*) trade to take place, and (*b*) the possibility of efficient trade. In terms of Fig. 9.5 these limits are $t_0 t_r$ and $t_0 t_s$.

Having established that there is a range of relative prices within which it is

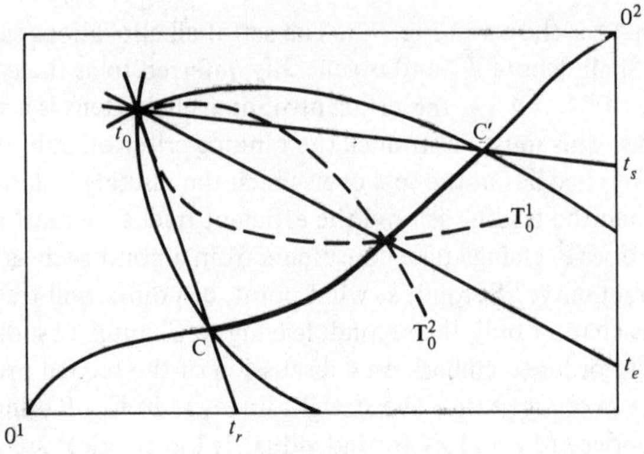

Fig. 9.5. Exchange Equilibrium

beneficial to trade we must next establish whether there exists a relative price ratio which will clear the market, i.e. whether there exists an equilibrium price ratio. To see whether this is so consider the price ratio $t_0 t_r$ swinging towards $t_0 t_s$ in Fig. 9.5. For each price ratio there will be a tangency point. The locus of such tangency points for individual 1 is the curve $t_0 \mathbf{T}_0^1$ which we shall call a *trading curve.* In a similar manner we generate the trading curve of individual 2, namely $t_0 \mathbf{T}_0^2$. It is apparent that $t_0 \mathbf{T}_0^1$ must lie wholly within the better set $\mathbf{B}_0^1$ associated with t_0. If we let $\mathbf{T}_0^1$ and $\mathbf{T}_0^2$ denote the *equilibrium trading sets* which are optimal for individual 1 and 2 respectively then $\mathbf{T}_0^1 \subset \mathbf{B}_0^1$ and $\mathbf{T}_0^2 \subset \mathbf{B}_0^2$. What we must establish is whether $\mathbf{T}_0^1 \cap \mathbf{T}_0^2$ is an empty set or not. If it is empty then no equilibrium price ratio exists. If it is not empty, does it follow that the elements in $\mathbf{T}_0^1 \cap \mathbf{T}_0^2$ also belong to the efficient set $\mathbf{T}^*$? It can be seen from Fig. 9.5 that whether this is so or not depends first of all on $\mathbf{T}$ being non-empty. Secondly, there are no restrictions placed on the shapes of the trading curves and so it is possible for $\mathbf{T}_0^1 \cap \mathbf{T}_0^2 = \boldsymbol{\emptyset}$; furthermore, and for the very same reason, $\mathbf{T}_0^1 \cap \mathbf{T}_0^2$ may contain more than one element. Third, since the trading curves are tangency points where these curves intersect, both indifference curves must also be tangential to each other which is the condition for an efficient point, thus if $\mathbf{T}^*$ exists and also $\mathbf{T}_0^1 \cap \mathbf{T}_0^2$ has at least one element then $\mathbf{T}_0^1 \cap \mathbf{T}_0^2 \subset \mathbf{T}^*$. Fig. 9.5 represents a situation where the two trading curves intersect only once giving rise to an equilibrium price ratio of $t_0 t_e$. That this is an equilibrium is clear because there are zero excess demands for both individuals, hence satisfying Definition 8.2.

What we have done in this section is to give a diagrammatic illustration of the existence of an equilibrium in a two-person two-commodity pure exchange model. We have also made reference to the possibility of multiple equilibria. Multiple equilibria is important because each represents a different allocation $\mathscr{x} \in \mathscr{X}$ and hence a different welfare level for each individual. We shall say more on this in the next chapter. Although this model supplies some information it is still restrictive. We cannot be sure that in a many-commodity many-person model such an equilibrium solution exists. If a solution does not exist our analysis must take a radically different form. We must now, therefore, turn to some of these more general models using the mathematical tools of the previous chapter. However, throughout our discussions it is worthwhile for the reader to keep in mind this simple version so that the symbolism does not detract from what we are attempting to do.

9.3 Pure Exchange Model – Neoclassical Version

In this section we shall carry out exactly what we have done in the previous section except we shall be considering an economy composed of m individuals and n commodities. Each individual k maximises his utility function $u^k(\mathbf{x}^k)$ subject to his budget constraint, i.e.

$$\max u^k = u^k(x_1^k, \ldots, x_n^k) = u^k(\mathbf{x}^k) \qquad k = 1, \ldots, m$$

$$\text{s.t.} \quad \mathbf{p}'\mathbf{x}^k = \mathbf{p}'\overline{\mathbf{x}}^k$$

where $\overline{x}_1^k, \ldots, \overline{x}_n^k$ are the initial endowments of the n goods which individual k possesses before transactions are undertaken. From our consumer analysis of Chapter 4 we have

$$x_i^k = x_i^k(p_1, \ldots, p_n; \overline{y}^k) \qquad i = 1, \ldots, n$$

i.e. $$\mathbf{x}^k = \mathbf{x}^k(\mathbf{p}, \overline{y}^k)$$

where $\overline{y}^k = \mathbf{p}'\overline{\mathbf{x}}^k$, and since this is fixed we may write $\mathbf{x}^k = \mathbf{x}^k(\mathbf{p}, \overline{y}^k) = \mathbf{g}^k(\mathbf{p})$.

We next define the excess demand for the ith commodity and k^{th} consumer as

$$z_i^k(\mathbf{p}) = g_i^k(\mathbf{p}) - \overline{x}_i^k.$$

Aggregating over individuals and letting $z_i(\mathbf{p}) = \sum_k z_i^k(\mathbf{p})$ we have

$$\left.\begin{aligned} \sum_k z_i^k(\mathbf{p}) &= \sum_k g_i^k(\mathbf{p}) - \sum_k \overline{x}_i^k \\ \text{or} \qquad z_i(\mathbf{p}) &= g_i(\mathbf{p}) - \overline{x}_i \end{aligned}\right\} \quad i = 1, \ldots, n,$$

If $\mathbf{z}(\mathbf{p})$ denotes the aggregate excess demand vector of the n goods,

$$\mathbf{z}(\mathbf{p}) = [z_1(\mathbf{p}), \ldots, z_n(\mathbf{p})]'$$

then we have by Walras Law (p. 217) that $\mathbf{p}'\mathbf{z}(\mathbf{p}) = 0$.

The existence of an equilibrium in this model has been elaborated by Gale and Nikaido and is sometimes referred to as the Gale–Nikaido theorem.

Theorem 9.1 (Gale–Nikaido Theorem) If $\mathbf{z(p)}$ denotes a vector of excess demand functions satisfying Walras Law $\mathbf{p'z(p)} = 0$ at any price vector $\mathbf{p}$ such that $\mathbf{p} \in \mathbf{S}_n = \{\mathbf{p}/\iota'\mathbf{p} = 1, \mathbf{p} > 0\}$ then there exists a price vector $\bar{\mathbf{p}} = (\bar{p}_1, \ldots, \bar{p}_n)'$ at which

(1) $\mathbf{z}(\bar{\mathbf{p}}) \leqslant 0$.

(2) $\bar{p}_i = 0$ if $z_i(\bar{\mathbf{p}}) < 0$.

Proof $\mathbf{S}_n = \{\mathbf{p}/\iota'\mathbf{p} = 1, \mathbf{p} > 0\}$ is a closed, bounded and convex set. Define the transformation $\mathbf{T(p)}$ by

$$\mathbf{T(p)} = \frac{\mathbf{p} + \mathbf{M(p)}}{1 + \iota'\mathbf{M(p)}}$$

where $\mathbf{M(p)} = \max\,[0, \mathbf{z(p)}]$. We have already shown in Section 8.6 that $\mathbf{T}$ maps $\mathbf{S}_n$ into itself. By the neoclassical assumptions we have $\mathbf{T(p)}$ continuous since $\mathbf{z(p)}$ is continuous. Hence all the conditions of Brouwer's fixed-point theorem (Theorem 8.2) have been met. Consequently there exists a $\bar{\mathbf{p}} = \mathbf{T}(\bar{\mathbf{p}})$, i.e.

$$\bar{\mathbf{p}} = \frac{\bar{\mathbf{p}} + \mathbf{M}(\bar{\mathbf{p}})}{1 + \iota'\mathbf{M}(\bar{\mathbf{p}})}.$$

First we demonstrate that if $\bar{\mathbf{p}}$ is an equilibrium price vector then $\iota'\mathbf{M}(\bar{\mathbf{p}}) = 0$. We then show that with $\bar{p}_i = 0$ if we are to satisfy Walras Law then $z_i(\bar{\mathbf{p}}) < 0$. Both are proved by contradiction. Suppose $\iota'\mathbf{M}(\bar{\mathbf{p}}) > 0$. From the fixed-point mapping we have for good i

$$\bar{p}_i[1 + \iota'\mathbf{M}(\bar{\mathbf{p}})] = \bar{p}_i + M_i(\bar{\mathbf{p}}),$$

i.e.

$$\bar{p}_i\,\iota'\mathbf{M}(\bar{\mathbf{p}}) = M_i(\bar{\mathbf{p}}).$$

But if $\iota'\mathbf{M}(\bar{\mathbf{p}}) > 0$ by assumption then $\bar{p}_i > 0$ if $M_i(\bar{\mathbf{p}}) > 0$; however $M_i(\bar{\mathbf{p}}) > 0$ implies $z_i(\bar{\mathbf{p}}) > 0$ and hence $\bar{p}_i z_i(\bar{\mathbf{p}}) > 0$. Furthermore, $\bar{p}_i z_i(\bar{\mathbf{p}}) = 0$ if $z_i(\bar{\mathbf{p}}) \leqslant 0$ because either $\bar{p}_i = 0$ if $z_i(\bar{\mathbf{p}}) < 0$, a free good, or else $z_i(\bar{\mathbf{p}}) = 0$ for $\bar{p}_i > 0$, which follows from Definition 8.2 of an equilibrium. To summarise so far. By assuming $\iota'\mathbf{M}(\bar{\mathbf{p}}) > 0$ we have

(1) $\bar{p}_i z_i(\bar{\mathbf{p}}) > 0$ if $z_i(\bar{\mathbf{p}}) > 0$.

(2) $\bar{p}_i z_i(\bar{\mathbf{p}}) = 0$ if $z_i(\bar{\mathbf{p}}) \leqslant 0$.

Summing over all goods we have $\bar{\mathbf{p}}'\mathbf{z}(\bar{\mathbf{p}}) > 0$. But this contradicts Walras Law which holds for any $\mathbf{p} \in \mathbf{S}_n$. Hence $\iota'\mathbf{M}(\bar{\mathbf{p}}) = 0$, since $\iota'\mathbf{M}(\mathbf{p}) < 0$ is ruled out by the definition of $\mathbf{M(p)}$.

Since $\iota'\mathbf{M}(\bar{\mathbf{p}}) = 0$ and $M_i(\bar{\mathbf{p}}) \geqslant 0$, $\forall i$ it follows $M_i(\bar{\mathbf{p}}) = 0$, $\forall i$. From this it follows $z_i(\bar{\mathbf{p}}) \leqslant 0, \forall i$. Now suppose $\bar{p}_i > 0$ for some i, then since $z_i(\bar{\mathbf{p}}) \leqslant 0$ we know there is at least one good for which $\bar{p}_i > 0$ and $z_i(\bar{\mathbf{p}}) < 0$, for all others $z_i(\bar{\mathbf{p}}) = 0$. Summing over all such goods we get $\bar{\mathbf{p}}'\mathbf{z}(\bar{\mathbf{p}}) < 0$ which contradicts Walras Law. Hence $p_i = 0$ for $z_i(\bar{\mathbf{p}}) < 0$. We have thus proved $z_i(\bar{\mathbf{p}}) = 0$ if $\bar{p}_i > 0$ and $\bar{p}_i = 0$ if $z_i(\bar{\mathbf{p}}) < 0$; hence

(1) $\mathbf{z}(\bar{\mathbf{p}}) \leqslant 0$.

(2) $\bar{p}_i = 0$ if $z_i(\bar{\mathbf{p}}) < 0$.

Q.E.D.

By means of Brouwer's fixed-point theorem we have demonstrated that in a general pure exchange model of the neoclassical type with all functions continuous that an equilibrium solution exists. In terms of the Edgeworth–Bowley box of the previous section we have demonstrated that there exists some relative price set at which there will exist no excess demands at positive prices or else some goods will be free in equilibrium.

Let us illustrate the general exchange model by taking a specific utility function.[3] Consider the utility function for the kth individual given by

$$u^k(\mathbf{x}^k) = \sum_{i=1}^{n} a_i \log x_i^k \qquad \sum_i a_i = 1, 0 < a_i < 1, \forall i.$$

Maximising this function subject to the budget constraint $\mathbf{p}'\mathbf{x}^k = y^k$ gives the following demand functions (see Exercise 5 of Chapter 4):

$$x_i^k = x_i^k(\mathbf{p}, y^k) = \frac{a_i^k y^k}{p_i} \qquad \forall i.$$

For the aggregate we have:

$$x_i(\mathbf{p}, Y) = \sum_k x_i^k = \sum_k \frac{a_i^k y^k}{p_i} \qquad \forall i.$$

Assume that all individuals have the same tastes then $a_i^k = a_i$, $\forall k$; hence

$$x_i = \frac{a_i}{p_i} \sum_k y^k = \frac{a_i Y}{p_i} \qquad \forall i$$

where $Y = \sum_k y^k$. But we are assuming income is the value of the initial allocation

so that $Y = \sum_{j=1}^{n} p_j \bar{x}_j$; consequently

$$g_i(\mathbf{p}) = \frac{a_i}{p_i} \sum_{j=1}^{n} p_j \bar{x}_j \qquad \forall i.$$

Now excess demands are $z_i(\mathbf{p}) = g_i(\mathbf{p}) - \bar{x}_i$ so that

$$z_i(\mathbf{p}) = \frac{a_i}{p_i} \sum_{j=1}^{n} p_j \bar{x}_j - \bar{x}_i$$

$$= \frac{a_i}{p_i} \left[\sum_{j=1}^{n} \left(1 - \frac{\delta_{ij}}{a_i} \right) p_j \bar{x}_j \right] \qquad \forall i$$

where $\delta_{ij} = 1$ if $i = j$ and $\delta_{ij} = 0$ if $i \neq j$.

If we can find a $\bar{\mathbf{p}}$ such that $z_i(\bar{\mathbf{p}}) = 0$, $\forall i$ then by Definition 8.2 this must be an equilibrium price vector. Consider $\bar{p}_j = a_j/\bar{x}_j$, $\forall j$ then

$$z_i(\bar{\mathbf{p}}) = \bar{x}_i \left[\sum_{j=1}^{n} \left(1 - \frac{\delta_{ij}}{a_i} \right) a_j \right] = \bar{x}_i \left(\sum_{j=1}^{n} a_j - 1 \right).$$

But $\sum_{j=1}^{n} a_j = 1$; hence $z_i(\bar{p}) = 0, \forall i$ and therefore at least one equilibrium exists. It readily follows that Walras Law is satisfied at any set of prices (see Exercises 5 and 6).

Notice an important feature of this example. It is assumed that $0 < a_i < 1, \ \forall i$ and since $\bar{x}_i > 0$ (since otherwise we would not be discussing its exchange) then $\bar{p}_i > 0, \ \forall i$. From this it follows $x_i^k > 0, \ \forall i$ and k so long as the individual has some income. Thus in this example the general equilibrium is characterised by all consumers maximising their utilities and consuming some of *every* commodity at positive equilibrium prices.

Whether the solution is unique has not yet been demonstrated nor have we discussed how the economy arrives at such an equilibrium (or equilibria). These issues will be discussed in later sections. Even so, the neoclassical model discussed above has two shortcomings. The first, which can be remedied, is the exclusion of production. The second is more fundamental because it would remain even if production were introduced. This is the strict convexity and differentiability of the excess demand functions. What, it may be asked, would occur if we had excess demand correspondences arising from better sets which are weakly convex? Even more to the point, what if this is also true of production? Could we in such a framework establish the existence of an equilibrium? The neoclassical framework cannot deal with this consideration and so we must turn to a more general framework. The undertaking is not easy because there are many interrelationships to keep in mind, but we cannot progress unless we know whether such an economy has an equilibrium solution at which all producers are operating at maximum profits and producing enough to satisfy consumer demands such that all consumers are maximising their utility.

9.4 Existence of Equilibrium in a General Exchange Model

The introduction of production, although making the discussion more realistic, does have its price and that price is greater complexity. Our aim will be to discuss the existence proof presented by Debreu [30], taking each step in the argument slowly. Although the mathematical specification becomes much more exacting than the pure exchange model the fundamental problem remains the same and this should not be lost sight of.

In earlier chapters we had $\mathbf{X}^k$ as the consumption set of the kth consumer. There are n commodities so that $\mathbf{X}^k$ lies in $\mathbf{E}^n$, and $\mathbf{x}^k \in \mathbf{X}^k$. Furthermore, again we shall denote the consumer's allocations by $\mathscr{X} = \underset{k}{\times} \mathbf{X}^k$ where $\boldsymbol{x} \in \mathscr{X}$ is a particular allocation. In our theory of production we let $\mathbf{Y}_j$ denote the production set of the jth producer. We shall assume there are l firms in the economy $j = 1, \ldots, l$. In general the production point $\mathbf{y}_j \in \mathbf{Y}_j$ is also in $\mathbf{E}^n$. Just as for consumption we shall let $\mathscr{Y} = \underset{j}{\times} \mathbf{Y}_j$ denote the set of production allocations. Finally, the economy is composed of r_ν $(\nu = 1, \ldots, s)$ resources. The total resource vector, $\mathbf{r}$, of an economy is given and are made available to the economy by those who own them. The point $\mathbf{r}$ lies in $\mathbf{E}^s$, which we shall assume to be a subset of $\mathbf{E}^n$, i.e. $s < n$.

An economy $\mathscr{E}$ is therefore characterised by:

(1) A consumption set $\mathbf{X}^k$ for each consumer.
(2) A preference relation P_k (or R_k) for each consumer.
(3) A production set $\mathbf{Y}_j$ for each producer.
(4) A given total resource vector $\mathbf{r}$.

So that we can progress with our argument we shall define a number of features of the $\mathscr{E}$ economy. First we shall consider some notation. We have already mentioned a consumption allocation set $\mathscr{X}$ and a production allocation set $\mathscr{Y}$. The $\mathscr{E}$-economy can be considered in terms of states $(\boldsymbol{x},\boldsymbol{y}) \in \mathscr{X} \times \mathscr{Y}$. Let $\mathscr{W} = \mathscr{X} \times \mathscr{Y}$ so that $(\boldsymbol{x},\boldsymbol{y}) = \boldsymbol{w} \in \mathscr{W}$. The point $\mathbf{x} = \sum_k \mathbf{x}^k$ and $\mathbf{y} = \sum_j \mathbf{y}_j$ are linear mappings of the allocations $\boldsymbol{x}$ and $\boldsymbol{y}$ respectively into the commodity space. So that to each state $\boldsymbol{w} \in \mathscr{W}$ there corresponds a commodity point $(\mathbf{x}, \mathbf{y}) \in \mathbf{X} \times \mathbf{Y}$ where $\mathbf{X} = \sum_k \mathbf{X}^k$ and $\mathbf{Y} = \sum_j \mathbf{Y}_j$.

Definition 9.3

A *state* of the economy $\mathscr{E}$ is the specification of each agent, i.e. for each consumer a point $\mathbf{x}^k$ and for each producer a point $\mathbf{y}_j$ in the commodity space. Thus a state is an $(m + l)$-tuple $(\boldsymbol{x},\boldsymbol{y})$ of points in $\mathbf{E}^n$, and can be represented by a point $\boldsymbol{w}$ in $\mathbf{E}^{n(m+l)}$.

Definition 9.4

Given $\mathbf{X} = \sum_k \mathbf{X}^k$ and $\mathbf{Y} = \sum_j \mathbf{Y}_j$ and given a state $(\boldsymbol{x},\boldsymbol{y})$ the point $\mathbf{x} - \mathbf{y}$ is the *net demand*, where $\mathbf{x} - \mathbf{y} \in \mathbf{X} - \mathbf{Y}$. Furthermore, the point $\mathbf{x} - \mathbf{y} - \mathbf{r}$ is the *excess demand*, where $\mathbf{z} = \mathbf{x} - \mathbf{y} - \mathbf{r} \in \mathbf{Z}$ and $\mathbf{Z} = \mathbf{X} - \mathbf{Y} - \{\mathbf{r}\}$.

Definition 9.5

A state $\boldsymbol{w} = (\boldsymbol{x},\boldsymbol{y})$ is a market equilibrium if $\mathbf{z} = 0$, i.e. $\mathbf{x} - \mathbf{y} = \mathbf{r}$. The set $\mathscr{W}$ satisfying $\mathbf{x} - \mathbf{y} = \mathbf{r}$ is denoted $\mathscr{M}$, i.e.

$$\mathscr{M} = \{\boldsymbol{w} / \mathbf{x} - \mathbf{y} = \mathbf{r}\}.$$

Definition 9.6

A state $\boldsymbol{w}$ is attainable if $\mathbf{x}^k \in \mathbf{X}^k, \forall k, \mathbf{y}_j \in \mathbf{Y}_j, \forall j$ and $\mathbf{x} - \mathbf{y} = \mathbf{r}$. The community's attainable set $\mathscr{A}$ is the intersection $\boldsymbol{w}$ and $\mathscr{M}$, i.e. $\mathscr{A} = \mathscr{W} \cap \mathscr{M}$.

It may help at this point to illustrate some of the conditions in these definitions. Although $\hat{\mathscr{X}}$, the feasible consumption set, is a Cartesian product, as we mentioned earlier we can present it in the more familiar form of an Edgeworth–Bowley box, as in Fig. 9.6 (*a*). The feasible production set, which we shall likewise label $\hat{\mathscr{Y}}$, unfortunately cannot be diagrammed. As mentioned above, to any $\boldsymbol{x} \in \hat{\mathscr{X}}$ there will correspond a consumption bundle $\mathbf{x} \in \hat{\mathbf{X}}$. Similarly, to any $\mathscr{y} \in \hat{\mathscr{Y}}$ there will correspond a production point $\mathbf{y} \in \hat{\mathbf{Y}}$ (in all cases we have placed a circumflex to show that given resource endowments produce bounded sets). As can be seen from Fig. 9.6 (*b*) both **x** and **y** belong to $\hat{\mathbf{Y}}$. Only points on the boundary of $\hat{\mathbf{Y}}$ employ all resources, but because resources are implicit the requirement of market equilibrium is $\mathbf{x} = \mathbf{y}$ and this occurs on the boundary of $\hat{\mathbf{Y}}$. For any other point $\mathbf{x}' \neq \mathbf{x}$ there will be excess demands, even if $\mathbf{x}'$ is on the boundary of $\hat{\mathbf{Y}}$. It is to be noted that what we have done here is to place the symbols used in the definitions in a familiar economic framework.

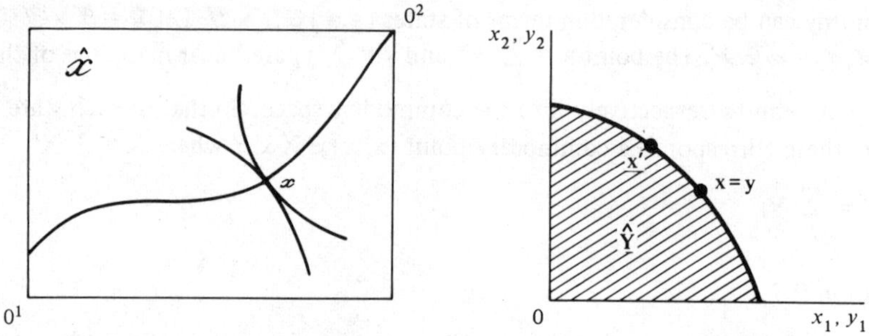

(*a*) Feasible consumption allocations

(*b*) Feasible production transformations

Fig. 9.6. Feasible consumption and production points

In order to take the analysis further we must make some assumption about how the given resources are distributed. This reveals at once that the results to be derived are crucially dependent upon the type of society we postulate (but see Exercise 7). In this regard we shall follow Debreu and consider a private ownership economy in which consumers own all the available resources and 'control producers'. Let $\mathbf{r}^k = (r_1^k, \ldots, r_s^k)$ denote the resources held by the kth consumer, $\sum_k \mathbf{r}^k = \mathbf{r}$.

Furthermore, each consumer owns part of the firms' profits. Let $\theta_{kj} \geqslant 0$ denote the share of profits in firm j held by individual k, where $\sum_k \theta_{kj} = 1$ for $j = 1, \ldots, l$.

A private ownership economy $\mathscr{E}'$ is therefore characterised by:

(1) A consumption set $\mathbf{X}^k$ for each consumer.

(2) A preference relation P_k (or R_k) for each consumer.

(3) The ownership $\mathbf{r}^k$ of the total resource endowment **r** such that $\sum_k \mathbf{r}^k = \mathbf{r}$.

(4) A share θ_{kj} in firm j by each consumer, $\theta_{kj} \geqslant 0$ and $\sum_k \theta_{kj} = 1, \forall j$

(5) A production set $\mathbf{Y}_j$ for each producer.

Since θ_{kj} is a share in profits we must next consider this in more detail. In the production chapters we established that for a given price vector **p** the producers will find a $\mathbf{y} \in \mathbf{Y}$ such that $\pi_j = \mathbf{p}'\mathbf{y}_j$ is maximised for all j. The profit π_j is distributed to all consumers since these are shareholders in all firms. Each consumer receives a total share of $\sum_{j=1}^{l} \theta_{kj}\pi_j$. The total wealth of the kth consumer therefore consists of the value of his initial stock holdings $\mathbf{p}'\mathbf{r}^k$ plus the share in all the profits. Let w^k denote the wealth of the kth consumer then

$$w^k = \mathbf{p}'\mathbf{r}^k + \sum_{j=1}^{l} \theta_{kj}\,\pi_j$$

$$= \mathbf{p}'\mathbf{r}^k + \sum_{j=1}^{l} \theta_{kj}\,\mathbf{p}'\mathbf{y}_j.$$

The budget constraint for the kth consumer is therefore $\mathbf{p}'\mathbf{x}^k \leqslant w^k$ or

$$\mathbf{p}'\mathbf{x}^k \leqslant \mathbf{p}'\mathbf{r}^k + \sum_{j=1}^{l} \theta_{kj}\,\mathbf{p}'\mathbf{y}_j.$$

Before we can establish whether an equilibrium exists in such a private ownership economy we must be clear on what constitutes an equilibrium.

Definition 9.7

An equilibrium of a private ownership economy $\mathscr{E}'$ is given by an $(m + l + 1)$-tuple $(\bar{\mathscr{X}}, \bar{\mathscr{Y}}, \bar{\mathbf{p}})$ of points in $\mathbf{E}^n$ such that

(1) $\bar{\mathbf{x}}^k R_k \mathbf{x}^k$, $\forall k$ such that $\{\mathbf{x}^k \in \mathbf{X}^k / \bar{\mathbf{p}}'\bar{\mathbf{x}}^k \leqslant \bar{\mathbf{p}}'\mathbf{r}^k + \sum_j \theta_{kj}\bar{\mathbf{p}}'\bar{\mathbf{y}}_j\}$.

(2) $\bar{\mathbf{p}}'\mathbf{y}_j = \max \bar{\mathbf{p}}'\mathbf{Y}_j$, $\forall j$.

(3) $\bar{\mathbf{x}} - \bar{\mathbf{y}} = \mathbf{r}$.

Hence, a point such as $(\bar{\mathscr{X}}, \bar{\mathscr{Y}}, \bar{\mathbf{p}})$ is an attainable state of the economy for which each consumer maximises his utility subject to his wealth constraint and each producer chooses an input–output combination which maximises his profit and both these situations exhaust available resources. The question now is: Given a private ownership economy $\mathscr{E}'$ does it have an equilibrium? First we consider $\mathbf{d}^k(\mathbf{p})$ and $\mathbf{y}_j(\mathbf{p})$ as correspondences. Using Definition 5.9 (p. 142) we have $s_j = \mathbf{s}_j(\mathbf{p}) = \{\mathbf{y}_j \in \mathbf{Y}_j / \mathbf{p}'\mathbf{y}_j = \max \mathbf{p}'\mathbf{Y}_j\}$ and we have shown in Section 5.5 that $\mathbf{s}_j(\mathbf{p})$ is homogeneous of degree zero in **p**. Also let $\mathbf{d}^k = \mathbf{d}^k(\mathbf{p})$ denote the set of most preferred points in the set $\{\mathbf{x}^k \in \mathbf{X}^k / \mathbf{p}'\mathbf{x}^k \leqslant \mathbf{p}'\mathbf{r}^k + \sum_j \theta_{kj}\,\mathbf{p}'\mathbf{y}\}$. Since $\mathbf{d}^k$ must belong to the budget line it follows that $\mathbf{d}^k(\mathbf{p})$ is a homogeneous of degree zero in **p**, a result we used frequently in earlier sections. It follows therefore that **d(p)** and **s(p)**, the aggregate demand and supply correspondences, are homogeneous of degree zero in **p**. Since $\mathbf{x}^k$ is an arbitrary point of $\mathbf{d}^k(\mathbf{p})$, $\forall k$ and $\mathbf{y}_j$ an arbitrary point of

$\mathbf{s}_j(\mathbf{p}), \forall j$ then $\mathbf{z} = \mathbf{x} - \mathbf{y} - \mathbf{r}$ is an arbitrary point in the set $\boldsymbol{\epsilon}(\mathbf{p}) = \mathbf{d}(\mathbf{p}) - \mathbf{s}(\mathbf{p}) - \{\mathbf{r}\}$ which is a subset of $\mathbf{Z} = \mathbf{X} - \mathbf{Y} - \{\mathbf{r}\}$. Let $\mathbf{C}$ denote the set of $\mathbf{p}$ for which $\mathbf{p} \in \mathbf{C}$, $\boldsymbol{\epsilon}(\mathbf{p})$ is non-empty and that $\mathbf{d}(\mathbf{p})$ and $\mathbf{s}(\mathbf{p})$ are defined and non-empty. Consequently, when $\mathbf{p} \in \mathbf{C}$ each consumer chooses a commodity bundle which is optimal for his wealth constraint and every producer chooses an input–output combination which maximises his profits for that price set. It follows that since both $\mathbf{d}(\mathbf{p})$ and $\mathbf{s}(\mathbf{p})$ are correspondences then $\boldsymbol{\epsilon}(\mathbf{p})$ is a correspondence, i.e. $\boldsymbol{\epsilon}$ is the aggregate excess demand correspondence which maps $\mathbf{C}$ into $\mathbf{Z}$, or $\boldsymbol{\epsilon}: \mathbf{C} \to \mathbf{Z}$.

Our problem now is to find a $\mathbf{p} \in \mathbf{C}$ for which the corresponding excess demand is zero. In other words, is there a $\mathbf{p} \in \mathbf{C}$ such that $0 \in \boldsymbol{\epsilon}(\mathbf{p})$? It readily follows that for $\lambda\mathbf{p} \in \mathbf{C}$, $\boldsymbol{\epsilon}(\lambda\mathbf{p}) = \boldsymbol{\epsilon}(\mathbf{p})$ because $\mathbf{s}(\lambda\mathbf{p}) = \mathbf{s}(\mathbf{p})$ and $\mathbf{d}(\lambda\mathbf{p}) = \mathbf{d}(\mathbf{p})$. We must now show for any $\mathbf{p} \in \mathbf{C}$ what condition is placed on the aggregate excess demand somewhat similar to Walras Law. For any actions $\mathbf{x}^k$ and $\mathbf{y}_j$ chosen by the agents for a given $\mathbf{p} \in \mathbf{C}$ the wealth constraint must satisfy:

$$\mathbf{p}'\mathbf{x}^k \leqslant \mathbf{p}'\mathbf{r}^k + \sum_{j=1}^{l} \theta_{kj}\,\mathbf{p}'\mathbf{y}_j \qquad \forall k.$$

Summing over all members in the community we get,

$$\sum_k \mathbf{p}'\mathbf{x}^k \leqslant \sum_k \mathbf{p}'\mathbf{r}^k + \sum_k \sum_j \theta_{kj}\,\mathbf{p}'\mathbf{y}_j$$

$$\mathbf{p}' \sum_k \mathbf{x}^k \leqslant \mathbf{p}' \sum_k \mathbf{r}^k + \sum_j \left[\sum_k \theta_{kj}\right] \mathbf{p}'\mathbf{y}_j.$$

i.e. $$\mathbf{p}'\mathbf{x} \leqslant \mathbf{p}'\mathbf{r} + \mathbf{p}'\mathbf{y}$$

or $$\mathbf{p}'(\mathbf{x} - \mathbf{y} - \mathbf{r}) \leqslant 0 \qquad \mathbf{p}'\mathbf{z} \leqslant 0.$$

Taking note that $\mathbf{p}'\mathbf{z}$ is the inner product of $\mathbf{p}$ and $\mathbf{z}$ these vectors are orthogonal if $\mathbf{p}'\mathbf{z} = 0$. Hence, for $\mathbf{p} \neq 0$ the set of points satisfying $\mathbf{p}'\mathbf{z} \leqslant 0$ is the set of points below and including the hyperplane through the origin and orthogonal to the given price vector, as illustrated in Fig. 9.7.

Debreu discusses the solution to the equilibrium in such an economy under the condition of free disposal. This is condition 6 under the axioms of the production set $\mathbf{Y}$ in Section 5.4 (p. 139) and is given by $(-\Omega) \subset \mathbf{Y}$. If this is satisfied then $\mathbf{s}_j(\mathbf{p})$ is non-empty if and only if $\mathbf{p} \geqslant 0$ (i.e. $\mathbf{p} \in \Omega$). This amounts to $\mathbf{z} \leqslant 0$, i.e. the equilibrium problem is now to find a $\mathbf{p} \in \mathbf{C}$ for which $\mathbf{z} \leqslant 0$ $(\mathbf{z} \in -\Omega)$, or alternatively, is there a $\mathbf{p} \in \mathbf{C}$ such that $\boldsymbol{\epsilon}(\mathbf{p}) \cap (-\Omega) \neq \emptyset$? If, in addition to free disposability, we require that at least one consumer satisfies the axiom of non-satiability (Axiom 9, p. 54) then the origin is excluded from the set $\mathbf{C}$. This allows us to define a unit simplex because $\boldsymbol{\epsilon}(\mathbf{p})$ is homogeneous of degree zero in $\mathbf{p}$; hence let

$$\mathbf{P} = \{\mathbf{p} \in \Omega \,/\, \iota'\mathbf{p} = 1, \mathbf{p} > 0\}.$$

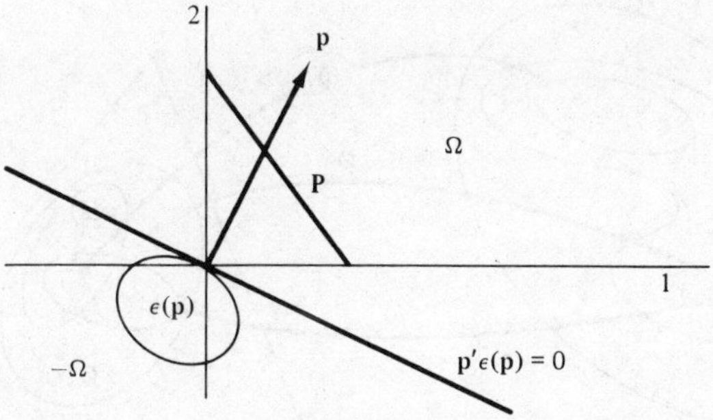

Fig. 9.7

To summarise so far. We have obtained a correspondence $\boldsymbol{\epsilon}$ from **P** to **Z** such that for every $\mathbf{p} \in \mathbf{P}$ we have $\mathbf{p'z} \leqslant 0$ or $\mathbf{p'}\boldsymbol{\epsilon}(\mathbf{p}) \leqslant 0$. The question now is what conditions must be placed on $\boldsymbol{\epsilon}$ and **Z** to ensure that there is a $\mathbf{p} \in \mathbf{P}$ such that $\boldsymbol{\epsilon}(\mathbf{p}) \cap (-\Omega) \neq \boldsymbol{\emptyset}$? It is to be noted there are two definitions of equilibrium: one without the non-satiation requirement which amounts to $\boldsymbol{\epsilon}(\mathbf{p})$ including the origin, and a more restrictive definition which incorporates the non-satiation requirement and amounts to $\boldsymbol{\epsilon}(\mathbf{p})$ intersecting the negative orthant only and not necessarily including the origin.

Debreu, in establishing the existence of a competitive equilibrium in the system so far outlined, accomplishes it by employing the following theorem.

Theorem 9.2 Let **Z** be a closed and bounded set in $\mathbf{E}^n$. If $\boldsymbol{\epsilon}$ is an upper semi-continuous correspondence from **P** into **Z** such that for every $\mathbf{p} \in \mathbf{P}$ the set $\boldsymbol{\epsilon}(\mathbf{p})$ is a non-empty convex set and satisfies $\mathbf{p'}\boldsymbol{\epsilon}(\mathbf{p}) \leqslant 0$, then there is a $\mathbf{p} \in \mathbf{P}$ such that $\boldsymbol{\epsilon}(\mathbf{p}) \cap (-\Omega) \neq 0$.

Proof **P** is a non-empty closed, bounded convex set. Since a condition of the theorem is that **Z** is a closed, bounded set we define a set **Z′** which is closed, bounded and convex and is such that $\mathbf{Z} \subset \mathbf{Z'}$ and belongs to $\mathbf{E}^n$. Since **P** is non-empty then **Z** is non-empty and therefore **Z′** is non-empty.

We first note there exists a real-valued function f defined on $\mathbf{P} \times \mathbf{Z'}$, i.e. $f(\mathbf{p}, \mathbf{z})$. Fig. 9.8 may be helpful in following the argument to be presented. For given $\mathbf{z} \in \mathbf{Z'}$ we have a real-valued function $\boldsymbol{\emptyset}(\mathbf{z})$ on **P**. Since **P** is a non-empty compact set then by Weierstrass's theorem (Theorem 3.6, p. 53) we know that there exists at least one maximum which is either on the boundary or in the interior of **P**. Let $\boldsymbol{\mu}(\mathbf{z})$ denote the subset of $\boldsymbol{\emptyset}(\mathbf{z})$ for which the values in **P** maximise $\mathbf{p'z}$ for given **z**. Then $\boldsymbol{\mu}(\mathbf{z})$ is non-empty, and by Theorem 5.5 (p. 149) since $\boldsymbol{\emptyset}(\mathbf{z})$ is continuous then $\boldsymbol{\mu}$ is upper semi-continuous on **Z′**. Since **P** is convex then $\boldsymbol{\mu}(\mathbf{z})$ is convex. The reason for this is as follows. If $\mathbf{z} = 0$ then $\boldsymbol{\mu}(\mathbf{z})$ is **P** itself since $\mathbf{p'z} = \mathbf{p'}0 = 0$, $\forall \mathbf{p} \in \mathbf{P}$. If $\mathbf{z} \neq 0$ then $\boldsymbol{\mu}(\mathbf{z})$ is the intersection of **P** and the hyperplane $\{\mathbf{p} \in \mathbf{E}^n / \mathbf{p'z} = \max \mathbf{p'Z}\}$, and since these are both convex their intersection must be convex.

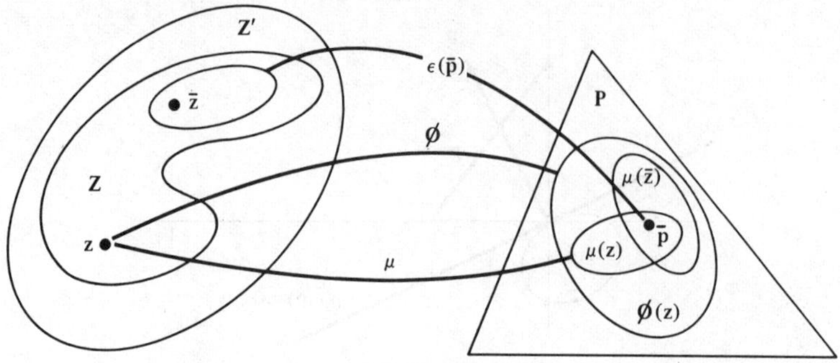

Fig. 9.8. The sets discussed in Theorem 9.2

Now define a correspondence $\boldsymbol{\psi}$ from $\mathbf{P} \times \mathbf{Z}'$ into itself defined by $\boldsymbol{\psi}(\mathbf{p}, \mathbf{z}) = \boldsymbol{\mu}(\mathbf{z}) \times \boldsymbol{\epsilon}(\mathbf{p})$. Thus $\mathbf{P} \times \mathbf{Z}'$ is the Cartesian product of two non-empty closed, bounded and convex sets in $\mathbf{E}^{2n}$ and is therefore closed, bounded and convex. Also since $\boldsymbol{\mu}(\mathbf{z})$ and $\boldsymbol{\epsilon}(\mathbf{p})$ are non-empty and convex then $\boldsymbol{\psi}(\mathbf{p}, \mathbf{z})$ is non-empty and convex. It also follows that $\boldsymbol{\psi}$ is upper semi-continuous because it is the product of two upper semi-continuous correspondences (Theorem 5.4, p. 149). Let us summarise the relevant conditions. We have a non-empty compact convex set $\mathbf{P} \times \mathbf{Z}'$ and an upper semi-continuous correspondence $\boldsymbol{\psi}$ which maps $\mathbf{P} \times \mathbf{Z}'$ into itself and is such that $\boldsymbol{\psi}(\mathbf{p}, \mathbf{z})$ is compact and convex. Then from Kakutani's fixed-point theorem we know there exists a $(\overline{\mathbf{p}}, \overline{\mathbf{z}})$ that $\boldsymbol{\psi}(\overline{\mathbf{p}}, \overline{\mathbf{z}}) \in \boldsymbol{\mu}(\overline{\mathbf{z}}) \times \boldsymbol{\epsilon}(\overline{\mathbf{p}})$ which is the same as $\overline{\mathbf{p}} \in \boldsymbol{\mu}(\overline{\mathbf{z}})$ and $\overline{\mathbf{z}} \in \boldsymbol{\epsilon}(\overline{\mathbf{p}})$, and is illustrated in Fig. 9.8.

If $\overline{\mathbf{p}} \in \boldsymbol{\mu}(\overline{\mathbf{z}})$ then this implies that for every $\mathbf{p} \in \mathbf{P}$ we have $\mathbf{p}'\overline{\mathbf{z}} \leqslant 0$. But if $\overline{\mathbf{z}} \in \boldsymbol{\epsilon}(\overline{\mathbf{p}})$ this implies that $\overline{\mathbf{p}}'\overline{\mathbf{z}} \leqslant 0$. Combining these two implications we can state that for every $\mathbf{p} \in \mathbf{P}$ we have $\mathbf{p}'\overline{\mathbf{z}} \leqslant 0$. Let $\mathbf{e}_h$ denote the hth column of the identity matrix, so that the vector $\mathbf{e}_h$ has unity in the hth position and zeros elsewhere. Also let $\mathbf{p} \in \mathbf{P}$ be defined $\mathbf{p} = \mathbf{e}_h$ then $\mathbf{p}'\overline{\mathbf{z}} = \mathbf{p}_h\overline{\mathbf{z}}_h = \overline{\mathbf{z}}_h \leqslant 0, \forall h$. Hence $\overline{\mathbf{z}} \in (-\Omega)$. Since $\overline{\mathbf{z}} \in (-\Omega)$ and $\overline{\mathbf{z}} \in \boldsymbol{\epsilon}(\mathbf{p})$ then $\overline{\mathbf{p}}'\boldsymbol{\epsilon}(\overline{\mathbf{p}}) \leqslant 0$ and $\overline{\mathbf{p}} \in \mathbf{P}$ is such that $\boldsymbol{\epsilon}(\mathbf{p}) \cap (-\Omega) \neq \boldsymbol{\emptyset}$.

Q.E.D.

Debreu then establishes the existence of equilibrium in a private ownership economy $\mathscr{E}'$ by making use of this theorem and the following nine assumptions

A. Assumptions on consumption
(1) $\mathbf{X}^k$ is closed, convex and bounded from below, $\forall k$.
(2) Each $\mathbf{X}^k$ possesses no point of satiation, $\forall k$.
(3) $\forall \mathbf{x}_0^k \in \mathbf{X}^k$ the sets $\mathbf{B}_0^k$ and $\mathbf{W}_0^k$ are closed in $\mathbf{X}^k$, $\forall k$.
(4) $\mathbf{B}_0^k$ is a convex set, $\forall k$.
(5) $\exists\, \mathbf{x}_0^k \in \mathbf{X}^k, \mathbf{x}_0^k \ll \mathbf{r}^k, \forall k$.

B. Assumptions on production
(6) $0 \in \mathbf{Y}_j, \forall j$.
(7) $\mathbf{Y}$ is closed and convex.

(8) $\mathbf{Y} \cap (-\mathbf{Y}) \subset \{0\}$.

(9) $(-\Omega) \subset \mathbf{Y}$.

We have after all this preparation the theorem

Theorem 9.3 The private ownership economy $\mathscr{E}' = \{(\mathbf{X}^k, R_k), (\mathbf{Y}_j), (\mathbf{r}^k), (\theta_{kj})\}$ has an equilibrium if assumptions (1)–(9) are satisfied.

Proof (Outline only). First consider assumption (1). Since $\mathbf{X}^k \subset \mathbf{E}^n$ it is closed and convex. However, it is not necessarily bounded from below. If we assume there is a basic minimum requirement of commodities which are necessary for human survival then there is no loss in assuming $\mathbf{X}^k$, $\forall k$ is bounded from below. The second assumption is no more than Axiom 9. Assumption (3) is ensuring that the indifference set is a boundary set to both $\mathbf{B}_0^k$ and $\mathbf{W}_0^k$. Assumption (4) is no more than Axiom 10. The fifth assumption attached to consumption is that there exists at least one commodity bundle which is strictly less than an individual's resource holdings, and this is true for all individuals. The assumptions concerning production are taken directly from those listed in Chapter 5 (p. 139).

Debreu first considers the possible unboundness of $\mathbf{X}^k$ and $\mathbf{Y}_j$ e.g. $\mathbf{Y}_j$ would be unbounded if constant returns to scale prevailed. He defines $\langle \mathbf{Y}_j \rangle$ to be the closed convex hull of $\mathbf{Y}_j$ (i.e. the smallest convex set formed from the set $\mathbf{Y}_j$). Similarly, $\langle \mathscr{E}' \rangle$ is the private ownership economy for which $\mathbf{Y}_j$ is replaced by $\langle \mathbf{Y}_j \rangle$. He then shows that an $\mathscr{E}'$-equilibrium is also an $\langle \mathscr{E}' \rangle$ -equilibrium. Now define two sets $\hat{\mathbf{X}}^k$ and $\hat{\mathbf{Y}}_j$ where $\hat{\mathbf{X}}^k$ satisfies assumptions (2) and (3) and $\hat{\mathbf{Y}}_j$ satisfies assumptions (6) and (7). Using these assumptions Debreu shows that $\bar{\mathbf{x}}^k$, $\bar{\mathbf{y}}_j$, the equilibrium of $\langle \mathscr{E}' \rangle$, are such that $\bar{\mathbf{x}}^k \in \hat{\mathbf{X}}^k$ and $\bar{\mathbf{y}}_j \in \hat{\mathbf{Y}}_j$. Furthermore, an $\langle \mathscr{E}' \rangle$ – equilibrium is an $\hat{\mathscr{E}}'$-equilibrium, hence an $\mathscr{E}'$-equilibrium is an $\hat{\mathscr{E}}'$-equilibrium For the usual reasons of homogeneity a price system for $\mathscr{E}'$ can be considered in terms of the normalised price set $\mathbf{P}$; thus we consider the $\hat{\mathscr{E}}'$-equilibrium problem where $\mathbf{p} \in \mathbf{P}$. Placing a superior mark $\hat{}$ on all the correspondences in an $\hat{\mathscr{E}}'$-economy he next establishes that just as $\mathbf{s}_j(\mathbf{p})$ and $\mathbf{d}^k(\mathbf{p})$ are upper semi-continuous on $\mathbf{P}$ so are $\hat{\mathbf{s}}_j(\mathbf{p})$ and $\hat{\mathbf{d}}^k(\mathbf{p})$. Having established this all the conditions of Theorem 9.2 are satisfied by $\hat{\mathbf{Z}}$ and $\hat{\boldsymbol{\epsilon}}$. Thus there exists a $\bar{\mathbf{p}} \in \mathbf{P}$ such that $\hat{\boldsymbol{\epsilon}}(\bar{\mathbf{p}}) \cap (-\Omega) \neq \emptyset$ and that $\bar{\mathbf{p}}$ is an equilibrium of $\mathscr{E}'$. That $\bar{\mathbf{p}}$ is an $\mathscr{E}'$-equilibrium can be seen as follows. From the application of Theorem 9.2 we have $\mathbf{z} \in \hat{\boldsymbol{\epsilon}}(\bar{\mathbf{p}})$. Then there is for each consumer an $\bar{\mathbf{x}}^k \in \hat{\mathbf{d}}^k(\bar{\mathbf{p}})$ and for each producer a $\mathbf{y}_j \in \hat{\mathbf{s}}_j(\bar{\mathbf{p}})$ such that

$$\bar{\mathbf{x}} - \mathbf{y} - \mathbf{r} = \mathbf{z}.$$

But $\mathbf{y} \in \mathbf{Y}$ and $\mathbf{Y}$ is convex and closed so that $\mathbf{y} \in \mathbf{Y}$ and $\mathbf{z} \in (-\Omega)$ implying that $\mathbf{y} + \mathbf{z} \in \mathbf{Y}$. Consequently there is a $\bar{\mathbf{y}}_j \in \mathbf{s}_j(\bar{\mathbf{p}})$ such that

$$\bar{\mathbf{y}} = \mathbf{y} + \mathbf{z}.$$

Subtracting these two results we get

$$\bar{\mathbf{x}} - \bar{\mathbf{y}} - \mathbf{r} = 0.$$

Hence, the state $(\bar{\mathscr{X}}, \bar{\mathscr{Y}}, \bar{\mathbf{p}})$ is an equilibrium of $\mathscr{E}'$.

So far we have concerned ourselves only with whether an equilibrium exists. It can readily be shown that if the weak axiom of revealed preference theory is invoked (Axiom RP.2, p. 73) then the $\mathscr{E}'$-equilibrium is a unique equilibrium. To show this is so suppose there are two equilibria $(\bar{\mathscr{x}}^1, \bar{\mathscr{y}}^1, \bar{\mathbf{p}}^1)$ and $(\bar{\mathscr{x}}^2, \bar{\mathscr{y}}^2, \bar{\mathbf{p}}^2)$. Throughout we shall consider only the aggregate elements $\mathbf{x} \in \mathbf{X}$ and $\mathbf{y} \in \mathbf{Y}$ corresponding to $\mathscr{x} \in \hat{\mathscr{X}}$ and $\mathscr{y} \in \hat{\mathscr{Y}}$. If $\bar{\mathbf{x}}^1$ and $\bar{\mathbf{y}}^1$ are equilibrium values at $\bar{\mathbf{p}}^1$ then

$$(\bar{\mathbf{p}}^1)'\bar{\mathbf{x}}^1 > (\bar{\mathbf{p}}^1)'\bar{\mathbf{x}}^2 \quad \text{and} \quad (\bar{\mathbf{p}}^1)'\bar{\mathbf{y}}^1 > (\bar{\mathbf{p}}^1)'\bar{\mathbf{y}}^2.$$

Similarly, if $\bar{\mathbf{x}}^2$ and $\bar{\mathbf{y}}^2$ are equilibrium values at $\bar{\mathbf{p}}^2$ then

$$(\bar{\mathbf{p}}^2)'\bar{\mathbf{x}}^2 > (\bar{\mathbf{p}}^2)'\bar{\mathbf{x}}^1 \quad \text{and} \quad (\bar{\mathbf{p}}^2)'\bar{\mathbf{y}}^2 > (\bar{\mathbf{p}}^2)'\bar{\mathbf{y}}^1.$$

But the first condition says that $\bar{\mathscr{x}}^1 RP \bar{\mathscr{x}}^2$ and $\bar{\mathscr{y}}^1 RP \bar{\mathscr{y}}^2$ whilst the second says that $\bar{\mathscr{x}}^2 RP \bar{\mathscr{x}}^1$ and $\bar{\mathscr{y}}^2 RP \bar{\mathscr{y}}^1$, where *RP* denotes the relation 'revealed preferred'. Thus if we include the weak axiom of revealed preference only one equilibrium is valid in the $\mathscr{E}'$-economy, i.e. the $\mathscr{E}'$-economy has a unique equilibrium.

9.5 Existence of Equilibrium in an Open Leontief Model[4]

In Section 6.3 (ii) we discussed the open Leontief model and established that on the production side a non-negative output vector $\mathbf{y} \geqslant 0$ of order $n \times 1$ maximises profits $\pi(\mathbf{p}, \mathbf{w})$ if

$$(\mathbf{I} - \mathbf{A})\mathbf{y} \geqslant \mathbf{c} \quad \text{s.t. } \mathbf{B}\mathbf{y} \leqslant \mathbf{r}$$

and
$$\mathbf{p}'(\mathbf{I} - \mathbf{A}) \leqslant \mathbf{w}'\mathbf{B}$$

where $\mathbf{A}$ and $\mathbf{B}$ are $n \times n$ and $s \times n$ respectively, s being the number of inputs. Hence $\mathbf{p}$ is an $n \times 1$ commodity price vector and $\mathbf{w}$ is an $s \times 1$ factor price vector. Now introduce the aggregate demand functions for goods and the aggregate supply functions for factors so that

$$c_i = c_i(p_1, \ldots, p_n; w_1, \ldots, w_s) \qquad i = 1, \ldots, n$$

or
$$\mathbf{c} = \mathbf{c}(\mathbf{p}, \mathbf{w})$$

and
$$r_v = r_v(p_1, \ldots, p_n; w_1, \ldots, w_s) \qquad v = 1, \ldots, s$$

or
$$\mathbf{r} = \mathbf{r}(\mathbf{p}, \mathbf{w}).$$

It is assumed that both functions are single-valued and continuous for all $\mathbf{p} \geqslant 0$ and $\mathbf{w} \geqslant 0$. The equilibrium set $\bar{\mathbf{y}}, \bar{\mathbf{c}}, \bar{\mathbf{p}}, \bar{\mathbf{w}}$, and $\bar{\mathbf{r}}$ must satisfy

$$(\mathbf{I} - \mathbf{A})\bar{\mathbf{y}} = \bar{\mathbf{c}}$$

$$\mathbf{B}\bar{\mathbf{y}} = \bar{\mathbf{r}}$$

$$\bar{\mathbf{p}}'(\mathbf{I} - \mathbf{A}) \leqslant \bar{\mathbf{w}}'\mathbf{B}$$

$$\bar{\mathbf{c}} = \mathbf{c}(\bar{\mathbf{p}}, \bar{\mathbf{w}})$$
$$\bar{\mathbf{r}} = \mathbf{r}(\bar{\mathbf{p}}, \bar{\mathbf{w}}).$$

Since the demand functions are homogeneous of degree zero in **p** and **w** we need only consider prices belonging to the unit simplex

$$\mathbf{S}_{n+s} = \{(\mathbf{p}, \mathbf{w})/\iota'\mathbf{p} + \iota'\mathbf{w} = 1, \mathbf{p} > 0, \mathbf{w} > 0\}$$

which is a closed, bounded convex set in $\mathbf{E}^{n+s}$. Our procedure is to establish an upper semi-continuous mapping which maps **S** into itself. Then we have met all the conditions of Kakutani's fixed-point theorem and so we have an equilibrium satisfying the above equations.

Consider a point $(\mathbf{p}^0, \mathbf{w}^0) \in \mathbf{S}$. The demand and supply functions map $(\mathbf{p}^0, \mathbf{w}^0)$ into points $(\mathbf{c}^0, \mathbf{r}^0)$. These must be points because we have assumed the functions $\mathbf{c}(\mathbf{p}, \mathbf{w})$ and $\mathbf{r}(\mathbf{p}, \mathbf{w})$ to be single-valued. Given that $(\mathbf{I} - \mathbf{A})^{-1}$ exists then we have a point $\mathbf{y}^0$ corresponding to $\mathbf{c}^0$, i.e. $\mathbf{y}^0 = (\mathbf{I} - \mathbf{A})^{-1}\mathbf{c}^0$. However, $\mathbf{y}^0$ may not be consistent with the given technology; in other words, $\mathbf{y}^0$ may lay outside the production set $\{\mathbf{y}/\mathbf{B}\mathbf{y} \leqslant \mathbf{r}, \mathbf{y} \geqslant 0\}$. This is illustrated in Fig. 9.9 (*a*), where we have considered two commodities and two factors. The production set is represented by the shaded region, and the vector $\mathbf{y}^0$ lies outside this set. Thus, we scale down

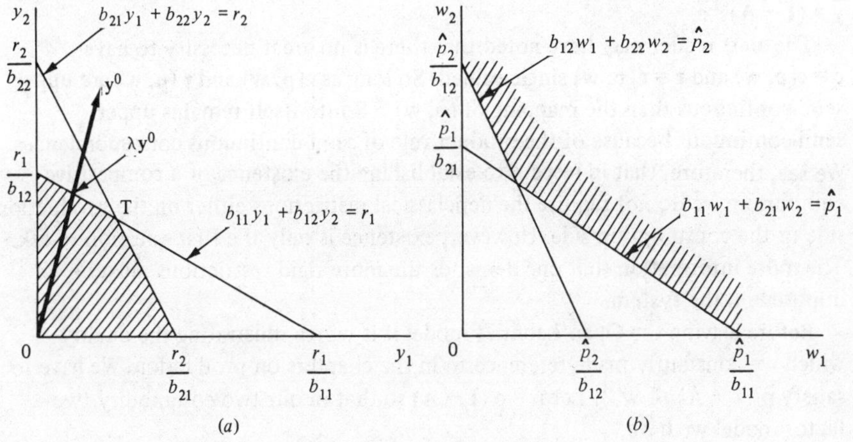

Fig. 9.9. Equilibrium in an open Leontief model

the vector $\mathbf{y}^0$ by a factor λ such that $\lambda\mathbf{y}^0$ belongs to the boundary of the production set. Given the vector $\lambda\mathbf{y}^0$ there is a set of prices associated with this output which constitute the normal to the hyperplane at $\lambda\mathbf{y}^0$. If $\lambda\mathbf{y}^0$ is not a vertex of the production set, as in Fig. 9.9 (*a*), then the price vector is unique. If, however, $\lambda\mathbf{y}^0$ is a vertex, such as point T in Fig. 9.9 (*a*), then there are a set of prices consistent with this output, specifically, the range of prices which lie between the normals of the adjacent sides of the vertex. Thus, let **P** denote the set of all such price vectors, i.e.

$$\mathbf{P} = \{\mathbf{p}/\lambda\mathbf{y}^0 \ \max \mathbf{p}'(\mathbf{I} - \mathbf{A})\mathbf{y} \quad \text{s.t. } \mathbf{B}\mathbf{y} \leqslant \mathbf{r}, \mathbf{y} \geqslant 0\}.$$

Now let **p** range over **P** then there will be an associated set of possible 'wage' vectors **w**. Let **W** denote the set of such 'wage' vectors, i.e.

$$\mathbf{W} = \{\mathbf{w}/\mathbf{w} \min \mathbf{w}'\mathbf{r} \quad \text{s.t.} \quad \mathbf{w}'\mathbf{B} \geqslant \mathbf{p}'(\mathbf{I} - \mathbf{A}), \mathbf{p} \in \mathbf{P}\}.$$

The set $(\mathbf{P}, \mathbf{W})$ is then defined as the normalised vectors

$$(\mathbf{P}, \mathbf{W}) = \{(\mathbf{p}, \mathbf{w}) \in \mathbf{S}/\mathbf{p} \in \mathbf{P} \;\&\; \mathbf{w} \in \mathbf{W}\}.$$

Thus if $\lambda\mathbf{y}^0$ is on the boundary and is not a vertex of the production set there is an associated **p** and **w** which are unique, and so $(\mathbf{p}^0, \mathbf{w}^0) \in \mathbf{S}$ is mapped into a point $(\mathbf{p}, \mathbf{w}) \in \mathbf{S}$. If, however, $\lambda\mathbf{y}^0$ is a vertex of the production set then we have sets **P** and **W** such that $(\mathbf{P}, \mathbf{W}) \subset \mathbf{S}$. Generally, $(\mathbf{p}, \mathbf{w}) \in \mathbf{S}$ is mapped into $(\mathbf{P}, \mathbf{W}) \subset \mathbf{S}$ and this mapping is upper semi-continuous.

We have, therefore, satisfied the conditions of Kakutani's fixed-point theorem. Letting ψ denote the upper semi-continuous point-to-set mapping, and letting $\Phi(\mathbf{S})$ denote the family of closed convex subsets $(\mathbf{P}, \mathbf{W})$ of **S** then we have an upper semi-continuous correspondence ψ of a compact convex set **S** into $\Phi(\mathbf{S})$. Hence there exists a $(\bar{\mathbf{p}}, \bar{\mathbf{w}}) \in \mathbf{S}$ such that $(\bar{\mathbf{p}}, \bar{\mathbf{w}}) \in \psi\,(\bar{\mathbf{p}}, \bar{\mathbf{w}})$, i.e. $(\bar{\mathbf{p}}, \bar{\mathbf{w}}) \in (\mathbf{P}, \mathbf{W})$. Thus, having established a $\bar{\mathbf{p}}$ and $\bar{\mathbf{w}}$ it readily follows that $\bar{\mathbf{c}} = \mathbf{c}(\bar{\mathbf{p}}, \bar{\mathbf{w}})$, $\bar{\mathbf{r}} = \mathbf{r}(\bar{\mathbf{p}}, \bar{\mathbf{w}})$ and $\bar{\mathbf{y}} = (\mathbf{I} - \mathbf{A})^{-1}\bar{\mathbf{c}}$.

The alert reader may have noted that there is no great necessity to have $\mathbf{c} = \mathbf{c}(\mathbf{p}, \mathbf{w})$ and $\mathbf{r} = \mathbf{r}(\mathbf{p}, \mathbf{w})$ single-valued. So long as $\mathbf{c}(\mathbf{p}, \mathbf{w})$ and $\mathbf{r}(\mathbf{p}, \mathbf{w})$ are upper semi-continuous then the mapping of $(\mathbf{p}, \mathbf{w}) \in \mathbf{S}$ into itself remains upper semi-continuous because of the product rule of semi-continuous correspondences. We see, therefore, that in respect to establishing the existence of a competitive equilibrium we do not require the neoclassical restrictions either on the production side or the consumption side. However, existence is only the first question to ask. The more information that one demands the more rigid restrictions must be imposed on the system.

Before leaving the Open Leontief model it is worth illustrating the duality which we constantly made reference to in the chapters on production. We have to satisfy $\mathbf{p}'(\mathbf{I} - \mathbf{A}) \leqslant \mathbf{w}'\mathbf{B}$. Let $\hat{\mathbf{p}} = \mathbf{p}'(\mathbf{I} - \mathbf{A})$ so that in our two-commodity two-factor model we have,

$$(\hat{p}_1, \hat{p}_2) = [(p_1 - p_2 a_{21}), (p_2 - p_1 a_{12})]$$

which are the profit conditions for firms 1 and 2 respectively. We require, therefore, $\hat{p}_1 \leqslant b_{11} w_1 + b_{21} w_2$ and $\hat{p}_2 \leqslant b_{12} w_1 + b_{22} w_2$. These relations are illustrated in Fig. 9.9 (*b*). The preference function in the primal problem is $\mathbf{p}'(\mathbf{I} - \mathbf{A})\mathbf{y}$, the total value of net output, of which the aim is to maximise. The preference function of the dual is $\mathbf{w}'\mathbf{r}$, and total payments is to be minimised. From the fundamental duality theorem of linear programming[5] we have that at the optimal solution the two preference functions are the same, i.e.

$$\bar{\mathbf{p}}'\bar{\mathbf{c}} = \bar{\mathbf{w}}'\bar{\mathbf{r}}.$$

In other words, the total value of final goods produced, national income, equals the total payments to factors of production, national income.

EXERCISES

1. To what extent is the trading set dependent upon the initial allocation? Construct a situation for a two-commodity two-person exchange model in which no trading set exists other than t_0 and t_0 *not* belonging to the efficiency locus.

2. Prove that all $x \in \mathbf{T}^*$ also belongs to $\mathscr{X}^*$.

3. Construct an exchange model for which the trading curves intersect on the contract curve three times. Discuss the economic significance of this result.

4. Explain the use of the mapping

$$\mathbf{T}(\mathbf{p}) = \frac{\mathbf{p} + \mathbf{M}(\mathbf{p})}{1 + \iota'\mathbf{M}(\mathbf{p})}$$

in the Gale–Nikaido theorem. Would the proof be any different if we used in place of $\mathbf{M}(\mathbf{p}) = \max\,[0, \mathbf{z}(\mathbf{p})]$ the modulated excess demand $\mathbf{M}(\mathbf{p}) = \max\,[-\mathbf{p}, \mathbf{z}(\mathbf{p})]$?

5. Walras Law states that $\mathbf{p}'\mathbf{z}(\mathbf{p}) = 0$, $\forall \mathbf{p}$. Given $u^k = \sum_{i=1}^{n} a_i^k \log x_i^k$, $\sum_{i=1}^{n} a_i = 1$, show that

$$\mathbf{p}'\mathbf{z}(\mathbf{p}) = \sum_{i=1}^{n} a_i \left[\sum_{j=1}^{n} \left(1 - \frac{\delta_{ij}}{a_i}\right) p_j \bar{x}_j \right]$$

and that this expression is zero for all $\mathbf{p}$.

6. The Stone–Geary utility function

$$u^k = \sum_{i=1}^{n} a_i^k \log (x_i^k - \gamma_i^k) \qquad k = 1, \ldots, m$$

gives demand functions

$$x_i^k = \gamma_i^k + \frac{a_i^k \left(y^k - \sum_{j=1}^{n} p_j \gamma_j^k\right)}{p_i} \qquad i = 1, \ldots, n.$$

(*a*) If every consumer has the same tastes so that $a_i^k = a_i$, $\forall k$ and $\gamma_i^k = \gamma_i$, $\forall k$ show that

$$z_i(\mathbf{p}) = m\gamma_i + \frac{a_i}{p_i}\left[\sum_{j=1}^{n} p_j(x_j - m\gamma_j)\right] - \bar{x}_i \qquad i = 1, \ldots, n$$

and establish that $\bar{p}_j = a_j/(\bar{x}_j - m\gamma_j)$ is an equilibrium price.

(*b*) Verify Walras Law with this excess demand function.

7. Consider the following two assumptions about distribution:

Assumption 1 Consumers are divided into two mutually exclusive and exhaustive groups C_1 and C_2 where C_1 denotes those consumers receiving a share of profits and C_2 those not receiving a share of profits. The wealth constraint for individual k is then

$$w^k = \mathbf{p}'\mathbf{r}^k + \sum_{j=1}^{l} \delta_k \delta_{kj} \pi_j \qquad k = 1, \ldots, m$$

$\delta_k = 1$ if $k \in C_1$ and $\delta_k = 0$ if $k \in C_2$.

Assumption 2 Consumers have a share in the total value of production. If this share is β^k and $\sum_k \beta^k = 1$ then the wealth constraint is

$$w^k = \mathbf{p}'\mathbf{r}^k + \beta^k \sum_{j=1}^{l} \mathbf{p}'\mathbf{y}_j \qquad k = 1, \ldots, m.$$

(*a*) Show that the results of Section 9.3 are unaffected.

(*b*) What other forms of distribution can be handled in this framework?

8. Explain the importance of fixed-point theorems in existence proofs of economic models.

10

WELFARE ECONOMICS

10.1 Introduction

Welfare economics can be considered as the normative branch of economics and in particular it attempts at a valuation of the policy goals. It is concerned with the well-being of a group or of society as a whole. This being so it must evaluate the various states in which an economy can find itself. Each state will involve a different consumption and production pattern, a different distribution of factors and a different distribution of income.

In discussing welfare we cannot escape making some value judgements; the best we can do is make our value judgements explicit. It must, therefore, be agreed from the outset whether we accept the statement that social preferences depend only and just only on the members which compose that society. This is the ethical postulate of Arrow which was discussed in Appendix 2B, which we shall repeat here.

Ethical Postulate Society's preferences depend upon the preferences of the individuals in that society and on none outside that society.

Although this belongs to ethics an economist cannot even begin to analyse the well-being of society without some such postulate. Even the Pareto ranking which appears the least objectionable is dependent upon this ethical postulate. But even accepting this postulate we still have a dilemma. Utility, as we discussed in Chapter 3, is an ordinal variable so we cannot say by exactly how much a person's welfare changes when a state of the economy changes. Even more than this, inter-personal comparisons are ruled out and this would be so even if utility was a cardinal variable.

Valfaredo Pareto realised that not all was lost. It is still possible to say that if someone gained and nobody lost by a change from one state to another then the change was beneficial to society and society would rank the second state higher than the first. We have, therefore, a Pareto ranking.

Definition 10.1

(Pareto Ranking) We have a Pareto ranking with P^*, R^*, and I^* if $\forall \mathbf{x}, \mathbf{y} \in \chi$

(1) $\forall k, \mathbf{x}R_k\mathbf{y}\ \&\ \exists h, \mathbf{x}P_h\mathbf{y} \Rightarrow \mathbf{x}P^*\mathbf{y}$.

(2) $\forall k, \mathbf{x}R_k\mathbf{y} \Rightarrow \mathbf{x}R^*\mathbf{y}$.

(3) $\forall k, \mathbf{x}I_k\mathbf{y} \Rightarrow \mathbf{x}I^*\mathbf{y}$.

It is clear that although R_k is complete for individual k, the relation R^* for society is not complete. There are elements of χ which cannot be compared. Thus if we have $\mathbf{x}^0$ and $\mathbf{x}^1$ such that $\mathbf{x}^0 P_1 \mathbf{x}^1$ and $\mathbf{x}^1 P_2 \mathbf{x}^0$ then society cannot rank the states $\mathbf{x}^0$ and $\mathbf{x}^1$, we say $\mathbf{x}^0$ and $\mathbf{x}^1$ are Pareto non-comparable. They may be comparable in some other sense, and it is for this reason we have placed an asterisk on P, R and I to make it clear that we are dealing with a Pareto ranking.

Even though R^* is not complete the question arises as to whether we can find another ranking which is complete. What we have is the following problem. If two states fall in the Pareto comparable region we rank them and we can make a clearly specified welfare statement. But are the states which are Pareto comparable large in number or small? In reality nearly every policy will make some members of the community better off and others worse off. If we are not to make any inter-personal comparisons how then do we overcome this impasse?

The answers sought have become known as the principles of compensation, at least in part. These principles have a long history and although still discussed it has generally been accepted that they do not constitute a useful path of investigation. We can reveal the essence of the debate very succinctly as follows. Suppose we have a state of nature $\mathbf{x} \in \chi$. Let $S(\mathbf{x})$ denote the set of all social states possible from a (potential) redistribution of $\mathbf{x}$. Obviously $\mathbf{x} \in S(\mathbf{x})$. The first compensation principle to be posed was that by Kaldor [63]. This says that a state $\mathbf{x}$ is better than a state $\mathbf{y}$ if we can attain a state $\mathbf{z}$ by redistributing $\mathbf{x}$ and if $\mathbf{z}$ is Pareto superior to $\mathbf{y}$.

Kaldor Compensation $\quad \forall \mathbf{x}, \mathbf{y} \in \chi \quad \mathbf{x} P \mathbf{y} \Leftrightarrow \exists \mathbf{z} \quad [\mathbf{z} \in S(\mathbf{x}) \ \& \ \mathbf{z} P^* \mathbf{y}]$.

It was realised by Scitovsky that under the Kaldor compensation it is still possible to redistribute $\mathbf{y}$ such that this is preferable to $\mathbf{x}$, which is inconsistent with the statement $\mathbf{x}P\mathbf{y}$. The proof of this is as follows. Let $\mathbf{x}, \mathbf{y} \in \chi$ be such that $\exists \mathbf{z} \in S(\mathbf{x}), \mathbf{z}P^*\mathbf{y}$ and that also $\exists \mathbf{w} \in S(\mathbf{y}), \mathbf{w}P^*\mathbf{x}$. From the former we have by the Kaldor test $\mathbf{x}P\mathbf{y}$ and from the latter that $\mathbf{y}P\mathbf{x}$, an inconsistency. Hence to rule out this inconsistency Scitovsky argued that for a state $\mathbf{x}$ to be preferable to a state $\mathbf{y}$ it must be possible to find a state $\mathbf{z} \in S(\mathbf{y})$ such that $\mathbf{z}P^*\mathbf{y}$ but not possible to find a state $\mathbf{w} \in S(\mathbf{y})$ such that $\mathbf{w}P^*\mathbf{x}$, i.e.

Scitovsky Compensation

$$\forall \mathbf{x}, \mathbf{y} \in \chi \quad \mathbf{x}P\mathbf{y} \Leftrightarrow [\ \exists \mathbf{z} \in S(\mathbf{x})\ \mathbf{z}P^*\mathbf{y} \ \& \quad \sim \exists \mathbf{w} \in S(\mathbf{y})\ \ \mathbf{w}P^*\mathbf{x}].$$

These tests are clearly an attempt to deal with the Pareto non-comparable states. Their essential defect is that it is supposed that the redistributions are only *potential* and not actual. But if they are not actual we are in the realm of the Utopias. Why not just say we can always find a Utopian state if we can redistribute income appropriately! This whole line of thought is doomed to failure.

Before leaving this discussion let us see Pareto comparability and non-comparability in terms of the theory of exchange outlined in Section 9.2. In Fig. 10.1 we have the familiar Edgeworth–Bowley box. Trading is beneficial if from a position t_0 we have $t_1 P^* t_0$. In the figure t_1 represents a state in which both individuals are better off relative to t_0. We established in Section 9.2 that the efficiency locus is the set of all Pareto optimal points denoted $\mathscr{X}^*$ and that the optimal trading set $\mathbf{T}^* \subset \mathbf{T}$ is also a

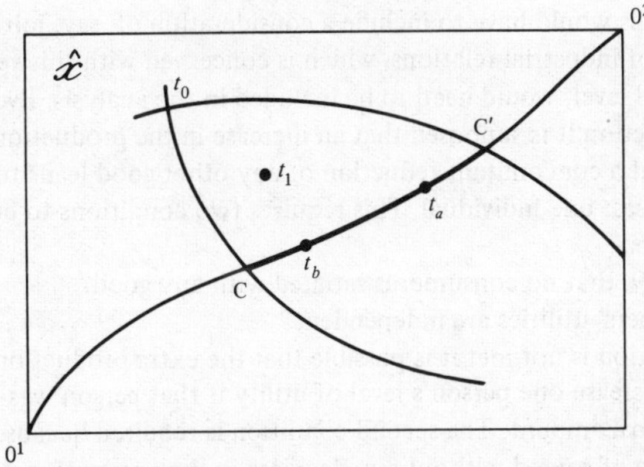

Fig. 10.1. Pareto comparable and non-comparable states in exchange theory

subset of the set of all Pareto optimal points. Consider the states t_a and t_b on the contract curve CC′. Both t_a and t_b are Pareto optimal. However, they are also Pareto non-comparable. We cannot establish whether $t_a P^* t_b$, $t_b P^* t_a$ or $t_a I^* t_b$. The Pareto comparable set is **T**—**T***, where **T** is the trading set, and the Pareto non-comparable set is **T***.

If we assume price-takers and a unique equilibrium there is no problem because the Pareto optimal point is preferable to every other point in **T**—**T*** and hence the competitive equilibrium point can be ascribed supreme. However, suppose even with perfect competition we have a situation of multiple equilibria of which say t_a and t_b represent two of these. The Pareto criterion is of no aid in saying which is preferable for clearly t_a is preferred by individual 1 and t_b by individual 2. The issues of welfare economics are directed at two areas therefore. First, in establishing the features of Pareto comparable states; second, considerations about how the ignorant set can be reduced if not eliminated. Thus Section 10.2 is concerned with the properties of Pareto comparable states.

10.2 Pareto Optimality

In so far as the economy consists of both producers and consumers, what matters for Pareto optimality is the allocation of production and its distribution, so that the utility of all consumers is not decreased but possibly increased for at least one member. The criterion, it is to be noticed, is based only on the utility of consumers because ultimately it is this which gives satisfaction. However, we even now are restricting the domain over which satisfaction is defined. The utility function of each consumer has only commodities as its arguments and satisfaction is therefore defined only over the commodity space $\mathbf{X}^k$, $\forall k$. Such a domain excludes from consideration satisfaction from snob appeal and such considerations as job satisfaction – a limitation which is a consequence of our abstraction. A more embracing analysis would have to include a consideration of, say, job satisfaction; and the subject of industrial relations, which is concerned with this very problem, but, at a practical level, would need to be included in the analysis. Even when discussing production it is supposed that an increase in the production of at least one good without a concomitant reduction of any other good leads to an increase in utility for at least one individual. This requires two conditions to be met on the side of consumers:

(1) Axiom 9, that no consumer is satiated with any good.
(2) Consumers' utilities are independent.

If the first condition is not met it is possible that the extra production of at least one good will decrease one person's level of utility if that person was already consuming the optimal amount. The second condition is required because an increase in the production of a good without any decrease in the production of all other goods may increase the utility of the first individual and because the level of consumption of the first individual has increased individual 2 feels worse off as a consequence – a manifestation of 'keeping up with the Joneses'. Such externalities in consumption are ruled out in the discussion of Pareto optimality; however, we shall see in Section 10.4 how this does effect the results of this section. It does mean, however, that the introduction of externalities introduces still further non-comparable states.

Classical welfare economics asserts the following central proposition: A necessary and sufficient condition for the distribution to be Pareto optimal is that the marginal rate of commodity substitution be the same for all individuals. This proposition requires that no consumer has a point of satiation with respect to any good, i.e. no consumer has a 'bliss point'; secondly, that the indifference curves are strictly convex to the origin so that no corner solutions are included, i.e. the Pareto optimal point must be an interior solution and not a boundary solution of the attainable set (cf. the Weierstrass theorem, p. 53). Only then is the classical condition a *necessary* condition. We now turn to a formal treatment of this proposition.

In demonstrating this result and that of production to follow we shall first list the notation to be used in this section.

Notation $\mathbf{x}^k = (x_1^k, \ldots, x_n^k)$ is the vector of n commodities consumed by individual k, $k = 1, \ldots, m$.

$\mathbf{y}_j = (y_{1j}, \ldots, y_{nj})$ denotes the production vector of n commodities by firm j, $j = 1, \ldots, l$.

$\mathbf{r}_j = (r_{1j}, \ldots, r_{sj})$ denotes the input vector of s inputs used by firm j, $j = 1, \ldots, l$.

We can write our central proposition in terms of the following theorem.

Theorem 10.1 (Pareto Optimality for Consumers). Given the classical assumptions of welfare economics and two individual utility functions $u^k(\mathbf{x}^k)$ and $u^h(\mathbf{x}^h)$ then for goods i and j a state of Pareto optimality is characterised by

$$\frac{\partial u^k/\partial x_i^k}{\partial u^k/\partial x_j^k} = \frac{\partial u^h/\partial x_i^h}{\partial u^h/\partial x_j^h} \qquad \forall\, k, h \text{ and } \forall i, j.$$

Proof Considering only individual k and assuming all other individuals $h \neq k$ have constant levels of utility, u_0^h. Let $x_i^0 = \sum_k x_i^k$, $\forall i$ denote the given availability of the n goods. Forming the Lagrangian expression for individual k we have

$$V^k = u^k(\mathbf{x}^k) + \sum_{h \neq k} \lambda^h [u^h(\mathbf{x}^h) - u_0^h] + \sum_i \mu_i(x_i^0 - x_i).$$

Differentiating we get

$$\mathbf{V}_x^k = \partial V^k/\partial \mathbf{x}^k = \delta^k \mathbf{u}_x^k + \epsilon^h \lambda^h \mathbf{u}_x^h - \boldsymbol{\mu} = 0 \qquad k, h = 1, \ldots, m$$

$$V_\lambda^k = \partial V^k/\partial \lambda^h = [u^h(\mathbf{x}^h) - u_0^h] = 0 \qquad h \neq k$$

$$\mathbf{V}_\mu^k = \partial V/\partial \boldsymbol{\mu} = (\mathbf{x}^0 - \mathbf{x}) = 0$$

where $\mathbf{u}_x^k = \partial u^k/\partial \mathbf{x}^k$ and $\mathbf{u}_x^h = \partial u^h/\partial \mathbf{x}^h$; $\delta^k = \left.\begin{matrix} 1 & k = h \\ 0 & h \neq k \end{matrix}\right\}$ and $\epsilon^h = \left.\begin{matrix} 0 \\ 1 \end{matrix}\right\} \begin{matrix} h = k \\ h \neq k \end{matrix}$;

$$\boldsymbol{\mu} = \begin{bmatrix} \mu_1 \\ \cdot \\ \cdot \\ \circ \\ \mu_n \end{bmatrix} \quad \mathbf{x} = \begin{bmatrix} x_1 \\ \cdot \\ \cdot \\ \cdot \\ x_n \end{bmatrix} = \begin{bmatrix} \sum_k x_1^k \\ \cdot \\ \cdot \\ \cdot \\ \sum_k x_n^k \end{bmatrix} \text{ and } \mathbf{x}^0 = \begin{bmatrix} x_1^0 \\ \cdot \\ \cdot \\ \cdot \\ x_n^0 \end{bmatrix}.$$

There are $mn + (m - 1) + n$ equations in $mn + m + n - 1$ unknowns.

We see from the expression for $\mathbf{V}_x^k$ that

$$\frac{\partial V^k}{\partial x_i^k} = \frac{\partial u^k}{\partial x_i^k} - \mu_i = 0$$

$$\frac{\partial V^k}{\partial x_i^h} = \lambda^h \frac{\partial u^h}{\partial x_i^h} - \mu_i = 0 \qquad h \neq k$$

for good i and the same expression for good j. This implies

$$\mu_i = \frac{\partial u^k}{\partial x_i^k} = \lambda^h \frac{\partial u^h}{\partial x_i^h} \text{ and } \mu_j = \frac{\partial u^k}{\partial x_j^k} = \lambda^h \frac{\partial u^h}{\partial x_j^h}.$$

Taking the ratio μ_i/μ_j gives our necessary result immediately. To demonstrate the sufficient condition, differentiate $\mathbf{V}_x^k$ with respect to the vector $\mathbf{x}^k$

$$\frac{\partial \mathbf{V}_x^k}{\partial (\mathbf{x}^k)'} = \delta^k \mathbf{U}^k + \epsilon^k \lambda^h \mathbf{U}^h.$$

If $\mathbf{U}^k$ and $\mathbf{U}^h$ are negative definite $\forall k, h$ (see Section 4.1 p. 79) then by Theorem 8.1 (p. 212) we have

$$\delta^k \mathbf{U}^k + \epsilon^k \lambda^h \mathbf{U}^h < 0 \ \text{ if } \lambda^h > 0$$

which ensures a maximum.

Q.E.D.

This result is illustrated in Fig. 10.2 in terms of the familiar Edgeworth–Bowley box.

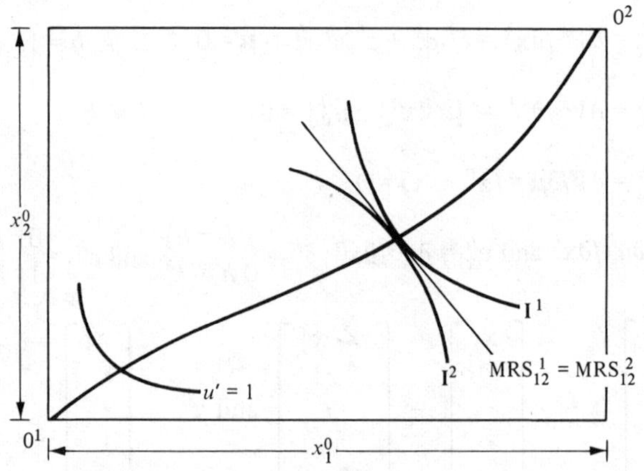

Fig. 10.2. Pareto optimality for consumers

The same line of reasoning applies to production. A necessary and sufficient condition for Pareto optimality in production is that the marginal rate of transformation for every pair of commodities is the same for all firms comprising the economy. This requires that the isoproduct set be strictly convex, and that the marginal product for any factor is never negative. If these are met then

Theorem 10.2 (Pareto Optimality for Producers). Given production functions $\mathbf{y}_j = f^j(\mathbf{r}_j), j = 1, \ldots, l$ and $\mathbf{r}_j = (r_{1j}, \ldots, r_{sj})$ and that the classical assumptions of welfare economics are met, then for inputs i and k a state of Pareto optimality is characterised by

$$\frac{\partial f^j/\partial r_{ij}}{\partial f^j/\partial r_{kj}} = \frac{\partial f^h/\partial r_{ih}}{\partial f^h/\partial r_{kh}}.$$

Proof Consider firm j and assume the outputs of all other firms are given at y_h^0 $(h \neq j)$. Inputs are assumed given $r_v^0 = \sum_j r_{vj}$, $\forall v$. Forming the Lagrangian expression for the jth firm we have

$$L^j = f^j(\mathbf{r}_j) + \sum_{h \neq j} a^h [f^h(\mathbf{r}_h) - y_h^0] + \sum_v \theta_v (r_v^0 - r_v).$$

Differentiating we get

$$\mathbf{L}_r^j = \partial L^j / \partial \mathbf{r}_j = \delta^j \, \mathbf{f}_r^j + \epsilon^h a^h \mathbf{f}_r^h - \boldsymbol{\theta} = 0 \qquad j, h = 1, \ldots, l$$

$$L_a^j = \partial L^j / \partial \underset{\sim}{a} = f^h(\mathbf{r}_h) - y_h^0 = 0 \qquad h \neq j$$

$$\mathbf{L}_\theta^j = \partial L^j / \partial \boldsymbol{\theta} = \mathbf{r}^0 - \mathbf{r} = 0$$

where $\mathbf{f}_r^j = \partial f^j / \partial \mathbf{r}_j$ and $\mathbf{f}_r^h = \partial f^h / \partial \mathbf{r}_h$; δ^j and ϵ^h as before,

$$\mathbf{r} = \begin{bmatrix} r_1 \\ \cdot \\ \cdot \\ \cdot \\ r_s \end{bmatrix} = \begin{bmatrix} \sum_j r_{1j} \\ \cdot \\ \cdot \\ \cdot \\ \sum_j r_{sj} \end{bmatrix} \qquad \mathbf{r}^0 = \begin{bmatrix} r_1^0 \\ \cdot \\ \cdot \\ \cdot \\ r_s^0 \end{bmatrix}$$

There are $ls + (l - 1) + s$ equations in that many unknowns.

For inputs i and k used by firm j we obtain immediately from $\mathbf{L}_r^j$ with necessary condition of the theorem

$$\frac{\partial f^j / \partial r_{ij}}{\partial f^j / \partial r_{kj}} = \frac{\partial f^h / \partial r_{ih}}{\partial f^h / \partial r_{kh}}$$

To obtain the sufficient conditions differentiate $\mathbf{L}_r^j$ with respect to r_j giving

$$\partial \mathbf{L}_r^j / \partial \mathbf{r}_j' = \delta^j \, \mathbf{Q}^j + \epsilon^h \, a^h \, \mathbf{Q}^h$$

where $\mathbf{Q}^j$ and $\mathbf{Q}^h$ are the Hessian matrices for firms j and h. Now if all firms operate in the relevant region (see Section 7.2) then $\mathbf{Q}^j$ and $\mathbf{Q}^h$, $\forall j, h$ are negative definite, hence by Theorem 8.1 (p. 212)

$$\delta^j \mathbf{Q}^j + \epsilon^h \, a^h \, \mathbf{Q}^h < 0 \text{ if } a^h > 0$$

which ensures a maximum.

Q.E.D.

This result is illustrated in Fig. 10.3.

The results of consumption and production are readily combined and this is left as an exercise. But the question is whether these conditions that must be met are at all reasonable? To quote Arrow [5].

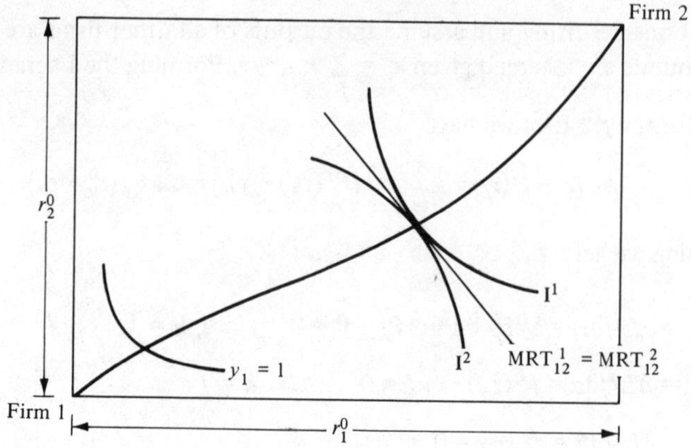

Fig. 10.3. Pareto optimality for producers

On the face of it, then, the classical criteria for optimality in production and consumption have little relevance to the actual world. From the point of view of policy, the most important consequence of these criteria . . . [is] that the use of the price system under a regime of perfect competition will lead to a social optimum allocation of economic resources [91, p. 509].

The assumptions in classical welfare economics are, particularly, the continuity and differentiability of functions, the strict convexity both of indifference curves and isoquants, and the non-existence of bliss points in both consumption and production. In our earlier analysis attempts were made to release the analysis from such rigidity. If this is done in the present situation the issue amounts to observing how a Pareto optimal solution is characterised. In undertaking this exercise we shall follow closely the analysis of Arrow [5]; however, the notation will be consistent with the remainder of this book as near as is possible.

As far as commodities, number of firms, number of consumers, etc., are concerned we shall adopt the notation laid out at the beginning of this section. In the

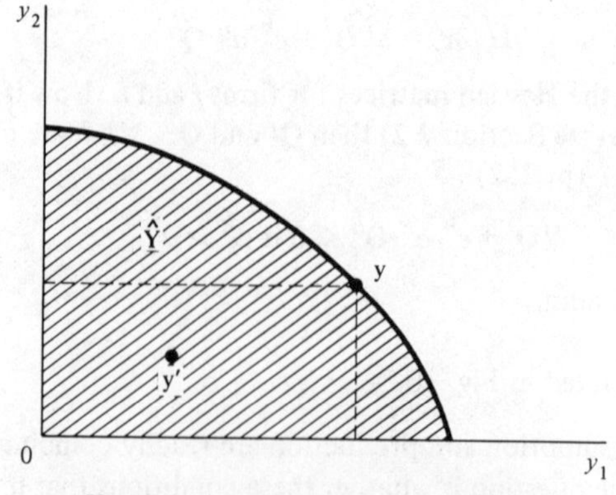

Fig. 10.4. Production possibility set

present formulation, however, the production function which converts inputs into outputs is only implicit. Once again we assume the input vector is given and this means we have a set of outputs which is bounded. Without loss of confusion we shall denote the feasible output set by $\hat{\mathbf{Y}}$, which denotes all the technologically feasible *output* vectors y for the economy, given the amounts of inputs. This production possibility set is illustrated in Fig. 10.4.

We can now state Arrow's assumptions.

Assumption 10.1 $x_i^k \geqslant 0, \forall i, k.$

Assumption 10.2 The desirability of distribution $x \in \hat{\mathscr{X}}$ by individual k depends only on $\mathbf{X}^k$.

Assumption 10.3 The preference ranking is strictly convex.

Assumption 10.4 The production possibility set $\hat{\mathbf{Y}}$ is non-null, convex and compact; furthermore, $\hat{\mathbf{Y}} \subset \Omega$.

Assumption 10.5 If $\mathbf{y} \in \hat{\mathbf{Y}}$ and $\mathbf{y}'$ is a vector such that $0 \leqslant y_i' \leqslant y_i$, $\forall i$ then $\mathbf{y}' \in \hat{\mathbf{Y}}$.

Assumption 10.6 Every commodity is perfectly divisible.

Assumption 10.1 rules out negative consumption. The second assumption asserts that given a distribution $x \in \hat{\mathscr{X}}$, the desirabilities of each individual is represented by $u^k(\mathbf{x}^k)$, $\mathbf{x}^k \in \mathbf{X}^k$, $\forall k$. In other words, it rules out externalities in consumption, such as utility functions of the form $u^k(\mathbf{x}^k, \mathbf{p})$ or $u^k(\mathbf{x}^k, \mathbf{x}^h)$, $k \neq h$. Assumption 10.3 amounts to saying that if $u^k(\mathbf{x}^k) = u^k(\mathbf{z}^k)$, $\mathbf{x}^k, \mathbf{z}^k \in \mathbf{X}^k$ then $u^k[\lambda \mathbf{x}^k + (1-\lambda)\mathbf{z}^k] > u^k(\mathbf{x}^k)$ for $0 < \lambda < 1$. The fourth assumption, which is illustrated in Fig. 10.4, says that $\hat{\mathbf{Y}}$ contains at least one feasible output vector y; that $\hat{\mathbf{Y}}$ is convex because $\forall\, \mathbf{y}', \mathbf{y}'' \in \hat{\mathbf{Y}}$ then $\lambda \mathbf{y}' + (1-\lambda)\mathbf{y}'' \in \hat{\mathbf{Y}}, 0 < \lambda < 1$; that $\hat{\mathbf{Y}}$ is compact because it is both bounded and closed; and finally that $\hat{\mathbf{Y}}$ is contained in the positive orthant. Assumption 10.5 is another way of stating the free disposal axiom (Axiom 5 of the economy set $\hat{\mathbf{Y}}$, p. 139). The difference is that this specification of the free disposal axiom is in terms of the output space alone. If the economy can produce y then it can also produce at any point in the south-west quadrant, as shown in Fig. 10.4. The purpose of introducing Assumption 10.5 is so that we can restrict the analysis to non-negative prices. Assumption 10.6 is included so that the proofs can be simplified at not too high a cost.

For an economy we have a distribution $x \in \hat{\mathscr{X}}$. Corresponding to this distribution there is a consumption vector $\mathbf{x} = \sum_k \mathbf{x}^k$. Given that $x \in \hat{\mathscr{X}}$ then $\mathbf{x} \in \hat{\mathbf{Y}}$ because both sets are constrained by the given resource endowment. We shall now define a Pareto optimum which incorporates both consumption *and* production, remembering that to a point $w \in \hat{\mathscr{W}}$ there corresponds an $\mathbf{x} = \sum_k \mathbf{x}^k$ and a $\mathbf{y} = \sum_j \mathbf{y}_j$.

Definition 10.2

(Pareto Optimum) A distribution $w^* \in \hat{\mathscr{W}}$ is said to be Pareto optimal in $\hat{\mathbf{Y}}$ if $\exists\, \mathbf{y}^* \in \hat{\mathbf{Y}}, \mathbf{y}^* = \mathbf{x}^*$ & $\sim [\exists\, w, \mathbf{y} = \mathbf{x}\ \mathbf{y} \in \mathbf{Y}\ \&\ u^k(\mathbf{x}^k) \geqslant u^k(\mathbf{x}^{*k}), \forall k$ and $u^h(\mathbf{x}^h) > u^h(\mathbf{x}^{*h})$ for at least one $h]$.

This is made clear in Fig. 10.5. The distribution $\overset{*}{\mathscr{x}} \in \hat{\mathscr{X}}$ uses up all the resources and both consumers exhaust the availability of both goods. The resources available to consumers and owned by them are used in production to enable the set $\hat{\mathbf{Y}}$ to be possible. If production is to be optimal all resources must be employed and so $\mathbf{y}^*$ belongs to the boundary of $\hat{\mathbf{Y}}$. But if the optimal consumption is to be met then $\mathbf{x}^*$ must equal $\mathbf{y}^*$ as shown.

In our earlier discussions we hinted at the fact that one issue of interest is whether a competitive equilibrium point(s) is also Pareto optimal. In this more general framework we must first make clear what is meant by a competitive equilibrium.

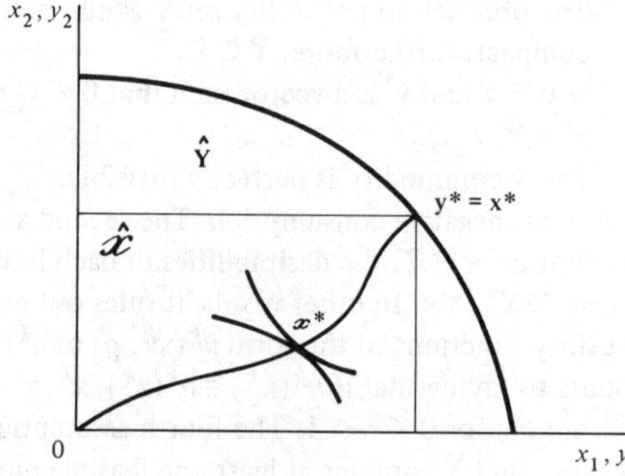

Fig. 10.5. Pareto optimality

Definition 10.3

(Competitive Equilibrium) A price vector $\bar{\mathbf{p}}$ and an output vector $\bar{\mathbf{y}} \in \hat{\mathbf{Y}}$ is a competitive equilibrium if

(1) $\forall k$, $\bar{\mathbf{x}}^k$ uniquely maximises $u^k(\mathbf{x}^k)$ subject to $\bar{\mathbf{p}}'\mathbf{x}^k \leqslant \bar{\mathbf{p}}'\bar{\mathbf{x}}^k$

(2) $\forall \mathbf{y} \in \hat{\mathbf{Y}}, \bar{\mathbf{p}}'\mathbf{y} \leqslant \bar{\mathbf{p}}'\bar{\mathbf{y}}$.

Hence competitive equilibrium requires all consumers to be utility maximising and all firms to be profit maximising.

A number of questions arise which are of interest. First, given that $\mathbf{x}^*$ is Pareto optimal in $\hat{\mathbf{Y}}$ is this point unique? The second question has already been raised elsewhere: In the present framework, can we say that any point which is a competitive equilibrium point is also a Pareto optimal point? Finally, if there exists a Pareto optimal point in the transformation set is there a non-negative price vector which gives rise to a competitive equilibrium? The remainder of this section is directed to the formal representation of these questions and their answers. What these results reveal is most important. Previously, Pareto optimality was characterised by the equality of marginal rates of substitution either in consumption or in production. Relative prices although present played a subordinate role.

However, in relaxing the classical assumptions we subordinate the marginal conditions and allow price relatives to play a more dominant role in the discussion of resource allocation. This can be observed when we recall that if a corner solution exists in, say, consumer demand there is no longer equality between marginal rates of substitution in consumption and relative prices and it is relative prices which consumers take account of in their decision-making in these circumstances.

Throughout our formal treatment we shall follow Arrow and consider only a single individual so that $k = 1$ (or $m = 1$). There is no loss, therefore, if we write $u(\mathbf{x})$ instead of $u^k(\mathbf{x}^k)$. The first question of whether $\mathbf{x}^*$ is unique can be posed as follows:

Theorem 10.3 There is a unique optimal point $\mathbf{x}^* \in \hat{\mathbf{Y}}$.

Proof $u(\mathbf{x})$ is a continuous function defined over a non-empty convex and compact set $\hat{\mathbf{Y}}$, hence by the Weierstrass theorem (Theorem 3.6, p. 53) there exists at least one $\mathbf{x}^* \in \hat{\mathbf{Y}}$ either in the interior of $\hat{\mathbf{Y}}$ or on the boundary of $\hat{\mathbf{Y}}$ and which maximises $u(\mathbf{x})$. Suppose that $\mathbf{x}^*$ and $\mathbf{z}^*$ are both optimal points, where $\mathbf{x}^*, \mathbf{z}^* \in \hat{\mathbf{Y}}$. Then $u(\mathbf{x}^*) \geqslant u(\mathbf{z}^*)$ and $u(\mathbf{z}^*) \geqslant u(\mathbf{x}^*)$ implying $u(\mathbf{x}^*) = u(\mathbf{z}^*)$.
Let $\mathbf{w}^* = \lambda\mathbf{x}^* + (1 - \lambda)\mathbf{z}^*, 0 < \lambda < 1$. Since $\mathbf{x}^*, \mathbf{z}^* \in \hat{\mathbf{Y}}$, then by Assumption 10.4 $\mathbf{w}^* \in \hat{\mathbf{Y}}$, and by Assumption 10.3 $u(\mathbf{w}^*) > u(\mathbf{w}^*)$. But this means $\mathbf{x}^*$ is suboptimal relative to $\mathbf{w}^*$ and both belong to $\hat{\mathbf{Y}}$, a contradiction to $\mathbf{x}^*$ and $\mathbf{z}^*$ being both optimal. Hence $\mathbf{x}^*$ is a unique optimum point.

Q.E.D.

A preliminary step in the proof of the theorems to follow is a consideration of four lemmas. Having proved these lemmas the proofs of the remaining theorems will be much simplified.

Lemma 10.1 For given k and a given number $\bar{u}$, the set of vectors $\mathbf{x}^k$ for which $u^k(\mathbf{x}^k) \geqslant \bar{u}$ is closed and convex; further if $\mathbf{x}'$ and $\mathbf{x}''$ belong to this set and $0 < \lambda < 1$ then $u[\lambda\mathbf{x}' + (1 - \lambda)\mathbf{x}''] > \bar{u}$.

Proof By Assumption 10.3 the utility function for individual k is quasi-concave. Then by Definition 3.11 (*ii*) p. 61 the set $\{\mathbf{x}^k / u^k(\mathbf{x}^k) \geqslant \bar{u}\}$ is a convex set. Since $u^k(\mathbf{x}^k)$ is continuous it follows that this set is closed. If $u^k(\mathbf{x}^k)$ is strictly quasi-concave then the set $\{\mathbf{x}^k / u^k(\mathbf{x}^k) \geqslant \bar{u}\}$ is a strictly convex set.

Q.E.D.

Lemma 10.2 Let $\mathbf{A}$ be any closed convex set and $\bar{\mathbf{x}} \in B(\mathbf{A})$, where $B(\mathbf{A})$ denotes the boundary of $\mathbf{A}$, then

$$\exists \bar{\mathbf{p}} > 0 \qquad \forall \mathbf{x} \in \mathbf{A} \qquad \bar{\mathbf{p}}'\mathbf{x} \leqslant \bar{\mathbf{p}}'\bar{\mathbf{x}}.$$

Proof If the dimension of $\mathbf{A}$ is less than the number of commodities then $\bar{\mathbf{p}}'\mathbf{x} = c$ since the vectors $\mathbf{x}$ must be linearly dependent. In particular $\bar{\mathbf{p}}'\bar{\mathbf{x}} = c$. Hence there exists at least one $\bar{p}_i > 0$ so that $\bar{\mathbf{p}} > 0$ and it follows $\bar{\mathbf{p}}'\mathbf{x} = \bar{\mathbf{p}}'\bar{\mathbf{x}}$. If the dimension of $\mathbf{A}$ is n, the number of commodities, then it must have at least two points. Let $\mathbf{B} = \{\bar{\mathbf{x}}\}$, then by the Minkowski theorem of separating hyperplanes (Theorem 4.1, p. 105) we have, for $\bar{\mathbf{x}} \in \mathbf{A}$, $\bar{\mathbf{x}} \in \mathbf{B}$ and $c = \bar{\mathbf{p}}'\bar{\mathbf{x}}$,

$$\bar{\mathbf{p}}'\mathbf{x} \leqslant \bar{\mathbf{p}}'\bar{\mathbf{x}} \qquad \forall \mathbf{x} \in \mathbf{A}.$$

Q.E.D.

Lemma 10.3 (Single individual case) If $\mathbf{x}^*$ is optimal in $\hat{\mathbf{Y}}$ but not a bliss point, then there is a vector $\bar{\mathbf{p}}$ such that

(1) $\bar{\mathbf{p}}'\mathbf{x} \geqslant \bar{\mathbf{p}}'\mathbf{x}^*$, $\forall \mathbf{x}$ such that $u(\mathbf{x}) \geqslant u(\mathbf{x}^*)$.

(2) $\bar{\mathbf{p}}'\mathbf{x} \leqslant \bar{\mathbf{p}}'\mathbf{x}^*$, $\forall \mathbf{x} \in \hat{\mathbf{Y}}$, $p_i \neq 0$ for at least one i.

Proof Let $\mathbf{V} = \{\mathbf{x}/u(\mathbf{x}) \geqslant u(\mathbf{x}^*)\}$. But from Theorem 10.3 we have that $\mathbf{x}^*$ is a unique optimal point in $\hat{\mathbf{Y}}$, hence $\mathbf{V} \cap \hat{\mathbf{Y}} = \{\mathbf{x}^*\}$. Let $I(\mathbf{V})$ denote the set of interior points of $\mathbf{V}$. Suppose $\mathbf{x}^* \in I(\mathbf{V})$ then $N_\epsilon(\mathbf{x}^*) \subset \mathbf{V}$, hence there exists at least two points $\mathbf{x}, \mathbf{z} \in \mathbf{V}$ such that $\mathbf{x}^* = \lambda\mathbf{x} + (1-\lambda)\mathbf{z}$ and $0 < \lambda < 1$. By Lemma 10.1 we have $u[\lambda\mathbf{x} + (1-\lambda)\mathbf{z}] > u(\mathbf{x}^*) \Rightarrow u(\mathbf{x}^*) > u(\mathbf{x}^*)$, a contradiction. Hence $\mathbf{x}^*$ belongs to the boundary set of $\mathbf{V}$, i.e. $\mathbf{x}^* \in B(\mathbf{V})$. It follows, therefore, that $I(\mathbf{V}) \cap \hat{\mathbf{Y}} = \boldsymbol{\emptyset}$. Since $\mathbf{x}^*$ is not a bliss point by assumption then $\mathbf{V}$ contains at least one point other than $\mathbf{x}^*$ and $\mathbf{V}$ is a non-empty closed convex set. By Assumption 10.4 $\hat{\mathbf{Y}}$ is also a non-empty closed convex set. By the application of the Minkowski theorem of separating hyperplanes (Theorem 4.1, p. 105) and remembering $\mathbf{x}^* \in \mathbf{V}$ and $\mathbf{x}^* \in \hat{\mathbf{Y}}$ we have $\bar{\mathbf{p}}'\mathbf{x}^* = c$ and

$$\bar{\mathbf{p}}'\mathbf{x} \geqslant c = \bar{\mathbf{p}}'\mathbf{x}^* \qquad \forall \mathbf{x} \in \mathbf{V}$$

$$\bar{\mathbf{p}}'\mathbf{x} \leqslant c = \bar{\mathbf{p}}'\mathbf{x}^*, \qquad \forall \mathbf{x} \in \hat{\mathbf{Y}}.$$

Q.E.D.

Lemma 10.3 for a single individual is illustrated in Fig. 10.6.

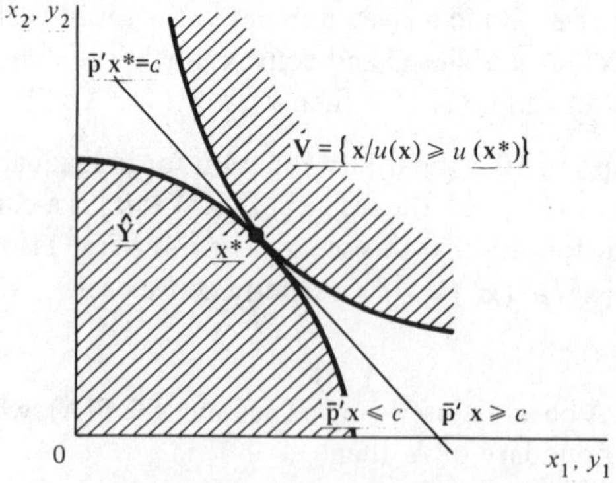

Fig. 10.6. Representation of Lemma 10.3

Lemma 10.4 For a given $\mathbf{x}^*$, let $\bar{\mathbf{p}}$ be such that $\bar{\mathbf{p}}'\mathbf{x} \geqslant \bar{\mathbf{p}}'\mathbf{x}^*$, $\forall \mathbf{x}$ such that $u(\mathbf{x}) \geqslant u(\mathbf{x}^*)$ and $\bar{p}_i x_i \neq 0$ for some i. Then $\mathbf{x}^*$ uniquely maximises $u(\mathbf{x})$ subject to $\bar{\mathbf{p}}'\mathbf{x} \leqslant \bar{\mathbf{p}}'\mathbf{x}^*$.

Proof Suppose to the contrary that for some $\mathbf{x} \neq \mathbf{x}^*$ we have $\bar{\mathbf{p}}'\mathbf{x} \leqslant \bar{\mathbf{p}}'\mathbf{x}^*$ and $u(\mathbf{x}) \geqslant u(\mathbf{x}^*)$. This latter condition implies $\bar{\mathbf{p}}'\mathbf{x} \geqslant \bar{\mathbf{p}}'\mathbf{x}^*$; hence these together imply $\bar{\mathbf{p}}'\mathbf{x} = \bar{\mathbf{p}}'\mathbf{x}^*$. Let $\mathbf{w} = \frac{1}{2}\mathbf{x} + \frac{1}{2}\mathbf{x}^*$ then

$$\bar{\mathbf{p}}'\mathbf{w} = \tfrac{1}{2}\bar{\mathbf{p}}'\mathbf{x} + \tfrac{1}{2}\bar{\mathbf{p}}'\mathbf{x}^* = \bar{\mathbf{p}}'\mathbf{x}^*.$$

By assumption $p_i x_i \neq 0$, i.e. $x_i > 0$; hence $w_i > 0$. Now define a vector $\mathbf{z}$ by $z_j = w_j$ for $j \neq i$ and $z_i = w_i + \epsilon$. For all ϵ sufficiently close to zero, $z_j \geqslant 0, \forall_j$. By Lemma 10.1 we have $u(\mathbf{w}) > u(\mathbf{x}^*)$, and hence for all ϵ sufficiently close to zero $u(\mathbf{z}) \geqslant u(\mathbf{x}^*)$. By assumption $\bar{p}_i \neq 0$. Choose ϵ sufficiently close to zero such that $u(\mathbf{z}) \geqslant u(\mathbf{x}^*)$ and such that if $\bar{p}_i > 0$ then $\epsilon < 0$ and if $\bar{p}_i < 0$ then $\epsilon > 0$. Then we have

$$\bar{\mathbf{p}}'\mathbf{z} = \bar{\mathbf{p}}'\mathbf{w} + \epsilon\bar{p}_i < \bar{\mathbf{p}}'\mathbf{x}^*$$

since $\epsilon\bar{\mathbf{p}}_i < 0, \forall \bar{p}_i$. This implies there exists a $\mathbf{z}$ such that $\bar{\mathbf{p}}'\mathbf{z} < \bar{\mathbf{p}}'\mathbf{x}^*$, $\forall \mathbf{z}$ such that $u(\mathbf{z}) \geqslant u(\mathbf{x}^*)$. But $u(\mathbf{z}) \geqslant u(\mathbf{x}^*)$ implies $\bar{\mathbf{p}}'\mathbf{z} \geqslant \bar{\mathbf{p}}'\mathbf{x}^*$, a contradiction. So the conditions of the lemma must be true.

Q.E.D.

We are now in a position to prove the remaining two theorems. The next theorem states that if there exists a price set at which excess demands are zero then the consumption–output combination is optimal. It is tempting to argue the converse, that if there is an optimal consumption–output combination then there exists a price vector for which all excess demands are zero. However, generally this is not true and Theorem 10.5 is an explicit statement of this. Before embarking on these, however, it is worth reminding the reader in what sense we have relaxed the classical assumptions. In all the theorems 10.3–10.5 the transformation set $\hat{\mathbf{Y}}$ is convex and this can be either weakly or strictly convex. For instance, Theorem 10.3, which states that there exists a unique optimal point $\mathbf{x}^* \in \hat{\mathbf{Y}}$, is true for $\hat{\mathbf{Y}}$ being weakly or strictly convex, as a perusal at Fig. 10.6 will indicate. If the set $\mathbf{V}$ is strictly convex whilst that of $\hat{\mathbf{Y}}$ is weakly convex then there will exist one optimal point. If both $\mathbf{V}$ and $\hat{\mathbf{Y}}$ are weakly convex, however, $\mathbf{x}^*$ is not necessarily unique. In that $\hat{\mathbf{Y}}$ can be either weakly or strictly convex all the forms of production outlined in Chapters 6 and 7 are permissible. So that Lemma 10.3 would hold under activity analysis as it would under neoclassical production theory.

We shall now turn to the final two theorems of this section.

Theorem 10.4 If there is a vector $\bar{\mathbf{p}}$ which equates supply and demand (i.e. is a competitive equilibrium) at $\bar{\mathbf{x}}$ then, given Assumptions 10.1–10.6, $\bar{\mathbf{x}}$ is a Pareto optimal point.

Proof Suppose the state $(\bar{\mathscr{X}}, \bar{\mathscr{Y}})$ is a competitive equilibrium state for a price vector $\bar{\mathbf{p}}$. Assume that $\bar{\mathbf{x}}$ is sub-optimal then there must exist a state $(\mathscr{X}, \mathscr{Y})$ such that $u(\mathbf{y}) > u(\mathbf{x})$. Since $\bar{\mathbf{x}}$ is a competitive equilibrium then it uniquely maximises $u(\mathbf{x})$ subject to $\bar{\mathbf{p}}'\mathbf{x} \leqslant \bar{\mathbf{p}}'\bar{\mathbf{x}}$, then it follows $\bar{\mathbf{p}}'\mathbf{y} > \bar{\mathbf{p}}'\bar{\mathbf{x}} = \bar{\mathbf{p}}'\bar{\mathbf{y}}$. But this contradicts condition (2) of Definition 10.3. Hence $\bar{\mathbf{x}}$ must be an optimal point.

Q.E.D.

Theorem 10.5 For any Pareto optimal point $\mathbf{x}^*$ there is a vector $\bar{\mathbf{p}} > 0$ such that

(1) $\bar{\mathbf{p}}'\mathbf{x} \geqslant \bar{\mathbf{p}}'\mathbf{x}^*, \forall \mathbf{x}$ such that $u(\mathbf{x}) \geqslant u(\mathbf{x}^*)$.
(2) $\exists \mathbf{y}^* (\geqslant \mathbf{x}^*), \bar{\mathbf{p}}'\mathbf{y} \geqslant \mathbf{p}'\mathbf{y}, \mathbf{y} \in \hat{\mathbf{Y}}$.
(3) If $\mathbf{x}^*$ is not a bliss point, then $y_i^* = x_i^*$, $\forall i$ in (2).
(4) If either $p_i x_i^* \neq 0$ for some i or $\mathbf{x}^*$ is a bliss point, then $\mathbf{x}^*$ uniquely maximises $u(\mathbf{x})$ subject to $\bar{\mathbf{p}}'\mathbf{x} \leqslant \bar{\mathbf{p}}'\mathbf{x}^*$.

Proof If $\mathbf{x}^*$ is not a bliss point, then (1)–(3) of this theorem are those proved in Lemma 10.3. Suppose $\mathbf{x}^* \in \hat{\mathbf{Y}}$ and is a bliss point, as illustrated in Fig. 10.7.

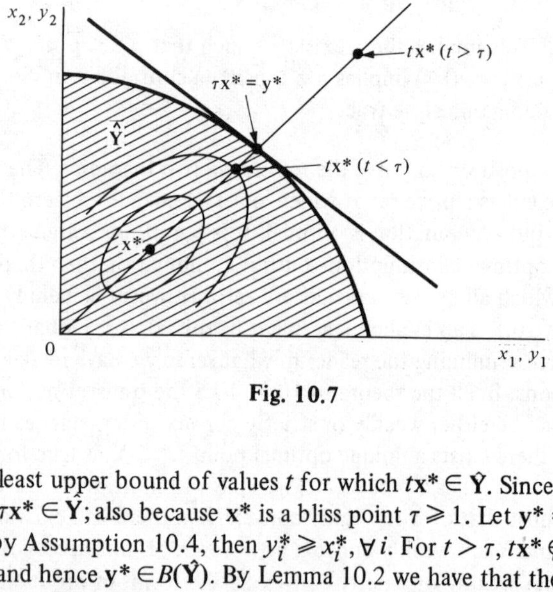

Fig. 10.7

Let τ be the least upper bound of values t for which $t\mathbf{x}^* \in \hat{\mathbf{Y}}$. Since $\hat{\mathbf{Y}}$ is closed it follows that $\tau\mathbf{x}^* \in \hat{\mathbf{Y}}$; also because $\mathbf{x}^*$ is a bliss point $\tau \geqslant 1$. Let $\mathbf{y}^* = \tau\mathbf{x}^*$. Since $x_i^* \geqslant 0$, $\forall i$, by Assumption 10.4, then $y_i^* \geqslant x_i^*, \forall i$. For $t > \tau$, $t\mathbf{x}^* \notin \hat{\mathbf{Y}}$. Therefore, $N_\epsilon(\mathbf{y}^*) \not\subset \hat{\mathbf{Y}}$ and hence $\mathbf{y}^* \in B(\hat{\mathbf{Y}})$. By Lemma 10.2 we have that there exists a price vector $\bar{\mathbf{p}}$ such that $\bar{\mathbf{p}}'\mathbf{x} \leqslant \bar{\mathbf{p}}'\mathbf{y}^*$, $\forall \mathbf{x} \in \hat{\mathbf{Y}}$, establishing condition (2) of the theorem. Now suppose $\mathbf{x} \neq \mathbf{x}^*$, $u(\mathbf{x}) \geqslant u(\mathbf{x}^*)$. Then if $\mathbf{w} = \frac{1}{2}\mathbf{x} + \frac{1}{2}\mathbf{x}^*$, $u(\mathbf{w}) > u(\mathbf{x}^*)$ by Lemma 10.1, which contradicts that $\mathbf{x}^*$ is a point of bliss. Thus the set $\{\mathbf{x}/u(\mathbf{x}) \geqslant u(\mathbf{x}^*)\} = \{\mathbf{x}^*\}$ so that condition (1) of the theorem is trivially true. Part (3) is excluded in this instance. Since for $\mathbf{x} \neq \mathbf{x}^*$, $u(\mathbf{x}) \geqslant u(\mathbf{x}^*)$ led to a contradiction, we have $u(\mathbf{x}^*) > u(\mathbf{x})$, $\forall \mathbf{x} \neq \mathbf{x}^*$, so that (4) follows trivially when $\mathbf{x}^*$ is a point of bliss. Having established (1), (2) and (4) for a point of bliss and (1), (2) and (3) for no bliss point, it remains to be shown that (4) holds for a situation where $\mathbf{x}^*$ is not a point of bliss. Since (1) has been shown to hold then by Lemma 10.4 condition (4) is met.

Q.E.D.

The requirements of Theorem 10.5 ensure the conditions under which a Pareto optimal state can always be reached by means of perfect competition. If, for example, the first individual is assumed to be satiated with respect to the first commodity as shown by the optimal allocation $\mathscr{x}^*$ in Fig. 10.8, then there is no relative price line through $\mathscr{x}^*$ which satisfies the optimum conditions for both consumers simultaneously. In other words, the optimum point $\mathscr{x}^*$ is such that both consumers are not maximising their utilities for some price set.

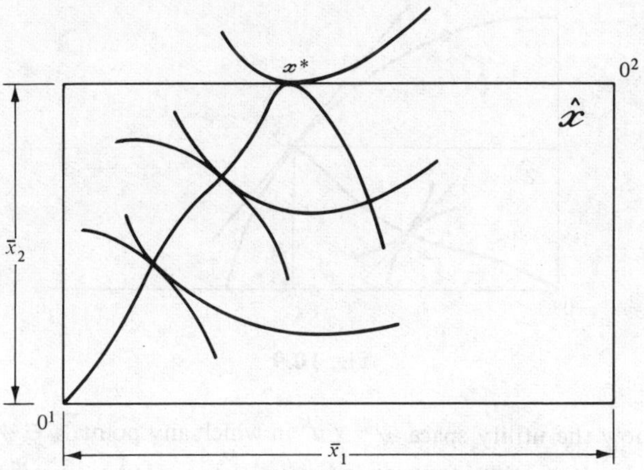

Fig. 10.8. Arrow's exceptional case

10.3 The Social Welfare Function

So far we have been considering only Pareto comparable points. There still remains the problem of Pareto non-comparable points. One attempted solution to this problem is the introduction of a social welfare function. Such a function is an ordinal-wise ranking of a society's welfare and is a function of all the members of that society. Just as for an individual, we can either deal with a ranking relation or with a form of utility function. If $R = \emptyset(R_1, \ldots, R_m)$ is a collective choice rule, in the sense used in Appendix 2B, Definition 2B.1, then there is also a social welfare function W which is a collective choice rule defined over the commodity space $\mathbf{X}$. Thus

$$\begin{aligned} W &= W(u^1, \ldots, u^m) \\ &= W[u^1(x_1^1, \ldots, x_n^1), \ldots, u^m(x_1^m, \ldots, x_n^m)] \end{aligned}$$

and W is a function whose k^{th} element $u^k(\mathbf{x}^k)$ is defined over $\mathbf{X}^k$. The social welfare function is the embodiment of Arrow's ethical postulate.

To see how the social welfare function overcomes the problem of non-comparable states we must look once again at the set of Pareto optimal points. In Fig. 10.9 we have the transformation set $\hat{\mathbf{Y}}$. Consider any point on the boundary of $\hat{\mathbf{Y}}$ such as $\mathbf{y}$, and construct the Edgeworth–Bowley box with these dimensions, as labelled by $\hat{\mathscr{X}}$

in Fig. 10.9. For any point $\mathbf{y} \in \hat{\mathbf{Y}}$ there will exist an efficiency locus consisting of all $\mathscr{x} \in \hat{\mathscr{X}}^*$. Along such an efficiency locus the level of the utilities for both individuals will vary.

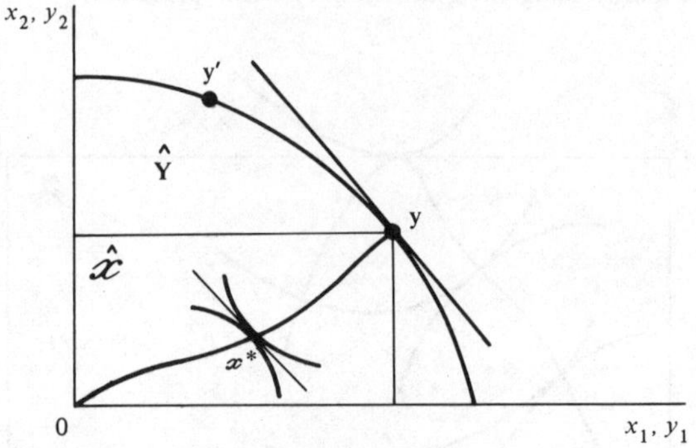

Fig. 10.9

Consider now the utility space $\mathscr{U} = \underset{k}{\chi}\, u^k$ in which any point $\mathscr{u} \in \mathscr{U}$ denotes the respective levels of utility for each individual, i.e. $\mathscr{u} = (u^1, \ldots, u^m)$. For any point $\mathbf{y} \in \hat{\mathbf{Y}}$ there will be an associated Edgeworth–Bowley box $\hat{\mathscr{X}}$ with the maximum possible dimensions $\mathbf{x} = \mathbf{y}$ and an associated utility set. The utility set denotes all $\mathscr{u}$ for points $\mathbf{x} \leqslant \mathbf{y}$ and such that all allocations $\mathscr{x}$ are Pareto efficient. Since this set is dependent upon the $\mathbf{y}$ we shall denote it $\hat{\mathscr{U}}(\mathbf{y}) = \{\mathscr{u} / \mathbf{y} \in \hat{\mathbf{Y}}\ \&\ \forall \mathbf{x} \leqslant \mathbf{y},\ \mathscr{x} \in \hat{\mathscr{X}}^*\}$, and where the circumflex is being used as before. To make this clear consider the point $\mathbf{y}$ in Fig. 10.9. If $\mathbf{x} = \mathbf{y}$ we have the set as shown and the set of efficient points $\hat{\mathscr{X}}^*$. In the utility space this particular combination of utility points must belong to the boundary of $\hat{\mathscr{U}}(\mathbf{y})$. Consequently, the point 0 in Fig. 10.9 is mapped into the point S in Fig. 10.10, whilst $\mathbf{y}$ is mapped into S′.

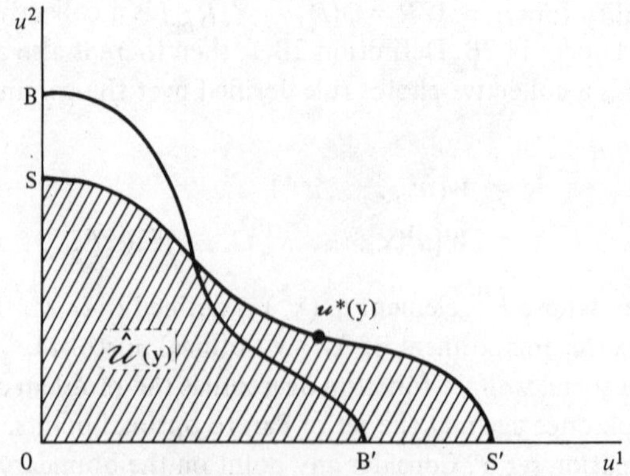

Fig. 10.10

Similarly, the point $\mathscr{x}^*$ is mapped into $\mathscr{u}^*(\mathbf{y})$. For any $\mathbf{x} < \mathbf{y}$ the utility point $\mathscr{u}$ must lie in the interior of $\hat{\mathscr{U}}(\mathbf{y})$. The curve SS′ is referred to as the *utility–possibility curve.*

Clearly for each point $\mathbf{y} \in \hat{\mathbf{Y}}$ there will be a different utility set, and in particular a different utility–possibility curve, such as BB′ in Fig. 10.10. Let us now consider the union of all such utility sets, i.e. $\hat{\mathscr{U}} = \bigcup_{\mathbf{y} \in \hat{\mathbf{Y}}} \hat{\mathscr{U}}(\mathbf{y})$. This set is shown in Fig. 10.11. The boundary of the set $\hat{\mathscr{U}}$ must consist of the 'envelope' of all the boundaries $\hat{\mathscr{U}}(\mathbf{y})$ by construction. Hence any $\mathscr{u}$ belonging to the boundary of $\hat{\mathscr{U}}$ must have an associated point $\mathbf{y}$ which belongs to the boundary of $\hat{\mathscr{U}}(\mathbf{y})$ and is such that $\mathbf{x} = \mathbf{y}$ and the allocation $\mathscr{x}$ associated with $\mathbf{x}$ is a Pareto optimal point. The boundary of $\hat{\mathscr{U}}$ denoted vv' in Fig. 10.11 is referred to as the *utility–possibility frontier.*

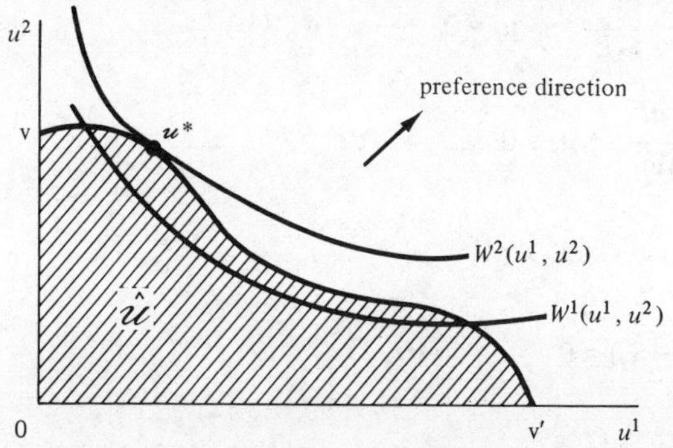

Fig. 10.11. Utility – possibility frontier

For any point in the interior of $\hat{\mathscr{U}}$ the allocation cannot be Pareto optimal taking both production and consumption into account, for even if $\mathscr{x} \in \hat{\mathscr{X}}^* \subset \hat{\mathscr{X}}$ for $\mathscr{u}$ to be interior means $\mathbf{x} \neq \mathbf{y}$, in which case there is at least one resource not being fully utilised, and hence there is no reason why the marginal rates of substitution in consumption should equal the marginal rate of transformation. However, all points on the boundary of $\hat{\mathscr{U}}$ are Pareto non-comparable. It is at this point we introduce the social welfare function. Since $\mathscr{u} = (u^1, \ldots, u^m)$ then $W = W(u^1, \ldots, u^m) = W(\mathscr{u})$. This can be considered in terms of a set of contours whose preference direction is away from the origin. Our problem amounts quite simply to

$$\max W = W(\mathscr{u})$$
$$\text{s.t. } \mathscr{u} \in \hat{\mathscr{U}}.$$

Notice the similarity between this and the maximisation problem given in Section 2.7. Fig. 10.11 gives a diagrammatic solution to this problem. Given all the Pareto non-comparable points the introduction of the social welfare function has allowed us to say that $\mathscr{u}^*$ is preferable over all other $\mathscr{u} \in \hat{\mathscr{U}}$ from society's point of view.

We can reveal the solution quite readily in the case of continuous single-valued functions. Denote the boundary of the production possibility set by $F(y_1, \ldots, y_n)$. Since $x_i = \sum_k x_i^k$, $\forall i$ then if there are to be no unused resources we must have $x_i = y_i$, $\forall i$. Thus our problem is

$$\max W = W[u^1(\mathbf{x}^1), \ldots, u^m(\mathbf{x}^m)]$$

$$\text{s.t. } (1) \quad F(y_1, \ldots, y_n) = 0$$

$$(2) \quad x_i = y_i \quad \forall i.$$

Form the Lagrangian

$$L = W[u_1(\mathbf{x}^1), \ldots, u_n(\mathbf{x}^n)] + \lambda F(y_1, \ldots, y_n) + \sum_i \mu_i(y_i - x_i).$$

Then

$$\frac{\partial L}{\partial x_i^k} = \frac{\partial W}{\partial u^k} \frac{\partial u^k}{\partial x_i^k} - \mu_i = 0 \qquad \forall i, k$$

$$\frac{\partial L}{\partial y_i} = \lambda \frac{\partial F}{\partial y_i} + \mu_i = 0 \qquad \forall i$$

$$\frac{\partial L}{\partial \lambda} = F(y_1, \ldots, y_n) = 0$$

$$\frac{\partial L}{\partial \mu_i} = (y_i - x_i) = 0 \qquad \forall i.$$

There are $mn + 2n + 1$ equations in $mn + 2n + 1$ unknowns.

Consider goods i and j then from $\partial L/\partial x_i^k$ we have

$$\frac{\partial u^k}{\partial x_i^k} \bigg/ \frac{\partial u^k}{\partial x_j^k} = \frac{\mu_i}{\mu_j} \qquad \forall k$$

and from $\partial L/\partial y_i$ we have

$$\frac{\partial F}{\partial y_i} \bigg/ \frac{\partial F}{\partial y_j} = \frac{\mu_i}{\mu_j}.$$

Hence

$$\frac{\partial u^k}{\partial x_i^k} \bigg/ \frac{\partial u^k}{\partial x_j^k} = \frac{\partial F}{\partial y_i} \bigg/ \frac{\partial F}{\partial y_j} \qquad \forall k$$

or

$$\text{MRS}_{ij}^k = \text{MRT}_{ij} \qquad \forall k.$$

This result is illustrated in Fig. 10.12.

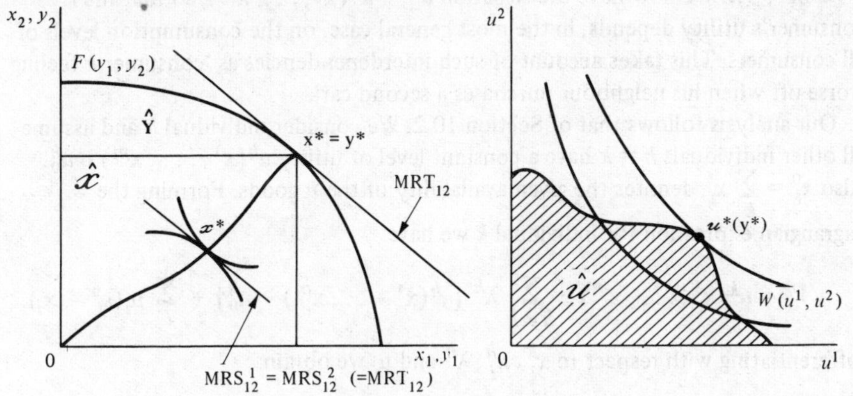

Fig. 10.12

The introduction of a social welfare function was for exactly the same reason as for the introduction of the compensation tests. It was pointed out earlier that because the compensations are potential then we are in a Utopian world. However, is the social welfare function any better? It does have a pedagogic appeal. But one can hardly conceive of any satisfactory social welfare function and it would appear that this approach to Pareto non-comparable states is equally Utopian.

10.4 Interdependent Utilities

There have been at least three discussions in the literature which direct attention to certain weaknesses of the Pareto optimal conditions; these are: (1) interdependence of utilities, (2) public goods, and (3) second-best optima. We shall take each in turn.

The first of these has been touched on but only to exclude it from consideration. The idea of interdependent utilities is not new as can be evidenced from Veblen's writings of which the *Theory of the Leisure Class* [122] is the best illustration. Duesenberry, however, supplied a formal framework within which to discuss the problem [32]. The obvious question is: Does the introduction of interdependence alter the Pareto optimal conditions? If so, in what way?

There are a number of formal ways one can approach such a question because it depends on how one considers 'interdependence'. For example, Duesenberry considers an individual's welfare dependent initially on his own income. This is different from our earlier analysis but is not unreasonable in that a given income defines the attainable set of commodities which this consumer can purchase. He then introduces interdependence by arguing that a person's welfare depends not just on his own income but also on other people's income. We shall not take this line of thought explicitly but rather say that interdependence manifests itself through the consumption levels of other consumers. Thus we initially had $u^k = u^k(\mathbf{x}^k)$, $\mathbf{x}^k \in \mathbf{X}^k$, $\forall k$. We now have the situation $u^k = u^k(\mathbf{x}^1, \ldots, \mathbf{x}^m)$, so that the kth consumer's utility depends, in the most general case, on the consumption levels of all consumers. This takes account of such interdependencies as 'consumer k feeling worse off when his neighbour purchases a second car'.

Our analysis follows that of Section 10.2. We consider individual k and assume all other individuals $h \neq k$ have a constant level of utility $u^h(\mathbf{x}^1, \ldots, \mathbf{x}^m) = u_0^h$. Also $x_i^0 = \sum_k x_i^k$ denotes the given availability of the n goods. Forming the Lagrangian expression for individual k we have

$$V^k = u^k(\mathbf{x}^1, \ldots, \mathbf{x}^m) + \sum_{h \neq k} \lambda^h \, [u^h(\mathbf{x}^1, \ldots, \mathbf{x}^m) - u_0^h] + \sum_i \mu_i(x_i^0 - x_i).$$

Differentiating with respect to x_i^k, x_i^h, λ^h and μ_i we obtain

$$\frac{\partial V^k}{\partial x_i^k} = \frac{\partial u^k}{\partial x_i^k} + \lambda^h \frac{\partial u^h}{\partial x_i^k} + \mu_i = 0 \qquad \forall k, i = 1, \ldots, n$$

$$\frac{\partial V^k}{\partial x_i^h} = \frac{\partial u^k}{\partial x_i^h} + \lambda^h \frac{\partial u^h}{\partial x_i^h} + \mu_i = 0 \qquad \forall h \neq k, i = 1, \ldots, n$$

$$\frac{\partial V^k}{\partial \lambda^h} = u^h(\mathbf{x}^1, \ldots, \mathbf{x}^m) - u_0^h = 0 \qquad \forall h \neq k$$

$$\frac{\partial V^k}{\partial \mu_i} = x_i^0 - x_i = 0 \qquad i = 1, \ldots, n.$$

There are a total of $2mn + m - 1$ equations in $2mn + m - 1$ unknowns.

From the first two expressions we have for good i

$$\frac{\partial u^k}{\partial x_i^k} - \frac{\partial u^k}{\partial x_i^h} = \lambda^h \left(\frac{\partial u^h}{\partial x_i^k} - \frac{\partial u^h}{\partial x_i^h} \right).$$

Hence, the marginal rate of substitution for goods i and j becomes

$$\frac{\dfrac{\partial u^k}{\partial x_i^k} - \dfrac{\partial u^k}{\partial x_i^h}}{\dfrac{\partial u^k}{\partial x_j^k} - \dfrac{\partial u^k}{\partial x_j^h}} = \frac{\dfrac{\partial u^h}{\partial x_i^k} - \dfrac{\partial u^h}{\partial x_i^h}}{\dfrac{\partial u^h}{\partial x_j^k} - \dfrac{\partial u^h}{\partial x_j^h}}$$

which clearly reduces to

$$\frac{\partial u^k}{\partial x_i^k} \Big/ \frac{\partial u^k}{\partial x_j^k} = \frac{\partial u^h}{\partial x_i^h} \Big/ \frac{\partial u^h}{\partial x_j^h}$$

when the utilities are independent.

To see the significance of the present result let us assume that there are only two individuals k and h and that individual k's utility depends on the consumption of good x_i^h consumed by h whilst individual h is independent of k. This means

$$\frac{\partial u^k}{\partial x_j^h} = \frac{\partial u^h}{\partial x_i^k} = \frac{\partial u^h}{\partial x_j^k} = 0.$$

The Pareto-optimal condition is now

$$\left(\frac{\partial u^k}{\partial x_i^k} - \frac{\partial u^k}{\partial x_i^h}\right) \Bigg| \frac{\partial u^k}{\partial x_j^k} = \frac{\partial u^h}{\partial x_i^h} \Bigg| \frac{\partial u^h}{\partial x_j^h}.$$

It is clear that equality of marginal rates of substitution for individuals k and h is sub-optimal. We can go a little further. Suppose consumer k feels worse off when his neighbour, individual h, purchases additional amounts of x_i^h, then $\partial u^k / \partial x_i^h < 0$. We have, therefore,

$$\frac{\partial u^h / \partial x_i^h}{\partial u^h / \partial x_j^h} = \frac{\partial u^k / \partial x_i^k}{\partial u^k / \partial x_j^k} - \frac{\partial u^k / \partial x_i^h}{\partial u^k / \partial x_j^k} > \frac{\partial u^k / \partial x_i^k}{\partial u^k / \partial x_j^k}.$$

For the altruist $\partial u^k / \partial x_i^h > 0$ and the opposite is the case. What this result says is that if marginal rates of substitution are equated then this position is sub-optimal because it is possible to redistribute (exchange) such that one person is made better off and the other person no worse off.

10.5 Public Goods

A natural type of externality occurs when goods are consumed collectively. My consumption (purchase of a ticket) to see the Blue Nile Falls does not reduce anyone else's consumption of the same good. The same applies to lighthouses and defence. There is a slight problem of interpretation here. Samuelson in his discussion of public goods [110] argues that if z is a public good then $z^1 = \ldots = z^m = z$ where z^k is the kth person's consumption of the public good z. This contrasts with private goods where $x = \sum_k x^k$. However, what matters when considering public goods is the supply and the fact that this is for all to consume if they so wish to do; this does appear a more sensible interpretation of defence [55].

Let $\mathbf{x}$ denote the vector of demands for private goods and $\mathbf{y}$ the vector supply of private goods as we have done in previous sections. We now introduce a vector supply of public goods, $\mathbf{q} = (q_1, \ldots, q_\nu, \ldots, q_g)$. This means the utility function of the kth individual is $u^k(\mathbf{x}^k, \mathbf{q})$, $\forall k$. On the supply side we consider the boundary of the transformation set as in the previous section but now it is a function of private goods and public goods, i.e. $F(y_1, \ldots, y_n; q_1, \ldots, q_g) = F(\mathbf{y}, \mathbf{q}) = 0$.

Because some goods are public goods we must introduce a social welfare function,

$$W = W(u^1, \ldots, u^m) = W[u^1(\mathbf{x}^1, \mathbf{q}), \ldots, u^m(\mathbf{x}^m, \mathbf{q})]$$

if we are to obtain any solution to our present problem. The economic problem is then

$$\max W = W(u^1, \ldots, u^m)$$
$$\text{s.t. } x_i = y_i \qquad \forall i$$
$$F(\mathbf{y}, \mathbf{q}) = 0.$$

Forming the Lagrangian expression

$$L = W[u^1(\mathbf{x}^1, \mathbf{q}), \ldots, u^m(\mathbf{x}^m, \mathbf{q})] + \sum_i \mu_i(y_i - x_i) + \theta\, F(\mathbf{y}, \mathbf{q})$$

and differentiating with respect to the vectors **x**, **y**, **q** and the Lagrangian constants $\boldsymbol{\mu}$ and θ, we obtain

$$\mathbf{L}_x = \frac{\partial L}{\partial \mathbf{x}^k} = \left(\frac{\partial W}{\partial u^k}\right) \mathbf{u}_x^k - \boldsymbol{\mu} = 0 \qquad \forall k$$

$$\mathbf{L}_y = \partial L/\partial \mathbf{y} = \boldsymbol{\mu} + \theta\, \mathbf{F}_y = 0$$

$$\mathbf{L}_q = \partial L/\partial \mathbf{q} = \mathbf{W}'_u\, \mathbf{U}_q + \theta \mathbf{F}_q = 0$$

$$\mathbf{L}_\mu = \partial L/\partial \boldsymbol{\mu} = \mathbf{y} - \mathbf{x} = 0$$

$$L_\theta = \partial L/\partial \theta = F(\mathbf{y}, \mathbf{q}) = 0.$$

This can be expressed in the form

$$\frac{\partial L}{\partial x_i^k} = \frac{\partial W}{\partial u^k} \frac{\partial u^k}{\partial x_i^k} - \mu_i = 0 \qquad \forall k, i = 1, \ldots, n$$

$$\frac{\partial L}{\partial y_j} = \mu_j + \theta \frac{\partial F}{\partial y_j} = 0 \qquad j = 1, \ldots, n$$

$$\frac{\partial L}{\partial q_\nu} = \sum_k \frac{\partial W}{\partial u^k} \frac{\partial u^k}{\partial q_\nu} + \theta \frac{\partial F}{\partial q_\nu} = 0 \qquad \nu = 1, \ldots, g$$

$$\frac{\partial L}{\partial \mu_i} = y_i - x_i = 0 \qquad i = 1, \ldots, n$$

$$\frac{\partial L}{\partial \theta} = F(\mathbf{y}, \mathbf{q}) = 0.$$

There are $mn + 2n + g + 1$ equations in $mn + 2n + g + 1$ unknowns.

Our analysis allows a number of features that Pareto optimality must satisfy. If goods i and j are private goods then from $\mathbf{L}_x$ we have

$$\frac{\partial W}{\partial u^k}\cdot\frac{\partial u^k}{\partial x_i^k}\Bigg|\frac{\partial W}{\partial u^k}\cdot\frac{\partial u^k}{\partial x_j^k} = \theta\,\frac{\partial F}{\partial y_i}\Bigg|\,\theta\,\frac{\partial F}{\partial y_j}$$

$$\frac{\partial u^k}{\partial x_i^k}\Bigg|\frac{\partial u^k}{\partial x_j^k} = \frac{\partial F}{\partial y_i}\Bigg|\frac{\partial F}{\partial y_j}$$

a result we obtained in Section 10.3. Suppose we now consider two goods r and s both of which are public goods. Then from $\mathbf{L}_q$ we have

$$\sum_k \frac{\partial W}{\partial u^k}\cdot\frac{\partial u^k}{\partial q_r}\Bigg|\sum_k \frac{\partial W}{\partial u^k}\cdot\frac{\partial u^k}{\partial q_s} = \frac{\partial F}{\partial q_r}\Bigg|\frac{\partial F}{\partial q_s}.$$

A more interesting result is the relationship between public and private goods. Consider a public good v and a private good i then we have from $\mathbf{L}_q$, $\mathbf{L}_x$ and $\mathbf{L}_y$

$$\sum_k \frac{\partial W}{\partial u^k}\cdot\frac{\partial u^k}{\partial q_v} + \theta\,\frac{\partial F}{\partial q_v} = \sum_k \mu_i\,\frac{\partial u^k/\partial q_v}{\partial u^k/\partial x_i^k} - \mu_i\,\frac{\partial F/\partial q_v}{\partial F/\partial y_i} = 0,$$

i.e. $$\sum_k \frac{\partial u^k/\partial q_v}{\partial u^k/\partial x_i^k} = \frac{\partial F/\partial q_v}{\partial F/\partial y_i}.$$

In other words, the sum of the marginal rates of substitution between a public good and a private good is equal to the rate of transformation between these goods. This means that we do not require the marginal rates of substitution between a public good and a private good to be equal for all individuals as is the case for the marginal rates of substitution between two private goods. Finally, we note that for individuals k and h and a private good i we require

$$\frac{\partial W}{\partial u^k}\cdot\frac{\partial u^k}{\partial x_i^k} = \frac{\partial W}{\partial u^h}\cdot\frac{\partial u^h}{\partial x_i^h}$$

$$\frac{\partial W/\partial u^k}{\partial W/\partial u^h} = \frac{\partial u^h/\partial x_i^h}{\partial u^k/\partial x_i^k}.$$

In other words, in the optimal state it is impossible to reallocate a private good between individuals without making one individual worse off. No such relation exists for a public good.

10.6 Theory of Second Best

Consider the familiar exchange problem once again as shown in Fig. 10.13. Rather than assume both individuals are price-takers suppose individual 1 acts as a

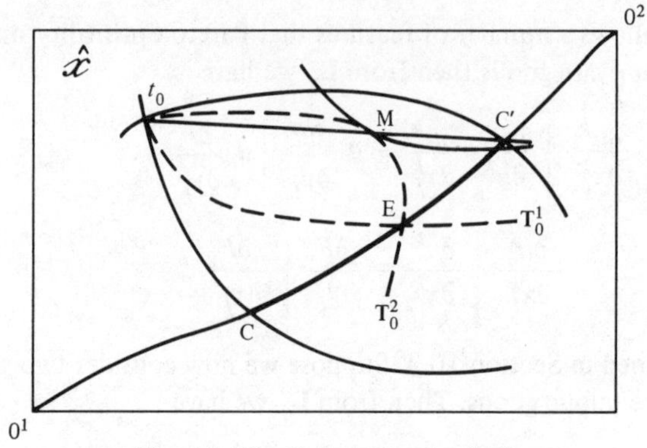

Fig. 10.13. Sub-optimal solution

monopolist and sets the price whilst individual 2 has to accept the price set by the first individual. If individual 1 allows the price to vary then individual 2 will move to points along the curve $t_0 T_0^2$. If the monopolist wishes to set a price ratio which maximises his utility he will set the ratio t_0M, at which the indifference curve of individual 1 is tangential to the trading curve of individual 2, at the point M. The point E is the perfect competitive point with the corresponding equilibrium price ratio of t_0E, which is Pareto-optimal. However, the solution M is clearly Pareto sub-optimal. The presence of taxes and subsidies will also lead to sub-optimal points. We have seen in previous sections that many conditions must be met for Pareto-optimality on the side of both production and consumption. The question arises that if a distortion of the sort just discussed is present does it follow that the remaining optimality conditions, say in production, are met? If they are not met, then the conditions for a second-best optimum, meaning the optimum in the presence of additional constraints on some of the first-best optimal conditions, are not those for the first-best optimum. This has the obvious implication, if true, that a movement towards competition in one sector when other sectors are not competitive does not necessarily lead to a more desirable state.

In stating the theory of second best we shall take a somewhat different line from Lipsey and Lancaster [77], which is more intuitive. We shall suppose that in some market i there is a distortion, e.g. monopoly power in one market, so that the optimal relationship does not hold.

Theorem 10.6 Let $F(x_1, \ldots, x_n)$ denote a continuous function and let $x_1, \ldots, x_n$ be constrained by $\emptyset(x_1, \ldots, x_n) = 0$. Furthermore, suppose $H^j(\mathrm{x}) = 0, j = 1, \ldots, n$ denotes the n equations obtained from $L = F(\mathrm{x}) - \lambda\emptyset(\mathrm{x})$, ignoring the equation L_λ. If an additional constraint of the form $H^i(\mathrm{x}) \neq 0$ for some i is now included then the optimal value of $F(\mathrm{x})$ subject to both $\emptyset(\mathrm{x})$ and $H^i(\mathrm{x}) \neq 0$ for some i will, in general, be such that none of the remaining optimal solutions $H^j(\mathrm{x})$ $(i \neq j)$ will be satisfied.

Proof In the absence of the constraint $H^i(\mathrm{x}) \neq 0$ we have for a maximum, say,

$$\max L = F(\mathrm{x}) - \lambda \phi(\mathrm{x}).$$

Differentiating we obtain

$$H^j(\mathrm{x}) = \frac{\partial L}{\partial x_j} = F_j - \lambda \phi_j = 0 \qquad j = 1, \ldots, n$$

$$\frac{\partial L}{\partial \lambda} = -\phi(\mathrm{x}) = 0,$$

Giving the optimal conditions

$$\frac{F_r}{F_s} = \frac{\phi_r}{\phi_s} \qquad r \neq s \, (r, s = 1, \ldots, n)$$

and some optimal $\lambda = \lambda^*$. Now suppose there is a distortion in the ith market so that $H^i(\mathrm{x}) \neq 0$. We can therefore find a $K \neq \lambda^*$ such that $H^i(\mathrm{x}) = 0$, i.e.

$$F_i - K\,\phi_i = 0 \qquad \text{for some } i.$$

Our problem is now to

$$\max V = F(\mathrm{x}) - \mu\phi(\mathrm{x}) - \theta(F_i - K\,\phi_i).$$

Differentiating

$$\frac{\partial V}{\partial x_j} = F_j - \mu\,\phi_j - \theta(F_{ij} - K\phi_{ij}) = 0 \qquad j = 1, \ldots, n$$

$$\frac{\partial V}{\partial \mu} = -\phi(\mathrm{x}) = 0$$

$$\frac{\partial V}{\partial \theta} = -(F_i - K\,\phi_i) = 0 \qquad \text{for some } i.$$

First note that $\theta \neq 0$ because if $\theta = 0$ then $F_i - \lambda\phi_i = 0$ or that $K = \lambda^*$. This follows from the Kuhn–Tucker conditions which says that if $\theta = 0$ then the constraint is not binding. This, of course, contradicts our assumption that the constraint is operating. Consider once again goods r and s.

$$\frac{F_r}{F_s} = \frac{\mu\phi_r + \theta(F_{ir} - K\phi_{ir})}{\mu\phi_s + \theta(F_{is} - K\phi_{is})} \qquad r \neq s$$

$$= \frac{\phi_r + \frac{\theta}{\mu}(F_{ir} - K\,\phi_{ir})}{\phi_s + \frac{\theta}{\mu}(F_{is} - K\,\phi_{is})}.$$

Generally, nothing is known about the signs of F_{ir}, F_{is}, ϕ_{ir} and ϕ_{is}. Thus if the marginal rate of transformation (F_r/F_s) is equated to the marginal rate of substitution (ϕ_r/ϕ_s) this will not be Pareto-optimal for the second-best situation where there is a distortion in the market for the ith good (see Exercise 10).

The theory of second best is somewhat negative and increases our area of doubt. However, it is important because the real-life situations always contain distortions of one kind and another and the solutions are always of a second-best nature. If, however, markets for goods r and s are not closely related to the market for good i then $(F_{ir} - K\phi_{ir})$ and $(F_{is} - K\phi_{is})$ will both be close to zero and so in formulating policy, the equality of F_r/F_s with ϕ_r/ϕ_s may not be too unreasonable. If the markets are related, however, knowledge of the cross-partials becomes important.

10.7 The Core of an Economy

A crucial consideration in the formation of prices in all markets is the number of individuals trading. It matters to the solution, as we shall show, whether the number is large or small and also whether there is any room for co-operation between participants in the market. The central theorem of this section is that if the number of traders is large and there is no room for co-operation then a competitive price system will emerge. Each individual acts selfishly with prices as parameters and 'the invisible hand' will ensure that all resources are fully utilised, all markets are cleared and the broad requirements of optimality will be met.

Other forms of competition met is that of co-operation and that of oligopoly in general (including duopoly). In the case of co-operation a number of outcomes are possible depending on the form the co-operation takes. In the case of monopoly the market form, although leading to a determinate solution (point M in Fig. 10.13), is none the less sub-optimal. Many of the various market forms have been unified in terms of the theory of games, particularly by Shapley and Shubik [113]. However, we shall closely follow the treatment by Arrow and Hahn [10] which frees the analysis from game theoretic concepts and particularly the necessity of an implicit cardinality arising from the payoffs of a game. Also, we shall use the pure exchange model of Chapter 9 to illustrate most of the concepts to be discussed.

Consider the pure exchange model in Fig. 10.13 (p. 272) where t_0 is the initial position. It has already been established that what the traders wish to do is to move to a point in the trading set $\mathbf{T}_0$, i.e. the trading set associated with t_0. If all participants act as price-takers then we have two equilibrium trading curves $\mathbf{T}_0^1$ and $\mathbf{T}_0^2$ which establishes a competitive equilibrium at E. The competitive equilibrium price ratio is given by the slope of t_0 E and E is Pareto optimal. If, however, individual 1 is a price-setter he will set a price t_0M at which his indifference curve is tangential at point M to individual 2's trading curve, as illustrated in Fig. 10.13. Two things are worth noting. First, the allocation M is not Pareto-optimal although it is a determinate solution. Second, point M is more favourable than point E to the price-setter and conversely more unfavourable to the price-taker. A third form of market behaviour is illustrated by Fig. 10.13 and it is the one considered by Edgeworth. Both participants can set prices and any negotiating is acceptable. The solution to this suggested by Edgeworth is any point on the contract curve CC′ because this determines the limits in which trade is beneficial to at least one participant and such that the solution is Pareto-optimal. Hence the solution set is **T***, i.e. all those points on CC′. We see, therefore, that the competitive equilibrium E is only one form, albeit a rigid form, of competition which establishes a solution.

We have taken the two-good two-person exchange model as far as we can. To derive any new results we must include more participants into the market situation. In doing this we follow Edgeworth by assuming there are two types, each type having the same preferences and the same initial holdings. In this situation perfect competition is readily analysed. If each is a price-taker then each pair, one from each type, will have the same trading curves and the same equilibrium point E, so that E will be the equilibrium point for the whole market.

To analyse other market forms we require some new concepts. The reader is reminded that corresponding to any feasible allocation $\mathscr{x} \in \hat{\mathscr{X}}$ there is an associated linear mapping $\mathbf{x} = \sum_k \mathbf{x}^k$. Our first task is to rule out certain allocations which cannot be equilibrium allocations. Given $\mathscr{x}, \mathscr{x}' \in \hat{\mathscr{X}}$ such that $(\mathbf{x}^k)' P_k \mathbf{x}^k$, $\forall k$ then we suppose $\mathscr{x}$ is not a bargaining equilibrium. We shall assume that, to be a bargaining equilibrium $\mathscr{x}$ must be Pareto-optimal. Furthermore, for $\mathscr{x}$ to be a bargaining equilibrium each individual must be better off at allocation $\mathscr{x}$ than at the initial allocation $\mathscr{x}_0$. What is new in the analysis is the fact that a subset of the market participants can get together and present a combined strategy. Definitions 10.4–10.6 give explicit meaning to the forms of coalition to be considered whilst Definition 10.7 uses the concepts of feasible and blocked coalitions to define the *core*, in the present case the core of a pure exchange economy only.

Definition 10.4

A *coalition S* is a set of households.

Definition 10.5

An allocation $\mathscr{x} \in \hat{\mathscr{X}}$ is *feasible for coalition S* if

$$\sum_{k \in S} \mathbf{x}^k \leqslant \sum_{k \in S} \mathbf{x}_0^k$$

where $\mathbf{x}_0^k$ is the initial stockholding of individual *k*.

Definition 10.6

An allocation $\mathscr{x} \in \hat{\mathscr{X}}$ is *blocked by coalition S* if

$$\exists \mathscr{x}' \neq \mathscr{x} \qquad (\mathbf{x}^k)' P_k \, \mathbf{x}^k \qquad \forall k \in S.$$

Definition 10.7

The *core*, **C**, of a pure exchange economy is the set of all allocations that are feasible and not blocked by any coalition, i.e.

$$\mathbf{C} = \{\mathscr{x} \in \hat{\mathscr{X}} / \sum_{k \in S} \mathbf{x}^k \leqslant \sum_{k \in S} \mathbf{x}_0^k \;\&\; \sim \exists \mathscr{x}' = \mathscr{x} \quad (\mathbf{x}^k)' P_k \, \mathbf{x}^k \quad \forall k \in S\}.$$

We see from Definition 10.7 that the contract curve in the two-individual model constitutes the core. With only two people the only coalitions are those of one individual and those of the whole group. By Definition 10.7 an allocation in the core cannot be blocked by the coalition of both households and is therefore Pareto-efficient. A competitive equilibrium, if it exists, satisfies the condition of belonging to the core. The obvious question is: What is the connection between the set of competitive equilibria and the set consisting of the core? This question only makes sense when there exists at least one competitive equilibrium and when the core is non-empty.

Even with multiple equilibria it is likely that the set of competitive equilibrium points is smaller than the set of points contained in the core. However, with the introduction of two more individuals, with preferences and initial allocations the same as the first two, it is possible for two-member coalitions to be formed which may give rise to blocked allocations. It would appear reasonable to suppose that some of those allocations formerly belonging to the core may now be blocked and so the core shrinks. It is this feature of formed coalitions and a shrinking core to which we now turn.

First we shall demonstrate that if a competitive equilibrium exists then the core is non-empty in that this competitive allocation belongs to the core.

Theorem 10.7 In a pure exchange economy, if $(\bar{\mathbf{p}}, \bar{\mathscr{X}})$ is a competitive equilibrium then $\bar{\mathscr{X}} \in \mathrm{C}$.

Proof Suppose $\bar{\mathscr{X}}$ is blocked by coalition S. If this is true then there exists an $\mathscr{X}'$ and a coalition S such that

$$\sum_{k \in S} (\mathbf{x}^k)' \leqslant \sum_{k \in S} \mathbf{x}_0^k$$

and

$$(\mathbf{x}^k)' P_k \, \mathbf{x}^k \qquad \forall k \in S.$$

But by the definition of competitive equilibria (Definition 10.3, p. 258) $\bar{\mathbf{x}}^k P_k \, \mathbf{x}^k$ if $\bar{\mathbf{p}}'\mathbf{x}^k \leqslant \mathbf{p}'\mathbf{x}^k$; hence it follows from the preference condition of the blocking coalition that $\bar{\mathbf{p}}'(\mathbf{x}^k)' > \bar{\mathbf{p}}'\bar{\mathbf{x}}^k$, $\forall k \in S$ and hence

$$\sum_{k \in S} \bar{\mathbf{p}}'(\mathbf{x}^k)' > \sum_{k \in S} \bar{\mathbf{p}}'\mathbf{x}_0^k.$$

Since $\bar{\mathbf{p}} > 0$ then from the condition of a blocking coalition we have, multiplying through $\sum_{k \in S} (\mathbf{x}^k)' \leqslant \sum_{k \in S} \bar{\mathbf{x}}_0^k$ by $\bar{\mathbf{p}}$,

$$\sum_{k \in S} \bar{\mathbf{p}}'(\mathbf{x}^k)' \leqslant \sum_{k \in S} \bar{\mathbf{p}}'\mathbf{x}_0^k$$

which contradicts our previous result. Hence $\bar{\mathscr{X}}$ belongs to the core, and if $\bar{\mathscr{X}}$ exists the core is non-empty.

Q.E.D.

We turn now to the two important theorems to come from this analysis. The first is the *parity theorem*, which basically says that at a final allocation all groups must be exchanging at the same rate; or alternatively, at a final allocation in the core the consumption allocation for consumers of the same type is identical. The second theorem, called the *limit theorem*, says that if the number in each group increases the core shrinks to the set of competitive equilibria points.

We shall not prove these theorems but rather outline why they appear to be so.

Theorem 10.8 (Parity Theorem) Given two types of traders, each containing *m* individuals where the members of each group have the same preferences and the same initial holdings, then any final allocation must be such that all members of the first group have the same quantities of all goods, and similarly for the second group, i.e. a final allocation belonging to the core must be such that all members of the first group are exchanging at the same rate with those of the second group.

Theorem 10.8 is illustrated in Fig. 10.14. Suppose we have two of type 1 which we shall call A_1 and A_2 and two of type 2 labelled B_1 and B_2. The initial allocation

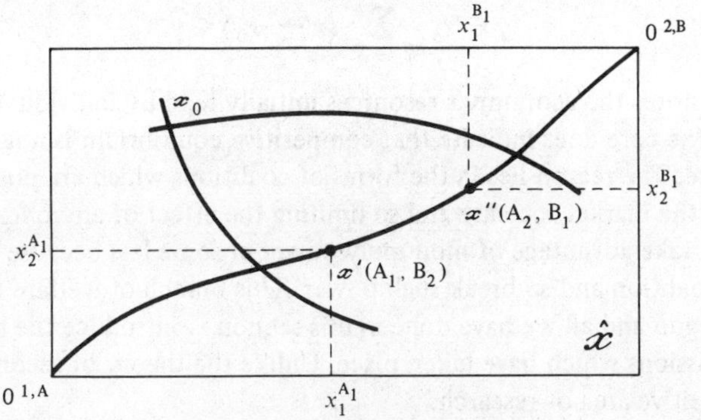

Fig. 10.14. Parity theorem

is $\mathscr{x}_0$ and since both A's are the same and both B's are the same then $\mathscr{x}_0$ represents both (A_1, B_1) and (A_2, B_2). Now suppose the final allocations are different so that

$\mathscr{x}' = (x_1^{A_1}, x_2^{B_2})$ and $\mathscr{x}'' = (x_1^{A_2}, x_2^{B_1})$ where the diagram shows only A_1 and B_1 marked off. As constructed it would be advantageous for A_1 and B_1 to form a coalition and recontract so as to finish at a point on CC′ lying between $\mathscr{x}'$ and $\mathscr{x}''$, since then both A_1 and B_1 would be better off. The same does not apply to A_2 and B_2 because for them any move to a point between $\mathscr{x}'$ and $\mathscr{x}''$ must make both worse off. Consequently some allocations along CC′ can, in the present case, be blocked by a coalition. Hence to be a final allocation and belong to the core requires that the allocation must be the same for any two, taken one from each group. There may of course be more than one such point.

Theorem 10.9 (Limit Theorem) If there are two types of traders each containing m individuals and where the members of each group have the same preferences and the same initial allocations then as m increases the core shrinks to the set of competitive equilibrium points.

The proof takes the following form. First demonstrate that the allocations $\mathscr{x} \in C$ are dependent upon m. The next step is to show that the core for $m + 1$ is contained in the core for m. This is intuitively so since a coalition that blocks for m certainly can block for $m + 1$, and there is likely to be a possible blocking coalition for $m + 1$ which is not present for m. The third step is to show that the competitive allocation(s) is (are) in the core for *any m*. Next it is necessary to demonstrate that the cores, which are functions of m, form a non-increasing sequence of sets, each of which contains the collection of competitive allocations. Finally, that no allocations other than the set of competitive allocations is in the core for *all m*. Hence, the core must shrink for increasing m to the set of competitive allocations.

We have in discussing the core remained in the pure exchange economy. However, generalisation to the inclusion of production is not difficult. For example, a consumption allocation $\mathscr{x}$ is feasible for a coalition S if for some

$$\mathbf{y} \in \hat{\mathbf{Y}}, \quad \sum_{k \in S} (\mathbf{x}^k - \mathbf{r}_0^k) \leqslant \mathbf{y}$$

where $\mathbf{r}_0^k$ denotes the economy's resources initially held by individual k. The analysis of the core does indicate that competitive equilibrium is not such an extreme case. The reason lies in the forms of coalitions which are possible as the numbers in the market increase and so limiting the effect of any one. In other words, attempts to take advantage of monopoly power become less because it is possible to form a coalition and so break such power. This branch of welfare economics has only just begun and all we have done in this section is introduce the reader to some of the discussions which have taken place. Unlike the theory of second best this does appear a positive area of research.

EXERCISES

1. Derive the Pareto conditions for production and consumption simultaneously.

2. Consider an economy composed of two individuals with utility functions $u^k = \frac{1}{2}\log x_1^k + \frac{1}{2}\log x_2^k$, $k = 1, 2$. Assume that total endowments are given by $x_1 = 5$ and $x_2 = 8$.

(*a*) Show that the efficiency locus is the diagonal of the Edgeworth–Bowley box by showing that its equation can be written $x_1^1 = 5x_2^1/8$.

(*b*) Suppose initial allocations are $\mathbf{x}^1 = (3, 3)$ and $\mathbf{x}^2 = (2, 5)$. Derive the equation for each individual's indifference curve through this point.

(*c*) Establish that trade will only take place if the relative price ratio $p = p_1/p_2$ lies in the range $1 \leqslant p \leqslant 2\frac{1}{2}$. Also show that for efficient trade the relative price must fall in the range $1{\cdot}2648 \leqslant p \leqslant 2$.

(*d*) Verify that $p = 1\frac{3}{5}$ is an equilibrium and hence show that the equilibrium allocation is $\mathbf{x}^1 = (2\frac{7}{16}, 3\frac{9}{10})$ and $\mathbf{x}^2 = (2\frac{9}{16}, 4\frac{1}{10})$.

3. Consider an economy composed of two individuals with utility functions $u^1 = \frac{3}{8}\log x_1^1 + \frac{5}{8}\log x_2^1$ and $u^2 = \frac{1}{2}\log x_1^2 + \frac{1}{2}\log x_2^2$. Assume that total endowments are given by $x_1 = 5$ and $x_2 = 8$.

(*a*) Show that the efficiency locus takes the form

$$x_1^1 = \frac{15x_2^1}{2(20 - x_2^1)}.$$

(*b*) If initial allocations are $\mathbf{x}^1 = (3, 3)$ and $\mathbf{x}^2 = (2, 5)$ show that the equations for each individual's indifference curve through this point are

$$\log 3 = \tfrac{3}{8}\log x_1^1 + \tfrac{5}{8}\log x_2^1$$

$$\log\sqrt{10} = \tfrac{1}{2}\log x_1^2 + \tfrac{1}{2}\log x_2^2.$$

(*c*) Establish that trade will only take place when the relative price ratio $p = p_1/p_2$ lies in the range $\frac{3}{5} \leqslant p \leqslant 2\frac{1}{2}$.

(*d*) Is $p = 1{\cdot}2$ an equilibrium price ratio?

4. Consider an economy with two commodities produced by two firms with production functions $y_1 = \gamma_1 r_{11}^{\alpha_1} r_{12}^{\alpha_2}$ and $y_2 = \gamma_2 r_{21}^{\beta_1} r_{22}^{\beta_2}$. If the economy has a resource endowment of r_1^0 and r_2^0, show that the production-efficiency locus takes the form

$$r_{11} = \frac{\alpha_1\beta_2 r_1^0 r_{12}}{[(\alpha_1\beta_2 - \alpha_2\beta_1) + \alpha_2\beta_1 r_2^0]}.$$

Under what conditions will this be a straight line through the origin?

5. In what way do the utility specifications $u^k(\mathbf{x}^k, \mathbf{p})$ and $u^k(\mathbf{x}^k, \mathbf{x}^h)$, $h \neq k$ deal with externalities in consumption? What problems arise in specifying the production sets $\mathbf{Y}_j$ and $\mathbf{Y}$ when there are externalities in production?

6. Consider an economy with a social welfare function expressible in terms of commodities 1 and 2 of the form $W = 3y_1^{1/2}y_2^{1/2}$ and a production-possibility boundary of the form $3y_1 + 3y_2 = 20$. This economy has only two individuals each with utility function $u^k = \frac{1}{2}\log x_1^k + \frac{1}{2}\log x_2^k$, $k = 1, 2$.

(*a*) Show that social welfare is maximised at $y_1 = 4$ and $y_2 = 4$.

(*b*) Given initial allocations $\mathbf{x}^1 = (1, 3)$ and $\mathbf{x}^2 = (3, 1)$ show that, although there are no aggregate excess demands, this allocation is *not* Pareto-efficient.

(*c*) Show that exchange will only take place in the relative price range ($p = p_1/p_2$), $\frac{1}{3} \leqslant p \leqslant 3$. Furthermore, establish that the competitive equilibrium allocation is $\mathbf{x}^1 = (2\frac{1}{5}, 2\frac{1}{5})$ and $\mathbf{x}^2 = (1\frac{4}{5}, 1\frac{4}{5})$.

7. Consider an economy with a social welfare function $W = u_1^\alpha u_2^\beta$, a production-possibility boundary $4y_1 + 3y_2 = 72$ and utility functions $u^k = \frac{1}{2}\log x_1^k + \frac{1}{2}\log x_2^k$, $k = 1, 2$.

(*a*) Show that welfare is maximised at $y_1 = 9$ and $y_2 = 12$.

(*b*) Verify that for such an economy the distribution of production between the consumers which maximises social welfare is indeterminate. Given $x_1^1 = 6$ show that the allocations which maximise social welfare are $\mathbf{x}^1 = (6, 8)$ and $\mathbf{x}^2 = (3, 4)$.

8. Consider an individual with a utility function $u^1 = x_1^1 x_2^1 + x_1^1 (x_1^2 - 5)$. This consumer is faced with a budget constraint $2x_1^1 + 3x_2^1 = 60$. Interpret the meaning of $(x_1^2 - 5)$ in the utility function. Show that if $x_1^2 = 9$ then the equilibrium for this consumer is given by $x_1^1 = 18$ and $x_2^1 = 8$. What would have been the equilibrium if individual 1's utility were independent of individual 2's?

9. Consider an economy which produces two private goods y_1 and y_2 and a public good q. The economy's production-possibility boundary is given by $3y_1 + 2y_2 + 2q = 18$. Assume that the social welfare function takes the form $W = u_1^\alpha u_2^\beta$ and that each individual has a utility function given by $u^k = \frac{1}{2}\log x_1^k + \frac{1}{2}\log x_2^k + \frac{1}{2}\log q$, $k = 1, 2$. Show that the values of y_1, y_2 and q which maximise social welfare are $y_1 = 2$, $y_2 = 3$ and $q = 3$. Further, show that if the first consumer has $x_1^1 = 1$ in equilibrium then both consumers have identical commodity bundles at the Pareto-optimal position.

10. Consider an economy composed of a single individual with utility function $u = \frac{1}{2}\log x_1 + \frac{1}{4}\log x_2 + \frac{1}{4}\log x_3$ and a budget constraint $3x_1 + 4x_2 + 2x_3 = 48$.

(*a*) Show that the optimal solution is $x_1 = 8$, $x_2 = 3$ and $x_3 = 6$.

(*b*) Suppose now there is a distortion in the first market so that $\partial u/\partial x_1 - 3K = 0$. Given $K = 1/72$ show that the second-best solution is given by $x_1 = 12$, $x_2 = 1\frac{1}{2}$ and $x_3 = 3$.

(*c*) Show that none of the Pareto-optimality conditions of the first-best solution are satisfied at the second-best optimum.

(*d*) Establish that welfare is lower at the second-best optimum relative to the first-best optimum.

Part V

INTRODUCTION TO DYNAMICS

11

STABILITY AND INTRODUCTORY DYNAMICS

11.1 Introduction

Nowhere in the discussion so far have we mentioned whether the equilibrium points are stable; by stability we shall mean, for the moment, a tendency back towards the equilibrium if disturbed from it. In fact, in places we have assumed that there is some dynamic mechanism which sets up market forces such that equilibrium is attained. There is a certain pedagogic value in not confusing the questions of comparative statics with dynamic considerations. But there must always come a point when we must turn to these dynamic considerations and see to what extent our conclusions are based on certain assumptions about adjustment behaviour.

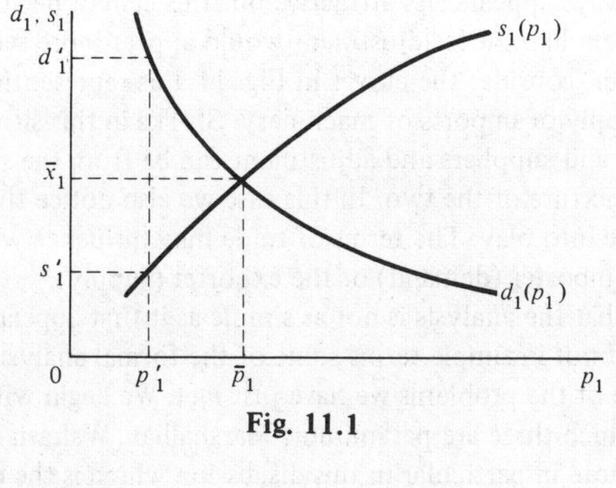

Fig. 11.1

Take, for example, the partial equilibrium analysis of Chapter 8. There we considered the demand and supply curve for a single good and each force was represented by an equation only in terms of that good's price. Such a market is represented in Fig. 11.1, with equilibrium solution $(\bar{p}_1, \bar{x}_1)$. Suppose that the price ruling is given by p'_1. At this price desired demand is d'_1 and suppliers are willing to supply s'_1. Hence we have a situation of excess demand and since the forces are not balanced something must happen. But what happens depends upon our assumptions as to the behaviour of demanders and suppliers when faced with such a situation. Let us just list a few possibilities. We could assume that there is an instantaneous adjustment. In such an 'ideal' world only transactions at $(\bar{p}_1, \bar{x}_1)$ would take place. (We shall see later that this is not the only assumption that will allow only transactions at $(\bar{p}_1, \bar{x}_1)$.) A more usual assumption is to introduce stocks into the problem. However, even this leads to a variety of possibilities. The simplest is to assume that *all demands* are met. This means transactions take place along the demand curve. For this to be so the excess demand $d'_1 - s'_1$ must be met out of stocks. Two assumptions are usually implicit in this argument. The first is that all stocks are held by suppliers. Second, suppliers when faced with falling stocks, will raise the price, and that the price will continue to rise until stocks remain unchanged. Conversely, when stocks are rising, as when there is excess supply, suppliers will reduce prices until stocks are unchanged.

An alternative analysis concerning stocks is that given the price p'_1 the excess demand will be met out of stocks, but that in the next period quantity will be increased so as to replenish stocks, the additional supply will be forthcoming at a higher price and this will continue until quantity no longer needs adjusting.

It is to be noticed that, so far, all the adjustment is on the supply side. It is possible to consider adjustment on the demand side, although this is less frequently contemplated. The simplest assumption is that *all supplies* are met. Thus at price p'_1 the excess demand $d'_1 - s'_1$ is left unsatisfied as transactions take place at s'_1. So long as there are demands not satisfied there will exist forces which will make it worth suppliers increasing supply and commanding a higher price. Adjustment on the demand side always appears less attractive but this cannot be stipulated for all problems. For an item like shoes adjustment would appear more sensible on the supply side. However, consider the curves in Fig. 11.1 as representing the import demand and the supply of imports of machinery. Stocks in this situation can be held by both demanders and suppliers and adjustment can be from the supply side, the demand side, or a mixture of the two. In this case we also notice that other considerations come into play. The terms of trade may influence who holds the greater stocks, the importer (demand) or the exporter (supply).

Already we see that the analysis is not as simple as it first appeared. The aim of this chapter is to set out in simple terms some of the formal analysis which allows us to consider some of the problems we have just met. We begin with a discussion of static stability of which three are paramount: Marshallian, Walrasian and Hicksian. The reader should note in particular in this discussion which is the dependent variable and which the independent variable of the dynamics. Section 11.3 turns to dynamic stability with discussions of the stability in the sense of Lyapunov and also the Lipschitz condition. Included here is the distinction between local and global stability. Finally, we shall discuss the dynamics of the open Leontief model as an illustration.

11.2 Static Stability

The earliest discussions on stability concerned itself with properties of the demand and supply curves rather than how explicitly price and quantity changed over time. Although the dynamics is not explicit we can say that two forms were clearly distinguished in the early literature. The first argued that if there was a positive (negative) excess demand then price rose (fell). This is the *price* adjustment model of Walras. The alternative was the *quantity* adjustment model of Marshall. If the demand price fell short (exceeded) the supply price then quantity would fall (rise). In discussing these two models, and they are distinct models, it is helpful to write out symbolically the demand and supply equations and the equilibrium conditions for both models.

Walrasian model	*Marshallian model*
$q^d = d(p)$	$p^d = D(x)$
$q^s = s(p)$	$p^s = S(x)$
$q^d = q^s = x$	$p^d = p^s = p$

The alternative stability conditions are made explicit in the following two definitions:

Definition 11.1

(Walrasian stability) Given a market demand and supply curve of the form $p^d = d(p)$ and $q^s = s(p)$ respectively, and an equilibrium price $\overline{p}$ then if

$$d(p) > s(p) \quad \text{for } p < \overline{p}$$
$$\text{and } d(p) < s(p) \quad \text{for } p > \overline{p}$$

the market is *Walrasian stable.*

Definition 11.2

(Marshallian stability) Given a market demand and supply curve of the form $p^d = D(x)$ and $p^s = S(x)$ respectively, and an equilibrium quantity $\overline{x}$ then if

$$D(x) > S(x) \quad \text{for } x < \overline{x}$$
$$\text{and } D(x) < S(x) \quad \text{for } x > \overline{x}$$

the market is *Marshallian stable.*

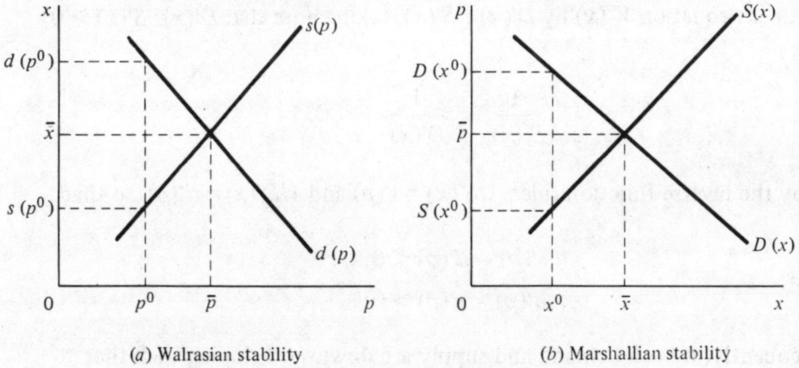

Fig. 11.2. Walrasian and Marshallian stability

These alternative definitions of stability are illustrated in Fig. 11.2. It is to be noticed how the axes are labelled. In each case the adjustment is with respect to the independent variable: price in the Walrasian model and quantity in the Marshallian model.

Although Definitions 11.1 and 11.2 refer to demand and supply for the independent variable being different from the equilibrium there is an implicit adjustment. In particular, for the Walrasian model, if there is a positive excess demand then it is assumed price will rise; if there is excess supply price falls. If $z(p) = d(p) - s(p)$ is the excess demand function for the Walrasian model the adjustment takes the form:

$$\frac{d[z(p)]}{dp} = \frac{d[d(p)]}{dp} - \frac{d[s(p)]}{dp} < 0,$$

i.e.

$$z'(p) = d'(p) - s'(p) < 0$$

where the prime denotes the first derivative. In the Marshallian model the adjustment takes the form:

$$\frac{d[V(x)]}{dx} = \frac{d[D(x)]}{dx} - \frac{d[S(x)]}{dx} < 0,$$

i.e.

$$V'(x) = D'(x) - S'(x) < 0,$$

that is to say, when there is excess demand quantity rises and the excess demand falls; when there is excess supply quantity falls and so too does excess supply (excess demand therefore increases).

The question arises whether these definitions of stability are just alternatives and that if the market is, say, Walrasian stable, is it also Marshallian stable? The answer is no! A market can be Walrasian stable but Marshallian unstable and vice versa. If we assume that the demand curve is always downward-sloping then both $d'(p) < 0$ and $D'(x) < 0$. However, suppose the supply curve rather than being upward-sloping is downward-sloping, then $s'(p) < 0$ and $S'(x) < 0$. Now divide the Marshallian adjustment equation $V'(x)$ by $D'(x) \cdot S'(x)$, taking note that $D'(x) \cdot S'(x) > 0$, giving

$$\frac{1}{S'(x)} - \frac{1}{D'(x)} < 0,$$

But by the inverse function rule[1] $1/S'(x) = s'(p)$ and $1/D'(x) = d'(p)$, so that

$$s'(p) - d'(p) < 0$$

or

$$d'(p) - s'(p) > 0.$$

Consequently, if both demand and supply are downward-sloping such that Marshallian adjustment is satisfied it cannot also satisfy the Walrasian adjustment.

The following table sets out the possibilities all in terms of $d'(p)$ and $s'(p)$. The Marshallian stability along with Walrasian instability is illustrated in Fig. 11.3 (see also Exercise 1).

		$d'(p) < 0$	
	$d'(p) < 0, s'(p) > 0$	$d'(p) < s'(p)$	$d'(p) > s'(p)$
Walrasian	stable	stable	unstable
Marshallian	stable	unstable	stable

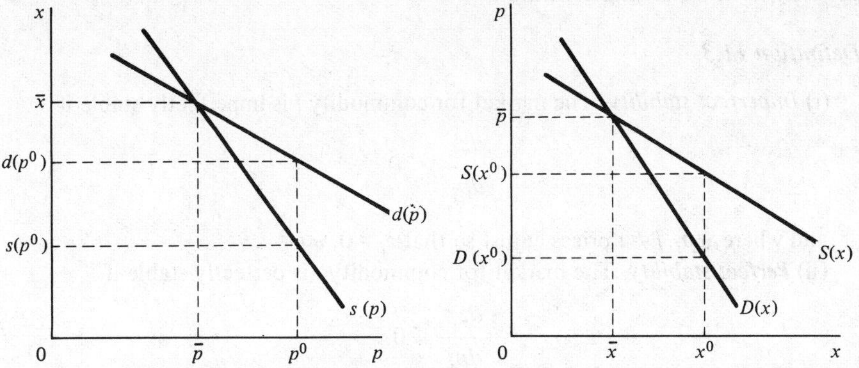

(*a*) Walrasian instability (*b*) Marshallian stability

Fig. 11.3

By the nature of the definitions these interpretations of stability only refer to a single market, i.e. to partial equilibrium. Hicks in *Value and Capital* attempted a definition of stability in the situation of many markets [52]. In doing this he utilised the Walrasian interpretation of excess demands. Hicks considered therefore $\mathbf{z(p)} = \mathbf{d(p)} - \mathbf{s(p)}$. We have already demonstrated that if $\mathbf{d(p)}$ and $\mathbf{s(p)}$ are continuous then $\mathbf{z(p)}$ is a homogeneous function of degree zero in prices, $\mathbf{z}(\lambda\mathbf{p}) = \mathbf{z(p)}$. In this analysis we shall suppose that the numeraire is $\lambda = 1/\boldsymbol{\iota}'\mathbf{p}$ so that $\mathbf{p}$ belongs to the unit simplex $\mathbf{S}_n$. It will be helpful to discuss this analysis in terms of the excess-demand price-response matrix $\mathbf{Z}_p$. Let

$$\mathbf{Z}_p = \frac{\partial \mathbf{z}}{\partial \mathbf{p}'} = \begin{bmatrix} \frac{\partial z_1}{\partial p_1} & \cdots & \frac{\partial z_1}{\partial p_n} \\ \vdots & & \vdots \\ \frac{\partial z_n}{\partial p_1} & \cdots & \frac{\partial z_n}{\partial p_n} \end{bmatrix} = \begin{bmatrix} z_{11} & \cdots & z_{1n} \\ \vdots & & \vdots \\ z_{n1} & \cdots & z_{nn} \end{bmatrix}.$$

If we differentiate at the equilibrium value we shall write $\mathbf{Z}_{\bar{p}}$ with the $(i, j)^{\text{th}}$ element $z_{ij}(\bar{\mathbf{p}})$.

Hicks has two interpretations of stability. The first says that a market is *imperfectly stable* if an increase in the price above the equilibrium price causes an excess supply of that good and a fall in price below the equilibrium price causes an excess demand of that good, *after all other market prices have adjusted so that all other markets are in equilibrium.* On the other hand, a market is *perfectly stable* if an increase (decrease) in the price above (below) the equilibrium price causes an excess supply (demand) of that good, after *any subset* of other market prices have adjusted so that in these markets equilibrium is established. We can formulate this precisely in the following definition:

Definition 11.3

(i) *Imperfect stability.* The market for commodity i is imperfectly stable if

$$\frac{dz_i}{dp_i} < 0$$

and where $\forall p_j, j \neq i$ prices adjust so that $z_j = 0, \forall j \neq i$.

(ii) *Perfect stability.* The market for commodity i is perfectly stable if

$$\frac{dz_i}{dp_i} < 0$$

and where for any arbitrary price set $(p_1, \ldots, p_s)$, not including p_i, these prices adjust so that $z_j = 0, j = 1, \ldots, s$; and all other prices, not including p_i, remain fixed.

Consider, therefore, $\mathbf{z} = \mathbf{z}(\bar{\mathbf{p}})$. Totally differentiating this with respect to p_i we have

$$\frac{\mathbf{dz}}{dp_i} = \mathbf{Z}_{\bar{p}} \frac{\mathbf{dp}}{dp_i}.$$

For imperfect stability we have therefore

$$\begin{bmatrix} dz_1/dp_i \\ \cdot \\ \cdot \\ \cdot \\ dz_i/dp_i \\ \cdot \\ \cdot \\ \cdot \\ dz_n/dp_i \end{bmatrix} = \begin{bmatrix} 0 \\ \cdot \\ \cdot \\ \cdot \\ z_i/d_i \\ \cdot \\ \cdot \\ \cdot \\ 0 \end{bmatrix} = \begin{bmatrix} z_{11} & \ldots & z_{1n} \\ \cdot & & \cdot \\ \cdot & & \cdot \\ \cdot & & \cdot \\ \cdot & & \cdot \\ \cdot & & \cdot \\ \cdot & & \cdot \\ \cdot & & \cdot \\ z_{n1} & \ldots & z_{nn} \end{bmatrix} \begin{bmatrix} dp_1/dp_i \\ \cdot \\ \cdot \\ \cdot \\ 1 \\ \cdot \\ \cdot \\ \cdot \\ dp_n/dp_i \end{bmatrix}.$$

By Cramer's rule we have

$$1 = \frac{|a_{ii}|}{|\mathbf{Z}_{\bar{p}}|} \cdot \frac{dz_i}{dp_i} \qquad \text{implying} \quad \frac{dz_i}{dp_i} = \frac{|\mathbf{Z}_{\bar{p}}|}{|a_{ii}|}$$

where $|a_{ii}|$ is the principal minor of order $(n-1) \times (n-1)$ of $\mathbf{Z}_{\bar{p}}$. For the ith market to be imperfectly stable we require that

$$\frac{dz_i}{dp_i} = \frac{|\mathbf{Z}_{\bar{p}}|}{|a_{ii}|} < 0,$$

i.e. the $(n-1) \times (n-1)$ principal minor must have a sign the opposite of $|\mathbf{Z}_{\bar{p}}|$, and this must have the sign of $(-1)^n$.

By the same reasoning, for the case of perfect stability all principal minors must alternate in sign. This readily follows. If we let $\mathbf{Z}^s_{\bar{p}}$ denote the partial response matrix for s commodities $s = 1, \ldots, n$ and including commodity i evaluated at the the equilibrium price vector $\bar{\mathbf{p}}$ then

$$\frac{dz_i}{dp_i} = \frac{|\mathbf{Z}^s_{\bar{p}}|}{|a^s_{ii}|}$$

where $|a^s_{ii}|$ is the principal minor of $\mathbf{Z}^s_{\bar{p}}$ of order one less than $\mathbf{Z}^s_{\bar{p}}$. Since s is arbitrary it must hold for all s that

$$\frac{dz_i}{dp_i} = \frac{|\mathbf{Z}^s_{\bar{p}}|}{|a^s_{ii}|} < 0$$

for perfect stability. For this to be true the principal minors $|a^s_{ii}|$ must alternate in sign.

Example 11.1 Let $\mathbf{Z}_{\bar{p}} = \begin{bmatrix} -10 & 2 & 1 \\ 1 & -3 & 0 \\ 2 & 8 & -1 \end{bmatrix}$. To see whether the first market is Hicksian imperfectly stable we must consider

$$\begin{bmatrix} dz_1/dp_1 \\ 0 \\ 0 \end{bmatrix} = \begin{bmatrix} -10 & 2 & 1 \\ 1 & -3 & 0 \\ 2 & 8 & -1 \end{bmatrix} \begin{bmatrix} 1 \\ dp_2/dp_1 \\ dp_3/dp_1 \end{bmatrix}.$$

First calculate $|\mathbf{Z}_{\bar{p}}| = -14$. Then we have by Cramer's rule

$$1 = \frac{\dfrac{dz_1}{dp_1} \begin{vmatrix} -3 & 0 \\ 8 & -1 \end{vmatrix}}{(-14)}, \quad \text{i.e.} \quad \frac{dz_1}{dp_1} = \frac{-14}{3} < 0.$$

Hence, the first market is imperfectly stable.

Now consider the situation where p_3 is held constant and market two is free to attain equilibrium. Then

$$\mathbf{Z}_{\bar{p}}^{s} = \begin{bmatrix} -10 & 2 \\ 1 & -3 \end{bmatrix} \text{ and } \begin{bmatrix} dz_1/dp_1 \\ 0 \end{bmatrix} = \begin{bmatrix} -10 & 2 \\ 1 & -3 \end{bmatrix} \cdot \begin{bmatrix} 1 \\ dp_2/dp_1 \end{bmatrix}$$

with $|\mathbf{Z}_{\bar{p}}^{s}| = 28$ and, applying Cramer's rule, we find

$$1 = \frac{\begin{vmatrix} dz_1/dp_1 & 2 \\ 0 & -3 \end{vmatrix}}{28}, \quad \text{i.e.} \quad \frac{dz_1}{dp_1} = -\frac{28}{3} < 0.$$

Finally, if we hold p_2 constant and assume market three is free to attain equilibrium. Then

$$\mathbf{Z}_{\bar{p}}^{s} = \begin{bmatrix} -10 & 1 \\ 2 & -1 \end{bmatrix} \text{ and } \begin{bmatrix} dz_1/dp_1 \\ 0 \end{bmatrix} = \begin{bmatrix} -10 & 1 \\ 2 & -1 \end{bmatrix} \begin{bmatrix} 1 \\ dp_3/dp_1 \end{bmatrix},$$

which gives, in exactly the same manner as before, $\dfrac{dz_1}{dp_1} = -8 < 0$. Notice that the principal minors alternate in sign with values -10, 28 and -14 respectively. Consequently, the system is both imperfectly and perfectly Hicksian stable. (See also Exercises 3 and 4.)

The stability condition of Hicks is also interpreted as $\mathbf{Z}_{\bar{p}}$ being negative definite because this means all its principal minors alternate in sign. Let $\mathbf{Z}_{\bar{p}}^{k}$ stand for the kth individual's excess-demand price-response matrix evaluated at the equilibrium price. Then we have for the aggregate

$$\sum_{k=1}^{m} \mathbf{Z}_{\bar{p}}^{k} = \sum_{k} \mathbf{X}_{\bar{p}}^{k} - \sum_{j=1}^{l} \mathbf{Q}_{\bar{p}}^{j} = (\sum_{k} \mathbf{S}_{\bar{p}}^{k} - \sum_{j} \mathbf{Q}_{\bar{p}}^{j}) - \sum_{k} \mathbf{x}_{y}^{k}(\mathbf{x}^{k} - \mathbf{x}_{0}^{k}),$$

where $\mathbf{X}_{\bar{p}}^{k} = \partial \mathbf{x}^{k}(\bar{\mathbf{p}})/\partial \mathbf{p}'$, $\mathbf{Q}_{\bar{p}}^{j} = \partial \mathbf{s}^{j}(\bar{\mathbf{p}})/\partial \mathbf{p}'$ and $\mathbf{x}_{0}^{k}$ is the original holding of commodities by individual k. Since $\mathbf{S}_{\bar{p}}^{k}$ and $-\mathbf{Q}_{\bar{p}}^{j}$ are negative semi-definite then by Theorem 8.1 (p. 212) $(\sum_{k} \mathbf{S}_{\bar{p}}^{k} - \sum_{j} \mathbf{Q}_{\bar{p}}^{j})$ is a negative semi-definite matrix. If we exclude the possibility that the determinant $|\sum_{k} \mathbf{S}_{\bar{p}}^{k} - \sum_{j} \mathbf{Q}_{\bar{p}}^{j}| = 0$ then $(\sum_{k} \mathbf{S}_{\bar{p}}^{k} - \sum_{j} \mathbf{Q}_{\bar{p}}^{j})$ is negative definite. If we further assume as Hicks did, that the income effects are symmetrical in the sense that $\mathbf{x}_{y}^{k} = \mathbf{x}_{y}\ \forall k$, then $\sum_{k} \mathbf{x}_{y}^{k}(\mathbf{x}^{k} - \mathbf{x}_{0}^{k})' = \mathbf{x}_{y}(\mathbf{x} - \mathbf{x}_{0})'$. But if all markets are in equilibrium then $\mathbf{x} - \mathbf{x}_{0} = 0$; hence the income term vanishes in the aggregate. It follows that under these assumptions $Z_{\bar{p}} = \sum_k Z_{\bar{p}}^k$ is negative definite and its principal minors alternate in sign. To state the converse of this result, a system can only exhibit instability if the income effect is asymmetrical.

The analysis above, which follows that of Hicks, shows that an equilibrium system, to be of any use, must be stable since only such systems when disturbed tend to approach equilibrium. The analysis attempts to show under what conditions such a system is stable. Unfortunately, the analysis makes no explicit reference to a dynamic system and so the link between statics and dynamics is incomplete. Samuelson presented the difference between dynamics and Hicksian statics. He presented a counter-example, and every economist now is given the cobweb as a case in point as Exercises 7 and 8 show. Even so Hicksian stability has two uses. First, it gives a set of stability conditions which are independent of the speed of response of prices to excess demands. In other words, if dynamic stability is to be independent of the speed of response it is necessary to satisfy the Hicksian condition of perfect stability. Second, in certain market conditions Hicksian perfect stability is necessary and sufficient for true dynamic stability.

11.3 Dynamics

Dynamics is concerned with the behaviour through time of all endogenous variables given arbitrary initial conditions [107, p. 260]. In terms of markets it concerns itself with an explicit statement of how prices change over time; in other words, with price-adjustment processes. In this section we will consider the definition of dynamic stability and the variety of price-adjustment processes which have been discussed. We shall also discuss the relationship between dynamic and static stability. Throughout we shall concern ourselves only with continuous time, but see Exercises 7 and 8.

In undertaking such an analysis the mathematical treatment is particularly concerned with differential equations because the price adjustment equation takes such a form. A differential equation takes the general form

$$\dot{x} = f(x, t),$$

where $\dot{x} = dx/dt$. Differential equations have played an important role in many branches of science and economics is no exception. In the early development of this branch of mathematics explicit integration techniques were evolved for handling standard types of differential equations. However, in general, the simple rules of integration failed and in practice numerical methods were used. But because of this shortcoming the question arose as to what conditions, or what particular restrictions, must be placed on the functions so that a solution does exist? One such condition, which is entering more and more into the literature of economics, is that of Lipschitz and is called the *Lipschitz condition*. The condition ensures that the solution to a differential equation is unique.[2] We shall consider this more formally below. A function which is considered along with differential equations, and is only now becoming increasingly used in economics, is the *Lyapunov function.*[3] This function gives a measure of deviation from equilibrium and is employed in establishing dynamic stability in the sense of seeing what happens to this deviation over time.[4] In discussing stability we inevitably must consider differential equations.[5] These equations are considered in terms of given initial conditions. We shall see that some of the requirements to be imposed, e.g. the Lipschitz condition, only hold for small neighbourhoods, and consequently the analyst's concern is only with the initial conditions being in this neighbourhood of equilibrium. Stability conditions for small neighbourhoods around equilibrium are referred to as *local*. For some problems we can say that regardless of the initial conditions the equilibrium will (eventually) be attained. Such a stability situation is referred to as *global* since the initial conditions can be any point in the whole domain. It is clear that if we can establish that a solution is globally stable then it must be locally stable but not conversely. Our problem then is to consider the global–local nature of the solutions to the price-adjustment equations.

Before we can discuss the dynamics and stability of our demand and supply model, therefore, we must have explicit notions of the terms we have discussed intuitively above. We can then state some important results of dynamic systems and then see how we can use them to discuss our present problem. It is important that the student of economics be aware of these concepts although they are not easy and the theorems have normally come from the impetus of other subjects, such as control engineering. Also the mathematics appears quite different from what has gone before so that the demands on the reader must inevitably become greater if this area is at all to be understood.

For a unique solution to a differential equation two conditions must be met. First the function must be continuous. This we discussed in Chapter 5, Section 6. The second condition is that of Lipschitz. Consider a differential equation of the form $\dot{x} = f(t, x)$. Given any two points (t, x) and (t, x') within the domain over which f is defined, then

$$\| f(t, x) - f(t, x) \| < K \| x - x' \|$$

where K is a constant. If these are satisfied then there exists a unique continuous function of t, say $\emptyset(t)$, which satisfies $\dot{x} = f(t, x)$.

We shall consider two very simple examples; in so doing we shall consider functions of a single variable only.

Example 11.2 Consider $g(x) = \sqrt{x/2}$. Let x be small and $x' = 0$. Consider the neighbourhood $N_e(x)$ including $x = 0$. To satisfy the Lipschitz condition we require

$$\| \sqrt{x/2} - 0 \| < K \| x - 0 \|.$$

$$\text{i.e.} \quad \sqrt{1/2x} < K.$$

But for any K positive we can always find a small enough x which violates this condition. If, for example, $K = 2$ then for $x < 1/8$ the Lipschitz condition is violated.

Example 11.3 Consider $g(x) = x^2 + 2$ and any two points x and y in the domain. Then we must have to satisfy the Lipschitz condition:

$$\| (x^2 + 2) - (y^2 + 2) \| < K \| x - y \|$$

$$\| (x - y)(x + y) \| < K \| x - y \|.$$

But from the Schwartz inequality[6] we have

$$\| (x - y)(x + y) \| < \| x - y \| \| x + y \|,$$

i.e. $\| (x - y)(x + y) \| < K \| x - y \|$

which is true for all $K > 0$. Thus the Lipschitz condition is not violated.

So far we have argued that if $f(t, x)$ is continuous and the Lipschitz condition is satisfied then for the differential equation $\dot{x} = f(t, x)$ there exists a unique continuous function $\phi(t)$ (which may also be written $x(t)$) which satisfies $\dot{x} = f(t, x)$. Now let us return to the n-normalised excess demands $z_i = z_i(p_1, \ldots, p_n)$, $i = 1, \ldots, n$. In terms of Walrasian adjustment where prices change we have the differential equations:

$$\frac{dp_i}{dt} = \dot{p}_i = f_i[z_i(p)] \qquad i = 1, \ldots, n.$$

Definition 11.4

Let $\bar{\mathbf{p}}$ denote the equilibrium normalised price vector such that $\mathbf{z}(\bar{\mathbf{p}}) = 0$. Equilibrium is characterised by the condition

$$\dot{p}_i = f_i(0) = 0 \qquad \forall i.$$

In other words, if the system is in equilibrium then no prices will change.

Suppose we have an initial set of prices $\mathbf{p}^0 \neq \bar{\mathbf{p}}$, then over time prices will change according to the above set of differential equations. Let $\psi(\mathbf{p}^0, t)$ denote such a time path of prices $\mathbf{p}$, given the initial set of prices $\mathbf{p}^0$. We have a variety of definitions of stability which must be distinguished.

Definition 11.5

An equilibrium $\bar{\mathbf{p}}$ is *locally stable* if for any $\mathbf{p}^0 \in N_\epsilon(\bar{\mathbf{p}})$, $\mathbf{p}^0 > 0$ then

$$\lim_{t \to \infty} \psi(\mathbf{p}^0, t) = \bar{\mathbf{p}}.$$

Definition 11.6

An equilibrium $\bar{\mathbf{p}}$ is *globally stable* if for any $\mathbf{p}^0 > 0$

$$\lim_{t \to \infty} \psi(\mathbf{p}^0, t) = \bar{\mathbf{p}}.$$

Thus local stability only refers to initial positions in the neighbourhood of equilibrium which will eventually converge on the equilibrium whilst global stability must hold for any price vector both 'near' to and 'far' away from the equilibrium price vector. It clearly follows that global stability implies local stability but not conversely.

Let us for a moment return to the system

$$\dot{\mathbf{p}} = \mathbf{f}[\mathbf{z}(\mathbf{p})].$$

Such a mathematical expression must have lying behind it a mode of dynamic behaviour which is embodied in the function **f**. One of the most widely discussed is that of the *tatonnement,* or the process of recontracting. This process is likened to an auction where the floor contains buyers and sellers. The auctioneer begins the bidding at, say, a price $\mathbf{p}^0$ which we take not to be an equilibrium. At such a price we suppose, unlike an auction, that the various demands and supplies are presented to the auctioneer. If these do not balance he will change the price upwards if there is excess demand and downwards if there is excess supply, *without having allowed any transactions to take place.* At the new price the same procedure is adopted. When a price is found for which all excess demands are zero the auctioneer allows transactions to take place. We can embody this process in the following definition:

Definition 11.7

A *tatonnement* process of price adjustment is such that if $\mathbf{p}(t)$ is not an equilibrium price vector at time t then it changes; furthermore, agents in the market can only transact at an equilibrium price vector $\bar{\mathbf{p}}(t)$.

As far as the auctioneer is concerned we have supposed he always acts in such a way that **f** is a sign-preserving function of **z**, i.e. price rises when $z_i > 0$ and falls when $z_i < 0$, with $p_i = 0$ when $f_i(0) = 0$, $i = 1, \ldots, n$. Now if for given $\mathbf{p}^0$ we have a time path $\mathbf{p}(t/\mathbf{p}^0)$ [$= \psi(\mathbf{p}^0, t)$, as used above in Definitions 11.5 and 11.6] problems would arise if a number of time paths arose in solving $\dot{\mathbf{p}} = \mathbf{f}[\mathbf{z}(\mathbf{p})]$. This is not to say that if we have a different initial condition we must have the same time path; on the contrary, we would expect with a different initial condition $\mathbf{p}^1 \neq \mathbf{p}^0$ the time path $\mathbf{p}(t/\mathbf{p}^1)$ would be different from $\mathbf{p}(t/\mathbf{p}^0)$. Furthermore, we would like $\mathbf{p}(t/\mathbf{p}^0)$ to be a continuous function.

Let us suppose for a moment $\mathbf{p}(t/\mathbf{p}^0)$ is continuous. Now it follows that $\mathbf{p}(t/\mathbf{p}^0)$ is unique if the Lipschitz condition is satisfied. This is the usual assumption. Neoclassical analysis is most fortunate in being able to invoke the Lipschitz condition. We have already shown that neoclassical theory always gives a strictly positive equilibrium price vector and also implied is that at no time does any price become negative. What this amounts to is a situation where the auctioneer will start from a positive price vector and he will never be in a position where he does not alter the price when excess demand is not zero. This latter situation would arise in the case of a free good where $p_i = 0$ and $z_i(\mathbf{p}) < 0$. In such a situation **f** is not continuous and the Lipschitz condition cannot be satisfied. This problem is difficult to handle and we shall leave this for the advanced student.[7] Thus we suppose $\mathbf{p}^0 \gg 0$ and so too is $\bar{\mathbf{p}}$.

We have said in Definition 11.6 that if for any $\mathbf{p}^0$, $\lim_{t \to \infty} \psi(t, \mathbf{p}^0) = \bar{\mathbf{p}}$ then the system is globally stable. It follows that if the economic system has a unique solution then global stability implies local stability. If, however, the economic system has multiple equilibria then we can only consider local stability. But how do we know whether an economic system is locally or globally stable when we are in a situation where the differential equations $f_i[z_i(\mathbf{p})]$, $i = 1, \ldots, n$ are typically non-linear and the number of equations is large. Under such circumstances one approach is to approximate the system by means of linear equations with constant coefficients. The method is as follows.

We begin with our vector of differential equations of order $n \times 1$

$$\frac{d\mathbf{p}}{dt} = \mathbf{f}[\mathbf{z}(\mathbf{p})].$$

Expanding $\mathbf{f}$ in a Taylor expansion about $\bar{\mathbf{p}}$ we have

$$\frac{d\mathbf{p}}{dt} \simeq \mathbf{f}[\mathbf{z}(\bar{\mathbf{p}})] + \frac{\partial \mathbf{f}[\mathbf{z}(\bar{\mathbf{p}})]}{\partial \mathbf{p}'}(\mathbf{p} - \bar{\mathbf{p}}).$$

But $\mathbf{f}[\mathbf{z}(\bar{\mathbf{p}})] = \mathbf{f}(0) = 0$ and letting $\mathbf{Z}^*_{\bar{p}} = \dfrac{\partial \mathbf{f}[\mathbf{z}(\bar{\mathbf{p}})]}{\partial \mathbf{p}'}$ we have[8]

$$\frac{d\mathbf{p}}{dt} = \mathbf{Z}^*_{\bar{p}}(\mathbf{p} - \bar{\mathbf{p}})$$

where $\mathbf{Z}^*_{\bar{p}}$ is an $n \times n$ matrix and $(\mathbf{p} - \bar{\mathbf{p}})$ an $n \times 1$ vector.

Since $(\mathbf{p} - \bar{\mathbf{p}})$ is purely the discrepancy from equilibrium, and denoting whether the initial position is above $(\mathbf{p} > \bar{\mathbf{p}})$ or below $(\mathbf{p} < \bar{\mathbf{p}})$ equilibrium, then whether the system is locally stable or not will depend upon the properties of $\mathbf{Z}^*_{\bar{p}}$. Suppose $dp_i/dt = k_i z_i(\mathbf{p})$, $\forall i$, and where $k_i > 0$ is the speed of response in the ith market, then

$$\frac{d\mathbf{p}}{dt} = \hat{\mathbf{k}}\mathbf{Z}_{\bar{p}}(\mathbf{p} - \bar{\mathbf{p}})$$

where $\hat{\mathbf{k}}$ is a diagonal matrix of order $n \times n$.

Given our result then

$$\frac{dp_i}{dt} = k_i z_{i1}(p_1 - \bar{p}_1) + k_i z_{i2}(p_2 - \bar{p}_2) + \ldots + k_i z_{in}(p_n - \bar{p}_n) \quad \forall i$$

$$= k_i \sum_{j=1}^{n} z_{ij}(p_j - \bar{p}_j)$$

where z_{ij} is the $(i, j)^{\text{th}}$ element of $\mathbf{Z}_{\bar{p}}$. A solution to this system takes the form:

$$p_i(t) = a_{i1}e^{\lambda_1 t} + a_{i2}e^{\lambda_2 t} + \ldots + a_{in}e^{\lambda_n t} + \bar{p}_i \qquad \forall i$$

$$= \sum_{j=1}^{n} a_{ij}e^{\lambda_j t} + \bar{p}_i$$

where a_{ij} are constants and λ_j are the n characteristic roots of

$$\begin{vmatrix} k_1 z_{11} - \lambda & k_1 z_{12} & \ldots & k_1 z_{1n} \\ k_2 z_{21} & k_2 z_{22} - \lambda & \ldots & k_2 z_{2n} \\ k_n z_{n1} & k_n z_{n2} & \ldots & k_n z_{nn} - \lambda \end{vmatrix} \equiv | k_i z_{ij} - \delta_{ij}\lambda | = 0.$$

Or in matrix notation

$$| \hat{\mathbf{k}}\, \mathbf{Z}_{\bar{p}} - \lambda \mathbf{I} | = 0.$$

It has been shown by Metzler [85] that only if the determinant $| \hat{\mathbf{k}}\, \mathbf{Z}_{\bar{p}} |$ has the same sign as $(-1)^n$ will the system be stable. But it is to be observed that the only difference between this result and that of Hicksian perfect stability is the presence of the speed of adjustment matrix $\hat{\mathbf{k}}$. Since for Hicksian stability we have sign $| \mathbf{Z}_{\bar{p}} |$ = sign $(-1)^n$ and in the present case for dynamic stability sign $| \hat{\mathbf{k}}\, \mathbf{Z}_{\bar{p}} |$ = sign $(-1)^n$ it follows that in the present case Hicksian perfect stability is necessary for local dynamic stability. But the result implies more than that; it says that if the Hicksian stability conditions are met they will be met independently of the speeds of adjustments in the various markets.

We shall now take a somewhat different route in analysing stability by combining our previous result with the modern approach, which we shall also use later. Consider the square of the Euclidean distance between the price vector $\mathbf{p}$ and the equilibrium price vector $\bar{\mathbf{p}}$, i.e.

$$D(t) = \sum_{i=1}^{n} (p_i - \bar{p}_i)^2 = (\mathbf{p} - \bar{\mathbf{p}})'(\mathbf{p} - \bar{\mathbf{p}}).$$

Thus when $dD(t)/dt < 0$, $\forall t$ the distance between $\mathbf{p}$ and $\bar{\mathbf{p}}$ is diminishing and will converge on $\bar{\mathbf{p}}$. Now differentiate this distance function with respect to time

$$\dot{D}(t) = \frac{dD(t)}{dt} = 2(\mathbf{p} - \bar{\mathbf{p}})' \frac{d\mathbf{p}}{dt}.$$

Substituting the result we obtained from the Taylor expansion we have

$$\tfrac{1}{2}\dot{D}(t) = (\mathbf{p} - \bar{\mathbf{p}})'\, \hat{\mathbf{k}}\, \mathbf{Z}_{\bar{p}} (\mathbf{p} - \bar{\mathbf{p}}).$$

It follows that if $\hat{\mathbf{k}}\,\mathbf{Z}_{\bar{p}}$ is negative definite then $\frac{1}{2}\dot{D}(t) < 0$ and local stability is assured. But it can be shown that if there exists a diagonal matrix **D** whose diagonal elements are all strictly positive then the product **DA** is stable and **A** is said to be **D**-stable [102]. In the present case it immediately follows from this result that $\mathbf{Z}_{\bar{p}}$ is **D**-stable because $\hat{\mathbf{k}}$ satisfies the conditions on the matrix **D**. Since $\hat{\mathbf{k}}\,\mathbf{Z}_{\bar{p}}$ is **D**-stable it follows that the real parts of the characteristic roots of $\hat{\mathbf{k}}\,\mathbf{Z}_{\bar{p}}$ are negative which amounts to $\hat{\mathbf{k}}\,\mathbf{Z}_{\bar{p}}$ being negative definite. Hence, $\frac{1}{2}\dot{D}(t) < 0$ and prices converge on the equilibrium.

We can illustrate some of the points made by means of a very simple example.

Example 11.4 Let the single-market system be represented by

$$q^d = 18 + 5p^{-1}$$
$$q^s = 4 + 3p$$
$$\frac{dz}{dt} = k\,z(p) \qquad k > 0.$$

Then $z(p) = 14 + 5p^{-1} - 3p$. For equilibrium $z(\bar{p}) = 0$ and solving this gives $\bar{p} = 5$. Hence $\partial z(\bar{p})/\partial p = (-5/p^2) - 3 = -3^1/_5$. The distance function then takes the form

$$\tfrac{1}{2}D(t) = k(p-5)(-3^1/_5)(p-5)$$
$$= \frac{-16k(p-5)^2}{5} < 0;$$

hence the system is locally stable.

So far we have discussed only local stability. The application of the distance function proves to be a most useful approach to considerations of global stability. The analysis employs what is referred to as *Lyapunov's direct method.* This method has the feature that an explicit solution to the differential equation is unnecessary. We begin by defining a Lyapunov function, $V(\mathbf{x})$.

Definition 11.8

A Lyapunov function $V(\mathbf{x})$ is a scalar function such that $\forall \mathbf{x}$,

$0 < \epsilon < \|\mathbf{x}\|$

(1) $V(\mathbf{x}) > 0$ if $\mathbf{x} \neq 0$.

(2) $V(0) = 0$.

(3) $V(\mathbf{x})$ has continuous partial derivatives; and

$$\frac{dV}{dt} = \mathbf{V}'_x \left(\frac{d\mathbf{x}}{dt}\right) = \sum_{i=1}^{n} \frac{\partial V}{\partial x_i} \cdot \frac{\partial x_i}{\partial t} \leqslant 0.$$

In employing this function to, say, the differential equation $\dot{\mathbf{x}} = \phi(\mathbf{x})$ all the variables are expressed as deviations from the equilibrium. We can then employ the following important theorem:

Theorem 11.1 If a Lyapunov function exists for the system $\dot{\mathbf{x}} = \phi(\mathbf{x})$ and $\phi(0) = 0$ then the system is stable. If in addition the Lyapunov function satisfies $dV/dt < 0$ then the system is said to be *asymptotically stable.*

We see from this theorem that our attention is switched totally away from the characteristic roots and towards finding a Lyapunov function. Once found we can discuss stability in the sense of Lyapunov.

The square of the Euclidean distance function $D(t) = V(\mathbf{p} - \bar{\mathbf{p}}) = (\mathbf{p} - \bar{\mathbf{p}})'(\mathbf{p} - \bar{\mathbf{p}})$ is a suitable Lyapunov function. For $\mathbf{p} \neq \bar{\mathbf{p}}$ it is clear that $V(\mathbf{p} - \bar{\mathbf{p}}) > 0$ and that $V(0) = 0$. The function is continuous. It is to be noticed that these conditions are independent of the final requirement concerning the differential equation. Given $\dot{\mathbf{p}} = \hat{\mathbf{k}}\mathbf{z}(\mathbf{p})$ we must demonstrate that $\dot{V} \leqslant 0$ or $\dot{V} < 0$. Differentiating the distance function with respect to time we have

$$\dot{D}(t) = \dot{V}(\mathbf{p} - \bar{\mathbf{p}}) = 2(\mathbf{p} - \bar{\mathbf{p}})' \frac{d\mathbf{p}}{dt}.$$

Substituting $\dfrac{d\mathbf{p}}{dt} = \hat{\mathbf{k}}\mathbf{z}(\mathbf{p})$ and multiplying through by ½ we obtain

$$\tfrac{1}{2}\dot{D}(t) = \tfrac{1}{2}\dot{V}(\mathbf{p} - \bar{\mathbf{p}}) = (\mathbf{p} - \bar{\mathbf{p}})'\,\hat{\mathbf{k}}\mathbf{z}(\mathbf{p}).$$

Let us suppose for simplicity that adjustments are the same in all markets. Then $\hat{\mathbf{k}} = k\mathbf{I}$; hence

$$\begin{aligned}\tfrac{1}{2}\dot{D}(t) &= k(\mathbf{p} - \bar{\mathbf{p}})'\mathbf{z}(\mathbf{p}) \\ &= k[\mathbf{p}'\mathbf{z}(\mathbf{p}) - \bar{\mathbf{p}}'\mathbf{z}(\mathbf{p})].\end{aligned}$$

But by Walras Law (see p. 217) $\mathbf{p}'\mathbf{z}(\mathbf{p}) = 0$; hence

$$\tfrac{1}{2}\dot{D}(t) = -k\,\bar{\mathbf{p}}'\mathbf{z}(\mathbf{p}).$$

In order to sign $\tfrac{1}{2}\dot{D}(t)$ we must sign $\bar{\mathbf{p}}'\mathbf{z}(\mathbf{p})$. At this point we invoke the weak axiom of revealed preference theory. If we have two prices, $\mathbf{p}$ and $\bar{\mathbf{p}}$, for a feasible solution we must have

$$\mathbf{p}'\mathbf{z}(\mathbf{p}) \geqslant \mathbf{p}'\mathbf{z}(\bar{\mathbf{p}}) \quad \text{implying} \quad \bar{\mathbf{p}}'\mathbf{z}(\mathbf{p}) > \bar{\mathbf{p}}'\mathbf{z}(\bar{\mathbf{p}}).$$

But $\mathbf{p}'\mathbf{z}(\mathbf{p}) = 0$ by Walras Law, hence $\mathbf{p}'\mathbf{z}(\bar{\mathbf{p}}) \leqslant 0$, which is true because for $\bar{\mathbf{p}} \gg 0$, $\mathbf{z}(\bar{\mathbf{p}}) = 0$. Hence it follows that $\bar{\mathbf{p}}'\mathbf{z}(\mathbf{p}) > \bar{\mathbf{p}}'\mathbf{z}(\bar{\mathbf{p}}) = 0$. Consequently, so long as $\mathbf{p} \neq \bar{\mathbf{p}}$, $\tfrac{1}{2}\dot{D}(t) < 0$ and we have asymptotic global stability. Global because this result holds for any arbitrary $\mathbf{p}$ and need not be in the neighbourhood of $\bar{\mathbf{p}}$.

Before continuing our analysis it is worth considering once again the tatonnement process. In doing this we shall concentrate on the pure exchange model discussed in Chapter 9. Suppose the initial allocation is given by $\mathscr{x}_0$, as shown in Fig. 11.4 (*a*). As far as tatonnement is concerned the auctioneering process is equivalent to establishing the trading curves $\mathbf{T}_0^1$ and $\mathbf{T}_0^2$. Where these trading curves intersect on the contract curve CC′ establishes the equilibrium price ratio, namely $\mathscr{x}_0$ E at which trading takes place and only at this relative price ratio. But what would happen if trading at 'false' prices were allowed [52]. Suppose the price ratio were $\mathscr{x}_0$ R as in Fig. 11.4 (*b*). At this price ratio individual 1 wishes to exchange at position S whilst individual 2 wishes to exchange at position Q. A variety of assumptions are now possible, but let us consider just one as an illustration. Suppose transactions take place in favour of individual 2 so that position Q becomes realised. The new allocation is Q and through this there will be a set of indifference curves, a new contract curve, which must be a subset of that for allocation $\mathscr{x}_0$, and a new set of trading curves. Let us now suppose that equilibrium is established at V where the trading curves emanating from Q intersect on the contract curve at V. It is clear that there is no *a priori* reason for supposing that V and E will be the same: in general we should expect them to be different, as illustrated in Fig. 11.4 (*b*).

We see, therefore, that the equilibrium price ratio in the case of tatonnement is $\mathscr{x}_0$ E whilst in the model allowing trading at 'false' prices it is QV in the present case. In all probability the ratios $\mathscr{x}_0$ E and QV will be different. In tatonnement the allocation goes from $\mathscr{x}_0$ to E whilst in the 'false' price version there is a set of allocations, e.g. $\mathscr{x}_0$, Q and V. However, we are generally concerned only with Pareto-efficient allocations such as E and V. Since E and V are both Pareto-efficient they are Pareto-noncomparable. If we must establish which final allocation is preferable we must invoke something like a social welfare function.

The importance of this brief discussion is to show very simply that a final equilibrium is dependent upon the dynamic model that lies behind the adjustment process. Our previous discussion concentrated on establishing whether an equilibrium was globally or locally stable. This applies equally to the trading under 'false' prices. What we have here shown is that the equilibrium we are establishing the stability of may be different from the tatonnement equilibrium. It is unfortunate that there has been little work on dynamics of non-tatonnement adjustment processes; this is an obvious area for future research.[9]

11.4 Stability in an Open Leontief Model

We can illustrate some of the above arguments by reconsidering the Open Leontief model. In so doing we shall consider the model in terms of equalities, i.e.

$$\mathbf{y} = \mathbf{A}\mathbf{y} + \mathbf{c}(\mathbf{p}, \mathbf{w})$$

$$\mathbf{B}\mathbf{y} = \mathbf{r}(\mathbf{p}, \mathbf{w})$$

$$\mathbf{p}' = \mathbf{p}'\mathbf{A} + \mathbf{w}'\mathbf{B}.$$

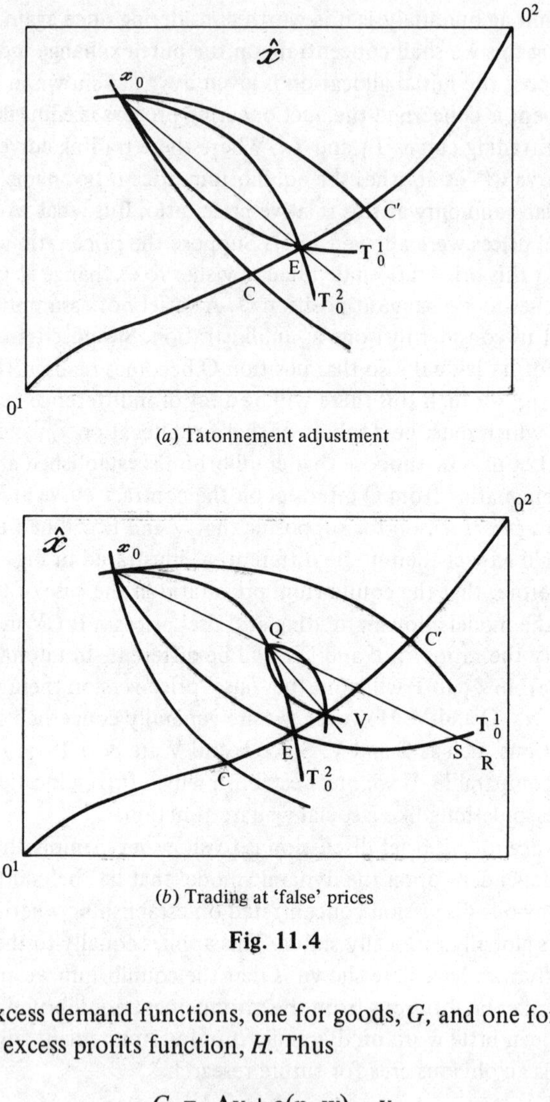

(*a*) Tatonnement adjustment

(*b*) Trading at 'false' prices

Fig. 11.4

We have two excess demand functions, one for goods, G, and one for factors, F; also there is an excess profits function, H. Thus

$$G = \mathbf{Ay} + \mathbf{c}(\mathbf{p}, \mathbf{w}) - \mathbf{y}$$
$$F = \mathbf{By} - \mathbf{r}(\mathbf{p}, \mathbf{w})$$
$$H = \mathbf{p}' - \mathbf{p}'\mathbf{A} - \mathbf{w}'\mathbf{B}.$$

If we denote $(\bar{\mathbf{y}}, \bar{\mathbf{p}}, \bar{\mathbf{w}})$ as the equilibrium set of vectors then by definition:

$$0 = \mathbf{A}\bar{\mathbf{y}} + \mathbf{c}(\bar{\mathbf{p}}, \bar{\mathbf{w}}) - \bar{\mathbf{y}}$$
$$0 = \mathbf{B}\bar{\mathbf{y}} - \mathbf{r}(\bar{\mathbf{p}}, \bar{\mathbf{w}})$$
$$0 = \bar{\mathbf{p}}' - \bar{\mathbf{p}}'\mathbf{A} - \bar{\mathbf{w}}'\mathbf{B}.$$

Subtracting so that we express the excess function in terms of deviations from equilibrium we have

$$G = \mathbf{A\Delta y} + \mathbf{\Delta c} - \mathbf{\Delta y}$$

$$F = \mathbf{B\Delta y} - \mathbf{\Delta r}$$

$$H = \mathbf{\Delta p'} - \mathbf{\Delta p'A} - \mathbf{\Delta w'B}.$$

In arriving at the stability conditions of this system we must be clear on the dynamic assumptions which can be made. First we shall consider Leontief's own version for which when excess demands are present output rather than prices are adjusted so that equilibrium is maintained between prices of goods and the costs of production. For simplicity, we shall assume that factor prices are held constant at the equilibrium level so that $\mathbf{\Delta w'} = 0$. Thus our adjustment equations take the form

$$\frac{\mathbf{dy}}{dt} = (\mathbf{A} - \mathbf{I})\mathbf{\Delta y} + \mathbf{\Delta c}$$

and

$$\frac{\mathbf{dp}}{dt} = \mathbf{\Delta p'}(\mathbf{A} - \mathbf{I}).$$

It is clear that from the dynamic equations the procedure is to determine first the time path of prices and then of outputs. First note that $d(\mathbf{\Delta p})/dt = \mathbf{dp}/dt$ so that

$$\frac{d(\mathbf{\Delta p})}{dt} = \mathbf{\Delta p'}(\mathbf{A} - \mathbf{I}).$$

Stability of this differential equation rests on the restriction which must be placed on the characteristic roots of

$$|\lambda\mathbf{I} - (\mathbf{A} - \mathbf{I})| = 0$$

or

$$|(1 + \lambda)\mathbf{I} - \mathbf{A}| = 0.$$

If $\mathbf{A}$ is non-negative and indecomposable then the dominant characteristic root satisfies $1 + \lambda^* < 1$ from the Perron–Frobenius theorem (Theorem 6.2, p. 173). This is equivalent to $\lambda^* < 0$. Since the general solution is

$$p_i(t) = \sum_{j=1}^{n} d_{ij}\, e^{(1+\lambda_j)t} + \bar{p}_i \qquad i = 1, \ldots, n$$

and this is dominated by the dominant root, λ^*, then it follows $p_i(t) \to \bar{p}_i,\ \forall i$ as $t \to \infty$.

In obtaining the path of output we must make some assumption about final demands, $\mathbf{c}$. If we assume that final demands increase over time at the same rate μ then $\mathbf{c} = \boldsymbol{\gamma} e^{\mu t}$, where $\boldsymbol{\gamma}$ is an $n \times 1$ vector of constants and μ is a scalar. Then we have

$$\frac{d(\mathbf{\Delta y})}{dt} = (\mathbf{A} - \mathbf{I})\,\mathbf{\Delta y} + (\boldsymbol{\gamma} e^{\mu t} - \bar{\mathbf{c}})$$

with a general solution

$$y_i(t) = \sum_{j=1}^{n} d_{ij}\, e^{(1+\lambda_j)t} + \gamma_i^*\, e^{\mu t} - \bar{c}_i + \bar{y}_i \qquad i = 1, \ldots, n.$$

Since we have assumed $\mathbf{w} = \bar{\mathbf{w}}$ then if $\mathbf{p} \to \bar{\mathbf{p}}$ it follows that $\mathbf{c}(\mathbf{p}, \bar{\mathbf{w}}) \to \bar{\mathbf{c}}$ as $t \to \infty$. Hence $y_i(t) \to \bar{y}_i$ as $t \to \infty$ if $\lambda_j < 0$. Consequently, if the price system is stable then the output system is also stable and this is true if the dominant characteristic root is less than unity (implying $\lambda^* < 0$).

The above specification of dynamic adjustment is not the only one to be investigated. An alternative to Leontief's is sometimes called the Walrasian–Samuelson specification. In this case it is assumed that if there is excess demand for good i then the price of that good will rise and vice versa for excess supply. Furthermore, when the price of good i exceeds its cost of production then output is increased and vice versa if price falls short of the cost of production. Formerly

$$\frac{d\mathbf{p}}{dt} = (\mathbf{A} - \mathbf{I})\,\Delta\mathbf{y} + \Delta\mathbf{c}$$

$$\frac{d\mathbf{y}'}{dt} = \Delta\mathbf{p}'\,(\mathbf{I} - \mathbf{A})$$

where again we have assumed $\Delta\mathbf{w} = 0$. With this alternative dynamics it is no longer the case that we can establish stability of prices and then turn to output. It is at this stage in the argument that we require the use of the Lyapunov function. We define two distance functions, one for displacement from equilibrium, V_1, and one for the differential equations, V_2. Hence

$$V_1 = \Delta\mathbf{p}'\Delta\mathbf{p} + \Delta\mathbf{y}'\Delta\mathbf{y} \geqslant 0$$

$$V_2 = \dot{\mathbf{p}}'\dot{\mathbf{p}} + \dot{\mathbf{y}}'\dot{\mathbf{y}} \geqslant 0.$$

It is to be observed that when equilibrium exists in both the price sector and the output sector then both V_1 and V_2 are zero. First we differentiate V_1 with respect to time:

$$\frac{dV_1}{dt} = \Delta\mathbf{p}'\frac{d(\Delta\mathbf{p})}{dt} + \frac{d(\Delta\mathbf{p}')}{dt}\Delta\mathbf{p} + \Delta\mathbf{y}'\frac{d(\Delta\mathbf{y})}{dt} + \frac{d(\Delta\mathbf{y}')}{dt}\Delta\mathbf{y}$$

$$= 2\left[\Delta\mathbf{p}'\frac{d\mathbf{p}}{dt} + \frac{d\mathbf{y}'}{dt}\Delta\mathbf{y}\right]$$

using the fact that $d(\Delta\mathbf{p})/dt = d\mathbf{p}/dt$ and $d(\Delta\mathbf{y}')/dt = d\mathbf{y}'/dt$. Now substituting in the dynamic adjustment equations we find

$$\frac{dV_1}{dt} = 2[\Delta\mathbf{p}'\mathbf{A}\Delta\mathbf{y} - \Delta\mathbf{p}'\Delta\mathbf{y} + \Delta\mathbf{p}'\Delta\mathbf{c} + \Delta\mathbf{p}'\Delta\mathbf{y} - \Delta\mathbf{p}'\mathbf{A}\Delta\mathbf{y}].$$

i.e. $$\frac{dV_1}{dt} = 2\Delta\mathbf{p}'\Delta\mathbf{c}.$$

Differentiating V_2 with respect to time we have

$$\frac{dV_2}{dt} = \dot{\mathbf{p}}'\ddot{\mathbf{p}} + \ddot{\mathbf{p}}'\dot{\mathbf{p}} + \dot{\mathbf{y}}'\ddot{\mathbf{y}} + \ddot{\mathbf{y}}'\dot{\mathbf{y}}$$

$$= 2[\dot{\mathbf{p}}'\ddot{\mathbf{p}} + \ddot{\mathbf{y}}'\dot{\mathbf{y}}].$$

Since $\dot{\mathbf{p}} = (\mathbf{A} - \mathbf{I})\boldsymbol{\Delta}\mathbf{y} + \boldsymbol{\Delta}\mathbf{c}$ then $\ddot{\mathbf{p}} = (\mathbf{A} - \mathbf{I})\dot{\mathbf{y}} + \mathbf{C}_p\dot{\mathbf{p}}$ where $\mathbf{C}_p = \dfrac{\mathbf{dc}}{\mathbf{dp}'}$ is a matrix of order $n \times n$. Also since $\dot{\mathbf{y}}' = \boldsymbol{\Delta}\,\mathbf{p}'(\mathbf{I} - \mathbf{A})$ then $\ddot{\mathbf{y}}' = \dot{\mathbf{p}}'(\mathbf{I} - \mathbf{A})$. Substituting we have

$$\frac{dV_2}{dt} = 2[\dot{\mathbf{p}}'(\mathbf{A} - \mathbf{I})\dot{\mathbf{y}} + \dot{\mathbf{p}}'\mathbf{C}_p\dot{\mathbf{p}} + \dot{\mathbf{p}}'(\mathbf{I} - \mathbf{A})\dot{\mathbf{y}}].$$

Consider $V = V_1 + V_2$ then for stability we require

$$\frac{dV}{dt} < 0 \text{ or } \frac{dV_1}{dt} + \frac{dV_2}{dt} < 0.$$

If $\mathbf{C}_p$ is negative semi-definite (which in terms of our earlier analysis amounts to $\sum_k \mathbf{X}_p^k$ being negative semi-definite which is true if the aggregate income responses are ignored, or cancel out as Hicks assumed) then

$$\frac{dV_1}{dt} = 2\,\boldsymbol{\Delta}\,\mathbf{p}'\,\boldsymbol{\Delta}\mathbf{c} \leqslant 0$$

and

$$\frac{dV_2}{dt} = 2\dot{\mathbf{p}}'\mathbf{C}_p\dot{\mathbf{p}} \leqslant 0.$$

It can be shown that if $dV_1/dt = 0$ then $dV_2/dt < 0$ and if $dV_2/dt = 0$ then $dV_1/dt < 0$. Thus if $\mathbf{C}_p$ is negative semi-definite then $dV/dt < 0$ and the Walras–Samuelson adjustment mechanism leads to a stable equilibrium.

This second analysis is similar to that of Jorgenson, who demonstrated in a different way that in the open Leontief system it was possible to have both output and price systems stable simultaneously [61]. In doing this stocks were introduced explicitly.

11.5 Conclusion

In earlier chapters we discussed the existence of an equilibrium in a variety of models. In this chapter we have been concerned with the stability of such equilibria, if they exist. Even when the equilibrium is unique there is no guarantee that the system will be dynamically stable. This result remains true even if it is statically stable. Also, when there is only one equilibrium there is still need of distinguishing between local and global stability since only the latter implies the former. If, however, there is likely to be more than one equilibrium it is possible only to discuss local stability.

One important consideration has been to clearly specify a dynamic adjustment which must link periods in the model together. This is not true of Walrasian stability, Marshallian stability and Hicksian stability. Even so these static stability conditions do give us some insights. Inevitably such dynamic specifications must manifest themselves in terms of difference or differential equations. Of particular note must be the often implied stock adjustments which are used to 'establish' equilibrium. One illustration of this within a cobweb model will be found in Exercise 8 where the result should be compared with that in Exercise 7.

Tatonnement has played a major role in discussions of dynamic behaviour. It must always be realised, however, that this does restrict trading to take place only at equilibrium prices. Models which incorporate non-tatonnement adjustments are recent and do appear fruitful lines of research. Hicks's fixed-price system was probably one of the earliest discussions of a non-tatonnement process.

We have here only touched on some aspects of dynamics. The recent developments have been particularly formulated in terms of properties of matrices and the interested reader may usefully consult Quirk and Saposnik [102]. It is hoped, however, that the elementary discussion of Lyapunov's function and the use of differential equations in specifying dynamic systems will aid the student and encourage his investigation into the more recent literature.

EXERCISES

1. For each of the following demand and supply systems (i) obtain the equilibrium price and quantity and (ii) specify which are Walrasian and which Marshallian stable.

(*a*) $q^d = 50 - \frac{1}{2}p$	(*b*) $q^d = 15 - 3p$	(*c*) $q^d = 40 - 2p$
$q^s = 35 + p$	$q^s = -10 + 2p$	$q^s = 50 - 4p$
$q^d = q^s = x$	$q^d = q^s = x$	$q^d = q^s = x$

2. In a two-market economy can there be any distinction between Hicksian imperfect and perfect stability? Consider an economy with the following demand and supply equations:

$$x_1 = 50 - \tfrac{1}{2}p_1 - 3p_2 \qquad x_2 = 10 + 2p_1 - 3p_2$$
$$s_1 = 35 + p_1 + 2p_2 \qquad s_2 = -p_1 + 2p_2.$$

Obtain the equilibrium prices and quantities. Verify that both markets are Hicksian stable.

3. Consider the equation $\dfrac{d\mathbf{z}}{dp_1} = \mathbf{Z}_{\bar{p}} \dfrac{\mathbf{dp}}{dp_1}$. If $\mathbf{Z}_{\bar{p}} = \begin{bmatrix} 10 & 2 & 1 \\ -1 & -3 & 0 \\ 2 & -8 & -1 \end{bmatrix}$

show that this system is neither Hicksian imperfectly stable nor Hicksian perfectly stable.

4. Consider the system

$$\begin{bmatrix} dz_1/dp_1 \\ dz_2/dp_1 \\ dz_3/dp_1 \end{bmatrix} = \begin{bmatrix} 5 & 4 & 2 \\ -1 & -3 & -4 \\ 1 & -1 & -2 \end{bmatrix} \begin{bmatrix} 1 \\ dp_2/dp_1 \\ dp_3/dp_1 \end{bmatrix}.$$

Show that the system is Hicksian imperfectly stable. Establish that if p_3 is held constant and market 2 is allowed to attain equilibrium then $dz_1/dp_1 = 11/3$. Also that if p_2 is held constant and market 3 is allowed to attain equilibrium then $dz_1/dp_1 = 6$. What do these results imply about Hicksian perfect stability?

5. Given the system

$$q^d = a + \beta p$$
$$q^s = \gamma + \delta p$$
$$\frac{dp}{dt} = kz(p) \qquad k > 0,$$

show that the time path of prices is given by

$$p(t) = (p^0 - \bar{p})e^{k(\beta-\delta)t} + \bar{p},$$

where $\bar{p} = (\gamma - a)/(\beta - \delta)$ and p^0 is the initial price. Show that the system is dynamically stable if $\beta - \delta < 0$. Also verify that, for the systems of equations in Exercise 1, (*a*) is dynamically stable, (*b*) is dynamically stable but that (*c*) is dynamically unstable.

6. Which of the following functions satisfy the Lipschitz condition?

(*a*) $f(x) = a + bx \qquad -\infty < x < \infty$

(*b*) $f(x) = 2 + x - x^2 \qquad -\infty < x < \infty$

(*c*) $f(x) = \frac{1}{2} \log x \qquad x > 0.$

7. Consider the following cobweb model:

$$q_t^d = a + \beta p_t$$
$$q_t^s = \gamma + \delta p_{t-1}$$
$$q_t^d = q_t^s.$$

(*a*) Is this system statically stable if $\beta < 0$ and $\delta > 0$?

(*b*) Show that

$$p_t = (p^0 - \bar{p})\left(\frac{\delta}{\beta}\right)^t + \bar{p}.$$

(*c*) Under what conditions is this system dynamically stable?

(*d*) Under what conditions will there arise explosive oscillations?

8. Consider the following cobweb model with stock adjustment:

$$q_t^d = a + \beta p_t$$
$$q_t^s = \gamma + \delta p_{t-1}$$
$$p_t = p_{t-1} - \lambda(S_{t-1} - S_{t-2}) \qquad \lambda > 0$$

(*a*) Explain why $S_{t-1} - S_{t-2} = q_{t-1}^s - q_{t-1}^d$ where S_t denotes stocks at the end of period t. Hence show that

$$p_t = (1 + \lambda\beta)p_{t-1} - \lambda\delta p_{t-2} + \lambda(a - \gamma).$$

(*b*) Show that equilibrium is still $\bar{p} = (\gamma - a)/(\beta - \delta)$ but that stability now depends upon the characteristic roots

$$b_1, b_2 = \tfrac{1}{2}[(1 + \lambda\beta) \pm \sqrt{(1 + \lambda\beta)^2 - 4\lambda\delta}\,].$$

(*c*) Discuss in what way this model differs in its predictions from that in Exercise 7.

9. Consider the system

$$q^d = 12p^{-1}$$
$$q^s = 2 + 2p$$
$$\frac{dp}{dt} = kz(p) \qquad k > 0.$$

Show that the only economically meaningful equilibrium price is $\bar{p} = 2$. Show that $\frac{1}{2}\dot{V}(p - \bar{p}) = -6k(p - 2)^2$ and hence establish whether the system is asymptotically globally stable or not.

10. Consider the system

$$q^d = 12p^{-1/2}$$

$$q^s = 2p$$

$$\frac{dp}{dt} = kz(p) \qquad k > 0.$$

Show that $\frac{1}{2}\dot{V}(p - \bar{p}) = -3k(p - \bar{p})^2$ and hence establish whether the system is asymptotically globally stable or not.

NOTES

CHAPTER 1

1. This view of 'successive approximation' has been forcefully argued by the late Lord Russell. B. Russell [106].
2. See, for example, C. G. Hempel [50].
3. This is further elaborated in Section 1.2(i).
4. The classification of the first kind has to my knowledge only been discussed in detail by N. Georgescu-Roegen [43, pp. 6–8]. The classification of the second kind has a long history.
5. The P_α set is the interpretation Koopmans gives to *postulates* [69, p. 132].
6. This interpretation is also held by K. Popper [10, p. 72].
7. See E. Nagel [88, pp. 92–4]; and E. Parzen [94, pp. 17–18].
8. Note that the correspondence is not unique, the classical school take $p(A)$ to be the degree of belief that A will occur. This gives rise to an alternative correspondence to that of the frequency school.
9. On operationalism in economics see D. F. Gordon [45].
10. See the discussion in P. Newman [90, pp. 10–11].
11. The α-class ideally is composed of the minimum number of fundamental propositions. One could conceive of convexity belonging to P_β being based on two or more fundamental propositions in P_α. But if two of the P_αs can be replaced by a single proposition then this is desirable.
12. But see the section below entitled 'Introduction of a γ-class'.
13. Scientific method can be considered as the general principles of procedure according to which scientific results are established and constantly revised. See, for example, M. R. Cohen [25].
14. For example, the discussions on the theory of the firm – whether it is behavioural or marginal, etc. See F. Machlup [81].
15. The analysis of Lionel Robbins [104, pp. 99–100] is consistent with this formulation.
16. The new-formed class would correspond to the ω-class of Georgescu-Roegen [43, p. 7].
17. There have been propositions stated in economic analysis which are impossible of refutation. The student should be careful to see these and eliminate them since they can never aid our understanding or further our knowledge.
18. Kepler's dissatisfaction with the error of up to 8′ between the hypothesised value and recordings of Tycho de Brahe of the planet Mars illustrates the exactness and small error which has been demanded by scientists. Kepler's

rejection of this error led to his laws of planetary motion. See A. Koestler [66].

19. In this respect statistical testing based on 5 and 1 per cent significance levels are purely arbitrary, and it is really up to the investigator, from his experience, to specify the tolerance he believes is permissible.

CHAPTER 2

1. See Section 8.6 below on free goods.

2. In mathematics a distinction is made between the *domain* and the *range* of a mapping $f\colon \mathbf{X} \rightarrow \mathbf{Y}$. f is a function if and only if for any $\mathbf{x} \in \mathbf{X}$ there is a unique $\mathbf{y} \in \mathbf{Y}$. The set $\mathbf{X}$ is referred to as the *domain* of the function f while the set $\mathbf{Y}$ is referred to as the *range*. Also the *image* of the function f, denoted $f(\mathbf{X})$, is the set of points in the range satisfying

$$f(\mathbf{X}) = \{\mathbf{y} \in \mathbf{Y}/\mathbf{y} = f(\mathbf{x}) \text{ for some } \mathbf{x} \in \mathbf{X}\}.$$

If the image is a proper subset of the range then the mapping is *into*, whilst if the image set is the same as the range then the mapping is *onto*.

3. Notice that asymmetry implies anti-symmetry but not conversely.

4. The relation R meaning 'at least preferred to' is reflexive, transitive, and complete and consequently gives rise to a complete quasi-ordering or weak ordering.

5. The axioms in this section follow closely those of V. C. Walsh [123].

6. See p. 51 for a strict definition of boundedness; and p. 50 for definitions of closed and open sets.

7. This section employs concepts which are expounded on more fully in Chapter 3.

8. This definition will have more meaning after the student has read Section 3.3 of Chapter 3.

9. For those readers familiar with Baumol's sales maximisation hypothesis [12, 15], it may be thought that the constraints do alter because of the choice of preference function since Baumol introduced a minimum profit constraint. This is not so. The introduction of a minimum profit constraint is in addition to, and not because of, the choice of preference function. This additional constraint falls into the γ-class referred to in Chapter 1.

10. We shall answer this below, Section 4.6.

CHAPTER 3

1. In two-dimensional space the non-negative orthant is the positive quadrant, including the origin. In n-dimensional space it is defined by the set $\mathbf{X} = \{\mathbf{x}/x_i \geqslant 0 \, \forall i\}$. Also there is a particular reason why we have written $\mathbf{X}$ rather than the more usual $\mathbf{X}^n$ which denoted the dimension of the space. In Chapters 8 and 9 when we come to aggregate demand and allocations of m consumers we reserve $\mathbf{X}^k$ to denote the consumption set of the kth consumer where $\mathbf{X}^k$ belongs to an n-dimensional space. Similarly $\mathbf{K}$ in Axiom 8 denotes a set of which $\mathbf{X}$ is a subset rather than writing $\mathbf{X}^k$.

2. We remind the reader we are using the following convention: $[a, b]$ is an interval *including* the points a, b; (a, b) is the interval excluding the points a and b; whilst $(a, b]$ and $[a, b)$ excludes from the interval a and b respectively, but includes b and a respectively.

3. See note 2 of Chapter 2 for an explanation of the terms 'domain', 'range' and 'mapping'. Continuity is discussed in Section 5.6 of Chapter 5.

4. The advanced student will find a proof of these theorems in H. Nikaido [92, ch. 1.2]. The student may also find it useful to consult J. C. Burkill and H. Burkill [20, ch. 3.6].

5. The reader is reminded of the convention we are employing concerning vector inequalities. Those in use are $\mathbf{x} \geqslant \mathbf{y}$, $\mathbf{x} > \mathbf{y}$ and $\mathbf{x} \gg \mathbf{y}$.

6. The two formulations of the attainable sets are:

(1) $p_1x_1 + p_2x_2 = y$, where p_1 and p_2 are given prices and y is income.

$$\mathbf{A} = \{(x_1, x_2)/p_1x_1 + p_2x_2 = y; x_1 \geqslant 0, x_2 \geqslant 0\}.$$

(2) $p_1x_1 + p_2x_2 \leqslant y$

$$\mathbf{A} = \{(x_1, x_2)/p_1x_1 + p_2x_2 \leqslant y; x_1 \geqslant 0, x_2 \geqslant 0\}.$$

7. Such indifference curves have been drawn by Edgeworth and more recently by K. Boulding [18, p. 605].

8. Throughout this book vectors will be written as column vectors and the transpose of $\mathbf{x}$ will be written $\mathbf{x}'$, thus $\partial f/\partial \mathbf{x}$ is a column vector.

9. Weight can be measured in lb. or grams, and the transformation of one into the other is of the form $y = bx$, where b is a multiplicative positive constant. Temperature can be measured, say, in either Centigrade or Fahrenheit, the transformation being of the form $F = 32^\circ + (9/5)C^\circ$, i.e. $y = a + bx$, which is a linear transformation. This latter transformation implies ratios are preserved, which implies the degree of change in intensity can be measured. This is true for temperature, but we must rule this out for utility. On these points the student should consult the lucid article by A. A. Alchian [2].

10. This result is obtained by totally differentiating $-dx_2/dx_1$ with respect to x_1.

11. See G. J. Stigler [118].

12. It is called direct to distinguish it from the indirect form discussed by Houthakker [57].

CHAPTER 4

1. The reader is reminded that $\mathbf{u}_x = \partial u/\partial \mathbf{x}$ is a column vector and $\partial \mathbf{u}_x/\partial \mathbf{x}'$ means you take each element in turn in the vector $\mathbf{u}_x$ and partially differentiate it with respect to each commodity, writing the result as a row vector, the rows then being stacked in the order they were differentiated. It may be helpful to think of $\partial \mathbf{u}_x/\partial \mathbf{x}'$ as

$$\begin{bmatrix} \partial u_1/\partial x_1' \\ \cdot \\ \cdot \\ \cdot \\ \partial u_n/\partial x_n' \end{bmatrix}.$$

On matrix differentiation see Johnston [60, ch. 4].

2. See R. G. D. Allen [4, ch. 14].
3. See the discussion of aggregate demand, Chapter 8.
4. The inverse of a partitioned matrix:

$$\begin{bmatrix} \mathbf{A} & \mathbf{B} \\ \mathbf{C} & \mathbf{D} \end{bmatrix},$$

where $\mathbf{A}$ is a square non-singular matrix, is given by:

$$\begin{bmatrix} \mathbf{A} & \mathbf{B} \\ \mathbf{C} & \mathbf{D} \end{bmatrix}^{-1} = \begin{bmatrix} \mathbf{A}^{-1} + \mathbf{A}^{-1}\mathbf{B}(\mathbf{D}-\mathbf{C}\mathbf{A}^{-1}\mathbf{B})^{-1}\mathbf{C}\mathbf{A}^{-1} & -\mathbf{A}^{-1}\mathbf{B}(\mathbf{D}-\mathbf{C}\mathbf{A}^{-1}\mathbf{B})^{-1} \\ -(\mathbf{D}-\mathbf{C}\mathbf{A}^{-1}\mathbf{B})^{-1}\mathbf{C}\mathbf{A}^{-1} & (\mathbf{D}-\mathbf{C}\mathbf{A}^{-1}\mathbf{B})^{-1} \end{bmatrix}.$$

5. A circumflex above a vector denotes a matrix which is diagonal and whose diagonal elements are those of the vector concerned.
6. This is proved by using the Schwartz inequality. Since $\mathbf{U}^{-1}$ is non-singular and symmetrical then there exists a matrix $\mathbf{B}$ such that $\mathbf{B}'\mathbf{B} = \mathbf{U}^{-1}$. Thus

$$[(\mathbf{q}'\mathbf{U}^{-1}\mathbf{q})(\mathbf{p}'\mathbf{U}^{-1}\mathbf{p}) - (\mathbf{q}'\mathbf{U}^{-1}\mathbf{p})^2] = (\mathbf{q}'\mathbf{B}'\mathbf{B}\mathbf{q})(\mathbf{p}'\mathbf{B}'\mathbf{B}\mathbf{p}) - (\mathbf{q}'\mathbf{B}'\mathbf{B}\mathbf{p})^2.$$

Let $\mathbf{u} = \mathbf{B}\mathbf{q}$ and $\mathbf{v} = \mathbf{B}\mathbf{p}$ then we have for the term in brackets:

$$(\mathbf{u}'\mathbf{u})(\mathbf{v}'\mathbf{v}) - (\mathbf{u}'\mathbf{v})^2 = \|\mathbf{u}\|\,\|\mathbf{v}\| - (\mathbf{u}'\mathbf{v})^2.$$

But from the Schwartz inequality we have $|\mathbf{u}'\mathbf{v}| \leqslant \|\mathbf{u}\|\,\|\mathbf{v}\|$. Hence

$$(\mathbf{u}'\mathbf{v})^2 \leqslant \|\mathbf{u}\|^2\,\|\mathbf{v}\|^2.$$

Hence

$$[(\mathbf{q}'\mathbf{U}^{-1}\mathbf{q})(\mathbf{p}'\mathbf{U}^{-1}\mathbf{p}) - (\mathbf{q}'\mathbf{U}^{-1}\mathbf{p})^2] \geqslant 0.$$

For $\mathbf{q} \neq c\mathbf{p}$ the strict inequality holds.

7. The reader may care to reflect back on the petrol shortage of 1974 when ration books in the United Kingdom were issued, but never used. Discussions on rationing occurred after the Second World War and the interested reader may usefully consult Samuelson [107, pp. 163–71], Tobin [120] and McManus [80].

CHAPTER 5

1. This section follows that of Walsh [123].
2. Walsh [123, p. 226].
3. $-\Omega = \{\mathbf{x} \mid x_i \leqslant 0, \forall i\}$.
4. In terms of the mathematics of convex cones, the cone $\mathbf{Y}_j$ in Fig. 5.2 is a pointed cone with vertex at 0.
5. In Chapters 9 and 10 we denote this set $\hat{\mathbf{Y}}$, the circumflex indicating that the outputs are bounded by the given inputs.
6. Suitable treatments will be found in D. Gale [42, ch. 2]; R. G. D. Allen [4].
7. This is closely associated with the theorem of separating hyperplanes and the Minkowski theorem. See Gale [42, pp. 44–6]; Roberts and Shultz [105, pp. 39–42].
8. This is basically taken from Debreu [30, pp. 38–9].
9. Those interested in which of the axioms concerning $\mathbf{Y}_j$ imply properties of $\mathbf{Y}$ may consult Debreu [30, pp. 39–42].
10. In this instance the profit function is defined $\pi_j(\mathbf{p}) = \sup_{\mathbf{y}_j \in \mathbf{Y}_j} \mathbf{p}'\mathbf{y}_j$.
11. An exception arises when we take account of resource constraints. In this case the production set $\mathbf{Y}_j$ is a finite convex set, which we shall call a *truncated production set.* When there is constant returns to scale we have a truncated convex cone. In the presence of such truncated cones the production sets are always bounded from above.
12. The concept of semi-continuity is due to R. Baire, *Annali di Mat.* (3A), III (1899).

CHAPTER 6

1. This section has been inspired by the brief section in Arrow and Hahn [10, pp. 54–5]. It has been called Ricardian because it is reminiscent of the labour theory of value which lies behind much of Ricardo's analysis, but also because it is the underlying basis of his theory of international trade. Pasanetti, however, in his mathematisation of Ricardo's model of growth and distribution gives wheat a

non-linear production function and gold a linear production function. See Pasanetti [95].

2. The notation has been so chosen that we can generalise immediately without bringing in any new subscripts.

3. A number of writers define **A** in gross terms so that $a_{ii} \neq 0$ and denotes the amount of good i used in the production of good i, e.g. the coal required for fuel to obtain coal from the pit face. The two approaches differ particularly in obtaining the characteristic roots of **A**, but one only needs to be careful on interpretation.

4. Given we have $\mathbf{B}\mathbf{x} = 0$, this holds trivially if $x_i = 0$ for all i. For a non-trivial solution of $x_i \geqslant 0$ for all i and at least one $x_i > 0$ we require $|\mathbf{B}| = 0$. See Hadley [47, pp. 173–8].

5. For a discussion on characteristic roots see Hadley [47, ch. 7].

6. This result has important implications from the point of view of computation.

7. *N.I.E.* 1971, table 19.

8. For proofs of the substitution theorem see Samuelson [109], Koopmans [68], Arrow [6] and Gale [42]. The proof by Gale is more elegant than the earlier proofs but it does require a knowledge of linear programming.

9. See Dorfman *et al.* [31, chs 9 and 10].

CHAPTER 7

1. See R. G. D. Allen [4, p. 478]; and Intriligator [59, ch. 8].

2. This is taken from Whitaker and McCallum [126, p. 58].

3. Homothetic functions also play a role in consumer demand. In Chapter 8.4 we demonstrate a result of consumer demand which does not require identical Engel curves but only the requirement that the preference function is homothetic.

4. This is true of the pure sciences in particular. Chemistry, for example, has recently gone through some changes by posing certain problems in a way which allows the application of group theory. This has led to a number of new insights.

CHAPTER 8

1. Independence in the sense used here must imply that trading only takes place at equilibrium. With all other goods in equilibrium the consumer has only, say, $\bar{y} - \sum_i p_i x_i$ to spend on good 1 so that equilibrium must be at this level of expenditure, unless the demand curve has unit elasticity *and* expenditure is always $\bar{y} - \sum_i p_i x_i$.

2. We shall use throughout the next few chapters the convention of a bar above a variable to denote competitive equilibrium and an asterisk after a variable to denote a Pareto-optimal point. The former should give no confusion with variables held constant.

3. We shall not attempt to prove these theorems although the mathematically inclined student may consult Courant and Robbins [26] for a simplified proof of Brouwer's fixed-point theorem and to Kakutani's original paper [62]. See also Arrow and Hahn [10, appendix C.4].

CHAPTER 9

1. We remind the reader that subscripts refer to commodities, superscripts to individuals and we shall prime bundles when we are refering to alternatives in the commodity space. Also note that standard **x** refers to commodities whilst cursive $\mathscr{X}$ refers to allocations.

2. Sometimes the literature uses contract curve and efficiency locus synonymously; however, it is more useful in the discussion of exchange to distinguish efficient *trades* from all other efficient points.

3. This example is taken from a delightful little book by E. Roy Weintraub [125, ch. 2].

4. This section follows that of Intriligator [59].

5. See Allen [4] and Gale [42].

CHAPTER 11

1. If $f(x)$ is continuous and single-valued then $\dfrac{dx}{dy} = 1/\dfrac{dy}{dx}$.

2. The Lipschitz condition plays a prominent role in discussions of demand theory, in particular the conditions under which the integrability conditions are satisfied. See Chipman *et al.* [25], particularly the article by Uzawa [121].

3. The Lyapunov function was first discussed in Russian *c.* 1907, later translated into French and only entered the English-speaking world after the Second World War.

4. The Lyapunov function is becoming prominent also in discussions of economic growth models, e.g. Burmeister and Dobel [21].

5. See Ince [58, pp. 62–3].

6. Given two vectors **u** and **v** the Schwartz inequality states that

$$|\mathbf{u}'\mathbf{v}| \leqslant \|\mathbf{u}\| \, \|\mathbf{v}\|.$$

7. See Arrow and Hahn [10, ch. 11].

8. $\mathbf{Z}_p^* = \dfrac{\partial f[z(\mathbf{p})]}{\partial \mathbf{p}'}$ and it is to be distinguished from $\mathbf{Z}_{\bar{p}} = \dfrac{\partial z(\bar{\mathbf{p}})}{\partial \mathbf{p}'}$. If, however,

$$f[z(\mathbf{p})] = \hat{k}z(\mathbf{p}) \text{ then } \mathbf{Z}_p^* = \hat{k}\mathbf{Z}_p.$$

9. Some work on non-tatonnement adjustment processes will be found in Hahn and Negishi [48].

BIBLIOGRAPHY

1. Afriat, S. A. (1966), *Economic Transformation.* Krannert Institute, Paper No. 152, Purdue University, Nov. 1966.

2. Alchian, A. (1953),'The Meaning of Utility Measurement', *American Economic Review,* vol. 43 (Mar 1953) pp. 26–50. Reprinted in W. Breit and H. M. Hochman (eds), *Readings in Microeconomics,* ch. 5, pp. 69–88.

3. Allen, R. G. D. (1938), *Mathematical Analysis for Economists.* London, Macmillan.

4. Allen, R. G. D. (1956), *Mathematical Economics,* 2nd ed. 1959. Macmillan.

5. Arrow, K. J. (1950), 'An Extension of the Basic Theorems of Classical Welfare Economics' in J. Neyman (1950) (ed.), *Proceedings of the Second Berkeley Symposium on Mathematical Statistics and Probability,* pp. 507–32. Reprinted in P. Newman (ed.) (1968), *Readings in Mathematical Economics,* vol. 1.

6. Arrow, K. J. (1951), 'Alternative Proof of the Substitution Theorem for Leontief Models in the General Case', in T. C. Koopmans (1951) (ed.), *Activity Analysis of Production and Allocation.* Cowles Commission Monograph 13. New York, Wiley.

7. Arrow, K. J. (1951), *Social Choice and Individual Values,* 2nd ed. 1963. Yale University Press.

8. Arrow, K. J. (1968), 'Economic Equilibrium', *International Encyclopedia of the Social Sciences,* vol. 4, pp. 376–86. Macmillan Co. of New York and The Free Press.

9. Arrow, K. J. (1964), *Aspects of the Theory of Risk-Bearing.* Helsinki, The Academic Book Store, 1965.

10. Arrow, K. J., and F. H. Hahn (1971), *General Competitive Analysis.* Edinburgh, Oliver & Boyd.

11. Barten, A. P. (1964), 'Consumer Demand Functions Under Conditions of Almost Additive Preferences', *Econometrica,* vol. 32, pp. 1–38.

12. Baumol, W. J. (1959), *Business Behaviour, Value and Growth,* revised ed. 1967. New York, Harcourt, Brace & World Inc.

13. Baumol, W. J. (1951), 'The Neumann–Morgenstern Utility Index – An Ordinalist View', *Journal of Political Economy,* vol. 59, pp. 61–6.

14. Baumol, W. J. (1958), 'The Cardinal Utility which is Ordinal', *Economic Journal,* vol. 68, pp. 665–72.

15. Baumol, W. J. (1958), 'On the Theory of Oligopoly', *Economica,* vol. 25, pp. 187–98.

16. Becker, G. S. (1962), 'Irrational Behaviour and Economic Theory', *Journal of Political Economy,* vol. 70, pp. 1–13.

17. Bilas, R. A. (1967), *Microeconomic Theory,* 2nd ed. 1971. New York, McGraw-Hill.

18. Boulding, K. E. (1941), *Economic Analysis,* 4th ed. 1966, vol. 1, *Microeconomics,* vol. 2, *Macroeconomics.* New York, Harper & Row.

19. Brown, A., and A. Deaton (1972), 'Models of Consumer Behaviour: A Survey', *Economic Journal,* vol. 82, pp. 1145–1236.

20. Burkill, J. C., and H. Burkill (1970), *A Second Course in Mathematical Analysis.* London, Cambridge University Press.

21. Burmeister, E., and A. R. Dobell (1970), *Mathematical Theories of Economic Growth.* London, Macmillan.

22. Chiang, A. C. (1967), *Fundamental Methods of Mathematical Economics.* New York, McGraw-Hill.

23. Chipman, J. S., *et al.* (1971), *Preferences, Utility, and Demand.* A Minnesota Symposium. New York, Harcourt Brace Jovanovich Inc.

24. Chipman, J. S. (1971), 'Consumption Theory without Transitive Preferences', in L. J. S. Chipman *et al.* (1971) (eds), *Preferences, Utility, and Demand,* ch. 11. New York, Harcourt Brace Jovanovich Inc.

25. Cohen, M. R. (1931), *Reason and Nature,* 2nd ed. 1953. London, Collier-Macmillan.

26. Courant, R., and H. Robbins (1941), *What is Mathematics?* Oxford University Press.

27. Davidson, D., and P. Suppes (1956), 'A Finitistic Axiomatization of Subjective Probability and Utility', *Econometrica,* vol. 24, pp. 264–75.

28. Debreu, G. (1958), 'Stochastic Choice and Cardinal Utility', *Econometrica,* vol. 26, pp. 440–4.

29. Debreu, G. (1959), 'Topological Methods in Cardinal Utility Theory', in K. J. Arrow *et al., Mathematical Methods in the Social Sciences 1959.* Stanford University Press.

30. Debreu, G. (1959), *Theory of Value: An Axiomatic Analysis of Economic Equilibrium.* Yale University Press.

31. Dorfman, R., P. Samuelson and R. Solow (1958), *Linear Programming Analysis.* New York, McGraw-Hill.

32. Duesenberry, J. S. (1949), *Income, Saving and the Theory of Consumer Behaviour.* New York, Galaxy Book, Oxford University Press 1967. Originally published by Harvard University Press, Cambridge, U.S.A.

33. Edgeworth, F. Y. (1881), *Mathematical Psychics.* London, Kegan Paul.

34. Edwards, W. (1954), 'The Theory of Decision Making', *The Psychological Bulletin,* vol. 51, no. 4, pp. 380–417. Also in V. Edwards and A. Tversky (1967) (eds), *Decision Making.* London, Penguin.

35. Edwards, W. (1961), 'Behavioural Decision Theory', *Annual Review of Psychology,* vol. 12, pp. 473–98. Reprinted in W. Edwards, and A. Tversky (1967) (eds), *Decision Making.* London, Penguin.

36. Ellsburg, D. (1954), 'Classical and Current Notions of Measurable Utility', *Economic Journal,* vol. 64, pp. 528–56. Reprinted in A. N. Page (1968) (ed.), *Utility Theory: A Book of Readings.* London, John Wiley.

37. Ferguson, C. E. (1966), (revised ed.) *Microeconomic Theory.* Homewood, Illinois, Richard D. Irwin, Inc.

38. Ferguson, C. E. (1969), *The Neoclassical Theory of Production and Distribution.* Cambridge University Press.

39. Friedman, M. (1953), *Essays in Positive Economics.* Chicago, University of Chicago Press, Phoenix ed. 1966.

40. Friedman, M. (1953), 'The Methodology of Positive Economics', in *Essays in Positive Economics* (1966), pp. 3–43. Reprinted in W. Breit and H. M. Hochman (1968) (eds), *Readings in Microeconomics*, ch. 2, pp. 23–47.

41. Frisch, R. (1959), 'A Complete Scheme for Computing All Direct and Cross Demand Elasticities in a Model with Many Sectors', *Econometrica,* vol. 27, pp. 177–96. Reprinted in A. Zellner (1968) (ed.), *Readings in Economic Statistics and Econometrics*. New York, Little, Brown & Co.

42. Gale, D. (1960), *Theory of Linear Economic Models.* New York, McGraw-Hill.

43. Georgescu-Roegan, N. (1966), *Analytical Economics: Issues and Problems.* Cambridge, Mass., Harvard University Press.

44. Goldberger, A. S. (1967), *Functional Form and Utility: A Review of Consumer Demand Theory.* Social Science Research Institute, University of Wisconsin, Systems Formulation, Methodology, and Policy Workshop Paper 6703.

45. Gordon, D. F. (1955), 'Operational Propositions in Economic Theory', *Journal of Political Economy,* vol. 63, pp. 750–61. Reprinted in W. Breit and H. M. Hochman (1968) (eds.), *Readings in Microeconomics,* ch. 3, pp. 48–59.

46. Graaff, J. de V. (1957), *Theoretical Welfare Economics.* Cambridge University Press.

47. Hadley, G. (1961), *Linear Algebra.* Addison-Wesley Publishing Co. Inc.

48. Hahn, F. H., and T. Negishi (1962), 'A Theorem in Non-Tatonnement Stability', *Econometrica,* vol. 30, pp. 463–9.

49. Hawkins, D., and H. A. Simon (1949), 'Note: Some Conditions of Macroeconomic Stability', *Econometrica,* vol. 17, pp. 245–8.

50. Hempel, C. G. (1945), 'On the Nature of Mathematical Truth', *American Mathematical Monthly,* vol. 52. Reprinted in H. Feigl and W. Sellars (1949) (eds) *Readings in Philosophical Analysis* pp. 222–37.

51. Herstein, I. N., and J. Milnor (1953), 'An Axiomatic Approach to Measurable Utility', *Econometrica,* vol. 21, pp 291–7. Also in P. Newman (1968), *Readings in Mathematical Economics,* vol. I. Baltimore, Johns Hopkins Press.

52. Hicks, J. R. (1939) *Value and Capital,* 2nd ed. 1946. Oxford University Press.

53. Hicks, J. R., and R. G. D. Allen (1934), 'A Reconsideration of the Theory of Value', *Economica,* vol. 1, pp. 52–76 and 196–219.

54. H.M.S.O. (1971), *National Income and Expenditure.*

55. Holtermann, S. E. (1972), 'Externalities and Public Goods', *Economica,* vol. 39, pp. 78–87.

56. Houthakker, H. S. (1950), 'Revealed Preference and the Utility Function', *Economica,* vol. 17, pp. 159–74.

57. Houthakker, H. S. (1960), 'Additive Preferences', *Econometrica,* vol. 28, pp. 244–57. Reprinted in A. Zellner (1968) (ed.), *Readings in Economic Statistics and Econometrics.* Boston, Little, Brown & Co.

58. Ince, E. L. (1927), *Ordinary Differential Equations.* London, Longmans.

59. Intriligator, M. D. (1971), *Mathematical Optimisation and Economic Theory.* London, Prentice-Hall.

60. Johnston, J. (1963), *Econometric Methods,* 2nd ed. 1972. New York, McGraw-Hill.

61. Jorgenson, D. W. (1960), 'A Dual Stability Theorem', *Econometrica,* vol. 28, pp. 892–9.

62. Kakutani, S. (1941), 'A Generalization of Brouwer's Fixed-Point Theorem', *Duke Mathematical Journal,* vol. 9, pp. 457–9. Reprinted in P. Newman (1968) (ed.), *Readings in Mathematical Economics,* vol. I, *Value Theory,* Baltimore, Johns Hopkins Press.

63. Kaldor, N. (1939), 'Welfare Propositions in Economics and Interpersonal Comparisons of Utility', *Economic Journal,* vol. 49, pp. 549–52.

64. Kaldor, N. (1972), 'The Irrelevance of Equilibrium Economics', *Economic Journal,* vol. 82, pp. 1237–55.

65. Kalman, P. (1968), 'Theory of Consumer Behaviour when Prices enter the Utility Function', *Econometrica,* vol. 36, pp. 497–510.

66. Koestler, A. (1959), *The Sleepwalkers.* London, Penguin (1964). Reissued in Pelican Books (1968).

67. Koopmans, T. C. (1951*a*), *Activity Analysis of Production and Allocation.* New York, Wiley.

68. Koopmans, T. C. (1951*b*), 'Analysis of Production as an Efficient Combination of Activities', ch. III of T. C. Koopmans (ed.), *Activity Analysis of Production and Allocation.* Cowles Commission Monograph 13. New York, Wiley.

69. Koopmans, T. C. (1957), *Three Essays on the State of Economic Science.* London, McGraw-Hill.

70. Kuhn, T. S. (1962), *The Structure of Scientific Revolutions.* Chicago, University of Chicago Press.

71. Kuhn, A. W., and A. W. Tucker (1950), 'Nonlinear Programming', in J. Neyman (ed.), *Proceedings of the Second Berkeley Symposium on Mathematical Statistics and Probability,* pp. 481–92. Reprinted in P. Newman (1968) (ed.), *Readings in Mathematical Economics,* vol. 1, ch. 1. Baltimore, Johns Hopkins Press.

72. Lamberton, D. M. (1971) (ed.), *Economics of Information and Knowledge.* London, Penguin.

73. Lancaster, K. (1968), *Mathematical Economics.* New York, Macmillan Company of New York.

74. Leontief, W. (1937), 'Implicit Theorizing: A Methodological Criticism of the Neo-Cambridge School', *Quarterly Journal of Economics,* vol. 51, pp. 337–51. Also in W. Leontief (1966), *Essays in Economics. Theories and Theorizing.* Oxford University Press.

75. Leontief, W. (1966), *Essays in Economics: Theories and Theorizing.* Oxford University Press.

76. Lipsey R. G. (1963), *An Introduction to Positive Economics,* 3rd ed. 1971. London, Weidenfeld & Nicolson.

77. Lipsey, R. G., and K. Lancaster (1956–7), 'The General Theory of the Second Best', *Review of Economic Studies,* vol. 24, pp. 11–32.

78. Luce, R. D. (1959), *Individual Choice Behaviour. A Theoretical Analysis.* New York, Wiley.

79. McKenzie, L. (1960), 'Matrices with Dominant Diagonals and Economic Theory', in K. J. Arrow *et al.* (eds), *Mathematical Methods in the Social Sciences,* 1959. California, Stanford University.

80. McManus, M. (1945–6), 'The Geometry of Point Rationing', *Review of Economic Studies,* vol. 22, pp. 1–14.

81. Machlup, F. (1967), 'Theories of the Firm: Marginalist, Behavioural, Managerial', *American Economic Review,* vol. LVII, no. 1, pp. 1–33.

82. Marschak, J. (1950), 'Rational Behaviour, Uncertainty, Prospects, and Measurable Utility', *Econometrica,* vol. 18, pp. 111–41.

83. Marshall, A. (1890), *Principles of Economics,* 8th ed. 1920. London, Macmillan, Papermac.

84. May, K. (1954), 'Transitivity, Utility and Aggregation in Preference Theory', *Econometrica,* vol. 22, pp. 1–13.

85. Metzler, L. A. (1945), 'Stability of Multiple Markets: The Hicks Conditions, *Econometrica,* vol. 13, pp. 277–92. Reprinted in P. Newman (1968) (ed.), *Readings in Mathematical Economics,* vol. I. Baltimore, Johns Hopkins Press.

86. Morishima, M. (1952), 'Consumer's Behaviour and Liquidity Preference', *Econometrica,* vol. 20, pp. 223–46.

87. Mosteller, F., and P. Nogee (1951), 'An Experimental Measurement of Utility', *Journal of Political Economy,* vol. 59, no. 5, pp. 371–404. Also in W. Edwards and A. Tversky, *Decision Making.* London, Penguin.

88. Nagel, E. (1961), *The Structure of Science.* London, Routledge & Kegan Paul.

89. Newmann, J. von, and O. Morgenstern (1944), *Theory of Games and Economic Behavior,* 3rd ed. 1953. Princeton University Press.

90. Newman, P. (1965), *The Theory of Exchange.* New Jersey, Prentice-Hall.

91. Newman, P. (1968) (ed.), *Readings in Mathematical Economics*, vol. I, *Value Theory.* Baltimore, Johns Hopkins Press.

92. Nikaido, H. (1968), *Convex Structures and Economic Theory,* vol. 51. London, Academic Press.

93. Page, A. N. (1968) (ed.), *Utility Theory: A Book of Readings.* London, Wiley.

94. Parzen, E. (1960), *Modern Probability Theory and its Applications.* London, Wiley.

95. Pasinetti, L. L. (1960), 'A Mathematical Formulation of the Ricardian System', *Review of Economic Studies,* vol. 27, pp. 78–98.

96. Patinkin, D. (1956), *Money, Interest, and Prices,* 2nd ed. 1965. London, Harper & Row.

97. Pearce, I. F. (1964), *A Contribution to Demand Analysis.* Oxford, Clarendon Press.

98. Pearce, I. F. (1970), *International Trade.* London, Macmillan.

99. Phelps, E. S. (1973), *Economic Justice.* London, Penguin. Readings in Economic Justice.

100. Plott, C. R. (1971) 'Recent Results in the Theory of Voting', in M. D. Intriligator (ed.), *Frontiers of Quantitative Economics*. Amsterdam, North-Holland.

101. Popper, K. (1934), *The Logic of Scientific Discovery*, English ed. 1959, rev. ed. *Discover* 1968. London, Hutchinson.

102. Quirk, J., and R. Saposnik (1968), *Introduction to General Equilibrium Theory and Welfare Economics.* New York, McGraw-Hill.

103. Richter, M. K. (1971), 'Rational Choice', in J. S. Chipman *et al.* (1971) (eds), *Preferences, Utility, and Demand.* New York, Harcourt Brace Jovanovich Inc.

104. Robbins, L. (1932), *An Essay on the Nature and Significance of Economic Science,* 2nd ed. 1935. London, Macmillan.

105. Roberts, B., and D. L. Schulze (1973), *Modern Mathematics and Economic Analysis.* New York, Norton & Co. Inc.

106. Russell, B. (1918), (Penguin 1953), *Mysticism and Logic*. London, Penguin.

107. Samuelson, P. A. (1947), *Foundations of Economic Analysis.* Harvard University Press. Harvard Economic Studies, LXXX.

108. Samuelson, P. A. (1949), *Economics,* 9th ed. 1973. New York, McGraw-Hill.

109. Samuelson, P. A. (1951), 'Abstract of a Theorem Concerning Substitutability in Open Leontief Models', in T. C. Koopmans (ed.), *Activity Analysis of Production and Allocation.* Cowles Commission Monograph 13. New York, Wiley.

110. Samuelson, P. A. (1954), 'The Pure Theory of Public Expenditure', *Review of Economics and Statistics,* vol. 36, pp. 387–9. Reprinted in R. W. Houghton (1970) (ed.), *Penguin Readings in Public Finance.*

111. Sen, A. K. (1970), *Collective Choice and Social Welfare.* London, Oliver & Boyd. Mathematical Economics Texts No. 5.

112. Sen, A. K. (1973), 'Balance and the Concept of Preference', *Economica,* vol. XL, no. 159, pp. 241–59.

113. Shapley, L. S., and M. Shubik (1967), 'Concepts and Theories of Pure Competition', in M. Shubik (ed.), *Essays in Mathematical Economics. Essays in Honor of Oskar Morgenstern*. Princeton University Press.

114. Simmons, G. F. (1963), *Introduction to Topology and Modern Analysis.* New York, McGraw-Hill.

115. Simmons, P. J. (1974), *Choice and Demand.* London, Macmillan.

116. Slutsky, E. E. (1915), 'On the Theory of the Budget of the Consumer', *Giornale degli Economisti,* vol. LI, pp. 1–26. Reprinted in *Readings in Price Theory,* ch. 2, pp. 27–56.

117. Sonnenschein, H. F. (1971), 'Demand Theory without Transitive Preferences. With Applications to the Theory of Competitive Equilibrium', in J. S. Chipman *et al.* (eds), *Preferences, Utility, and Demand,* ch. 10. New York, Harcourt Brace Jovanovich Inc..

118. Stigler, G. J. (1950), 'The Development of Utility Theory', *Journal of Political Economy,* vol. LVIII, pp. 307–27, 373–96. Reprinted in A. N. Page (1968) (ed.), *Utility Theory: A Book of Readings.* London, Wiley.

119. Theil, H. (1967), *Economics and Information Theory.* Amsterdam, North-Holland Publishing Co.

120. Tobin, J. (1952), 'A Survey of the Theory of Rationing', *Econometrica,* vol. 20, no. 4, pp. 521–35.

121. Uzawa, H. (1959), 'Preferences and Rational Choice in the Theory of Consumption', in K. J. Arrow *et al., Mathematical Methods in the Social Sciences.* Also an adapted version in J. S. Chipman *et al.* (1971), *Preferences, Utility, and Demand.* A Minnesota Symposium. New York, Harcourt Brace Jovanovich Inc.

122. Veblen, T. (1899), *The Theory of the Leisure Class.* London, Macmillan.

123. Walsh, V. C. (1970), *Introduction to Contemporary Microeconomics.* London, McGraw-Hill.

124. Ward, B. (1972), *What's Wrong with Economics?* London, Macmillan.

125. Weintraub, E. R. (1974), *General Equilibrium Theory.* London, Macmillan. Macmillan Studies in Economics.

126. Whitaker, J. K., and B. T. McCallum (1971), 'On Homotheticity of Production Functions', *Western Economic Journal,* vol. 9, pp. 57–63.

127. Worswick, G. D. N. (1972), 'Is Progress in Economic Science Possible?', *Economic Journal,* vol. 82, pp. 73–86.

128. Zellner, A. (1968) (ed.), *Readings in Economic Statistics and Econometrics.* New York, Little, Brown & Co.

AUTHOR INDEX

Afrait, S. N., 151
Alchian, A., 311
Allen, R. G. D., xi, 82, 312, 313, 314, 315
Arrow, K. J., 20, 21, 33, 35, 38, 39, 40, 41, 42, 214, 249, 255, 256, 257, 269, 263, 274, 313, 315, 316

Baire, R., 313
Barten, A. P., 78, 82, 84, 87
Baumol, W. J., 29, 310
Becker, G. S., 33
Bilas, R. A., xi
Boulding, K. E., 311
Bowley, A. L., 151, 228, 229, 230, 237, 250, 254, 263, 279
Brahe, T. de, 309
Brouwer, L. E. J., 201, 221, 222, 234, 235, 315
Burkill, H., 311
Burkill, J. C., 311
Burmeister, E., 315

Chiang, A. C., xi
Chipman, J. S., 32
Cobb, C. W., 81, 184, 190, 191, 192, 200
Cohen, M. R., 309
Courant, R., 315
Cournot, A. A., 87, 88, 89, 91, 95, 118, 211
Cramer, H., 289, 290

Davidson, D., 34
Debreu, G., 20, 21, 28, 34, 35, 126, 236, 238, 240, 241, 242, 243, 313
Dobell, A. R., 315
Dorfman, R., 314
Douglas, P. H., 81, 184, 190, 191, 200
Duesenberry, J. S., 267

Edgeworth, F. Y., 151, 202, 228, 229, 230, 235, 237, 250, 254, 263, 264, 274, 275, 279, 311
Edwards, W., 37
Ellsburg, D., 36
Engel, E., 83, 87, 88, 89, 91, 95, 118, 207, 210, 211, 213, 225
Euclid, 5, 6, 43, 46, 47,61, 64, 296, 298
Euler, L., 89, 212

Ferguson, C. E., xi, 122
Fisher, F. M., 93
Friedman, M., x, 6, 8, 9, 11, 12
Frisch, R., 82, 87
Frobenius, G., 122, 170, 172, 173, 301

Galbraith, J. K., 125
Gale, D., 234, 247, 313, 314, 315
Geary, R. C., 87, 88, 89, 90, 117, 118, 247
Georgescu-Roegen, N., 309
Giffen, R., 92, 93, 118, 225
Goldberger, A. S., 78
Gordon, D. F., 309
Graaff, J. De V., 69

Hadley, G., 314
Hahn, F. H., 274, 313, 315, 316
Hawkins, D., 170, 173
Hempel, C. G., 309
Herstien, I. N., 35
Hicks, J. R., 63, 67, 82, 93, 218, 284, 287, 288, 289, 290, 291, 296, 303, 304, 305
Houthakker, H. S., 69, 73, 74, 82, 87, 311

Ince, E. L., 315
Intriligator, M. D., 314, 315

Johnston, J., xi, 312
Jorgenson, D. W., 303

Kakutani, S., 201, 203, 222, 223, 224, 225, 242, 245, 246, 315
Kaldor, N., x, 250

Kepler, J., 309
Keynes, M., 218, 222
Koestler, A., 310
Koopmans, T. C., 125, 309, 314
Kuhn, H. W., x, 16, 95, 97, 98, 99, 102, 111, 112, 113, 115, 116, 194, 273
Kuhn, T. S., x

Lancaster, K., 21, 170, 192, 272
Leontief, W., 11, 121, 122, 127, 153, 160, 161, 162, 165, 166, 172, 173, 177, 179, 201, 206, 207, 227, 244, 246, 284, 299, 301, 302, 303
Lipschitz, R., 284, 291, 292, 293, 294, 306, 315
Lipsey, R. G., 17, 55, 272
Luce, R. D., 37
Lyapunov , A. M., 284, 292, 297, 298, 302, 304, 315

McCallum, B. T., 192, 314
Machlup, F., 309
McKenzie, L., 170
McManus, M., 313
Marschak, J., 29, 35
Marshall, A., 4, 215, 284, 285, 386, 289, 304, 305
Marx, K., 218
May, K., 43
Metzler, L. A., 296
Mill, J. S., 122
Milnor, J., 35
Minkowski, H., 105, 106, 260, 313
Morgenstern, O., 35, 37
Morishima, M., 72

Nagel, E., 309
Negishi, T., 316
Neumann, J. Von., 35, 37
Newman, P., 309
Nikaido, H., 170, 234, 247, 311

Pareto, V., x, 41, 42, 45, 69, 93, 202, 224, 230, 249, 250, 251, 252, 253, 254, 256, 257, 258, 261, 262, 263, 265, 267, 269, 271, 272, 273, 274, 275, 276, 279, 280, 299, 315
Parzen, E., 309
Pasinetti, L. L., 313, 314
Patinkin, D., 72, 218
Pearce, I. F., 10, 29, 208, 210
Perron, O., 122, 170, 172, 173, 301
Phelps, E. S., 42
Philips, A. W., 27
Popper, K., 309

Quirk, J., 304

Ricardo, D., x, 11, 122, 153, 154, 155, 156, 159, 160, 161, 180, 181, 206, 207, 313
Richter, M. K., 33, 39
Robbins, H., 315
Robbins, L., 5, 29, 309
Roberts, B., 313
Russell, B., 309

Samuelson, P. A., 17, 73, 74, 180, 269, 302, 203, 313, 314
Saposnik, R., 304
Schwartz, H. A., 293, 312, 315
Scitovsky, T., 250
Sen, A. K., 20, 21, 42, 74
Shapley, L . S., 274
Shubik, M., 274
Shultz, D. L., 313
Simmons, P. J., 71
Simon, H. A., xi, 170, 173
Slutsky, E. E., 82, 85, 86, 87, 95, 118
Smith, A., 203
Sonnenschein, H. F., 32
Stigler, G. J., 311
Stone, R., 87, 88, 89, 90, 117, 118, 247
Suppes, P., 34

Taylor, B., 295, 296
Theil, H., 78, 82, 84, 87
Tobin, J., 313
Tucker, A. W., x, 16, 95, 97, 98, 99, 102, 111, 112, 113, 115, 116, 194, 273

Uzawa, H., 29, 73, 109, 315

Veblin, T., 267

Wald, A., 29
Walras, L., 215, 217, 233, 234, 236, 240, 247, 284, 285, 286, 287, 293, 298, 302, 303, 304, 305
Walsh, V. C., 124, 310, 313
Ward, B., x
Weierstrass, K., 53, 54, 241, 252
Weintraub, E. R., 315
Whitaker, J. K., 192, 314
Worswick, G. D. N., x

SUBJECT INDEX

α-class, 4–7, 8, 9, 10, 11, 13, 14, 24, 121, 123
activities, 121, 122, 124, 127–8, 131, 138, 153, 174–80
activity model of production, 122, 127, 153, 174–80
Arrow Possibility theorem, 40–1
attainable set, 18–19, 25, 26, 27, 29, 30, 31, 43, 54–5, 76, 105, 106, 124
average product, 185–6
axiom, 5–7, 12–4, 15, 18, 24–8, 32–3, 35–7, 39–42, 43, 54–6, 61–3, 64, 65, 66, 67, 73–4, 75, 78, 109–10, 121–2, 123–31, 137–9, 142–3, 151, 155, 174, 198–9, 206, 227–233, 252, 310
  of asymmetry, 24
  of comparability, 7, 24, 32, 35, 39
  of constant returns to scale, 126, 127, 141, 143, 156
  of convexity, 7, 12, 61–3, 67, 127, 229
  of exchange, 227–33
  of insatiability, 54, 56, 65, 67, 75, 217, 241, 252
  of probability, 36
  of production, 123–31, 139, 240
  of rationality, 25–8, 33, 108
  of revealed preference, 5, 73–4, 109–10
  of society, 39–40
  of transitivity, 24, 32, 43, 125

β-class, 4–7, 9–11, 13–14, 309
bargaining equilibrium, 275
better set, 61–3, 65–7, 106, 212, 228, 232
boundary point, 50, 51, 58, 63

γ-class, 9–11, 13–4, 123, 198–9, 309, 310
choice, 6, 7, 8, 9, 15–16, 17–19, 24–33, 34–42, 43–4, 45–7, 49, 54–56, 73–4, 123, 125
coalition, 275–8
cobweb model, 304, 306
collective choice rule, 39
commodity space, 15, 45–7, 54, 55, 59, 65, 72, 103, 311
compensated demand, 91–2, 117
complements, 92–4, 118, 119
cone
  convex, 128, 129, 132–7, 138, 143, 151, 174, 176, 206, 313
  convex polyhedral, 134–7, 140, 141, 143, 157, 174–5, 176, 177, 179
  dual, 133–4, 143, 157–8, 169
  truncated, 159, 167, 179, 313
constraints, 15, 16, 18, 25, 29–32, 44, 55–6, 95–100, 101–3, 112–113, 125, 159–60, 310
contract curve, 151, 230, 274–5, 229, 315
core of an economy, 202, 274–8
corner solution, 63, 96, 99, 259
correspondences, 142, 143–50, 155, 158, 176, 194, 205, 206, 223–4, 239–44
cost, 5, 11, 12, 30, 44, 97, 153, 181, 182, 183, 193, 195, 206–7
Cournot aggregation, 87, 88, 89, 91, 95, 118, 211

decomposability, 122, 170–4, 182, 301
decreasing returns to scale, 127, 129, 190, 191, 193
demand functions, 203–6, 207–13, 225, .
  input, 194, 200
  modulated excess, 201, 203, 217–218, 225, 247
dimension, 68, 203
diminishing returns, 186, 188

&-economy, 237–8
&′-economy, 238–44

economic region, 186, 188, 193, 199
efficiency locus, 151, 247, 250, 264, 279, 315
efficient trade, 201, 231–2, 279, 315
elasticity of substitution, 191–3
Engel aggregation, 87, 88, 89, 91, 95, 118, 211
Engel curves, 83, 88, 207, 210, 213, 225
equilibrium, 214–18, 221–4, 232–3, 235–6, 239–43, 244–6, 274, 293–4, 314
  competitive, 201–2, 224, 241, 242–244, 246, 251, 258–63, 274–6, 279, 280, 315
  consumer, 78–82
  firm, 193–6
  general, 215–17, 236
  partial, 214–15, 283–4
  stability of, 284–91, 293–7, 298, 299–304
ethical postulate, 38, 40, 249
excess demand equations, 201, 203, 215–17, 225, 233, 240, 261, 287, 293
exchange model
  general, 236–244
  pure, 233–6, 247, 250–1, 271–2, 274–8, 299
exchange rate, 231
externalities, 7, 125, 126, 138, 252, 257, 269–71, 279

facet, 129, 136, 137, 175–6
fixed-point theorems, 201, 203, 221–4, 225, 315
  Brouwer, 201, 203, 221–2, 225, 234, 235, 315
  Kakutani, 201, 203, 221, 222–4, 225, 242, 246, 315
functions
  concave, 56, 59–60, 65–6, 67, 75, 76
  convex, 56, 59–60, 65, 75
  distance, 47, 49, 77
  homogeneous, 189–90, 192–3
  homothetic, 189, 191–3, 207, 213, 314
  Lyapunov, 292, 297–8, 302, 304, 315
  quasi-concave, 56, 61, 64, 65–6, 67, 75
  quasi-convex, 56, 61, 75

Gale–Nikaido theorem, 234, 247
generalised substitution theorem, 107–109
Giffen good, 93, 118, 225

half-line, 132, 134–5, 138, 154, 157, 160, 162, 175
half-space, 103–4, 106, 108, 132, 134, 136
Hawkins–Simon conditions, 169, 170, 173
homogeneity, 89–90, 109, 117, 118, 142, 211–12, 217, 218, 239, 240, 245
hyperplanes, 103–7, 108–9, 118, 119, 136–7, 139, 140–3, 217

income effect, 82, 85, 86, 87, 107, 204
income flexibility parameter, 86–7
indifference, 6, 7, 22–3, 24–8, 35, 36, 39, 41, 43
indifference curves, 7, 16, 45, 54–6, 61–3, 64–8, 74, 75, 76, 78, 79, 93, 205, 207, 225, 228–30, 231, 232, 252
inferior goods, 92, 94, 107, 204
input substitution, 174, 177–80
integrability, 74, 208, 209, 210, 225, 315
interior point, 50, 53, 58, 62–3, 105, 106
isoquants, 7, 130–1, 187, 191–2
isoproduct set, 129–77, 182, 187, 254
isoprofit curves, 140–2

Kuhn–Tucker conditions, 16, 95–103, 111–16, 194, 273

Lagrangian multiplier, 79, 80–1, 91, 97, 98, 100–1, 117, 253, 255, 266, 268, 270
Leontief production model, 121, 122, 127, 153, 160–70, 173, 174, 177, 179, 201, 227, 244–6
  stability of, 299–303
limit point, 52
limit theorem, 278
Lipschitz condition, 284, 291–3, 294, 306, 315
Lyapunov function, *see* functions

marginal
cost, 196, 199, 207
product, 183, 185, 186, 194
rate of commodity substitution, 67–8, 69, 70, 79, 80, 81, 107, 183, 252, 258, 265, 266, 268–9, 271, 273
rate of technical substitution, 183, 254, 265, 271, 273
utility of money-spending, 80–1, 83, 85, 86, 102, 117
Minkowsi theorem, 105, 260

neighbourhood, 49–50
neoclassical production theory, 97, 122, 127, 131, 177, 183–200
normalised price set, 201, 203, 218–20, 226, 245
normative propositions, 7–9, 249

oligopoly, 10, 12
operational, 6, 12, 45, 73, 309
opportunity cost, 17
ordering, 18, 19–22, 23, 24–28, 32, 34–7, 39, 43, 71, 310
anti-symmetric, 20, 21, 23, 43, 310
asymmetric, 20, 21, 23, 24, 43, 310
complete, 20, 21, 22, 23, 24, 32, 35, 39, 42, 73, 310
lexicographic, 43
quasi-ordering, 20, 21, 22, 23, 27, 43, 310
reflexive, 20, 21, 22, 23
symmetric, 20, 21, 22, 23
subordering, 71
transitive, 18, 19, 20, 21, 22, 23, 24, 32, 43–4, 74

Pareto
efficiency, 230–1, 264, 276, 280, 299
optimum, 41–2, 202, 224, 230, 251–263, 265, 269, 271–4, 275, 315
Pareto ranking, 41, 42, 202, 230, 249–50
Parity theorem, 277
perfect competition, 12, 154, 156, 193, 200, 251, 262, 275
Perron–Frobenius theorem, 122, 172–3, 301
positive propositions, 7–9
preference, 5, 15, 18, 19, 22–3, 24–9, 38–42, 54, 62, 64–7, 73–4, 124, 238
continuity of, 24, 28–9, 35, 54
function, 29–31, 49, 54, 64–7, 246
in the sense of Pareto, 40–2
social, 22, 38–42
stochastic, 34–7
primitives, 5, 6, 15, 22, 23, 25, 28, 39, 43, 121, 123, 124
probability, 6, 12, 24, 34–7
production function 56, 121, 154, 183–193, 198
Cobb–Douglas, 184, 190, 192, 200
CES, 184, 191, 192, 200
homogeneous, 189–93, 200
production possibility boundary, 17, 169, 179, 180, 226
production set, 56, 123, 126, 127, 131, 137–40, 141, 142, 157, 159, 167, 254, 237–40
production possibility set, 129, 164, 169, 245, 257
profits, 29, 30, 31–2, 44, 131, 140–3, 149, 154–7, 166, 175, 178, 193, 244, 310
profit function, 31, 97, 140–3, 149, 150, 154–5, 157, 160, 164, 166, 167, 175, 181, 193, 313
programming, 31, 126
public goods, 202, 267, 269–71, 280

rational behaviour, 15, 16, 19, 25–8, 33, 39–40, 73, 108
rationing, 16, 96, 102–3, 119, 313
refutation, 11–3, 309
relation, 6, 15, 18, 25–3, 28–9, 69
equivalence, 22, 23, 25, 43, 56
revealed preference, 73–4
social, 38–42
relevant region, 187–8, 191, 193, 194, 199, 206
revealed preference theory, 5, 16, 45, 73–4, 109, 110, 244, 298
revenue, 30, 193, 198
Ricardian production model, 122, 153–60, 161, 164, 180, 181, 313
ridge lines, 188, 193

second-best, theory of, 202, 267, 271–4, 278, 280
semi-continuity, 143–50, 207, 215, 220, 221, 223–4, 241, 242, 246, 313

semi-transitive, 43–4
separability, 69–72, 77
sets
  bounded, 26, 51, 52, 54, 310
  closed, 51, 52, 54, 104, 105, 310
  closure of, 51
  open, 26, 29, 47–8, 50, 51, 310
simplex, 201, 203, 218–20, 226, 245
simplifying propositions, 10, 13, 67
Slutsky decomposition, 82, 85, 86, 95, 118
social welfare function, 39, 40, 69, 97, 202, 207, 263–7, 280
spaces
  compact, 47, 49, 52, 53, 105
  connected, 47, 48–9, 59, 67, 77, 104, 105
  metric, 47, 50, 51, 52, 64
  Euclidean, 46, 47, 64
stability, 215, 283–307
  asymptotic, 298, 307
  dynamic, 291–307
  global, 292, 293–8, 299, 303–4, 307
  local, 292, 293–8, 299, 303–4
static stability
  Hicksian, 284, 287–91, 296, 304, 305
  Marshallian, 284, 285–7, 304, 305
  Walrasian, 284, 285–7, 304, 305
Stone–Geary function, 87–91, 117, 118, 247
substitutes, 92–4, 118, 119
substitution effect, 82, 85–6, 87, 107, 204, 205
supply, 142, 155–6, 158, 160–1, 176, 181, 197, 199, 203, 206–7

Tatonement, 294, 299, 304, 316
total product, 185, 188
trading curve, 232–3, 274, 299
trading set, 228–33, 247, 251, 274
transformation relation, 121, 123–6, 151

utility
  interdependence of, 202, 267–9, 280
  marginal, 64, 68, 69, 75, 78, 80, 95, 102, 183
  measurability of, 36–7, 46–7, 64, 311
utility function, 16, 35–7, 54, 56, 64–72, 74, 75, 76, 78–95, 198, 233, 235
  Cobb–Douglas, 75, 81, 117
  separability of, 69–72, 77
  Stone–Geary, 75, 76, 87–91, 117, 118, 247

verification, 11–13

Walrus law, 217, 233, 234, 236, 240, 247
Weierstrass theorem, 53–4, 241, 252, 259
welfare, 249–80
  compensation tests, 202, 250–1 267
worse set, 62–3, 66